National Intelligencer Newspaper Abstracts 1840

Joan M. Dixon

HERITAGE BOOKS
2015

HERITAGE BOOKS
AN IMPRINT OF HERITAGE BOOKS, INC.

Books, CDs, and more—Worldwide

For our listing of thousands of titles see our website at
www.HeritageBooks.com

Published 2015 by
HERITAGE BOOKS, INC.
Publishing Division
5810 Ruatan Street
Berwyn Heights, Md. 20740

Copyright © 2003 Joan M. Dixon

All rights reserved. No part of this book may be reproduced or transmitted in any form or by any means, electronic or mechanical, including photocopying, recording or by any information storage and retrieval system without written permission from the author, except for the inclusion of brief quotations in a review.

International Standard Book Numbers
Paperbound: 978-0-7884-1733-7
Clothbound: 978-0-7884-6198-9

DAILY NATIONAL INTELLIGENCER
WASHINGTON, D C
1840

TABLE OF CONTENTS

Daily National Intelligencer
  Washington, D C, 1840--1

Index--404

Dedicated to my great grandparents
George B Boland and Winifred [Maher] Boland
1839-1901   1837-1896

PREFACE

National Intelligencer Newspaper Abstracts
1840
Joan M Dixon

The National Intelligencer & Washington Advertiser is hereafter the Daily National Intelligencer. It was the first newspaper printed in Washington, D C; Samuel H Smith, the originator. The same was transferred to Jos Gales, jr on Aug 31, 1810; on Nov 1, 1812, the paper was under the firm of Jos Gales, sr, & Wm W Seaton. The Library of Congress has microfilm of the paper from the first issue of Oct 31, 1800 thru Jan 8, 1870, the final paper. The Evening Star Newspaper of Jan 10, 1870 reports: The Intelligencer is discontinued: the proprietor, Mr Delmar, says that having lost several thousand dollars, & being in poor health, he has resolved to discontinue its publication.

Included in the extractions are advertisements; appointments by the President; Hse o/Rep petitions; passed Acts; legal notices; insolvent debtors; marriages; deaths; mscl notices; tax lists; military promotions; court cases; deaths by accident; prisoners; & maritime information-crews. Also, items or events which might be a clue as to the location, age or relationship of an individual are copied.

No attempt has been made to correct the spelling. Due to the length of some articles, it was necessary to present only the highlights of same. Copy of the complete news item, letter, Chancery record, etc, is recommended.

The index contains all surnames and *tracts of lands/places*. Maritime vessels are found under barge, boat, brig, frig, schn'r, ship, sloop, steamboat, or vessel.

ABBREVIATIONS:

AA CO	ANNE ARUNDEL COUNTY
CO	COMPANY/COUNTY
CMDER	COMMANDER
CMDOR	COMMANDOR
D C	DISTRICT OF COLUMBIA
ELIZ	ELIZABETH
ELIZA	ELIZA
MICHL	MICHAEL
MONTG CO	MONTGOMERY COUNTY
NATHL	NATHANIEL
PRSNL	PERSONAL
PG CO	PRINCE GEORGES CO
WASH	WASHINGTON
WASH, D C	WASHINGTON, DISTRICT OF COLUMBIA

BOOKS IN THE NATIONAL INTELLIGENCER NEWSPAPER SERIES: 1800-1805 /1806-1810/1811-1813/1814-1817/1818-1820/1821-1823/1824-1826/1827-1829/1830-1831/1832-1833/1834-1835/1836-1837/1838-1839/1840//
SPECIAL: CIVIL WAR 2 VOLS, 1861-1865

DAILY NATIONAL INTELLIGENCER
WASHINGTON, D C
1840

WED JAN 1, 1840
Senate: 1-Ptn of Thos D Morrison; of John Paul; from John Hall; of Francis Martin & Chas G Livermore. 2-Bill for relief of John J Jacox; of John McCloud. 3-Cmte on Finance: bill for relief of Wm H Robertson, J H Garrow, & J W Simonton; & for relief of W A Whitehead, late collector of the port of Key West, recommending their passage. 4-Ptn from W P Hunt, praying confirmation of a title to land in Missouri. 5-Ptn from J S Sturgis, of revenue service, praying to be placed on the same footing with the ofcrs of the Navy. 6-F A Harrison, praying that he may be secured from the loss occasioned by the destruction of the post ofc, by fire. 7-Wid/o Maj Weed, stating that the pension which she receives is not that which she ought to receive under law, & praying that some proper provision may be made. 8-Memorial of the heir of Thos Powers: from the legal reps of Richd Harrow.

Estray black mare was taken up on Mon, with a common saddle, half worn, & an old bridle. Can be seen at Mr Clarvoe's stable, on 7th st. Owner to prove property, pay charges, & take her away. –Saml Garner, near Brandywine, PG Co, Md.

Cash for negroes, of both sexes, for the Louisiana & Mississippi markets. Letters to Wm H Williams will be attended to promptly: call at his jail, on 7th st, between the Centre Market & the Long Bridge.

THU JAN 2, 1840
Charlottesville, Dec 21. We learn with much regret that *Enniscothy*, the splendid mansion of Col Isaac A Coles, on the Green mountains, in Albemarle Co, Va, was on Mon last, discovered to be on fire. Everything, even the shrubbery, was entirely destroyed. This mansion was built by Col John Coles, about the time of the first settlement of this part of the country, long before the Revolutionary war, & occupied by him for the balance of his life. The principal part of the valuable furniture, library, & paintings, were saved. It was the family mansion of its worthy proprietor & he devoted the best part of his life in beautifying & rendering it comfortable.
-Adv

$20 reward for a bay horse supposed to be stolen from the stable of Mr Zachariah Walker, on the 26th ult. I will pay the reward if brought to Marlborough.
-Wm A Wallace, Upr Marlboro, PG Co, Md.

Senate: Cmte on Pvt Land Claims: 1-Bill issuing a patent to the heirs or legal reps of Francis Rivard, dec'd. 2-Bill authorizing a patent to be issued to Jos Campan, for land in Mich. 3-Bill for relief of the heirs of Pierre Batin; of the heirs & legal reps of Wm Conway; of Danl Marsaqui; of Alvarez Fisk; of Juan Belgar; of Jos Bogy; of Jos Cochran. 4-Bill for relief of the legal reps of Philip Barbour, dec'd. 5-Bill for relief of Chas Morgan, of La. 6-Bill for relief of Sebastian Butcher, & heirs & legal reps of Bartholemew Butcher, Michl Butcher, & Peter Bloom. 7-Bills for relief of Jas Basset; of Saml Collins; of Jno S Billings; & a bill granting a pension to Hannah Laighton.

Comfortable rooms for rent: residence about 200 yards north of the Capitol. Rooms can be seen by applying to Mr D M Wilson, in the Rotundo, or to either of the police of the Capitol. –J E Whailes

Mrd: on Mon last, in Wash City, by Rev Geo G Cookman, Mr Wm E Church to Miss Eleanor A Scarce, of Alexandria.

Zachariah Poulson has of late relinquished the labor attending the publication of a daily paper, &, as John Poulson, his eldest son, who has spent the greater portion of his days aiding as a assist, declines retaining the establishment, the American Daily Adv, [the first newspaper which appeared daily on the American Continent] has been transferred to Messrs S C Brace & T B Newbold. –Zachariah Poulson, who has, for more than 39 years, been its proprietor. Phil, Dec 28, 1839.

A writer in Boston computes that there are 30,000 persons in the U S of the name of John Smith.

N Y, Dec 30. An attempt was made a day or two ago to poison the family of Mr Jesse Hoyt.

FRI JAN 3, 1840
Ofc of the Potomac Ins Co: Wm J Goseler, sec.

Mortality among newspapers: the old estate of these was Poulson's American Daily Adv, now no more. We can remember as far back as to when it was in the hands of Mr Poulson's predecessors, Dunlap & Claypoole, 45 years ago: had the widest circulation in Phil, [then the seat of Gov't.] Two other daily papers have also ceased to exist in Cincinnati, Ohio: the Cincinnati Whig, & the other the Evening Post. Regret & surprised at the extinction of the Balt Chron. The Columbia Telescope, published at Columbia, S C, has fallen a victim to changes in the politics of that state, & has expired.

Strayed or stolen or Tue, a dark sorrel horse: Reward-$10 for the return of said horse. –Franklin Little

Fort Towson, Ark, Nov 7, 1839. Today we buried Gen Geo Culvert, the head chief of the Choctaw nation, the greatest of warriors, & the white man's friend. He was a Revolutionary veteeran; served under Gen Washington in our struggle for independence, from whom he received a commision of Major of Militia in the U S service, & a sword. He served under Gen Wayne, & also under Gen Jackson in the Fla war in 1814 against the Seminoles; Gen Jackson presented him with a Col's commission, & afterwards a sword, when Pres of the U S. Although 95 years of age, he walked as upright as a man of 25. He was interred with his saddle & bridle, his 2 swords, & the U S flag. He was a planter, & his fields of cotton whitened the hills & dales near the fort. He educated his sons & located them on plantations among his people. [Part from a letter of an ofcr in the U S Army.]

For sale: a tract of land in Montg Co, Md: about 400 acs, with 3 small dwlgs on it. –Jos Forrest

SAT JAN 4, 1840

In Chancery: Darius Clagett, cmplnt, vs, Benj K Morsell, adm of Sarah McDowell, Virginia, & Geo McDowell, infant chldrn of said Sarah McDowell, dec'd, dfndnts. Person having claims against Sarah McDowell, dec'd, are to produce them to the Clerk of this Court on or before the first Mon in Feb next. -Jos Forrest, auditor

$50 reward for 2 horses stolen from the stable of Peyton & Dorsey, on Dec 26. Address Peyton or Dorsey, Alexandria, or the subscriber, Philemont P O, Loudoun Co, Va. –Geo Gregg

Appointments by the Pres: Coll of Customs: Chas C P Hunt, Dist of Miami, Ohio, from Jan 13, when his commission expires. John W Dough, Dist of Teche, La, from Dec 30, v Edwin L Cockle, dec'd. Land Ofcrs: Anthony W Rabb, Receiver of Public Moneys, Wash, Miss, from Dec 31, when his commission expired. Registers: Jas McGoffin, St Stephen's, Ala, from Dec 31, when his late commission expired. Alanson Saltmarsh, Cahaba, Ala, from Feb 24, 1840, when his present commission will expire.

Mrd: on Thu last, by Rev Geo G Cookman, Mr Wm J Bland to Miss Mary E Davis, of Gtwn, D C.

Old members of Congress. Mr C F Mercer, of Va, who has just resigned his seat, has been in Congress since 1817, [22 years,] having been elected 10 times. Mr Lewis Williams, of N C, who is called "the father of the House," being the oldest member, was first in the House in 1815, 24 years since. Mr John W Taylor, of N Y, was in Congress 20 years; Mr Newton, of Va, 30 years; Mr John Randolph, about 26 years; Mr Macon, of N C, 28 years; Mr S Smith, of Md, 39 years; Mr Findlay, of Pa, 28 years, the latter four in both Houses.

Louisiana: appointments by the Gov'n'r, Dec 17, 1839: Levi Peirce, to be Sec of State, v, Henry A Bullard, resigned. Henry A Bullard, to be Judge of the Supr Court, v Geo Strawbridge, resigned.

N Y Jrnl of Commerce: Edwin W Moore, Cmdor in the Texan Navy, & Cmder of the brig *Colorado*, now at that port, was arrested on Tue by the U S authorities in that city, & held to bail in sum of $1,000 to answer a charge of having enlisted men in that city for the Texas army or Navy. Rufus Hughes, a butcher in Fulton market, Benj W Benson, a tailor, & Robt Tolford & Jas Jackson, watermen, were also arrested, charged with the same offence, & all held to bail in similar sums.

The U S corvette *Lexington*, Capt Clack, arrived at Valparaiso on Aug 23, said to be last from Callas.

Upper Marlborough, Jan 2. Jas Robinson, of Piscataway district, for a number of years Surveyor of PG Co, Md, was found dead on Dec 22. He was returning home on the 21st, but probably owing to the darkness of the night, lost his way. He lingered but a few hours. -Gaz

Three women burnt to death. Mrs Hannah Langdon, d/o Rev Jos Langdon, of Portsmouth, N H, on Sun week. A widow, Crockett, aged 70, was found nearly consumed. Mrs Lyman, aged 78, w/o Luke Lyman, of Northampton, Mass, on Fri last, when her dress took fire while toasting bread.

Cincinnati, Dec 26, 1839. Messrs David Cline & Hiram Barber, who resided in Newport, & P Brooks, all drowned while crossing the river into Ky Christmas day, when on a hunting excursion. –Republican

MON JAN 6, 1840
Lt Grafton, of Co D, 1st Regt, U S Artl, was not, as stated in a letter from Portsmouth, on board the brig *Virginia*, which sailed thence 11th ult for N Y. He was at Bangor with a detachment of the Company, & arrived in Boston a day or 2 since, on his way to N Y to meet the brig in that place.

Mrd: on Jan 1, by Rev Dr Laurie, Mr Louis Gottheil to Mrs Eliz Woodward.

Died: yesterday, after a short illness, Jas Francis, infant s/o Francis & Mary Riley, [Navy-yard hill.] Funeral this afternoon at 2 p m.

Died: on the 29th ult, at Millstone, Somerset Co, N J, at the residence of her son-in-law, Dr J B Elmendorf, Mrs Ann Frelinghuysen, wid/o Gen Frelinghuysen, of N J.

Death due to exposure: Letitia Snowden, an aged & respectable colored woman, on Jan 2. She did not die in the street, but was found in a state of insensibility. [Local]

Army of the U S: Gen Order #67: Adj Gen Ofc, Wash, Nov 11, 1839. Q M Dept:
[Corr in Jan 7 paper: date should be Dec 31, not Nov 11.]
Maj Thos F Hunt, Q M, to be Deputy Q M Gen, with rank of Lt Col, Nov 8, 1839, v Brant, resigned.
Capt Saml McRee, Asst Q M, to be Q M, with rank of Maj, Nov 8, 1839, v Hunt promoted.
1st Lt Abram C Myers, of 4th Infty, to Asst Q M, with rank of Capt, Nov 21, 1839, v McCrabb, dec'd.
1st Lt Saml L Plummer, of 1st Infty, to Asst Q M, with rank of Capt, Nov 22, 1839, v McRee promoted.
1st Lt W M D McKissack, of 5th Infty, to Asst Q M, with rank of Capt, Dec 19, 1839, v Peyton, dec'd.

Pay Dept:
Benj Walker, Capt of 3rd Infty, to be Paymstr, Dec 17, 1839, v Forsyth dismissed.
Eugene Van Ness, of N Y State, to be Paymstr, Dec 18, 1839, v Lytle, dec'd.

Corps of Engrs: To 1st Lt, Jul 1, 1839:
2nd Lt Jas H Trapier; 2nd Lt Stephen H Campbell; 2nd Lt J M Scarritt

Ord Dept:
2nd Lt Lewis A B Walbach, to be 1st Lt Nov 16, 1839, v Temple resigned.
Brvt 2nd Lt Franklin D Callender, to be 2nd Lt Nov 16, 1839, v Walbach promoted.

2nd Regt of Dragoons:
1st Lt Geo A H Blake, to be Capt, Dec 3, 1839, v Bryant resigned.
2nd Lt Wm J Hardee, to be 1st Lt, Dec 3, 1839, v Blake promoted.
Ephraim M Thayer, of Ohio, to be 2nd Lt Dec 29, 1839.

2nd Regt of Artl:
2nd Lt Arnold E Jones, to be 1st Lt Nov 12, 1839, v Peyton dec'd.
Arthur B Lansing, late Lt 1st Artl, to be 2nd Lt Nov 13, 1839.

3rd Regt of Artl:
2nd Lt W A Brown, to be 1st Lt Nov 6, 1839, v Rodney dec'd.
2nd Lt Henry A Bruton, to be 1st Lt Nov 10, 1839, v Poole dec'd.

1st Regt of Infty:
Brvt Maj Greenleaf Dearborn, Capt of 2nd Infty, to be Maj Nov 27, 1839, v Garland promoted.
1st Lt Sidney Burbank, to be Capt Nov 8, 1839, v McRee promoted Q M.
1st Lt Seth Eastman, to be Capt Nov 12, 1839, v Barker dec'd.
2nd Lt W E Prince, to be 1st Lt Nov 8, 1839, v Burbank promoted.
2nd Lt S E Muse, to be 1st Lt, Nov 12, 1839, v Eastman promoted.
2nd Lt G W T Wood, to be 1st Lt Nov 16, 1839, v Storer resigned.
John C Terrett, of Va, to be 2nd Lt Nov 16, 1839.
Benj H Arthur, of Vt, to be 2nd Lt Dec 1, 1839.

2nd Regt of Infty:
Maj Bennet Riley, of 4th Infty, to be Lt Col Dec 1, 1839, v Cummings promoted.
1st Lt A Riviere Hetzel, to be Capt Nov 27, 1839, v Dearborn promoted.
2nd Lt Chas E Woodruff, to be 1st Lt Nov 27, 1839, v Hetzel promoted.
R J Powell, of N C, to be 2nd Lt Dec 1, 1839.

3rd Regt of Infty:
1st Lt Nathl C Macrae, to be Capt Dec 18, 1839, v Walker appointed Paymstr.
2nd Lt Josiah H Voss, jr, to be 1st Lt Dec 18, 1839, v Macrae promoted.
Robt D Stephen, of Va, to be 2nd Lt Dec 30, 1839.
4th Regt of Infty:
Lt Col Alex Cummings, of 2nd Infty, to be Col Dec 1, 1839, v Cutler resigned.
Maj John Garland, of 1st Infty, to be Lt Col Nov 27, 1839, v Foster dec'd.
Brvt Maj Thos Staniford, Capt 8th Infty, to be Maj Dec 1, 1839, v Riley promoted.
2nd Lt M C M Hammold, to be 1st Lt Nov 7, 1839, v McCrabb dec'd.
Granville D Haller, of Pa, to be 2nd Lt Nov 17, 1839.
Wm Brownwell, of Conn, to be 2nd Lt Dec 31, 1839.
8th Regt of Infty:
1st Lt Edmund A Odgen, to be Capt Dec 1, 1839, v Staniford promoted.
2nd Lt Lucius O'Brien, to be 1st Lt Dec 1, 1839, v Ogden promoted.
Grafton D Hanson, of D C, to be 2nd Lt Dec 1, 1839.
Casualties: Resignations:
Col Enos Cutler, 4th Infty, Nov 30, 1839.
Lt Col Joshua B Brant, Dpty Q M Gen, Nov 7, 1839.
Capt Thos S Bryant, 2nd Dragoons, Dec 2, 1839.
1st Lt W H Storer, 1st Infty, Nov 15, 1839.
1st Lt R E Temple, Ord, Nov 15, 1839.
Deaths:
Brvt Col Wm S Foster, 4th Infty, at Baton Rouge, La, Nov 26, 1839.
Capt Thos Barker, 1st Infty, Tampa Bay, Fla, Nov 11, 1839.
Capt R HPeyton, Assist Q M, Tampa Bay, Fla, Nov 11, 1839.
Capt John W McCrabb, Assist Q M, St Augustine, Fla, Nov 6, 1839.
1st Lt Benj Poole, 3rd Artl, St Augustine, Fla, Nov 9, 1839.
1st Lt Jas M Bowman, 1st Dragoons, Fort Wayne, Ark, Jul 21, 1839.
1st Lt Geo C Rodney, 3rd Artl, St Augustine, Fla, Nov 5, 1839.
2nd Lt Constant Freeman, 4th Infty, Fort Wayne, Ark, Nov 17, 1839.
2nd Lt R S Jennings, 3rd Artl, St Augustine, Fla, Nov 12, 1839.
Paymstr John S Lytle, N Y, Dec 10, 1839.
Dismissed: Paymstr R A Forsyth, Dec 6, 1839.
By order of Alex'r Macomb, Maj Gen Cmder-in-Chf: R Jones, Adj Gen

$50 reward: I Henry Eubanks, collector of Taxes in Dover Hundred for the years 1836 thru 1838, have ascertained by the proceedings before the Judges of the Protestant Episcopal Church that Archibald T K McCallum while a preacher of that church, & at the last genr'l election in Brandywine Hundred, presented a forged receipt of a pretended tax which he alleged had been paid to the undersigned, & that the Inspec & Judges of that election, in spite of all objections, allowed him to vote upon that false receipt. Said McCallum never paid a tax in Kent Co in his life, & was never assessed there. Reward to any person who will leave the receipt with me, properly indentified, so that I may prosecute for this fraud & forgery of my name all who were guilty of it. -H Eubanks, Wilmington, Del

TUE JAN 7, 1840
Hse o/Reps: members of the Hse will wear crape on the left arm for 30 days in memory of the dec'd, the Hon Jas C Alvord, a member elect from Mass.

Senate: 1-Ptn from Jas Glentworth, a soldier in the Revolutionary war, praying for a pension on account of his services. 2-Cmte on Commerce: referred the memorial of Geo Taylor, of Va, in relation to property taken by the French prior to 1800, moved to be discharged from the same: referred to the Cmte on Foreign Relations. 3-Also, same on ptn of Josiah Thucker: referred to the Cmte on Naval Affairs. 4-Cmte on Pensions: bills for the relief of Saml White; granting a pension to David Waller; relief of Mgt Barnes; relief of John McCloud. 5-Cmte on Pensions: unfavorable report on ptn of Dr Palmer. 6-Bills referred: bill for relief of Thos L Winthrop & others, dirs of the New England Mississippi Land Co. Also, a bill for relief of Jos E Nourse. 7-Ptn from Hannah Allen, & from David Green. 8-Ptn from J B Hancock, in relation to a reservation of land by the treaty of Dancing Rabbit Creek. 9-Ptn from Wm Ferguson, from Fred'k Sammons, & from Elisha Bentley.

Criminal Court-Wash: Judge Dunlop took his seat this morning. Jury: Thos Carbery, foreman

John Cox	John Boyle	Wm Hayman
Jos Forrest	Geo Parker	Wm Murdock
Wash Berry	Walter Smoot	John Mason, jr
Jehiel Brooks	John Carter	Francis Dodge
Chas R Belt	Jacob Gideon, jr	Raphael Semmes
Wm Gunton	Benj K Morsell	Thos Munroe
Joshua Peirce	Chas A Burnett	Henry McPherson
John F Cox	Lewis Carbery	

In the course of the morning, Edw T Merton, the young man arrested under charge of robbing Lewis H Sands, a few days ago, at one of the principal hotels, was arraigned, & pleaded not guilty. Mr J H Bradley appeared as cnsl for the prisoner & his trial was fixed for Thu next.

WED JAN 8, 1840
Criminal Court-Wash. 1-Mariah Dougless, free negro, not guilty of assault & battery on negro Sam, slave of Thos R Riley. 2-Harriet Jones & Letty Clarke, free colored women, proved to be united in the practice of fraud. 3-Frederic Clitch, guilty of selling snuff boxes with obscene paintings under the lid in the Centre Market: merely fined because he was a foreigner & an ignorant man.

Senate: 1-Ptn from Jos Sawyer, a Capt in the revenue service, in relation to pay. 2-Ptn from the heirs of Christopher Tompkins & from Enoch Baldwin. 3-Motion that the papers of Isaac Colyer, & those of John Lang, be referred to their appropriate cmte. 4-Cmte on Public Lands: bill for relief of J S Silsbee, & a bill for the relief of Wm Jones, without amendment. 5-Cmte on Roads & Canals: relief of Jos Baxter. 6-Bill for relief of J M Strader.

In the matter of Geo Sinclair, insolvent debtor: ptn in the case states that Geo St Clair was discharged under the insolvent law of this dist, on Jan 11, 1826, & Enoch Bryant was appointed the trustee for the benefit of his creditors; that said trustee sold to one John Dobbyn 89 acs of land for $913, for which he gave 2 promissory notes, each for $456.50, payable in 3 & 5 months after date; that at the time Dobbyn purchased from the trustee, he was a creditor of the said St Clair to a much greater sum than the amount of his purchase, but, for want of proper attention, Dobbyn neglected to exhibit his claims to the trustee, & set them off against the notes which he executed; that the trustee died without executing a deed to Dobbyn, & said Dobbyn was afterwards appointed the trustee of said insolvent, who also died without adjusting his individual & trustee accounts. Subsequently Chas R Belt was appointed trustee of said insolvent, & is now invested with the said ofc; that the said Dobbyn was, at the time of his death, in the peaceable possession of said property; & there was appointed by the Crct Court of this county a trustee to sell his real estate for the benefit of certain creditors; that, among other property, the said trustee sold to Matilda Dobbyn, the petitioner & admx of said Dobbyn in this cause, the lands purchased by said Dobbyn as aforesaid. Object of the ptn is, that Belt be ordered to answer this ptn, & to settle said accounts, & to cancel & give up said notes to the said admx, & as exec a sufficient deed in the trustee of said Dobbyn's estate of said lands, to hold the same subject to the trusts imposed on him by said trust. It is ordered that the trustee & creditors of Geo St Clair appear before the Hon Jas S Morsell, Assist Judge of the Crct Court of D C, at this Court rm, on Jan 16 next, to show cause, if any they have, why the prayer of the said ptn should not be granted. -Wm Brent, clk

Died: on Dec 18, at his residence in Surry Co, N C, Hon Meshack Franklin, in his 67th year; formerly a Rep in Congress from N C for 8 years, embracing the epoch of the war of 1812.

Died: on Dec 20, at Francestown, N H, Mrs Mary Woodbury, aged 69, mother of the Sec of the Treas.

Died: on Jan 6, Mr John Mount, in his 52nd year, of a lingering & painful disease. His bereaved companion & his chldrn mourn his loss. Funeral from his late residence, Elliot's Bldgs, Pa ave, today at 1 p m.

THU JAN 9, 1840
Delicate health & indifferent hearing admonish me to close my transactions & to lessen my agricultural pursuits. For sale: my residence, containing about 1,200 acs, on Mountain run, 4 miles from Stevensburg: dwlg house & most out houses are of brick or stone. I wish to rent a small farm, say from 150 to 400 acs of good land, on the Chesapeake bay. –John Thorn, Berry Hill, Stevensonburg, Va

Died: on Jan 7, at his residence on Capitol Hill, Ignatius Wheatley, in his 70th year. His funeral will be from his late residence, today at 2 p m.

Orphans Court of Wash Co, D C. Letters of administration de bonis non, with will annexed, on personal estate of Edw Murphy, late of said county, dec'd. –Mary Murphy, John Porter, adm de bonis non w a

P Kinchy, Confectioner: at his old stand on Pa ave, between 10th & 11th sts. [Ad]

FRI JAN 10, 1840
The Md Republican is offered for sale by its proprietor, Jeremiah Hughes.

Shocking murder on Jan 4, on the Eastern Shore, of Md: letter from Geo Town Cross Rd, Kent Co: victim was Mr Jas P Wroth, & the perpetrator was Edgar Newman, s/o a widow lady now residing in Phil. Cause was jealousy over Lavinia Piner, d/o the late B Piner, of Kent Co, Md. Newman was arrested & taken to Chestertown jail.

Mr J S Gallagher has retired from the firm by whom the Richmond Whig is conducted, & the paper in the future be conducted by Messrs Pleasants & Mosely. Intimate the paper will be enlarged.

Fayeteville, N C, Jan 1. On Mon last, altercation took place between Mr Duncan MacRae, jr, & Mr John W Ochiletteree, 24, in which the latter received a pistol ball in his head. Wound is feared to be mortal.

The dwlg house of Col Saml W Davies, Mayor of the city of Cincinnati, Ohio, was burnt to the ground a few days ago. Its distance, & situated some hundred yards up a steep hill prevented the engines from reaching the scene in time to be of any particular service.

The Hon Benj Ferguson, of Clark Co, Ind, shot himself on Fri week. He had just been called on by a lawyer, in relation to a security debt of several thousand dollars. He put the muzzle of his gun in his mouth. –Lou Jou

Senate: 1-Ptn from Joshua Howard, of Mich, praying for the passage of an act confirming his claim to a tract of land south of the river Rouge, in that state. 2-Ptn from Saml Nords, asking that his claim to certain lands may not be invalidated by the treary with the Caddo Indians. 3-Ptn from Zadock Smith, for remuneration for work done on the Cumberland road. 4-Ptn from citizens of Milwaukie, asking that the confirmation of the titles of F Laventure & others may not be confirmed. 5-Cmte on the Judiciary: bills for the relief of the heirs of Francis Newman, & for the relief of Agnes Dundas, without amendment. 6-Bills introduced for the relief of Wm Berry; of John L Scott; of Alfred Westfield; of Jacob Hank; of John Ritchie; of Saml Ferguson; of Denis Quinliman; & of Jas L Robertson.

Criminal Court-Wash. Jesse Bates, free negro, acquitted for an assault & battery on John Douglass, a slave of Mrs Cannon, of Pr Wm Co, Va. Douglass was shot in the knee & amputation was necessary.

A T Harrington & Chas Anderson guilty for riot: Harrington to pay fine of $20; Anderson-$10.

For rent: 2 story brick hse on H st, between 18th & 19 sts. –David Hines, agent, residing in the adjoining house.

Wash City Ord: Act for relief of Ulysses Ward: fine for selling wood & lumber without a license: remitted: provided, he pay the costs of prosecution.

SAT JAN 11, 1840
Senate: Cmte on the Judiciary: unfavorable report on the ptn of J S Rowlette.

Having made such improvements in the crossing of the ferry at Nottingham, the width of the Ferry being reduced to 100 years by construction of a safe & permanent causeway: it was heretofore, 1 mile. Persons travelling from the lower counties to Annapolis will find this the most direct road; those from this county to Calvert will find great advantage in crossing at Nottingham. –Geo Calvert, Nottingham, Md

L A Thompson & T H Hagner, Attys & Cnslrs at Law, Tallahassee, Fla. [Ad]

Orphans Court of Wash Co, D C: ordered that John McElroy be appointed adm, with will annexed, on personal estate of Wm McSherry, dec'd, unless cause to contrary be shown. –Nath P Causin -Ed N Roach, reg/o wills

For rent, the Globe Tavern, in Hagerstown, now in possession of Otho H W Stull. Possession on Apr 1 next. Inquire of Eli Beatty, or Fred'k Dorsey, in Hagerstown, Md, or John Harry, Gtwn, D C.

Died: yesterday, Wm Bruce, s/o Mr L A Gobright, in his 5th year. His funeral is today at 2 p m, from the residence of his parents on E st, between 9th & 10th sts.

Little Rock, Ark, Dec 18. By Col T J Pew, who arrived here late last evening, 4 days from Fort Smith, we learn that Jack Nicholson, one of the murderers of Maj Ridge, & an Indian named Terrell, & 2 others charged with being concerned in the disturbances in the Cherokee nation, have been arrested by the commands under Lt Porter, 4th Infty, & Northrup, 1st Dragoons. Prisoners are now on way to this city, under charge of the U S Mrshl, Maj E Rector. The Super of Indian Affairs, Capt Wm Armstrong, received instructions to withhold all annuities & payments to the Cherokees, except mere subsistence until affairs become more settled. -Gaz

U S Hotel, n w corner of public square, Martinsburg, Va: new & commodious: brick erected on King st. –B Oden

MON JAN 13, 1840
Hse o/Reps: 1-Ptn of Margaretta Askins, for pension & relief; 2-Ptn of Mathews, Wood & Hall, for compensation for marble furnished the custom-hse in N Y. 3-Ptn of Solomon J Lee, for pension. 4-Ptn of T M Jacquelin, for return of duties paid by him to the custom-hse. 5-Ptn of Chas G Ridgely, for expenses incurred by him in the service of the U S. 6-Ptn of Maria E Ballagh, Sarah Woodruff, & Harriet Plinter, heirs at law of Peter Shackerty, for pension & relief. 7-Ptn of Lewis H Bates & Wm Lacon, for a return of duties & relief. 8-Ptn of Sarah Hildreth, wid/o John Hildreth, for pension.

Appointments by the Pres: Reg of Land Ofc-
John J Colemen, at Huntsville, Ala, from Dec 31, 1839, when his late commission expired.
Albert Badeolet, for land subject to sale at Vincennes, Ind, from Jan 14, 1840, do.
John C Pedrick, to be Cnsl of U S for the port of Rio Grande, Brazil.
Jesse D Bright, to be U S Mrshl for dist of Ind, for term of 4 years from Jan 19, 1840, when the term of service of the present Mrshl will expire.
Saml Allison, to be U S Cnsl at Lyons, France.
Chas S McCauley, to be Capt in the Navy, from Dec 9, 1839.
Harrison H Cocke, to be Cmder in the Navy, from Mar 3, 1839.
Wm J McCluney, John B Montgomery, & Horace B Sawyer, to be Cmders in the Navy, from Dec 9, 1839.
Geo McCreery, to be Lt in the Navy, from Mar 3, 1839.
John A Winslow, Benj Moore Dove, Jas R Sully, Bernard J Moeller, Ferdinand Piper, Henry Walke, Thornton A Jenkins, & Jos C Walsh, to be Lts in the Navy, from Dec 9, 1839.
John C Mercer & Saml C Lawrason, to be Surgeons in the Navy, from Dec 9, 1839.
Edw Bissell, to be Purser in the Navy, from Dec 30, 1839.
John O Connor Barclay, Jas B Gould, Chas H Wheelwright, Richd W Jeffey, & Thos M Porter, to be Assist Surgons in the Navy, from Oct 17, 1839.
Wm A Nelson, Wm G G Willson, & John H Wright, to be Assist Surgeons in the Navy, from Dec 9, 1839.

Mrd: on Thu last, by Rev J P Donellan, Mr John Daery to Miss Mary Lyons, all of Wash City.

Died: after a few days illness, Mrs Juanna Ryland, consort of the Rev Wm Ryland. Her funeral will be from her late dwlg, near the north end of the Marine Garrison, on Tue, at 2 p m. [No date-current item.]

Died: on Jan 12, at his mother's residence, on Capitol Hill, Terence Martin, in his 25th year. His funeral is today at 2 p m.

Died: a short time since, at Lancaster, Ohio, Gen Philemon Beecher, aged 63, a pioneer of Ohio, who had served as a member of the Hse o/Reps for several years, ending in 1821.

Cincinnati Gaz: died in this city, on the 22nd ult, Robt Burts, of the U S Navy, in his 24th year: author of the novel "the Scourge of the Ocean," & Jack Marinspike's Yarn. A few months ago he became a Passed Midshipman. Suddenly he was seized with consumption, which previously had taken his beloved & lovely sister. Two months since, he returned home, to die in the bosom of his family.

To the editors of the Ntl Intell for publication. How & why is it that the heirs of Gen Thos Nelson, of Yorktown, can receive nothing for his actual disbursements & expenditures for his country, nothing for services rendered at a time when his country was too poor to pay, & he too proud & rich to receive them; & now, whilst the heirs of hundreds are being made rich for the services of their ancestors in the Revolution from an overflowing treasury, in the receipt of lands or commutation pay, they are denied their just claim of actual expenditures by their sire, in his country's great hour of want & peril? Could the true chapter of those times, & incidents of 10 years subsequent to 1781, having an important bearing upon his name & glorious nature, be made manifest, a tale of wrongs & injustice done to his great name would be revealed that would sink into shade & nothingness many of the would be great men of modern, yes, & of ancient days. I am his representative head, & yours truly. Yorktown, Jan 8, 1840 [The letter below followed.] Phenix, Chesapeake Bay, Sep 14, 1777. Letter from T Parker, Senior Capt of H M ships at the entrance of the bay- to Brig Gen Thos Nelson. I am favored with your proposal upon the exchange of prisoners, confined to the exchange of the ofcrs & seamen belonging to the Solebay. In answer to which I beg leave to observe, that the distinction which Govn'r Henry is pleased to make between people taken in arms & those taken in merchant vessels is the first instance of the kind ever made in war, as all subjects are supposed to be involved in the same predicament with the leaders that rule over them. From this idea, every man taken, carrying on any sort of trade for the benefit of that state, must be ever looked upon in the same light as those carrying arms. I must herefore beg that this distinction may be abolished, & I am ready to treat upon the terms you propose, but cannot engage particularly for Capt Travis; that must be left to the decision of Lord Howe. I must call to your remembrance the number of natives of these colonies that have been released from H M ships upon this station since Dec last; which never can be the case in the future, unless something permanent is now fixed upon. Sorry I am to say that an ofcr belonging to the ship *Raisonable* was very near being killed some few days since, with a flag of truce flying, by some people at Cheriston, upon the eastern Shore. Am to request, for the advantage of us both, that care may be taken that nothing of this sort ever happens in future.

Masonic meeting of Fed Lodge #1, this evening. By order of the W M. -J P Van Tyne, sec

I O O F-the Grand Lodge of D C will hold a meeting at 7 p m, this evening. –Jno H Clarvoe, sec

Criminal Court-Wash: Jan 10. Matthew Starks, convicted of petty larceny: fined $1 & to be imprisoned in the county jail for the space of 1 month. Alex'r Watts, petty larceny: fined $1 & 2 months in county jail.

Miniature Painting: Miss E J Bayne: room on Pa ave & 11th, over the store of Messrs Ricards, Gibbs, & Co.

We commend the series of "Lectures on Popular Education", by Mr Geo Combe, of Edinburgh: & "The Teacher Taught, or the Principles & Modes of Teaching", by Mr Emerson Davis, of Boston.

Double murder: at Americas, in Sumpter Co, on Dec 9. Geo Robertson, a candidate for shrf, struck John Kimmey, the present shrf, across the head with a Bowie knife, wounded him severely. Kimmey then shot Robertson thru the body, escaped into the yard of Mr Gore's htl. He was pursued by Jas Shearn, with a pistol. Kimmey begged him not to kill him, but Shearn shot him deliberately. Robertson died of his wounds a few hours later, & Kimmey about 2 days later. Shearn escaped, & also Wm Sims, who was involved. -From the Georgia Messenger

TUE JAN 14, 1840
Reward for lost part of a gold watch chain: leave same with A B Claxton, at the ofc of the Army & Navy Chron, or at Mrs Gibson's brdg hse, 11th & E st.

Mrd: on Dec 26, in Boston, Robt Jas Mackintosh, of H B M's Legation, to Mary, d/o the Hon Nathan Appleton.

The wills of Shakespeare, Milton, & Napoleon, are tied up in one sheet of foolscap, & may be seen at Dr Commons'. The will of the Bard of Avon is an interlineation in his own handwriting. "I give unto my wife my brown best bed, with the furniture." Proved by Wm Buyarde, Jul 22, 1616. The will of the minstrel of Paradise is a nuncupative one, taken by his dght, the great poet being blind. The will of Napoleon is signed in a bold style of writing; the codicil, on the contrary, written shortly before his death, exhibits the then weak state of his body. -Globe

Mrd: on Jan 7, by Rev John Hodges, Mr Jeremiah Townshed to Miss Eliz Moore, of Chas Co, Md.

Mrd: Jan 9, by Rev John Hodges, Mr Wm N Burch to Miss Louisa E M Parker, both of PG Co, Md.

Mrd: on Jan 5, in Portsmouth, Va, by Rev W Moriarty, Capt Duveyrier, of the Royal French Navy, to J R Palmer, only child of B O'Neil, of Portsmouth, Va.

Died: on Jan 13, Mrs Cecilia Billmyer, in her 50th year, after a long & severe illness. Her funeral is from the residence of her brother-in-law, Mr Richd Hendley, today, at 2 p m.

Died: on Nov 17, at Fort Wayne, Ark, Lt Constant Freeman, of the 4th Infty U S Army, only s/o the late Ezekiel Freeman, of Wash.

Mr F Cooke has located himself in Wash City, & will give lessons on the piano, violin, & guitar. Recommended by Mr H Dielman. Apply at F Taylor's Bookstore, near Gadsby's.

Any information relative to the heirs of Mr Thos Ballard, who formerly lived near Princess Anne, Somerset Co, Eastern Shore, Md, will be gladly received. He removed, about 1775, to Windsor, N C, & there mrd. His descendants are now living in either N C, S C, Ga, or Ky. Address to C D Prince, Fredericktown, Calvert Co, Md. Some of the members of Congress may be in possession of the desired information.

Hse o/Reps: 1-Ptns of N Masters, Danl Ingolls, & Thos W W Godbold: for pensions. 2-Ptn of H Stevens & others, for the revisal of the law protecting the revenue against frauds: referred to the Cmte on Mfgrs. 3-Ptn of Sally Stanley, for a pension: referred to the Cmte on Revolutionary Pensions. 4-Ptn of Thos H Perkins & 212 others, Merchants of Boston, for a revenue cutter for the coast of Mass, to be propelled by steam. 5-Ptn of Henry Hatch, of Boston, to be indemnified for spoliations committed by the French previous to 1800. 6-Ptn of John Eddy & others, of Fall river, mfgrs of wool, for the passage of a law to protect the mfgrs of wool from frauds committed upon the revenue by foreigners in the importation of woollen goods.

Trustees of the Upper Marlboro Academy wish to employ a gentleman teacher.
--Jno B Brooke, Pres

WED JAN 15, 1840
U S Supreme Court: Jan 13, 1840: met this morning at the Capitol, agreeable to law. Present:
Hon Roger B Taney, Chief Justice. Assoc Justices: the Hons Jos Story, Smith Thompson, John McLean, Henry Baldwin, Jas M Wayne, Philip P Barbour, John Catson. Albion K Parris, of Maine, & C P Van Ness, of Vt, were admitted Attys & Cnslrs of this Court.

The dght & only child of Lord Brougham is dead. She was interred in the burial ground of the Benchers of Lincoln's Inn, on Dec 4. This is the only instance on record of the interment of a female in this burying ground. –Foreign News

The packet ship *Philadelphia*, Capt Morgan, arrived at Portsmouth on Nov 28. Jos Bonaparte & suite were passengers in her. Capt M was presented with a most splendid gold dessert service by that gentleman.

Fire yesterday originating in a chimney on the house of Mrs Gassaway, on so side of Pa ave, between 10th & 11th sts: extinguished with only trifling damage to the bldg. Another alarm of a chimney fire yesterday, in the house of Mr Dunn, printer, corner of 9th & E sts.

Senate of the U S, Jan 10, 1840. Cmte on Public Lands, to whom was referred the memorial of John A L Norman, of Fla, actg under the resolutions of the Leg Cncl of said Territory, asking Congress to grant a township of land for the establishment of the Dade Instit of Fla. Our desire is to hand down to posterity the names of those who have met death for their country, in its most horrid forms, & now lie buried in the wilds of Fla. Bill was read & ordered to a 2nd reading.

THU JAN 16, 1840
Preston B Elder, editor of the Columbia Spy, died on Mon last, at that place, in his 30th year.

A suit for an alleged defalcation of $69,000 is pending at New Orleans against W H Kerr, late postmaster at that city.

U S Supreme Court: Jan 15, 1840. #16-Ambrose Walden, plntf in error, vs John Craig's heirs et al. #19-Bank of Met, plntf in error, vs E Guttachlick. #49-Geo Wildes & Co, cmplnts, vs Theodore D Parker et al.

A full length portrait of Mr Van Buren painted by H Inman, engraved by J Sartain, is in the hands of an agent, now in Wash City, for sale.

Senate: 1-Cmte on Public Lands reported bills for: relief of Peter Warner of Ind; relief of legal reps of Jos Barnard; relief of Ben Parsons. 2-Cmte of Claims made an adverse report on the case of J H Piatt. Same cmte reported a bill for the relief of the legal reps of Jno J Bulow, dec'd. Also, bills for relief of Gad Humphreys, of Malachi Hagan, of Converse & Reeves, & of E W & H Smith. 3-Cmte on P O & Post Red: bill for relief of Ira Day, of Vt. 4-Cmte on Revolutionary Claims: bill for relief of Pierre Menard & Col Francis Vigo.

Mrd: Jan 11, in N Y, Jas Bayard Whittemore to Jeannette Eliza, only d/o Capt J D Sloat, U S Navy.

Mrd: on Jan 5, at Louisville, Ky, Wm B Whiting, U S Navy, to Miss Mary Lee Nicholls, adopted d/o the late Jas Bruce Nicholls, of Alexandria, D C.

Mrd: on the 25th ult, in Brooklyn, N Y, Wm W Hurlburt to Eliz W, d/o the late Silas Butler, formerly Purser in the U S Navy.

Mrd: on Jan 31, at Columbia, by Rev Wm B Yates, Wm D Porter, of Charleston, to Miss Emma A Haraden, of Greenville, Tenn, y/d/o the late Capt Nathl Haraden, of the U S Navy.

Died: on Dec 11, at his residence near Pearlington, Miss, Judge P Rutilius R Pray. He was Pres of the convention which framed the Constitution of the state of Miss; was elected a member of the bench of the High Court of Errors & Appeals, which ofc he held at the time of his death.

Cmte appointed by the Nat'l Demo Whig Convention, at Harrisburg: nomination as candidate for the Presidency, Gen Wm Henry Harrison; for V P, the Hon John Tyler, of Va. Your obedient servants:

John Owen, of N C, chrmn
Elisha W Allen, of Maine
Jas Wilson, of N J
Isaac C Bates, of Mass
Jas F Simmons, of R I
Wm Henry, of Vt
Chas Davis, of Conn
Robt C Nicholas, of N Y
Ephraim Marsh, of N J
Richd Mansfield, of Dela
J Andrew Shultz, of Pa

Reverdy Johnson, of Md
Jas W Pegram, of Va
Thos Metcalf, of Ky
Jacob Burnett, of Ohio
Douglass McGuire, of Ind
G Mason Graham, of La
T C Tupper, of Miss
Wm H Russel, of Mo
Geo W Ralph, of Ill
Henry W Hilliard, of Ala
Geo C Bates, of Mich

[Part of the reply from Harrison :]
Should I be elected to the Presidency, I will, under no circumstances, consent to be a candidate for a second term. Reply from Govn'r Tyler-Wmsburg, Va, Dec 16, 1839. I have the honor to be, gentlemen, your obedient servant. --John Tyler

FRI JAN 17, 1840
All persons indebted to the Boot & Shoe establishment conducted by me, from Jan, 1839, to Jan, 1840, will please pay their accounts to Mr Andrew Hoover, at the old stand, #10, Pa ave. --T B Griffin. [Hoover will continue the business.]

Senate: 1-Cmte on Pensions: adverse reports on the ptns of John Qunicy, Danl Riol, & John Paul. Also, bills for relief of Saml Collins & Hannah Leighton. 2-Cmte on Naval Affairs: adverse reports on the claim of Irvine Shubrick, & the ptn of Ann Eliza Ball. 3-Cmte on Pensions: discharged from further consideration of the ptns of Nathl Jacobs, John R Midwinter, Eliz Monroe, Thos D Morrison, Abraham Cook, & Aaron Fitzgerald. 4-Cmte of Claims: memorial of John Kurtz: to lie on the table.

The remainder of the passengers in the ship *Ville de Lyon* reached our shores in safety, from Bermuda, tho after a tedious voyage. They arrived at Savannah on Jan 9 in the British barque *Mary*, Capt Godfrey, from Bermuda. They are: Mrs Orne & son; Mrs Langlois; Miss Langlois; Mr Chasterlain & lady & 5 chldrn; Mrs Walsh; Mrs Caradeur; Miss R Gavean; Miss M Gavean; Rev Mr Kerney, of Balt; Messrs Gordon, of N Y; Miesegas, of Phil; A Garvean; V Durant; A Caradeur, of Charleston; H Vibeit, of Lyons; David.

Capt Jackson Gould, of Rahway, N J, drowned-Jan 9: broke thru the ice while skating on the Sound.

Nantucket Inq: indebted to Geo Winslow, Keeper of the Light, for the vessels to pass the Light Vessel stationed in the Vineyard Sound: in 1838, 12,686 passed: in 1839, 14,665 passed.

Mrd: on Jan 8, at Norristown, by Rev Mr Stem, Saml Nixon, M D, of Greenwood, [Caddo Parish,] La, to Miss Emily, d/o Edw Magee, of the former place.

Died: on Sat last, at Richmond, Va, Chas Shirley Carter, a Mbr of the Bar, formerly of Pr Wm Co, which he formerly represented in the Hse of Dels: whose death has excited the sympathies of the whole city.

Died: on Dec 27, at his residence, in Livingston Co, N Y, Col Wm Fitzhugh, in his 79th year. He was formerly of Md, a patriot of Washington school in the war of independence, a Lt of Dragoons at the siege of Yorktown, & aid-de-camp of Gen Fish, of Md. He was an early settler in the valley of the Genesee, where he laid a foundation of affluence for a large family that survives & mourn the loss of an affectionate & venerated parent.

Died: on Tue week, at Norwich, N Y, in his 36th year, Elias P Pellett, editor of the Chenango Telegraph. The Albany Evening Jrnl says: we have known him from his early youth; 20 years since, when we published a paper in Norwich, the dec'd, in his boyhood, was residing near the village, on his father's farm. He had an unquenchable thirst for information. He spent his leisure hours reading of exchange papers in our ofc.

SAT JAN 18, 1840
Notice to creditors: the undersigned has ample means in his possession to pay every debt he owes in Wash City & Gtwn. –Danl Pierce

Orphans Court of Wash Co, D C: ordered that Jas Williams be appointed adm on the estate of Wm Hallard, dec'd, unless cause to the contrary be shown. –N P Causin -Edw P Roach, reg/o wills

Public sale: order of the Orphans Court of Chas Co, Md: sale of several valuable negroes, on Feb 5. [Was set for Jan 1, 1840.] -Jos M Adams, adm or G A Adams, dec'd. Followed by this: Public sale: Orphans Court of Chas Co, Md: sale on Feb 5, in Port Tobacco, all the remaining negroes, 11 or 12 slaves for life, belonging to the estate of the late Gustavus A Adams. –Jos M Adams, adm of G A Adams, dec'd, Port Tobacco, Md.

By 2 writs of fieri facias, issued by Gilbert L Giberson, a J P of Wash Co, D C, at the suit of Boteler & Dunn, against Danl Peirce, I shall sell all the estate, right, title, interest, property, claim, & demand, at law & in equity of Danl Peirce, in 2 small brick tenements in Wash city, on Pa ave, between 12th & 13th sts, in sq 292: so seized & taken in execution, by public auction, to the highest bidder, for cash.
–Thos C Wilson, cnstbl

Dreadful disaster: the steamboat *Lexington* burnt & nearly 200 of the passengers & crew destroyed. Ofc of the Republican Standard, Bridgeport, Jun 14. It left N Y for Stonington on Mon: large quantity of cotton on her deck: 2 miles from Easton's Neck, the cotton took fire. Capt Chester Hilliard, of Norwich, a passenger on board, lashed himself to a cotton bale & was taken up this morning by the sloop *Merchant*, of Southport. The following were thought to have perished: Robt Blake, of Wrentham; Mr Fowler, of N Y; Wm A Green, firm of Allen & Green, Providence; Saml Henry, of Boston; Chas H Phelps, of Stonington; R W Dow, firm of Dow & Co, N Y; Capt Vanderbilt. Balt American received letters stating that Mr John W Keirle, & Mr G W Walker, Mr Keirle's son-in-law left N Y in the steamboat *Lexington* on the day of her fatal disaster; that there are strong grounds for belief that Mr Church, formerly of the firm of Messrs A Lilly & Co, & Mr A Weston, of Weston, Pordexter & Co, of Balt, were on board. This article was followed by: N Y, Wed: slip containing an account of the passengers & crew who were on board, in addition to those who perished, & which you thereby are at this time only possessed of:

Dr Follen & lady, formerly Prof of German lit at Harvard Univ
J Corley, Providence
S Henry, Manchester, Eng
Henry Craig, of the hse of Maitland, Kennedy, & Co
Chas Lee, of Boston
H S Finn, of Newport, the comedian
John Brown, of Boston
Chas Woolsey, of Boston, some say with a wife & 7 chldrn
Mr Mason, of Gloucester
Geo Child, of Stonington, Cmder
Jesse Comstock, of Providence, clk
N P Newman, steward

Ed Therber, mate
D Crowly, 2nd mate
Courtland Hempstead, engr
Wm Quimby, 2nd engr
Martin Johnson, wheelman
Jos Robinson, colored, cook
Oliver Howell, colored, 2nd cook
R Peters, colored, 3rd cook
Job Sands, colored, head waiter
Susn Hulcomb, chambermaid
Chas H Phelps, of Stonington
John Cosely, of Providence
[See paper of Jan 20.]

U S Supreme Court-Jan 17, 1840. #29: Thos Evans, adm, plntf in error, vs Sterling H Gee. #23: Wm & Jas Brown & Co, plntfs in error, vs, Thos McGraw.

MON JAN 20, 1840
On Thu, Mr Thos Kirby, of the firm of Kirby & Miller, Galena, Ill, shot himself thru the heart, with a pistol, at Mrs Jones' boarding house, in St Paul's st, Balt, & died immediately. He was an Englishman by birth, & formerly lived in Balt.

Senate: 1-Ptn of Luke Woodbury & others, praying the establishment of a mail route 2-Additional documents submitted in relation to the ptn of Jubal B Hancock. 3-Cmte on Patents: asked to be discharged from further consideration of the ptns & memorials of Stephen McCormic, F A Chevalier De Geerston, & Chauncey Hall: which was agreed to. 4-Same cmte: referred a bill for relief of Chas M Keller & Henry Stone, & for relief of Hazard Knowles. 5-Cmte of Claims: ptn of Jas Williams, for his relief: ordered to a 2nd reading.

The schn'r *Amistad* case: in the Dist Court of the U S for the Dist of Conn, Judge Judson gave his decision on Mon last: 1-The Dist Court of Conn has jurisdiction, the schn'r having been taken possession of, in a legal sense, on the "high seas". 2-Libel of Thos R Gedney & others is properly filed. 3-Seizors are entitled to salvage. 4-Green & Fordham, of Sag Harbor, who claim to have taken original possession of the vessel & cargo, cannot sustain their claim, & their libels dismissed. 5-Ruiz & Montez, thru the Spanish Minister, have established no title to the Africans, as they are undoubtedly Bozal negroes, or recently imported from Africa in violation of the laws of Spain. 6-The demand of restitution, to have the question tried in Cuba, made by the Spanish Minister, cannot be complied with, as, by their own laws, it is certain they cannot enslave these Africans, & therefore, cannot properly demand them for trial. 7-That Antoine, being a Creole, & legally a slave, & wishing to return to Havana, a resolution will be directed under the treaty of 1795. 8-These Africans be delivered to the U S Pres, to be transported to Africa. Court stands adjourned til Jan 23, & meantime the decree will not be entered, to give an opportunity to the parties to appeal, if they see fit.

The death of Gen Robt T Lytle, of Cincinnati, Ohio, announced in New Orleans papers several days ago, as having taken place at the Verandah Htl-we had hoped was an error, due to the recent death of his bro, in N YC, Maj J S Lytle, Paymstr-Army. The news is confirmed: he died on the 21st ult, when arrested in New Orleans by the disease which ended his life. He was on his way to seek a new home in Texas.

Hse-keeper wanted in a small family where there are no chldrn, to do the hse work. Inquire at the store of J & G F Allen, Pa ave, between 9th & 10th sts. Wanted, a genteel colored woman of the above description, to cook & wash. Apply as above.

Little Rock, Ark, Dec 25. The steamboat *De Kalb*, Capt Tomason, with a btln of 3 companies of the 3rd Regt U S Infty, from Fort Jesup, La, en route for Fort Gibson, passed up on Mon last. Ofcrs: Capt A Lewis, commandng; Capt B Walker, Co D; 2nd Lt J Currier, Co K; 2nd Lt W H Gordon, Co F; 2nd Lt John B Peyton, A A Q M & AA C S; attending Surgeon, Dr J H Andrews, of Natchitoches, La. The non-com ofcrs, musicians, & pvts amounted to 178. -Gaz

Some 6 weeks since Serg Young, of the Marine Corps, stationed at Bedlow's Isl, had suddenly disappeared. It appears he wandered away under some aberration of intellect. –N Y Courier

Passengers on the steamboat *Lexington* [burnt & nearly 200 of the passengers & crew destroyed.]
[See Jan 18, 1840 newspaper.] Capt Chas Hilliard, the only passenger known to be saved.
Mr Isaac Davis, Mr John Brown, Mr Chas W Woolesy, of Boston
Mr John Corey, of Rosboro, Mass
Mr J Porter Felt, jr, of Salem
M Fowler, Mr Robt Schultz, Mr Ballou, or Bullard, Mr E B Patten, of N Y
Alphonse Mason, of Gloucester, Mass
Mr Jesse Comstock, clk of the boat
Mr Chas H Phelps, of Stonington
Mr Saml Henry, firm of A & S Henry, Manchester, Eng
Mr R W Dow, firm of Dow & Co, N Y
Mr Wm A Green, firm of Allen & Green, Providence
Mr Robt Blake, of Mass, Pres of Wrentham Bank
Capt Foster, of Providence, late of the John Gilpin
Mr Chas Bracket, clk to N Bracket, N Y
Capt J D Carver, of Plymouth Mass, of bark *Brontes*
Mr H C Craig, firm of Maitland, Kennedy, & Co, N Y
Mr Abraham Howard, firm of Howard & Merry, Boston
Rev Dr Follen, Mr John Brown, Mr White, of Boston
Mr Adolphus Harnden, super of Harden's express
Mr Pierce, of Portland, mate of the bark *Brontes*
*Capt E J Kimball
*Capt B T Foster
[*Recently returned after several years absence & were on their way to visit their families in the east.]
Mr Royal T Church, Mr John W Keirle, of Balt
Capt Low, agent of the Boston underwriters
Capt Theophilus Smith, of Cartmouth, Mass
Mrs Chas S Noyes, clk to C B Babock, N Y
Mr Albert E Harding, of the firm of Harding & Co, N Y
Mr John Hoyt, mail contractor
Mr Henry J Finn, comedian

Mrs Russell Jarvis, of N Y & 2 chldrn
Mr Weston, firm of Weston & Pendexter, Balt
Mr John G Brown, firm of Shall & Brown, New Orleans
Mr Walker of Balt, with Mr Keirle
Mr Stephen Waterbury, firm of Mead & Waterbury, N Y
Mr J A Leach, s/o Leach & Lovejoy, Boston
Mr N F Dyer, of Pittsburg, formerly of Braintree
John Brown, a colored man
Mr H C Bradford, of Boston, from Kingston, Jamaica
Mr Nathl Hobart, Mr Chas Lee, Mr John G Low, Mt Stuyvesant, of Boston
Mr John Lemist, Treas of the Boston leather Co of Roxbury, Mass
Mr Jonathan Linfield, Stougton, Mass
Mr Philo Upton, Egremont, Mass
Mr Van Cott, Stonington, Conn
Capt Mattison
Mr Robt Williams, of Cold Spring, N Y
Mr Richd Picket, of Newburyport
Mr Everett, of Boston, returning from the burial of a brother, who died here last week.
*Wid/o Henry A Winslow, firm of Winslow & Co, of N Y
*Mr John Winslow, of Providence
*Mr Wm Winslow, of Providence, father of the above
[*They were returning to Providence with the corpse of Mr H A Winslow, who died in N Y a few days ago.]
Boat's Co: Capt Geo Childs, Cmder
H P Newman, steward
E Thurbur, 1st mate
Mr Manchester, pilot, saved
Job Sand, head waiter
Cortland Hemsted, Chief engr
Wm Quimby, 2nd engr
Martin Johnson, wheelman
R B Schultz
Benj Cox & Chas Smith, [saved,] firemen
5 colored waiters
Susan C Hulcumb, colored, chambermaid
Jos Robin, colored, cook
Oliver Howell, colored, 2nd cook
Robt Peters, colored, cook
Capt Hilliard & a fireman succeded in getting on the same bale: the fireman began to despond, talked to his wife & chldrn, & told Capt H that his name was Cox, & he resided in Oak st, N Y: Capt H endeavored to cheer him up, but in the morning he expired. Among those lost is Mr Saml Henry, of Manchester, Eng, an eminent merchant, nephew of our townsman Alex'r Henry. Mrs Follen was mentioned with her husband as among the lost. It would seem from the above that Mrs F was not

with her husband. Addition to the lost: John G Stone, of Boston; & a s/o Mr Chas Woodward, of Phil. U S Gaz: Mr Sheafe, of Portsmouth, N J, who is said to have been on board, has gone to New Orleans. Mr Henckley, of Portland, & Mr H W Warner, of N Y, who were also said to have been on board, were not there; neither was the lady of Prof Follen, she was being kept here by indisposition; but in addition to those mentioned, there were: Elias Brown, jr, of Stonington; H C Bradford, lately arrived from Jamaica; Patrick McKenna, a clk to Messrs Donnelly & Wyatt, of this city, John Walker & Isaac Howes, both of Cambridgeport, seamen, recently arrived from New Orleans; Mr Wilson, of Wmsburg; Mr J B Smith, of Brooklyn; & Chas Bosworth, of Royaltown, Windsor Co, Vt.

TUE JAN 21, 1840
F St Academy: Classical & Mathematical: on 12th st. Of whom may be seen at his Academy, he refers to Messrs Al Dimitry, J H Offey, & Jos S Wilson.
--Chas Kraitisr, M D

Senate: 1-Memorial from John Hatton. 2-Ptn from Mary Brush, an indigent widow, stating that her late husband had assisted, by an invention of his, to heat & ventilate the Hse o/Reps, for which he had never been compensated: praying remuneration might be made: referred to the Cmte for D C. 3-Ptn from Chas Blight, on account of the heirs of Robt Fulton. 4-Ptn from Thos B Parsons & Silence Elliot. 5-Ptn from Ed Fanning, in relation to the Exploring Expedition. 6-Ptn from Polly Clough. 7-Ptn from Lewis Feuchtwanger, asking to be allowed to issue $20,000 worth of cents in German silver. 8-Cmte on Naval Affairs: unfavorable report on the ptn of Wm Hebb. Same cmte: adverse report on the ptn of Saml Warner. 9-Cmte on Pensions: inquire into granting a pension to Ebenezer Swan, on account of a disability incurred by him in the military service of the U S.

Death in the Debtor's Prison: the last N H Aegis, printed at Haverhill, announces that on Jan 3, Mr Ebenezer Eaton, aged 65 years, a soldier of the last war, whose valor won for him the scars which ensured from his country a pension of $48 a year, was retained as security for the payment of his board bill. "Shame, where is thy blush?" "Law, where lingereth thy justice?"

Died: on Jan 17, in Wash City, Mariah, y/d/o the late Thos Waggaman, of the Gen Post Ofc Dept.

Chambersburg Whig: on Jan 2 the dwlg & store-hse of Jas Brewster, in Shirleyburg, Huntingdon Co, Pa, were destroyed by fire, & Mrs Mgt Brewster, the mother, a young woman named Mgt Mitchell, & a boy-s/o Henry Brewster, perished in the flames.

Appointments by the Pres: Jos Redue, Surveyor & Inspec of Revenue for the port of Chester, Md, from Jan 6, when his commission expired. J R Hardening, Surveyor for the dist of Perth Amboy, & Inspec of Rev for the port of New Brunswick, N H, from Jan 6, when his commission expired. Hiram Perry, Surveyor & Inspec of the Rev for the port of Albany, N Y, from Jan 6, when his commission expired. Benj Stiles, Collector of the Customs for the dist of Hardwicke, Geo, from Jan 6: do. Thos Nelson, Collector of the Customs at Richmond, Va, from Jan 6: do. John Dangerfield, jr, Collector of the Customs for the dist of East River, Va, from Jan 13: do. Jas Dell, Collector of the Customs for the dist of St John's, Fla, from Jan 13: do. Wm Milburn, to be Surveyor of Public Lands, in Ill & Mo. Matthew Birchard, at present Solicitor of the Genr'l Land Ofc, to be Solicitor of the Treas, v Henry D Gilpin, appointed Atty Gen. Edmund Christian, to be U S Mrshl for the Eastern Dist of Va, from Dec 28, 1839, when his former term of service expired. Norris Wilcox, to be U S Mrshl for Conn, from Jan 28, 1840, when his present commission expires.

WED JAN 22, 1840

Senate: 1-Ptn from P J Peterson, asking permission to purchase a certain island in the mouth of the Miss. 2-Ptn from John C Worthington. 3-Ptn from John Diell, a citizen of Sandwich Islands, praying that a certain work of his in relation to said Isls might be admitted duty free. 4-Ptn from John Crawford, for arrears of pension. 5-Ptn from Chas D Connor; from Jacob Denham; from John Johnson. 6-Cmte on Public Lands: ask to be discharged from further consideration of the ptn of Chalon Gerard & others, praying to be permitted to enter a quantity of land on credit. 7-Cmte on Indian Affairs: unfavorable report on the ptn of Jos Burke.

The *Glebe* mansion house in Alexandria Co, owned by Gen Van Ness, of Wash, & occupied by Maj J W Minor, accidentally took fire on Fri last, & was burned down.

On Fri, Mr Hale Young, of Brookfield, Mass, was passing the railroad track in that town in a sleigh, when he was run afoul of by the locomotive, & the cars took his head off instantaneously.

Mrd: on Sept 19 last, at the residence of the U S Minister at Paris, Henry Ledyard, of N Y, Sec of the U S Leg in Paris, to Matilda Frances Cass, y/d/o Gen Cass, Envoy Extra & Minister Pleni from the U S to the Court of France.

Died: on Jan 17, in Wash City, after an illnes of 7 weeks, Mr Jas Bowan, aged about 73 years. The writer of this notice can say, with melancholy pleasure, that he gave manifest evidence of a full belief in the Saviour of mankind, & was in possession of his senses to the last moment of his life.

Died: on Jan 18, at Ellicott's Mills, Sarah Ellicott, relict of the late Jonathan Ellicott, in her 75th year.

Died: on board ship *Wm Penn*, on her passage from Balt to Montevideo, Caroline L H Delas Carreras, consort of Ruperto Delas Carreras, of the latter place, & d/o Mr John Moore, of Balt. [No date-current item.]

Reward for stray bay colt, 2 years old: strayed about Dec 28. --A Naylor, Wash

THU JAN 23, 1840
Senate: 1-Ptn from Ira Sabin, asking for a pension. 2-Ptn from certain settlers of Milwaukie, asking that the titles to lands of Francis Laventure & others be not confirmed.

U S Supreme Court: Jan 22, 1840. Joshua A Lowell, of Maine, & Elijah Vance, of Ohio, admitted attys & cnslrs of this Court. #29: Francis West et al appellants, vs Walter Brashear.

The undersigned. Passengers in Messrs Neil, Moore & Co's line of Post Coaches from Wheeling to Cincinnati, feel it their duty to the Public, to express their entire satisfaction of their late trip, which was accomplished in 48 hours.

Amos Clark, Evansville, Ind	Aug Kennedy, St Louis
L Lantz, Pa	L B Hanchett, Natchez
D Haviland, N Y	Edw Collins, Ire
John Cooke, Ire	R G Hickey, Wash

Obit-died: on Nov 30 last, at Lancaster, Ohio, the Hon Philemon Beecher, in his 64th year. He was one of the few remaining early pioners of Ohio: emigrating to there from Litchfield, Conn, at an early age: Rep in Congress for the years 1817 to 1827. He died as he lived, a Christian & a Philosopher.

Orphans Court of Wash Co, D C: in the case of Wm Moulder, adm of John N Moulder, dec'd: Feb 11 appointed for the settlement of said estate. --Ed N Roach, reg/o wills

FRI JAN 21. 1840
Senate: 1-Ptn from Jno De Treville. 2-Ptn from John Nantz & others, praying a continuation of their pensions. 3-Ptn from Jas Caldwell. 4-Ptn from Lewis Gordon, asking a pension. 5-Ptn from Thos Elibert, asking remuneration for a horse lost in the military service of the U S. 6-Cmte on Finance: bill for the relief of the legal reps of H J Pickering & others: majority of the cmte, when it came up in its order, to recommend its indefinite postponement. 7-Same cmte: asked to be discharged from further consideration of the ptn of Saml Law: referred to the Cmte on the Judiciary. 8-Cmte on Pensions: adverse report on the ptn of Arthur Mathews. 9-Cmte on Commerce: adverse report on the ptn of Nathl Gunnison.

Partnership between R France & Jas B Phillips, under firm of R France & Co, expired by limitation on the 10th proximo. Jas B Phillips will continue the Lottery & Exchange business on his own account, at the old stand, near Brown's Htl. Richd France will continue business as heretofore, between 9th & 10th sts.

U S Supreme Court: Jan 23, 1840. #39-P E Frevail, appellant, vs, Franklin Bache, adm of J Dabadie.

N Y, Jan 21. Return of missionaries: Rev Cephas Bennet, his wife, & 4 chldrn, who have been connected for several years with the Baptist Mission in Burma, arrived yesterday in the ship *Champlain* from Calcutta. Mr B's health having failed. Dr Judson, connected for 28 years with that mission, is in a very feeble state.
–Jour of Commerce

Dr Chas Follen, who was lost in the steamboat *Lexington*, was born at Ramrod, in Hesse Darmstadt, in 1796. His elder bro, Augustus Follen, is now a Prof in the Univ of Zurich, in Switzerland, & an eminent poet. Previous to 1824, Dr Follen was a Prof of the civil law in the Univ of Basle, in Switzerland.

Died: on Jan 17, in Wash City, after an illness of 7 weeks, Mr Jas Cowan, aged about 73 years.

Died: on Jan 15, at the residence of Jos Clarke, near Princeton, N J, Hannah White, wid/o Robt White, within one day of completing her 91st year; an aged & respectable member of the Soc of Friends. She was one of the two sisters who aided in nursing & assisting the gallant Gen Mercer, who fell mortally wounded at the battle of Princeton on Jan 3, 1776, & who was carried to their father's house, adjoining the field of battle, where he lingered & died about 10 days after the battle.

Died: Dec 28, 1839, in Moorefield, Hardy Co, Va, Mrs Lucy Williams, consort of Dr M Williams, after a short & severe illness. It is in the breast of her husband & numerous offspring where the desolation will be felt. To her venerable parent, this additional stroke comes with peculiar force, this being the 3rd child she has followed to a premature tomb within a few months. –Moorefield, Dec 30.

$10 reward for gray mare that broke away from the cart on Dec 11. Return to me or Richd Osborne, Gtwn. -Benj Stockett, near Upr Marlboro, Md

SAT JAN 25, 1840
At Rev Mr McLain's Chr, [late Mr Poor's,] on 4½ st, at 11 a m, tomorrow, a Discourse on the claims of Africa will be delivered by Mr Elliot Creason.

Jos Gales, lately resident in Wash City, has been elected Intendant of the city of Raleigh, N C, which ofc he formerly filled for several years before his tempo residence here.

Hse o/Reps: 1-Ptn from Chas J Ingersoll, contesting he seat of Chas Naylor, a member of this Hse, & asked that it be read by the Clk. Mr Keim claimed it as a right, on the ground of privilege. Mr Ramsey supported the motion. Hse referred it to the Cmte of Elections.

The French Pill! Of all remedies ever yet discovered for the cure of Gonorrhea, Gleets, female cmplnts, these pills are the most certain. –R S Patterson, successor to W Gunton

MON JAN 27, 1840
The brig *Genr'l Scott*, of Portland, Capt Littlejohn, reported as lost on her passage from Portland to Balt, is safe in the port of Balt, having arrived there on Jan 14, after a long passage of 35 days, with no injuries.

Appointed by the Pres: Jos A S Ackein to be U S Atty for the northern & middle dists of Ala, v Jeremiah Clemens, elected to the Leg of Ala. Geo W Churchill, to be U S Atty for the dist of E Tenn.

Brunswick [Geo] Adv: from a passenger by the stage line from Tallahasse, we learn that an assault was made by Mr Willis Alston on Gen L Read in that place on Jan 5, in the dining-room of the principal hotel, while the inmates were at supper. Mr A fired 2 pistols at Gen R & then attacked & cut him severely with a Bowie knife. The Gen was alive at last account, & expected to survive. It will be remembered that a duel took place a few weeks since, between Gen R & a brother of Mr A, in which the latter was killed.

Mrd: on Jan 16, at Montmorency, Balt Co, by Rev Mr Anster, Chas Grosvenor Hanson, of Belmont, to Anne Maria, eldest d/o the Hon J T H Worthington.

Died: on Jan 19, at *Morven*, his residence near Leesburg, Loudoun Co, Va, in his 75th year, Thos Swann. He was born in Md, but at an early period of life removed to Alexandria, where he studied law in the ofc of Col Simms: commenced practice in Leesburg, & became the lgl preceptor of the late Wm Wirt: from Leesburg he removed to Alexandria, & was appointed, by the elder Pres Adams, U S Atty for D C; to which ofc he was again, in 1821, on the resignation of Gen Jones, appointed by Pres Monroe; filled the ofc until Jan, 1833, when he returned to Va. In early life he mrd Miss Jane Byrd Page, whom he survived more than 25 years.

Died: on Jan 19, at the residence of Col Washington Owen, in Montg Co, Md, Lyles Robinson, of Winchester, Va, in his 17th year.

Died: on Jan 26, Mordecai Foy, a native of the county of Roscommon, Ire, aged 50 years. Funeral from his late residence tomorrow, at 1 p m.

Senate: 1-Cmte of Claims: bill for relief of the legal reps of David Stone. Also, for relief of John J McIntosh. Adverse report on the ptn of Geo Whitman. 2-Adverse report on the ptn of Isaac Collier. 3-Cmte of Claims: adverse report on the ptn of Abel Pennington. 4-Bill for relief of Saml R Slaymaker was taken up in cmte of the whole: engrossed for a 3rd reading.

U S Supreme Court: Jan 24, 1840. #40: Bank of Alexandria, plntf in error, vs Edw & F C Dyer. #44: Geo Holmes, plntf in error, vs Silas H Jennison, Governor.

Caution: persons are warned not to purchase or take any lien upon the real estate of John B Steenbergen, in Va, Pa, Ind, Mich, Ill, Wisc, or Iowa, or any part of it; & further not to purchase or take any lien upon his personal estate or any part of it. The reason for this caution is, that his whole estate, real & personal, pledged by several written contracts to secure a debt due to the U S Bank of Pa, which contracts will be enforced by law. Information from the undersigned or the ofcrs of the Bank of the U S of Pa. –Jas M H Beale, of Va

Orphans Court of Wash Co, D C. Letters of administration on the estate of Jarred Gossage be granted to Jas H Causten, unless cause to the contrary be shown. –Nathl P Causin -Ed N Roach, reg/o wills

Coal & Hay: for sale. –Wm H Edes, Water st, Gtwn.

TUE JAN 28, 1840
John Sullivan & Son, late of Sullivan & Locke. Genr'l Commission Merchants of Balt, Md. [Ad]

Election for dirs of the Balt & Potomac Steam-packet Co, for ensuing year, will be held at the store of Saml Wilson, McEldery's Wharf, Balt, Md, on Feb 3, between 12 & 1 o'clock. –Godfrey Meyer, pres

Wash Co, D C: certify that Victor Beyer brought before me a stray bay horse. –Jas Marshall, J P [Owner of the above to come forward, prove property, pay charges, & take him away. –V B-near Eastern Branch]

For sale: valuable tract of land belonging to John R Cooke, of Richmond, Va, which, before his departure for Richmond, was advertised for sale by him, & prevented offering it for sale in the first instance, by the illness of his family. It will be sold at public auction at the residence of Lewis A Smith, on the premises, on Feb 29 next. Tract contains about 800 acs & will be sold in 2 parcels.
–A S Tidball, trustee: Winchester

$50 reward for run away, a yellow man named Pompey Jackson, about 30 years of age. –A B Simms, residing near Newport, Chas Co, Md.

Senate: 1-Ptn from Pamela Allen, wid/o Saml Allen, a soldier of the Revolution: praying for a pension. 2-Ptn from Henry Wood, asking remuneration for goods seized while he was a licensed trader among the Indians. 3-Ptn from Jas Williams, asking to be relieved from a judgment obtained against him as surety of Henry Ashton, late mrshl of D C. 4-Ptn for the relief of Miguel Esclava.

Southern Reporter [Grenada, Mi] A G Weir, mrshl of the Northern Dist of Miss, was killed a few days since in an encounter with Gordon D Boyd, in Kosciusko, Miss. –Ripley Free Press

Died: yesterday, in Wash City, Cmdor Isaac Chauncey, one of the senior ofcrs of the Navy, & Pres of the Brd of Navy Com'rs. Funeral on Thu at 11 a m, precisely.

Cut flowers for sale: Wm Buist, proprietor of the 12th st Green-Houses. No admittance on the Sabbath.

Wash Co, D C: insolvent debtor, Christopher Gill, has applied to be discharged from imprisonment. -Wm Brent, clk

To let-2 story frame hse on 6th st, between E & F sts. –J L Harbaugh, 7th st

WED JAN 29, 1840
Mrd: on Mon last, by Rev Geo G Cookman, Mr Emmerick W Hansell, of Phil, to Miss Eliz Ann Robinson, of Wash.

Mrd: on Tue, by Rev Geo G Cookman, Mr Jas R Watson to Miss Susanna Johnson, all of Va.

Mrd: on Tue, by Rev Geo G Cookman, Mr Mathew Cook, of Wash, to Miss Sarah E Hutton, of Montg Co, Md.

U S Supr Court: Jan 28. #51-Theresa Keene, plntf in error, vs W Whitaker. #72-John Foy, plntf in error, v John D Powell: writ of error to the U S Crct Court for Ala was docketed & dismissed with costs. #73-Wm B Cook, appellant, vs Camp & Grigg: appeal from the Crct Court of the U S for Mississippi was docketed & dismissed with costs. #53-Wm Remington, plntf in error, vs O M Linthicum. Court adjourned.

Senate: 1-Ptn from Susan R Picket: asking to be allowed a pension. 2-Ptn from the heirs of Henry Eckford. 3-Cmte on Indian Affairs: bill for relief of John C Reynolds. 4-Cmte on Public Lands: bill for relief of Wm Ostein. 5-Cmte of Claims: bill for relief of Jos N Hernandez. 6-Ptn from Jacob Greaves: asking a pension. 7-Ptn from Jos Smith, Rigdon Higbee, & others, of the Mormon faith, setting forth grievances under which they labored while in Mo, & asking the interposition of Congress in their behalf.

Died: on Jan 23, at Mercersburg, Pa, Mrs Harriet B Henry, wid/o the late Rev Robt Henry, & sister of the Hon Jas Buchanan, of the U S Senate.

Died: on Wed last, in the city of Brooklyn, N Y, of sudden illness, Mrs Eliz B Randolph, w/o J B Randolph, U S Navy.

THU JAN 30, 1840

Orphans Court of Wash Co, D C. Letters of administration on personal estate of Jas Cole, late of said county, dec'd. −Saml Stott, adm

Advices from Galveton, received at New Orleans, are to Jan 14th. Advices from Austin to the 1st state that Col Burleson had defeated the Indians at Pecau Bayou, with a loss of 6 killed, & 25 prisoners. Capt Lynch fell in combat. Ascertianed also that Col Ross had been killed in a street fight in Gonzales. Congress was to adjourn on Jan 17th, after passing a law to sectionize the Cherokee lands. In the Burleson fight, Egg, a noted Chief, fell. The wife of Bowles was among the captured. Some time since, the British vessel *Agnes*, arrived at Galveston with emigrants. It appears that John Woodward, the Texian Cnsl at N Y, sold to Mr Iken, an Eng capitalist, lg quantities of Texian lands, to which he had not the shadow of a title, & that these emigrants who had come out had purchased their lands of Iken. Congress will donate land to these emigrants in addition to their head rights.

Greenway, the residence of Chas J Catlett, in Loudoun Co, Va, accidentally caught fire & was burned down on Fri last. It was but a few days ago that we announced the destruction, by fire, of the residence of Maj Minor, Mr Catlett's son-in-law, in this county. −Alex Gaz

Senate: 1-Cmte on the Judiciary: bill for relief of Thos L Winthrop & others, dirs of the New England Mississippi Land Co. 2-Adverse report on the bill of the adms of Jos Edson.

Mrd: on Jan 23, by Rev Dr Hawley, Mr F Hamilton Southworth, of St Louis, Mo, to Miss Emma D N Nevitt, of Wash City.

Mrd: on Thu last, in Balt, by Rev Dr Henshaw, Rev Lancelot B Minor to Miss Mary Stewart. [Mr Minor is one of the Misionaries of the Protestant Episcopal Church at Capt Palmas, West Africa, to which station, accompanied by his wife & the Rev Mr Smith, he intends to return in a vessel about to sail from Norfolk. −Arena]

Died: on Jan 16, Juliana Patterson, in her 6th month, only d/o Thos R Gedney, U S Navy.

Died: on Jan 15, at Mt Carmel, Wabash Co, Ill, Robt Philip, s/o Richd H Day, M D, & Eliz, his wife, aged 10 months & 5 days.

Orphans Court of Wash Co, D C: Jas Long, administrator of Wm Moody, dec'd: appointed Feb 25 for the settlement of the estate. −Ed N Roach, reg/o wills

JAN 31, 1840
Nov Term, 1839: Talbot Co Court, Court of Equity. Wm Willson & Sarah his wife, vs, Jos Ferris & Deborah his wife, Danl Atwell, John B Atwell, Jos Atwell, Ann Atwell, Wm W Anderson, Mary E Anderson, Ann J Anderson, John A Anderson, & Mgt Anderson, chldrn of Mgt Anderson, dec'd, formerly Mgt Atwell, heirs at law of Wm Atwell. Case: Wm Atwell, of Talbot Co, died intestate, seized in fee at the time of his death to land in King's Creek hundred, in said county, called *Oxford*, part of another tract of land called *Oxford Resurveyed*, part of another tract called *Rich Farm*; part of *Rich Farm Add*, & part of *Mill Land*, otherwise called *Dixon's Lot*, containing the whole of 428 acs of land, more or less; that the said Wm Atwell left the following his heirs at law & legal reps: Sarah A Willson, w/o the cmplnt, & one of the sisters of the intestate, Deborah Ferris, w/o Jos Ferris, another sister of the intestate, & the following persons, chldrn of his dec'd sister, Mgt Anderson, formerly w/o Wright Anderson; that is to say, Wm W Anderson, Mary E Anderson, Ann J Anderson, John A Anderson, & Mgt Anderson, all which said chldrn are infants under 21 years of age. The bill also states that the aforesaid heirs at law of the dec'd intestate, Wm Atwell, have interest in common, by descent in the land, & that it will be for the interest & advantage of both infant reps & those of full age to sell the aforesaid land. The bill further states that Jos Ferris & Deborah his wife resided in Milton, Wayne Co, Ind, Danl Atwell, Ann Atwell, & Jos Atwell reside in Logansport, Cass Co, Ind, John B Atwell resides in N Y C, N Y, Wm W Anderson, Mary E Anderson, Ann J Anderson, & John A Anderson, chldrn of Mgt Anderson, dec'd, reside near Milton, Wayne Co, Ind, & that all the before named heirs at law & legal reps are beyond the reach of the process of this Court, & out of the state of Md. Same to appear on or before Apr 1, 1840. –P B Hopper -Jas Parratt, clk

Chas Francis Adams, the only living s/o the venerable ex-Pres, addressed the N Y audience on Thu last, on the "Influence of Domestic Feeding upon Public Conduct During the Rev."

Mr Jas Thompson, of Phil, formerly an ofcr of the steamboat *Pizarro*, was shot & killed on Wed last, at Bellview, by Mr Jas C Mitchell, merchant of that place. Mr M is in confinement. –Galena Demo, Jan 10

Mrd: on Jan 28, by Rev Mr Stringfellow, Mr Chas R Beale to Miss Rebecca R Butt.

Mrd: on Thu, in Wash City, by Rev Geo G Cookman, Jos Mathews to Eliz W Brooks, all of Balt.

Senate: 1-Ptn from B G Mackall. 2-Ptn from Jos & Wm N Steed, asking to be relieved from certain liabilities as sureties. 3-Cmte on Indian Affairs: adverse report on the ptn of Robt Grignon. 4-Cmte on Pensions: unfavorable reports on the ptns of Louisa M Rivard, Mary Blakesale & Eunice Stearn, & Betsey Booth.

Wash Corp: 1-Nomination of Geo McNaughton for Superintendent of Chimney Sweepers for the 2nd ward: rejected. Same for Nathan Moore for the 1st Ward.

SAT FEB 1, 1840
For sale: valuable estate called *Glymont*: 646 acs, on so side of Potomac river, 30 miles from Wash. Can be seen by applying to Jas B Pye, living on the place, or address a line to Pomonky P O, Md:

For rent: 2 story frame hse on 9th st. Apply to J Fugitt, at the Lumber & Coal Ofc adjoining the premises.

Franklin Fire Co: First Annual Ball on Feb 3, 1840. Mgrs:

Wallace Kirkwood	Henry Howison	Geo M Davis
Jno A Blake	W Ogden	E L Hamilton
C S Coltman	Wm Ridall	Jno V Shields
Wm M McCauley	Francis Hill	Geo Furtney
A W Denham	Jno C Rives	A Sessford
Jno T Given	Thos Smallman	W Nailor
Geo Lamb	Geo C Whiting	Jno Willey
J E Given	Geo Hilbus	N B Van Zandt
J H Stewart	Wm Duer	

Farm on which I reside for sale due to precariour nature of circumstances: about 450 acs, in Chas Co, Md: with tolerable good frame house, & kitchen. Apply in writing to me at Allen's Fresh, or to Minchin Lloyd, Milton Hill. –J Philip Stuart

It appears that among the passengers in the ill-fated steamboat *Lexington*, on her last trip, were Mr John Martin & Mr Gilbert Martin, father & son, lately from England. –Jrnl of Commerce [Feb 3 paper: investigation by Capt Stephen Manchester.]

U S Supreme Court: Jan 31. #36-Wm A Carr, appellant, vs S H Duval et al.

Died: at Dumfries, Va on Jan 25, in her 35th year, Mrs Cath Ann Thomas, w/o Wileman Thomas, of Dumfries.

MON FEB 3, 1840
New goods just received & for sale: goods usually kept in variety stores.
–Jno H Drury, opposite 7 Bldgs, Wash.

Danl A Wilson chosen to be a judge of the Genr'l Court of Va for 8th judicial dist, v Judge Wm Daniel, dec'd.

Mr John McMillan, of Mercer township, Butler Co, Pa, was frozen to death on Thu last, on his return home from business in Harrisville, in the same township. His body was found the next morning.

Mrd: Sat last, by Rev Geo G Cookman, Mr Edw Eiglehart to Miss Martha Ann Duvall, of PG Co, Md.

Died: on the 23rd ult, at Leesburg, Va, Mrs Anna Rose, w/o Capt John Rose. She was the last surviving child of the late Col Geo Beall, of Gtwn, D C, & had resided in Loudoun since her marriage in 1792.

Greenville Academy, S C: teacher of Math wanted. Address Wm B Leary, Greenville C H, S C.

TUE FEB 4, 1840
Senate: 1-Ptn from John Compton, asking compensation for a tract of land. 2-Ptn from Aaron Fane, in relation to his pension. 3-Ptn from Geo W Oldner. 4-Cmte of Claims: bill for relief of Duncan L Clinch, with a special report. Bill for relief of Jas Tongue, with a report. 5-Cmte of Claims: bill for relief of Hezekiah Cunningham.

Appoinments by the Pres: [Commission-cms.]
Robt Ezell, Coll of Customs for Edenton, N C, v Duncan McDonald, whose cms will expire Feb 29.
Marcus Derkheim, to be U S Cnsl for Hanseatic free city of Breman, v Joshua Dodge, resigned.
Franklin Clinton, to be Lt in the Navy from Dec 11, 1839.
Jas K Bowie, to be Lt in the Navy from Jan 17, 1840.
Custom-hse Ofcrs-Collectors:
Nicholas Willis, Dist of Oxford, Md, v John Willis, dec'd.
Wm F Haile, for Champlain, Plattsburg, N Y, v D B McNeill, resigned.
Dennis Prieur, for Mississippi, La, v J W Breedlove, resigned.
Thos A S Donephain, for dist & port of Natchez, Miss, v Jas Stockman.
Geo D Hale, for Gloucester, Mass, v Wm Beach, resigned.
Jas R Pringle, Charleston, S C, from Jan 29, 1840, when his late cms expired.
Surveyors:
Jas R Thompson, for port of Town Creek, Md, v Wm B Scott, resigned.
Alex'r K Phillips, Fredericksburg, Va, v Adam Cooke, dec'd.
Ely Moore, N Y, v Hector Craig, removed.
Wm Williams, East Rvr, Va, v Francis Armstead, dec'd.
Jos Litton, Nashville, Tenn, v Joel M Smith, resigned.
Nathl P Porter, Louisville, Ky, v Edw S Camp, dec'd.
Aaron Hart, Pittsburg, Pa, v John Clark, removed.
Jefferson L Sangston, Wheeling, Va, v Thos P Norton, resigned.
Appraisers:
Chas J F Allen, Boston, Mass, v John Crowninshield, resigned.
Edw A Raymond, Boston, v Levi B Lincoln, removed.
Land Ofcrs: Registers-
Marvellous Eastham, at Springfield, Ill, v S A Douglass, resigned.

Benj R Petrikin, at Dubuque, Iowa, v J W Worthington, resigned.
Geo R Girault, at Chocchuma, Miss, v Wm Van Norman, resigned.
Henry P Womack, at Greensburg, La, v Nicholas Baylis, resigned.
Receiver:
Woods Mabury, at Jeffersonville, Ia, v D W Sloane, dec'd.
Edwin McName, at Helena, Ark, v David Thompson, resigned.
A S Lewis, at New Orleans, La, v Thos H Kennedy, resigned, who was appointed during the recess of the Senate, v R M Carter, resigned.
Jonathan Kearsley, at Detroit, Mich, from Feb 10, 1840, when his present cms will expire, agreeably to the nomination.
Geo W Cole, at St Augustine, Fla, v John C Cleland, removed.
Md State Appointments: copied from the Annapolis Herald:
Sec of State: Cornelius McLean
State Librarian-David Ridgely
Topog Engr: J H Alexander
State Geologist: Julius T Ducatel

Shocking accident last week at the Carrollton mills, on Franklin rd, about 2 miles from Balt, nearly caused the death of Mr Benj Shakespeare. His legs were broken when his overcoat caught in the machinery. He is a much respected man, & has a wife & 9 chldrn. His life is in a very precarious situation. -Sun

Mrd: on Sabbath last, by Rev Geo G Cookman, Mr Edw Ward to Miss Susanna Pierce, of Wash City.

Hse o/Reps: nominated to be Chaplain: number of votes given 184; necessary to a choice 93.

Rev J N Danforth-29	Rev Mr Balch-31	Rev T Braxton-24
Rev Mr Wilmer-19	Rev F W Boyd-20	Rev Mr Donnelly-4
Rev Mr Babbitt-19	Rev Levi R Reese-9	

Names of Donnelly & Reese were then withdrawn. The Hse adjourned.
[Paper of Feb 10: a card from Rev John Philip Donelan, Assist Pastor of St Patick's Cath Chr, F st, Wash City: His nomination was without his knowledge: his numerous perplexing daily duties, under any circumstances, could not accept the ofc.]

Wash, Pa, Feb 1. 1-On the 18th ult, Mr Henry Donnell, a respectable farmer near Cannonsburg, had one of his arms torn off above the elbow while attending a thrashing mach. However, we understand he is doing well. 2-John Hamilton was found, last Sun, between Sandy Flack's Tavern, in Munntown, Nottingham township, in this co, & Mr Benj Williams residence, having perished in the snow. He was the father of a family, who are mostly grown up, however. -Reporter

Mrd: on Sun last, by Rev Mr Hamilton, Mr Jos Shepherd to Miss Caroline Heyser, all of Wash City.

Valuable land at auct: the devisees of Weedon Sleet will sell, on Feb 20, on the premises, the tract of land on the S W Mountain, in Orange Co, upon which said Weedon Sleet resided at the time of his death. The land adjoins *Linden*, the late residence of J Morton: about 600 acs. –Geo Sleet, on behalf of himself & other devisees.

Mrd: on Jan 8, at Norristown, Pa, by Rev Mr Stem, Saml Nixon, M D, of Greenwood, La, formerly of Loudoun Co, Va, to Miss Emily, d/o Edw Magee, of the former place.

WED FEB 5, 1840
John Varden has now got possession of the 1st & 2nd floors of the Masonic Hall on 4½ st, for the purpose of establishing his Museum permanently in Wash City.

Senate: 1-Cmte of Claims: adverse reports on the following bills: relief of Dennis Quinlican; of Chas A Dodd; of Wm Bennett; of Jas H Ralston; of David McNair; of Jacob Hanks; of Alfred Westfall; of Saml Ferguson; of Jacob Dunham. 2-Cmte of Claims: relief of John L Scott; relief of John Richey. 3-Cmte on Public Lands: bill for relief of Zadoc Martin. Same cmte, to be discharged from the further consideration of the memorial of Saml Massey & Thos James.

Political meeting on the Western Reserve, Ohio, at Chardon, on Jan 22: gathering of the people to respond to the nomination of Harrison & Tyler. Delegation from Astabula Co floated a banner, with the following inscription: "Don't give up the ship." Harrison & Tyler. "The Union of the Whigs for the sake of the Union." The hero of Tippecanoe. "Is he honest? Is he capable." The car from Centreville, with 6 Revolutionary vets, & many of the oldest inhabitants of Madison township: waved a banner with the following: "The Old Whig Banner of '76" Harrison & Reform. Wm Henry Harrison. "Is he honest" Is he capable? Is he faithful to the Constitution?" On the inverse: Harrison & Tyler. The Ohio farmer & the Constitution. "Liberty & Union, now & forever." Credit & Commerce. Large sleigh manned by the citizens of Painesville: flag painted by Mr Single for the occasion: following memoranda: Wm Henry Harrison

Appt'd an Ensign by Washington, 1791.	Appt'd Cmder-in-Chief N W Army, 1812.
Appt'd Sec N W Terr by Adams, 1797.	Appt'd Minister to Colombia by Adams, 1827.
Appt'd Indian Com'r by Jefferson, 1801.	Battle of Miami, Aug 24, 1794.
	Battle of Tippecanoe, Nov 7, 1811.
Appt'd Govn'r of Indiana by Madison, 1809.	Battle of Fort Meigs, May 1-6, 1813.
	Battle of Thames, Oct 15, 1813.
	Harrison & Reform

Orphans Court of Wash Co, D C. The case of Chas G Wilcox, adm of Chas G Wilcox, dec'd. Feb 18 appointed for settlement of estate. –Ed N Roach, reg/o wills

Greenfield [Mass] Courier says that it is now ascertained that Miss Sophia T Wheeler, about 18, of this town, was on board & among the lost, on the steamboat *Lexington*. She was on her return from teaching in Middletown, N J, to her father's, for the purpose of being married. Dr J G Davenport, of Middleton, was with her, on a visit to his father's family in Colerain. Mr Davenport's name was not given with the list of pasengers, as originally published.

Balt museum for sale: large & valuable collection of rare, curious & interesting objects. It was originally got up by Rubens Peale, whose family is identified with the great Establishment in Phil, whose experience enabled him to make the Balt Museum second only to that of which his father was the founder. Property may be seen by applying to Mr De Selding, at the Museum: or to-John H B Latrobe, Thos Wilson, Wm Hamilton, trustees

Wash Corp: 1-Communication received from the Mayor nominating Wm M Robinson, super of chimney sweepers in the 1st Ward, & Richd Pierce, for the 2nd Ward, was considered & confirmed. 2-Ptn of Alfred Wallingsford: to take out a lottery license, in lieu of his billiard & shop license: laid on the table.

Died: on Mon last, in Wash City, Mrs Susan H Tolson, in her 32nd year: after a long & painful pulmonary disease. Funeral today at 10 a m, from her house over Mr Slade's Hardware store, Pa ave, between 8th & 9th sts.

THU FEB 6, 1840
St Mary's Co, Md: Taxes due on the following:
1837: Cole, Eleanor: *Hopewell's Dance*: 20 acs
1837: Killburn, Eliz: part of *St Jerome's Plains*: 3 acs
1835, 36 & 37: Aisquith, Geo-heirs: The *Flower of the Forest*: 100 acs
1837: Armstrong, Henry: 100 acs
1836: Greenwell, Jos of Thos-heirs: part of *Truth & Trust*: 56 acs
1837: Hellen, Thos F-heirs: part *Burdett's Neck*: 98½ acs
1837: Hammett, Robt McK: *Ishmael's Right, Stiles' Chance, Pleasant Levels*, part bought of Wm Heard, *Well Close*, part *Wild Cat*, part *Ishamel's Right, Mill Pond*: 436½ a s
1834, 35: Key, Henry G S: part *Burdett's Neck*: 98½ acs
1837: Leigh, Geo S: *Piney Neck, Depford*, part *St Jos' Manor*: 330 acs
1837; Leigh, John-heirs: *By the Mill*, the *Mill*, part *St Jos' Manor, Mill & Mill Seat*, last part of *Ripe, Poverty Hills, Abell's Lot, Abell's Chance, John's Dread & John's Ramble*, the *Mill Race, Water Mill*: 417½ acs
1837: Partridge, Wm J: pt *Honey Creek*: 76½ acs
1835, 36, 37: Sumerville, Wm C-heirs: *Woolsey Manor, Sarah's Retreat*: 432 acs
1837: Sewall, Robt: part *Leh Manor Head, Friend's Discovery with add, Leh Manor Head, Summer Field*, part *Hopewell's Delight & Bachelor's Hopewell*: 417½ acs

1837: Tabbs, Barton-heirs: *Craton*, part *Salem*, *Addition*, part *Hard Bargain*, part *Wood's*, part *Chas' Chance*, part *Brick Kilns* & part *Addition*: 694 acs
1837: Walker, John-heirs: Bought of John Redman over the rd: 84¾ acs
1837: Abell, Enoch B: *Leak's Purchase*: 120 acs
1837: Abell, Jas: part *Crackburn's Purchase*: 100 acs
1837: Abell, Thos: A*bell's Scuffle, Addition*: 157½ acs
1837: Anderson, Jos-heirs: part *Workington Park*: 81½ acs
1837: Anderson, Jane: part *Workington Park*: 41 acs
1837: Ashcom, Geo G: lot in Leonardtown with improvements
1834: Bennett, Wm of Richd: part *Piles' Woodland*: 180 acs0
1835, 36, 37: Brewer, Richd: *Good Luck*, part *Goldsberry's Race*: 101½ acs
1836, 37: Brown, Susanna-heirs: *Wales, Susanna, Gaynard's Lot, Somerset Add, Yoke by Chance, Maiden's Fair*, part *Workington Park*, part *Delabrooke*: 2,263 acs
1836, 37: Bowes, Christopher: *Ferney Hills*: 130 acs
1836, 37: Blackistone, Wm J: lot in Leonardtown
1836: Booth, Leonard T: part *Hopton Park*: 35 acs
1836: Bradburn, Edw R: *Knotting, Bachelor's Rest, Joshua's* Plains, part of *Bachelor's Rest*: 253 acs
1837: Betts, John-heirs: *Farthing's Fortune & Three Friends, First Vacancy*, part *Three Friends*: 96¼ acs
1837: Brewer, Wm: *Three Corners*: 160 acs
1837: Brown, Wm H: *St Ann's Freehold, Hanover, Gough's Level, Four Square*: 205 acs
1837: Brown Henry, F B: *Roseland & Add, Roseland & Add, Mt Vernon*: 277¼ acs
1834: Clarke, Jas: *Beaver Dam*: 139 acs
1835, 36: Cooper, Jos: part of *Doe Park* & *Doe Park with Addition*: 208 acs
1836: Carpenter, Geo, F B: part of *Vowles Purchase*: 20 acs
1836: Carpenter, Thos, F B: part of *Vowles Purchase*: 20 acs
1836: Carpenter, Lewis, F B: part of *Vowles Purchase*: 20 acs
1836: Carpenter, Eliza, F B: part of *Vowles Purchase*: 20 acs
1835, 36, 37: Drury, Peter, adm large *Hayden*: part *Yieldingberry & Perch Hole Marsh*: 53¼ acs
1836, 37: Davis, Richd, Washington: *St Giles*, part of *Pomfret Fields*: 173 acs
1835, 36, 37: Drury, F Desales-heirs: *No Name, Neviles, St Ann's*: 187 acs
1835: Dougherty, Thos: *Edinborough*: 1 ac
1837: Dorsey, Clement: part of *Delabrooke Manor*: 7¾ acs
1837: Davis, Thos S: *Wilderspool & Green Hills*: 154½ acs
1837: Davis, Jos-heirs: *New Design*, part of *New Design*: 265½ acs
1836, 37: Ford, Henry-heirs: *Kirby's Choice, Truth & Trust, Bachelor's Comfort*: 225¼ acs
1836, 37: Ford, John F-heirs: part of *Downham*: 63 acs
1837: Fenwick, Ignatius: part of *Resurrection Manor*: 37 acs
1837: Fenwick, Enoch-heirs: half of *Trent Marsh*, half bought of John Booth, half *Booth's Endeavor*: 127½ acs

1836, 37: Graves, Justinian: *Beaver Dam, Danbury, Security*, part of *Ford's Security & Ramble*: 242¼ acs
1838: Greenwell, Saml of Wilfred: part of *Heard's Friendship & Two Friends*: 50 acs
1837: Graves, John A: part *Botton*, part of *Maiden's Lot*, part of *Wathan's Disappointment*, part the *Ramble*, part of *Hardship's Addition*: 338¼ acs
1834, 35, 36: Hammet, Bennet: *Wheatley's Content*: 50 acs
1836: Howard, Jas: *Baptist's Hope, Poplar Point, Chas' Srvy & Rolly*: 200 acs
1837: Howard, Jas & others: *St Oswald's*: 112 acs
1837: Johnson, Wm: part of *Broad Neck*: 90 acs
1836, 37: Joy, Edw: *Rackoon Hills, Neighbor's Fare*: 223 acs
1836, 37: Johnson, John, of Leonard: *Cissell's*: 99¼ acs
1837: Jarboe, Jos: part *St Peter's Hills*, part *Dryadocking*: 125 acs
1835, 36: Maryman, Jas-heirs: *Vowles' Purchase*: 75 acs
1835, 36: Mattingly, Geo-heirs: part of *Twitnam, St Wm's*: 183¾ acs
1835, 36, 37: Maryman, Benonia: part of *Richd Maryman's Lands, Vowles' Purchase & White Acre, Maryman's Lot & Vowles' Purchase*, part of *White Acre, Vowles' Purchase, Cissell's Venture*, part of *Long Neck, Cissell's Venture*: 205½ acs
1835, 36: Moore, Warring F-heirs: *Green Hills, Wilderspool & Green Hills*: 290½ acs
1836, 37: Morgan, Eliz, Dorothy, & Caroline: part of *Hard-fortune*, part *Chas' Chance, Tradesman's Lot, Yoke by Chance, St Jos'*: 235 acs
1837: Mattingly, Geo: part of *Washington Park*: 110½ acs
1836: Martin, Henry B: lot in Leonardtown
1836, 37: McWilliams, Jas: *Gardner's Chance, Meadows*: 215 acs
1837: Magaw, John: *Small Hope & Redman's Hardship, Hopewell's, Coxen's Rest, Branch & Chas' Victory, Flood's Qrtr, Redman's Hardship*
1837: Martin, Thos N: part of *St Mgt's*: 90 acs
1837: Moore, Maria M: *Green Hills*: 136 acs
1836, 37: Nelson, Obadiah: *Hopewell, Hardship's Addition*: 183 acs
1835, 36, 37: Norris, Athanasius: *Logan's Plains*: 65 acs
1837: Norris, Chas G: part of *Wheatley's Meadows*, part *Norris' Venture*, part of *Sandy Levals*, & part *Last Shift*: 96 acs
1837: Norris, Stephen: *Tauston Dean, St Mgt's, Rochester, St Mgt's*: 234 acs
1837: Neale, Geo W-Chas Co: *Delabrooke*: 153½ acs
1837: Neale, Henry C: *Scotland*, part of *Dock*, being part of *Scotland*: 121 acs
1835: Payne, Jos-heirs: *Long Neck*: 50 acs
1837: Plowden, Wm H-minor: part of *Enclosure, Beaver-dam & Delabrooke*: 257 acs
1835: Russell, John B: *Woodpecker*: 91½ acs
1836: Reeder, Susanna: *Jas' Additon*, part of *Linstead*, part of *Hard Fortune*: 169 acs
1837: Reeder, Thos-heirs: lot #1, being part of *Delabrooke*: 192 acs
1837: Raley, Saml, Celestia Joy, & others: *Rackoon Hills, Neighbor's Fare*: 223 acs
1835: Stone, Joshua: *Manning's Purchase, Drayden's Hills*, part of *Graden, Aberdeen, Wilkinson's Industry*: 353¼ acs

1835, 36, 37: Stone, Glovina, & Thos J: *Curry-glass*, being part of *Rocky Point, Vowles' Purchase*: 363 acs
1835, 36, 37: Shirley, Ignatius-heirs: *St Mgt's, Last Shift*: 203 acs
1837: Stone, Bennet: part of *Goldsberry's Acre*: 67¾ acs
1836: Spencer, Jas-heirs: part of *Resurrection Manor*, & 2 parts of same: 332 acs
1836: Saxton, Jos, F B: *Green Meadows*: 117 acs
1836: Smith, Clement, [D C]: *Blackland & Spalding's Venture*: 607 acs
1836: Spencer, Jas & others: *Newton's Rest, Wm's Endeavor, Locust Thicket*, part of *Harm-watch-harm-ketch*: 171 acs
1837: Stone, Jos: *Thompson's Expense*, part of *Vowles' Purchase, Edinborough with Add, Hog Island*: 328 acs
1835, 36: Thomas, Edw-heirs: *Pleasant Levels*, part of *Truth & Trust*: 110 acs
1836: Turner, Philip: part of *Yieldingberry*, part of *Hopton Park*: 157½ acs
1834, 35, 36, 37: Winsatt, Saml: *Hardtimes*: 100 acs
1837: Woodland, Primus: part of *Doe Park with Add*: 100 acs
1835, 36, 37: Walker, Jas-heirs: part of *Walker's Venture, Landing Neck*, part of *Hopton Park, Farthing's Fortune*, part of *Farthing's Fortune & Additon*, part of *St John's Mill Seat, Edinborough*, part of same by plot: 439½ acs
1835, 36, 37: Williams, Lewis: *Revel's Backside & Mark's Venture, St Mgt's, Revel's Backside, Mark's Venture*: 302 acs
1835, 36, 37: Welsh, John-heirs: *Nimboquint*: 100 acs
1835, 36, 37: Walker & Alvey: part of *Hopton Park*: 23½ acs
1835: Wheeler, Wm: *Logan's Plains*: 50 acs
1836, 37: Wilkinson & Brewer: *Industry*, part of *Graden*: 76½ acs
1837: Woodward, Thos-heirs: *Reader's Purchase, Hampstead, Lancaster's Discovery*, part *Hopton Park, Forest Land, Names not Known*: 373 acs
1837: Wheatley, Jos-heirs: *Hickory Thicket, Hanover*: 93 acs
1836, 37: Winsatt, Eliz-heirs: part of *Peace & Quietness, Hickory Hills, Spink's Rest*: 258¾ acs
1837: Weaklin, Jas H: *Hopewell*: 151 acs
1836, 37: Yates, Alex'r: part of *Yieldingberry*: 60 acs
1836: Yates, Chas, minor: *Long Neck*: 50 acs
1837: Yates, Edw: *Scrubby Oak, Stoy Hill, Swamp Island*, part of the *Ramble*: 142 acs
1834, 35, 36: Booth, Jeremiah-heirs: *Basford Berry Gleaning*, lot at *Llewellen's*: 200 acs
1835: Blakistone, Nathl: part of *White's Neck*: 49 acs
1835: Bowling, Wm W: *St Clement's*: 50 acs
1835: Barber, Eliz M: *Chaptico Manor*: 70 acs
1834: Cheseldine, Washington: part of *Catharine's Isl*: 20 acs
1835, 36, 37: Clements, Wm & Wash Chaseldine: part of *Hacket's Thicket*: 60 acs
1835, 36, 37: Compton, Wm: lot #7: 431¼ acs
1836: Hayden, Jas-heirs: *Beverly, Mill Lot*, part of *Ingsbeth, Water Mill, Garner's Lot* & part of *East Gift, Nichol's Hope*, & *Cawood's Inheritance*, part of *Garner's Lot*: 665½ acs

1834, 35: Llewellen, John & Wm: *Penryn*: 169 acs.
1834, 34: Mattingly, Alex'r: *Beverly & Ingsbeth*
1834, 35: Stone, Wm M: *Berwick, Reeder's Adventure, Carroll's Gift, Strife*: 207 acs
1834, 35: Saxon, Bennet: part of *Bachelor's Rest, Joshua's Addition*: 129.9 acs
1834: Thompson, Henry: *Suttle's Range*: 112 acs
1835: Tarlton, Eliz-heirs: part of *Mattapony*, part of *White's Neck*; 148 acs
1835: Turner, Josiah & Philip: *Manor, Dearbought*: 359
1835: Thompson, Wilfred-heirs: *Hagden's Discovery*: 53¾ acs
1835: Tubman, Francis: part of lot #2: 27 acs
1834: Woodward, Mgt: *Constantinople*: 100 acs
1836: Watson, John: *Partnership, Addition to Partnership*: 172 acs
1834: Cartwright, Wm [Ch Co]: *Chisom*: 96 acs
1834: Carseley, Littleton: lot #4: 124 acs
1837: Carrico, Gustavus: Chas' Lot: 162 acs
1837: Childs, Saml: lot & improvements in *Charlotte Hall*
1837: Davis, Briscoe-heirs: part of *Recompense*: 36¾ acs
1837: Edelen, Eugenius F: lot #1: 221¾ acs
1837: Fernandes, Walter: *Westham & Cawood's Inheritance, Westham & Cawood's Expense*: 228 acs
1837: Gardiner, Jas, [Chas Co]: part of *Freeman's Lodge*, part of *Enclosure with Addition*, part of *Hope* & part of *Burrough's Gift*: 198 acs
1837: Harrison, Aquilla: *Arabia*: 20 acs
1837: Harrison, Arthur: *Wood's Enclosure*: 82 acs
1835: Kilgour, Wm-heirs: half *Satisfaction*: 255 acs
1835: Kennock, Geo: *Good Luck*: 100 acs
1835: Kilgour, Wm: *Town Neck, Remainder*, part of *Price's Rest, Kilgour's Addition, Best Land*, part of *Offield, Ludgate*, part of *Dryden, Widow's Down*, in Jno Keech's land, lot #3: 515 acs
1837: Keech, Philemon-heirs: *Price' Rest, Freeman's Lodge*: 196 acs
1837: Kilgour, Chas J: ½ *Satisfaction*, ½ *Satisfaction*
1837: Love, Chas R-heirs: *Formby, Partnership, Love's Adventure, Formby*: 215 acs
1834, 35: Mills, Wm-heirs: *Good Luck, Barber's Enclosure*: 206 acs
1836, 37: Mills, Wm-heirs: *Good Luck*: 136 acs
1837: Reeder, Susanna: *Long Looked-for-come-at-last, Trueman's Hunting Qrtr, Good Lucks, Edw'd Discovery, Lock's Meadows, Keeche's Folly*: 391¾ acs
1835: Sothoron, Wm Gude Julis C & E D Tiner: *Plains of Jerico, Good-pennyworth, & Dent's Venture*: 240 acs
1837: Turner, Philip: *Barber's Enclosure*: 70 acs -A Wilhelm, late collector

Ga News: Gen Read was not killed in his recent rencontre with Mr Willis Alston, at Tallahassee, on Jan 5 as reported. Tho very severely wounded by a pistol shot & a Bowie knife, he was, at last accounts, slowly recovering, & his life is supposed to be out of danger.

Among the passengers lost in the ill-fated steamboat *Lexington* was Mr Geo O Swan, of Columbus, Ohio, who was on his way to join the law school at Cambridge. He accompanied Mr Justice McLean, of the Supr Court, as far as Phil, where he met Judge Story, who gave him letters of introduction to gentlemen in Cambridge. He is represented to have been a young man of much promise. Another-among the passengers, it is now ascertained that Mr John Ricker, of Monroe, Maine, was one.

Mrd: on Thu last, at Barnsfield, by Rev Mr Goldsmith, Alex'r Harrison to Mary Ann, d/o A B Hose, sen, all of King Geo Co, Va.

Died: on Feb 4, Camsadel, an interesting little girl, aged 5 years & 6 months, eldest d/o Otho & Ruth Gattrell, of Wash City.

Waterloo for sale: virtue of a deed of trust from Needham H Washington: which deed is recorded in the clk's ofc of King Geo Co, Va: sale on the premises on Apr 10 next, all the right, title, & interest of said Washington in the estate called *Waterloo*, lying on the Potomac river, in King Geo Co, Va. The title is unexceptionable: tract contains between 800 & 1,000 acs, & has on it many valuable improvements. –Geo Fitzhugh

For rent: that beautiful residence on I st, belonging to Col Geo Bomford, & in the occupancy of the subscriber, to whom, while on the place, reference may be had for particulars. –Jas Laurie

FRI FEB 7, 1840

Hse o/Reps : 1-Ptn of Josiah King, of Norton, Mass: on the commencement of the Revolutionary war, his father & himself resided in Nova Scotia; that they immediately returned to the U S, & were in the U S army during the whole war. He asks that Gov't would grant him land on his own account & on the account of his father, to which he is equitably entitled: referred to the Cmte on Revolutionary Claims. 2-Ptn of Levi Eldridge, of Harwick, Mass, & of Josiah Holmes, asking for an allowance on fishing vessels lost at sea: referred to the Cmte on Commerce. 3-Ptn of Henry Defrees & Stephen Jenny, of Nantucket, Mass, bondsmen of Purser Fanning, dec'd, they ask for relief: referred to the Cmte on the Judiciary. 4-Ptn of Danl Fellows & others, inhabitants of Edgartown, Mass, for rebldg a light-hse & pier at Edgartown: referred to the Cmte on Commerce. 5-Ptn of Danl Weed & 76 others, citizens of Ipswich, Mass, praying that the exportation of ardent spirit to the Sandwich Islands may be prevented, & for the prohibition of ardent spirit into the U S: referred to the Cmte on Commerce. 6-Memorial from Lemuel W Wheelock & others, contesting the right of Osoryn Baker to a seat in the Hse o/Reps: referred to the Cmte on Elections. 7-Ptn of Eliz Stockwell for a Revolutionary pension; of Mary Reed for the same; of Lucy Tugalla for the same; of Wm Kilhour & others of Saxonville, Mass, for security against frauds in duties on woollens. 8-Ptn of Joel Knight & 75 others praying that the exportation of opium to China in American vessels may be prohibited; of Benj Hawkes for regulation of pay; of Ellery Brown for Revolutionary pension: all appropriately referred. 9-Ptn of Ira W Barton & many citizens of Worcester Co, Mass, representing that there are outstanding warrants for bounty lands, & no lands set apart for satisfying the same; & praying Congress to appropriate good & available land for that purpose. 10-Ptn of Aaron Tufts & others of Dudley, Mass, praying a reduction of the rates of letter postage. 11-Ptn of Asa Rand & citizens of Pompey, Onondaga Co, N Y, praying Congress to pass an act to prohibit furnishing intoxicating drinks to the Army & Navy & to the Indians within the jurisdiction of the Gen Gov't, & to increase the duty on ardent spirits. 12-Ptns of Sarah Adams, Arnold Straton & others, John C Russel & others, H Marsh & others, the heirs of Gilbert Deach, Lemuel Pomroy & others, Saml Rosseter & others, David N Dewey & others, Amos Proctor & of W A Howard. 13-Ptns of Hetty Fassett, John Magraw, Isaac McMaster, & Lewis Chandler, praying for pensions: referred to the Cmte on Pensions. 14-Ptn of Zenas Jones, an invalid pensioner, for an increase & arrears of pension: referred to the Cmte on Invalid Pensioners. 15-Ptns of Carlos Cooledge & others, praying for a mail route from Danville to Woolcott; of J R Skinner & others, for the same; of Isaac Pennock, jr, for a mail route, & of Isaac Pennock for a mail route. 16-Ptn of Chas Payae & others, relative to mfgr, & of Lyman King. 17-The following ptns were referred to cmte, viz: Ephraim Bowes, to Cmte on Revolutionary Claims; David Bartlett, to Cmte of Claims; Elisha Dillingham, to Cmte on Revolutionary Pensions; Saml Warner, to Cmte on Invalid Pensions: Allen Wardwell, to Cmte on Revolutionary Pensions: Darius Hawkins, to Cmte on Invalid Pensions. 18-Ptn of Saml Slater & Sons, mfgrs of wool in the U S for relief against frauds in importations of foreign mfgrs of wool, & of Saml Almy & Co for the same object: both referred to the Cmte on Manufactures. 19-Ptn of Wm Sigourney, postmaster, for post route from Providence to N Brookfield: referred to the Cmte on the P O & Post Roads. 20-Ptn of Stephen Cornell, for pay as 1st Lt in the Navy: referred to the Cmte on Naval Affairs. 21-Ptn of Seth Chapin, heir of Seth Chapin, dec'd: referred to the Cmte on Revolutionary Pensions. 22-Ptn of Mrs Susan Rogers, wid/o Rev Wm Rogers, of the heirs of John Weeden: referred to the Cmte on Revolutionary Pensions. 23-Ptn of Edw W Lawton & 10 others, of Newport, Newport Co, R I, mfgrs of Wool, praying Congress that the laws for the collection of duties may be reviewed, effectual to prevent frauds. 24-Ptn of O M Stillman & 6 others, of Westerly, Wash Co, R I, mfgrs of wool, praying Congress that the laws of the duties may be revised. 25-Ptn of Eliz Mayes, of Newport, R I, for renewal of pension. 26-Ptns of John Vroman & Saml Hunt, of Niagara Co, N Y, for Revolutionary pensions. 27-Ptn of Gilbert Howel, of N Y, for claim growing out of services performed during the last war. 28-Ptn of Godfrey Clair, of N Y, for a Revolutionary pension. 29-Ptn of Geo Williams & others, of Portage, Allegany Co, N Y, for establishment of a mail route. 30-Ptn of Wm Parker, a Seneca Indian, for an increase of pension. 31-Ptn of Saml Gilman, of Genesee Co, N Y, for relief by pension or otherwise, on account of Revolutionary services. 32-Memorial of Edmund Fanning, praying for a loan of money from the U S for the support & advancement of commerce, the fisheries, & by exploration of the South Seas. 33-Memorial of Noah Brown & others, in behalf of the owners, ofcrs & crew of the pvt armed brig *Warrior*, praying to be paid certain money arising out of the sale of the captured brig *Dundee* & her cargo, the proceeds of which were paid into the Dist Court of the U S for the southern dist of N Y. 34-Memorial of Gorham A Worth, praying for relief from certain alleged liability to the U S as surety. 35-Memorial of Meigs D Benjamin, praying that certain overcharged duties paid on damaged goods may be refunded. 36-Memorial of Chas Kohler, praying remuneration for services in Fla as pilot, & for salvage due to him from the U S. 37-Memorial of Mary W Thompson, wid/o Alex'r R Thompson, late Lt Col in the U S Army, for compensation for extra services rendered the U S by her late husband. 38-Memorial of Boggs & Thompson, J G & R B Forbes, John Levale, Cotheal & Hoff, Jacob Ritter, Jos Simmons, Robt & John F Hutchinson, for drawback duties. 39-Memorial of Wm Steele, for a pension for services as a soldier of the Revolutionary war. 40-Memorial of Henry Beamish, for remission of a forfeiture. 41-Memorial of J & T S Winslow, praying that certain duties paid by them may be refunded. 42-Memorial of John McColgan, praying that he may be remunerated for advances of money made by him for the maintenance of the capt & crew of the American brig *Phenix* while imprisoned in Ire. 43-Memorail of Henry Ely, praying the allowance of drawback upon a quantity of Canadian flour exported by him in 1838 & 1839. 44-Memorial of Robt Roberts, praying for relief. 45-Memorial of Elias Nixsen & others, grangers in the N Y custom-hse, for relief. 46-Ptn of Christiana Fisher & others, widows of the ofcrs of pvt armed vessels, praying for renewal of pensions. 47-Ptn of John Fisher, of Naples, N Y, praying for a pension. 48-Memorial of F S Boyd & others, of N Y, mfgrs of putty, praying that a duty be laid upon imported putty: referred to the Cmte on Mfgrs. 49-Memorial of Sarah Hazard, wid/o Maj Wm Hazard, of Beauford dist, S C, praying for a pension: referred to the Cmte on Revolutionary Pensions. 50-Memorial of Truman Wright & others, of Racine, Wisc Terr, praying for the construction of a harbor at Racine: referred to the Cme on Commerce. 51-Memorial of the heirs of Dr Mordecai Hale, for 5 years' pay as surgeon's mate in the Revolutionary war, & for invalid pension: referred to the Cmte on Revolutionary Claims. 52-Memorial of Jos Howard, jr, J Sprague & others, citizens of N Y & Brooklyn, praying for the consurction of a dry dock at Brooklyn: referred to the Cmte on Naval Affairs. 53-Memorial of John Whitehead & others, owners of Key West, asking for remuneration for losses incurred by the Gov't having occupied a part of the island for naval purposes: referred to the Cmte on Naval Affairs. 54-Memorial of Goodhue & Co, Jas Lee & others, of N Y, praying for the passage of an explanatory law to an act passed in Jun, 1838, to remit duties on goods destroyed by fire in said city in Dec, 1835: referred to the Cmte on Commerce. 55-Memorial of S E Glover & other ship-mstrs, ship-owners, & merchants, of N Y, praying for an investigation into the official conduct of N P Trist while cnsl at Havana: referred to the Cmte on Commerce. 56-Ptn of Pollen & Colgate, praying for a return of duties: referred to the Cmte on Commerce. 57-Ptn for relief of Eli Darling: referred to the Cmte on Naval Affairs. 58-Ptn of Josiah Hunt, for a pension for wounds received during the Revolution: referred to the Cmte on Invalid Pensions. 59-Ptn of Wm A Wousten, for arrears of pension: referred to the Cmte on Invalid Pensions. 60-Ptn of Peleg Clark for giving compensation to privateersmen during the time they were prisoners of war during the last war: referred to the Cmte on Naval Affairs. 61-Ptn of Letitia Hatfield, wid/o Lt Hatfield, for pension & relief: referred to the Cmte on Revolutionary Pensions. Also, ptn of Amos Rooke, for pension for Revolutionary services: do. 62: Ptn of Reuben Steeves, for relief, under resolution: referred to the Cmte on Revolutionary Claims. 63-Ptn of Mrs Cath Telfair, for bounty land, on account of the Revolutionary services of her father, Capt Isaiah Wood: referred to the Cmte on Revolutionary Claims. 64-Ptn of Henrietta Barnes, an heir of Col Lathrop Allen, for Revolutionary services: referred to the Cmte on Revolutionary Claims. 65-Ptn of the heirs of Capt Thos Park, dec'd, for compensation for pvt property sold for the use of the Gov't during the Revolutionary war. 66-Ptn of Saml Hutchinson, a soldier of the Revolution, praying to be inscribed upon the pension roll. 67-Ptn of Jos Hall, for a pension as an invalid. 68-Ptn of Geo Putnam Farrington, of Chautauque Co, N Y, praying for a pension. 69-Ptn of Eunice Abell, praying for a pension. 70-Ptn of Jas Gee, for a pension as an invalid. 71-Ptn of Casper M Rouse, for remuneration, for losses sustained by his father in the Revolutionary war. 72-Ptn of D Raymond, respecting the currency of the U S. 73-Ptn of Geo H Noble & 99 others, of Otsego Co, N Y, for a reduction in the rate of letter postage. Also, the ptn of Jos Peck & 122 others, of New Lisbon, Otsego Co, N Y, for the same object. 74-Ptn of Robt O Robertson & others, of Jersey City, in favor of the application of Capt Hiram L Wuker for compensation for clearing out the channel in the Dela. 75-Ptn of Lindley W Woolley & citizens of N Jersey, on the subject of the public lands: referred to the Cmte on Public Lands. On the same subject: ptn of Simeon McCoy & others; of Silas C Cook & others; of W S Johnson & others. 76-Ptn of W Abraham S King praying for a pension: referred to the Cmte on Revolutionary Pensions. Ptn of Mrs Jane Vreeland for a pension: referred to same. 77-Ptn of Abigail Dumas, wid/o John F Dumas, dec'd, praying for relief on account of damages sustained by the capture of a Spanish privature: referred to the Cmte on Ways & Means. 78-Ptn of Edw Caleby & others, coach lace makers of Phil, praying for imposition of duties on silk coach lace: referred to the Cmte on Ways & Means. 79-Ptn of Geo Curloch & others, coach lace weavers of Bridgeport, Conn, for the same purpose. 80-Ptn of Mary Kelsey, sister of the late Capt John Pearson, a Revolutionary ofcr, praying for relief on the ground of losses & services of her brother: referred to the Cmte on Revolutionary Claims. 81-Ptn of John J Smith, for a pension for wounds received during the late war with Great Britain: referred to the Cmte on Invalid Pensions: 82-Ptn of Robt Taylor, of Phil, for payment of drawback: referred to the Cmte on Commerce. 83-Ptn of Capt John Smith, claiming for Revolutionary services. 84-Ptn of Lt Scott Ketchum, of the U S army, for relief. 85-Ptn of the heirs of Matthew Armor, dec'd, for relief. 86-Ptn of Thos Stratton, of Beaver Co, Pa, a soldier of the Revolution, praying for remuneration for services in the Revolutionary war: referred to the Cmte on Revolutionary Claims. 87-Ptn of John Spier, of Mercer Co, Pa, praying to be placed on the pension list on account of services in the Indian war under Gen Wayne, by which his health was impaired & is now old & poor, & unable to support himself by labor: referred to the Cmte on Invalid Pensions. 88-Ptn of the heirs of Capt Robt Vance, dec'd, who served as a capt in the Revolutionary war, in the Va line, from 1776 to the end of the war, praying for commutation pay & interest, to which their father was entitled: referred to the Cmte on Revolutionary Claims. 89-Ptn of Simon Carley, of Beaver Co, Pa, a Revolutionary soldier, praying for a pension on account of his services: referred to the Cmte on Revolutionary Pensions. 90-Ptn of Wm Scott, of Beaver Co, Pa, praying for a pension on account of extraordinary exposure & loss of health in the service of the U S in the late war: referred to the Cmte on Invalid Pensions. 91-Ptn of Jas Scott, of Mercer Co, Pa, praying to be placed on the invalid pension list, on account of disability occasioned by exposure in the service of the U S in the late war: referred to the Cmte on Invalid Pensions. 92-Ptn of John Butts, of Dauphin Co, Pa, on behalf of himself & other heirs of Capt Hawkins Boon, an ofcr of the Revolution, praying for commutation under the resolution of Congress of 1780: referred to the Cmte on Claims. 93-Ptn of Robt Doak, praying remuneration for loses sustained in the Revolutionary war: referred to the Cmte of Claims. 94-Ptn of Josiah Westtake, of Mercer Co, Pa, praying for additional pension, which has been withheld from him from Mar 4, 1824, to Sep 4, 1831: referred to the Cmte on Invalid Pensions. 95-Ptn of Thos Hall, of Beaver Co, Pa, a soldier of the Revolutionary war, praying to be placed on the pension list, on account of Revolutionary services: referred to the Cmte on Revolutionary Pensions. 96-Ptn of John Killenger, of Mercer Co, Pa, a soldier of the late war, praying for a pension in consequence of loss of health, occasioned by exposure when in the service of his country: referred to the Cmte on Invalid Pensions.

In Chancery: Clk's ofc of the County Court of Pr Wm Co, for Feb 1840. Wm Dean, Aaron D Harmon, & Jos H Miller, joint merchants, mfgrs, & partners, trading under the firm of Dean, Harmon, & Miller, plnts, vs, Wm Sexsmith & Jas D Tennille, dfndnts. Wm Sexsmith, not having entered his appearance & given security: & not an inhabitant of this Cmnwlth, to appear here on May 1, 1840. –J Williams, Co Clk

SAT FEB 8, 1840
The Classical & Math Academy, in Gtwn, to be conducted by Wm R Abbot, late Principal of the Hagerstown Academy, will be opened on Feb 12th, in the brick house on Montg st, adjoining Mr Robt Ould's residence.

Senate: 1-Ptn of John S Morton, asking relief from liability of surety given for a certain paymstr in the army. 2-Ptn from Robt K McLaughlin. 3-Cmte on Pensions: asked to be discharged from the memorial of Saml Crapin, & that it be referred to the Cmte on Naval Affairs: expressing at the same time, an opinion of its justice. Also made adverse reports on the ptns of Abraham White & Wareham Kingsley. 4-Ptn from Sarah Ralston, asking remuneration for certain negroes. 5-Ptn from Jos Whipple, asking for payment for services in the ship *John Adams*. 6-Ptn from Messrs Quackenboss, Birdsall, & Chas L Livingston, sureties of Saml Swartwout, late collector of N Y, asking for an act to authorize a compromise with the Gov't of claims against them. 7-Cmte on Pensions: adverse report on the ptn of John Crawford. 8-Cmte of Claims: Adverse report on the ptn of W Hawkins. 9-Cmte on the Judiciary: bill for relief of John H Shepherd. 10-Bill for relief of John E Bisham.

Com'rs appointed by Montg Co Court, Md, to divide the land held & seized by the late Edw Burgess, sen, dec'd, of said county, give notice that they shall proceed on Apr 13 next, to divide: a tract called *Henry & Elizabeth*, & a tract adjoining called *Henry & Elizabeth Enlarged*: lying in said county, & a part of the land is in the occupancy of Elisha Etcheson, & part in the occupancy of Jeremiah Watkins.
–Henry Gaither, Thos Griffith, Remus Riggs

F Pettrich, Sculptor, having completed a statue of a Fisher Girl, in marble, invites the members of Congress & the public generally to call at his studio, near the Treas bldg, & examine, before its removal.

Lecture on Greece will be given by Mr C Plato Castanis, a native of Athens, at the Hall of the Medicine College, Feb 8, at 8 o'clock.

Appointments by the Pres: Geo W Jones, to be Surveyor of the Public Lands for the Terrs of Wisc & Iowa, from Apr 1, 1840. Wm E Sawyer, Receiver of Public Moneys at Mardisville, Ala, v Levi W Lawler, whose commission expired on Dec 31, 1839.

MON FEB 10, 1840
Dept of State: Wash, Feb 7, 1840. Information received that an adjustment has been effected with the British Gov't of the amount to be paid to owners of the slaves in the cases of the ship *Comet* & the ship *Encornium*, payment has been made to the U S bankers at London. Slaves shipped in the *Comet*, in D C, was 164, with a child born on passage-165. 19 deducted when no passage was allowed; 11 escaped as fugitives; 5 returned to servitude in the U S, 3 died, including the infant born on passage, leaving 146 of the *Comet's* cargo to be paid for. Insurance on that number, valued at $70,000, amount was taken as value of the 146 slaves for whom compensation was to be made of the *Comet's* cargo. Slaves on board the *Encornium* was 45: only 33 had comp made, on the ground that 12 had returned with their owners to the U S. Of the whole number, 13 only had been insured, at the value of $6,200. Amount allowed for the cargo was $15,739. To these sums interest at 4%, from the time of seizure until the probable time of payment, estimated at $27,360, was added, & for expenses at Nassau $1,900. Those interested in the cargoes of the above vesels will transmit to the Dept of State the evidence necessary to establish their right to indemnity, & to enable the Dept to make an apportionment of the money to be paid.

Mr Owen Downey, an elderly man, was taking his supper at the hotel of Mr Christy, in Wilmington, Dela, on Sat last, when he suddenly fell dead, as supposed, with an apoplectic fit. It was found a piece of beef steak, about 2 inches in length, of which he was eating, had lodged in his throat, & choked him to death. He was in perfect health at the time.

Mrd: on Sabbath last, by Rev Geo G Cookman, Mr Edw Ward to Miss Susanna Pierce, of Wash City.

36 years ago today, on Dec 25, at noon, says the New Orleans Courier, the flag of the U S replaced the flags of France & Spain on the Public Square & in the 5 forts which then defended New Orleans. The first house built in New Orleans was in 1717; but no plat was made of the city until 1729.

Hse o/Reps: 1-Ptn of John H Russell, & also of Knott Martin 3rd & Arnold Martin, for an allowance of bounty upon fishing vessels lost at sea. 2-Ptn of Sarah Graves, Thos Cloutman, Edw Brooks, Sarah Bean, Lucretia Brown, Rebecca Widger, & Eliz Converse, for pensions. 3-Ptn of Jos Janes, late inspec of Salem, for an allowance of a claim for services. 4-Ptn of Saml G Perkins & others, praying that measures be taken to procure indemnity for a large amount of property sequestered by the Gov't of Hayti, by order of Christophe. 5-Ptn of Timothy Powers for a pension: referred to the Cmte on Revolutionary Pensions. 6-Ptn of Isaac Chapman & 3 others, for claims as enlisted sldrs under the act of 1812: referred to the Cmte of Claims. 7-Memorial of Cadwalader Evans, of Pittsburg, regarding his invention of a safety-guard to prevent the explosion of steam-boilers. 8-Ptn of S Witherow & others, of Adams Co, Pa, praying for a duty on imported silk: referred to the Cmte on Mfgrs. 9-Ptn from Henry Gitt & others, of like import; from Henry W Slagle & others; from Saml S Forney & others; from Geo Hick & others; from Jas Cunningham & others. 10-Ptn of Geo W Wright & others, praying for a post route from Gettysburg to Arendtsville, & thence to Wilsonville, Adams Co, Pa. 11-Ptn of Cath Snyder, wid/o Geo Snyder, a soldier of the Revolution, praying for a pension. 12-Ptn of John Caldwell, a citizen of Phil, praying Congress to redeem certain depreciated paper money issued by the Continental Congress; one from Jas Cunningham, of like import. 13-Ptn & documents of Cath Rinker, wid/o of a Revolutionary soldier, for a pension. 14-Ptn of Mary Taylor & Mary Ann Bury, chldrn of a Revolutionary sldr. 15-Ptn & documents of Mary Campbell, wid/o John Campbell, a Revolutionary soldier, asking for a pension. 16-Ptn of Thos R Fisher & others, of Pa, mfgrs, asking Congress to adopt measures to prevent fraud in the importation of foreign goods. 17-Ptn from Edwin F Shoenberger & others, of Bedford Co, Pa, to revise the laws of the collection of duties, & make them more effectual in preventing frauds. 18-Ptn of Danl Young & others, of same county & state, of similar import. 19-Ptn of Robt Graham, of Westmoreland Co, Pa, to confirm his right to certain lands in Ill. 20-Ptn from Pliny Hayes, a Revolutionary soldier, for increase of pension. 21-Ptn of Abram Bean & others, on the rate of postage on letters. 22-Ptn from Wm Kellar, of Bedford Co, Pa, a soldier in the late war, for a pension. 23-Ptn from the heirs of Lt Col Jas Piper, for compensation for the services rendered by their ancestor. 24-Ptn from Abraham Morrison, of Cambria Co, Pa, one of the sureties of the late Capt Webster, Postmaster at Somerset, Pa, to refund money unjustly collected. 25-Memorial signed by Jos Henderson, of Wash Co, Pa, who is one of the heirs & atty in fact for the other heirs of Richd Dalliner, late of Dela, dec'd. Ptn sets forth that R Dalliner, as Capt in the militia, in the state of Dela, served during the whole of the Revolutionary war, & requests that the ptnrs may be allowed 5 years pay & the usual quantity of land granted to Capts of the Continental Army: referred to the Cmte on

Revolutionary Claims. 26-Ptn of Robt Haysham, for arrears of compensation for services in the Custom-hse in Phil. Of C G Childs & others, for a light-hse on Brandywine shoal. Of Wm Singleton, for a pension. Of John Girard Ford, for compensation for 2 years servicex in the Custom-hse in Phil. Of Strickland, Gill & Co, for remission of duties on plates for engravings. Of Robt Brady, a claim for a vessel destroyed during the late war. Of Edw Thomas & others, for duty on silk imported. Of Dr R Coates & W R Johnson, for compensation for services & losses connected with the Exploring Expedition. Of John W Randall, for the same. Of Dr J F Caldwell, for compensation under a mail contract. Of Mrs Susan Bainbridge, for arrears of pension due the late Com Bainbridge. 27-Memorial of John Spaulding & others, for compensation for a large number of hogsheads of tobacco taken by the British during the late war with Great Britain: referred to the Cmte on Foreign Affairs. 28-Memorial of Thos C Lyles & others, for remuneration for property destroyed during the Revolutionary war: referred to the Cmte on Revolutionary Claims. 29-Memorial of Theodore Middleton, a Revolutionary sldr. 30-Memorial of Augustus Willet, rep of Jos R Willett. 31-Ptns from Thos, exc of John Barnes, from Saml Atcherson, from Rector Mitchell, from Wm Hebb, of D C, & from the reps of Nathl Davis: referred to appropriate cmtes. 32-Memorial of W A Bradley, Pres of the Patriotic Bank of D C: praying for renewal of its charter. 33-Memorial of Isaac Lea, recommending Dauphin, Pa, as a suitable site for the establishment of a Nat'l Foundry. 34-Memorial of Wm Lyman, on the subject of a Nat'l Foundry & iron. 35-Ptn of Capt Wm Quantrill, for a pension for wounds received in the last war with Great Britain. 36-Ptn of Robt Moncrief, for a pension. 37-Ptn of Saml Quarles, of Bedford Co, Va, for an allowance for carrying the mail from Pittsylvania C H, Va, to Patrick C H, Va: referred to the Cmte on the P O & Post Roads. 38-Ptn of Clayton & Mitchell, of Franklin Co, Va, to be paid the arrears of pension of Wm Kemplin, dec'd, a Revolutionary sldr: referred to the Cmte on Revolutionary Pensions. 39-Ptn of John Murcheson, of Campbell Co, Va, praying compensation for Revolutionary services: referred to the Cmte on Revolutionary Claims. 40-Ptns of the heirs of Maj Thos Massie, Capt Jas Dillard, Capt Thos Thweat, Capt Tarpley White, & of Capt John Mark, for commutation pay. 41-Ptn of the heirs of Lt John Piper, to be relieved against a forged land warrant. 42-Ptn of Jos Scott, for Revolutionary services. 43-Ptn of the heirs of Col Wm Lewis, & the heirs of Col Chas Lewis, for commutation pay. 44-Ptns of John Thompson, Neil Shannon, Peter Ambler, & Jos Cubberly, asking to be placed on the invalid pension list. 45-Ptn of Adam Floeher, an old soldier, praying to be released from a judgment obtained against him in the U S court for the western dist of Va. 46-Ptn of Chas Collins, Pres of Emory & Henry College, with 95 other citizens of Western Va, praying for a reduction of letter postage: referred. 47-Ptn from Jas S Calhoun, of Columbus, Ga, asking remuneration for losses & damages sustained by the acts of the military ofcrs & authorized agents of the Genr'l Gov't, by impressing his property for public use, & violating, for the public interest, certain contracts solemnly entered into between the said Jas S Calhoun & the Gov't: referred to the Cmte of Claims, with accompanying documents. 48-Ptn from Gen Duncan L Clinch, of St Mary's, Ga, asking pay for supplies furnished, taken, & used by the ofcrs & sldrs of the Gen'l

Gov't, belonging to him, all of which were used during the Fla campaigns: referred to the Cmte of Claims. 49-Ptn from John McKennie, of Augusta, Ga, praying compensation for securing a certain debt due the U S: referred to the Cmte of Claims. 50-Letter from Jas Edmondson, Postmaster at Cohuttah Springs, Murray Co, Ga, in relation to a mail route. 51-Ptn of John Dennis, a superannuated ofcr of the custom-hse in Savannah, asking additional pay for his long services: referred to the Cmte on Commerce. 52-Ptn of Wm Mosely & others, of Ga, asking the establishment of a post route: referred. 53-Ptn of Sutherland Mayfield, asking a pension for the loss of a limb whilst in the U S army in the war of 1812: referred to the Cmte on Invalid Pensions. 54-Papers on the files of the Hse on the claim of the late Col Simeon Knight, Paymstr in the U S army, were referred to the Cmte of Claims. 55-Ptn from M Gregory & others, for a new post route from Portsmouth, Scioto Co, via Locust Grove, to Hillsoborough, Highland Co, Ohio: referred. 56-Ptn from D C Carson & others, praying for the reduction of postage: referred. 57-Ptn from John Peebles, of Scioto Co, Ohio, praying for increased compensation for certain services as collector of taxes: referred to the Cmte of Claims. 58-Ptn from Chas H Smith, for some adequate compensation for a certain tract of land entered by him within the Va miltary dist in Ohio, but improvidently sold by the U S to others: referred to the Cmte on Public Lands. 59-Ptn from Cadwallader Wallace, of Ross Co, Ohio, praying for adequate compensation for lands entered by claimants in satisfaction of Va military continental land warrants within the Va military dist in Ohio, but which have been improvidently sold by the U S: referred. 60-Ptn of Merrifield Vickory, of Clark Co, Ohio, praying that certain arrears of pension may be allowed & paid to him. 61-Ptns of Timothy Cook, John Metcalf, Isaac Cook, & Philip Riker, all for indemnity for property lost in the war of 1812: referred to the Cmte of Claims. 62-Ptn of Thos Richmond, for leave to enter public lands: referred. 63-Ptn of Ruel Stanton & others, for a post route: referred. 64-Ptn of P Ramsey & others, & B B Hunter: reduce postage: referred.

The d/o the Rev Gilbert Mason, of Wash, Ky, was recently burnt so as to cause death by her clothes catching fire.

Henry Bishop, 10 years a messenger of the Patent Ofc, writes a card explaining his removal from ofc. A dead letter had been received from the G P O, addressed to his son David J Bishop, at Cincinnati, Ohio, in his hand-writing, bearing the Com'rs frank. As the Com'r said he never franked the letter, he wished an explanation. Bishop said he did wrong in making use of the frank without the Com'rs knowledge, but from the very liberal manner in which the franking privilege had been used in the ofc, he was not aware that it would be considered as so great an offence. The subscriber being out of employment, & having a large family to support, offers his services to any person or persons that may wish to employ him. --Henry Bishop

On Thu last, Mr P Haas, Lithographer, of Wash City, was attacked on Pa ave, cruelly by 3 persons. Fri last the accused were arrested. Mr Haas is recovering from his wounds.

TUE FEB 11, 1840

Hse o/Reps: 1-Ptn of the chldrn & other heirs of Lt Danl Starr for pay for their father's services as a Lt on board the U S ship *Trumbull*. 2-Ptn of Griswold Avery, asking for a pension for Revolutionary services. 3-Ptn of Mrs Esther Colver, late the wid/o Moses Jones, for a pension. 4-Ptn of the heirs of Lt Nathl Fanning, dec'd, asking that a medal be given for his act of bravery on board the ship *Good Man Richard*, under Cmdor John Paul Jones, & for prize money arising from said service. 5-Ptn of Jas Williams for compensation for services & expenses in arresting a deserter from the U S army in 1834. 6-Ptn of Nathan Smith & others for allowance of bounty on a fishing voyage to the Straits of Belle Isle. 7-Ptn of O J Loy & others of Lyme, Conn, mfgrs of wool, asking that the laws for the collection of duties, in order to prevent frauds to the prejudice of the honest mfgrs, be revised. 8-Ptn of Asa & Jabez L White, of Bolton, Conn, praying a release from their contracts for carrying the U S mail. 9-Ptn of Mary Ripley, of Coventry, Conn, wid/o Jabez Ripley, a soldier of the Revolution, for a pension. 10-Ptn of Eliz Hill, of Sterling, wid/o Parker Hill, a Revolutionary soldier, for a pension. 11-Ptn of Esther Sawyer, of, wid/o Azariah Sawyer, a soldier of the Revolution, for a pension. 12-Ptn of Desire Jolly, wid/o Wm Jolly, a soldier of the Revolution, praying for an increase of pension. 13-Ptn of Martha McMasters, wid/o Hugh McMasters, a soldier of the Revolution, praying for arrears of pension. 14-Ptn of Effe Van Ness, wid/o Garret Van Ness, an ofcr of the Revolution, praying for a pension. 15-Ptn of Geo Newton, of Fulton Co, N Y, a soldier of the last war with Great Britain, praying to be restored to the invalid pension roll. 16-Ptn of Mary & Eliz Odill, only surviving chldrn of A W Odill, who was a Capt & Maj in the last war, & died of wounds received in said war, praying for 5 years full pay for the services of their father. 17-Ptn of Chas Nukirk, stating that he held a commission in the U S army in 1814, & that in the battle of Oswego, N Y, in said year, the enemy took from him all his effects, consisting of money, & clothing, for which he prays relief. 18-Ptn of the heirs at law of Jellis Fonda, praying compensation for property belonging to said Fonda, which was destroyed in the Mohawk Valley, N Y, by the common enemy, in the Revolutionary war. 19-Ptn of Esther Lefferts, late wid/o Wm S Thom, dec'd, a Lt in the Revolutionary army, praying payment of the commutation of half pay to which her said husband was entitled. 20-Ptn of Joshua Webster & others, citizens of N Y, praying that Simon D Kittle, of Montg Co, N Y, be released from a judgement of $20,000, obtained against him by the U S as surety for Alphonso Wetmore, late paymstr in the U S army. 21-Ptn for relief of Brig Gen Peter C Fox, & of Mrs Eliz Davidson; the former for services, in the late war with Great Britain, & the latter for a pension for services of her dec'd husband, G Davidson, in the Revolutionary war. 22-Ptn of F Pellicer & others, praying relief from an award of the Sec of the Treas, under the law of 1834, for the loses sustained by the operations of the U S troops in Fla. 23-Ptn of John P Baldwin, of Key West, praying compensation for property lost by order of the commandng ofcr, to prevent said property, being mostly land, from falling into the hands of the Indians. 24-Ptn of Capt J Y Smith, praying compensation for the loss of steamboat *Hyperion*. 25-Claim of Dr Weedon for property taken by militia in service of the U S: & for medicine furnished by Hewlett as ast surgeon, & for medical services to the U S. 26-Claim of Mr McDonald for a horse. 27-Claim of J Elzuardi, asking remuneration for a slave taken by the U S as Indian interpreter & sent to Arkansas. 28-Claim of Dr Turner for a horse. 29-Claim of W G Saunders for property destroyed by the U S army. 30-Ptn of J Croskey & others. 31-Claim of the heirs of Manuel Domingues to a tract of land. 32-Claims of Capt T C Rudolph; of Capt Clark; of Capt Peters. 33-Ptn of Capt Jacob Houseman for pay for military services. 34-Claim of Dr Clarke & Dr Forry vs U S for medical services. 35-Claim of Dr Worrell vs U S for medical services.

Mrd: on Feb 4, in Gtwn, by Rev Mr Hoff, Laurason Riggs, of Ill, to Miss Sophia Theresa, d/o Joel Cruttenden.

Mrd: on Feb 6, at Gtwn, D C, at the residence of Capt Boyce, by Rev Mr Slaughter, Geo W Peter to Jane, d/o the late Roger Boyce, all of Md.

Mrd: on Jan 28, at Holly Grove, Northampton Co, Va, by Rev Mr Jackson, Mr Tully W Parker, of Accomack, to Miss Mgt T Evans, of the former place.

Died: on Sun last, at his residence, in Gtwn, Mr Francisco Pizarro Martinez, late Envoy Extra & Minister Pleni of the Republic of Mexico. His funeral is this morning at 10 a m.

Died: Jan 31, Winchester, Va, Col Geo Orrick, many years Cashier of the Farmers' Bank there.

$10 Reward for strayed horse: return to Levi Pumphrey, of Wash City, or Jesse Lipscomb, of Gtwn. -Robt Balding

WED FEB 12, 1840
Hse o/Reps: 1-Cmte on the P O & Post Roads to inquire into establishing a post route from Perry C H, Ky, to Harlan C H, Ky, passing by Breshear's Salt Works in Perry Co, & Capt John Lewis' hse, upon the Poor fork of Cumberland river, in Harlan Co: a horse mail, weekly. 2-Cmte on Revolutionary Pensions to inquire into granting pensions to:
Mrs Eliz Christer, wid/o Danl Christer
Mrs Mary Millbank, wid/o John Millbank
Mrs Eliz Adkins, wid/o Jas Adkins
Mrs Sally Sanders, wid/o Nathl Sanders
Wm Bowier
Mrs Mary Biggs, wid/o Randolph Biggs
Mrs Susan Catlett
John Casey
Mrs Mgt Smith, wid/o Jared Smith
Solomon Jarvis

Mrs Mgt Penn, wid/o Maj Shadrach Penn
Jeremiah Adams
Mrs Rhody Polk, wid/o Ephrain Polk
Mrs Lydia Rogers, wid/o Kinsley Rogers
Mrs Franky Quinn, wid/o Benj Quinn
Mrs Janet McClure, wid/o Thos McClure
Mrs Jane Johnson, wid/o Saml Cooper
Mrs Mgt McCaw, wid/o Michl Downes
Mrs Martha Conly, wid/o Ensign Arthur Conly
Mrs Frances Chandler, wid/o Lt Danl Chandler
Mrs Martha Lemon, wid/o Ensign John Lemon
Mrs Eliza Hampton, wid/o Preston Hampton
Mrs Mgt Hamilton, wid/o Lt Chas Hamilton
3-Cmte on Revolutionary Pensions to inquire into placing Delila Morris, the wid/o Holloway Morris, dec'd, a Revolutionary soldier, on the pension roll. 4-Cmte on Invalid Pensions: to inquire into allowing Nicholas Darnel, an invalid pensioner, of Carroll Co, Tenn, a pension from the commencement of his disability. 4-Cmte on Revolutionary Claims: to inquire into allowing the claim of Benj Sammons for services during the Revolutionary war: papers on file.

Senate: 1-Ptn from Abner Jones, of La, asking improvements at the mouths of the Ohio & Mississippi rivers. 2-Cmte on Pvt Lands: bill for relief of Gregoire Sarpy. 3-Letter of Jacob Olinger, a Revolutionary soldier, of Carroll Co, Ind, praying a law allowing pensions to all Revolutionary sldrs who served 3 months in the Revolutionary army: referred. 4-Cmte on Revolutionary Pensions: to inquire into placing Thos Fulton, a resident of Lawrence Co, Ala, on the pension roll of Revolutionary pensioners. 5-Cmte on Invalid Pensions: to inquire into allowing a pension to Madison Collins, of Warren Co, Ind. 6-Claim of Francis Malone for compensation for Revolutionary services be referred to the Cmte of Claims. 7-Cmte of Claims: to inquire into allowing additional comp to Capt John Nelson, of Ind, & others, who were made prisoners during the late war with Great Britain, & that the letter of said Nelson in favor of said claim be referred.

Balt-on Feb 7: Augustus Rackel, a young man in the employ of Mr Baxter, gunsmith, in Pratt st, accidentally shot & killed himself. Mr Baxter was so affected, it caused his own death, very shortly after. –Patriot

Mrd: on Sabbath last, by Rev Geo G Cookman, Mr Emmanuel Longson to Miss Mary Irvine, all of Wash City.

Died: Feb 7, at the residence of her son-in-law, Wm B Kibbey, in her 73rd year, Mrs Susan Rinker, a native of St Mary's Co, Md, a resident of Alexandria for 50 years, & of this city for the last 7 years, of a lingering illness, leaving her 3 dghts & 1 son, & numerous relatives, to mourn their irreparable loss.

Died: on board U S frig *Constitution*, 3 days before her late arrival at Valparaiso, Lt Pinkham, U S N.

City Ord-Wash. Act of relief: Jas Phalen & Co & P H Borland: issue licenses for vending lottery tickets.

THU FEB 13, 1840
Senate: 1-Ptn from Jas M Morgan, asking compensation for acting as bearer of despatches. 2-Ptn from Simeon Givin, asking to locate a certain tract of land. 3-Ptn from John P Kunklee, asking compensation for carrying the mail. 4-Documents relating to the claim of Sarah McKay. 5-Cmte of Claims: adverse reports on the memorials of: Jos Ratcliffe, of John Morton & John Lancaster, of David Taylor, of Thos Elliot & of Britton Evans. 6-Cmte on Public Lands: bill for relief of Jos Roby. 7-Cmte of Claims: adverse report on the ptn of Seymour Treat.

Notice: The creditors of Nathan Smith, provided for in a deed of trust to the subscribers, as trustees, are notified that further dividend is now ready to be made. –Edw Dyer, Thos Blagden, trustees

The *Chain bridge* across the Potomac, at the Little Falls, has been entirely carried away, & its timbers have come down river.

Sale of valuable real estate: by decree of the Crct Court of Wash Co, D C: Anthony Preston, & Rosina, admx of Archibald Cheshire, vs, Mary Linsey Cheshire & others, heirs at law of A Cheshire. –In Chancery By decree of Jan 6, 1840, public sale of the title & estate of Archibald Cheshire, dec'd: real estate in Wash City: pt of lot 1 in sq 267 on Md ave, with frame tenement thereon. Also, lot 2 in sq 267, beginning on Md ave. Also, lot 16 in sq 267, on 13½ st, with 2 frame bldgs thereon. –J B H Smith, trustee -Edw Dyer, auct

For sale: storehse, dwlg, & houses, with some land, near Goshen, Montg Co, Md. –B Magill, Goshen

Died: on Feb 5, at his residence in Caroline Co, Md, John Boon, a Senator in the Leg of Md for the dist in which he resided. His illness was of a short duration, as he had only just arrived at home on a visit from Annapolis, Md.

FRI FEB 14, 1840
Supreme Court of the U S: Feb 13: #56-Lessee of Henry E Sloat, plntf, vs, John Haughwout et al. By consent of parties this cause, from the Crct Court of the U S for the southern dist of N Y, was dismissed.

Mrd: on Tue last, in Wash City, by Rev Geo G Cookman, Mr John Greaves to Miss Amanda Boyd.

For the South: first rate steamboat will leave the end of Spear's wharf, Balt, every Mon, Wed, & Fri mornings, at 10 a m. for Norfolk & Charleston. This line connects with the Portsmouth R R & the Jas river boats for Petersburg & Richmond. –J W Brown, agent

Steamboat line for Phil, via New Castle & Frenchtown Trnpk & R R: leaving Bowly's wharf, Balt, at 6 p m daily, except Sun. Passage through $4. Meals as usual. –T Sheppard, agent, Balt.

SAT FEB 15, 1840
Senate: 1-Memorial of Saml E Coves & 159 others, citizens of Portsmouth, N H, upon the subject of a Congress of Nations.

Edenton Sentinel: on Jan 24, the dwlg house of Miss Patsey Ward, near Windsor, Bertie Co, was consumed by fire together with all its inmates, consisting of an elderly lady, 3 chldrn, & Miss Ward herself. Two sons of the elderly lady reached the scene only in time to see their only parent buried beneath the burning timber.

Boston Patriot: Mrs Eliza Jarvis, the lady of Russell Jarvis, who, with her 2 chldrn, perished in the last casualty of the steamboat *Lexington*, was the only surviving d/o Thos Cordis, & grand-dght of the late Thos Kemble, of your city. She was a niece of the late Caleb Bingham & a cousin of the wife of Gen Towson, of the U S army, a lady most highly respected at Washington, & of Col H K Oliver, of Salem. Mr Cordis has again been subjected to the deepest affliction, having followed to the tomb 2 wives, &, with the exception of Mrs Jarvis, [now, alas] added to the melancholy list, the entire family by his first wife. Mrs Jarvis was about 37 years of age, her elder dght 13, & her younger 7.

Trustee's sale: by decree of the Court of Chancery of Md: at Good Luck, in PG Co, Md: a tract of land in said county called *Arthur's Seat Enlarged*, being part of the real estate of John Contee, late of said county, dec'd: contains about 237 acs, & adjoins the lands of Chas Duvall, Trueman Lanham, & others. Improvements consist of a good dwlg house, & out-houses. –J Johnson, trustee [Subscriber is also authorized to sell a parcel of land belonging to the estate of the dec'd, about 25 acs, in D C, & adjoins the property of Col Bomford, called *Kalorama*. Direct mail to Annapolis.]

Orphans Court of Wash Co, D C. Letters of administration on personal estate of Mordecai Foy, late of said county, dec'd. –Ann Foy, admx

Died: on Feb 14, Gracey Ann Bowin, of a lingering illness. Funeral from her late residence on 11th st, between F & G sts, this morning at 11 a m.

Died: at his late residence on 6th st, in his 54th year, Dr Benj Thompson, late of Concord, N H, an eminent Botanical Physician. [No date-current item.]

MON FEB 17, 1840
Orphans Court of Wash Co, D C. Letters of administration on personal estate of Saml Hamilton, formerly of England, & late of Wash Co, dec'd. Persons with claims are to exhibit them to John H Sherburne, of Wash City, on or before Feb 11 next. —Geo Actland, adm

Appointments by the Pres: Henry Ulshoeffer, to be U S Cnsl for Trinidad de Cuba. Manuel Alvarez, to be U S Cnsl for Santa Fe, Mexico. Philip A de Creny, to be U S Cnsl for the Isl of Martinque. John Wm Van den Broeck, to the U S Cnsl for Amsterdam. Wm Harrison H Griffiths, to be Commercial Agent of the U S for the Isl of Mauritius. John Henry Young, to be Clk to the Com'r for marking the boundary line between the U S & the Republic of Texas. Robt J Hackley, Register of the Land Ofc at Tallahassee, Fla, from Dec 31, 1839, when his late commission expired. John A Cavedo, Surveyor & Inspec of the Rev at Fernandina, Fla, v Domingo Acosta, resigned.

Indian murders in Fla: St Jos, Jan 29. Express received Tue from Iola, with letter from Mr J L Smallwood, merchant of that place, stating that on Mon the family of Mrs Harlan, about 6 miles from Iola, were all murdereed & the premises burnt, by a party of Indians. A company under the command of Col Fitzpatrick, has gone in pursuit of them.

$150 reward for runaway negro man Moses, about 6 feet high. He left Mr Sheckelford, in Charlotte Hall, St Mary's Co, Md, to whom he was hired.
—Ann Posey, near Gtwn

Article headed by *old member of Congress* had 2 errors: the venerable W Findley, of Westmoreland Co, Pa, served in Congress only 22 years, but was never a member of the Senate; he died on Apr 7, 1821. Wm Findlay, of Franklin Co, Pa, was elected to the Senate in 1821, & served 6 years; his time of service commencing with the 1st session of the 17th Congress, after the decease of the former. You will observe their names are differently spelled, tho pronounced the same. —John Findley, Springfield, Mercer Co, Pa: Feb 6, 1840.

Mrd: on Feb 13, in Balt, by Rev Mr Duncan, N Fred'k Blackbock to Sarah E B, 2nd d/o John Dushane, all of that city.

Died: on Jan 30 last, in St Louis, Miss Mary H Mauro, 3rd d/o Col P Mauro, formerly of Wash City.

We learn on Fri, that Baptista Gluck was one of the persons lately committed to the jail of this county, in default of bail, to answer to the charge of assaulting & cruelly wounding Mr Philip Haas. [We learn that Mr Gluck was released from prison, having found satisfactory bail to the amount of $1,000.]

Information wanted: if the Rev Geo R Parburt is living he will confer a favor by letting the subscriber know his place of residence. –John Lacy

Jos Francis, inventor of Francis' Patent Life Boat, has been asked to give genr'l information as to the proper method of using the boat.

Obit–died: on Feb 6, at Feeding Hills, in Springfield, Mass, Levi H Clarke, of N Y: graduate of Yale College, came early to the bar of Conn: his residence was at Middletown, Conn: appointed to the ofc of State's atty. About 1816 he emigrated, with some friends, to the then infant city of Rochester, where he invested his money partly in wild land, but mostly in the Carthage bridge: a disastrous speculation. In a single night he was deprived of the greater portion of his property. On the organization of Monroe Co, he was app't one of the judges of the county, but did not long continue there. Quitting the bar, he resorted to his pen for support. While the late Johston Verplanck was the editor of the American, Mr Clarke was his assistant. In 1825 & 26 he traveled to England, returning in 1827, to which time he purchased the Morning Herald. Later he was incapacitated with several repeated strokes of paralysis. –N Y Com [Mr Clarke was a Reporter for the Nat'l Intell in the Hse o/Reps during the session of 1821-22.]

Information wanted of my husband, John M Johnson, who has been absent from his disconsolate wife & 5 chldrn upwards of 4 years. Mr Johnson was raised in Conn: is a slender man, about 6 ft high, about 45 years of age. I have reason to believe he was in N Y C last spring. Should this reach his eye, I would once more solicit his return to his helpless wife & little chldrn. Any information directed by letter to me, Berryville, Clark Co, Va, will be thankfully received. –Mary Johnson

House to rent: with or without the furniture: at corner of Gay & Green sts, Gtwn, well known as the property of the late Wm Williamson, & recently occupied by the Mexican Minister. For terms apply to Mrs Kennedy's, Pa ave. Possession on Mar 15. –Jane W Williamson

Training stable on the Wash Race-course will open in a few days. Services of a good trainer will be engaged. -Wm Holmead

For sale, or to let: the undersigned, throught the kindness of his landlord, having the privilege of redeeming the pair of small tenements lately sold under the bell by a pair of his creditors in the dead of winter, would offer them for sale or to let on favorable terms. –Danl Pierce

TUE FEB 18, 1840
The Rt Rev Bishop Meade, of Va, will preach in Trinity Chr this evening at 7 o'clock, p m.

In Chancery: Walter F Boarman, vs, Walter Jamison & others. Object of the bill in this case is to obtain an injunction to restrain proceedings at law against the cmplnt, to compel the dfndnts to interplead & to settle their several claims & demands as the legatees, reps, & next of kin of Benedict Jamison & Saml Jamison, late of Chas Co, dec'd. Benedict Jamison died in 1837, having, by his will, appointed the cmplnt & Walter Jamison his excs; that Walter renouncing, letters testamentary were granted to the cmplnt, who has made considerable progress in settling the estate; that the test bequeatherd his personal estate, in certain proportions, to his brother Walter Jamison, his nephew John H Mudd, his niece Emily Mudd, his sister Mary Mudd, & his nieces Sally Maria Jamison & Josephine Jamison; that the testator, Benedict Jamison, was one of the sons of Saml Jamison, who died in 1830 intestate, & leaving as his heirs at law & personal reps the said Benedict, Mary mrd to Ignatius Mudd, Chas Jamison, since dec'd, leaving the said Sally Maria & Josephine Jamison his infant dghts, & Walter Jamison, chldrn of his first marriage; that he also left Rosella, since mrd to John L Lancaster, & Saml D Jamison, chldrn by his 2nd marriage; that shortly before the death of the said Saml Jamison he conveyed to the said Benedict Jamison a consideralbe number of negroes, & that they constitute a portion of the property distributable among his personal reps; that John L Lancaster & wife & Saml D Jamison allege that the said conveyance, whatever may have been its form, was intended as mere trust for the use of the grantor, & that, consequently, the said Benedict called not dispose of the property therein contained by his will, but that upon the death of Saml it was distributable among his personal reps, including themselves; that Lancaster & wife & Saml D Jamison also allege that Benedict Jamison was, from mental imbecility, incapable of making a will, [under which they take no interest,] & that they, as a portion of his personal reps, are entitled to participate in the distribution of his estate, which allegations of the said Lancaster & wife & Saml D Jamison are denied by the aforesaid legatees of the said Benedict; that the cmplnt, tho ready & willing to pay whatever surplus may remain in his hands, when the same shall be ascertianed, to the parties entitled, cannot, in consequence of these conflicting claims, do so with safety to himself; that some of the parties have sued him, & that he apprehends others will do so, unless restrained by the intervention of this Court; that said Ignatius Mudd & Mary his wife, John H Mudd, & Mary Mudd, chldrn of said Mary, reside in D C, out of the jurisdiction of this Court. Same to appear on or before Jul 7 next. –Ramsay Waters, reg c c

Great sale of real estate: on the premises, the whole of the *Montpelier Estate*, including the mansion of the late John Thomson Mason, in Wash Co, Md, containing 3,500 acs of prime limestone land. Estate conveyed to the subscribers, in trust, by Abraham Barnes & others. Lands are already divided into compact & well-arranged farms, but will be sold in still smaller tracts if desired by purchasers. Title to these lands has been judicially settled by the highest tribunal in the state, & is therefore undoubted. –Wm Price, D G Yost, trustees. Persons wishing to view the lands are to call on Dr Wharton or Melchor B Mason, on the premises, or either, in Hagerstown, Md.

Monsieur Piotr Kowalewski informs he is at Mrs Middleton's brdg-hse, Pa ave, & ready to open a school for the instruction in the knowledge of the French language.

Thu last, an eulogium on the character of the late Robt Y Hayne, of Charleston, was delivered there by Gen McDuffie. The whole city united in the ceremonies & business was suspended for the day.

Mrd: on Feb 13, by Rev Mr Dubison, Mr Wm P Pumphry to Miss Anne Maria Palmer, d/o John Palmer, all of PG Co, Md.

Died: on Feb 13, at Sandy Spring, Md, Jas P Stabler, in his 44th year.

The steamboat *Fredericksburg* will commence her route between Balt & the Dist, on the 22nd, leaving Balt every Sat at 4 o'clock. Geo Guyther, master

WED FEB 19, 1840
Firemen's Convention on Wed next, at half past 7, at the Hall of Franklin Fire Co. –Edm Hanly, sec

The broad pennant of Cmdor Warrington was shifted on Fri from the U S ship *Java* to the ship *Delaware*, of 80 guns, Capt C W Skinner, the receiving ship at that port.

Senate: 1-Ptn from Jas Delano, in relation to French spoliations prior to 1800. 2-Ptn from Alex'r Vattemere, proposing a plan for interchange of copies of valuable books, specimens of natural history & fine arts, between this Gov't & other civilized nations of the world. 3-Memorial of Hall J Kelly, in relation to the establishment of a colony at Oregon, & a grant of land to the said Kelly, may be favorably considered. This memorial seemed to take an active interest in promoting the views of Mr Kelly, & shows forth the the services he has rendered in exploring the trackless wilds of Oregon. 4-Ptn from the heirs of R K Meade. 5-Cmte on Revolutionary Claims: bill for relief of the heirs of Danl Pyatt. 6-Cmte on Pvt Land Claims: bill for relief of the heirs of Miguel Esclava. Also, adverse report on the ptn of the heirs of Anderson Lane. 7-Cmte on Pensions: adverse report on the ptns of Ebenezer Swann, Susannah R Pickett, & Avan Cramp. 8-Cmte of Claims to inquire into comp for N G Hamilton for a horse pressed into the U S service in Fla. 9-Bill for relief of John H Shepherd, adm of Abiel Wood: considered in Cmte of the Whole, ordered to be engrossed for a 3rd reading. 10-Papers on the files relating to the heirs of Wm Walker: referred to the Cmte of Claims. 11-Cmte of D C: bill for relief of Adam G Stewart. Also to be discharged from further consideration of the ptns of Thos L Bone, Gilbert Walker, N B Hill, & Wright Groom. 12-Cmte of Claims: bill for relief of Jas B Morgan. Also, adverse report on the ptns of Abraham Williamson, John G Mackall, & Fleming Wood. 13-Cmte on Public Lands: bill for relief of John W Monette; also, for the relief of David B Bush. 14-Cmte on Pvt Land Claims: to inquire into granting 80 acs of land to Chas M'Kenzie in lieu of a similar quantity sold to him by the land ofc at Monroe, Mich, the tract so sold being overspread by the lake.

For sale: the bldg formerly occupied by the under signed as a Cabinet & Chair Mfgr, on La ave: to the highest bidder, without restriction. Business carried on at the new stand on Pa ave. –Jas Williams

U S Supr Court, Feb 10, 1840. Honors paid to the memory of Jos M White, of Fla. Chief Justice Taney present: the Hon Saml L Southard called to the chr, Gen Walter Jones appointed sec. Resolution by Jos R Ingersoll to wear the usual badge of mourning during the residue of the term.

Mrd: on Feb 16, by Rev Mr Smith, Jos W Walker, formerly of Fred'k, Md, to Miss Sarah Frances Lee, of Balt, Md.

Mrd: on Feb 13, at Gtwn, by Rev Mr Hamilton, Mr Jas W Doughty, of St Louis, Mo, to Miss Mgt, d/o Wm S Nicholls.

Reward of $2 for return of my lost free papers, that I lost on Mon, in going from E st down 12th st. They were given from the Clk's ofc in Alexandria. To the best of my knowledge they were given in 1832. Age 19 years, with a scar in the middle finger of the right hand, 5 feet 7¾ inches high. I was born free, as will be seen by the evidence of Cath Gray. –Jas Butler

THU FEB 20, 1840
Appointments by the Pres: A H Hall, Receiver of Public Moneys at Augusta, Miss, from Feb 17, v Jas L Jolly, who did not qualify. Isaac W Jewett, Collector of the Customs for the dist of Pearl river, Miss, v Saml Learned, resigned. Wm Halloway, Surveyor & Inspec of Rev, at North Kingston, R I, Feb 15, when his late commission expired. John M Moriarty, Surveyor & Inspec of the Rev, at Gloucester, Mass, v Alphonso Mason, dec'd.

Died: on Feb 10, at the residence of Dr Richd S Culbreth, in Caroline Co, John H Culbreth, formerly Sec of State of Md, & s/o the Hon Thos Culbreth.

Died: Feb 14, at Balt, Ann Odle Hilleary, infant d/o Wm & Mary Hillman, at PG Co, Md, aged 11 months.

Appointments of Deputy Postmastr:
Azariah C Flagg, at Albany, N Y
Saml Workman, at Wash, Pa
Jas S Gunnell, at Wash, D C
Alex'r Galt, at Norfolk, Va
Abraham Coryell, at Easton, Pa
Chas K Miller, at Bangor, Maine
Wm McQueen, at New Orleans, La
Jos Blair, at Columbus, Miss
Allen Romlin, at Galena, Ill
John W Townsend, at Mobile, Ala
John H Lord, at Oswego, N Y
Geo L Douglass, at Louisville, Ky
Nathl Mitchell, at Portland, Maine
Chas W Woodbury, at Salem, Mass, v Ebenezer Putnam, removed

Senate: 1-Ptn from Capt E Shaler, asking a pension. 2-Cmte on the Judiciary: adverse report on the ptn of the heirs of Silence Elliot. 3-Cmte of Claims: bill for the relief of John E Bispham. 4-Cmte on the Judiciary: adverse report on the memorial of the assignee of David Beard. 5-To be engrossed for a 3rd reading: relief of Chas Morgan, of La; relief of Jos Cochran; relief of Alvarez Fish, & the legal reps of Thos P Eskridge; relief of the heirs & legal reps of Wm Conway; relief of Pierre Babin; relief of the heirs of Madam de Lusser; relief of Jos Campau.

Crct Court of Wash Co, D C: Nov Term, 1839. Robt Oliver's excs, vs, Susan Decatur: in Chancery. Jas Dunlop & Jno Marbury, trustees in the cause, having reported to the Court, pursuant to the decree, they have sold land called *The Long Meadows*, to Wm A Bradley, for $1,230, & lot 5 in sq 170 in Wash, to B O Tayloe, for $832.27: ordered & decreed that the sales be ratified. -Wm Brent, clk

The barn of Col Thos N Burwell, about 3 miles from Fincastle, Va, was destroyed by fire on Jan 30, together with its contents of grain, hay, horses, oxen, & cows.

Mrs Cath Yohe, long known as the proprietor & conductor of some of our most noted & finest hotels, died suddenly & unexpectedly early on Mon morning.
–Phil U S Gaz

FRI FEB 21, 1840
Tribute to the memory of Rufus King: born in the town of Scarborough, Maine, in 1755, eldest s/o Richd King: read law at Newburyport, in the ofc of Judge Parsons, was admitted to the Bar in 1789. Public life thus chronologically ememberaced: 1778-Aid to Gen Sullivan in the Revolutionary war. 1781-Mbr of the Mass Assembly for Newbury. 1784-Del to Congress. 1788-Mbr of the Mass Convention that ratified the U S Constitution. 1789-Mbr of the N Y Leg. Elected in conjunction with Gen Schuyler to the U S Senate, under the Fed Constitution. 1796-Appt'd Minister Pleni to Great Britain by Pres Washington, in which station he continued till 1803. 1813-Elected to the U S Senate, & held the ofc till 1825 or 26. 1826-Appt'd Minister to Great Britain. He was several times in nomination for Govn'r of N Y, & for U S Pres. In 1786 he mrd Miss Alsop, of N Y C, whither he removed in 1788. In 1808 he settled permanently on his farm at Jamaica, where he died in 1827.

Senate: 1-Ptn from Willis McDonald, for a pension. 2-Cmte on Pensions: adverse report on the ptn of John Briggs. Also, asking to be discharged from consideration of the ptn of A P King & Henry Lucas, & that it be referred to the Cmte of Claims. 3-Cmte on Pensions: ask to be discharged from further consideration of the memorial of Aaron Payne. Also, from the ptn of Lucy Easton. 4-Cmte on Military Affairs: to inquire into affording Saml Colt such aid as may enable him to make further experiments in his late discoveries & improvements in munitions of war. 5-The Senate took up the adverse report made by the Cmte on Indian Affairs on the claim of Jubal B Hancock.

The name printed Thos Curver, in our N Y correspondent's letter in our last, should be Wm Carver.

Appointments by the Pres: Wm Selden, of Va, to be U S Treas, v John Campbell, superseded. Geo Washington Montgomery, to be Cnsl of the U S for the port of Tampico, Mexico. Franklin Peale, to be Chief Coiner of the U S Mint at Phil. Jonas R McClintock, of Pa, to be Melter & Refiner of the U S Mint at Phil.

Died: on Dec 27 last, at his residence in Phillips Co, Ark, after a short illness of typhus fever, Mr Hatch Turner, formerly of St Mary's Co, Md.

Whigs & Conservatives of D C: Cmte resolved, Wm Henry Harrison for Pres: John Tyler for V P.
Republican Cmte: Walter Jones, chrmn

Thos Allen	Alex McWilliams	Willard Drake
David A Hall	Jos Bryan	Benj Ogle Taylor
Jacob A Bender	John Purdy	Wm Easby
Jos Harbaugh	Benj Burns	Thos L Thruston
Chas Boteler	John G Robinson	P R Fendall
Josh L Henshaw	Richd S Coxe	Geo Waterston
Jos H Bradley	Wm W Seaton	Stephen P Franklin
Seth Hyatt	Geo Crandell	John F Webb
Wm A Badle	Saml Harrison Smith	Jacob Gideon, jr
Dr Wm Jones	Harvery Courtitenden	Wm Wilson
Wm L Brent	Thos Stanley	R C Weightman
Jas Marshall	Richd Cutts	
Jenry J Brent	Geo Sweeny	

Gtwn:

Henry Addison	Bennett Sewell	Wm Jewell
John Myers	John Carter	Dr P Warfield
Philip T Berry	John L Smith	O M Linthicum
Wm S Nicholls	Chas E Eckell	John Wilson
Robt J Brent	Walter Smith	Saml McKenney
Raphael Semmes	Wm Hayman	
Lewis Carbery	Dr Wm Sothoron	

Alexandria:

Harrison Bradley	Thos Semmes	Cassius F Lee
Saml Messersmith	Jas Irwin	Robt I Taylor
Henry Daingefield	Stephen Shinn	John Lloyd
Robt H Miles	Saml Isaacs	John Withers
Benj T Fendall	Hugh C Smith	John W Massie
John Roberts	Benj Kinzey	
Benj Hallowell	Edgar Snowden	

U S Supreme Court, Feb 20. #43-Lessee of Wm Pollard's heirs vs Gaius Kibbe; in error to the Supr Court of Ala: opinion of the Court in this case: reversing the judgment of said Supr Court, with costs, & remanding the cause for further proceedings. #49-Jos Smith vs the C & O Canal Co; on appeal from the U S Crct Court for Alexandria, D C. Opinion of this Court: affirming the decree of the Crct Court in this cause, with costs.

Hse o/Reps: 1-Ptn of Constantine F Rafinesque, Prof of Historical & Natural Sciences, in relation to the Smithsonian bequest: referred. 2-Ptn of Joshua Drew, for a remittance of $253, which he paid the Collector of New Orleans for a supposed violation of the law relative to the returns of seamen: referred to the Cmte on Commerce. 3-Ptn of Alex'r Vattemare, Elector of the Dept of the Seine & Oise, France, in relation to an interchange among nations of works relating to the arts & sciences: referred to the Cmte on the Library. 4-Ptn of Mrs Anne Royall, of Wash City, for compensation due her late husband: referred to the Cmte on Revolutionary Claims. 5-Ptn of Robt White, of Cincinnati, for a pension: referred to the Cmte on Invalid Pensions. 6-Ptn of J L & T Hedge, merchants, & other citizens of Plymouth, Mass, praying for the erection of a custom-hse & public store-hse in Plymouth: referred to the Cmte on Commerce. 7-Ptn of Josiah Brigham, & other citizens of Quincy & Braintree, Mass, praying for an appropriation to remove obstructions in the channel of Weymouth Fore river, near its mouth: referred to the Cmte on Commerce. Same for the ptn of Jos Load, & others of Braintree & Weymouth, Mass. 8-Ptn of Chas Blight, in behalf of the heirs of Robt Fulton, for relief. 9-Ptn of Wm Rice, of Mass, for an allowance of $500, loss sustained by him in erecting a monument on Bowditch Ledge, in Salem harbor: referred to the Cmte of Claims. 10-Ptn of O T Hinde, of Ill, to adopt measures to effect the restoration of the Jews of the Holy Land: referred to the Cmte on Indian Affairs. 11-Ptn of Chas W Macomber, of Mansfield, Mass, to be paid the amount of certain bills of credit issued by resolution of Congress during the Revolution: referred to the Cmte of Ways & Means. 12-Ptn of Stephen R Riggs, Alex'r G Huggins, Gideon H Pond, & Danl Gavin, missionaries among the Sioux Indians, for a suppression of wars between the Indian tribes.

Mrs Maeder, [late Miss Clara Fisher,] a very celebrated & popular actress, is now under engagement by the mgrs of the Nat'l Theatre. Her singing & acting alike are excellent.

SAT FEB 22, 1840
Battle of Monmouth, Jun 28, 1778. Cmder-in-Chief Washington proceed slowly toward Monouth C H: cncl of war had 2 risking a general engagement-Cadwallader, a gallant fellow, & Anthony Wayne, who always said ay when fighting was to be had on any terms. The American Chief determined, happen what would, to fight Sir Henry Clinton, so that he should not evacuate Phil, & reach his stronghold in N Y unscathed. As Washington approached near Monmouth, a fifer boy tells him that our boys are coming, & the British right behind them. 5,000 picked ofcrs & men were in full retreat, closely pursued by the enemy. Washington inquired for Maj Gen Lee,

who commanded the advance. During this interview, Lt Col Hamilton, aid to Wash, leaped from his horse, &, drawing his sword, addressed the Genr'l with, we are betrayed. Washington ordered Col Stewart & Lt Col Ramsay, with their regts, to check the advance of the enemy. The spirited horse of Washington sank under his rider, & expired on the spot: Washhington instantly remounted. Memorable day on the part of the British, was the death of the Hon Col Monckton, a brother of Earl Galway. On the part of the Americans: the fate of the young & brave Capt Fauntleroy, of the Va line, was remarkable. He was on horseback, at a well near a farm house, waiving his turn, while the sldrs were rushing to the well, imploring for water. The Capt, with the point of his sword resting on his boot, his arm leaning on the pommel, continued to waive his turn, when a cannon-shot bonding down the lane , struck the ofcr near the hip, & hurled to the ground a lifeless corpse. Among the incidents of the battle, was the achievement of the famed Capt Molly, a nom de guerre given to the w/o a matross in Proctor's Artl. While serving some water to the men, Capt Molly's husband received a shot in the head & fell lifeless. She grasped the ramrod, sent home the charge, & called to the matrosses to prime & fire. It was done. The amazonian fair one kept to her post till night closed the action, when she met Gen Greene, who presented her to the Cmder-in-Chief. Washington gave her a piece of gold & assured her that her services should not be forgotten.

Orphans Court of Wash Co, D C. Letters of administration on personal estate of Saml Hamilton, late of England, & late of Wash Co, gentleman, dec'd. –Geo Actlard, adm [Note: this appears to be the same as a previous notice with Actland as adm.]

Orphans Court of Wash Co, D C. Letters of administration on personal estate of Horatio Plant, late of said county, dec'd. –Enoch Moreland, exc

Supr Court of the U S, Feb 21, 1840. #7-the U S vs E Wiggins: appeal from the Supr Court for East Fla. Reversing the decree of the said Supr Court, & dismissing the ptn of the claimant. #52-Jas Taylor vs Nicholas Longworth et al: appeal from the U S Crct Court for Ohio: opinion of this Court, affirming the decree of the said Crct Court in this cause, with costs.

Mrd: on Thu last, by Rev Geo G Cookman, Mr Washington Wallingsford, of Gtwn, to Miss Mary Ann Turner, of Wash.

Mrd: on Feb 17, at North Guilford, New Haven Co, Conn, by Rev Mr Whitmore, Ira J Fenn, Atty at Law, of Lacon, Ill, to Miss F E Dudley, of the former place.

Died: on Feb 20, Mrs Eliza Brunet, consort of the late John Brunet, of Wash City, in her 40th year. Funeral from her late residence on 7th st, on Sun, at half past 9 a m.

MON FEB 24, 1840

Senate: 1-Ptn from Zachariah Williams &Robt W Williams, citizens of Ala & Ga, asking remuneration for prop impressed by the Gov't during the late war, & for provisions furnished, for which they have never been paid. 2-Cmte on the Judiciary: asked to be discharged from further consideration of the ptn of John Johnson, late Indian agent, & that the report therefore be printed. Also, a special report on the ptn of Jacob Kern, adverse to the same: & an unfavorable report on the ptn of John Johnston. 3-Cmte of Claims: adverse reports on the ptns of Wm Morgan, Adam How, Wm Mondes, & the heirs of John Ireland. 4-Adverse report made on the claim of Jubal B Hancock was re-committed to the Cmte on Indian Affairs.

The Hon Osmyn Baker, Rep in Congress from Mass, is at present from his seat, in consequence, we regret to learn from the Eastern papers, of the death of his wife.

The Md Republican, which has been published at Annapolis, Md, for nearly 20 years past by Jeremiah Hughes, has been transferred to Geo S McKiernan, by whom it will be hereafter published. Mr Hughes hopes to devote himself to the mgmnt of Niles's Nat'l Reg, of which he became proprietor by purchase some time ago.

Mrd: on Feb 20, by Rev Mr Donelan, Mr John Allen to Miss Eleanor A Hughes, both of Wash City.

$50 reward for runaway negro man Nelson, about 35 years of age.
--M Lloyd, Milton Hill, Md

TUE FEB 25, 1840

U S Supr Court, Feb 24. #30: John Peters et al, vs, The Warren Ins Co: on a certificate of division, from the U S Crct Court of Mass: Justice Story delivered the opinion of this Court, that in this case the contributory amount paid by the Paragon on account of the collision was a direct, positive, & proximate effect from the accident, in such sense as to tender the dfndnts liable therefor upon this policy. #54: Phil & Trenton R R Co, vs Jas Stimpson: in error to the U S Crct Court for Pa. Justice Story delivered the opinion of this Court, affirming the judgment of the said Crct Ct in this cause, with costs.

Appointments by the Pres: Robert J Chester, to be U S Mrshl for West Tenn. John Mills, to be U S Atty for Mass, for term of 4 years from Jan 13, 1840, when his former term expired. H L Holmes, to be U S Atty for dist of N C. Edw McCrady, to be U S Atty for S C. Chas Walker, to be U S Atty for southern dist of Fla. Robt M Charleton, to be U S Atty for Ga. Henry W McCorry, to be U S Atty for West Tenn. Chas Weston, U S Atty for Territory of Iowa.

WED FEB 26, 1840

The venerable Jas Maury, aged 95, the first American Cnsl at Liverpool, appointed by Washington, died last evening. [N Y-Feb 24.] [See Feb 20 paper.]

Hse o/Reps: 1-Resolved, that the application of Eliz Young, for the allowance of a claim of her dec'd husband against the Gov't for services rendered under the order of the Gov't, in taking the number of Cherokees in Ark, be referred to the Cmte on Indian Affairs. 2-Ptn of Tarlton Ellege & Jas White, for a grant of a certain quantity of land: referred to the Cmte on Public Lands. 3-Ptn of Jas Evans, Jacob Groom, & Jas Alcorn, for an appropriation for depredations committed by the peace party of the Sac & Fox Indians on their property in Mo during the late war: referred to the Cmte on Indian Affairs. 4-Ptn of H S Chalmers, in relation to a claim on the Gov't, as heir of his fatherr, for property burned in Wash during the late war: referred to the Cmte of Claims. 5-Ptn of Saml Gladney, for a special pre-emption: referred to the Cmte on Public Lands. Ptn of Henry Underhill for the same: do. 6-Cmte of Claims: to inquire into paying the claim of John W Read for certain services rendered the U S. 7-Cmte of Claims to inquire into allowing the claim of John Wilson, of Ind, for a horse lost in the U S service in 1813. 8-Cmte on Revolutionary Pensions: to inquire into paying the heirs of Barnet Barnes the amount due him as a Revolutionary pensioner up to the time of his death. 9-Cmte on Foreign Affairs to inquire into allowing compensation to Wm D Jones, for extra services while cnsl for the U S at Mexico, & during the absence of the regularly accredited minister at that Court; that his letter to Mr Duncan, member of this Hse, be referred to said cmte.

Maj Chas Warley, a respectable citizen of Charleston, S C, was thrown from his horse & killed on Feb 18. [Feb 29 paper: alleged death of Maj Warley was utterly unfounded. He is in good health.]

Mrd: on Feb 23, by Rev Mr Mathews, Mr Peter Blasinger to Miss Cath Brown, all of Wash City.

Mrd: on Mon last, in Wash City, by Rev Geo G Cookman, Mr Jas H Powers to Miss Eliz S Davis.

Wash Corp: 1-Ptn of Louis Beeler, praying the remission of a fine: referred to the Cmte of Claims. 2-Ptn of Wm Dougherty, for same: do. 3-Ptn of Geo Lambright & others, for a curbstone & footway paved on I st north, between 9th & 10th sts: which was read. 4-Ptn of John B Blake & Owen McCue was, on motion of Mr Hanly, taken up for consideration.

Senate: 1-Ptns to be engrossed: relief of Juan Belgar; of Danl Marsaque; of Jos Bogy. Also, of Sebastian Butcher, & the heirs & legal reps of Bartholomew Butcher, Michl Butcher, & Peter Bloom. 2-Ptn by Mr Clay, of Ala: from John & Jas Scraggs, asking commutation. 3-Ptn from Jas Rhinehart.

City Ord-Wash. Act to authorize John Varden to exhibit his museum without taking out a license thereof: & can charge & receive pay for such exhibitions, without a license, for 2 years.

U S Supreme Court, Feb 25. #55: Leasee of Henry Brewer, vs, Jacob & Danl Blougher: in error to the Crct Court of the U S for Md: Mr Chief Justice Taney delivered the opinion of this Court, affirming the judgment of the Crct Court in this cause, with costs.

Snowhill, Md, Feb 18. Mr Purnell Bennett, formerly of this county, put an end to his existence, by cutting his throat, in that city. It is stated that the misery he endured in consequence of having accidentally killed a friend, caused this act of self-destruction. Bennett was displaying a dirk knife when it went into the heart of his friend Latchum, in his own [L's] hse. Bennett has a wife & 2 chldrn. -Banner

THU FEB 27, 1840
Senate: 1-Ptn of Wm Rand, a soldier of the Revolution, asking for a pension. 2-Several ptns from Joshua Kennedy, relating to land claims. 3-Ptn from Wm Rathbone, late a paymstr & contractor. 4-Papers of the heirs of Ed Buncombe in relation to Revolutionary services. 5-Cmte on Pvt Land Claims: bill for relief of Geo De Passan, of La. Also, adverse reports on the ptns of Wm Barclay & of Jos Wallace. Asked to be discharged from further consideration of the ptn of Wm D Ferguson. 6-Cmte of Claims: bill for relief of Francis Gehon, Mrshl of the Terr of Wiskonsin. Also, asked to be discharged from further consideration of the ptn of Francis Young. 7-Cmte on Naval Affairs: bill for relief of the heirs of Henry Eckford, dec'd. Also, a bill for the relief of Reynell Coates & Walter R Johnson. 8-Cmte on Public Lands: bill for relief of Francis Laventure, Ebenezer Childs, & Linas Thompson, with a special report thereon. 9-Ptns from Madeline Sassin, & from A C Surlls; from Robt Hilton & others.

Furnished rooms to let: corner of 6th st & La ave. –M G Handy

U S Supr Court, Feb 26. #74: J L Edmonds et al, vs, A Crenshaw; appeal from the Crct Court of the U S for Ala. Opinion of this Court: reversing the judgment of the said Crct Court in this cause, with costs. #61: H A Suydan, vs, W Boyd & D Newton's adms; on certificate of division from the U S Crct Court for Ala: opinion of this Court, that the plea that the estate of the said decedent is insolvent is not sufficient in law to abate the said action. #28: M Martin et al, plntfs, in error, vs, Wm C H Waddell. The argument in this cause was continued by Mr Wood for the plntfs in error.

Notice to fishermen: a complete outfit, emembracing every thing necessary for immediate fishing for both shad & herring may be purchased by applying to: J & H Thecker, Water st, Gtwn.

Orphans Court of Wash Co, D C. Letters of administration the personal estate of Wm Mackey, late of said county, dec'd. –Alex'r Mackey, adm

For sale: improved property in Wash City, prime cost about $10,000, which I wish to sell or exchange for U S Bank of Pa, or any of the incorporated stocks of D C, or a farm well improved. Owner is about closing his business, & wants to leave here about May 1 next; until which time he invites all indebted to him or King & Pickrell to call & close their accounts. –John Pickrell, Water st, Gtwn

Phil Gaz announces the death of Capt David Deacon, of the U S Navy, on Sat, at his residence in Burlington, N J: after an illness of about 6 weeks, but he had long been in very feeble health, suffering much from rheumatism & general debility. His last active service was the command of the frig *Brandywine*, during her 3 years cruise & station on the Western coast of South America.

FRI FEB 28, 1840
Death of Jas Maury: age 95, a Virginian, appointed by Gen Washington the first American Cnsl at Liverpool: superseded by Gen Jackson, & soon after returned to his native country. His life was gentle, & his end with peace. But that only dght, who has been so long the property of her father's declining years, the mainstring angel, watchful & unwearied that seemed to live only in his life, verily, she shall have her Reward. –N Y Amrcn

Newark Daily Adv of Mon: we record the death of the Hon John Rutherford, who died at his residence, [Edgerston.] on the Bergen side of the Passaic, yesterday, after a painful illness of some months, with dropsy in the chest. He was a native of N Y C, where he was educated for the Bar. He was, we believe, a grandson of Wm Alexander, Earl of Stirling, whow is distinguished in the early annals of N J, & soon after his majority, removed to this state, where he has resided ever since. By inheritance, he became the largest land-holder in the state; elected to the U S Senate in 1790, to fill the seat vacated by Judge Patterson. He left a large family circle to cherish the ennobling virtues of his character. He had completed his 80th year.

There has been some difficulty, row, or mutiny, on board the ship *Ohio 74* in the Mediterranean, which required the aid of Cmdor Hull & Marines to quell–but we have not learned the particulars. –Phil Gaz [Feb 29 paper: appears, upon examination, to have been nothing serious: leave to go on shore was given to the crew, which is what they wanted.]

Died: Feb 26, Mrs Mary Smoot, consort of Jos Smoot, of Wash City: in her 35th year.

SAT FEB 29, 1840
Accidental deaths on the C & O Canal on Feb 23: skiff upset & drowned were: Luke Burk, Anthony Ferguson, Patrick Boland, & Patrick Oger.

Richmond papers announce the decease of Wm D Hodges, a member of the Hse of Dels of Va from Nansemond Co, in his 28th year. Though so young, had already 3 years as a Mbr of the Leg.

Senate: 1-Ptn from Thos Frayley. 2-Ptn from Wm Blake, asking to bring from Canada, free of duty, a quantity of shot, or sprue iron, for reasons set forth in a communication to Mr Williams. 2-Adverse report on the memorial of Wm Lefever. 3-Cmte on Patents: bill for relief of Chas L Fleischmann. 4-Cmte on Pvt Land Claims: bill for relief of the heirs of Madam De Lusser & their legal reps, which was ordered to be printed. 5-Cmte on Pvt Land Claims: adverse report on the memorial of Simeon Given. Also, to be discharged from the ptn of Chas McKenzie: referred to the Cmte on Public Lands.

Appointments by the Pres: to be U S Judge: 1-Isaac S Pennybacker, for dist west of the Alleghany mountains, in Va. 2-John C Nicoll, for the dist of Ga. 3-R B Gilchrist, for the dist of S C. 4-To be Sec in & for the Terr of Fla-Jos McCants. 5- For the Terr of Iowa, Jas Clarke. 6-Wesley Jones, of N C, to be U S Mrshl for the dist of N C from Apr 26, 1840, when the term of service of the present Mrshl will expire.

Mrd: on Jan 30, by Rev Mr Kerr, Mr Zadok Robinson to Miss Eliza S Baden, all of PG Co, Md.

MON MAR 2, 1840

$100 reward for runaway negro man John, purchased of Wm Bernard, who lives near Fredericksburg, Va, where he may have gone. Age about 21. –Wm A Harrison, Hampstead P O, King Geo Co, Va.

Letter from a gentleman in Texas to a gentlemen in Balt, which states that Mr Miller, the confidential clk of Mr Steenbergen, who disappeared so mysteriously last spring, arrived lately in Galveston, from New Orleans, bringing with him 57 negroes. It was his intention to settle in Brazil. –Balt Sun

U S Supreme Court, Feb 28, 1840. Saml B Walcott, of Mass, admitted an Atty & Cnslr of this Court. #67: The U S vs Isaac Morris; on a certificate of division, from the Crct Court of the U S for N Y: Chief Justice Taney delivered: negative for the 1st & 2nd questions, & affirmative for the 3rd & 4th. #76: The U S, plntf, vs John B Gratiot et al: cause argued by Col Benton for the dfndnts. #82: the U S, plntf, vs S B Stone: Mr Atty Gen for the plntf. Feb 29, 1840. #22: Albert P De Valengin's adm, plntf in error, vs John H Duffy. Mr Johnson for the plntf in error, & Mr Williams for the dfndnt in error. #89: Jas Atkins, appellant, vs, N & J Dick &Co. Mr Coxe for the appellant, & Mr Crittenden for the appellee. #11, 12, 13, 14: The U S appellant, vs J Rodman; J Delespine's heirs; E Watterman's heirs; & J Forbes' heirs.

Georgia Journal: Mr Colquitt, Rep in Congress from Georgia, was called home by the illness of his wife, & her death took place before he arrived there.

Destructive fire Wed in Wilmington, Dela: Judge Milligan's residence, & the Union Bank, destroyed.

Mrd: on Jan 26, at Bloomsbury, Harford Co, Md, by Rev R L Goldsborough, Maskell C Ewing to Cornelia, d/o the late Wm M Lansdale.

Died: on Feb 10, at his residence, in the village of Aurora, N Y, Mr John Morgan, [brother of the Hon Chr Morgan, of the Hse o/Reps,] in his 28th year. For 6 months prior to his death he was confined to his bed with consumption: was a graduate of Amherst College, Mass: returned to his native village & united with the Presby chr. In relations of a son, a brother, a husband, a father, a friend, & a citizen, & above all, a Christian, causes deep bereavement. He has left an amiable wife & 1 child, a tender mother & 5 brothers, with numerous relatives.

Died: on Feb 29 last, at her residence near the Navy Yard Hill, Mrs Ann J Deneale, w/o Jas C Deneale, aged 53 years, after a long & painful illness. She has left a large family of chldrn to lament her death.

Died: on the 23rd ult, Edw Maxwell, s/o Washington Evans, late editor of the Martinsburg Gaz, aged 1 year, 4 months & 24 days.

Pittsburg Advocate: passengers on board the steamboat *Monongahela*, Capt Chas Stone, for about 10 days, on her trip from New Orleans to Pittsburg, take this method to thank him for his gentlemanly conduct, attention of the servants, accommodations & comforts. [Capt Stone has 2 brothers, cmders of boats on the western waters. Passengers should endeavor to get on board the *Pennsylvania*, the *Monongahela*, or the *Loyal Hanna*, all of Pittsburg.]

Jas Burrows, Cincinnati, O
Jas A Patterson, Decatur Ala
Saml G Stevenson, Louisville, Ky
John Dalzell, Phil
P A White, Cincinnati, O
R B Getling, West Tenn
J M Stukey, Vicksburg, Miss
J W Butler, Pittsburg
R H Gardner, Nashville
J F Morgan, Columbia
John Middleswarth, Newport, O
L J Iddings, Warren, O
W P Lucas, Nashville

B R Harris, Mt Pleasant, Tenn
J C Reynolds, Pittsburg
W W Lapsley, Natchez
Robt Matthews, Shelbyville, Tenn
Thos Darvis, Shelbyville, Tenn
Jas Martin, Louisville
S Hemphill, Ala
Jas Dalzell, Pittsburg
Lucius L Johnson, Phil
Archimedes Robb, Westchester, Pa
J M Long, Beaver
Freeman Borden, Hartford, Va
J C Loomis, Hartford, Conn

For rent: dwlg house at present occupied by the subscriber on the Hill, 5 minutes walk of the Capitol. Apply to the subscriber, residing on the premises, or Griffith Coombe. Possession now. –J B Rooker

Hse o/Reps: 1-Ptn for relief of Louis H Bates & Wm Lacon. 2-Bill for relief of Jas W Osborne. 3-Bill for relief of Andrew Low; of Benj Adams & Co; of Saml D Walker; & of Zachariah Jellison. 4-Bill for relief of Chastelain & Ponvert. All bills were read twice & committed. 5-Cmte of Claims: ptns of Israel H Baker, Christopher Werner: referred. Ptn of Wm Nicholas rejected. Unfavorable reports on the ptns of Wm Bryden, Dr Jas Reynolds, Simon Green, Richd Hathaway & others, David Beard's assignees, Peter Mitts, Lyman King, Stephen Arnan, Raymond A Henderson, Geo Gale, John Byington, John Kelley, Lewis Bissell, & Thos Simpson: ordered to lie on the table. Bills for relief of Ebenezer A Lester; of Nicholas Hedges; of Ebenezer Lobdell; of Richd Booker & others; of John Howe; of the legal reps of John Wilkinson; of Thos W Taylor; of Jas Cox; to amend the act for the relief of Chauncey Calhoun; of Gamaliel E Smith; of Garret Vliet; of Nathl Goddard & others: bills read twice & committed. Bill for relief of Cornelius Tiers: committed. Unfavorable report on the ptn of Dr Thos Cort: ordered to lie on the table. Bill for relief of John Underwood, & a bill for relief of Josias Thompson, late Super of the Cumberland Rd between Brownsville & Wheeling: committed. Unfavorable report on the case of Thos Crown: laid on the table. Bill for relief of Wm Bailey, survivor of Bailey & Delord: committed. Report on the cases of J & N Hamlin; which, on this report, were referred to the Sec of the Treas, to be disposed of according to the act of Feb 12, 1825. Unfavorable reports on the cases of Archibald McCallum, Dr Wheeler Randall, Jos Hernandez, on behalf of the estate of Francis Pelicer; Isaac Auland, John McIntire & others, Thos Holder, Preston Frazier, John R Allen, Richd J Jones, Wm Hunter: laid on the table. Unfavorable reports on cases of Thos Harrison & Jas McCuthcen: referred to the Cmte of the Whole. Bills for relief of Thos Fillebrown, jr; of Sylvester Philips & heirs & legal reps of Chas Langdon, dec'd; of the legal reps of John Addoms; of Capt John Downes; & of Benj C Roberts. committed. Unfavorable report on the case of the heirs of Septa Fillmore: laid on the table. Same for Elisha Britton. 6-Cmte on Commerce: Bill for relief of John H Jacocks. committed. Bill for relief of Boggs & Thompson, Robt & Thos Hutchinson, Cothel & Hoff; Jas G & R B Forbes, Jos Simmons, Jacob Ritter, jr, John Laval & Robt Taylor. committed. Bill for relief of Meiga J Benjamin & Co; relief of Wm Widsham; of John M Jacquelin: committed. Bills for relief of Geo Willis; of Elliot Smith & Nathan Farnsworth: committed.

TUE MAR 3, 1840
Senate: 1-Ptn from R J Heaton. 2-Ptn from Sarah Bishop, wid/o Colvin Bishop. 3-Adverse report on the ptn of John Nantz. 4-Cmte on Pensions: to inquire into placing John McClanahan, of Mo, who served in the regular U S army & was wounded in the battle when Gen St Clair was defeated by the Indians in the Northwest, on the pension roll.

Com'rs appointed by Somerset Co Court to divide the real estate of Wm Roach, sen, dec'd, late of said county, according to the will of the dec'd: shall meet on the *Little Bolton Farm*, in Annamessin Neck, Somerset Co, Md, on May 4 next. –Theodore G Dashiell, Thos Robertson, Levin Ballard, Nathl Dixon, Geo Hargis, com'rs

Orphans Court of Wash Co, D C. Letters of administration, with will annexed, be granted to David Young, on the estate of Eliz Greenfield, unless cause to the contrary be shown. –Nathl P Causin –Ed N Roach, reg/o wills

Mrd: on Sat last, in Wash City, by Rev Geo G Cookman, Mr Edw J Shaw to Miss Eliza Ward, of Norristown, Pa.

Died: Sun, of a severe illness, in her 63rd year, Mrs Eliz Young, relict of the late Gen Robt Young, of Alexandria. Her funeral is at residence of her son-in-law, Philip R Fendall, on La ave, tomorrow at 8 a m.

Died: Sun, at his residence in Wash City, Jos Thaw, of the Treas Dept, in the 65th year of his age. He had been a clk in the same Dept more than 40 years. He was for many years an exemplary member of the Bapt Chr: a benevolent neighbor, affectionate father, devoted husband. Funeral on Wed at 11 a m.

WED MAR 4, 1840

Senate: 1-Ptn of John Hadley, asking to be allowed to enter one section of land in place of another. 2-Ptn from the heirs of John Forbes, praying the confirmation to a tract of land. 3-Ptn from John Thomas, a Revolutionary sldr. 4-Papers relating to the claim of John McClanahan. 5-Cmte of Claims: to be discharged from further consideration of the memorial of R B Mason.

Florida's Rancho, Jan 29, 1840 Filesola appt'd commander-in-chief of the invading army, & is in advance of his division. He left Mexico City on the 23rd of last month, with 1,500 infty. They are now approaching the Rio Grande in 4 grand divisions There is no longer any doubt about the murder of Col Johnson & his men by a party of Centralists under Cordova. Their bodies were seen hanging to a tree by some Americans who came into camp

Spec order, #9: Adj Genl Ofc, Wash, Feb 25, 1840. By direction of the Sec of War, a Med Brd to consist of: Surgs T G Mowar, C H Finley, H S Hawkins & [W L Wharton-supernumerary member] will convene at Phil, Pa, on May 1: to examine applicants for appointment in the Med Staff of the Army. By order of Maj Gen Macomb: R Jones, Adj Gen.

Wanted: a journeyman tailor: immediate employment & a permanent situation. Apply to C Cammack's, F st, near the Treas Bldg.

THU MAR 5, 1840

U S Supr Court: Mar 3, 1840. #48-Geo Wildes & Co, vs, Theodore D Parker et al; on a certificate of division in opinion from the U S Court for Mass. #64-Jos Swift, vs, Geo W Tysen; on a certificate of division in opinion between the Judges of the Crct Court for N Y.

To the ladies: dress-cutting & fitting taught in 4 lessons. Mrs Edwards, from London, at Mrs Shields, near the City P O, Pa ave, Wash.

Raleigh Reg: Gen Beverly Daniel, who has served as a U S Mrshl since Mr Jefferson's adm, has been removed from office. In appointing persons to take the census, he did not appoint all Van Buren men, but selected some Whigs.
—Petersburg Intell

Died: on Mar 3, after a severe illness, Mr John B Gorman, aged 43 years, late of Boston, Mass, & a resident of Wash City for many years, leaving a large & disconsolate family. Funeral from his late residence on Pa ave, this day, at 11 a m

Died: on Mar 2, at Hagley, King Geo Co, Va, Jas Garnett Taliaferro, sen, [only bro/o the Hon John Taliaferro,] in his 73rd year, after a short but severe illness

At Blawenburgh, N Y, on Feb 19, the 8 year old dght of Capt Geo Sortor was killed in a thrashing machine accident, which caused instant death.

For sale: a lot of fine horses from the west: can be seen at the Livery Stable of F Golding, 8th st.

FRI MAR 6, 1840

A new paper, The Tippecanoe, is about to be established at Greencastle, Ind. It is to be edited by Jas McAchran, one of Harrison's old sldrs, now upwards of 71 years. He served his country under Harrison in the battlefield & is now ready to serve his old General, who freed the soil now occupied by himself & his chldrn from the grasp of America's enemies.

U S Supr Court: Mar 4, 1840 #44-Geo Holmes, vs, Silas H Jennison, Govn'r of Vt, et al. This writ of error to the Supr Court of Vt was dismissed for the want of jurisdiction. Adjourned till tomorrow.

The Observer of Trieste states there is a man at present living at Hildgausen, in Silesia, named Hans Herz, in his 142nd year. He has not been able to speak for 6 years, but his grandchildren understand him. All his sons are dead: smokes 3 pipes: has not gone outside for the last 37 years. He still takes 2 or 3 turns in his chamber every day.

Senate: 1-Ptn from Jno Gibson, adm of John Judge, in relation to an improvement in the mode of trying the strength of cables. 2-Ptn from Wm McMahon, asking compensation for provision afforded to the Va & Md militia at Cumberland, during the whiskey insurrection in 1794. 3-Cmte on the Judiciary: bill for relief of Wm P Rathbone. Relief for the heirs of Thos Cooper, dec'd. Relief of the sureties of Archibald Snead.

Mrd: on Mar 3, by Rev Jos White, Dr Richd H Edwards, of Monroe Co, Ala, to Ann Eliza, d/o Dr Chas G Edwards, of Loudoun Co, Va.

Died: yesterday, Wm Anderson, infant s/o Wm & Only P Burger. His funeral is today at 3:30 p m, at the residence of his grandfather, Wm Anderson, 12th & G sts.

Died: on Mar 3, Amanda, aged 3 months, y/d/o Otho & Ruth Gattrell, of Wash City.

Died: on Mar 4, after a short but severe illness, Mary Eliz, 2nd d/o Jas P & Harriet Ann McKean, aged 6 years & 8 months.

Died: on Mon last, at N Y, Benj Clark, aged 66 years. He had ever been known as "the Quaker lawyer"-the only lawyer of that peaceable sect whom we have ever known. —Com Adv

Theophilus R Fisk, editor of the Old Dominion, having been appointed by the Demo Assoc of D C to deliver an address, will perform on Mar 6, at Carusi's Saloon, Mar 6, at 7½ p m.

SAT MAR 7, 1840
By virtue of a writ of fieri facias, issued by G L Giberson, & to me directed, I shall sell a small frame house on lot 2 in sq 381, fronting on C st, on Mar 12, seized & taken as the property of Chas Lafon, & will be sold to satisfy a judgment due to G C Grammer. —H B Robertson, cnstbl

To let: a 2 story frame house on 7th st, between E & F sts. Apply to J S Barbaugh, on 7th st.

The partnership heretofore between Geo Mattingly & Thos Hughes, late contractors on the B & O R R, is this day, Mar 7, dissolved by mutual consent. Settle accounts with Mattingly. —Geo Mattingly, Thos Hughes. [Charlestown Free Press, Va.]

Hse o/Reps: presentation by members of Congress from the slave states, of abolition memorials, viz: By Mr Rhea, of Tenn, Jan 14, 1822, for the gradual abolition of slavery in D C. By Mr Saunders, of N C, Dec 13, 1824, from citizens of N C, for the gradual abolition of slavery in the U S. By Mr Barney, of Md, Feb 11, 1828, from citizens of Balt, for the abolition of slavery in D C. By Mr A H Shepperd, of N C, Mar 30, 1828, from citizens of N C, for entire abolition of slavery in D C. By Mr Washington, of Md, Mar 5, 1830, from inhabitants of Fred'k Co, Md, for the same object. Add that of Alex'r Smyth, of Va, in the debate on the Missouri question, in Jan, 1820: produce a bill to emancipate the slaves in D C, or, if you prefer it, to emancipate those born hereafter.

M Anelli's paintings are now on exhibition at the Museum on 4½ st. Two fine Egyptian mummies are added to the collection, & also 2 live eagles from Mt Vernon

MON MAR 9, 1840
Taken up-Mar 5-a large Seine boat about 36 ft long & 7 ft wide, with 8 rowlocks. Owner can have same by proving property & paying charges —John Bridges, near White Warehse, Eastern Branch

Proposals will be received for furnishing 6 horses, 2 carryalls, with harness complete, & 4 saddles & bridles for the use of the Hse o/Reps —Jos Follansbee

Hse o/Reps: 1-Cmte on Commerce: bill for relief of Isaac Champlin & others, owners, ofcrs, & crew of the schn'r *Buffalo*, of Stonington, Conn; a bill for relief of Robt Milnor, late gauger in the custom-hse at Phil; bill for relief of Robt Milnor & John Thompson, bill for relief of Nathan Levy. Bills for the relief of the owners of the schn'r *Three Bros*, of John L Bowman & Enoch J Noyes, & of Gilbert Smith & Nathan Stork. 2-Cmte on Commerce: bill granting 2 townships of land for the use of the Univ in the Terr of Iowa; & a bill to authorize Jas Alexander to relinquish certain land, & to locate other land in lieu thereof. 3-Cmte on Public Lands: discharged from the further consideration of the case of Benj Elliott, & it was laid on the table. 4-Bill for relief of Jas Brewer, of Ohio; & a bill granting a right of pre-emption to certain lots in the town of Perrysburg, in Ohio. 5-An act for relief of Alvarez Fisk & the legal reps of Thos P Eskridge: without amendment. 6-Bill for relief of Jas L Cochran, & an unfavorable report on the ptn of Harrison R Blanchard. The latter was laid on the table. 7-Unfavorable report on the ptn of John Cole, which was laid on the table, & a bill for relief of the legal reps of Wm Williams, dec'd. 8-Bills for relief of Mary Tucker, & of the heirs & legal reps of John Grimball, dec'd. 9-Cmte on the P O & Post Roads: an act for the relief of A G S Wright, reported without amendment. 10-Cmte on the Judiciary: bill for the relief of the heirs & reps of Thos Atkinson, dec'd. Reported, without amendment, the Senate bill entitled: An act for the relief of John H Sheppard, adm of Abiel Wood. 11-Cmte on the Judiciary: bill to refund a fine imposed on the late Matthew Lyon, under the sedition law, to his heirs & legal reps; & a bill for the relief of Jos Willis & the heirs & legal reps of Robt Leckie & Jeremiah D Hayden, dec'd. 12-Bill for relief of Benj Fry. 13-Bill for relief of Sarah H B Stith & her chldrn. 14-Unfavorable report on the ptn of the reps of Peyton Randolph, dec'd: laid on the table. 15-Bill for relief of Wm Saunders & Wm R Porter, sureties of Wm Estes. 16-Cmte on Revolutionary Claims: bill to authorize the payment of 7 years half pay on account of the death of Capt Wm Gregory to the person or persons entitled to the same. Bill to authorize 7 years half pay of a Lt due on account of the death of Lt Jonathan Dye, who was killed in the battle of Brandywine. Unfavorable reports on the cases of the heirs of Capt Jacob Cohen, the heirs of Capt Leighton Yancey, & the heirs of Richd Epperson: case of the heirs of Capt Abraham Livingston: laid on the table. 8-Unfavorable reports on the cases of the heirs of Capt Clough Shelton, the heirs of Capt Garland Burnley, the heirs of Patrick Coyle, the heirs of Capt Danl McNeil, & the heirs of Capt Wm

Langborne: laid on the table. 9-Cmte on Revolutionary Claims were discharged from the case of Geo Townley: laid on the table. 10-Cmte on Pvt Land Claims: bill for relief of Oliver Welsh; bill confirming the claim of Augustine Lacoste to a certain tract of land therein named. Same cmte: discharged from the cases of the reps of Gregory Sarpey & the reps of Chas Brown's heirs: laid on the table. 11-Bill for relief of the heirs & legal reps of Don Carlos de Villemont. 12-Report on the cases of Pierre Molaison, Pierre Richoux, Francis Martin, Alice Foley, & Alex'r Comeon, accompanied by a bill for the relief of Pierre Molaison & others. 13-Bill for relief of Chilton Allan & others; of Wm Marbury, of La, of Hyacinthe Lassel, of Mary Sroufe, & of chldrn of Stephen Johnston, dec'd. 14-Cmte on Pvt Land Claims: discharged from the ptn of Saml Myers: laid on the table. 15-Report upon the memorial of Gen Danl Parker, with a bill for his relief; ordered to be printed. Report on the ptn of Nathl Offutt & others, citizens of Hampshire Co, Va, asking the release of Valentine Cowgill from service in the U S Army, adverse to the same: laid on the table & to be printed. 16-Cmte on Naval Affairs: bill for relief of the sureties & heirs of Melancthon W Bostwick. 17-Cmte on Foreign Affairs: bill for relief of Alex'r H Everett. 18-Cmte on Revolutionary Pensions: bills for relief of John H Genther; of Eliz Davidson; of Wm Lomax; of Jacob Becker; of Jabez Collins; of Phebe Dickman; of Jas Phelps; of Wm B Winston; of Eliz Jones; of Thompson Hutchmion, of Cath Allen, of John England, of Jas Dealty; of Hugh Davs; of Chauncey Rice. Discharged from the ptn of Polly Hale: referred to the Cmte on Revolutionary Claims. 19-Bills for the relief of Wm A Cuddeback & of Eliz French; & a bill granting a pension to Eliza Fooches. 20-Bills for the relief of Jos Bailey; of Geo Morris; of John Lathram; of Benj Mitchell, of Reuben Murray, of Wealthy Baker; of Jas Boylan; & of Job Halsey. 21-Bills for relief of Leonard Smith; of Nathan Baldwin; of Sarah Oakley, of Ichabod Bearsley, & of Jacob Adams. 22-Bills for relief of Eliz Case, of Thruston Cornell, & of the adm & heirs of John Lindsay, dec'd; also, bills granting pensions to Martha Strong, to Benj Price, to David Sleeth, & to Jas J Coffin. 23-Bills for the relief of Conrad Widrig, of John Davis, & of Jas Francher. 24-Bills for relief of Thos Bennett, of John Lybrook, of David Mellon, of Ann Bloomfield, of Henry Rush, of Israel Parsons, of Philip Hartman, of Mathew Wiley, of Wm York, of Isaac Austin, of John Black, of Helen Miller, of Stephen Olney, of Wm Andrews, of Christian Brougher, of Peter Hedric, of Erastus Pierson, of Michl Seitsinger, of Wm Neel, & of Asenath Campbell. Unfavorable reports on the ptns of: Stephen Freeman; Eliz Rowe, wid/o Squire Ambler; Timothy Shays; & Saml Campbell. 25-Unfavorable reports on the following ptns, & the Cmte on Revolutionary Pensions was discharged from their further consideration, viz:

Henry Ethel	Peter Haas	Elisha Dillingham
Joshua Bailey	Jacob Miller	John H Fallen
John Cottrel	Mgt Lawrence	Eliz Rowe
Thos Harvey	Isaac Fowler	Danl Woolsey
Phebe Peck	Saml Gray	Sarah Decker
Mary Pike	Calvin Goodno	Jacobus Swaitwood
Saml Pettingel	Ann Knephly	Tunis Swart
Mrs J Smith	Sarah Callender	John Croft

Chas L Broad	Jacob Gist	Mgt Askins
Azubah Harrington	Wm Jenkinson	Peter Catlett
Gaius Paddock	John Whitman	Thos Hall
John Hasey	Jeremiah Odell	Chas Watts
Lettis Pond	Henry Peyton	John Magoon
Susan Borden	Evan Thomas	Sarah Parsons
Mary Hickman	Susan Titus	John Atherton
John Boyd	Eliz Allen	Menfield Vickory
Justice Artman	Timothy Shay	Martha Lamore
Jane Burgess	Saml Campbell	Jacob Ford
Michl Bock	John Reed	Richd Raines
Eleazer Allen	Thos Ramsay	Susan Campbell
Jos B Brooke	Winney Porter	Oliver Peck
Danl W Kenney	Benj Pierce	Pliny Hays
Maria Hornbeck	John Snow	John Voorhees
John Brower	Wm Amy	Saml Dean
Jos Wood	Sophia Delesdernier	Susan Rodgers
Wm Meade	Phebe Smith	Polly Hamilton
Valentine Miller	Cath Rinker	John H Schenk
David Mallory	Saml Jordan	Jos Parker
Ann Goldsbery	Stephen Freeman	Dorcas Colly
Isaac Haviland	David Mason	Ensign Mitchell
John Seigleman	John Edmondson	Mgt & Mary Daring
Newcomb Blodget	Eliz Truax	Benj Chappell-heirs
Amasa Dunbar	Jas Reed	wid/o Caleb Faxon

26-Cmte on Invalid Pensions: bills for relief of Peter A Myers, of John Piper, of Job Wood, of Mary Hunter, of John Keeler, of Fielding Pratt, of Jas Fleming, of Saml M Asbury, of Neil Shannon, of Elijah Blodgett, & of Thos Collins. 27-Bills for the relief of Jas Bailey, of Stephen Appleby, of Danl W Goings, & of Hiram Saul. 28-Bills for the relief of John H Lincoln, of Jared Winslow, of Nathl Davis, of Wm Hughes, of Jas Cummings, of John E Wright, of Thos Wilson, & of Saml B Hughes. 29-Bills for the relief of Levi Johnson, of Barton Hosper, of Isaac Justice, of Gideon Sheldon, of Robt Frazier, of Myron Chapin, of Medad Cook, of Lyman Bristol, & of Chas Riley. 30-Bills for the relief of Pamela Brown, of Sylvester Tiffany, of Jas Smith, of Wm Sloan, of Robt Whitlet, of Jos W Knipe, & of Levi M Roberts. 31-Bills for relief of Lyman N Cook, of Wm Butterfield, of Geo Hommel, of Jacob Euler, of David Wilson, of Saml Brown, of Emanuel Shrofe, of Isaac Boyd, of Wm Bowman, of Benj McCulloh, of David A Baldwin, of Lt John Allison, of Levi Collmus, of Wm Poole, of Josiah Strong, of Seneca Rider, of Peter W Short, of Jehosphaphat Briggs, & a bill to repeal so much of the act for the relief of certain invalid pensioners therein named, passed Mar 2, 1833, as grants a pension to Jesse Cunningham. 32-Bills for the relief of Simeon Knight, of Robt Lucas, of John Brown, of Wilfred Knott, & of Wm Glover. 33-Ptns of the citizens of Wythe Co, Va, praying Congress to relieve Jos Ramsay, a surviving ofcr of the Revolution, from a judgment recovered against him at the suit of the U S: referred to the Cmte on the Judiciary. 34-Ptn of Jas Seaburn, praying that certain tonnage duty paid by him at Wilmington, N C, in 1815, may be refunded: referred to the Cmte of Ways & Means. 35-Mr Garland, of La, said he hoped the resolution reported by the Cmte on Indian Affairs would be adopted, & that the cmte would proceed to exam the charges contained in the ptn of Saml Norris, alleging fraud & misconduct against Jehiel Brooks, the com'r who negotiated the treaty with the Caddo Indians in 1835, by which, Norris alleges he has been injured, & the Gov't defrauded out of a valuable tract of land. 36-Cmte on the Expenditures in the Treas Dept to inquire & report to this House, whether Lund Washington, who is & has been from the commencement of the present session a Reporter for the Globe, & as such has been occupying one of the privileged seats in this Hall, is the same Lund Washington who is reported by the Sec of the Treas in his report made to this hse on Feb 14, 1840, as a clk in his ofc at a salary of $1,200 a year. 37-Report of the Cmte of Elections: regarding: Philemon Dickerson, Peter D Vroom, Danl B Ryall, Wm R Cooper, & Jos Kille: entitled to take their seats in the Hse o/Reps as members of the 26th Congress. Resolved-subject of said election be postponed until the 2nd Mon of Apr next.

Persons indebted to the subscriber are requested to settle their accounts, on or before Mar 15, or they will be placed in a legal course to close them immediately.
–Wm Emack

Orphans Court of Wash Co, D C. Letters of administration bonis non on personal estate of Geo McCauley, late of said county, dec'd –Hugh McCormick, adm

Furnished rooms to let: 2 or 3 comfortable rooms: inquire F, between 11th & 12th sts.
–Louis Galabran

Balt, Mar 7. Fire last night in a large 4 story hse in South Liberty st, occupied by Mr F Scholmeyer, upholsterer, who, we regret to say, was burnt to death, & his wife & child so much injured by the fire & suffocation as to leave little hope that they can survive. –American [Mar 11 paper: Mrs S, rendered childless & a widow, is in a favorable way today, & likely to recover. Fred'k Hilden & Abram P Hilden, were this morning arrested by the Police Ofcr Chany, who are charged with the awful crime of setting fire to the dwlg & store of the late Mr S. They were apprentices to Mr S & slept in the room where the fire originated, & had possession of the keys.
–Patriot.]

Two flatboats were consumed by fire at Pulaski on Feb 19, & 2 young men, John Kelley & Andrew C Browning were consumed.

Explosion on Fri: the drying hse attached to the powder works of Jas Beatty, about 5 miles from Balt, blew up: no injury to any person.

Mrs Gassaway, corner of Pa ave & 10th st, south side, has 3 very pleasant rooms vacant.

Senate: 1-Cmte on Pvt Land Claims: bill for relief of John Compton. 2-Cmte of Claims: adverse report on the ptn of Wm McMahon. 3-Cmte on the Judiciary: bill for relief of Saml Lord. 4-Cmte on Foreign Affairs: to inquire into the justice & propriety of allowing comp to Wm D Jones, for extra services while Cnsl of the U S at Mexico, & during the absence of any accredited agent near the Govn'r: letters & docs accompany: referred to the same cmte.

Francis Bloodgood, one of the oldest & most respectable citizens of Albany, died yesterday. He was at the time of his death, Pres of the State Bank, & had been several years Mayor of the city, & was long a Clk of the Supr Court.

Mrd: on Thu, by Rev Geo G Cookman, Mr Chas Davis, of Phil, to Miss Mary Cockrell, of Wash City

Died: on Mar 4, Wm Naylor, of Romney, Va. He left home on the 2nd to visit his farm on the North Branch, & in returning was attacked with a disease under which he has labored at times for years past, which terminiated his existence at the house of Mr Keller, in Frankfort.

Died: on Wed last, at the residence of her father in Jacksonville, Montg Co, Md, Miss Caroline Farre, d/o J S Farre, aged about 30 years.

Died: Mar 4, after a short but severe illness, Mr Geo C Thompson, in his 40th year.

Died: on the 28th ult, at his residence in Columbus, Gen Wm Doherty, formerly Mrshl of the Dist of Ohio, in his 50th year.

Richmond Whig: Gen Carrington's Tobacco Factory, at Halifax C H, was destroyed by fire last week. His loss is estimated to be from $8,000 to $10,000.

For sale: 5,000 morus multicaulis trees, none less than 6 feet high, stout, well branched, & in perfect preservation, at 10 cents ea. Apply thru the P O. –A D Washington

TUE MAR 10, 1840
Stolen or strayed, from rack opposite the Patriotic Bank, a bay mare, with saddle bags, bridle, & some groceries. Reward: $10. –Philip Davis, Sup't for Mr T Taugett, near Marlborough, PG Co, Md.

For rent: 2 story brick hse on Capitol Hill, with stable attached to it. Inquire of S Bassett, corner of E Capt & 2nd sts east, or at the Senate Chamber.

Edgar Snowden has been elected Mayor of the city of Alexandria for the ensuing year.

Public sale of valuable real estate: in Nottingham, on Mar 20 next, the Plantation on which the subscriber now resides, belonging to the heirs of Thos Baden, dec'd, about 270 acs. Adjoins the lands of Elisha Skinner, Jos N Baden, W B C Worthington, & Wm Harvey. Tolerable frame dwlg, with necessary out-hses. Posession will be given immediately or next fall, at option of the purchaser. The title is indisputable. On Mar 25th, sale of oxen, furniture, & utensils. —T M D Baden, PG Co, Md

Chas K Wagler gives public notice that he is neither able nor willing to pay any debts hereafter contracted by the woman called his wife. All debts previously contracted his father will liquidate, if proper time be allowed. If any one trusts said woman hereafter, he may do so at his own risk.

Passengers in the steam-ship *Great Western*:

Manuel Blandin	Wm E Shaw	Mott Williams
Edw Fletcher	Wm Porcher	Mr Renard
Mrs E Fletcher	Geo Bailey	Philip Physick
John Middleton	Philip Schleslinger	Geo Usborne
Abm Goodman	John Alcock	Chas Dayton
Weston Craycroft	John Duer	Wm Livingston
Henry Bohlem	Chas Best	Wm Crossman
Henry Samuel	Mrs C Best	Dominic Pope
Edw Kennard	Thos Storrow Leipezig	Thos Cringem
Jas Patterson	Fred'k Homer	Wm Cummins
John Fehrman	Edw Ingelby	Edw Whitney
Chas Miller	Wm Ritchie	Richd Lowndes
Wm Pollitz	Mrs C Shaw	Geo Ives
Jas Buckley	Mrs M Freeman	Thos Dewing
Richd Muspral	B Howell	Henry Collman
Thos Faile	B Larhan	Fred'k Lennig
Saml Storrow	Geo Hurst	A T Cipriant
Tule Gavelle	Jas Hay	Wm Bent
Jos Wiggens	Saml Dyer	Mr Pattison
Joshua Freeman	Saml Brown	Mr Durand
Wm Parrington	Hy Shaw	Mary Andrews
Wm Alwood	R Ker	Lorenzo de Venturo
Wm Davidson	Wm Brownell	H Cheves
Ame Legoux	C Lowther	Mrs Fletcher Wilson
Felix Collinard	Wm Baldwin	Prince Lucien Murat
Henry Glenard	G Christ	
Jas Newman	Jas Bates	

For sale: now receiving wood & lime, a large quantitiy of Oak, Ash, & Pine wood, at the lowest prices, for cash, or to punctual customers. —Walter Warder, 12th near the Canal.

45 days later from England: the Queen of England was mrd to Prince Albert of Saxe Coburg on Feb 10. The Duke of Wellington has had 2 or 3 alarming fits of illness: daily bulletins are issued from Apsley Hse.

WED MAR 11, 1840
Appointments by the Pres: Collectors: [commission-cmn]
Gershom Mott, Burlington, N J, from Mar 28, when his present cmn expires
Jas N Roach, St Mary's, Md, from Apr 14, do.

Surveyors:
Thos Armstrong, Carter's crk, Va, from Mar 31, when his present cmn expires
Henry G S Key, Lelewellensburg, Md, from Feb 19, do.
Isaac Pipkin, Murfreesbroough, N C, from Mar 23, do.
Nathl Jackson, Newburyport, Mass, from Apr 30, do.
Lewis B Willis, New Orleans, La, from Apr 14, do.
Felix G H Long, St Andrew's Bay, Fla, v T F Lofton, who has vacated the ofc.

Naval Ofcrs:
Thos M Newell, to be a Capt in the Navy, from Jul 27, 1840.
Cornelius K Stribbling, to be a Cmder in the Navy, from Jul 28, 1840
John Rodgers, to be a Lt in the Navy, from Jan 28, 1840.
John B Marchand, to be a Lt in the Navy, from Jan 29, 1840.
Wm Rogers Taylor, to be a Lt in the Navy, from Feb 10, 1840.

Longevity: in South Kingston, R I, with population of 3,700, there are 45 between the ages of 80 & 100, 6 of them between 90 & 100, & one over 102. The remainder of the 45 are between 84 & 90.

Senate: 1-Cmte on Naval Affairs: bill for relief of Wm Hogan, adm of Michl Hogan, dec'd. 2-Cmte on Pvt Land Claims: bill for relief of Jean Baptiste Corneau. 3-Cmte on P O & Post Roads: bill for relief of Francis A Harrison. 4-Select Cmte: bill authorizing the publication, by Saml Forry, of certain papers: meterological & statistical register: & 2nd-a collection of facts in relation to the med topog of the military posts, & the vital stats of the troops. 5-Ptn from Maj Gen Gaines, of the U S Army, proposing a system of nat'l defence. 6-Ptn from Olivia Cannon, asking for a pension. 7-Ptn from Mrs Wiley, wid/o a Revolutionary soldier, asking for a pension. 8-Cmte on the Commerce: bill or relief of Jacob Pernel & others. 9-Cmte for D C: bill for relief of Caspar W Wever. 10-Cmte on Pensions: bill for relief of Mary Neal. Also, a bill for relief of Tyler Spafford. 11-Ptn from Jas M Schoolcraft, asking the payment of money guaranteed by a treaty with the Ottoway & Chippeway Indians. 12-Ptn from John Bradish, assignee of certain claimants, & claiming interest on the amount. 13-Cmte on Pvt Land Claims: bill for relief of legal reps of Pierre Bonhommie, with a report, which was ordered to be printed. 14-Cmte of Claims: adverse report on the ptn of the heirs of Robt Fulton. 15-Cmte on Indian Affairs: bill for the relief of Saml McKay. 16-Cmte on Pensions: adverse report on the claim of Fred'k Sammons for a pension. 17-Bill for the relief of Jos Campau.

For sale: lot 17 in sq A, in Wash City: fronts on Pa ave: with a very neat 2 story brick bldg, sufficient for a small family. Terms easy. Apply to T L Thruston.

Orphans Court of Wash Co, D C. Letters of administration on personal estate of Geo B Cropley, late of said county, dec'd. —Robt Barnard, adm

Crmnl Court, Wash: Grand Jury.

Peter Force- foreman
John F Cox
John Boyle
John McClelland
Lewis Johnson
Geo B Magruder
Walter Smoot
Griffith Coomb
Jos Forrest
Robt White
Saml McKenney

Otho M Linthicum
Geo W Young
Washington Berry
Adam Lindsay
Wm S Nicholls
John Lutz
Chas A Burnett
Thos Blagden
Abner C Pierce
Edw Simms

Trustee sale: decree of the high Court of Chancery of Md: sale at Morton's store, in Benedict, Chas Co, Md, on Apr 1, valuable real estate in said county, near Benedict, being the same estate upon which Zachariah Southoron lived, & which John Southoron aferwards sold to his brother Henry Southoron. —John Scott, trustee

U S Supreme Court: Mar 9, 1840. #22: Albert P Devalengin's admx et al, vs, John H Duffy, in error to the Crct Court for Md. Mr Chief Justice Taney delivered the opinion of the Court, affirming the judgment of said Court Court in this cause, with costs & 6% damages. #10: S L Fowler vs H Brantley et al; in error to the Crct Court U S for southern dist of Ala. Mr Justice Catron delivered the opinion of the Court, affirming the judgment of the said Court in this cause, with costs. #27. John F Games et al, vs Lesse of Walter Dun's heirs; in error to the Crct Court U S for Ohio: Mr Justice McLean delivered the opinion of the Court, affirming the judgment of said Court in this cause, with costs. #31: Saml Sprigg, vs, Bank of Mt Pleasant; on appeal from the Crct Court U S for Ohio: Mr Justice Thompson delivered the opinion of this Court, affirming the judgment of the said Crct Court in this cause, with costs. #76. The U S, vs John P B Gratiot et al; on a certificate of division from the Crct Court U S for Ill; Mr Justice Thompson delivered the opinion of this Court, ordering it to be certified to said Crct Court, that the Pres had power, under the act of Mar 3, 1807, to make the contract set forth in the declaration. The Court adjourned to the term in course.

Orphans Court of Wash Co, D C. Letters of administrationd bonis non on the personal estate of Nicholas Barber, late of said county, dec'd. -Robt Barnard, adm de bonis non

Hse o/Reps: 1-Cmte on the P O & Post Roads: to examine & report upon the accounts of Wm B Jenkins, late Postmaster at Clinton, Ken, with the Gen P O Dept. 2-Cmte on Revolutionary Pensions: to inquire into granting a pension to Andrew Loskey, for Revolutionary services

Wives Wanted! The subscriber has been authorized to issue an advertisement for wives for the Stone-Cutters at the Treas Bldg who still remain unmrd. They are about 28 in number, & between the ages of 23 & 35. A good opportunity is now offered to those young ladies who wish to enter the matrimonial state. Applicants must be between the ages of 17 & 33 years, of good moral character, & good disposition. Applications sent thru the P O, before Sat next at 12 M, addressed to the subscriber, will be thankfully received, & immediately attended to. —John L Taggart, sec: Wash, Mar 10, 1840

Governess wanted: subscriber wishes to employ in his family a Governess to take charge of 4 young ladies: a competent teacher, vocal & instrumental music, drawing & painting, & worsted work, teaches the Eng & French languages, a liberal salary. — Benj Lee, Upr Marlboro, PG Co, Md.

THU MAR 12, 1840
Senate: 1-From E Littell, a plan for the absorption of the banking capital of the country, without injury to the community. 2-Papers in relation to the case of Jas Williams. 3-Ptn from Conrad Waters, for a pension. 4-Ptn from A C Hollinger, asking remuneration for services. 5-Ptn from John Barnard, adm on the estate of John Barclay Flemming, late purser in the Navy. 6-Bill for relief of John P Bispham was considered in the Cmte of the Whole, & ordered to be engrossed.

The brig *Northumberland*, Capt Watts, which arrived at Balt on Mon, brought as passenger Lt Wm H Kennon, of the frig *Constitution*, Com Claxton, bearing of despatches to our Gov't from Lima. Capt W learned that the new Gov't of Peru would not receive our Charge d'Affaires. The American Cnsl was acting as Charge.

Lt Cmndnt G H Talcott, in a card in the Troy Daily Whig, renders thanks to the firemen of West Troy, for their assistance when a fire broke out in a blacksmith's shop in the arsenal, on Thu. By them the principal range of shops was saved.

Died: on Jan 28 last, at Vienna, Mrs Frances Ann Sophia Clay, w/o John Randolph Clay, Sec of the Leg of the U S at Vienna, aged 26 years.

FRI MAR 13, 1840
From Annapolis, we learn that the Govn'r & Senate appointed new Reps of Md in the Canal & R R Cos, viz: Wm Carmichael, Henry G S Key, & Benj C Howard.

Miss Janette White, age 17 years, died at Millersburgh, Ohio, Feb 25, from inflammation caused by a puncture with a pin.

The frig *U S*, off Sandy Hook, Feb 13, 1840. Mr Chas White, a Jersey pilot, has brought this ship out over the bar by way of Gedney's Channel; average sounding at half tide was 5 fathoms, the least cast of lead might be stated at a qrtr less five. –Lawrence Kearney, Cmndng the frig *U S*: to Cmdor Jas Renshaw, Naval Sta, N Y. 2-From the New Era of Feb 21 N Y, Feb 18, 1840. I beg leave to state that it is false, as she was piloted out by Mr Jas Kelso, one of the oldest & most experienced of the N Y Pilots, who was well acquainted with the channel now called Gedney's Channel, thru the usual ship channel.. –Candour 3-N Y Feb 25, 1840: My assoc, Mr Jas Kelso, objected in my going thru the channel, & left the poop deck, & did not return to duty until the ship had passed the bar. –Chas White, Jersey Pilot, & Pilot of the frig *U S*, Feb 13, 1840, thru Gedney's Channel. To Lt R W Meade, N Y, N Y.

Criminal Court-Wash Mar 12, 1840. The U S vs Baptista Gluick: indicted for assaulting & beating Philip Haas, Lithographer, in Wash City, on Feb 6, 1840. Mr Haas swore positively that the dfndnt, with Lewis Nagle & Christopher Cummings, was one of the persons who assaulted him. An alibi was set up for Mr Gluick by several witnesses, the Hon C H Williams & J W Crockett. Verdict-not guilty. Wm A Baker, also tried today for grand larceny, stealing $60 in bank notes, the property of Wm E Andrews, was acquitted.

Mrd: on Feb 13 last, at *Fulton Grove plantation*, by Rev Mr Daniel, Mr P Vitallus Duflon, Merchant, of New Orleans, formerly of N Y, to Miss Eliz, only d/o Edw Poole, of La.

Died: on Mar 8, in Wash City, of hemorrhage, Mr Gabriel Bradley, in his 40th year.

Died: on Mar 11, after a long & protracted illness, Mrs Mary Webb, in her 83rd year.

Farm & country seat for sale: little farm of 90 acs. Apply to the owner, Dr C Streater, Stemmer's run, near Balt, Md.

Hse o/Reps: 1-Cmte on Revolutionary Pensions to inquire into granting a pension to Cath Shannon, wid/o Robt Shannon, a soldier of the Revolution; also, to Diana Moore, wid/o Wm Moore, a soldier of the Revolution; also, to Isabella Gulion, wid/o Jeremiah Gulion, a soldier of the Revolution; also, to Frances Green, wid/o Robt Green, a Lt of the Va Line of the Rev; also, into the propriety of increasing the pension of Wm Merriweather, a Lt of the Ill Regt, who is now receiving pay as a Sgt only. Also, that the papers in the Pension Ofc to support said claims be referred to said cmte. 2-The papers of the heirs of Geo Pursell, dec'd, in relation to a pension, be referred to the Cmte on Revolutionary Pensions. 3-Cmte on Pvt Land Claims: to inquire into granting to Andrew Johnson, of Scott Co, Ky, any military bounty lands to which Capt John Johnson, of the Va Line of the Rev, may be entitled; & official transcript of the papers filed by him in the Exec Dept of Va in support of his claim be referred to said cmte. 4-Cmte on Invalid Pensions: to inquire into restoring to Mrs Frances L Pratt, only d/o Col Wm Pratt, an invalid pensioner, the pension relinquished by him to the Gov't, but which he subsequently devised to his said dghtr; & that the will of Col Pratt & papers on file in the Pension Ofc be referred to said cmte. 5-Ptns presented: of Stephen Richardson, of Ky, praying to be allowed arrears of pension: referred to the Cmte on Invalid Pensions. 6-Ptn of Andrew Craig, praying compensation as a mail contractor: referred: to the Cmte on the P O & Post Roads. 7-Ptn of Moses Wright, praying for a pension: referred to the Cmte on Revolutionary Pensions. 8-Cmte on Revolutionary Pensions: to inquire into granting a pension to Isaac Levan, of N C, for services in the Revolutionary war. 9-Cmte of Claims to inquire into allowing to Alex'r H Saunders, late a soldier of the U S army, such balance of pay as may appear to be justly due him from the evidence produced. 10-Cmte on Invalid Pensions: to inquire into increasing the pension of Jas Roberts, an invalid pensioner of the U S. Also, to inquire into increasing the pension of Maj Chas Larrabee, who lost an arm in battle in the last war with Great Britain. 11-Cmte on Revolutionary Pensions: to inquire into allowing Jos McMilton, a soldier of the Revolution, a pension. Also, to inquire into increasing the pension of John Grimm. Also, to inquire into placing the name of Benj Chapman upon the list of Revolutionary pensioners. Also, to inquire into allowing to Ebenezer Stow, of Gorham, Maine, his pension from Mar 4, 1820, to Mar 3, 1826. Also, to inquire into increasing the pension of Mrs Lydia Hoard, & also of Jacob Jackson, of N Y. Also, to inquire into granting a pension to John Hoover, a Revolutionary sldr. Also, to inquire into placing the name of Abigail York on the list of pensioners under the act of Jul 7, 1838. Also, to inquire into granting pensions to Wilmot Maraden & Lois Smith, wids/o Revolutionary sldrs. Also, to inquire into allowing a pension to Penelope Plunket on account of the Revolutionary services rendered by her former husband, Jos Davis. Also, to inquire into allowing to Elijah Borden the arrears of a pension from Sep 25, 1820, when he was stricken from the pension roll, until Jan 19, 1832, when his name was restored to the roll. Also, to inquire into placing the name of Wm Wallace, of Phippsburg, Maine, on the list of Revolutionary pensioners. Also, to inquire into granting a pension to Lucy Whitmore, of Lincoln Co, Maine, wid/o Andrew Whitmore, a soldier of the Revolution. 12-Cmte on Invalid Pensions: to inquire into allowing a pension to Jos Mayse. Also, to inquire into granting a pension to Geo Whitue for injuries received in the late war with Great Britain. Also, to inquire into granting a pension to John Woods, of Jeff Co, Ky. 13-Ptn of S G Simmons, of the U S Army, praying compensation for services rendered by him in 1838, as Sec to Com'rs appointed by the U S to treat with Creek & Osage Indians; which ptn was referred to the Cmte of Claims. 14-Cmte on P O & Post Roads to inquire into granting relief to Thos McMuster, jr, in relation to a mail contract entered into by him. 15-Cmte on Naval Affairs: to inquire into granting a pension to Polly Clough, under the act of Mar 3, 1837, entitled "An act for the more equitable adm of the Navy Pension Fund. 16-Cmte on Commerce: to inquire into reporting a resolve in favor of John Throop, of Bristol, Maine, for the amount of fishing bounty upon the schn'r *Pacific*.

"Historical Account of Massachusetts Currency," by Jos B Felt. Just received at the Book & Stationery Store of W M Morrison, 4 drs west of Brown's Htl. Also, the American Swine-breeder, by Henry Ellsworth.

SAT MAR 14, 1840
Notice to bridge builders: invite plans & proposals for the construction of a bridge at the site of the late Chain Bridge: its length to be 300 feet, with sufficient width for 2 wagons to pass each other thereon: abutment on the Va side is still standing secure. –O M Linthicum, John Pickrell, Thos Turner, com'rs: Gtwn, D C

Orphans Court of Wash Co, D C. Letters of administration on estate of Jas L Anthony, late of said county, dec'd, be granted to Thos Carbery, unless cause to the contrary be shown. –Nathl P Causin –Ed N Roach, reg/o wills

Strayed or decoyed from my residence on Pa ave, a large white pointer dog, 3 years old, named Dash. Suitable Reward for return of said dog to my residence, or at the Capitol.. –John L Wirt

To carpenters & masons: will receive proposals for bldg a mill-hse in Gtwn, D C, on the Canal: 62 feet x & 70 feet, 4 stories high. –Thos J Davis, Greenfield Mills, Md

Mrd: on Jan 15 last, by the Hon Judge Jenkins, Mr Wm J Beall, of Shreveport, Caddo, La, [formerly of Md,] to Miss Julia, d/o the late Thos Welsh, of Grand Cane, Parish of Caddo, La.

Geo Wolf, Collector of the Port of Phil, died suddenly at the Phil Custom-Hse, on Wed last; age about 70 years. He had been laboring under an affection of the heart for some time, but was well enough to walk down to the ofc. On passing to his pvt room, he asked some one to assist him in taking off his cloak. This done, he laid down on a settee, & shortly expired. He had previously filled the ofcs of Rep in Congress, Govn'r of Pa, & First Comptroller of the U S Treas.

On Feb 25, the dwlg of Matthias Engler, in Newport township, Luzerne Co, Pa, was destroyed by fire, & 2 chldrn & a brother of Mr Engler perished in the flames. Mr Engler, his wife, & a Miss Weiss, were badly burnt.

Capt M C Perry appointed to the command of the steam frig bldg at the Navy-yard, Brooklyn: experimental gun practice will be continued during the present year. The steamer *Fulton*, under command of Capt John T Newton, will still be engaged on that service, the whole under the direction of Capt Perry.

MON MAR 16, 1840
Cabinet-making: shop on Pa ave, between 12th & 13th sts. Prepared to attend funerals. –John A Aniba

Appointments by the Pres. Isaac H Bronson, of N Y, to be U S Judge for the E Dist of Fla, for 4 years, v Robt R Reid, appointed Govn'r of that Terr. Alfred Balch, of Tenn, to be U S Judge for the Middle Dist of Fla, for 4 years, v Thos Randall, whose term expired. Jas S Green, to be U S Atty for the Dist of N J, for 4 years, from Jan 18, 1840, when his former commission expired.

Senate: 1-Ptn from Clements, Bryan & Co, asking remuneration for losses sustained in a contract, & that the Sec of War be allowed to settle the claim on the principles of equity & justice. 2-Ptn from J F Hall & John Francis, asking to have life-boats placed at certain locations on the maritime border, where they might be useful in cases of shipwreck. 3-Ptn from R & S Dorr & Co, asking that a duty on silk may be imposed. 4-Ptn from the widow of John Dickman, for a pension. 5-Ptn from Wm Lefevre. 6-Cmte on Indian Affairs: bill for relief of legal reps of John Scott, dec'd. 7-Cmte on Naval Affairs: asked to be discharged from the further consideration of the ptn of Jos Whipple. Also, an adverse report on the claim of J B Parsons. 8-Bill for relief of John E Bispham was read a 3rd time & passed. 9-Ptn from John Martin, asking to be allowed arrears of pension. 10-Ptn from Chas K Watson & others, of Seneca, asking passage of a uniform bankrupt law. 11-Cmte of Claims: asking to be discharged from further consideration of the ptn of H H Brown. 12-Ptn from Etienne Lefebre.

The N Y Express says that the estate of the late Robt Lenox is the largest ever left by an individual in that city: personal estate alone amounts to $2,443,566.85, or nearly 2 & a half millions. By his will, his son will receive, it is believed, over 2 millions, & each of his dghts about a hundred thousand dollars. This immense estate was accumulated by the industry of one man, & that, too, without ever taking a dollar over lawful interest.

Mrd: on Thu last, in Wash City, by Rev Geo G Cookman, Mr Jos Stephenson to Miss Mary Ann Harris, d/o Wm A Harris, all of this place.

Died: Mar 15, in Wash City, Lt Wm Lambert, U S Navy. His funeral is today, from his late residence, at 4 p m.

Died: on Jan 27 last, in Paris, Mrs Eliz Kortwright Hay, d/o the late Pres Monroe, & relict of Judge Hay, of Va.

City Ord-Wash. Resolution to authorize John B Ferguson to keep a fish dock on the wharf owned by the heirs of Col Wharton, for the ensuing season, under the laws-as regulated in this city.

TUE MAR 17, 1840
Steamboat for Phil, via New Castle & Frenchtown Trnpk & R R. Passage through $4, with meals as usual. -T Sheppard, agent, Balt, Md.

Moses Dawson's Life of Gen Harrison, pg 216. [The following is a part of what is copied in the paper.] The Indians left 38 warriors dead on the field: the troops under Gen HarrisonH amounted on the day before the battle to more than 800. At Tippecanoe they rushed up to the bayonets of our men. Should our country again require our services, to oppose a civilized or savage foe, we should march under the command of Gov Harrison with the most perfect confidence of victory & fame.

Joel Cook, Capt 4th Infty
Josiah Snelling, Capt 4th U S Infty
R C Barton, Capt 4th Infty
O G Burton, Lt 4th Infty
Nathl P Adams, Lt 4th Infty
Chas Fuller, Lt 4th Infty

A Hawkins, Lt 4th Infty
Geo Gooding, 2nd Lt 4th Infty
Josiah D Foster, Surgeon 4th Infty
H Burchstead, Ensign 4th U S infty
Hoses Blood, Assist Surgeon 4th Infty

Letter to his Excell Wm Henry Harrison, Cmder-in-Chief of the Northwestern Army: on his retiring from service: signed-

Edw W Tupper, Brig Gen
Simon Perkins, Brig Gen
Chas Miller, Col
John Andrews, Lt Col
Wm Rayen, Col
Robt Spafford, Lt Col 2nd Regt Ohio quota

N Beasely, Maj
Jas Galloway, Maj
Solomon Bentley, Maj
Geo Darrow, Maj
Jacob Frederick, Maj

[Dawson's Life of Harrison, pg 277.] [Note-there was a W W Cotg, Maj, that was difficult to read.]

One of the cheapest newspapers in the U S: the Gleaner: issued from the ofc on Wall st, N Y C, at he unusual low price of $2 per annum in advance. –W Van Benthuysen, Publisher, N Y C

Wm Henry Harrison: in 1791, at age 19, appointed by Washington an ensign in our infant army. 1792: promoted to the rank of Lt, & in 1793 joined the legion under Gen Wayne, & in a few days hereafter was selected by him as one of the Aids. On Aug 24, 1794, distinguished himself in the battle of the Miami, & elicited the most written approbation of Gen Wayne. 1795: made a Capt, & placed in command of Fort Washington. 1797: appointed by Pres Adams Sec of the Northwestern Terrr, & ex officio Lt Govn'r. 1798: chosen a delegate to Congress. 1801: appointed Govn'r of Indiana & in the same year Pres Jefferson appointed him sole com'r for the treating with the Indians. 1809: appointed Govn'r of Indiana, by Madison. On Nov 7, 1811, gained the victory of Tippecanoe. On Sep 11, 1812, the siege of Fort Meigs commenced-last 5 days, & terminated by the brilliant sortie of Gen H. Oct 5, 1813: gained the victory of the Thames, over the British & Indians under Proctor. 1814: appointed by Madison one of the Com'rs to treat with the Indians, & in ths same year, with his colleagues, Govn'r Shelby & Gen Cass, concluded the treaty of Greenville. 1815: again appointed such Com'r, with Gen McArthur & Mr Graham, & negotiated a treaty at Detroit. 1816: elected to Congress. Jan, 1818: he introduced a resolution in honor of Kesciusko, & supported it in one of the most feeling & classical, & eloquent speeched ever delivered in the Hse o/Reps. 1819: elected a member of the Ohio Senate. 1824: elected a Senator in Congress, & was appointed, in 1825, Chrmn of the Military Cmte, in place of Gen Jackson, who had resigned 1827: appointed Minister to Colombia, & in 1829 wrote his immortal letter to Bolivar, the deliverer of S America. Gen H is descended from one of the oldest & most respectable families in Va. his father, Benj Harrison, rendered himself particularly conspicuous by his prompt adoption of the cause of the colonies. Gen H has always been a Democratic Republican of the school of Washington, Jefferson, & Madison. His father was one of the signers of the Declaration of Independence

Mrd: on Mar 12, at N Y, by Rev R K Rogers, Richd S Coxe, of Wash City, to Mrs Susan R R Wheeler, of N Y, d/o the late John G Warren, of that city.

Mrd: on the Sabbath last, in Wash City, by Rev Geo G Cookman, Mr Saml Wise, of Alexandria, to Miss Jane Ann Jacobs, of Wash City.

Died: on Mar 15, in Wash City, Mr John Rugg, of Heath, Mass, in his 22nd year.

Orphans Court of Wash Co, D C. Letters of administration the personal estate of Thos Magnier, late of said county, dec'd. -J F Callan, adm

WED MAR 18, 1840

Hse o/Reps: 1-Ptn of Alex'r Thompson, of N Y, a Revolutionary soldier, praying to be inscribed on the pension roll. 2-Ptn of Richd Reynolds, of N Y, an invalid soldier of the late war, praying for a pension. 3-Ptn of Alex'r Hill, of Wash Co, Pa, praying for a pension, with an accompanying doc. 4-Ptn of Jas Burleigh & others, praying an appropriation for opening a road from the mouth of the Iowa river to the city of Iowa, in the Terr of Iowa. 5-Ptn of Saml Stout, praying compensation for certain damages sustained by him in the war with the Sac & Fox Indians. 6-Ptn of G S Hubband & others, citizens of Chicago, Ill, praying the construction of a harbor at Racine, Terr of Wiskonsin. 7-Ptn of Benj Beckford & others, citizens of Pike Co, Ill, praying the privilege of locating other lands in lieu of a 16th section therein named. 8-Ptn of R C Robertson & others, for the relief of Mr Ames. 9-Ptn of Thos J Wilcox, praying a mail route therein described. 9-Ptn of the legal reps of Michl Brisbois, for remuneration for property taken at Prairie du Chien, in 1816, by order of an ofcr of the U S Army. 10-Ptn of John Hacket & other citizens of Wiskonsin, praying appropriation for a harbor at Milwaukie, & for a road from Milwaukie to Beloit. Also, of Legrand Rockwell & others, citizens of Walworth Co, Wiskonsin, for the same. 11-Ptn of R Wheeler, H B Towslee, Geo Batchelder, Ephraim Perkins, & others, citizens of Wiskonsin, praying appropriation of $4,000 for a road from Southport to Bulington. 12-Ptn of F A Wingfield, Clinton Walworth, & others, praying a reduction in the price of the canal lands to $1.25 per ac, & a right of preference to the actual settlers in the purchase of said lands. 13-Ptn of Cath Williams, asking for a pension. 14-Memorial of Francis Kendig & 148 others;

Abraham Kauffman & 90 others; Thos Himea & 37 others; Andrew Griffin & 25 others; Jas Barber & 25 others; Jas Cottrell & 26 others, all citizens of Lancaster Co, Pa, praying for an increase of duty on imported silks. 15-Remonstrance from Wm F Mackay & other citizens of Pa, against the annexation of Texas. 16-Ptn of Wm Jones, late Postmaster at Wash, praying compensation for services rendered. 17-Ptn of Lund Washington, for a qrtr's salary, [$200.] as a clk in the War Dept, due to his son, Wm J Washington, minor. 18-Ptn of Wm Doutherty & 196 other workmen on the public bldgs, stating that the money appropriated is exhausted & they are now out of employ until Congress makes appropriation. 19-Ptn of Jas Collins, Jas Maxwell, Ebenezer Brigham, & others, for an appropriation for a r r from Lake Mich to the Miss. 20-Ptn of Wm M Jackson, Carlisle Hastings, A B Coon & other inhabitants of the 5th subdivision of the Northwestern Terr into states, for the repeal of so much of the act of Apr 18, 1818, as conflicts with the ord of 1787. 21-Ptn of C Hall, A D Soper & others, for improvement of the navigation of the Neenah & Wiskonsin rivers. Ptn of John S Horner, John Lowe, John P Arnot & others, for the same purposes. 22-Ptn of Henry Phoenix, Wm H Bruce, L G Calkins & others, for an appropriation for a harbor at Racine. 23-Ptn of Rufus S Reed, Capt Danl Dobbins, Chas M Reed, & other citizens, of Erie, Pa, for an appropriation for a harbor at Milwaukie. 24-Ptns from Saml Rockwell, Wm Hansell, & Wm H Underwood, asking of Congress the payment of certain claims against the Cherokee Indians as a tribe, & assumed by the Genr'l Gov't under the late treaty with that tribe. 25-Ptn from Dr R R G Lee, of Ala, for relief for an injury sustained in the service of his country. 26-Ptn from Peter Grennell, former Postmaster at Monticello, Ga. 27-Ptn from Benj F Hard, of Charleston, S C, asking the payment of certain arrearages from the P O Dept. 28-Ptn of R R McNemar & others, for a post route therein mentioned. 29-Ptn of Hugh Hamill, praying for a pension. 30-Ptns of Bishop McIlvaine & others, & of O H Knapp & others, for a reduction in the rate of postage. 31-Ptn of S Fuller & others, C S Rhodes & others, Robt Chappel & others, & H H Johnson & others, praying Congress to pass a bankrupt law. 32-Memorial of Nathl Hull, of Dela Co, Ohio: prays Congress to pass an act granting to Ohio a tract or gore of land containing about 60 acs, to be appropriated to the use of schools, as provided for in such cases by the laws of Ohio. 33-Affidavits of Ira Carpenter, of Dela, Ohio, in support of certain claims which he holds against the U S for the loss of property during the late war with Great Britain. 34-Ptn of Byron Kilbourn & others, from Wiskonsin Terr, for construction of a harbor at the mouth of the Milwaukee river. 35-Ptn of John Brundage & 40 other citizens of Marlborough, Ohio, praying the Congess to recognize the Republic of Hayti: laid on the table. 36-Ptn of Jos Eaton & 21 others, remonstrating against the annexation of Texas to the U S: laid on the table. 37-Memorial of Edmund Pendleton Gaines setting forth a system of nat'l defence, of which he claims to be the inventor & author. 38-Ptn of Mittis F Lowe, asking compensation for a horse lost in the Fla campaign.

Union Bank of Gtwn: John Marbury, Pres: meeting of stockholders on Apr 20.

Adm's sale of furniture & slaves: on Mar 20, at the late residence of Walter C Williams, dec'd, in Foxall's Row, all household furniture. Also, 2 valuable negro women, slaves for life-one a cook, the other a house servant & chamber-maid. —Clement Cox, adm -Thos C Wright, auct, Gtwn

Crml Court-Wash: Mar 16 John Magar, a county cnstbl, was indicted & tried for an assault & battery on Jos Johnson, in Wash City, on Feb 22, 1840: cnstbl was much intoxicated at the time-Johnson was being taken in for disorderly conduct. Jury found the dfndnt guilty. Fined $25 & costs of prosecution, & find security in $200 for his good behavior for one year.

Mrd: on Mar 17, by the Very Rev Dr Matthews, Mr Geo C Whiting to Miss Eliz, d/o John T Sullivan, of Wash City.

Died: on Mon, in Wash City, Edmund Henri James, in his 33rd year. His funeral is from the residence of his mother, corner of 14th & E sts, on Thu, at 10 a m.

Died: on Mar 16, in Wash City, Mrs Jane Crandall, formerly of Alexandria, in her 56th year, after a long & painful illness. Her remains will be interred at 10 a m. Her funeral is at the residence of her dght, Mrs L C Denny, in Third St.

Died: on Mar 16, Sarah Jane, infant d/o Fred'k & Maria Speiser. Her funeral is this afternoon at 3 p m.

Died: on Mar 15, in Alexandria, Colin Auld, aged 74 years. Mr Auld was a native of Scotland, & for the last 14 years a respectable citizen of Alexandria.

Died: Mar 13, in Alexandria, Mr Jas Johnston, a native of that place, aged 43 years.

THU MAR 19, 1840

J Johnson is authorized by Mrs Ann L Contee to sell a portion of the real estate which she derived from her father, the late Richd Snowden. The land lies in PG Co, adjoining the property of Mr Fitzhugh, within 1 mile of Balt & Ohio R R: about 60 acs, being part of a tract called *Friendship Enlarged*. -J J

Proposals will be received for grading & gravelling H st north. —Thos J Belt, com'r 3rd Ward. Perez Packard, Jas Towles, assist com'rs.

Died: on Tue, in Wash City, at Brown's Hotel, Mr Nathl Ray Thomas, aged 27 years, of Marshfield, Mass. He was on his way to the Western country, having been detained here some time by business.

Died: on Mar 14, at Richmond, Va, in his 14th year, Jas Lyons, jr, eldest s/o Jas Lyons. He leaves bereaved parents & a large circle of friends. —Whig

Died: on Mon, at the residence of her father, Mr Robt Gwathmey, in Richmond, Mrs Mary Ann Barney, w/o Mr Chas R Barney, of Balt.

The Hon John Lowell died of apoplexy on Fri, at his residence in Roxbury, Mass, aged 70: lawyer, statesman, politician, & a writer.

FRI MAR 20, 1840
Sale of grocs, crockery, china, & glass ware at the store of Mr J Danford, the balance of his stock in trade. —Edw Dyer, auct

For sale: on Mar 21, in front of the premises, that very valuable house & lot on Pa ave, now occupied by Mr Jas Riordan as a bookstore & lottery ofc. Lot fronts 16 feet on Pa ave: with excellent well finished 3 story brick house, covered with slate. —E Dyer, auct

Appointments by the Pres: Harmanus Bleecker, of N Y, to be Charge d'Affaires of the U S to the Netherlands. Geo H Flood, of Ohio, same, to the Republic of Texas, v Alcee Labranche, resigned. Henry Ledyard, of N Y, to be U S Sec of the Leg at Paris. Horace C Cammack to the U S Treas of the Branch Mint at New Orleans. Jos M Kennedy, to be Superintendent at same. John L Riddel, to be Melter & Refiner at same. Philos B Tyler, to be Coiner at same. Saml McRoberts, of Ill, to be Solicitor of the Gen Land Ofc, v Matthew Birchard, appointed Solicitor of the Treas. Jas S Green, to be U S Atty for the dist of N J, for 4 years, from Jan 13, 1840, when his former commission expired. John F Bacon, of N Y, to be U S Cnsl at Nassau, in the island of New Providence, v Geo Huyler. Js L Edwards to be Com'r of Pensions. Duncan B Graham, to be Register of the Land Ofc at Montg, Ala, v John H Sommerville, dec'd. Thos Johnson, to be Register of the Land Ofc at Batesville, Ark, v John Miller, who declines the appointment. Danl Ashby, to be Receiver of Public Moneys at Lexington, Mo, v Edwin M Ryland, superseded.

Senate: 1-Ptn from Thos Coates, asking to change a location of land, which is found to conflict with a Spanish grant. 2-Ptn from Philip Wheney, asking for a pension. 3-Ptn from John P Thompson, asking payment for a wagon & team. 4-Ptn from Edw S Wright, in relation to a contract. 5-Cmte on Pvt Land Claims: report in the case of Gregoire Sarpy. 6-Bill for relief of Capt Snodgrass' company of Missouri vols was taken up, & ordered to be engrossed for a 3rd reading. 7-Ptn from John Piper, a soldier of the Revolution. 8-Cmte on Pvt Land Claims: bill granting pre-emption rights to Enoch Evans. 9-Cmte on Revolutionary Claims: bill for the relief of Eliza Causin & the heirs of John Stone, dec'd. Also, for the relief of the legal reps of Capt Wm Williams, of N C. 10-Cmte of Claims: bill for the relief of Clements, Brian, & Co. 11-Bill introduced to confirm the claim of John Baptiste Lecompte to a tract of land in La. 12-Bill for relief of Zachariah & Robt Williams.

On Mar 6, the boilers of the steamboat *Commerce*, which left Appalachoochie, exploded, destroying the lives of 2 engrs, a passenger, Mr John Burton, of Appalachicola, & 3 deck hands

Died: on Mar 18, in Wash City, Thos Whelan, in his 35th year. His funeral is at Mr P Kinchey's at 11 a m.

Mr John Dal_arn, long a resident of Jeff Co, Va, was accidentally killed on Mon last, at his residence near Smithfield. He was leading a wild young horse with a rope halter, which was wrapped around his wrist, when the animal took fright & ran furiously some distance, dragging Mr D. He was so seriously injured, that he died instantly. He was about 55 years of age, & has left a wife & numerous relatives to lament his unexpected death. –Charlestown, Va. –Free Press

For rent: 2 story frame dwlg, west of Dr Buck's bldgs, fronting the Mall. Apply to Edmund Brooke

On Sat last, there was an exhibition at the Arsenal in this city of Cochran's Patent Repeating Cannon.

SAT MAR 21, 1840
Wash & Alexandria boat: steamboat *Jos Johnson* in complete order: departures from Wash & Alexandria. -Ignatius Allen, Capt

Lost: $80, which I laid for a moment on the window in the R R Ticket Ofc, while making change for another person. There were 3 $20 Va bills, one $20 Ga, payable at Augusta. Reasonable Reward. –T B Hamlin

Teacher: a young lady who is an experienced teacher wishes to form an engagement. Address: Danl Cumming, 4 So Gay st, Balt.

Drone, this high-bred stallion will make his season for the present year at the Kendall Course, near Balt, at $30 the season. –Jas B Kendall

Libel Case: in the case of the State of Md, vs, the Rev Robt J Breckenridge, for a libel upon Jas L Maguire, which has for a number of days been under trial at Balt, the Jury on Thur stated that they called not agree upon a verdict. They were then discharged. Ten were for acquittal, & 2 for conviction.

Died: on Mar 20, after a long & painful illness, Mr John Duke Emack, in his 38th year. Funeral from his late residence, C st, on Sun, at 3 p m.

MON MAR 23, 1840
For rent: store at present occupied by Mr Wm Egan, opposite Todd's apothecary shop. Apply to the occupant of the dwlg.

Exeter, N H: died in this town, on Sabbath night, Miss Martha Rogers, aged 78: d/o the late Rev Danl Rogers, of Exeter, who was the s/o Rev John Rogers, of Ipswich, Mass, who was the s/o Pres John Rogers, of Harvard Univ, a preacher of the gosepl, who was the s/o Rev Nathl Rogers, of Ipswich, who was the s/o Rev John Rogers, of Dedham, Eng, who was the grandson of Rev John Rogers, the martyr, who was burnt at Smithfield, Eng, Feb 5, 1555, nearly 3 centuries ago.

Amos G Thomas, who was acquitted before the Sup Court at Middletown, Conn, a few days since, on charge of murdering Mr Jared Burr, of Haddam, & robbing him of a considerable sum of money, we learn from the New Haven Herald, has since been arrested & committed to prison for highway robbery. The money of Mr Burr was found on his person, concealed in his coat collar.

War Dept, Jan 26, 1840. Letter to Brig Gen Z Taylor, commandng Army of the So Fla, from J R Poinsett. Subject: authorities of the Terr of Fla have imported a pack of bloodhounds from the Isl of Cuba: their use be confined altogether to the tracking the Indians.

Obit-died: on Feb 28, at the Albion Hotel, city of Boston, Wm Lee, late 2nd Aud of the U S Treas. In his relations as father, husband, brother, & friend, his character was distinguished by kindness & devotion.

Rufus H King elected Pres of the N Y State Bank, v Francis Bloodgood, dec'd.

Sudden illness of Mr Speaker Williams, Speaker of the Hse of Dels of Md, has been visited by a stroke of paralysis, from which it is feared he may not recover. Mr Giles elected Speaker for remainder of session.

Southern Patriot: the Navy Dept determined to make Charleston a naval station, & have appointed Capt Edw R Shubrick the first, & Lt Knight the 2nd ofcr on the station.

Passengers in the steam-ship *Great Western* for Bristol: Of N Y:

H H Leeds & lady	H H Dutilh	Mr Guire
Jos Sands	H Schultz	P S Forbes
H W Livingston	Henry Placide	Edw Fitzgerald
John Wallis, jr	Dr Julien Chabert	John Muir
Jas L Moore	H A Taylor	

Of Paris: Mr Devaraigne & lady, S Chuard, & C Demotte
Of Phil: J Morley, F A Packard, H Bohlen
Of London: Edw O Hornby, J Aspden, W H Ropas, G O Davenport
Of Ire: Edw Gammen   Of Balt: Mr Barney
Of Canandaigua: John Grieg &   Of Prussia: Mr Dyhrenforth
servant   Of Va: Andrew Leitch

Of Charleston: H Frazer
Of Natchez: Jas Ferguson
Of Montreal: Capt Douglass
Of St John, N B: John Wisbart
Of Mexico: Francisco Andraole
Of Havana: M de Mora & lady & Miss Mora
Of Grenada, W I: Thos Burgs
Of Eng: Mr Harrison
Of Glasgow: Mr Mills
Of Frankfort: Mr Roch
Of Trieste: G H Buckler
Of Leeds: John Terry

On Mar 5, while crossing the bridge over Venable's mill dam, near Barren Creek Springs, Somerset Co, Md, Mr Jas K Lewis & his wife, of this county, were precipitated down a precipice of about 20 feet, when the horse took fright: neither were injured. —Cambridge [Md] Chronicle

Appointments by the Pres: 1-Calvin Blythe, Collector of the Customs for the Dist of Phil, v Geo Wolf, dec'd. 2-Thos Turner, Chas Scott, Henry Naylor, Joshua Pierce, Saml Smoot & Henry Howison, to be J Ps for Wash Co, D C. 3-Wm N Mills, to be J P for Alexandria, D C.

Mrd: on Mar 22, by Rev Mr Nixon, Mr Jno McCauley to Miss Eliz Castel, both of Wash City.

Mrd: on Mar 8, in Balt, by Rev Mr Nardell, Mr Chas W Boteler, jr, of this city, to Miss Cath, d/o John Jos Pentz, of Balt.

Mrd: on Feb 26, in N Y, Lt Geo Pegram, of the U S Army, to Miss Susan Spencer, d/o the late Oliver H Spencer, of Eliz, N J.

Died: on Mar 20, in Wash City, of an affection of the liver, Mrs Paulina E Kinchy, a native of Belfort, France, w/o Paul Kinchy, in her 30th year. Her funeral is at 10 a m, this morning.

Died: on Mar 19, after a few days sickness of congestive fever, Mr Chapman F Newton, aged 21 years, late of Louisville, Ky, y/s/o Mr Augustine Newton, of Wash City. A devoted son & brother.

Died: on Mar 8, at New Orleans, after a protracted & lingering illness, Chas J D Freeland, recently arrived from Richmond, Va, aged 31 years. He was a practical printer, of good capacity & highly respectable character, who had many friends in Wash. Disease threatened his life for many months.

Died: on Wed last, at Phil, Dr Jos Parrish, in his 63rd year, well known as a physician of eminence & respectability.

Senate: 1-Ptn from Prudence C Loring, asking for a pension. 2-Ptn from the heirs of Gen Ezra Meade. 3-Cmte on Pvt Land claims: bill for relief of the heirs of Jos

Thompson, dec'd, confirming a tract of land in Missouri. 4-Cmte of Claims: unfavorable report on the ptn of Wm C Hollinger.

Hse o/Reps: 1-Bills to be engrossed for a 3rd reading: relief of Bates & Lacon; of Jas W Osborne; of Danl D Walker; of Balt; of Chastelain & Pouvert; of Ebenezer A Lester; of Nicholas Hedges; of Ebenezer D Lobdell; of Richd Booker & others; of John Howe; of John Wilkinson; of Thos W Taylor; of Jas Cox; of Chauncey Calhoun; of Gamaliel E Smith; of Garret Vliet; of Cornelius Tiers; of John Underwood; of Josiah Thompson; of Sylvester Phelps & heirs of Chas Landon; of John T Addoms; of Capt John Downes; of Benj C Roberts; of Boggs & Thompson; of Thos Fillebrown; of Robt & Thos Hutchinson, & others; of Meigs D Benjamin & Co; of Wm Wickham; of John M Jacquellin; & of Geo Willis.

A sub-Treas before the Revolution: from the History of N Y, from the first discovery to the year 1732, by Wm Smith, A M, with a continuation to the year 1840. In 1691, under the adm of Gov Henry Sloughter, the Genr'l Assembly established a revenue. Gov Fletcher was succeeded by Richd, Earl of Bellamont, who in his opening speech, gave the Assembly his word of honor that he would not steal the public money. Bellamont was a man of his word. His successor was Lord Cornbury, who was removed in Jun, 1721. In 1741, Lt Gov Clark complained of the encroachment of the Legislature upon his prerogatives. –Watertown Reg

Tuscaloosa, Ala: on Mar 5-difficulty between Washington Moody & Maj John Cantley, both of this city, led to Mr Moody shooting a dbl-barrelled gun at Maj C, hitting him in the stomach, & as he turned to make his escape, the other barrel was discharged to the back of his head. Maj C instantly fell to the ground. Mr Moody delivered himself to the civil authorities.

TUE MAR 24, 1840
Students of Richmond, [Va] Academy, held on Mar 17, a meeting to pay respect to the sudden & untimely death of their late fellow-student, Jas Lyons, jr. Thos Jeff Peyton was called to the chair, & John R Thompson appointed sec. Students to attend the funeral today & wear the badge of mourning on the left arm for 10 days.

Notice: Whereas my wife, Eliz A Markins, on Mar 15, left my bed & board without any just cause or provocation, I hereby forewarn all persons from harboring or trusting her on my account, as I am determined not to pay any debt she may contract. Persons offending against this ad will be proceeded against according to law.
–John S Markins

A fair will be held at the residence of Mrs Lethe Tanner, corner of H & 14th sts, with a view to defray the expenses of the Colored Israel Conference, which will take place on Apr 17 next.

Mr Custis, of Arl, has presented to the Hon J K Paulding, to Washington Irving, & to Mrs Sigourney, each a case with slips from the descendant of Pope's Willow. the slips to be distributed by the distinguished authors above named, & charming poetess, to the most worthy of Littérateurs, male & female, in the U S. History of Pope's Willow, implanted in the American soil, is as follows: In 1775, John Park Custis, the father of Mr Custis of Arl, while on duty as Aid-de-Camp to the Cmdr-in-Chief, at the siege of Boston, had an opportunity of showing some civilities to a British ofcr, made prisoner in a transport. Upon the evacuation of Boston, & march of the American forces toward N Y, the Briton, grateful for the kindnesses he had received, presented to the Aid-de-Camp a small oil-skin case, hermetrically sealed, containing slips, cut by the ofcr's own hand, from Pope's celebrated Willow at Twickenham, the ofcr believing that the troubles in America would soon cease, & he should remain with his regt for a good many years in the colonies, he had brought over the willow to adorn some little establishment he proposed to purchase near Boston, & thus implant the descendants of the great poet's favorite tree in the Western hemipshere. Mr C brought with him, in his portmanteau, the British ofcr's present: & 65 years ago, planted the Willow of Twickenham on the banks of the Potomac, some magnificent specimens are now flourishing near Arlington house. The Weeping Willow is said to be of Asiatic origin, & first introduced in England from a ship found in a pkg of Smyrna figs. When Pope's Willow decayed, it was dug up by the roots, & conveyed into the Grotto, & innumerable were the relics cut from the lifeless substance, to be preserved in veneration of the illustrious Bard.

Hse o/Reps: 1-Ptn of Jesse Willis & others: referred. 2-Ptn of Vincent J Strickland, asking compensation for cattle taken by the U S army. 3-Ptn of P Kennon, asking a pension for a wound received in the Indian war. 4-Ptn of Col Wm Wyatt, praying remuneration for losses sustained on a contract with the U S for brick. 5-Proposal of Jacob Houseman to end the Fla war, & catch the Indians for $200 a head. 6-Claims of Augus M Crawford & Saml Carter for horses. 7-Ptn of widow Garcia, a murdered post rider's widow. 8-Ptn of Isaac S Middleton, for compensation for extra service at the Navy yard, Pensacola. 9-Ptn of Wm Walton, for compensation for lost horses. 10-Ptn of Jas & Geo Anderson, asking remuneration for losses sustained by the Indians. 11-Ptn of Mr Hamburgh, for losses sustained by the murder of his partner at Coozahatchie. 12-Ptn of J & N Hamblin, for compensation for wood purchased & used by the U S steamboats. 13-Ptn of Col Fitzpatrick, proposing to end the Fla war by contract. 14-Papers of T W Dabney & Alex'r Watson, in relation to their claims for property destroyed by the Indians. 15-Ptn of Jas Roan, claiming a pre-emption right granted to Donalson, which is since covered by Forbes' grant & asking to locate it elsewhere. 16-Additional evidence in the case of Col Tucker, presented. 17-Memorial of R K Call.

Died: on Mar 22, Mary Emma, 2nd d/o Buckner & Cath B Bayliss, aged 1 year, 9 months & 10 days.

Died: on Mar 8, at Louisville, Ky, in her 53rd year, after an illness of several months, Mrs Jane Martin Johnson, consort of Francis Johnson. Mrs Johnson was a native of Ky, & the d/o Col Richd Young.

Died: on Mar 17, at the residence of her father, Dr Francis W Hawkins, in her 40th year, after a long & tedious illness, Mrs Susanna Jane Matthews, w/o Gen John Matthews, near Port Tobacco, Chas Co, Md.

WED MAR 25, 1840

Lexington [Ky] Intell: On the 13th, the extensive flouring mills & cotton factory belonging to Mr A Caldwell were destroyed by fire: supposed to be the work of an incendiary. Loss estimated at $30,000.

Mrd: on Wed last, in Wash, by Rev Mr Hawley, Col Wm Nichols, of La, to Miss Adelaide Jackson, d/o John F Jackson, of Pr Wm Co, Va.

Died: on Feb 13, at Savannah, Ga, Mr Benj A Childs, of D C, leaving numerous relations & friends to mourn his untimely departure. His death was caused by an injury sustained by the running away of the horses attached to an omnibus in which he was a passenger.

Died: on Mar 23, after a short but painful illness, Mrs Mary J Kennedy, w/o Wm H Kennedy, of Fredericksburg, & d/o Mr Fred'k Golding. Funeral at her father's residence, on 7th st, at 4 p m today.

Crct Court for Wash Co, D C: in Chancery. Pres, Dirs, & Co of the Farmers' Bank of Md, vs, Jas Murray & Charlotte W his wife, & Keturah Rackliffe. On Mar 17, 1835, the dfndnts joined in a mortgage to the cmplnts of lots 8, 9, & 10 in sq 166, in Wash City, to secure a certain debt owing to the cmplnts by the dfndnts, & one Sarah E Murray, of whom said Jas Murray was the principal debtor; that of said debt there remains unpaid & now due & in arrears, the sum of $3,563, on interest from Aug 9, 1839, until paid, &, by reason of the failure of said Murray to pay the same, the mortgage has become absolute at law, but is subject to the dfndnt's equity of redemption. Object of the bill is to have a short day limited for the payment to the cmplnts of said sum, with interest. It appears that the dfndnts reside out of D C: same to appear on or before the first Mon in Aug next. -Wm Brent, clk

Senate: 1-Memorial of Wm E Kennedy. 2-Cmte on Pensions, to which was referred the ptns of the wid/o John Vial; of the wid/o Jonathan Tewgood; of the wid/o Geo Hood;, the memorial of Joel Leftwich;, & the ptn of Jas Pierce: made unfavorable reports thereon. 3-Cmte on Commerce: bill for relief of the legal reps of Aaron Vail, late Cnsl at L'Orient: ordered to a 2nd reading. 4-Bills for the relief of Elliot Smith & Nathan Farnsworth: referred to the Cmte of Claims.

One cent Reward & no thanks, for the apprehension & delivery to the undersigned Barbara Ann Mattingly, an indented apprentice, who ran away from my house late Dec, without any reason whatever. All persons are hereby warned against harboring, employing, or in any other way encouraging said runaway, as I intend to enforce the law in relation to such cases. –Francis Morun

Wash Corp: 1-Ptn of Mrs M Mechlin: referred to the Cmte of Claims. 2-Ptn from Lewis Carusi: referred to the Cmte of Claims. 3-Ptn of A Casenove & others, on the subject of the wharfage on fish: referred to the Cmte of Ways & Means. 4-Ptn of Wm W Seaton & others, praying for improvement of 6th st west: referred to the Cmte on improvements. 5-Ptn of Jos Wimsatt, remonstrating against a reduction of the wharfage on fish: referred to the Cmte of Ways & Means. 6-Ordered that Fred'k Dawes have leave to withdraw his ptn, presented on Nov 18 last. 7-Ptn of Henry Johnson, praying permission to enclose certain sts adjacent to sqs 174 & 188: referred-to Cmte on Police.

For sale: a farm-about 300 acs, on the B & O R R. To view the property call on the subscriber, Horace Capron, at the Laurel Factory, or to the person having charge of the farm.

Hse o/Reps: 1-Cmte on Revolutionary Pensions: to inquire into compensating Sally Stanby for the Revolutionary services of her husband. 2-Case of Polly Hamilton for a pension, on which an adverse report was made by the Cmte on Revolutionary Pensions on Mar 5, be recommitted to the same cmte. 3-Cmte on Military Affairs to inquire into purchasing of John W Cochran his six-pounder brass cannon model for a large garrison gun for seaboard defence.

THU MAR 26, 1840
Senate: 1-Ptn from Benj Homans & Alfred B Claxton, of Wash City, praying to be released from the penalty of a certain bond. 2-Cmte on Claims: adverse reports on the memorial of John W Thompson, & the memorial of Jas Morgan. 3-Bill reported for the relief of Hugh Stewart: ordered to a 2nd reading. 4-Cmte on the Judiciary: adverse report on the claim of Jas Williams: ordered to be printed. 5-Bill for relief of Jas Herron introduced.

Public sale at *Good Luck*, PG Co, Md, on Apr 3, the following tracts of land: *Expedition, Addition to Hope Enlarged, & Parcel Enlarged:* 300 acs more or less, which was mortgaged by the late Jas Beck to Walter Smith & Clement Smith: land is about 12 miles from Wash. –N C Stephen, D C Digges, Bladensburg, Md

Trustee's sale of valuable improved property: deed of trust executed by Hon Buckner Thruston, of Wash City, dated Jan 1, 1839: lot 18 & 19 in sq 16; brick house & lot on So B st, in sq 690, with all bldgs. –Dean James, trustee. –E Dyer, auct

Protection Ins Co: Seth Hyatt, of Wash Co, agent for the Co of Hartford, Conn. —J M Goodwin, sec, Hartford, Conn

Mrd: yesterday, in St John's Church, by Rev Dr Hawley, Chas Willing, M D, of Phil, to Rebecca, d/o the Hon Jos L Tillinghast, Mbr of Congress from R I.

FRI MAR 27, 1840

Hse o/Reps: 1-Cmte on Naval Affairs: to inquire into paying to Jas Fenasye, late a pvt in the Marine Corps, the sum of $19.66, which he claims as prize money for assisting in the capture of certain Algerine vessels in the Mediterranean sea in 1815, & letters from the Sec of the Navy & the said Fenasye, be referred to the said cmte. 2-Resolved that the Cmte on Pvt Land Claims: to inquire into a reissue of land warrant #1161, for 300 acs, issued on Feb 21, 1826, in the name of Jas Erwin & other heirs at law of Jos Evin, which said warrant is lost. 3-Cmte on Revolutionary Pensions: to inquire into granting a pension to Mgt McIntire. 4-Cmte on Invalid Pensions: to inquire into allowing a pension to Jacob Jackson, of N Y. 5-Resolved that the report of the Sec of the Navy as relates to the claim of arrears of pension of Maria Harrison, only child of John Garde, dec'd, late a sailingmaster on board the U S ship *Insurgent*, together with the proof & other papers therewith submitted, be referred to the Cmte on Naval Affairs. 6-Cmte on Revolutionary Pensions: to inquire into allowing the heirs of Dr Saml Kennedy interest on the 5 years half pay granted to his heirs by an act of Congress passed in 1832. 7-Cmte on Naval Affairs: to inquire into granting a pension to the wid/o Capt Philemon Gatewood, of the Revenue service, who died from disease contracted in the U S service, whilst co-operating with the naval forces on the coast of Fla.

On Tue last, an inquest was held by Thos Woodward, coroner, & a jury, in view of the body of a negro woman, Hannah Datcher, who was found in Rock Creek, near Gtwn, on Mar 24. Verdict: dec'd accidentally fell into the creek & was drowned, the night being very dark.

Wm C Orme: dry goods, at his store. [Ad]

Senate: 1-Papers in relation to the claims of the heirs of Robt Fulton. 2-Paper in relation to the claim of Dr Manser for services in Fla. 3-Cmte on Naval Affairs: an adverse report on the memorial of the adm of John B Fanning, late purser in the U S Navy.

Horrid events: Mr John B Austin's large dwlg, 4 miles from Yonkers, was burnt down on Mar 21, & 6 of his 14 chldrn perished in the flames: 3 sons & 3 dghts, all under 20, were in an upper room, & called not be reached. The house of Mr Ebn Trip, at Schoharie, was destroyed by fire, & his dght, 13, & an infant grand-dght, perished in the flames. —N Y Star

Died: on Mar 18, at her residence in Phil, in her 73rd year, Mrs Ann Cheavens, a native of Yorkshire, Eng, & mother of Wm Easby, of Wash City.

Early corn, garden & flower seeds, just received a supply. On hand, a quantity of Silk Worms' Eggs. -Ann Gardiner, nearly opposite the Catholic Chr.

SAT MAR 28, 1840
Senate: 1-Ptn from John McClenahan, asking to be placed on the pension roll. 2-Ptn from Mary Linn, asking remuneration for the services of her late husband in the Revolutionary war. 3-Cmte of Claims. the bill for the relief of Don Carlos Dehault Delassaus, without amendment, & gave notice that when it came up he should move for its indefinite postponement.

Balt Annual Conf of the Meth E Chr. holding its session the past 10 days at Gtwn, adjourned on Tue. The following are the appointments for:
Potomac Dist: Edwin Dorsey, P E
Alexandria, Geo G Cookman, & Jos Plotner
Wesley Chapel, John Davis
Lancaster: Wm Hank
Gtwn: W B Edwards
Rock Crk: Wm H Laney
Fredericksburg: Thos C Hayes
Fairfax: Thos Wheeler, Geo W Israel
Warrenton: Littleton F Morgan
Stafford: Nelson Head, Robt T Nixon
Loudoun: Robt Cadden, Thos Sewall, jr
Lancaster: Wm Hank, Layton I Hansberger
Westmoreland: Wm O Lumsden, E McCollum
Leesburg: Stephen G Roszel, Stephen A Roszel
Foundry: Thos C Thornton, Jas M Hanson, sup

Mission to colored people in Westmoreland: Jas Berkley

N Y Times: Donald McLeod has retired from the post of Assoc Editor of that paper, having connected himself with another political journal of the highest character for ability & usefulness.

Duff Green proposes to publish in the city of Balt a newspaper to be called "The Pilot". Born & educated in the West, he has known Gen Harrison personally, & he has known Mr Van Buren since 1826.

Died: on Mar 19, in St Mary's Seminary, Balt, the Rev John Tessier, in his 82nd year.

Died: on Mar 15, at Pawling, Mr John Wooden, aged 83 years.

Died: on Feb 23, at St Andrew's, U C, Alex'r McDonald, partner in the Hudson Bay Co.

Died: on Mar 20, at Sodus, Wayne Co, N Y, Rev W. Stone, aged 83 years.

Suicide: Saml Grafton, aged 18 years, in Kings Co, N Y, from a self inflicted shot to the heart. He formed an attachment for a young lady, which was not reciprocated.

Boots, shoes, store fixtures at auct: on Mar 30: at my store, the 2 story brick house on the north side of Pa ave, between 3rd & 4th sts. –R Brooke –Ed Dyer, auct

MON MAR 30, 1840
Hse o/Reps: 1-Mr Lincoln presented, by leave, a memorial of Edw S Wright, surety of Benj Homans & Alfred B Claxton, of Wash City, praying to be exonerated from his liability as surety in a bond: referred to the Cmte on the Judiciary. 2-Bills read a 3rd time & passed: for the relief of Lewis H Bates & Wm Lacon; of Jas W Osborne, of Balt; of the legal reps of Jas Wilkinson, dec'd; of Saml D Walker; of Zachariah Jellison; of Chastelain & Ponvert; of Ebenezer A Lester; of Nicholas Hedges; of Ebenezer Lobdell; of Richd Booker & others, of John Howe; of Thos W Taylor; of Jas Cox; of Chauncey Calhoun, of Gamaliel E Smith; of Garret Vleit; of Cornelius Tiers; of John Underwood; of Josias Thompson, superintendent of the Cumberland road between Brownsville & Wheeling; of Sylvester Phelps & the heirs or legal reps of Chas Landon, dec'd; of John T Addoms, exc of John Addoms; of Capt John Downes; of Benj C Roberts; of Boggs & Thompson, Robert & Thos Hutchinson & others; of Meigs D Benjamin & Co; of Wm Wickam; of Geo Willis, & of Thos Fillebrown, jr. 3-Bill for the relief of John M Jacquelin was ordered to be engrossed & read a 3rd time today. 4–Bill for the relief of Wm Bailey, survivor of Bailey & Delord, was postponed to Apr 3.

We learn that Capt Thos H Stevens has been appointed Cmndnt of the Yard, v Cmdor Patterson, dec'd. He is a resident of this city, so favorably known to them during his former service at that Yd.

Texas: J W Eldridge, editor of the Houston Star, is dead.

Died: on Sat last, Jane Laura Eleanor, d/o J B & J J Wingerd, aged 3 years, 1 month & 29 days. Funeral today at 11 a m, from their residence on D, between 7th & 8th sts.

At New Orleans in Mar 16 last, Capt St Clair was stabbed to death by a Mr Reilly, the keeper of the Commercial Hotel, Girod & Levee sts. He attacked him with a Bowie knife.

Arrested on Sat by R R Burr, cnstbl, Addison Brown, a fugitive from justice, charged with being concerned in several robberies in Wash City, in the dwlg house of Mr Gregory Ennis, & Mrs McDaniel.

Wash Navy Yard: attached to the Navy Yard: Mar 1, 1840: Capt, Thos Holdup Stevens, Cmndnt
Cmder, John H Aulick
Lt, Robt B Cunningham
Surg, David S Edwards
Assist Surg, Chas A Hassler
Purser, Dudley Walker
Chaplain, Wm Ryland
Mstr, Marmaduke Dove
Gunner, Thos Barry
Navy Agent, Ellis Kane
Navy Storekeeper, Cary Selden
Mstr Blacksmith, Jas Tucker
Mstr Blockmkr, Amon Woodward
Mstr Engr, Wm M Ellis
Mstr Joiner, John H Smoot
Mstr Plumber, John Davis of Abel
Clk of the Navy Yard, Richd Barry
Inspec & measurer of timber, Jas Carbery
Clk of Cmndnt, Wm H Bayne
Clk of Cmndnt, David M Comb
Clk of Storekeeper, Geo Herold
Clk of Mstr Bldr, Francis Barry, sen
Porter, Thos Ward
Keeper of the Magazine, Wm Hebb

Henry Bishop appointed a constable in Wash Co, D C: can generally be found or heard of in the ofcs of W Thompson, B K Morsell, & C T Coote, in the 3rd Ward. –H B

TUE MAR 31, 1840
Mrd: on Mar 24, at Phil, Capt Chas F Smith, of the 2nd Regt U S Artl, to Fanny, d/o the late Henry Mactier, of Balt.

Retention of defaulters in Ofc. 1-Jos Reckless, Collector at Perth Amboy, N J: willfully withheld from the U S a credit for tonnage money received for a vessel: his excuse was, that he retained it to meet various claims against the vessel, for which claims he had, as he pretended, made himself liable. He also exhibited fraudulent receipts-sum charged was $447, & amount paid only $145. 2-The case of Wm Linn, Receiver of Public Money at Vandlia, Ill. He wound up a defaulter: & was permitted to resign, a peculator in the sum of $55,962.06. 3-Wiley P Harris, Receiver of Public Money at Columbus, Miss: went on treading in his own footsteps, until in 1836, the balance of public money in his hands amounted to $128,884.70: on Aug 31, in a letter to the Pres, he resigned. He recommends Col Gordon D Boyd, of Attala Co, his successor. 4-Boyd was appointed. The amount of Mr Harris' defalcations was $109,178.08, about $20,000 less than the amount stated in Mr Sec Woodbury's letter of Jun 6, 1836. Geo D Boyd: pecuniary part alone of his defalcation was $55,965.54. 5-John Spencer, Receiver of Public Moneys at Fort Wayne, Ind: failed to make the returns of public money required by law: defaulter to the amount of $5,206.84. He is still in ofc.

WED APR 1, 1840
Washington Branch Railroad: Saml Stettinius, Agent. [Ad]

Hse o/Reps: 1-Memorial of G Stow & others, citizens of Keeseville, N Y, praying for the passage of uniform laws on bankruptcy. Like memorial from H K Averill & others, citizens of Plattsburg, N Y. 2-Ptn of Ezra Thurber praying that a certain suit instituted against him by the U S be dismissed. 3-Ptn of Slocum Howland, Allen Thomas, & others, for a repeal of the rule rejecting anti-slavery ptns. 4-Ptn of Geo B Throop & others, for an improvement of the harbor at Little Sodum, N Y. 5-Ptn of Horace Hills & others for a bankrupt law. 6-Ptn of Humphrey Howland & others for a Congress of Nations. 7-Ptn of Abijah Fitch & others, for abolishing the use of ardent spirits in the army, the Capitol, & among the Indian tribes. 8-Ptn of Jos Tallcott & others, against the use of bloodhounds. 9-Ptn of W H Noble & others, for the relief of Jacob McDonald. 10-Ptn of Benj Waterman, praying compensation for carrying the mail from Buffalo to Lodi, N Y. 11-Ptn of John Van Horn, asking compensation for grist-mill & house burned during the last war on the Eighteen-mile creek, Niagara Co, N Y. 12-Ptn of Edw Putnam for a pension: referred to the Cmte on Revolutionary Pensions. 13-Ptn of Amos Green & others, heirs-at-law of John Green, dec'd, asking for arrearages of pension due the dec'd: referred to the Cmte on Revolutionary Pensions. 14-Ptn of David Barlett, for interest on balance of account. 15-Ptn of Wm A Howard & others, for a duty on imported cigars. 16-Ptn of S P Child & others, for a light-house on Sandy Point, Prudence Isl, Narragansett Bay. 17-Ptn of Riley Steene & others, for the recognition of the independnce of Hayti: laid on the table. 18-Ptn of Saml Brown, for increase of compensation as naval ofcr. 19-Ptn of Phebe Moore & others, of Newport, R I, Hannah Sisson & others, Asa Simon & others, Asa Simon, jr, & others, Patience Hall & others, Alfred Goldsmith & others, Abraham Wilkinson & others, Geo Taft & others, Louisa Jencks & others, Edw Mason & others, Sarah W Harris & others, Ruth Ingraham & others, Riley Steene & others, praying for the abolition of slavery & slave trade in D C & Territories, & of slave trade between the states, & against the admission of new states recognizing slavery. 20-Ptn of J M Broadhead, claiming an allowance for apprehending certain deserters from the Marine corps. 21-Ptn of Stephen Livingston & Richd Livingston, only heirs of Richd Livingston, who served as Lt Col during the Revolutionary war, praying for the commutation of 5 years full pay. 22-Ptn of Casper B Cook & others, members of a band of music attached to the 19th Regt 11th Brig & 14th Div of N Y Inf, which was ordered to Sackett's Harbor in 1814, during the late war with England, praying for compensation for service. 23-Ptn of Jos McIntyre, Lemuel Wilcox, & Jas Stewart, for relief for losses sustained on a contract with the U S in 1818. 24-Ptn of Eli Benedict & others, against the annexation of Texas: ordered to be laid on the table. 25-Memorial of Ebenezer Disbrow & others, remonstrating against the rule adopted by the Hse on Jan 28, 1840: laid on the table.

The aged Matron of the Revolution: the wid/o Brig Gen John Paterson, late of N Y state, & a Gen ofcr of the Mass Continental line, is now living at Ogden, N Y. One of her grandsons writes of visiting his grandmother, who is near 100 years old, & found her sprightly & in perfect health. She is the oldest female in this state, & amongst the last of our Revolutionary mothers. --Charleston Courier

Sgt-Maj Geer, while superintending the ball practice of the Coldstream Guards, imprudently stood in front of the division while giving orders. He had given the word "Present!", &, while obeying the order, a hair trigger caught on his cuff of the coat of one of the men, & sent the ball thru the ofcr's head. Verdict, "accidental death."

Mrd: on Oct 28, by Rev Mr Donelan, Jas Pilling to Susan E Dalton, all of Wash City

Mrd: on Jan 30 last, at the Leg of the U S, at Constantinople, Mr John P Brown, Dragoman of the U S Leg, to Miss Mary Ann Porter, niece of Com Porter

Harrisburg, on Mar 27, the only d/o Gen Evans, member of the Hse o/Reps from Armstrong Co, drowned in the river. She was about 7 years old.

Senate: 1-Ptn from Jno Johnson, former Indian agent, praying to be released from a certain judgment obtained against him by the Gov't. 2-Ptn from Mrs Mary Thompson, wid/o Lt Col Thompson, late an ofcr in the army, asking remuneration for expenditures made by her husband. 3-Ptn from a number of citizens of the county & city of Phil, asking that Congress remit the remainder of the imprisonment of Wm Lyon Mackenzie, held in durance for a breach of the U S neutrality laws: suggestion sent to the U S Pres. 4-Cmte on Pensions: adverse on the claim of John Bosworth. 5-Cmte of Claims: bill for relief of Henry Lucas & A C King. 6-Cmte on Naval Affairs: adverse report on the claim of Ben L Carleton. Also, an adverse report in the case of Wm Ramsay. 7-Cmte on Pensions: bill for relief of Hannah Allen, wid/o Saml Allen. Adverse report on the claim of T R Saunders. Adverse report on the claim of Wm Ross. Also, on the claim of Lewis Newnsha. 8-Cmte on Patents: bill for relief of Jas Herron.

$200 reward for runaway negro woman Eliz Dover, or Fillman. Believe she was taken off by a colored hackman. —Wm Thos Carroll

For rent & possession immediately: 2 story brick house, with basement to it, being on I st, adjoining Dr McWilliams'. Apply to V Pulizzi.

THU APR 2, 1840
Benj Lowndes, late of Md, Atty & Cnslr at Law, New Orleans. [Ad]

Atty's at Law, Mobile, Ala: Chas E Sherman & John A Chambers. [Ad]

For sale at public auction: the Hygeia Hotel, at Old Point Comfort, Fortress Monroe, Va. It is now under rent of $1,500 per annum, clear of all taxes, payable qrtrly. —John G Colley, adm of Marshall Parks -Jno H Nash, auct

Valuable property for sale: located in Bladensburg, Md. about 2 acs with a frame store-hse & dwlg. Possession immediately. –B L Jackson, Wash City, or Thos Ferrall, Bladensburg, Md.

$50 reward for a new Seine-boat & the sails of the schn'r *Archimedes*, which were taken from said schn'r off St Geo's Isl, in the Potomac river, where she was sunk, on Mar 28. Information to Perry & Shepherd, Nanjemoy, Chas Co, Md, or J & E T Sanders, Balt, Md, or A Shepherd, Wash, D C.

Died: Apr 1, Eliz, infant d/o Robt & Jane Farnham, aged 2 years & 7 months. Her funeral is today at 3 p m.

Mrd. on Feb 25, at Goshen, Orange Co, Va, by Rev David Wood, Mr Wm T Eliason, of Madison Co, to Miss Susan G, d/o Geo Pannill.

Orphans Court of Wash Co, D C. Letters of administration on the personal estate of Eliza Brunet, late of said county, dec'd. –B L Bogan, exc.

Teacher wanted in his family: J O Wharton, Avondale, near Clear Spring, Wash Co, Md.

FRI APR 3, 1840

Died: on Apr 2, Mr Gabriel Suter, in his 43rd year, after a short illness. Funeral from his late residence on G st, between 5th & 6th sts, Sat, 2 p m.

St Patrick's Day, Wash City: friends of Ireland assembled for dinner at Carusi's saloon. Among the guests were Geo Washington P Custis, of Arl, the adopted s/o Washington; & the V P of the U S, the Hon Richd M Johnson. Also attended: Jas Carson; Jas Hoban-V P of the U S; Mr Edw Stubbs; Mr Chas Murray; Theophilus Fisk; John Boyle, P Fred'k White; Ambrose Lynch; M Wall; Dr Boyd Reilly; John H Shea, of Balt; Jas Handley; Jas Maher; John Foy; Philip Ennis; Lt Maguire; A Ager; Michl Ryan; Barney Kelley; Michl O'Brian; John Boyle; Thos Jordan; Wm Devereux; John Joyce; Wm Hughes; Michl Hughes.

Senate: 1-Ptn from Thos Goin, a resident of N Y C, asking remuneration for time & money spent in aiding the naval school apprenticeship system. 2-Ptn from the nephews of the late Gen Herkimer, asking Congress to renew an appropriation of $500, passed by the old Congress in 1777, to erect a monument to the memory of their departed uncle. 3-Ptn from Owen McCue, a citizen of D C, asking Congress to take some steps to secure him the payment of a prize of $10,000, drawn under the authority of Congress in Wash some number of years since. 4-Cmte of Claims: adverse report on the Hse bill for the relief of Thos Fillebrown.

For rent: large room over John Sheahan's Fruit Store, opposite Gadsby's. Apply to John Sheahan.

Appointed by the Pres: Hiram P Hastings, of N Y, to be Cnsl of the U S for the port of Trinidad de Cuba, v Henry Ulshoeffer, dec'd. Allen Wardwell, Surveyor & Inspec of the Rev at Bristol, R I, from Mar 28, when his late commission expired. Wm McNides, Collector of the Customs at Edenton, N C, v Robt Ezell, who declined the appointment. E A F Lavallette [formerly Vallette] to be a Capt in the Navy from Feb 23, 1840. Joshua R Sands to be Cmder from Feb 23. H J Hartstene to be Lt from Feb 23. Benj F Sands to be Lt from Mar 16.

The brig *Escambia*, Capt Dunham, belonging to Messrs E D Hurlbut & Co was lost at sea on Mar 25, while on her passage from Charleston to N Y, & out of 16 persons who were on board only one is known to be saved. Persons on board: Capt Rufus Dunham; the mate, Wm Bulkley; 2nd mate, Edwin Hull; J Chamberlain, cook & steward; Isaac Tradle, Henry Johnston, John Williams, John Peters, Jas Lucas, & Allen Jackson, seaman; Mr Wilber of Newport, R I, & 2 others, names unknown, passengers

Jas Wills, the eccentric low comedian, well known in this city, in Boston, & in N Y, as an excellent actor of the Reeve school, committed suicide a short time since at Natchez.

Hse o/Reps: 1-Mr Custis, of N Y, presented the memorial of Jas A Stevens & others, proprietors of the steamboats *Albany* & *De Witt Clinton*, & about 28 others, who desire that practical knowledge may form the basis of legislation in the practice of steam navigation. 2-Ptn of A P Smith & others, citizens of N Y C, praying for the passage of a bankrupt law. 3-Ptn of David Prouty & others of Spencer, Mass, praying the reduction of the rate of letter postage. 4-Ptn of Persia Morgan, wid/o Maj Abner Morgan, an ofcr of the Revolution army, praying that she may be placed on the pension list: referred to the Cmte on Revolutionary Pensions. 5-Ptn of Jacob Jackson, of China, N Y, for a pension, & futher papers from Sylvester Tiffany, relating to a pension.

Senate: 1-Memorial from J J Robertson, praying that the chldrn of American foreign missionaries, born abroad, may be accounted native American citizens. 2-Memorial of the heirs of John Chalmers, praying compensation for property destroyed by the enemy during the last war. 3-Memorial of Mathew Winslow & others, praying remuneration for errors in land surveys. 4-Bill for relief of Jacob Greaves was taken up, & to be engrossed for a 3rd reading.

Caution: there are no copies of the works, either in marble or plaster, yet for sale in the U S: productions of Hiram Powers, the American sculptor, now in Florence, Italy. —Boyd Reilly

SAT APR 4, 1840
Senate: 1-Ptn from Preston Starrit, asking compensation for losses sustained under a certain contract. 2-Leave obtained for John Nantz to withdraw his ptn & papers. 3-Bill for relief of Jacob Greaves, & the bill to file claims to lands in the dist between Rio Hondo & Sabine Rivers, passed

Mrd: on May 31, in Balt, by Rev Dr Wyatt, Lt Wm H French, 1st Regt U S Artl, to Caroline, d/o the late Geo Read, of Dela.

Hse o/Reps: 1-Ptn of Jos Balch, pres of the Merchants' Ins Co, & ofcrs of numerous Ins Cos, merchants, ship-mstrs & owners, & pilots, asking for erection of a light-hse on Minot's Rock, Boston harbor: referred to the Cmte on Commerce. 2-Ptn of John Lilly & others, mfgrs of umbrellas & parasols, asking to have the duty restored which, by the adjudication of the Courts, has been held not to be applicable to those articles imported into the U S: referred to the Cmte of Ways & Means. 3-Ptn of Phoebe Rogers, of Charlestown, Mass, setting forth that her husband was a head rigger in the employ of the Gov't in the Navy Yard in Charlestown, when he fell from the fore-yard of the ship *Independence*, & was killed, representing also her extreme poverty & distress, & asking a provision in her favor: referred to the Cmte on Military Affairs. 4-Ptn of Eliz Sweatt, only surviving child of Benj Richards, representing that her father was in the service of his country on board the U S brig of war *Pickering*, in 1800, when the vessel was lost with all on board, & praying that she may be admitted to a participation in the Navy Pension Fund, to which she has been advised that she is entitled: referred to the Cmte on Naval Affairs. 5-Ptn of heirs of Bartholomew Trore, late of Charlestown, Mass, setting forth the meritorious services of their ancestor in the Revolutionary war, & praying compensation therefor: referred to the Cmte on Revolutionary Claims. 6-Ptn of Benj Lyon, of Dorchester, Mass, representing his Revolutionary services, & asking to be put upon the roll of Revolutionary pensioners: referred to the Cmte on Revolutionary Pensions.

Boarding: Mrs Jane Taylor, commodious house on Pa ave: terms being moderate.

Sale of very genteel furn. order of Orphans Court sale at late residence of the late John Duke Emack, on C st: all his household & kitchen furniture -Johnson Hellen, adm -Ed Dyer, auct

For rent: large 3 story brick house, on E st, 2 doors east of C James' Apothecary Store, corner of 14th st & Pa ave. Inquire of C Hayden, 2 doors east, or to Wm Cammack, on G st, between 13th & 14th sts.

Notice: committed to the jail of King Geo Co, Va, on Feb 24, a negro man named Sam, who says he belongs to Mr Wm Vaugh, or Vaws, of St Mary's Co, Md. He is about 20 years old. Owner to prove his property, pay charges, & take him away. –Jas Arnold, keeper of the jail of King Geo Co, Va.

Wash Library-on 11th st: Geo Sweeny, G M Head, & Wm McL Cripps appointed Judges of Election. –J F Haliday, sec

Tobacco Convention held at Port Tobacco, Md, on May 24: Col Francis Thompson appointed Pres: Judge Ferguson & E J Hamilton, V Ps Dr Thos Davis & Geo Dement, Secs. Appt'd delegates:

Danl Jenifer	Robt Gray	General John
John B Wills	Wm Thompson	Matthews
Hugh Cox	Robt Brawner	C Jenkins
Henly Smoot	Walter H Robertson	J H Digges
John Briscoe	Geo W Barnes	J Johnson
W F Lancaster	John M Muschitt	John Hamilton
Geo W Neale	John D Freeman	Henry H Hawkins
Menchin Lloyd	Ussiel Nalley	C Jenkins
Johama Stark	Jos Brummett	Josias H Hawkins
Robt Digges	Alex'r Matthews	Theodore Mudd
Jas Neale	W B Stone	Henry Mudd
John Hughes	Gustavus Brown	John D Bowling
Dr Jno Fergusson	Walter Mitchell	Wm C Dyer
Wm Fergusson	Francis C Green	Alsur Gardiner
John T Stoddert	John Spalding	Jas Morton
Josias Hawkins	Geo R Spalding	Dr Wm Green
Wm Penn	Silvester F Gardiner	Hawkins Jameson
F H Digges	Allison Bealle	Valentine Miles
Henry Neale	Thos Berry	Wm Matthews
Jno Chrismond	Farnley Robey	Aquilla Turner
John Barnes	Chas Wills	Francis Bowling
Walter M Miller	Richd Dement	Dr Benedict Gardiner
Henry C Bruce	Allison Roberts	Dr Walter Boarman
Jos Young	Richd Gardiner	John F Gardiner
Richd Barnes	G H Gardiner	Aloysius Bowling
Dr Francis Neale	John G Chapman	Alex'r Middleton
Chas A Pye	John J Jenkins	
Francis E Dunnington	H Brawner	

MON APR 6, 1840
Storm at Mobile on the 24th ult. dwlg of Mr Jacob Page, father-in-law of one of the editors of the Mobile Chron, a good 2 story frame bldg, was unable to withstand the blast, & buried 3 of the family beneath its ruins. The wife of Mr Page was killed; one of his dghts was badly wounded, one of his sons badly injured. A part of the nunnery of Spring Hill was blown down several of its inmates were injured. The warehouse occupied by C A Gilbert, on Water st, was overthrown, report says that the house of Col Smoot received great damage by the storm.

Hse o/Reps: 1-Engrossed, read a 3rd time, & passed: Act for relief of John H Jacobs. Relief of Alvarez Fisk, & reps of Thos P Eskridge. 2-Bills of the Hse, included in those reported this day from the Cmte of the Whole, & ordered to be engrossed, read a 3rd time, & passed, viz: relief of Smith & Farnsworth; of Isaac Champlin & others; of Robt Milnor & John Thompson; of Nathan Levy; of Gilbert A Smith & Nathan Stark; bill to authorize Jas Alexander to relinquish certain lands, & to locate other lands in lieu thereof; bill for relief of Jas Brewer; relief of the reps of John Gremball, sen, dec'd. 3-Engrossed bill for the relief of Robt Milnor, late gauger of the customs at Phil, was postponed till this day week. 4-Engrossed bill for the relief of Bailey & Delord coming up for a 3rd reading. 5-Engrossed bill for the relief of Mary Tucker was postponed. 6-Bill for relief of John L Bowman & Enoch J Noyes-question being: shall the bill pass? 7-Memorial of F L Smith, asking the establishment of an Agric & Educ Dept of Gov't: ordered to be printed. 8-Ptn of Marshal Preston & others, for a post route from Lowell, Mass, to Woodsocket Falls, in R I. 9-Ptn of Wm H Fessenden & others, of Sandwich, Mass, for reduction of rates of postage. 10-Ptn of Geo Thompson & others, of Milton & Dorchester, Mass, for reduction of postal rates. 11-Ptn of A Jones & others, of Otis, Mass, praying for a duty on foreign silk, or a bounty on domestic silk. 12-Ptn of Jas Hewins, of Sheffield, Mass, for increase of his pension as a Revolutionary sldr. 13-Ptn of John White & others, of Acton, & of Susan Haywood & other women, of Acton, praying that the rule refusing to receive abolition ptns may be rescinded. 14-Ptns praying for the recognition of the Haytien Gov't: Judith Smith & others, of Waltham; of Jas Lewis & others, of same; of Maria Driver & others, of Malden; of Robt Oliver, jr, & others, of same; Jas B Woodbury & others, of Acton; of Augusta Woodbury & others, of Acton; of Maria J Bartlett & others, of Chelmsford; of Lucy A Browne & others, of Sudbury; of E C Stowell & others, of Townsend, all of Mass.

Gen Wm Lambert elected Mayor of the city of Richmond, Va.

The coroner held an inquest on Sat week on the body of Noah Talcott, of N Y, who died from internal hemorrhage, caused by a fall. Verdict accordingly.

The Hon Christopher G Champlain, late of Newport, R I, whose death has been lately announced, was a graduate of Harvard Univ, class of 1786. He was a Rep in Congress from 1798 to 1806, & afterwards a Senator in the U S from R I.

Wanted immediately: a white nurse to take charge of a young infant. Apply to Dr F May's, Capitol Hill. None need apply without the highest recommendations.

The bill for the annuity of 300,000 francs to Louis Philippe's 2nd son continues to excite lively attention in the Chambers & jrnls.

Cochran's Patent Bomb Cannon, for throwing hollow shot & shells, is attracting the attention which it is said by those who best understand those matters eminently to deserve.

Crct Court of Wash Co, D C in Chancery. B Henri Lubrez Klimkiewiez, vs, Kousciusko Armstrong, Hypolitus J A Estko, Cath Estko, wid/o Thadeus Estko, dec'd, & Romanus, Martina, & Louis Estko, chldrn of Thadeus Estko, dec'd, & Geo Bomford, adm de bonis non, of Thadeus Kosusciusko, the exc of B L Lear. Bill, the cmplnt is the nearest living relative of the late Gen Thadeus Kousciusko; that the Gen retuned to Europe in 1798, & lived in France from that time until the year 1814 or 1815; about that time he visited Vienna, & from there to Switzerland, arrived in Jul, 1815, & remained until Oct 15, 1817, when he departed this life; that his residence in Switzerland was intended to be tempo, & he contemplated a return to France when he died. When he was about to leave America in 1798, he left a large personal estate in the hands of Thos Jefferson, his exc thereof, & directed the disposition of the property as therein ordained; that Mr Jefferson, after the death of Gen K, declined his execution, & the paper was admitted to record in the Orphans' Court of Wash Co, D C, & adm thereof, with the will annexed, committed to Benj L Lear, since dec'd; that said Lear received from T Jefferson, in cash & stocks a fund amounting to more than $20,000; the fund remained undisposed of & largely accumulated until the death of said Lear; that on the death of Lear, adm de bonis non, with the will annexed, was granted to Geo Bomford by the said Court. The bill further charges that the said test paper is void, & that, as to said property, said Kousciusko will be held to have died intestate. That Kousciusko died leaving no lineal heir, & the cmplnt is his nearest collateral heir; that said property will descend to such person as would be entitled, under the laws of the domicil of the intestate, & that, by the laws of France, & also of Switzerland, the cmplnt would be entitled to the said property; that Kousciusko Armstrong, after the death of Gen Kousciusko, claimed the sum of $3,704 out of said fund, & brought his suit in this Court to compel the payment thereof, but the cmplnt denies his right to it, ever if the paper on which he claims it be genuine, because it was not proved in such way as to give it validity. Gen K did leave 2 wills, duly executed copies of which are filed, but they do not dispose of the aforesaid fund; that these, & the test paper left with Mr Jefferson, constitute only papers in reference to the disposition of his estate; that the lengh of time which has elapsed since the death of Gen K is sufficient to prove his intestacy as to the funds in the hands of Bomford; that persons named Estko have instituted in this Court their suit, claiming to be descendants of Anna, the sister of Gen K, [at some time,] & at others creditors of the Gen, whereas the cmplnt charges that the said Anna was the cousin of the said Gen K; the said Etkos' claim as creditors on account of an alleged mortgage made by Gen K to Anna & her husband, but they file no deed or evidence thereof; he denies the justice & legality of the claim on account of its staleness. The bill seeks to compel Geo Bomford to exhibit an account showing what assets came into his hands of the estate of Gen Thadeus K, the nature thereof, & the disposition he has made of them; that Kousciusko Armstrong, Hypolitus J A Estko, Cath Estko, & Romanus Martina, & Louisa Estko, may exhibit their claims forthwith, & that the amount of assets in the hands of said Geo Bomford be decreed to be paid over to the cmplnt. The bill avers that the said H J A Estko, Cath, Romanus, Martina, & Louisa Estko, reside in Poland, in Europe, beyond the jursdiciton of this Court; F S Key make his affidavit that Kousciusko Amstrong also resides beyond the jurisdiction of this Court. Ordered, said dfndnts to appear in the Clks ofc of this county, at the rules to be held on the first Mon in Oct. –F S Key, Solicitor for cmplnts -Wm Brent, clk

The Howard Society of Wash City acknowledges the receipt of $5.13 from Messrs Thos Scrivener & Wm Mockbee, being the balance in their hands of the money collected in Ward 4 of the city, during last winter, for the relief of the poor of that Ward. –Mary Joy, super

Senate: 1-Ptn from Thos Haskins & Ralph Haskins, asking a compensation with the U S. 2-Cmte of Claims: bill from the Hse o/Reps without amendment: act for relief of Richd Booker; of Gamaliel Smith; of Jas Cox; & of V G Hamilton. 3-Cmte on the Judiciary: adverse report on the claim of the adm of Jos Edson.

Ofcrs on board U S ship *Independence*, lately arrived at N Y from a long cruise: Cmdor-John B Nicholson. Lts: John Pope, Amasa Paine, Chas Henry Davis, Chas M Armstrong, Chas A Poor, Theodore P Green
Capt of Marines-Thos S English   Actg Mstr-Wm Lewis Herndon
Fleet Surgeon Walter Smith   Cmdor Sec-Lyde Goodwin McBlair
Purser-Thos Breese   Prof of Math-Thos H Perry
Assist Surgeons-Augustus J Bowie, J Howard Smith
Passed Midshipmen: John P Decatur, Edw F Beale, Chas R Slade, Thos H Stevens, John Brooks, Henry Rolando, John Wilkinson,   Henry Rodgers, Andrew Weir
Capt's Clk-Littleton R Polk   Actg Btswn-Wm B Forrester
Steward-Saml F Hooper   Actg Sailmkr-Isaac Whitney
Actg Gunner-Thos Robinson   Mstr's Mate-Henry N Lundt
Carpenter-John Gree

Among those lost in the ill-fated brig *Escambia*, on the 25th ult, was Jas Edmund Gladd, in his 16th year, s/o David Gladd, of N Y. He was a youth of great promise, & has left many relatives to mourn his untimely death.

Mrd: on Mar 25, at Providence, R I, by Rev Dr Crocker, Saml Larned, late Charge d'Affaires at Lima, to Celia, eldest d/o Albert C Grumne, Atty Gen of Rhode Island.

Died: on Mar 18, at Ft Monroe, after a long & painful illness, Mr Wm Armistead, aged 67 years.

Died: on Apr 7, at Knightly, Talbot Co, Md, Capt Edw S Winder, of the 2nd Regt Dragoons U S A in his 42nd year.

Died: on the 11th *inst*, at Waterborough, Maj Gen Malachai Ford, of the 2nd Div of S C Militia. He was successor of Gen Hayne, & much esteemed as a man & an ofcr.

Died: on the 24th ult, in Calvert Co, Md, at the residence of her nephew, Mr Richd Beckett, in her 70th year, Miss Mary H Blake, a lady highly respected & esteemed.

The remains of Capt John W McCrabb, late of the U S Army, will be interred in the Eastern Branch Burying Ground this day [Mon.] The funeral will move from the house of Saml Humphrey's, in Gtwn, at 12 o'clock precisely. Ofcrs of the Army, of the Navy, & the Marine Corps, & other friends of the dec'd, are respectfully invited to attend.

TUE APR 7, 1840
The Log Cabin Advocate is the title of a weekly political paper issued at Balt by John F McJilton, which will be published until the close of the Presidential election. It will be continued thereafter if it meets with public approval.

Young men of the U S. your Democratic Harrison brethren of Balt send and address, there is ample room for you in our hearts & homes-Baltimoreans await you at the Convention.

Joshua M Hall	John Buck	Wm A Talbott
Thos C Monmonier	Elisha Lee	Thos Carroll
Jesse D Reid	Neilson Poe	Chas H Pitts
David Creamer	A Rich, jr	Brantz Mayer

To let: new 3 story brick house on Pa ave, between 9th & 10th sts. The key can be got at the Wash Coffee-house, corner of 9th st. Apply for info-C Alexander, upholsterer, Pa ave.

For sale, cheap, 50 tons best Anthracite coal. Inquire of J P Pepper, Pa ave.

Furnished apts to let in the brick bldg on 7th st, between D & E sts. —J C McKelden, on the premises.

Mrd. on Mar 29, by Rev Dr Connor, Thos Jefferson Smith, of Fla, to Miss Sienna E Simms, d/o Edw Simms, of Wash.

Mrd: on Apr 1, at Norfolk, Va, Geo Brooke, of Brooke Grove, Montg Co, Md, to Miss Eliza Jordan, of Norfolk.

Died: on May 4, in Gtwn, D C, at the residence of her sister, Mrs Hobbs, Mrs Sybilla Carbery, relict of the late Col Henry Carbery, aged about 64 years. Her numerous relations & friends will long remember her great kindness & sincere affection for them.

Died: Mar 23, at his residence, near Colesville, Montg Co, Md, Mr Jas Lazenby, sen, in his 61st year.

Died: on Mar 31, at Ogdensburg, N Y, in Christian peace, after a long & most painful illness, Virginia, d/o Dr Thos Henderson, U S Army.

WED APR 8, 1840
Hse o/Reps: 1-Ptn of Isaac Sawyer, of Piscataquia Co, Maine, a soldier of the late war with Great Britain, praying for a pension. 2-Ptns of Joshua B Harvey; & of John Campbell, each of Penobscot, Maine, sldrs of the late war with Great Britain, praying for a pension. 3-Ptn of John Stevens, of Somerset Co, Maine, who served during the Revolutionary war, in privateering service, praying for a pension: referred to the Cmte on Revolutionary Pensions. 4-Resolved: that the Cmte on Invalid Pensions inquire into allowing to Henry Overly a pension from the time he was disabled [being about the beginning of Nov, 1777,] to the time he was placed on the penison roll, under the act of Mar 3, 1809. 5-Resolved that the Sec of War communicate to this Hse a copy of the charges preferred against F L Dancey, for alleged frauds against the U S as special super of the Sea-wall at St Augustine, Fla, with all the evidence on said charges, the reports of Capt Mansfield & Lt Benham in relation thereto, & all other information in the possession of the War Dept. 6-Memorial from Moses Gilman & others, of Sangersville, Maine, praying that the standing rule adopted by the Hse o/Reps of the U S on Jan 20, 1840, may be rescinded. 7-Ptn of Ann Reddington, Robt P Dunlap, & Ed Kent, a cmte of the State Temperance Soc in Maine, praying that the spirit ration in the Navy may be discontinued. 8-Ptn of Allen Rogers, of Maine, stating that a brig belonging to him brought in from Rio Janeiro to Phil a number of men attached to the U S exploring expedition, & that, on the voyage, said vessel was compelled to stop at Bahia for a supply of provisions; for which, & other incidental expenses, he prays remuneration. 9-Memorial of Harvey & Flagg, of N Y, for the drawback on 14 cases of merchandise: referred to the Cmte on Commerce. 10-Memorial of Wm E Churchil, J R Pitkin, & others, of N Y, praying for a general bankruptcy law: referred to the Cmte on the Judiciary. 11-Memorial of Henrietta Davenport, of N Y, praying for a pension: referred to the Cmte on Revolutionary Pensions. 12-Wiskonsin: inquire into establishing a post route from Prairie du Chien, by Wingville, Belmont, Elkgrove, Millseat Bend, New Diggings, Gratiot's grove, Waddam's grove & Bald knob, to Boonsboro. From Milwaukee, by Lisbon, Hatch's mill, & Piperville, to Watertown. 13-Cmte on Revolutionary Claims: to inquire into granting pensions to Susan Ellwood & Lydia Lockwood: referred. 14-Cmte on Revolutionary Pensions: to inquire into paying the heirs of Col John H Stone the arrears of a pension to which he was entitled under the resolution of Congress of 1776, & that the memorial & papers of the heirs of the late Maj Benj Stoddert be taken form the files of the Hse & referred to the Cmte on Revolutionary Claims. 15-Cmte on Revolutionary Pensions: to inquire into restoring to the pension roll the name of Wm Pepper, of Va. 16-Resolved: that the papers connected with the claim of the heirs of Peter Moore, dec'd, be referred to the Cmte on Revolutionary Claims, with instructions to report by bill or otherwise.

Dissolution of the business, in Wash City, under the name of Cards, Gibbs, & Co, by mutual consent. —John R Ricards, Andrew C Gibbs, P A Ricards

Message received from the Senate, announcing the death of the Hon Thaddeus Betts, a member of that body, that his funeral would take place tomorrow at half past 12 o'clock. His wife has lost in him a kind & devoted husband, the childrn a fond & affectionate father. [He died on Apr 7.]

Senate: 1-Ptn from Henry Bradley & others of Yates Co, N Y, against the admission of Fla as a slave state: ordered to lie on the table. 2-Ptn from Wm T Winn, adm of T Winn, late a purser in the U S Navy. 3-Cmte on Commerce, reported the bill from the Hse o/Reps for the relief of Meigs D Benjamin & Co, without amendment. 4-Cmte on Pensions: to inquire into causing the name of Benj Owens, a Revolutionary soldier, to be placed on the roll of Revolutionary pensioners. 5-Cmte on Indian Affairs: a bill for relief of Geo Duvall, without amendment: referred. 6-Cmte of Claims: bill for relief of Capt John Downes: referred. 7-Bill for relief of Jno Underwood: recommended that it be rejected. 8-Adverse report on the ptn of Jas Ryland.

The remains of Capt John W McCrabb, late of the U S Army, who died in Fla on Nov 6, 1839, were this day consigned to their last resting place near the Eastern branch of the Potomac. He has left a widow & an infant son. Capt McCrabb was the only child of Capt McCrabb, of the army, who died of yellow fever at Baton Rouge, in his 29th year, leaving an infant son, the subject of this memoir: both having died at the same age, held the same rank in the army, were cut off by the same disease in the Southern climate, each leaving an infant son. Capt J W McCrabb was an 1833 graduate of West Point.

Wash, Pa: from a citizen of Somerset township, in this county, we learn that Saml Marshall, committed suicide one day last week by hanging. He was the father of a numerous family: a reputable citizen. Pecuniary embarrassments is said to be what induced him to this rash act. –Reporter

Elkton Gaz: on Wed last, as Mrs Karsner, w/o Mr Danl Karsner, of Cecil Co, Md, was crossing the Frenchtown & Newcastle R R, in a vehicle, in company with her dght, the horse which they were driving was run over by the cars, & instantly killed, & Miss K severely tho no dangerously injured.

Wash Corp: 1-An Act for the relief of Mrs M Mechlin: read 3 times & passed. 2-Cmte of Claims: reported a bill for the relief of Eliz Thomas: read 3 times & passed. 3-Cmte of Claims: ptn for the relief of Jas E Thumlert. 4-Cmte of Claims: to be discharged from further consideration of the ptns of
Wm B Wilson & of John R Watson.

THU APR 9, 1840
Col Jas Gadsden elected Pres of the Charleston & Cincinnati R R Co, vice V W Bee, resigned.

Winchester, Mar 11, 1840. Invitation to a dinner to the Hon W C Rives: at the first gun that was fired at the established institutions of the country, you threw yourself in to the breach, & have nobly battled in ther defence. Your obedient servants:

A S Baldwin	J H Sherrard	Robt V Baldwin
P Williams, jr	John F Wall	Chas J Brent
H M Brent	Benj Bushnell	R V Barton
A S Tidball	J S Carson	Thos S Sangster
T A Tidball	E C Breedin	John Anderson
J Kean	Robt Y Conrad	H M Baker
Nathan Parkins	Bus Tayor	A Nolen
M B Cartmell	Lemuel Bent	Henry W Baker
Chas H Clark	Thos Servery	Jas P Risby
P McCormick	C B Hite	Hugh H McGuire
Geo Aulick	H S Machn	Taliaferro Stribbling
Jas H Burgess	Isaac F Hite	

Meeting of the friends of Gen Wm H Harrison was held at Port Tobacco, Chas Co, Md, on Mar 24, to app't Dels to meet in the Convention at Charlotte Hall, on May 16. John Barnes, chrmn, assisted by Theodore Mudd & Francis C Green: John J Jenkins & Silvester F Gardiner appointed Secs. Appt'd:

Jos Young	Alex'r Penn	Richd Adams
Edw R Wheeler	Dr Thos Maddox	Geo P Jenkins
Robt W Hanson	Jas M Saunders	Peter W Crain
Hawkins H Robertson	Henry Harris	Chas Jenkins
Dr John F Price	Geo T Smoot	Dennis Spalding
Robt S Reeder	Columbus Lancaster	Dr Ferdinand Spalding
Saml T Dent	Danl Jenifer	John R Robertson
Geo Taylor	Dr John H Boarman	John W Jenkins
Richd Price	Dr Benj J Gardiner	Saml Tarleton Berry
Saml H Beall	Thos J Gardiner	Richd Gardiner
Geo Brent	Stanislaus Ferrall	Pearson Chapman
John A Matthews	Edw Gardiner	
Dr Robt Ferguson	Peter Wood	

For Charlotte Hall Convention on May 16:

Col John Hughes	Jas Morton	John D Freeman
Menchin Lloyd	H H Hawkins	Gen John G Chapman
Col Hugh Cox	John Hamilton	Gen John Matthews
Dr T Hanson	Walter M Millar	Peter W Crain
Dr S W Dent	Robt Gray	Francis C Green
Benj Adams	Wm F Rennoe	John J Jenkins
Henry J Bowling	Henry C Bruce	

Appointment by the Pres: Asa R Cassidy, to be Deputy Postmaster at Zanesville, Ohio, from Apr 1, vice Wm Blocksom, resigned.

Died: on Apr 3, at Cincinnati, Ohio, Chas Hammond, a learned Mbr of the Bar, & for many years the able & independent editor of the Cincinnati Daily Gaz.

E S Thomas, who is on his way to visit Charleston, S C, where, some 30 years ago, he published the Charleston City Gaz, intends putting to press his *Reminiscences* of the last 65 years, with sketches of his own life.

Notice: If Susanna White, formerly Susanna Jordan, d/o Wm Jordan, dec'd, of Nottoway Co, Va, is living, or, if she is not living, then her descendants are entitled to a portion of the estate of Edw Jordan, dec'd, late of Brunswick Co, Va, who was an idiot; which they can get by applying to me. Address Union Level, Mecklenburg, Va. -Crawford Hughes, adm of Edw Jordan, dec'd.

Frostburg Hotel: Alleghany Co, Md: L W Stockton property, leased by Nathan Parker, Frostburg, Md. [Ad]

Obit-died: on Mar 18, at the residence of his son-in-law, Mr Geo Carter, near Warrenton, Fauquier Co, Va, Ambrose Walden, in his 89th year, a gallant ofcr of the Revolutionary war. He was born in Caroline Co, Va, on Jan 3, 1752. His ancestor, of a highly respectable family of Lincolnshire, Eng, had emigrated in 1715, & settled at Layton's, Richmond Co: subject had the honor of the private friendship of Pendleton, Page, & Taylor: in 1776 he served a tour of 8 months in the militia at Hampton & Portsmouth in the minute service in a company commanded by Capt Jas Dabney, of Louisa, attached to a Regt command of Col Chas Dabney, of Hanover; in 1777, he recruited the number of men entitling him to the commission of ensign & marched them from Caroline Co, Va, to Phil, where he joined the Continental Army Feb 9, 1777, & was attached to the Pa line & to a Regt called Congress's own Regt, commanded by Col Moses Hazen, Sullivan's division; & tho absent from the army on recruiting service at the battle of Brandywine, he was at the battle of Germantown, having been previously promoted to Lt, he commanded a company, his Capt being absent. He remained in the Continental Army upwards of 2 years. In 1780, he went to Ky, then the scene of Indian warfare-when the Indians made an incursion & took Martin's & Ruddle's stations with a number of prisoners, Ambrose Walden, then at Bowman's station, went express thru the wilderness to Col Logan, some 20 to 30 miles distant, to give him the information & ask for aid. The force that called be assembled was placed under the command of Col Geo Rogers Clark, then at the falls of Ohio on his return from Vincennes & the capture of Hamiton. In Sept, 1780, he returned to Caroline Co, & was, by the Court of that county, appointed to a command in the militia, with which he assisted Wayne's army in crossing the Rappahannock in order to form a junction with Lafayette, shortly afterwards effected at Racoon Ford. He again volunteered, & was at the surrender of Cornwallis at Yorktown. —Va Times

Died: on Mar 17, at his residence in the Northern Liberties, Phil, in his 79th year, John Kessler, sr. He was an ofcr under Cmdor Barry, in the frig *Alliance*-the first vessel of war that bore "the stripes & stars" across "the ocean wave;" & had the satisfaction of bearing to his native home the immortal Lafayette, on his first return to France, after the signal services he had rendered to our infant Republic. On retiring from the Navy, Mr K entered into the mercantile business: was appointed Magistrate by the late Govn'r McKean, which commission he held for 37 years: elected to the Leg of Pa. –U S Gaz

Died: Mar 23, at his residence near Nashville, Tenn, aged 83 years, Dr Morgan Brown, a native of Anson Co, N C: removed to S C, & resided near the Cherawa on Pedee river until he emigrated to this state, in 1795. Service in the Revolutionary war-first a volunteer under Col Thompson: was at the defence of the city of Charleston from the attack made by the British fleet under Sir Peter Parker: afterwards as Lt of Infty in the North, having been present at the battle of Brandywine, & some other engagements. Later period of the war, he acted as Assist Commissary to the Southern army under Baron de Kalb, Gates, & Gen Greene, & as superintendent of transports under Greene; was in the partisan warfare carried on in that section between the Whigs & Tories. After the war, he served several sessions in the Leg of S C. –Nashville Banner

FRI APR 10, 1840
$30 reward for negro Arnold Jackson, about 21, who broke jail on Apr 7. –Horatio N Steele, jailor

Hse o/Reps: 1-Bill allowing rations to Brig Gen John E Wood, Adj & Inspec Gen of the U S Army: ordered to the Cmte of the Whole. 2-Cmte on Military Affairs: unfavorable report upon the memorial of Chas Newkirk, of the state of N Y, which was laid upon the table.

Mrs M W Plant has removed her school to E st, near 6th: for terms apply to M W Mrs Plant.

The commodious steamer *Columbia* commenced running on the line between the Dist & Balt in place of the old steamer *Fredericksburg* last week. She is commanded by Capt Guyther: engr-Martin Rudolph: in service for the last 6 years, during which time he never lost a trip, or met with an accident. –Gtwn Adv

On Sun, a young man named Yerkes, about 19, the s/o Harman Yerkes, had his head cut off by being run over by 2 railroad cars, in Broad st, a short distance above Market.

$100 reward for negro man Thysan, about 23: had lived for some time both at Gadsby's & Fuller's Hotels. –B F Middleton

Senate. 1-Ptn from a number of citizens of Mo, asking that Wm Triplet may be confirmed in his land title. 2-Ptns from Chandler Sherman & Benj Campbell, representing that they had taken possession of island #111 in the Miss river, & put improvements theron-they ask to be allowed to purchase at a fair price. 3-Ptn from Thos Daniel, a soldier under Gen Wayne, asking remuneration for services under that commander. 4-Ptn from Jno L Messereau, asking remuneration for services of his father in the Revolutionary war. 5-Cmte on the Judiciary: adverse report on the ptn of John Johnson, asking to be released from the payment of a certain judgment. 6-Cmte on Commerce: bill from the Hse o/Reps for the relief of Nathan Levy, without amendment. 7-Cmte on Indian Affairs: bill for relief of Jubal B Hancock. 8-Cmte on Pensions: adverse report on the ptn of the wid/o David Lynn, an ofcr of the Revolution army. 9-Resolved, that the Sec of the Treas be asked to send the papers relating to the claims of Jas Allen to a pre-emption right in Missouri.

Mrd. on Apr 9, in Gtwn, D C, by Rev Mr Johns, His Excellency Alex'r De Bodisco, Chamberlain of His Majesty the Emperor of all the Russias, his Actual Cnslr of State, & Envoy Extra & Minister Plen to the U S to Miss Harriett Williams, d/o Brook Williams.

SAT APR 11, 1840

Valuable lots & lands for sale: order of the Crct Court of Wash Co, D C, in Chancery: real estate of Walter S Chandler, late of said county, died seized & possessed: lot 11 in sq 16; lots 14, 15, 31, & 32 in sq 24; lots 1, 2, 3, 10 thru 16, & 25 thru 28, in sq 36; lots 15 & 19 in sq 102; lot 1 in sq 122, lot 1 in sq 409; lot 2 in sq 978. Also, 2 portions of sq 952 on Ga ave, adjoining the property of Mr Gaddes. Lots in Gtwn: lots 145, 146, & 147, on 3rd st, opposite the residence of Mr Horatio Jones. Lands near to & adjoining Gtwn: about 2¼ acs, part of a larger tract called *Pretty Prospect*, adjoining the residence of C Swartz, & lands late the property of Gen John Mason. 2 acs, more or less, near the Corp of Gtwn, adjoining the lands of Mrs Poor & Wm Homiller. All that tract being part of the tract called *Pretty Prospect*, & adjoining to *Woodley*, the late residence of Philip Barton Key, & to *Rosedale*, the present residence of Mr John Green, about 39 acs, more or less. Plans will be exhibited, & any further information given by Mrs Chandler, in Gtwn. Com'rs: Nathan Lufborough, J W Bronaugh, Wm D C Murdock, Chas A Burnett. –Thos C Wright, auct

Obit-died: on Mar 25 last, at her residence in Accomac Co, Va, Mrs Susan Parker, the wid/o Wm O Parker, dec'd, in her 49th year. She has left a family of 2 sons & many relatives & friends. She had lingered long in pain, & died as she had received, a Christian. -W

Senate: communication signed by Danl Two Guns & others as chiefs & sachems, of the Seneca nation of Indians, alleging that unfair means were practised in obtaining the asset of those Indians to a treaty concluded with them, of which they have proof, & requesting that no acton be had on said treaty until their arrival at Wash.

MON APR 13, 1840

The Empire State: a weekly newspaper published in N Y: edited by J B Moore & Russell Jarvis. –J Gregg Wilson & Co, 162 Nassau st, N Y.

We learn by the Eastern papers that Peter Edes, the vet printer, died at Bangor, Me, on the 29th ult, at the advanced age of 83. He is believed to be the oldest printer in the U S. Till within a few years he resided in Balt, & assisted his son, the late Col Edes, in his ofc, in the capacity of proof-reader.

Paris. New Cabinet formed under Thiers, the Inevitabel: took place. Mr Thiers was born at Marseilles in 1797: s/o a simple mechanic. At 18, he went to Aix & became a student of the Law. Colleagues of Thiers: Vivien, Minister of Justice & Public Worship; a Deputy of the Left Centre, & a Cnslr of State; born 1799, originally a lawyer. Gen Cubieres, Minister of War: in capacity he may be ranked above his predecessor, Gen Schneider; but he cannot be popular with the French army. Louis Philippe will have not reason to complain of this dispositions or measures. Adm Roussin, Minister of Marines: held the post of Ambassador in Constantinople for several years. Count Jaubert, Minister of Public Works: born in 1799, once a lawyer. Chas De Remusat, Minister of Interior: born in 1797, s/o a former Chamberlain of Napoleon, grandson of Lafayette, & nephew of the famous Casimir Perier. Alexandre Gouin, Minister of Commerce: a banker of Tours, born there in 1792, a deputy since 1831. V Cousin, Minister of Public Instructions: the translator of Plato: no one can exceed him in self-conceit & dogmation.

Jos Gilpin, of Preble Co, Ohio, beat his wife, then cut his own throat as to cause his death. Mrs Gilpin is likely to recover.

Daily newspaper & printing ofc for sale: The Balt Post & Commercial Transcript. For terms apply to Geo W Wheelwright, trustee of the mortgagees

Young Men's Nat'l Convention: will meet in Balt on May 4. Cmte of reception:

A Herald	John Buck	Oliver Norris
Jas P Stafford	Edw Mitchell	Geo Cox
Nicholas L Dashiells	Wm Stuart Appleton	St Geo W Teackle
B W Herring	Elisha Lee	Jos C Manning
A W Bradford	Neilson Poe	Thos G Pitts
Jesse D Reid	Joshua Jones	O Horsey, jr
Wm P Cole	Thos Sheppard, jr	Wm P Stewart
Thos Mullen	Alex Gould, jr	Dr Jno R Piper

–T Yates Walsh, chrmn –John W Woods, Rufus B Gallup, secs

Caution: ran away on Fri, Euphemia Bedford, mulatto servant girl, about 17 years old. She is commonly called Phene. –M Ball, Pa ave

W W Corcoran has associated with him in a copartnership, in the Stock & Exchange business, Mr Geo W Riggs, jr, of N Y It will be conducted under the firm of Corcoran & Riggs —W W Corcoran

Proclamation by the Govn'r of Va: it has been represented to the Exec that Wm B Dabney, late first teller of the Bank of Va, has feloniously embezzled funds of that bank entrusted to his charge, & has fled from justice. I therefore, Thos W Gilmer, Govn'r of Va, offer a Reward of $200 for his apprehension, & to convey him to Richmond

Md State Convention: the Hon R W Bowie, of P G Co, appointed chrmn, & Col Jos H Nicholson, of Annapolis, acted as sec. Cmte recommended the appointment of the following: Robt W Bowie, Pres
V Ps: John McKim, jr, Thos Hood, Col Goldsborough
Secs: Dr Lemmon, Jos H Nicholson., W B Clark
State Central Cmte:

Saml Jones, jr	Wm R Jones	Thos Yates Walsh
Nathl L Williams	Geo W Krebs	Wm H Gatchell
John P Kennedy	Geo R Richardson	Gustav W Lurman
Jas L Ridgely	Jas Frazier	Chas H Pitts
Abraham G Cole	Jas Harwood	Geo M Gill
Jas Grieves	Wm Chesnut	Saml McClellan
Hugh Birckhead	Asa Needham	Neilson Poe

Destructive fire early last Sat morning: broke out in the bldg formerly used as the Telegraph printing ofc, & last occupied by Mr S D Langtree & Mr Thos Allen, as printing ofcs for the Democratic Review & the Madisonian. Efforts made to save the hse of Mrs Ironsides, the Baptist Chr, the hse of Mr Chas Bell, [a frame bldg,] & the Med College were all in imminent danger. Slate roof on Mrs Ironsides' aided in its preservation. The soap factory of Mr Ellis, a frame bldg, was totally consumed.

Senate: 1-Ptn from John Scarborough & Nancy his wife, asking a grant of land on the ground of having raised 20 chldrn for the benefit of the Republic. They state they migrated from N C about 8 years ago to the far West; that they have reared 20 chldrn, the oldest not 25, & the youngest not weaned. referred to the Cmte on Public Lands. 2-Ptn of Wm H Smith, of Miss, asking to be confirmed in his title to land. 3-Ptn from Griffin Ross, Geo Read, & others, praying pre-emption rights to certain designated lands. 4-Ptn from Jos Phillipson, asking confirmation of title to a tract of land. 5-Document in support of the claim of Preston Starritt. 6-Cmte on Public Lands: bill for relief of Jos L Cochran with an amendment. 7-Bill from the Hse o/Reps for the relief of Sutton Stephens without amendment. 8-Bill for relief of Jas Alexander; of Jas Brewer; of the reps of Wm Williams, sen: without amendment. 9-Cmte of Claims: bill for relief of John J Adams. Adverse reports on: bill for relief of Josias Thompson; of Benj C Roberts; of Garret Vliet. 10-A bill for relief of Wm Bayley, survivor of Bayley & Delord.

Trustees of the First Baptist Chr tender thanks to the firemen & citizens who were the means of saving, from total destruction, their meeting-hse. John Wilkinson, Saml Grubb, Edmund F Brown, & Geo M Kendall.

Card from Mrs Ironsides: heartfelt thanks to the Fire Companies, & her friends & neighbors, who kindly volunteered in removing & returning the furniture of her house, the destruction of which, at one time, seemed inevitable.

TUE APR 14, 1840
Sale at public auction: Apr 16, in borough of Norfolk, the steamer *Old Dominion*, built in this place in 1834. Sale at Colley's Yd. –John G Colley, adm of Marshall Parks, dec'd. –John M Nash, auct

Orphans Court of Wash Co, D C: insolvent debtors Christopher Cummings & Lewis Nagel, have applied to be discharged from imprisonment. -Wm Brent, clk

Senate: 1-Ptn from Jas Allen, asking the passage of a special law granting the right of pre-emption. 2-Ptn from Susan Murphy, asking remuneration for property destroyed by the U S troops in 1812. 3-Cmte on the Judiciary, bill for relief of Thos Hastings & Ralph Hastings. 4-Cmte on Finance: unfavorable report on the following: bill for relief of Jas W Ward, of Balt; of J D Walker, of Balt; of Chastelain & Ponvert; of Jas W Osborne. 5-Cmte of the Whole: relief of Geo W Paschall; of Mgt Barnes, wid/o Elijah Barnes, of Clements, Bryan, & Co.

Died: on Apr 12, at Giesborough, the residence of her mother, Miss Sarah Ann Young. Her funeral is at 12 o'clock today. Her illness was brief. She was a lovely sister & dght.

The mansion at *Dalecarlia*, near the Little Falls of the Potomac, the residence of Mrs Smith, accidentally took fire on Sun morning, & was entirely consumed.

While the steamer *Gen'l Brady* was on her passage from Pittsburgh to Wheeling, on Wed last, Mr Wm Mull, the bar-keeper, in attempting to dip a bucket of water, lost his balance & fell overboard, at Browne's Isl, a few miles from Steubenville, & was drowned.

For sale: *Buckland Mill*, Prince Wm Co, Va. on Broad Run: with miller's house, & lot & garden; about 66 acs. Also, woolen factory-34 by 60 feet. Also, the farm on which Smith resides: about 290 acs. Also, a town lot in Buckland. For information refer to Mr Wm Dean, Alexandria, D C. –Thos Smith

WED APR 15, 1840
New Spring goods-just received. –Jas B Clarke, #2 8th st, opposite Centre Market.

Newly m'd couple, Mr & Mrs Chas Gibney, were drowned in Paint Creek, Ohio, on the 25th ult. They had been m'd at Portsmouth on the 23rd, & started for Newwark, on board a canal boat, the water being drawn off the canal below Paint Creek, they left the boat, in a wagon, with several other persons, & in attempting to cross that stream, they were thrown out. Others in the wagon escaped.

Mlle Herbele, who became the w/o Mr Falconet, a banker of Naples, but who still lives under the former name in recollection of thousands of admirers of her dancing in the theatres of Italy & Germany, & who was also a short time in the opera in London, died lately at Naples.

Fire at Gtwn yesterday in a stable attached to the residence of Dr Bohrer, & a splendid saddle mare, the property of Mr John Taylor, perished in the flames.

Died: on Mar 6 last, at Glasgow, Scotland, Jas Macleod, M D, 2nd s/o John Macleod, of Wash City.

Dr M was a native of this district: educated at the Univ of Glasgow-received the degree of Dr of Med in 1829: resided in Glasgow, from that period. He died after a short but severe illness.

THU APR 16, 1840

All the genteel household furniture at auction, at the late residence of Mr Edmund James, on Pa ave, over Mr John France's Lottery ofc. -Ed Dyer, auct

Sale of part of lot 5 in sq 229, at public auctioon: decree of the Crct Court of Wash Co, D C: in the case of D Clagett, cmplnt, vs Benj K Morsell, adm, & Wm McDowell & Geo McDowell, infant chldrn of Sarah McDowell, dec'd: corner of 15th & Pa ave. --Benj K Morsell, trustee --Edw Dyer, auct

Residence for sale or rent: dwlg house, 14th & H sts, occupied by Mr L B Hardin.

FRI APR 17, 1840

The Southern Mail brings news of the death of the Hon Patrick Noble, Govn'r of S C, who died at his residence in Abbeville, Dist, Apr 7, of dropsy in the chest being the disease of which he died. In Dec, 1818, he succeeded to the chair of Speaker of the Hse o/Reps, on the transfer of Gen Hayne from the Speaker's chair to the ofc of Atty Gen of the state. He was in his 50th year.

Brd of Ofcrs: Cmdor Jas Biddle, of the Navy, Maj Geo W Walker, of Marine Corps, & Capt W C DeHart, of the Army, assembled at the naval asylum near Phil, on Mar 10, to prepare a code of regulations for the Marine corps; adjourned on the 30th.

Jos W Parkins, ex-sheriff of London, died suddenly, at Newark, on Sun. He had been ill for some weeks, but thought to be on his way to recovery. --N Y Dispatch

Benj S Bulfinch, an aged journeyman printer, was drowned in the south fork of the Licking river, near Newark a few days ago. He expected his verses would be published as soon as he died. —Wheeling Times

For sale or rent: 2 story brick dwlg on E Capitol st, adj the residence of Mr J H Hausten: corner of N J ave & E st south. -Michl Dooley

For rent: the south half of the hse on the corner of Md ave & 12th st. Inquire of Mr Rumph, occupying the north end of said hse, or Edw Mattingly, near the Navy Yard.

Senate: 1-Bills to be engrossed: relief of John McCloud; of Wm Jones; of John S Wilson, of Cheorkee Co, Ala. 2-Bill for relief of Isabella Hill, widow, & John Hill, Eliz Hill, & Saml Hill, chldrn & minor heirs-at-law of Saml Hill, dec'd. 3-Bills for relief of Jos Paxton; relief of the heirs of Francis Newman, heirs of Agnes Dundas. 4-Memorial of David McMullen, of Wash Co, Pa, praying for a pension: referred to the Cmte on Revolutionary pensions. 5-Memorial of Wm Cain, of Wash Co, Pa, for a pension. referred to the Cmte on Invalid Pensions. 6-Ptn of John Van Slyck, of Minden, N Y, who during the late war with Eng [1814] was ordered to Sackett's Harbor, & whilst there on duty as a soldier, from exposure, became afflicted with disease which has hitherto rendered him decrepit & unalbe to labor, praying for a pension. 7-Ptn of Rhineboldt Trangott, of Root, N Y, who in 1780 came to the U S with Count Rochambeau, & served as a soldier in the Cntnl Army from thence until the capture of Lord Cornwallis, praying for a pension 8-Ptn of Fred'k Smith, of Johnstown, N Y, praying for a location of a sldr's grant in one of the Northern states, instead of Ark. 9-Cmte on Public Lands: reported a bill for relief of Chas McKinsey 10-Ptn from the widow of Jas Howard, asking a pension. 11-Ptn from Messrs H Langtry & B W Jenkins, praying indemnity for losses sustained by a contract for the supply of the Cherokees. 12-Ptn from the reps of Robt Moore. 13-Cmte on Public Lands: ptn of Wm Tracy, late a soldier in the U S Army, praying for an allowance of bounty lands: resolution that the prayer of the ptn ought not to be granted.

Disaster at Johnston: from the Providence Herald of Mon. The first reservoir gave way & so sudden was the crash, that even persons in their dwlgs had not time to escape. Names of the sufferers:
Franklin Randall, aged 2½ years, s/o Mr Benj Randall.
Mr Philip Angell & his wife
Mrs Sarah Rogers, w/o Mr Abner Rogers
Mr Oliver Angell, aged 18 years
Emily Ann Angel, aged 6 years, & Benj Angell, aged 4 years, chldrn/o Mr Philip Angell.
Mr John W Haull, aged 31 years.
Mrs Lucinda Hull, aged 28 years
Mr Wm McAnsland, aged 26 years
Mrs Matilda Whitmore, aged 46 years.

Miss Julia Ann Whitmore, aged 10 years
Miss Laura J Whitmore, aged 7 years
The above are the family of Mr Brayton Whitmore, who is absent on a visit to Conn.
Mrs Martha Whitmore, aged 20 years, w/o Mr Russell Whitmore.
Mrs Sarah Whitmore, aged 25 years, w/o Mr Nelson Whitmore.
Jenetta Whitmore, d/o the above, aged 8 months.
The bodies have all been recovered, many of them very much mutilated. The rest of Mr Randall's family were saved by taking refuge in the upper part of the hse, by the timely warning of Mr Randall, who, standing, without, saw the rolling tide advancing in time to give them notice of its approach. The body of Julia Ann Whitmore is missing. The widow Eddy was carrried down the stream but was found covered up with leaves. She was much exhausted, but is likely to improve.

Mrd: on Apr 9, at St Paul's Chapel, N Y, by Rev Mr Higbee, Capt Alex'r S Macomb, of the U S Army, to Susan, only d/o Philip Kearney, of that city

Died: yesterday, Miss Eliza Robertson, in her 20th year. Funeral at 3 p m today, from the residence of her sister on D, between 10th & 11th sts.

SAT APR 18, 1840
Hse o/Reps: 1-Memorial of Hugh A Garland, the Clk of the Hse, requesting the appointment of a select cmte, with powers to enter into the fullest exam of all transactions between himself & Mr Langtree on the subject of contracts for stationery & lithography. 2-Ptn of Wm W Snowden & others, proprietors & publishers of Magazines, praying that their publications may be place, as respects postage, on the same footing with newspapers.

Senate: 1-Ptn of John H Hagedorn & Adolph Cramer, merchants in New Orleans, praying to be allowed a drawback on certain articles of merchandise exported by them. 2-Docs submitted in relation to the claim of Jas Crooks & Wm Crooks, citizens of Great Britain, to indemnity for illegal seizures of their vessel & cargo by a U S ofcr in 1812. 3-Cmte on Pvt Land Claims: bill for relief of Thos P Copes. 4-Cmte on Commerce: in which was referred Hse bill for relief of Robt Milnor & John Thompson, reported it without amendment. 5-Cmte on Finance to which was referred Hse bill for relief of Lewis H Bates & Wm Lacon, recommended that it do not pass. 6-Cmte on Commerce, to which was referred Hse bill for relief of Wm Wickham, reported same without amendment. 7-Bill for relief of Avery, Saltmarsh & Co was taken up. postponed for the present. 8-Bill for relief of J M Strader. 9-Following were considered & ordered to be engrossed: bill for relief of Benj Parsons; of reps of Jos Barnard; of E W & H Smith; of Converse & Rees; of Hazard Knowles; of Chs M Keller & Henry Stone, of Sutton Shepherds; of John C Reynolds; & of Wm Osteen. 10-A bill to refund to Noah Miller & others a part of the proceeds of the sale of the British sloop *Mary*, & cargo, captured by them, & libelled & sold for the benefit of the U S.

Dedication of the new church in Alexandria: recently finished for the use of the Second Presby Congregation in Alexandria, dedicated on Sabbath morning next at 11 a m. Sermon by Rev Thos T Waterman, of Phil. —J N Davenport, pastor

Mrd: on Apr 17, by Rev Mr Watson, Mr Geo W Ranson, of Jeff Co, Va, to Miss Amelia C Winrott, of Gettysburg, Va.

Died: on Apr 12, in Phil, of apoplexy, Francis Anthony Chevalier De Gerstner, of Austria.

Died: on Apr 10, at Alexandria, Mrs Charlotte Vowell, w/o Thos Vowell, in her 73rd year.

Died: on Apr 6, at Leesburg, in her 42nd year, Mrs Mgt Hannah Douglas, w/o Dr John H McCabe, & d/o the late Chas Binns.

Died: on Apr 6, at Fairview, Fauquier Co, Va, in her 24th year, Miss Eliza B Hampton, eldest d/o the late John Hampton, of said county. The dec'd had for some time been laboring under pulmonary symptoms, but her last illness was believed by her physician to have been of bilious fever. Miss Hampton was principal teacher of the female dept of the New Balt Academy, until her declining health rendered it necessary to decline the duties. At her funeral the semon was preached by Elder John Ogilive, principal of the institution.

Died: Jan 8, in London, Madam D'Arblay, [better known as Miss Burney,] the author of Evelina, & the contemporary & favorite of Johnson, Garrick, Reynolds, Boswell & Goldsmith, in her 88th year.

MON APR 20, 1840

Capt Jas Riley, the well known author of an interesting personal narrative of adventures among the wild Arabs, died on Mar 15, on board of his brig *Wm Penn*, bound to Mogadore, in his 63rd year. His accounts included the testimony of Judah Paddock, who had been wrecked, & experienced cruelties from the savages.

Senate: 1-Ptn from John Jones & others, in relation to claims for services. 2-Ptn from Sherburne Dearborn, asking a pension. 3-Documents in support of the claim of Walter Hayne. 4-Ptn from John Moore, in relation to a claim. 5-Cmte on Revolutionary Claims: bills for relief of John Jordan; of the heirs of Dr John Ramsay; of Jas McCrory; of Fred'k Seigle. 6-Bills considered in the Cmte of the Whole-to be engrossed: bill for relief of Hezekiah Cunningham; of Jas Smith, of Ark; of John L Scott; of Zadoc Martin, of Miss; of Gregoire Sarpy, or his legal reps; of Danl B Bush; of John W Monette; & of Saml Crapin. 7-Senate to take up the bill for the relief of Brig Gen John E Wool & Col Croghan, which having been granted, an animated discussion ensued on the merits of this case.

Massacre in Texas: from correspondence of the Balt Patriot: New Orleans, Apr 8. The steamship N Y came in yesterday after a passage of 46 hours from Galveston, Texas. Residents of San Antonio have had a serious quarrel with the Cumanche Indians, in which 33 were slain. On Mar 19, 65 Indians arrived at St Antonio, bringing Miss Lockhart, a girl taken by them a year & a half since, from the Guadaloupe, for the purpose of holding a council with the agents of our Gov't. They wanted a high price for her, & if so, would bring all the other prisoners, one at a time. Miss Lockhart said she had seen all the other prisoners at their camp a few days before she left. Col W G Cooke, actg Sec of War, being present, thought it proper to take hostages for the safe return of the prisoners, & Col Fishers was ordered to march 2 companies & place them in the vicinity of the council rm. After some parleying, the chiefs were then told they were prisoners, & would not be liberated until they restored their white prisoners. They made a rush for the door: Capt Howard received a severe stab wound. The whole 12 chiefs were immediately shot. Capt Reed's company was attacked by the warriors in the rear of the yard: they were pursued & all were killed with the exception of 1 renegade Mexican. Our loss-killed: Lt W M Dunnington, Pvts Kammiski & Whitney, Judge Thompson of Houston, Judge Hood of Bexar, Mr Cayce of Matagorda, & a Mexican. Wounded: Capt G T Howard, 1st Infty; Capt Matthew Caldwell, 1st Infty; Lt E A Thompson, Pvt Kelly, Co 1, Judge Robinson, Mr Higginbotham, Mr Morgan, & Mr Carson. From Mr Durkee, who arrived from Austin yesterday, that Col Burleson has been called to organize an expedition to operate against the Cumanches. He is to raise one co on the Colorado, & at Austin, & take with him the company which left Houston a short time since, under Capt Pearce, & a body of Tonkwa Indians. Houston, Mar 30. Paper of Sat: the Cumanche fight in the public sq at San Antonio: 83 Cumanches & 6 Americans were killed, & a number wounded. Judge Robinson was severely wounded with an arrow, & Mr J C Morgan, after receiving 2 shots from the bow, siezed hold of an axe, & revenged himself by killing 2 Indians.

Mrd: on Wed week, in Newbern, N C, Hon Chas Shepard to Miss Mary, d/o the Hon John R Donnell.

Mrd: on Apr 15th, at Phil, by Rev Dr Ducachet, Edw S Norris to Rosalie Letitia, d/o R Hassler, of Wash City.

Died: on Apr 14, in Boston, Mrs Martha Ann, w/o Mr Thos P Cushing, & d/o John Cargell, of Sussex Co, Va, aged 39 years.

Died: on Apr 15, at Providence, R I, aged 73, Mrs Anna Tillinghast, relict of the late Jos Tillinghast, & mother of the Hon Jos L Tillinghast, Rep in Congress from R I.

Mr Jas Cowles, of Va, committed suicide by cutting his throat, on Mon last, at the Globe Inn, Balt. He died instantly.

St Augustine, Fla: Apr 10. The late long-talked of expedition has been up to the Ocklawaha, & again returned to qrtrs. This expedition consisted of nearly 300 men, a large portion of them mounted. Maj Childs & Lt Tompkins, of the artl, arrived in the steamer *Wm Gaston* from the Southern posts. The garrisons are all in good health. The long drought, it is feared, may operate against the exam of Pi-haiokee, or Grass-Water, as intended by Lt McLaughlin, U S Navy. Indian fires are numerous, & the confidence of the enemy continues the same.

Whig Cmte of D C· meeting Apr 14, 1840: Noble Young, chrmn. A McDonald Davis, actg sec.

Dels: Wm B Magruder	Wm P Elliot	Danl Mabin
Henry May	Thos Owen	Geo W Stewart
Henry J Brent	Wm Bates	Jas E Given
Thos H Havenner	John T Given	Leonard Harbaugh
A B Claxton	Wm M Addison	E Miller
Alex'r McCormick	Leonidas Coyle	Henry Winters
Walter Lenox	Geo Clarke	F Hagar
Thos Allen	Saml Smoot	Wm E Crossfield
Alex'r McD Davis	Chas W Boteler, jr	M J Gilbert
Jas F Halliday	Danl Campbell	Lewis R Denham
John T Towers	John Walker	Geo F Allen
Jos Borrows	Wm B Todd	J T Ellwood
John C McKelden	John Y Catlett	John T Ryon
F Howard	Richd Nalley	Geo H Plant
G W Harkness	V Harbaugh	Henry Dillenger
Geo S Gideon	Jos Etter	Fitzhugh Coyle
Walter Hellen	Robt A Waters	Wm J Rawlings
Wallace Kirkwood	Saml G Kneller	John C F Digges
Saml Bacon	Chas Bradley	Henry Holiday
Noble Young	John H Lang	Eugene Laporte
Hugh B Sweeny	Geo Stettinius	A W Turner
John H Noyes	John H Kirkwood	Theodore Harbaugh
Richd Wallach	Benj E Gittings	Silas Moore
Chas L Jones	John Sexsmith	Henry F Byrne
J M Carlisle	Wm T Dove	Wm Duer
J B H Smith	John F May	Geo M Grossard, jr
Thos H Bowen	P Havener	Chas H Lane
Wm McLeod	Levi C Bootes	J P McKean
Jas H Stewart	John McClelland, jr	H A Weeden
Jos Thomson	Thos K Gray	J Hepburn
Jos B Ford	Dennis C Hare	John Bates
Jos B Tate	J C Burch	Wm Hoover
Josiah Goodrich	Chas Edmundson	Josiah Essex
Robt Clarke	Hamilton Clements	John B Morgan
Robt S Patterson	Saml Hoover	Stephen P Franklin

Richd France	Wm Mockbee	R M Coombs
Josiah Melsin	R H Stewart	Wm T Porter
R W Bates	Chas P Wannall	Thos Miller
Robt U Hyatt	Robt Dyer	Wm Force
Jos H Bradley	Jas Nevitt	Jos Beardsley
J A Blake	Francis Hill	Saml Stott
Jos Butler	R C Washington	Nathan Hammond
Wm Bates	Wm Howard	Geo Talbot

On Apr 13, as an engine was returning from a fire at Cincinnati, Mr Chas Taylor was run over by it, & so much injured that he died in about 15 minutes

The large oyster taken up by Zavier Francois while oystering on Mon last, was brought up from the wharf on a dray: measuring 3 feet 1 inch in length & 23½ inches across the widest part of it. Ayres, the purchaser, will exhibit it at Alhambra this day at 11 o'clock —Mobile Chron

TUE, APR 21, 1840
Senate: announcement of the death of Judge Hugh L White: had been in enfeebled health: member of this body during the early part of this session: emigrated at any early day to Tenn, while yet a youth, & settled near the town in which his remains are now deposited: was a descendant of a father who participated in the Revolutionary war, & who, in transferring his residence to Tenn, brought with him the spirit of enterprise & love of country. In private life he was amiable & ardent: died at his residence at Knoxville, on Apr 10

Imported John Bull will stand, Apr 1 thru Jul 1, at his stable, in Upr Marlboro. Letters addressed to Mr Fielder Suit, Upr Marlboro, will be attended to.

Hse o/Reps: 1-Ptns presented: of Geo Randall & John C Haskell, for the payment of a balance due them for work done at Big Sedus Bay, N Y: referred to the Cmte of Claims. 2-Ptn of S H Weed, for establishment of a home for our seamen while in port: referred to the Cmte on Commerce. 3-Ptn of Job Chase & 421 others, of Harwich, Dennis & Chatham, Mass, for a light-hse on Kill-pond Bar: referred to the Cmte on Commerce. 4-Ptn of Jas Fox, for a pension: referred to the Cmte on Naval Affairs. 5-Ptns of Arnold S Congdon & 309 other citizens of New Bedford, Mass, to repeal all laws respecting slavery in D C. 6-Ptn of Robt R Crosby & others, of Brewster, Mass; of Freeman Ryder & others; of Jos Bates & others; of Susan Allen & other women; of Solomon Rich & others of Provincetown, Mass; of Mary T Hatlett & 109 other women, of Barnstable, of Jos Marsh & others, of Sandwich, Mass; of David Long & others, of Nantucket; of Susan Dew & 452 others, of Nantucket; all praying for the abolition of slavery & the slave trade in D C. all refused to be received. 7-Ptn of Andrew M Macy & 151 others, of Nantucket, of Eunice C May & 451 others: all against the admission of Fla as a slave state: refused to be received.

Mrd: on Apr 14, at *Woodland Plains*, by Rev Robt Prout, Mr R Winder Hanson to Miss M Frances Speake, all of Chas Co, Md.

Died: on Sun last, Mrs Sarah Ann Evans, aged 33 years, of a tedious illness [consumption,] leaving a disconsolate husband & 4 helpless infants to bewail their loss. Funeral from her late residence in the rear of the Catholic Church, on G st, today at 10 a m.

Appointments by the Pres: John S Hacker, Register of the Land Ofc at Kaskaskia, Ill, v Miles Hotchkiss, whose commission will expire on Apr 30, 1840. Wm Armistead Terrell, Register of the Land Ofc at Augusta, Miss, v Wm Howze, dec'd. Robt N Kelley, Register of the Land Ofc at Opelousas, La, V Edw V Davis, dec'd.

WED APR 22, 1840

Wash Corp: 1-Ptn of W C Orme & others, praying the conveyance of water thru the alley in sq A to Missouri ave: referred to the Cmte on Improvements. 2-Ptn of Jas Holledge, praying permission to keep a portion of north P st enclosed for a reasonable time: referred to the Cmte on Police. 3-Cummunication from Wm Hebb, police magistrate of the 4th Ward, respecting certain statements in the ptn of Philip Reilly: referred to the Cmte of Claims. 4-Cmte on Improvements: referred the ptn of John A Smith & others-bill authorizing the curb stone to be set & footway paved on the north side of Mass ave, between 4th & 5th sts: passed. 5-Same cmte was referred the ptn of K H Lambell: regarding-forming & gravelling west side of 9th st, from Md ave to so H st: passed. Similar ptn from J T Frost & others: which was read. 6-Cmte of Claims: act for relief of John R Watson: was passed.

Senate: 1-Memorials presented & referred: from citizens of Mich, asking the release of Wm Lyon Mackenzie from imprisonment: referred to the Pres of the U S. 2-Asking to withdraw the papers of Webster Hayne. 3-From Levi Owen & other citizens of Ky, asking grants of land in Oregon, & permission to take their negroes with them, & that John Rowan, of Ky, be appointed Govn'r of Ky. 4-From Rev S G Winchester, asking that duties paid on certain theological books imported by him be refunded. 5-From John Bruce, praying relief for loss sustained by a contract. 6-Cmte on Foreign Relations: asking to be discharged from the memorial of John M Clayton & others, in relation to making a navigable communication between the Atlantic & Pacific oceans at the isthmus of Darien: referred to the Pres of the U S, to whom it was originally directed. 7-Cmte on Indian Affairs: asking to be discharged from further consideration of the ptn & papers of Geo C Johnson. 8-Cmte on Pensions: adverse report on the ptn of Willis McDonald. 9-Cmte on Pvt Land Claims: bill for relief of Elihu Hall Barry, without amendment. 10-Cmte of Claims: bill for relief of John Moore. Also, an adverse report on Hse bill for relief of the heirs of John Wilkinson, dec'd. Also, Hse bill for the relief of Cornelius Tiers, with an amendment.

Wm B Laub has recently taken the store lately occupied by Mr C E Upperman, corner of F & 15th sts: gen'l assortment of groceries & liquors. Mrs E A L will resume the tuition of the piano on May 1, having declined for some months past, thru indisposition.

Naval Court Martial: to assemble at the Navy yard in Phil on May 25: trial of Cmdor Jesse D Elliott. Cmdor Jacob Jones, Pres.
Members:
Cmdor Lewis Warrington   Capt David Conner
Cmdor Wm M Crane   Capt John D Sloat
Cmdor Jas Renshaw   Capt Geo W Storer
Capt Chas W Morgan
Judge Advocate: John M Read, of Phil

The out-bldgs of the Cragie Mansion hse at Cambridge, Mass, were destroyed by fire on Wed last. By great exertions of the fireman, & an abundant supply of water from the fish-pond on the premises, the venerable Mansion was saved. This was the head-qrtrs of Gen Washington in 1775.

Bank of Chambersburg: Geo Chambers has resigned the Presidency of this bank, & T G McCullon,, has been elected to the ofc thus rendered vacant.

Wanted immediately: a female hse servant, who can cook, wash, & iron for a small family. One from the country would be preferred. Recommendations required. –W Fischer

For rent: a 2 story brick hse on north side of Bridge st, Gtwn. Apply for the key at Mr Saml Wardle's store, a few doors above the premises.

Potatoes for sale. J & H Thecker, Water st, Gtwn.

Just arrived: new style Paris dress muslins. Also, have a large assortment of ladies' best quality Phil slippers constantly on hand. –Jas B Clarke, #2 from 3th st, opposite Centre Market.

THU APR 23, 1840
Crct Court of Wash Co, D C: in Chancery: Farmers' & Mechanics' Bank of Gtwn, vs, Mary Jackson et al. Ratify trustee report of sale of lots 9 thru 11, in sq 449, in Wash City, to Henry Naylor, for three & a qrtr cents per sq foot, making the sum of $654.03. -Wm Brent, clk

In Chancery: John Mountz & the Corp of Gtwn, cmplnts, vs, Thos K Wilson & others, heirs of Isaac Wilson, dfndnts. All those having claims against the estate of Isaac Wilson, dec'd, are notified to produce the same with vouchers on or before May 16 next, at the Auditor's ofc in Wash City. -Jos Forrest, aud

Mrd: on Apr 22, by Rev Mr Hawley, Alex'r Lee to Miss Henrietta P Barcroft.

Mrd: on Mar 14, at Van Buren, Ark, by Rev Mr Stiggins, Mr Hobart Key, formerly of PG Co, Md, to Mrs Abigail Jones, of New Madrid, Mo.

Died: on Apr 16, Mr Philip Alexander, Teller of the Farmers' Bank of Va at Fredericksburg.

Notice to the creditors of John Nicholason, dec'd: genr'l meeting in Phil city, at Evans' tavern, Geo st, on May 12, at 4 p m. Assessment of one mill per cent upon their claims [without interest] should be sent by them forthwith to Wm W Haly, So 6th st, Phil, Pa, [no payment to exceed $50 on any one claim,] in order to defray the necessary expenses of the cmte. –T B Freemen, chrmn -W T Elder, sec

Priam, the celerated imported Racer & Stallion, will cover the present season, at my stables, eighty pay mares, at $150 cash, with a dollar to the groom. [More information was included pertinent to Priam.] -A T B Merritt, Hick's Ford, Va

FRI APR 24, 1840
Chas Co Equity Court, Mar Term, 1840. John T Berry, vs, Eliz J Dixon, Wm Dixon, & Eveline Dixon, heirs of Wm Dixon Ratify sale by the trustee, Wm B Stone, of the real estate in the proceedings, & given notice thereof to Saml Sheriff, for the sum of $4 per ac, at 6, 12, & 18 months. –Edmund Key -John Barnes, Clk Chas Co Court, Md

Senate: 1-Cmte on Indian Affairs: adverse report on the ptn of J L Schoolcraft. 2-Cmte on Naval Affairs: adverse report on the ptn of Jas Ware. 3-Cmte on Pvt Land Claims: report in favor of the claims of Miguel Eslava, & recommending the passage of the bill for his relief.

City of Wash, the capital of the U S, is in D C, in that part which was formerly a part of Md. city comprehends all the lands beginning on the east side of Rock creek, at a stone standing in the middle of the road leading from Gtwn to Bladensburg, thence along the middle of said road to a stone on the east side of the Reedy branch of the Tiber, [at 9th st west,] thence southeasterly, to a stone in the road leading from Bladensburg to the Eastern [Anacostia] Branch Ferry. It was planned under the direction of Geo Washington, then Pres of the U S, [from whom it takes its name,] by Pierre C L'Enfant, in 1791. The area of the city, according to a statement made by Wm Elliott, late Surveyor, in 1835: circumference 14 miles, containing 310,838,235 sq feet: or-7,134 acs: length of sts, deducting intersections-199 miles: length of avenues-65 miles. Total of present bldg grounds-132,947,416 feet. The bldg belonging to the U S are, first, the Capitol: the wings were nearly completed when the British army, under Gen Ross, [who was afterwards slain in battle near Balt,] in Aug, 1814, set fire to the Capitol, the President's House, & Public Ofcs:

reduced all to ashes, even the Library of Congress. The foundation of the north wing was laid by Washington on Sep 16, 1793, & the centre on Aug 24, 1818, the annivesary of its destruction. The sq contains about 36 acres, having been extended in 1836. The Capitol & grounds are well supplied by spring water brought in iron pipes from a spring 2 miles north: in the centre is a monument to the memory of those who fell before Tripoli in 1804. Waste water is conveyed to form 2 jets in the low grounds of the garden. The colonnades in the Rep Hall are a species of breccia obtained from the banks of the Potomac by the then architect, B H Latrobe. The Tiber runs through the middle of the city from the north, entering into the canal west of the Capitol The Act of Congress for locating the seat of Gov't was approved & signed by Geo Washington, then Pres, Jul 16, 1790, & the Gov't removed here in 1800, during the Presidency of John Adams. Legal jurisdiction was assumed Feb 27, 1801, & the laws of Md & Va then existing declared to be in force. The city was incorporated by act of Congress dated May 3, 1802, by which act the appointment of Mayor was vested in the Pres, yearly, & the 2 branches of Council by the people in general ticket. By supplemental act of May 4, 1812, the Corp was made to consist of a Mayor, Aldermen, & Common Council-the Board of Aldermen to consist of 8 members, chosen for 2 years, & a Council of 12 for 1 year- & the Mayor, by joint ballot of the 2 boards, yearly. The number of inhabitants were, at different periods, as follows:

Year:	White:	Slaves:	Free colored:	Total:
1800	2,464	623	123	3,210
1803	3,412	717	223	4,352
1807	4,198	994	500	5,692
1810	6,292	1,436	892	8,620
1820	9,606	1,945	1,696	13,247
1830	13,379	2,319	3,130	18,837
1840 estimate				24,508

3,954 dwlg houses, of which 1,804 are brick, & 2,150 are frame, & 422 bldgs for shops, besides public bldgs, making a total of about 4,500.

Henry Hatch Dent, Atty & Cnslr, Wash, will practice in the several Courts for D C & in the U S Supreme Court. Ofc 4½ st, very near the City Hall.

For sale: the steamboat *Chesapeake*, at public auction on May 23, at Bradley's Wharf, Wash City. She has been newly coppered, & the amount of her bill of repairs, is over $10,000. She is the most economical boat now to be found.
—L W Stockton, D Barnum, Balt; or to Purman Black, Wash City.

Among the passengers who sailed from N Y for Liverpool on Tue last, was R J Mackintosh [Attache of the British Legation] & his lady.

Vicksburg Whig of Apr 11 states that Jos W Wade & H D Robertson, both formerly of Hinds Co, Miss, & more recently of La, met a few days since on the west of the Miss a little above Vicksburg, & killed each other.

Hon Richd Biddle intends to retire from Congress. In addition for many reasons for wishing to retire, of which you are already aware, that my health has continued to suffer, more & more, under a residence here. –R Biddle: Wash , Apr 11, 1840.

Died: on Apr 22, after a long & painful illness, in her 36th year, Mrs Matilda Lee Bean, w/o Benj Bean, of Wash City. Funeral from the residence of her husband, 3rd & L sts east, Fri, at 1:30 p m.

Reward for strayed or stolen red yearling heifer: taken from my enclosure about 2½ miles from the Capitol, near the Balt turnpike. –W Hickey

Farm for sale: about 70 acs, with a handsome cottage-built house, adjoining the farm of Mr Wm Hickey. –Andrew Forrest, residing near the Navy Yard.

SAT APR 25, 1840
The Court Martial in the case of Cmdor Elliott is ordered to assemble on the 1st Mon in May, & not the 4th as mentioned. Cmdor Crane & Cmdor Renshaw have been excused from serving as members & Cmdor E P Kennedy & Capt Foxhall A Parker been ordered in their stead. –A & N Chron

Brig Gen Taylor relieved, at his own request, from the command of the troops in Fla, & Brig Gen W K Armistead, of the 3rd Artl, ordered to succeed him. The change to take place on May 1. A & N Chron

Mrd: on Apr 23, in Wash City, by Rev G G Brooke, Mr Jas B Davis to Miss Mary Ann Bennett.

Died: on Apr 11, at Mt Vernon, Ohio, after a short illness, in his 24th year, Wm A M Brooke, late of PG Co, Md: native of Md, left in 1830 to pursue his studies at Kenyon College, where he graduated with the highest of honors. He then became a resident of the first named place: was a gentleman highly esteemed for his many virtues, & has left numerous relations & friends who deplore his loss.

For sale: flour, cement, whiskey, & bacon. –C Hogmire, Water st, Gtwn

MON APR 27, 1840
$100 reward for runaway negro girl Jane Taylor, about 21. May have changed her name, as she wanted a free negro for her husband, Henry Botler, a brick-moulder by trade, & who has been living at the Savage Factory, A A Co, Md; has since left there, & supposed to be in Balt. She was living with Mr Thos Lansdall, Savage Factory, A A Co. Address letter to me at Good Luck P O. –Richd G Brashears

A letter in the N Y Observer, this morning, states that 2 English missionaries, named Williams & Harris, have been eaten by the savages in New Zealand; a third escaped by flight.

Senate: 1-Ptn from Jonathan H Cobb, of Dedham, & Saml Cobb, of Needham, Mass, mfgrs of silk, praying that a duty may be imposed on imported foreign silks. 2-Ptns referred: ptn of the heirs of Joshua Bishop, for horses stolen by the Indians in 1812. 3-Ptn from John Turner, for horses taken in 1812. 4-Ptn from Francis Roy, Antoine Foy, Jos Reves, & Jno P Donoyer, for Indian depredations. 5-Ptn from the adm of Sarshall Cooper. 6-Ptn from David McQuintly, adm of Wm Head, praying remuneration for Indian depredations. From Robt A & John G Heath, for the same. 7-Depositions from Robt Hancock & Francis Cooper. 8-Ptn from Elisha Todd, for property taken by the Sac & Fox Indians in 1814. Same for Jos Boggs. Same for David Magill. Same for Abraham Brown. 9-Ptn from John A Bannon, praying remuneration for Indian depredations. Same for Jos Roy; Jesse Watkins, Jas Turner, & Benj Coton. Same for Joshua Truman; from Lewis Bartholet; Jos Austin; John P Roy; Thos Wasson; Thos Wood; from R E Gentry, & Wm Monroe & others. 10-Ptn from Wm Monroe & Jos Wolfskill, for losses sustained in Boonslick settlement by the friendly Sacs during the war. 11-Ptn from Geo Jackson, for Indian depredations. 12-Cmte of Claims: reported a bill for the relief of Langtry & Jenks; & made an adverse report on the claim of John Bruce.

Hse o/Reps: 1-Bills taken up, considered as in Cmte of the Whole, to be engrossed for a 3rd reading: relief of:

Jos Basset	Thos P Copes
Jos S Billings	Alfred P King
Henry Wilson	Henry Lucas
Rep of G Flaujac	Jubal B Hancock
Geo de Passau, of La	Chas McKinzie
N G Hamilton	Jas H Rolfe
Saml Lord	Thos & Ralph Haskins
Tyler Spafford	Lgl reps of John Scott
Casper W Wever	Mary Neal, wid/o Saml Neal, dec'd
Francis A Harrison	John Compton, assignee & Saml
Jean Baptiste Comeau	Mackay
Lgl reps of Pierre Bonhomme	Lgl reps of Geo Duval & others

Francis Laventure, Ebenezer Childs, & Linus Thompson
Lgl reps of Aaron Vail, dec'd, late Cnslr at L'Orient
Jacob Pennel & others, owners of the vessel *Eliza*, of Brunswick
2-Bill granting a pre-emption right to Enoch Evans. 3-Bill confirming the claim of the heirs of Jos Thompson, dec'd, to a tract of land in Missouri. 4-Bill granting a pension to Pamela Allen, wid/o Saml Allen, a soldier of the Revolution. 5-Further consideration of the following bills indefinitely postponed: relief of:

Rich Booker & others	Gamaliel E Smith
Thos W Taylor	Nathan Levy

Wm Wickham
Geo Willis
Jas L Cochran
Heirs & legal reps of John Grimball, sr

Meigs D Benjamin & others
John T Addoms, exc of John Addoms
Jas Brewer, of Ohio
Robt Milnor & J Thompson

5-Act to authorize Jas Alexander to relinquish a tract of land, & to locate other land in lieu thereof. 6-Bills from the Hse considered as in Cmte of the Whole, & their further consideration indefinitely postponed: relief of:

Jas Cox
Jas W Osborne
Wm Bailey, survivor of Baily & Delord
John Howe
Nicholas Hedges

Benj C Roberts
Lewis H Bates
W Garret Vleit Lacon
Owners of the schn'r *Three Bros*

Josias Thompson, superintendent of the Cumberland road between Brownsville & Wheeling.

7-Cmte of Claims: unfavorable reports on the cases of Matthew J Keith, Jas W Anderson, & Jos P & Jos W Johnson. Also, reported back to the Hse, without amendment, bill from the Senate entitled: An act for the relief of Geo W Paschal. Also, an act for the relief of Chas M Keller & Henry Stone. Unfavorable report on the case of Britton Evans. Also, on Wm Jennings, ex'r of John S Westwood. An amendatory bill for relief of Gen Duncan L Clinch. 8-Cmte on Public Lands: cmte discharged from further consideration of the ptns of Hugh Riddle, of Alex'r Grant; of Henry Brandenburg; of Wm Davis, of Chas H Smith, Benj Pegg, Thos Richmond, Brice Wilson: ordered to lie on the table. Act for relief of Wm Jones; a bill for relief of Wm Leblanc. 9-Cmte on P O & Post Roads: unfavorable report on the ptn of Saml N Burnett.

On Sat, a wooden bldg, used as a stable, in the occupancy of Mr F Golding, tavern-keeper, at 7th & I sts, was struck with lightning, & burst into flames.

Public examination of the pupils in the school under the superintendence of Miss Mary Wannell will take place in the 4th Presby Chr, 9th st, today at 11 o'clock.

$10 reward for strayed or stolen on Apr 21 from the premises of the subscriber, living adjacent to the *Adelphia Mills*, near the Montg line, PG Co, Md, a bay mare. —Walter Chew N B: information directed to Bladensburg, PG Co, Md.

Died: on Sat last, of consumption, after a lingering illness, Mrs Dorothy Moore, aged 33 years, leaving a disconsolate husband & 4 small chldrn to lament their loss. Funeral from her late residence on 6th st, this day at 10 a m.

TUE APR 28, 1840
Died: on Sun last, Mrs Maria Lousa Williams, w/o Mr John Williams, of Wash City, aged 28 years. Her funeral will be from the residence of her father, John Wells, jr, on Bridge st, Gtwn, today at 10 a m

Senate: 1-Ptn by Mr Pierce, asking that the papers of Huldah Tucker, now on file, be referred to the Cmte on Pensions. 2-Ptn for an account from Chas Gordon. 3-Cmte on Pensions: bill granting a pension to Molly Willey. Same cmte: adverse report on the ptn of John Martin; of Martin Burke; of the wid/o Benj French, of Jos Dunham. Bills were severally read a 3rd time & passed. 4-Cmte of Claims: recommending that the Hse o/Reps for the relief of Thos Filebrown, jr, be indefinitely postponed, was taken up, when Mr Southard went into a succinct history of the facts connected with this claim, & advanced the bill from the Hse on the merits of the case. 5-Cmte of Claims: recommending the indefinite postponement of the bill for the relief of John Underwood, clk in the ofc of the 1st Auditor: which having been agreed to; the Senate adjourned.

Appointments by the Pres: Wm Marin, to be U S Judge for the S Dist of Fla. Vinton Butler, of Fla, to be U S D A for the Dist of Fla, v Geo Walker, resigned. J G Searcy, to be U S Mrshl for the Middle Dist of Fla, v S W Duvall, dec'd. Chas F Ryan, to be U S Cnslr for the port of Copenhagen, v Chas J Hasbro, resigned. Chas S Wallach, of Ohio, to be U S Cnslr for the port of Matagorda, in the Republic of Texas, v John A Morgan, dec'd. Jas E Freeman, of N Y, to be U S Cnslr for the port of Ancona, in the Roman States. Wade H Greening, Register of the Land Ofc at Sparta, Ala, from Mar 14, 1840, when his present commission will expire.
Surveyors of the Rev: Nathan Bardin, Bristol, R I, v Allen Wardwell, dec'd. Geo Forbes, Wheeling, Va, v Jefferson L Sangston, resigned.

San Antonio de Bexar, Mar 26, 1840. Comanche Indians proposed a treaty of peace with this Republic, & offered to surrender all our citizens held by them in captivity. Finally, on Mar 19, 65 of their tribe arrived, with but one of the several captives: council was held. At the close of the talk, the Indians attempted to rush thru the door of the room-Capt Howard seized one of them & was stabbed. A sentinel was also stabbed, & a citizen killed by one thrust with a knife. In this conflict 6 were killed on our part, & several wounded. The Camanches' common practice is to approach individuals, settlements, & forts with a white flag, &, when they are fairly in possession of the ground, murder all in their power. It excites the regrets of us all that such a fatal catastrophe resulted from the well-intended efforts of this Gov't to cause this most perfidious race to have some regard for their plighted faith. No one dreamed of anything but submission on the part of the Indians: their resisstance induced the bloody result. We have now, 31 prisoners-2 blind men, & the balance are women & chldrn; the warriors were all killed. One or two of the Indians escaped.

We observe that our late respected fellow townsman, Jas R M Bryant, has, in conjunction with Mr J B Johnson, taken charge of a Whig paper published at Crawfordsville, Ind, called the Indiana Record, which his fine talents will render an able auxiliary in the Whig cause.

New Orleans, Apr 16, Mr A H Weatherby, formerly a printer, but for some years collector of Marine intelligence for the jrnls of New Orleans, fell from a window in the Bulletin ofc & died 3 hours later. He was a native of Mass, but for many years resided in this city, where he had a large number of friends & asquaintances, by whom he was universally esteemed. –Sun

WED APR 29, 1840
Trustee's sale of real estate: under the power of a deed of trust, executed to me by John Lynch: sale on the premises, on May 21, all that parcel of ground in Wash City, upon the plat of Wash City: lot 26 in sq 729: with frame dwlg & store upon the lot, & heretofore owned & occupied by the late Wm Emack, dec'd. –J P McCormick, trustee -E Dye, auct

The schn'r *Byron*, Capt Pearsall, arrived last night from Matamoras, which place she left on Apr 14, with confirmation of the defeat of the Feds on Apr 1 by the Centralists: battle fought at Lerado. Feds had 200 men killed, 150 wounded, & 170 made prisoners. Gen Zapata, being made prisoner, was shortly afterwards shot, & his head sent to Guerera as an example. -Bee

Charleston, S C: Apr 25, 1840: appointed Dels to the Balt Convention. Hon W Thompson & Jas H Adams, for the state, & G S Bryan, E Gamage, Thos Corbett, Jacob Delamotta, T H Read, jr, D Hamilton, [s/o Gen Hamilton,] & G D Miller.

Died: on Apr 2, in Fred'k Co, Md, after a long & painful illness, Wm W Farquhar, in his 26th year.

Died: yesterday, after a short illness, Mary, infant d/o Mr John Evans.

The Veterans of Boston: the oldest person living in Boston-so far as we know-is Mistress Eliz Chase, who was 100 on Oct 28, 1839: constant worshipper at St Paul's Chr: widow of 3 husbands, & might survive a fourth. The oldest man living in Boston is Wm Abrams, who was born Jan 16, 1742, & completed his 98th year in Jan last: tailor, by trade: made the clothes he now wears when 96. He has 124 descendants, namely 9 chldrn, 54 grchldrn, 60 great grchldrn, & 1 great great grchld. Simon Willard, clock maker, was 87 on Apr 3: just completed a clock with his own hand: which, with his own hands he has put up in the turret of the new Unitarian Chr at Medford. Wm Pierce, the Revolutionary barber, was born on Christmas Day, 1747, & is now in his 93rd year: hears well, but has lost his sight. He considers himself one of he last survivors of the Boston Tea Pary. –Boston Transcript

The trial of Edgar P Newman, formerly of Phil, for the murder of Wroth in Jan last, came on before the Superior Court in Chestertown, Md, Chambers, Pres, Ecleston & Hopper, Assist Judges. Verdict: murder in the 2nd degree. 18 years imprisonment in the Md Penitentiary at Balt. -Pa

We take pleasure in nominating another individual for the ofc of Mayor, who is now, we believe, the oldest citizen of Wash, & has been 20 years in the cncls of Wash City: Mr Geo Watteeston. He is a gentleman of leisure; intimately acquainted with the business & wants of the Corp. -Several voters

THU APR 30, 1840

For Madeira: passage only: fine fast-sailing coppered brig *Otho*, Small, mstr, will sail about the 1st prox, has comfortable accommodations for a few passengers. Apply to Lambert & McKenny, Alexandria.

Senate: 1-Ptn from Henry Goodyear & others, asking grants of land in Fla for the purpose of raising tropical plants. Also, from Jacob Housman, asking pre-emption or grant for the same purpose. Also, from Wm C Bethel, in relation to the same, at Key Bacas, Fla reef. 2-Cmte on Pensions: unfavorable report on the ptn of Phoebe Nestor. 3-Cmte of Claims: adverse reports on the ptns of Wm James & of Susanna Murphy. Also, asked to be discharged from further consideration of the ptn of D S Gardiner. Also, adverse report on the claim of Wm & Jas Crooks. 3-Cmte on Pvt Land Claims: asked to be discharged from further consideration of the ptn of Robt McCarty. 4-Cmte on Revolutionary Claims: reported a bill for the relief of the heirs-at-law of Ed Wade, dec'd. 5-Cmte on Pensions: adverse report on the claims of Hester Hill & of Wm Coley. 6-Adverse report on the ptn of the owners of the steamboat *John McLean*, was referred back due to some additional test received.

Boston papers announce the death of Rev John Kirkland, D D, formerly, for many years, Pres of Harvard Univ. He was the s/o the celebrated missionary to the Six Nations-the Rev Saml Kirkland. He was the author of several papers, particularly upon Indian subjects, published in the Mass Historical Collections. —Com Adv [No date-current item.]

St Mary's Hall, Green Bank, Burlington, N J: summer term of this institution will begin on May 6. -E J Germain, Chaplain, principal teacher, & Head of the Family

Mrd: on the 31st ult, at the Univ of Va, Geo Rives, of Albemarle, to Miss Maria F, d/o Prof Tucker, of the Univ.

Mrd: on Apr 21, at West Point, by Rev Dr Cutler, Lt Thos Tingey Craven, U S Navy, to Emily, d/o Dr Thos Henderson, U S Army.

Died: on Apr 16, at Clinton, Hunterdon Co, Pa, Mrs Eliza Manners, w/o Dr John Manners, & d/o the late Thos Cooper, L L D, of S C, aged 49 years, much regretted.

Caution: to all whom it may concern. All persons are warned not to trust any one on my account or that of my brothers. We are determined not to pay for anything that may be obtained by word or order, as we will give no orders. This step is taken in consequence of some impositions already practised in this way. Either of my brothers, Lewis & Henry, or myself, will transact all business for the future in person. -John Walker

Trespassing cow has taken up on my enclosure, on Capitol Hill. Owner to prove property, pay charges, & take her away. She has been trespassing since Mar 8 last. -Jas Spurling

Sale of genteel furniture: on the 30th inst: at the late residence of the late Jos Thaw, dec'd, on N Y ave, near the Fourth Presby Chr -Edw Dyer, auct

Trustee's sale by virtue of a decree of PG Co Court, in Equity: sale on May 29 next, that part of the real estate, about 200 acs, more or less, of which the late Richd Duvall died seized & possessed, which by his last will & testament, he devised in trust for his sons, Alex'r Duvall & Gabriel Duvall, described in his will as lying on the west side of *Best's Marsh*, or Branch, in PG Co, adjoining the estate on which the said dec'd resided, it being part of the land devised to the said Alex'r & Gabriel Duvall, that was conveyed to the said Alex'r by a certain deed of partition of said land, executed by the said devisees, Aug 15, 1836. -C C Magruder, trustee, Upr Marlboro, Md

FRI MAY 1, 1840
Senate: 1-Cmte on Foreign Relations: adverse report on the case of Wm G Jones 2-Cmte on Pvt Land Claims: adverse report on the ptn of Joshua Kennedy 3-Bill for relief of the heirs of the late Robt Fulton, dec'd: was made the special order for May 6 next.

To let: well built & convenient house in Franklin Row. Inquire of Anthony Preston, 12th st.

Sale of valuable real & personal estate: by the power in the will of the late Jas M Bell: sale on the premises, tract of land, whereof he died seized, in Culpeper Co, near the *Glebe*, lately held by Rev John Woodville: about 700 acs. Also, on May 28, property known as *Bell Park*, near the Culpeper Court Hse: about 545 acs. Also, on May 18, at the front door of Wm G Allan's Tavern, at Culpeper C H, another 194 acs of land, the property of the late Jas M Bell. Tract will be sold in 2 parcels: one of 40 acs, under the will; the other of 154 acs, under a deed of trust for the benefit of Philip Lightfoot. The purchaser of the latter, will have to pay cash, unless Maj Lightfoot will relend the money to him, which he probably will be willing to do -Wm Green, exc of Jas M Belt

Mr H R Robinson, on Pa ave, Wash City, is agent for the Log Cabin Adv, where it can always be obtained on the day of publication.

Appointed by the Pres: Henry D Peire, Naval Ofcr, at New Orleans, La, from Apr 1, 1840, when his late commission expired. Aloysius Thompson, Surveyor & Inspec of the Rev at Llewellersburg, Md, v H G S Key, resigned.

SAT MAY 2, 1840

Statement of some of the defaulters to the Gov't, whose defalcations have occurred since Jan 1, 1830.

Defaulter:	Residence:	Amount of defalcation:	When due.
*S Swartwout	N Y	$1,225,705	
Wm M Price	N Y	75,700	1837, 38
A S Thruston	Key West, Fla	2,822	Jan 22, 1838
Gen W Owen	Mobile	11,173	Jul 25, 1838
I T Canby	Crawfordsville, In	39,013	
A McCarty	Ind	1,388	Jul 18, 1836
W L D Ewing	Vandalia, Ill	16,754	Apr 9, 1830
John Hays	Jackson, Miss	1,386	Dec 31, 1834
W M Green	Palmyra, Miss	2,312	Dec 31, 1835
S S Chambers	Little Rock, Ark	2,142	Aug 4, 1836
D L Tod	Opelousas, La	27,230	Apr 11, 1832
B R Rogers	Opelousas, La	6,624	May 25, 1837
M Cannon	New Orleans	1,259	Jun 25, 1836
A W McDaniel	Wash, Miss	6,000	Oct 6, 1830
John H Owen	St Stephen's, Ala	30,611	Nov 1, 1836
G B Crutcher	Choctaw, Miss	6,061	Mar 31, 1832
G B Dameron	Choctaw, Miss	39,069	Apr 1, 1835
S W Dickson	Choctaw, Miss	12,229	Sep 16, 1837
W P Harris	Columbus, Miss	109,178	Nov 9, 1835
Wm Taylor	Cahaba, Ala	23,116	Jun 30, 1836
U G Mitchell	Cahaba, Ala	54,626	Feb 28, 1837
J W Stevenson	Galena, Ill	43,294	May 5, 1837
L Hawkins	Helena, Ark	100,000	Nov 9, 1835
S W Beall	Green Bay	10,620	Jun 29, 1837
Jos Friend	Washita, La	2,551	May 25, 1835
Wm H Allan	St Augustine	1,997	Oct 17, 1836
G D Boyd	Columbus, Miss	50,937	Aug 31, 1837
R H Sterling	Chocchuma, Miss	10,733	Feb 28, 1837
P Childers	Greenbury, La	12,449	Feb, 1838
Wm Lina	Vandalia, Ill	55,962	do
S T Scott	Jackson, Miss	12,550	do
J L Daniel	Opelousas, La	7,280	do
J T Pollock	Crawfordsville, Ill	14,981	do
M Neville	Cincinnati, Ohio	13,781	do

M J Allen   Tallahassee, Fla   25,691   do
B T Brown   Springfield, Ill   3,600   do
*Commenced in 1830, increased till 1838.

Wash Co, D C: insolvent debtor, Richd Eaton, has applied to be discharged from imprisonment. -Wm Brent, clk

For sale: flour, whiskey & hay. In store: W T Compton, Water st, Gtwn. [Ad]

Wanted to hire: a plain cook, that can come well recommended for honesty & good conduct. A slave from the country would be preferred. Apply at Dr Gunton's, 9th & Pa ave.

For rent: 3 story brick hse on Pa ave, Ward 1, nearly opposite the residence of the Hon John Forsyth. It is at present occupied by Maj Wm B Scott, who will relinquish on May 20. -Thos Cissell, a few doors down.

MON MAY 4, 1840

Notice: to the creditors of the Commercial & R R Bank of Vicksburg. By a deed of assignment made by said bank to us, recorded Feb 15, 1840, the affairs of said bank are placed in our hands for liquidation & payment. -W W Frazier, Thos E Robins, Wm S Bodley, assignees

$200 reward for runaway negro man Wm Turpy, about 35: supposed he rode a yellow bay horse, belonging to Mr Bassford of the neighborhood, which horse he advertised. -Wm D Bowie, Queen Anne P O, PG Co, Md.

Senate: 1-Cmte on Military Affairs: bill for relief of the legal reps of John D Treville, dec'd. 2-Bill for relief of the reps of Capt Wm Williams, late of N C: further consideration postponed.

City Ord-Wash. 1-Act for relief of Mrs M Mechlin, that the fine imposed on her, for an alleged violation of the law relating to wooden bldgs, be, & the same is hereby remitted: provided she pay the cost of prosecution. 2-Act for relief of Eliz Thomas: fine imposed for keeping a dog without obtaining a license, remitted: provided she pay the cost of prosecution.

Mrd: on Apr 30, in Wash City, by Rev G G Brooke, Mr Arivuel D Collingsworth to Miss Rebecca Dixon, both of Alexandria.

Mrd: on the 21st ult, by Rev Mr Roloff, Dr Hillery P Mudd, of St Chas, Mo, to Miss Clarecy, d/o Maj Theodore Mudd, of Chas Co, Md.

Died: on Sun last, at Boston, the Rev John Thornton Kirkland, formerly pastor of the New South Church, Boston, & subsequently Pres of Harvard Univ. His funeral was on Tue

Died: May 3, after an illness of about 7 weeks, Mrs Sarah Shephed, in her 65th year.

TUE MAY 5, 1840
Notice to teachers: a single gentleman, well qualified to take charge of a neighborhood school, where chldrn of both sexes are taught, may obtain a desirable situation by making immediate application. -John W Milburn, Clifton Factory, St Mary's Co, Md

Governess wanted: a lady to teach English education, French, drawing & painting, music, & ornamental needlework. Liberal salary. Letter to me, post paid, Queen Anne, PG Co, Md-John B Mullikin.

From Fla: St Augustine: 1-One Indian killed & one taken prisoner, by Capt Holmes, of the 7th Infty, about a week ago, who struck upon their trail. 16 horses were captured. 2-A Court Martial has been ordered to assemble at this post on Mon next, of which Beig Gen Armistead is Pres, & Col Walbach, Col Gates, Majors Churchill, Payne, McClintock, Ashby, Capt Fulton, & Lt T P Ridgeley are members. 3-It is said that overtures have been made to Gen Taylor, by the chief Indians who figured in the massacre at Caloosahatchie, to permit them to come in, & be transported westward.

A patent has been recently issued for improvements in the manner of constructing the tracks of railroads, invented by Jas Herron, Civil Engr, a gentleman of much experience in this field.

Mrd: on Apr 28, by Rev Septimus Tuston, Thos H Fowke, late of Pr Wm Co, to Miss Anne Weaver, d/o Jos Weaver, of Fauquier Co, Va.

Mrd: on Apr 28, at New Haven, Conn, by Rev Saml Mervin, the Rev Geo J Wood, of Wash City, to Susan T, d/o the Rev Saml Mervin of the former place.

Music teacher wanted: M D Elmore, Zanesville, Muskingum Co, Ohio.

WED, MAY 6, 1840
Disappearance of Mr Jacob May, of Lawrenceville, Ill, who arrived in Phil, on Mar 26 last, & put up in the Red Lion Hotel, in Market st. Mr May is a partner in 2 commercial houses in the West. He stated he had been quite sick on his passage, once in Cincinnati & once in Pittsburg. He wrote a letter: N Y, Apr 1, 1840. *Dear Jesse, David, & wife: I got here on Sunday. If I never see you again, do, Dubois & David, take care of my family.* On receipt of this letter, Mr McLean [partner,] proceeded to N Y, via Phil. Reason to fear that a foul murder has been committed.

$500 reward to the citizens & police of N Y: Mr Jacob May, of the firms of May & Dubois, & Dubois, Pain, & Co, merchants & millers, of Lawrenceville, Ill: Reward for the detection & arrest of the supposed murderers, & recovery of money stolen. Information can be left with Mr J M McLean, at 88 Pearl st house, N Y, or with either of us: -Bray, Bancroft, & Co: 163 Market st -Allen R Reeves & Co: 177½ Market st -Cooledge & Wyeth, 181 Market st Phil, Apr 30, 1840

Mr John Scudder, a respectable farmer at Four Mile Ferry, above Trenton, accidentally shot himself in the head on Sat last. He was the brother of the former Pres of the Mechanics' Bank at Trenton, now a merchant of that city

Rockville, Md, May 1. A young man, Saml Miles, near Clarksburg, in this county, made a violent assault upon his brother-in-law, Mr Young, by attempting to shoot him. They had quarrelled over some land. S Miles' father followed after him, but it was too late. Miles fired a pistol, 2 shots hitting Young in the breast. The wound is not yet fatal, but little hope of his recovery. Miles fled. -Jrnl & Free Press

Among the passengers arrived at N Y from Liverpool, are Mr N P Willis & his lady.

THU MAY 7, 1840
Balt, May 6. On Mon last, a gang of half-grown boys were carrying a pole with a figure representing Gen Harrison as a petticoat hero: Mr Laughlin stepped out of the ranks with the view to stop them, when he received the blow over the head from a stick which deprived him of life. Inquest was held by A H Greenfield, coroner. Mr L has left a widow & 4 chldrn-one an infant. He was a respectable mechanic, a carpenter, residing on Federal Hill. The solemn duty of committing the remains of Mr Laughlin to the grave was yesterday performed by the Dels to the Convention. Chief Marshl, Capt Jas O Law, supported the weeping & bereaved wife of the dec'd. Burial was in the Meth Episc congregation burial ground. We learn that the Massachussetts Delegation yesterday paid over $1,000 to the widow & orphans of the murdered Laughlin. -American

Capt Jos Smith has been relieved from the command of the U S ship of the line *Ohio*, now in the Mediterranean, in consequence of ill health; & Capt E A F Lavallette ordered to succeed him.

Pvt sale of house & lot on Pa ave, #29 sq B, with 2 story brick bldg, with back kitchen, now occupied by Mr Michl McCarty as a tailor's shop. It is a leasehold for 99 years, renewable forever, with certain ground rent. Apply to Mr McCarty, or to myself. -Edw Dyer, auct

Mrd: on Feb 27, at *White Cottage*, the residence of Jonathan H Lawrence, Holmes Co, Miss, by Rev John West, John Walker Wood, of Gtwn, Key, [formerly of Albemarle Co, Va] to Miss Mgt, 2nd d/o Maj Jas Catling.

FRI MAY 8, 1840
Boarding: Mr & Mrs Aborn having taken the house adjoining Mr D Clagett's store, Pa av, can accommodate a few genteel boarders.

H V Hill's patent cemented refrigerator made & sold by Henry Lee, agent: in use for 4 years, & since my last alteration, they have given universal satisfaction to those that have observed the printed directions. For info. Wm A Bradley, Col Wm L Brent, Com Stephen Cassin, Maj R T Mason, or Mr Isaac Beers. --Henry Lee, agent

Race over the Kendall Race Course, Balt, on May 12, for 4 days. --Jas B Kendall, proprietor

Largest gun yet: cast at the works of the West Point Foundry Assoc, Cold Spring, N Y, on the 30th ult-a cannon of 12 inches bore, for projecting either shells or solid shot, the former weighing 160 & the latter 240 lbs. The gross weight of this, the largest casting ever made in this country, is 13½ tons. Time required in pouring was 12½ minutes. It was cast by order of & for account of Capt Robt Stockton, U S N

Citizens of St Augustine, in testate of the services of Lt W K Hason, U S Army, at Fort Mellon, Aug 3, 1839, resolved on tendering him a sword, in token of their approbation of his conduct at that post. Sword arrived Sat last, & immediately forwarded to that ofcr. The kilt, of solid silver richly gilt, is in the shape of a cross, with a gradual swell of its grip, & its ear, bearing the appropriate devices of the knife, the bow, & the tomahawk. The scabbard is of similar material, surmounted by a star, & its end embossed with leaves & acorns. The blade bears on its side: "The Citizens of St Augustine to Lt W K Hanson, U S A" & on the reverse, "For Meritorious Services at Fort Mellon, August 3, 1839." -St Augustine Herald

Died: on May 5, Wm Duddington, aged 2 years & 4 months, only s/o Henry I & Eliz Brent. Our Saviour has emphatically said, "Let little chldrn come unto me."

N Y May 5-the sloop *Palmyra*, of Newark, bound to Newark, when off Fort Washington Point, struck with a sudden squall & went down. Lost: Miss Ophelia L Goodell, Miss Sarah Osborn, & Mr Parkerson Springsted, of Rockland Co. One of the two saved: Capt Jas Potter. The women were from 15 to 17.

City Ord-Wash: 1-Act of relief of John R Watson, for failing to provide a box to his privy be, & the same is remitted: provided he pay the cost of prosecution. 2-Act for relief of Jas E Thumlert. for keeping a dog without obtaining a license therefor be, & the same is remitted: provided he pay the cost of prosecution.

SAT MAY 9, 1840
J H Coxe, David Saunders, Nathan Lufborough, Joshua Peirce, John Cox, Lewis Carbery, & Robt White, appointed members of the Levy Court of Wash Co, D C.

Hse o/Reps: 1-Cmte on Military Affairs: bill for relief of Enoch Hidden. 2-Cmte of Claims: recommending the indefinite postponement of the Hse bill for relief of Ebenezer A Lester. Also, a favorable report on the Hse bill for relief of Ebenezer Lobdell. 3-Cmte on Military Affairs: to inquire into authorizing experiments to be made upon the application of steam vessels to harbor defence.

John B Brooke appointed by the Govn'r of Md to be Clk of PG Co Court, v Aquila Beall, dec'd.

Mr Wm A Pratt had published an accurate isometrical view of the Pres' House & grounds, the surrounding public bldgs, & private residences. They may be procured at Mr Fisher's & Mr Morrison's bookstores.

Accident several days ago in the family of Mr Moses Boone, residing near Dundee, Kane Co, Ill: a 5 year old d/o Mr Boone was struck & killed, when caps exploded, bursting the canister. His 8 year old son was playing with some damaged caps-he was severely injured, but could recover. —Chicago American

Appointments by the Pres: Jas B Sheppard, of N C, to be U S Atty for the dist of N C, v H L Holmes, resigned. Robt M Noxon, Collector of the Customs at Edenton, N C, v Wm McNider, declined the appointment. Seth Driggs, of N Y, to the U S Cnsl for Cumana Barcelona & the Isl of Margarita, in the Republic of Venezuela, to reside at Cumana.

Mrd: on May 5, at Indiantown, Chas Co, Md, by Rev A Mudd, Gen Moses Marshall Rawlings, of Ill, to Mrs Ann H Tyar, of Chas Co, Md.

Died: on Mar 25 last, at his residence, Mont Axile, PG Co, Md, Augustus W Preuss, aged 60 years, a native of Dantzic, Prussia, who emigrated to this country about 30 years ago. His poetic pieces, published in the Nat'l Intell were generally over the signature of Sylvanus. -E

Crct Court of Wash Co, D C-in Chancery. The Western Bank of Balt, vs, Wm Prout, John Hoover, & John B Steinbergen. Bill charges that Steinbergen, of Va, assigned to the complnt, on May 17, 1838, 6 bonds of John Hoover, one of the dfndnts, all dated Apr 23, 1834, & each bond to said Steinbergen, his certain atty, execs, adms, or assigns, in the penal sum of $4,600, with this condition, to pay the sum of $2,300, with interest, from the date until paid; bonds are now due & all of them unpaid, amounting to $27,600. Further charged in said bill that John Hoover made a deed of trust of certain real estate, in D C to Wm Prout, Apr 23, 1834, recorded among the land records of Wash Co, D C, directing said Prout to sell & dispose of said property, to pay the several sums of money, if unpaid, upon said bonds. Same have not been paid. Prout ought to be removed & another appointed in his place. Steinbergen resides out of the jurisdiction of this Court: same to appear on or before the 4th Monday in Nov, 1840. –W Cranch, judge -Wm Brent, clk

Senate: 1-Ptn from Ambrose Case, for a pension. 2-Ptn from Jacob Hull 3-Cmte of Claims. asked to be discharged from the further consideration of the ptn of Timothy Nye. Also, for indefinite postponement of Hse bill for relief of R _ Hall. Also, from the same cmte, reported a bill for the relief of Preston Storris.

MON MAY 11, 1840

Charleston, May 7. Crct Court of U S: sentence passed yesterday, by Judg Gilchrist, on John J Lamb, clk & assist postmaster, at Gtwn, in this state, for stealing $260 in bank bills from a letter in the post ofc at that place, & on Jas Sanderlyn, for aiding & abetting the former in perpetrating the offence. Penalty imposed by Congress, in such cases, is imprisonment, not less than 19 years nor more than 21 years. Lamb being but 17, he was sentenced to 10 years imprisonment, Sanderlyn, of mature years, was sentenced to 15 years. High praise is due to Mr A S Grosvenor, the gentleman injured by the theft, for the promptness & energy with which he pursued the felons. -Courier

Two cantos of *Cabiro*, a poem just published in Balt by Geo H Calvert, written in the ottava rima, & done with great spirit in style & language

The Boston papers announce the death of Rev Dr Tuckerman, late a distinguished Unitarian clergyman of Boston. He died in the island of Cuba, whither he had gone for the benefit of his health.

Savannah, May 5. Indians in Fla. We learn from an ofcr arrived here on Sun, in the ship *Genr'l Clinch*, from Garey's Ferry, on the 27th or 28th ult, as Capt Rains, 7th Infty, with 18 men, [all mounted,] was returning from a scout, & he & his party were fired upon near Fort King by a large party of Indians: 4 of his men killed, & Capt Rains severely wounded. This new outbreak is presumed to be owing to the destruction, by Maj Loemis' command, of some of the crops of the savages, near Annuttalliga & Hamosassa, 130 acs of corn, 4 feet high, having been destroyed by the troops. Capt Rains, previously to leaving the fort, had concealed in the hammock a shell, covered with blankets, which the Indians removed, & the shell exploded, some of them it is presumed lost their lives. A volunteer, Sanders, of Capt Hinly's company, was killed about the same time by Indians, 4 miles from Newnansville. -Georgian

Mr Jacob Gideon, sen, a Revolutionary vet, was at the great Whig festival, the venerable guest of Gen Medtart. The venerable sire of '76 was ordered by Gen Washington to bear the Flag of Truce to Lord Cornwallis, at the surrender at Yorktown, Va, & is now in his 86th year. He had a grandson in the procession, a Delegate from the District [Mr G was in the grand Whig Procession of May 4, in Balt, Md.]

Mrd: on May 5, by Rev Wm Hawley, Mr Jos Etter to Miss Rachel Hyde, all of Wash City.

Mrd: on Thu last, by Rev Mr Matthews, Mr Chas Schley to Miss Mary Long, all of Wash City.

Mrd: on May 7, by Rev J N Danforth, Mr John Post, of Wash, to Miss Harriett Brown, of Alexandria.

Mrd: on May 5, by Rev C B Dana, Rev K J Stewart, of Wash, to Miss Hannah, d/o E I Lee, of Alexandria.

Mrd: on the 21st inst, by Rev B C Robert, Wm Ashe Alston, of S C, to Anne, d/o the Hon Alex'r Porter, of La.

Died: on May 9, Lewis Chism, in his 32nd year. Funeral today at 4 p m, from his residence on G st, between 18th & 19th sts.

Partnership under the firm of E H & C H James dissolved by the death of E H James. Business in the future will be conducted by C H James, at the old stand, 14th & E st

Trustee's sale of real property: decree of Crct Court of Wash Co, D C: Court of Chancery: case of Thos Blagden & Abraham B Waller against Mary Pancoast & others: public auct on Jun 1 next of: lot 7 in sq 768; also, lots 16 & 17 in sq 687, with improvements thereon, consisting of a 2 story brick bldg on lot 17. -J W Beck, trustee -Edw Dyer, auct

TUE MAY 12, 1840
Orphans Court of Wash Co, D C. The case of Lewis Johnson, adm of Wm Otis, dec'd: the adm has appointed the first Tue in Jun next for settlement of said estate. —Ed N Roach, reg/o wills

Select Cmte of Congress to witness the practical operation of the invention "Raub's Double Self-acting Safety Valve, on board the steamer *Columbia*, as she proceeds down the Potomac for that purpose on May 12: leaving Foulke's & Lambell's wharf at 3 p m. Tickets at the Drug Store of Mr Patterson, or of the Capt. Refreshments & the Marine band will be on board. —Geo Guther, Capt

Albert Pike, Atty at Law, resides at Little Rock, Ark, & will attend to business in the several Courts in any part of the state.

Senate: 1-Ptn from Alex'r J Williams, asking for a remuneration for military services. 2-Cmte of the Whole & engrossed: bill for relief of Saml Collins. Bill for relief of Hannah Leighton was discussed at great length.

Destructive fire on May 2 in the beautiful village of Springfield, Cumberland Co, Pa: originated in a stable belonging to Mr Saml McNeal-13 houses & 10 barns & stables destroyed. Col Josiah Hood has been the principal sufferer.

Mysterious disappearance: of Mr Benj Smith, book-keeper in the Bank of Pa, who left him home in Phil, on May 2. was seen in Balt during the past week: age about 45 years. He is a most estimable man, in whom the bank places every confidence Information will gladly be received at the Nat'l Htl.

Murder committed near the Point of Rocks on May 6: a woman named Davis & her child, a boy about 11 years, living in the family of her brother, at one of the locks of the canal, were both found murdered in their bed-room. At least the woman was left insensible, & not expected to recover. –Fred'k Herald

Mrd: on May 11, by Rev Mr Davis, Mr Nicholas G Nichols to Miss Martha Ann Austin, all of Wash City.

Letter to the editors of the Richmond Whig from Henry L Brooke: subject-address of the Van Buren Central Cmte to the People of Va. [He is a member of the Central Whig Cmte.]

WED MAY 13, 1840
Corp of Wash: before any license for a tavern or ordinary shall be granted, the person making application shall produce to the Mayor a certificate signed by 6 respectable freeholders, residing in the neighborhood of the premises for which application for a license is made, that the public convenience requires a tavern of ordinary to be established in such neighborhood.
By whom the premises were examined & certified. By whom recommended:
Thos Baker, 3rd Ward, sq 431, 8th st

Edw Dyer	Thos Donoho	Theodore Harbaugh
Thos Lloyd	Raphael Jones	Leonard Harbaugh

Chas Borremans, 1st Ward, sq 74, Pa ave: By whom recommended:

Saml Smoot	Geo Krafft	A Hoover
John C Reimily	L Kervand	Thos Conner

Lloyd Brown, 2nd Ward, sq 226, Pa ave & 14th st:

Jos Abbott	C H James	Christopher Cammack
Allison Nailor	Robt Cruit	John Daly

Richd Brooks, 6th Ward, sq 928, 8th & K sts:

John Costigan	John Smith	Jas Barry
Chas Miller	Alex'r Forrest	Stanislaus Tench

Jesse Brown, 3rd Ward. Sq 460, Pa ave:

Wm Prout	Jos Ingle	Wm Stettinius
A Coyle	Wm Ward	Wm C Orme

J Boulanger, 3rd Ward, sq B, Pa ave:

Saml Bacon	Jos S Clarke	Wm C Orme

Wm Stettinius   Wm Prout   Jno Purdy
Abr Butler, 2nd Ward, sq 24, north F st:
Allison Nailor   Henry Howison   Jos Abbott
Jno France   Jas McClery   Elexius Simms
Jno H Clarvoe, 3rd Ward, sq 461, 7th st:
Peter F Bacon   W G W White   Jos S Clarke
Thos Lloyd   R G Briscoe   Saml Bacon
John B Cornwall, 3rd Ward, sq B, 4½ st & Pa ave:
Thos Lloyd   M McCarty   Benj Bean
Th Burch   B F Middleton   J Fitzgerald
Jas Cuthbert, 2nd Ward, sq 224, north F st:
Elex Simms   Robt Cruit   Nicholas Callan
Wm Dowling   Christopher Cammack   Wm H Stewart
John Douglass, 3rd Ward, sq 490, La ave:
S Hyat   T F Semmes   John Hoover
Michl McDermott   J A Donohoe   Philip Ennis
Wm Dowling, 2nd Ward, sq 254, north F st:
Nicholas Callan   Elexius Simms   Michl Ward
Christopher Cammack Jos Abbott   John Daly
John W Dexter, 2nd Ward, sq 226, Pa ave:
Allison Nailor   Jos Abbott   Grafton Powell
John Daly   Robt Cruit   John C Rives
John H Eberbach, 2nd Ward, sq 291, Pa ave:
P Kinchy   Nicholas Travers   John France
C Eckloff   Wm M McCauley   Henry Ault
Mary Fagan, 6th Ward, sq 906, L st:
Philip Inch   Geo Duckworth   Martin King
Matthew Trimble   Thos Bayne   R M Combs
Frere & Eno, 1st Ward, sq 86, 20th st:
A K Parris   Chas A Clements   F Godfrey
John Walker   Wm Serrin   Thos Lundy
A Favier, 1st Ward, sq 119, 19th st:
Saml Redfern   Thos Smith   A Hoover
L Kervand   Geo Krafft   Saml Stott
Jas Fitzgerald, 3rd Ward, res 10 Pa ave:
Philip Ennis   John Sinon   P W Browning
Walter Jones   Isaac Beers   John M Farrar
Fossett & Fletcher, 3rd Ward, sq B Pa ave:
Edw Simms   B F Middleton   Thos Cookendorfer
I Mudd   Alex'r Lee   John Brown
John Foy, 2nd Ward, sq 348, D & 10th sts:
Michl Ward   E Dyer   Wm Orme
Michl Sardo   Clement Woodward   Jas Fitzpatrick
E H Fuller, 2nd Ward, sq 225, Pa ave:
Wm Orme   Jos Abbott   C H James

E H James   Robt Cruit   Allison Nailor
Bernard Giveny, 3rd Ward, sq 343, 7th st:
Ambrose Lynch   J H Goddard   Stanislaus Murray
Thos Macgill   Saml Brereton   Philip Ennis
Henry Gooding, 4th Ward, sq 729, E Capt st:
Wm Magill   D Homans   Robt Beall
John Lynch   Thos J Barrett   Z Hazell
B Guttschlick, 3rd Ward, sq 490, La ave:
R Burdine   John Wilkinson   Chas Pettit
Jos Borrows   R R Burr   Chas Bell
Lewis Goldsmith, 3rd Ward, sq 455, 7th st:
J H Goddard   E G Emack   H B Robertson
Jas H Shreeve   Jas Williams   Thos Macgill
Jas S Hall, 2nd Ward, sq 226, Pa ave:
John France   E Simms   Wm M McCauley
John A Brightwell   Jos Abbott   John Daly
John Hancock, 3rd Ward, s 491, Pa ave:
Thos Lloyd   B F Middleton   Alex Lee
Saml Bacon   Martin Murphy   Solomon Drew
R H Harrington, 6th Ward, sq 930, K st:
John Costigan   R M Combs   Philip Otterback
Edw W Clark   Chas Miller   D M Coombe
Jacob Hess, 2nd Ward, sq 254, F st:
J M Krafft   Grafton Powell   C Eckloff
Andrew Noer   Wm Dowling   Nicholas Callan
John Hyde, 4th Ward, sq 688, Va ave:
Jas Young   D Homans   Wm Magill
Chas T Krebs   W J McDonald   C W Steuart
Dennis McInnerny, 3rd Ward, sq 491, Pa ave:
Philip Ennis   Edw Simms   Jas Hoban
Stans Murray   M Foy   Jas Fitzgerald
Susan Joyce, 4th Ward, sq 732, B st:
D Homans   Henry Gooding   John Johnson
Geo Phillips   Thos J Barrett   Wm Magill
Geo Kensett, 2nd Ward, sq 291, 13th st:
John C Rives   John France   A Carothers
Henry Ault   Elexius Simms   W H Stewart
Lucy Laskey, 3rd Ward, sq 461, 7th st:
J A Donohoo   B F Middleton   W G W White
Thos Lloyd   Mich McDermott   Thos Burch
Thos Lloyd, 3rd Ward, sq 461, 7th st:
P F Bacon   S Hyatt   Jas T Clarke
R G Briscoe   Saml Bacon   W G W White
Jas Lynch, 4th Ward, sq 729, E Capt st:
Thos J Barret   Henry Gooding   Wm Magill

D Homans   Z Hazell   John Lynch
Patrick Magee, sq 101, on I st:
A K Parris   John Mullikin   John Walker
Louis Vivans   Thos Lundy   A Hoover
Jas Maher, 2nd Ward, sq 256, E & 13½ sts:
Lewis Thompson   Wm M McCauley   Allison Nailor
John France   Richd Travers   Isaac Cooper
Patrick Moran, 3rd Ward, sq 475, Pa ave:
M Foy   Jas Fitzgerald   Stans Murray
Philip Ennis   Thos Lloyd   Gregory Ennis
Martin Murphy, 3rd Ward, res 10, Pa ave:
J Fitzgerald   Thos Lloyd   B F Middleton
John Sinon   Mich McCarty   Th Burch
Newton & Gadsby, 3rd Ward, sq 491, Pa ave:
J H Bradley   E G Emack   Wm C Orme
Enoch Tucker   W Prout   B F Middleton
Christopher O'Neal, 6th Ward, sq 907, 7th st:
Geo Duckworth   Philip Inch   Wm M Ellis
Jas Tucker   Jno H Smoot   Jno Keithley
Grafton Powell, 2nd Ward, sq 254, E st:
Nicholas Callan   J A Brightwell   Jas McClery
Elexius Simms   Christopher Cammack   Allison Nailor
Ann Powers, 3rd Ward, sq 461, 7th st:
J A Donohoo   B F Middleton   W G W White
Thos Lloyd   Michl McDermott   Th Burch
Jno Purdon, 2nd Ward, sq 292, Pa ave:
C Eckloff   F Burch   C L Coltman
C Alexander   Jno France   N Travers
H W Queen, 2nd Ward, sq 355, G & 11th sts:
Jas Mitchell   A Shepherd
W W Stewart   Wm Radcliff   Peter Hepburn
J E Thumlert   Geo Hercuss
Francis Reily, 6th Ward, sq 928, 8th st:
Robt Clarke   Jas Barry   Matthew Jarboe
Jno Costigan   Thos Bayne   Thos Thornley
Henry Rochat, 1st Ward, sq 74, Pa ave:
Jno Mullikin   L Kervand   A Hoover
A K Parris   Jno Walker   Louis Vivans
Chas Rosenthal, 2nd Ward, sq 322, 11th st:
A Noer   D Munro   W H Stewart
Wm Orme   P Kinchy   A Carothers
A Ruppert, 3rd Ward, sq 408, 9th st:
Wm Uttermuhle   N Shanks   J L Peabody
C Eckloff   Thos Lloyd   John Hoover
John Smith, 3rd Ward, sq 458, 7th st:

J A Donohoo	Theodore Harbaugh	D S Waters
John Hoover	Raphael Jones	Solomon Drew
Wentin Sauter, 1st Ward, sq 119, Pa ave		
A Hoover	Thos Smith	L Kervand
Saml Redfern	A K Parris	Geo Krafft
B O Shackell, 3rd Ward, sq 461, 7th st		
Thos Lloyd	Saml Bacon	S Hyatt
Peter F Bacon	B F Middleton	John A Donohoo
Richd Smith, 2nd Ward, sq 256, E st		
Nathan Plant	And Carothers	Michl Ward
Allison Nailor	John France	W H Stewart
Jeremiah Sullivan, 2nd Ward, sq 225, 13th st		
C L Collins	Elexius Simms	Christoper Cammack
Nicholas Callan	Wm Dowling	Michl Ward
H W Sweeting, 3rd Ward, sq 490, C st		
Alex Lee	Saml Bacon	Jas Hoban
S Hyatt	J P Pepper	Edw Simms
Michl Ward, 2nd ward		
Henry Ault	Wm Steward	Wm M McCauley
Wm Dowling	Nicholas Callan	Wm B Walker
Cornelius Wells, sq 267, Md ave & 14th st		
P G Howle	J S Harvey	Isaac Hills
Peter Cazenave	Jos King	Patrick Green
John West, 3rd Ward, sq 461, Pa ave		
S Hyatt	J B Gorman	Carey Selden
Thos Burch	Thos Cookendorfer	T H Bowen
Voltaire Willett, 3rd Ward, sq 490, C st		
Stans Murray	B F Middleton	Edw Simms
Carey Selden	E G Emack	Danl Campbell

Drug store for sale: subscriber, wishing to leave the city, [on account of ill health,] is desirous of disposing of his store: nothing called induce the property to dispose of it but the necessity of travelling for his health. —Wm F Bender, 6th & Pa ave

The Globe says Amos Kendall has resigned the ofc of Postmaster Gen; to take effect as soon as a successor's e appointed. Mr K says that he retires on account of ill health; that he has not accumulated wealth in his ofc, & has arranged to undertake the editorship of the Extra Globe until Nov.

The Albany Argus of Sat states that the Pres has remitted the fine of $250 imposed upon Rensselaer Van Rensselaer for a violation of the neutrality laws, it having been shown that he was unable to pay it. The residue of the punishment imposed upon Wm Lyon Mackenzie, who was sentenced to 18 months imprisonment from Jun 20 last, & a fine of $10, has also been remitted.

Mrd: on May 12, by Rev Mr Hawley, Capt Fred A Smith, U S Corps of Engr, to Agnes Maria, d/o the late Jos Mechlin, of Wash City.

Law Notice: N C Stephen, Bladensburg, & D C Digges, Upr Marlboro, Attys at Law & Solicitors in Chancery. [Ad]

Senate: 1-Ptn from Eliz Garrabrantz, asking for a pension. 2-Ptn from Jos Hampton & others, remonstrating against the use of bloodhounds. 3-Ptn from Saml W Hill & others, asking that land patents may issue to Francis Laventure. 4-Ptn of David McCaleb, asking confirmation of a land title. 5-Ptn from Fred'k Counts & others, asking the right of pre-emption to land settled & cultivated by them. 6-Ptn from citizens of Natchez, praying the release of Wm Lyon Mackenzie. 7-Ptn of Alex'r McCullogh, asking to locate lands derived from certain Spanish confirmations. 8-Cmte of Claims: asking to be discharged from the claim of Alex'r Lee, & that he have leave to withdraw his papers.

A public meeting of the voters of the 5th Ward is requested at Capt John Cryer's, at the old Brew Hse, on Sat, at 7 p m, to nominate a suitable candidate for the Mayoralty.

Nominations from the Mayor for Guardians of the Poor: Danl H Haskell, 1st Ward; John McClelland, 2nd Ward; Leonard Harbaugh, 3rd Ward; Henry J Stone, 4th Ward; John B Ferguson, 5th Ward, Noble Young, 6th Ward. Same were considered & confirmed.

Wash Corp: 1-Memorial from John Thos Clements & others, Cmte of the Columbian Journeyman Hse Carpenters' Soc: referred to Messrs Maury & Randolph. 2-Claim of Geo Adams, late Collector of Taxes: referred to the Cmte of Claims.

Germans attend! Meeting of the Germans friendly to the election of Gen Harrison will be held this evening at the Perseverance Engine Hse, at half past seven. Mr Francis J Grund, of Phil, editor of the Pa German, will address them in the German language.

Sale by order of the Crct Court-in Chancery: Anthony Preston & Rosina Cheshire, adms of Archibald Cheshire, dec'd, vs, Mary Lindsey Cheshire & others, heirs at law of A Cheshire. Sale of lot 2 in sq 267 in Wash City: lot fronts on Md ave. –J B H Smith, trust. -Edw Dyer, auct

THU MAY 14, 1840
500,000 bricks for sale at the Patent Brick Press, near the Navy Yard, warranted to be at least equal to other bricks, & at the lowest prices. –Jasper Du Flon, agent

Wanted: a farm adapted for grazing, about 2 to 400 acs, near the city: bldgs must be good. –John F Webb, broker

Senate: 1-Ptn from Alex'r Colman, asking to locate a certain section of land. 2-Cmte of Claims: asked to be discharged from further consideration of the ptn of Mr Watkins.

Gen J A Quitman, of Miss, has declined being a candidate for Elector on the Van Buren ticket. The "honest Nullifier" is evidently dissatisfied with the coalition between the leaders of his party & the spoils men —Alex Gaz

Fredericksburg Arena, May 12. Wm B Dabney, First Teller of the Bank of Va, has returned to Richmond, & emphatically declares he did not take a cent of the money of the bank.

Mrd: on the 30th ult, at Brooklyn, Long Island, by Rev Mr Spencer, Lt Wm Rogers Taylor, U S Navy, to Caroline A, d/o Gold S Silliman

Died: on May 13, after a short illness, Mr Wm Ward, a native of the county of Monahan, Ire, in his 50th year. Funeral from his late residence on F st, between 6th & 7th sts, today at 4 p m.

Died: on Wed, Wm Dunawin, aged 19 years. Funeral from the residence of his father, on 8th between G & H sts, today at 3 p m

Died: on Apr 25th, of pulmonary consumption, at Newcastle, Ky, Mrs Clarissa Kerr, w/o Rev Andrew H Kerr, & d/o Archibald Van Horn, dec'd, of Md. Hers was a calm, peaceful, & triumphant death

FRI MAY 15, 1840

The Fred'k Herald states that David Linton has been sentenced to the penitentiary for 2 years, for stealing sapling trees suitable for hoop poles

Senate: 1-Cmte on Pensions: unfavorable report on the ptns of Richd Elliott & Shearborn Dearborn. 2-Ordered to a 3rd reading, bill for relief of the legal reps of David Stone; relief of Richd Robinson. 3-Bill for relief of Wm Bennett: indefinitely postponed.

N Y, May 14. The slave schn'r *Sarah Ann* arrived here yesterday from Sierra Leone in charge of Lt J C Williamson, of the U S Navy. She was seized on the coast of Africa for dabbling in the slave trade. was owned in New Orleans, & commanded by Capt Raymond: was seized in one of the small rivers on the coast by the English brig of war *Bonita*, & delivered to Lt Com Payne, of the U S schn'r *Grampus*, on Mar 12 last. He placed her in charge of Lt Williamson, with a prize crew of 8 men, & ordered her home for trial. She sailed under American colors, & had all the implements for a slave expedition; no slaves were on board when captured. Most of her crew are on board the *Grampus*. The Capt died on Apr 8. -Herald

Frankfort, Ky, Yeoman observes: last week, Dr Hawkins, well know in this community, was waylaid in Mercer Co, & shot & killed, by an individual named Mayfield, who has been taken into custody.

Mrd: on May 13, at Sandy Spring, Roger Brooke to Sarah T Gilpin, d/o Bernard Gilpin, all of Montg Co, Md.

Died: on Tue last, at his residence in Rockville, Montg Co, Md, Benj Stoddert Forrest, for many years Pres of the Md Senate, & a distinguished member of the bar.

SAT MAY 16, 1840

Valuable land for sale: on Jun 10, the tract of land of which Capt John Crain died seized & possessed. It is in Fauquier Co, Va, 1½ miles from Middleburg. farm contains 400 acs, laid off into 9 fields; with a commodious mansion house, built of stone, with all necessary out bldgs, also a grist mill. Title is unquestionable. -Mary Sullivan, admx de bonis non, with will annexed of John Crain, dec'd.

Woodlawn for sale: subscriber, being desirous of relieving himself from the trouble of a large landed estate, offers for sale his farm, called *Woodlawn*, on Dogue creek once a part of Mt Vernon estate: upwards of 2,000 acs of land: large brick barn, farm house, corn houses, & outbldgs. Also, a large stone mill upon the creek. The dwlg house is not surpassed by any in Va in construction, style or finish, & situation, being on a high hill, in a grove of fine oaks, commandng a beautiful view of the river in front. The house is built of brick with freestone sills & lentils to windows & door, coping of the basement also of stone, slate roof, 2 stories high, 4 rooms on a floor, spacious cellars under the house, portico in front, paved with marble, & confined by freestone, all the out hses of brick. The subscriber would prefer, if the purchaser was willing, retaining the house & from 200 to 250 acres around it. Apply at Audley, near Berryville, Clarke Co, Va, of L Lewis. To view the premises, apply to Mr A Remington, lvg on the farm, or to Wm H Foote, of *Hayfield*, adjoining *Woodlawn*, will have every facility afforded them. –L Lewis

"The Bro Jonathan," a periodical published weekly in N Y, has engaged the pen of N P Willis.

Mrd: on May 4, at New Haven, Conn, Hon David Daggett, Prof of Law in Yale Univ, to Miss Mary Lines, of New Haven.

Mrd: on May 7, at New Haven, Conn, Lt Jas T McDonough, of the Navy, to Laura, eldest d/o the Hon Saml J Hitchcock, Instructor of Law in Yale College.

Died: on Apr 24, at Northeast, Cecil Co, Md, of consumption, Sarah, y/d/o the late John Maffit, of that place.

The brig *Susan Mary*, bound to Matagorda, has on board a church with all its appendages, pulpit, & pews. This bldg has been erected & shipped by Mr Jas N Wells, bldr, of this city, ready for putting up. —N Y Jour of Com

Copartnership under firm of E Waters & Co is this day dissolved by mutual consent. Settle accounts with E Waters. corner of 12th & E sts. —E Waters, J S Harvey & Co

Orphans Court of Wash Co, D C. Letters of administrationd de bonis non on the estate of John Peters be granted to Robt Barnard, unless cause to the contrary be shown on or before Jun 5. —Nathl P Causin -Ed N Roach, reg/o wills

MON MAY 18, 1840

Phil, May 16. Our readers will rejoice that Mr Jacob May, whose disappearance created anxiety, is among the living, & now in the care of our hospitable Sanderson of Merchants' Htl. —Sentinel

Vicksburg Sentinel: Wm H Shelton, Pres of the Brandon Bank, & S M Pucket & Richd Hobson, directors of same, have left Miss for Texas: took with them 300 negroes. Shelton armed 50 or his negroes, & procured 10 white men to enable them to force their way out of the state. The marshal is in pursuit. -N O Bulletin

Among the passengers in the ship *Stephen Whitney*, which sailed from N Y a day or 2 since for Liverpool, were J Hare Powell, lady, & 2 servants, Julia Powell, Saml Powell, Deveaux Powell, Baring Powell, Hare Powell, & Matthew T Miller, all of Phil

Mr Sherrod Williams, of Ky, who has been confined to his room about 8 weeks with a severe illness, is now recovering his health, & will soon, be able to answer the calls of his friends & constituents

Troy, N Y, May 13. On Mon, in a house near the Catholic Chr, Jonathan H Kendrick, sexton of Rev Mr Hopkins' Soc, a cabinet-maker, killed his wife by choking her. This was his 2nd marriage, & threatened her with death should she dare leave him. —Daily Mail

Appointments by the Pres: Benj Bytewood, Collector of the Customs at Beaufort, S C, v David Turner, removed. John French, Surveyor of the Revenue at New London, Conn, from Jun 21, 1840, when his present commission will expire. J P B Wilmer, to be a Chaplain in the Navy from May 7, 1839. Rodman Lewis, to be a Chaplain in the Navy from Mar 13, 1839. Thos B Nalle, to be a Purser in the Navy from Oct 17, 1839. Thos P McBlair, to be Purser in the Navy from Nov 11, 1839. Thos Eastin, to be Navy Agen for the port of Pensacola, West Fla, for 4 years from May 10, 1840, when his present commission will expire. Jos W Curtis, to be a 2nd Lt in the Marine Corps from May 4, 1840.

Mr Abraham Reddick, aged 89 years, was recently united in wedlock to Miss Mary Hodges, aged 15 years, all of Gates Co, N C.

Mrd: on May 14, in Wash City, Mr Saml M Semmes, of Cumberland, Md, to Elenora Nelson, d/o Jonathan Guest, of D C.

Mrd: on May 7, by Rev T C Thornton, Mr Wm T Clarke to Miss Amelia Hunt, of Fairfax Co, Va.

Mrd: on May 7, by Rev T C Thornton, Mr Jas N Davis to Miss Eliz S O'Neale, all of Wash City.

Mrd: May 14, by Rev T C Thornton, Mr Henry Miffleton to Miss Almey Allison, of Alexandria, D C.

Mrd: on May 14, by Rev T C Thornton, Mr Jacob Jackson to Miss Ellen Burke.

Died: on Apr 5 last, at Holly Springs, Miss, after a few hours illness, Alfred H Powell, Atty at Law, in his 33rd year. He was a native of Loudoun Co, Va, & emigrated west early in life to pursue his profession. After a residence of several years in Tenn he removed to Miss, where he resided till the time of his death, having formed a professional partnership with his father-in-law, the late Judge Humphries.

Nicolas Warner will at all times be found at his ofc on 8th st, near Pa ave, to wait upon all who may employ him as Boot-black & Porter. 2nd hand clothing bought & sold on commission. –N W

Mr Wm M Price & family arrived yesterday in the packet-ship *Garrick*. He says he is prepared to prove that he is not a defaulter.

Fanny Elssler has taken the city by storm. The Park Theatre is crowded nightly.

The Duke of Nemours was mrd on the 27th to the Princess Victoria of Coburg, on which occasion the King would extend the amnesty of May.

Passengers in the steam-ship *British Queen*, from London:

Mstr Spencer	J C Sinton
Miss Spencer	G Brooking
Mr H Simpson	R Gosher
C Kirkby	M Cemmerling
G Gillespie	Jas Drake
C G Taylor	L Drake
E Lane	A Sanderman
G R Robinson	W Chapman
Col John Heth	H Chapman

J Holford
R L Davis
Mrs Mott
F Hoole
R Hemmingway
V M Hoffman
B Flint
J E Rofferstein
W H Holmes
J Frosts
W Jackson
J Carter
Robt Taylor
J W Kawksley
J W Owens
W Laing
Baron de Tuylle
Mrs Ericsson
Capt Sandaman
Mr Blakiston
Adam Hope
R Bell
A Kennedy
A Hogge
G Tunscott
J Cennacher
R W Gray & servant
J Montavo & servant
Dr Turnpenny & lady
L Woolley & lady
W S Fearing & lady
Mrs Harman & child
J W Duncombe & lady

J Hoisey
Mr Durant
Mrs Peck
H A Rose
J Hughes
Miss Hughes
J D Gregg
G Hepburn
W M Westmacott
Miss M Young
Thos Y Hall
Mr Welchman
Dr Bernard
Mrs Furniss
Mrs Holland
Mr Barry
E Fitzgerald
W M Brown, jr
Mr Artault
B Levi
Mr Silden
Mrs Johnson
Mr Davis
W H Reynolds
J H Buchanan
Miss Chace
Lord Mulgrave & servant
A M Laurence, lady, child, & servant
Mr & Mrs Van Schaick & servant
Mr S Magnus, lady, & servant
Mr Churchill, lady, & child
Mrs Newsted, 2 chldrn, & servant
Mrs Roberts, child, & servant

Passengers in the packet-ship *Garrrick* arrived at N Y from Liverpool:
Of N Y: E Palmer & lady
E Cary, lady & servant
W M Price & lady
Mr Price
Mstr A Price
Miss C Price, & servant
Mr W F Post

Miss Susan Babcock, of Stonington
Mr A Harvey & lady, of Canada
Lt Staunton, of Royal Artl
Mr G S Minor, of Va
Mr D H Tucker, of Va
& 320 in the steerage

Ordination: the Presbytery of D C will meet in the 2nd Presby Chr, on N Y ave, near 13th st: Rev Geo J Wood will preach, & be installed Pastor of said church. All invited: today at 8 p m.

Senate: 1-Ptn for relief of Mary W Thompson. 2-Cmte on Pensions: relief of Danl Steinrod.

TUE MAY 19, 1840
To let: well built & convenient house in Franklin Row. Inquire of Anthony Preston, 12th st.

Senate: 1-Cmte on Commerce: asking to be discharged from the further consideration of the ptn of David E Brocket. 2-Cmte on the Judiciary: was referred the bill for the relief of Thos L Winthrop & others, an elaborate report setting forth all the facts: ordered to be printed. 3-Cmte on Pensions: a bill for the relief of Wm Rand. 4-Cmte on the P O & Post Roads: bill for relief of Avery, Saltmarsh & Co, with an amendment

Hse o/Reps: 1-Memorial of Wm A Griswold, Pres of the Champlain Transportation Co, & of John Griffiths & others, owners of steamboats, in relation to the existing steamboat laws, & to the proposed change or amendment of those laws. 2-Ptns of Phoebe Burrill, & of Hannah Strong, & of Hannah Brooks, praying for pensions. 3-Additional papers in support of the claim of Robt Graham, of Westmoreland Co, Pa, to a tract of land in Ill: referred to the Cmte on Pvt Land Claims. 4-Ptn of Lt Peter Huston, an ofcr in the Northwestern army during the late war, for a pension. 5-Ptn of Wm Slicke, of Bedford Co, Pa, a soldier of the Revolution: for a pension. 6-Ptn of Saml D Rose, in relation to money stolen from the U S mail, & now in possession of the P O Dept. 7-Ptn of Geo Williams, of Crawford Co, Ohio, a descendant of Capt Isaac Williams, jr, dec'd, for relief by the grant of a tract of land. 8-Ptn of Jos Ellery, for a pension: referred to the Cmte on Invalid Pensions. 9-Ptn of Stephen Howard, a Revolutionary soldier, for a grant of land: referred to the Cmte on Pvt Land Claims. 10-Ptn of Alex'r Ferriole & others, praying for indemnity for losses in the Revolutionary war: referred to the Cmte on Revolutionary Claims. 11-Ptn of John Clark, for a pension: referred to the Cmte on Revolutionary Pensions. 12-Ptn of Jos Plumb, for arrears of pension: referred to the Cmte on Revolutionary Pensions. 13-Ptn of chldrn of Mary Addoms, for arrears of pension: referred to the Cmte on Revolutionary Pensions. 14-Ptn of Jeremiah McCreedy, praying for reimbursement of moneys advanced by 2 companies of U S troops during the last war: referred to the Cmte of Claims. 15-Ptn of Jos F Gibbs, praying for a pension: referred to the Cmte on Revolutionary Pensions. Papers of Squire Ferris referred to same.

For rent: the house on Capitol Hill occupied at present by the Vice President Possession will be given on Jun 18 -Henry Daingerfield, Alexandria

Boarding: Mrs Auld on the south side of Pa ave, near 4½ st, has several pleasant rooms vacant.

John M Niles, of Conn, appointed by the Pres, to be Postmaster Gen of the U S, v Amos Kendall, resigned.

Churchill C Cambreleng, of N Y, nominated by the Pres of the U S to the Senate as Minister Pleni to the Court of St Petersburg.

Natchez in ruins: horrible storm on May 8, raged for half an hour with most dreadful power. Mrs Alexander was rescued from the ruins of the Steamboat Hotel, much injured, with 2 chldrn in her arms, both dead. The Court-house at Vidalia, Parish Concordia, is low with the earth: Judge Keeton was dug from the ruins horribly mangled & dead; only person in the bldg. [May 25 paper: The splendid villa of Andrew Brown, is totally ruined: the mansions of Peter Little & Mrs Linton, escaped with the loss of chimneys: Messrs Farish & Bemiz were dug alive, after 2 hours confinement, in the ruins of Parker's Southern Exchange, & the dead body of Moses, a valuable servant, was found. 11 bodies taken from the ruins of the Steamboat Hotel, which have all been removed by the gangs of slaves of Col Surget, Mr Crossgrove, & others, generously sent in by those wealthy planters. 35 killed by the storm were interred up to 12 o'clock yesterday. Full particulars in the Weekly Courier, by next Thu or Fri.]

From Arkansas: Michl J Stock, late co-editor of the Times, was drowned on May 2, while generously essaying to help a friend across Town Branch.

Mrd: on May 14, by Rev Mr Dana, J Murray Forbes, of Falmouth, Va, to Miss Mary Eliz Semmes, d/o the late Dr Thos Semmes, of Alexandria, D C.

Died: May 12, at his late residence, in Princeton, N J, at age 73 years, Saml Bayard, V P of the Ameircan Bible Soc, in the formation of which he took an active part.

In consequence of the death of Thos Detter, Conrad Hess has been appointed scavenger of that part of the 3rd Ward lying east of 7th st & north of D St.
St Augustine, May 8. During the last week the highest offence known to military law occurred at Pilatka. Brvt Maj Ashby, commandng ofcr of the post, was absent, & the command devolved on Lt Merrill. Order was issued to a non-com ofcr respecting the removal of prisoners, who peremptorily refused to carry it out. Lt M was subject to personal violence. Dr Hitchcock knocked down several of the mutineers, although not before a carbine was levelled at the Dr, & missed fire. - News

Sir Robt Seppings, distinguished naval architect of Eng, died at Taunton, Eng, on the 25th ult, at age 72 years. The Royal Soc & the Royal Soc of Arts both awarded him their gold medals.

Citizens of Raleigh, N C, on May 9, gave a complimentary dinner to their respected fellow-townsman, Gen Beverly Daniel, who was lately superseded by the U S Exec in the ofc of Mrshl of N C, an ofc which he received from Pres Jefferson, & which he filled with honor, until the successor thought fit to supesede him by the appointment of a devoted partisan. Jos Gales, sr, & John Devereux, sen, were called on to preside. Toasts given by: Geo E Badger, Chas Manly, Gen S F Patterson, Gen Jas Iredell, Geo W Mordecai, Geo W Polk, & H W Miller.

On Sun, the large flouring mill, the property of Mr Nathan Tyson, about 3 miles from the city of Balt, on the Falls rd, was completely destroyed by fire: communicated from one of the kilns by accident.

Trustees of Charlotte Hall School, in St Mary's Co, Md, announce the appointment of Dr Chas Kraitair as principal, with the able assistance of Mr Shaw & Mr Barnes. –H G S Key, chrmn

Recommended by:

John Quincy Adams	Geo M Keim	J N Barker
S Cooper	J R Poinsett	Jas Whitcomb
S Burche	A Mouton	Jos S Wilson
Wm R King	Wm S Fulton	S P Dornenburg
Henry Clay	D Jenifer	J H Offey
Thos H Benton	T L Smith	B Klimkiewicz
J N Nicollet	John M Moore	J T H Worthington
W Matthews	J Miller	

Extensive sale of groceries: with a view of entering more extensively into the Grocery business, in Richmond, Va, the coming fall. Public auction at their store on Pa ave, on May 22. –Howison & Jackson -Ed Dyer auct

WED MAY 20, 1840
Balt, May 19. Lorenzo Dow, alias Pablo, was yesterday sentenced in the murder of Capt Wm B Langdon, of the brig *Francis*, of Boston. Delivered by Chief Justice Taney, & was that of death. The prisoner is to be hung upon the walls of the jail. He is a Malay, & his appearance very unintellectual & insane. –American

Wash Corp: 1-Act for relief of Osborne Turner: read 3 times & passed. 2-Ptn from Stanislaus Rigsby: referred to the Cmte of Claims. 3-Cmte of Claims: asked to be discharged from the ptns of Wm Lomas & Andrew Noerr: discharged accordingly. 4-Ptn of J G Robinson & others, a cmte on the part of the Northern Liberties Fire Co, for use of a certain space as a site for an engine-house, & also for such pecuniary aid as the Corp may be disposed to extend: referred to the Cmte on Improvements. 5-Ptn of John Jarboe, praying permission to continue a frame bldg on an alley in sq 726: referrred to the Cmte on Improvements. 6-Cmte on Police: to whom was referred the ptn of Henry Johnson, asked to be discharged from its further cosideration. 7-Cmte on Claims: for relief of Clement Woodward, reported the same without amendment: passed.

Dr W R Rose offers his services to the citizens of Wash in the different branches of his profession. Ofc in the wing of Gadsby's, near the corner of C st.

Chas S Boker was, on Mon last, elected Pres of the Girard Bank, at Phil, vice Mr Schott, resigned.

Andrew Newell, a Justice of the Peace in Binbrooke, Upr Canada, says the Buffalo Commercial Adv, was thrown from a horse which he was racing, & received such wounds as to cause his death in an hour afterwards.

The Phil Commercial Herald, unable to make head-way against the pressure of the times, has been united to & consolidated with the Pennsylvania Inquirer.

Letter to the editor of the Balt Patriot: Balt, May 18, 1840. Contributions for the relief of the family of the late Thos H Laughlin amount, in the whole, only to $2,430.12½: state of Mass sent $1,000; nearly $500 from Va. –John V L McMahon

The late Dr Parrish, of Phil, who died last month, made an express provision in his will that $150 of his estate be annually expended in making his old horse comfortable as long as he lives. He shall be quartered in Burlington, be liberally fed, have a bed of straw every night, be regularly curried & kept clean, & used just enough for his own agreeable & healthy exercise; no more than this.

Murder in Kent Co: letter dated Chestertown, May 15, states that Mr Jas Woodall, formerly deputy shrf, was killed last Wed by a man named Swartha, at New Market, of which place both were residents. Some ill feeling existed between them: a dispute arose, during which Swartha struck Woodall with a stick, & cleft his skull completely from the forehead to the chin. Swartha is awaiting trial.

Senate: 1-Ptn from Fielder Dorsey, a messenger in the Pension ofc, asking additional compensation for extra services rendered. 2-Ptn from T W Marlow & others, of Wash City, praying that the banks of D C may be compelled to resume specie payments, or that they be forced to wind up their concerns & surrender their effects to their creditors. 3-Cmte on Revolutionary Claims: asking to be discharged from the further consideration of the ptn of Maj Farrar, & that it be referred to the Cmte on Pensions. 4-Cmte on Naval Affairs: adverse report on the ptn of the wid/o Jos S Cannon.

Albert G Moon shot Hamilton Bussey in Memphis last Wed. Moon made his escape. -Ibid

Balt, May 18. On Sat the lady of our Chief Justice Taney, met with an accident. While with her dght, when in the drug store of Mr Andrews, she unknowingly stepped into an opened trap door, behind the counter, while admiring some flowers. Mrs Taney fractured one of her legs above the knee & seriously injured her back. –Sun

Mrd: on May 12, by Rev Mr Berry, L Warrington Gillet, of Balt, to Ann Isabella, d/o Conrad Hogmire, of Gtwn.

Died: on May 11, at Athens, Ga, Gen Burwell Pope, in his 50th year, a citizen distinguished as well by his public spirit as his merits as a private citizen.

Died: on Mon last, Ellen, y/d/o W A & C E Williams.

Wm Hunton, late of Fauquier Co, Va, died in Aug, 1838. By his last will he declared: should provision be made by either the Colonization Soc or the Gov't, at any time between this & the year 1850, for sending emancipated slaves to Africa, it is my desire that all those that I now have in possession, & their increase, be set at liberty & sent to Africa under the direction of the Board, provided they are willing & will go in families, & that the offer to them, in case provision be made, shall be given by my excs in a friendly manner. Robin & Richd, slaves, refused to accept their freedom; Lewis & Peter, slaves, absconded from the agent of the American Colonization Soc at Norfolk, & voluntarily returned to the family of the said Wm Hunton, dec'd. Such is slavery in Va.

Holly Springs, Miss: May 5. On Apr 29, Solomon B Isaacs, State's Atty for this dist, was attacked & killed in his ofc by a young man, Thos Westbrook, who inflicted mortal wounds upon him, with a Bowie knife, & he died immediately. The prisoner was committed for trial. –Conservative

The tornado at Natchez, on May 7: crossed the point below the plantation of David Barland: opposite the plantations of P M Lapice, in the parish of Concordia: slighly injured the mansion called the *Briers*: swept the mansion late of Chas B Greene, called the *Bellevue*, & the ancient forest in which it was embosomed into a mass of ruins: Court-house at Vidalia is torn down, also the dlwg houses of Dr M'Whorter, & of Messrs Dunlap & Stacey. Judge Keeton was instantly killed while at dinner at the house of Mr Stacey. Public meeting held at which Col Jas C Wilkins presided, & F L Claiborne was sec. Addresses by J M Hewitt & J M Duffield. Noah Barlow, proprietor of the City Hotel, threw open his doors to the wounded. Dr Pollard used the Tremont House for an additional hospital, Stephen Duncan having offered to be responsible for the rent. Mr Ruffner & S J Boyd made a practical estimate of the damages.

Wash City News. Mr Anthony R Fraser, of Four-mile creek, south of the Potomac, sent to our ofc yesterday a bowl of the finest strawberries we have ever seen: orders will be received at his stall in the south shed of the new Centre Market.

Hse o/Reps. 1-Ptn from John P Lewis & a large number of the citizens of Monmouth Co, N J, asking an appropriation to improve the navigation of the Shrewsberry river: referred to the Cmte on Commerce. 2-Ptn of Christopher Niswanger & Wm S Sullivant: petitioners state that in Nov 1837, they entered into a contract with the Commissary Dept to furnish & deliver provisions for the U S Army at Fort Towson public landing, they purchased & shipped, but, within a few miles of said landing, the boat in which the shipment was made was snagged & sunk, & a portion of the provisions were lost, they were assured by the agents of the Gov't at the time that it would not be expected that they, the petitioners would fulfil the residue of their contract. The petitioners state the supplies to be in the amount of $5,454.48: they received $4,000 from the Gov't; petitioners protest: referred to the Cmte of Claims. 3-Ptn of Ebenezer Byers, of Mercer Co, Pa, a soldier of the Revolution & Indian wars, praying for a pension: referred to the Cmte on Revolutionary Pensions. 4-Ptn of Wm Saward, of Dorchester Co, Md, asking compensation for services in transporting troops & provisions in the Revolutionary war. 5-Ptn from Lt F M Maury, asking compensation for services rendered the Gov't in srvyng the Southern harbors: referred to the Cmte of Claims. 6-Ptn from Robt Harkney, of Wilkes Co, Ga, asking to be placed on the pension roll as a Revolutionary sldr: referred to the Cmte on Pensions. 7-Ptn from Barnabas Stewart, of Ga, asking pay for a wagon & team: referred to the Cmte of Claims. 8-Ptn from Gen H H Tower, of Ga, asking to be compensated for the transportation of baggage, of volunteers in Fla: referred to the Cmte of Claims. 9-Ptn from Saml Glemar & others, of Ga, asking establishment of a post ofc at Woodstock, Oglethorpe Co: referred to Cmte on the P O & Post Roads.

On Mon last, the grocery store of Mr Carothers, on F st, was burglariously entered, & robbed of $20.

Heavy storm on the Lakes last week. The steamboat *U S* had a narrow escape while attempting to make the port of Huron. The schn'r *Kewanne* in attempting to make the same port was driven ashore, & one man drowned. Wm Pierce, of Boston, Mass, was lost overboard from the brig *Illinois*. The steamboat *Champlain* was run ashore high & dry on the beach of Lake Mich. The schn'r *Gen Warren*, high & dry at Presque Isle.

Stray cow trespassed on my enclosure: owner to prove property, pay charges, & take her away. -Dorothy Wales, near Navy Yard

Wm A Williams has this day received a few first quality Mantel Clocks, which he will dispose of at the reduced price of $15, all of which he warrants to keep first rate time, or no sale.

THU MAY 21, 1840

Balt College of Dental Surgery: commences on the first Mon in Nov, for 4 months –Chapin A Harris, Dean of the Faculty

Bill for the disposal & management of the fund bequeathed by Jas Smithson to the U S, for the establishment of an institution for the increase & diffusion of knowledge among men. The sum of $508,318.46, placed in the Treas of the U S on Sep 1, 1838, as the proceeds, in part, of the bequest, with all sums which have been or may be realized, shall be passed hereafter to the credit of the fund, to the denominated the Smithsonian fund, in the U S Treas. No part of the fund, principal or interest, shall be applied to any school, college, university, institute of education, or eccleslastical establishment. $30,000, part of the first year's interest accruing on the same fund, be, & the same is appropriated for erection of the establishment, at Wash City, of an astronomical observatory, adapted to continual observations of the phenomena of the heavens, to be provided with the necessary, best, & most perfect instruments & books, for the periodical publication of the said observations, & for the annual composition & publication of a nautical almanac. $60,000 from the 2nd & 3rd year's interest, is appropriated, to be invested so as to yield a yearly income at the rate of 6% a year; from which yearly income shall be paid the compensation of an astronomical observator, to be appointed by the Pres of the U S, & the incidental & contingent expenses of repairs upon the bldgs, as they may be required.

Senate: 1-Report of the Cmte of Claims on the subject of the claim of Wm & Jas Crooks, owners of the British vessel *Lord Nelson*, was postponed until tomorrow.

Hse o/Reps: 1-Ptn from R P De Silver, of Phil, asking Congress to authorize the purchase of a number of copies of "A Concise system of Instructions & Regulations for the Militia & Vols of the U S." 2-Ptn of Geo G Sill & others, praying the establishment of a mail route from Peoria to Farmington, via lower bridge of Kickapoo. 3-Ptn of Jas M Goodhue & others, citizens of Ill, praying the reduction of the rates of postage. 4-Ptn of D B McKinney & a large number of citizens of Ill, praying the release of Wm L Mackenzie by the interposition of Congress. 5-Ptn of Jos Keith & others, citizens of Ill, against granting a pre-emption to Warfield & Williams. 6-Memorial of Wm Whitlock, jr, Balton Fox Livingston, & other merchants of N Y, praying a reduction in the fees of the marshal, clerk, & other ofcrs of the U S Dist & Crct Courts for the Southern Dist of N Y: referred to Cmte on Commerce. 7-Memorial of Chas Stoddard, of N Y, praying for the return of duties overcharged on chain cables & anchors imported in the ship *Ville de Lyon*: referred to Cmte on Commerce.

Convention of the Protestant Episcopal Church in the diocese of Ga, held at Clarksville, May 4, Rev Stephen Elliott, Prof of Sacred Lit in the College at Columbia, S C, was elected Bishop of the diocese.

St Louis, May 7: Mr Chas C Lacy & his wife & child were drowned on Sat last, in attempting to cross Merrimack river in a skiff at Dougherty's Landing: 2 other persons were saved.

FRI MAY 22, 1840

The N J case-conspiracy exposed. Affidavits, leading one from Ellis, the Locofoco Clk of Monmouth, & the use made of it in Congress, caused those which succeeded it. The gist of his affidavit was, that Gov Pennington sent for the *returns* of the Congressional election *after the election*, & before he was required by law to make the returns. The other affidavits prove not only that Ellis swore falsely, entirely so, but that Gov Pennington sent for the *list of nominations*, merely *before* the election, & that the *returns*, instead of having been hastily sent for by the Govn'r, were transmitted to the Sec of State [Jas D Westcott] by Ellis himself, & that Gov P D Vroom, when the charge was made against Gov Pennington, with a view of impeaching that ofcr's character, knew that it was false, & yet silently permitted it to go in favor of himself & against an innocent & faithful ofcr. [The false depositions filled the next 2 cols. Names included in same were: Nathl Hilliard, innkeeper in the township of So Amboy, Middlesex Co, Mar 20, 1840, before Jas M Hartshorne, Mstr in Chancery, in the presence of Garret Adrain, agent for Danl B Ryall, Peter D Vroom; & Jas McDowell, agent of Wm Halsted. Isaac W Lanning-lawyer; John B Aycrigg; Mr Danl H Ellis; John S Darcy-of full age; Geo Haywood; Alex'r W Ball-age 22 years; Mr Ryerson; Theo Freylinghuysen, jr-Mstr in Chancery; s/o David Ball, Judge Haywood, of Mount Holly. After these conclusive affidavits, viz Apr 13, Ellis came forward & made another deposition, confessing that he had made a "mistake!" Thus the conspiracy to defame Gov Pennington ends in the disgrace of its authors. –Madisonian]

Senate: 1-Memorial from Messrs Ally, Stanton, & Co, merchants of N Y C, importers of woollen goods, asking a remission of duty on goods destroyed by fire. 2-Cmte on Pensions: unfavorable report on the ptn of Jacob Hall. 3-Cmte on Pensions: asked to be discharged from the further consideration of the memorails of: Wm Ferguson, of Eliz Garrabranta; of the wid/o Saml Walker; of Thos Farrar; of Conrad Walter, & of E Shaler.

Farm for sale: desirous of removing to the South: sale of the farm on which I reside: about 1 mile of Wash City: within a fraction of 100 acs: with frame dwlg. Inquire of Messrs B L Jackson & Brother, south side of Pa ave, or to Jos Hughes, on the premises. –J H

Mrd: on May 1, in Balt, Lt J Stockton Keith Reeves, of the 1st Regt of Artl, U S A, to Annie Dorsey, d/o the late Geo Read, of Dela

Mrd: on May 6, in Phil, Capt A N Brevoort, of the U S Marine Corp, to Mrs Eliza Sharpe.

Mrd: on Apr 30, in Brooklyn, N Y, Thos W Cumming, of the U S Navy, to Mgt, d/o Robt Bach.

Mrd: on May 19, in Wash City, by Rev Mr H Stringfellow, Mr Benj Cross to Miss Eliz F Saunders.

Died: on May 6, at Loretto, Pa, after a short illness, the Rev Demetrius Augustine Gallitzin, who for 42 years exercised pastoral functions in Cambria Co. He was born in 1770, at Munster, in Germany. His father, Prince de Gallitzin, ranked among the highest nobility in Russia. His mother was the d/o Field-Mrshl Gen de Schmeltan, a celebrated ofcr under Fred'k the Great.

N Y: U S Mrshl yesterday arrested Wm M Price at the suit of the Gov't. After a short detention he was liberated, on giving bail of $82,000. Newcomb, the absconding teller of the Manhattan Bank, voluntarily surrendered yesterday at the police ofc. He was discharged on $10,000 bail.

Public sale of valuable improved property: on Jun 20: by deed of trust from Josiah Colston, dated Nov 14, 1839, & recorded in the land records in this county, in Book W B #77, folios 338 to 343, the south half of lot 24 & all of lot 25 in sq 457, in Wash City, with 2 brick bldgs -Edw Dyer, auct

SAT MAY 23, 1840
Laws of the U S passed at the first session of the 29th Congress-R M T Hunter, Speaker of Hse o/Reps -Rh M Johnson, V P of the U S & Pres of the Senate. Approved Mar 31, 1840-M Van Buren

Wash, May 13, 1840. Resignation letter of R Biddle: severe indisposition with which I have been visited in the course of a 3 years' residence at Wash, & under which I now labor, forces upon me the conviction that I shall not be able to discharge satisfactorily, during the next winter, my duties as a Rep. I have been reluctantly impelled, therefore, after mature reflection, to resign; remaining, however, at my post until the end of the present session. -R Biddle

Senate: 1-Cmte of Claims: adverse report on the ptn of Fielder S Dorsey, & reported a bill for the relief of Edw Criddle, recommending its indefinite postponement.

Died: on May 20, at Richmond, Va, Danl Call, one of the oldest & most respected citizens. Mr Call, was, while at the Bar, an eminent member, & he has left behind him sterling professional mementoes of the high rank of which he had attained in his profession.

Died: on May 21, at Bellefield, her late residence, in PG Co, Md, Mrs Harriet B Oden, wid/o the late Benj Oden, in her 61st year

Hse o/Reps. 1-Bills laid aside to be reported: relief of Thos Atkinson, dec'd; of John H Sheppard, adm of Abiel Wood; of A G S Wight; of Jos Wallace & the heirs & reps of Robt Leckie & J D Hayden, dec'd; of Benj Fry; of Saunders & Porter, sureties of Estes; of the heirs of Capt Wm Gregory; of the heirs of Lt Jonathan Dye; of Oliver Welch; of Augustin Lacoste; of Pierre Molaison, sen; of Jos Cochran; of Chilton Allan; of Wm Marbury; of La; of Hyacinth Lassel; of Mary Sroufe; of the heirs of Stephen Johnston, dec'd; of Gen Danl Parker; of the sureties & heirs of Melancthon Bostwick, dec'd; of Alex'r H Everett; of John H Genther; of Eliz Davidson; of the reps of Wm Lomax; of Jacob Bocker; of Jabez Collins; of Phebe Deckman; of Jas Phelps, of Eliz Jones & others; of Cath Allen, of John England; of Jas Deatley; of Hugh Davis; of Chauncy Rice

The Hon Edw Everett, late Govn'r of Mass, & a Rep in Congress from Mass for a number of years, is about to leave the U S on a visit to the old world.

Public are hereby cautioned & warned against trading for, or in anywise receiving, a due-bill drawn by the undersigned in favor of T A Donaphin, for $150, As I have claims in bar of said due-bill, which will require settlement before said due-bill can be paid. The above due-bill was drawn about 12 months ago   -A Shepherd

Jas Wood, of Phil, the murderer of his dght, [acquitted upon trial on the ground of insanity.] has been delivered by the Court of Oyer & Terminer of that city into the custody of his bail. The penalty of the bail bond is $6,000, & the sureties are justified in upwards of $18,000 It is stated in the Phil Ledger "that he is now on his way to a distant part of the Union, in company with one of his bail."

We regret to learn that inquiries for Mr Benj Smith, late of the Pa Bank, have not been successful-he has not been heard of since the day before the Balt Convention. -U S Gaz

Trustee's sale: in Port Tobacco, Chas Co, Md: Court of Equity: all those tracts & parts of tracts of land of which Alexius Edelen died seized, called *Simpson's Supply & Calvert's Hope*, together 320 acs, more or less: land lies in the forest of Newport, Chas Co: has comfortable dwlg house. -Peter W Crain, W Mitchell, trustee

MON MAY 25, 1840
Stations of the U S Revenue Cutters: [15]

Alert: Capt Nones, Eastport, Me
Morris: Capt Walden, Portland, Me
Madison: Capt Currier, Portsmouth, N H
Hamilton: Capt Sturgis, Boston
Vigilant: Capt Connor, Newport, R I
Wolcott: Capt Mather, New Haven, Conn

Jackson: Capt Bicker, N Y
McLane: Capt Hunter, Wilmington, Del
Van Buren: Capt Prince, Balt
Taney: Capt Webster, Norfolk
Dexter: Capt Day, Charleston, S C

Crawford: Capt Rudolph, Savannah
Jefferson: Capt Foster, Mobile
Woodbury: Capt Jones, New Orleans
Erie: Capt Dobbins, Erie, Pa
–Army & Navy Chron

From the York Express, May 22: a visit to the North Bend. This is the home of Genr'l Harrison.

Joshua Monroe, of Shaftsbury, Vt, well known in Troy, & a large stockholder in some of the Troy banks, we understand, comitted suicide last week: particulars are not known. –Troy Mail

At a Naval Gen Court Martial, at the Navy Yard, at Phil, on May 4, Lt Chas H McBlair was tried on the following charges: 1-Contemptuous treatment of his superior, being in the execution of his ofc. 2-Unofficerlike conduct, in having used provoking words, gestures, & menaces towards Capt Henry E Ballard, an ofcr in the U S Navy. 3-Same to Capt Chas G Ridgely. The Court finds only the 1st charge proved: the Court does therefore fully acquit the accused. –Army & Navy Chronicle

Buffalo Republican: murder of Mr Ransford Otis, in Concord, Erie Co, on the 23rd ult, by Maj McEllroy. McEllroy was employed by Otis on his farm. McE set the barn on fire to cover-up the murder: said the blood on his pantaloons was from a woodchuch he had killed. Mrs Otis said that he put the pantaloons on clean that morning. He was committed, & is now in jail in this city.

The Hon D B V_ger, upwards of 70 years of age, has been released from prison in Montreal: he was one of the most distinguished lwyears in the country: many years a member of Parliament: a man of property & unstained character. He was thrown into prison, where he insisted on being tried, but neither a trial called be obtained nor charges made out. He has, however, been offered his liberty, if he would ask it! Having asserted his innocence, & refused to make any concession, he would not sue for acquittal. He is at length released unconditionally.

Salisbury for sale: valuable grazing farm in Va, of 1,300 acs, with large dwlg house. Mr Freeman, the present occupant, who has been in possession the last 8 years, will show the premises. Also, several small farms, from 1 to 300 acs, on the Little Rvr Trnpk Rd, about 9 miles from D C. Apply to the subscriber, in Alexandria, D C, by mail or otherwise. –John Lloyd

Died: on Apr 1, at Weathersfield, Conn, Mrs Eunice Tryon, aged 85, widow of the late Moses Tryon, Capt in the U S Navy.

The steamboat *Grampus* blew up on May 13, about 25 miles inside of the Bar, at the Balize. John Sprigg, 2nd engr, died in 2 hours after the explosion, from being scalded. Wm Walker, missing. Wm T Knight, mate, slightly scalded. Capt Kenton, of the boat *Victoria*, sent his boat to the wreck & had the wounded brought on board. The engineer was buried at Balize.

Mrd: on Thu last, by Rev Mr Davis, Mr Landon Thompson to Miss Eliz Tilley, all of Wash City.

Mrd: on May 7, in Rochester, N Y, Capt Martin Scott, of the 5th Regt of Infty, U S Army, to Miss Lavinia, d/o Gardner McCracken, of that city.

Mrd: in St Paul's Chr, Phil, by Rev T R Lambert, Chaplain U S Navy, Lt Wm Wade Bleecker, U S Navy, to Miss Lucretia Ann Badger, of Phil. [No date-current item.]

Died: on Apr 29, at Ogdensburg, N Y, at the residence of his son-in-law, Geo N Seymour, Louis De Vilers, in his 83rd year. He was a native of Abbeville, in France: at any early age entered into the service of Louis XVI as Lt in the btln of Vermandois: after several interviews with Dr Franklin, then our minister at Paris, he was transferred in 1783 to a regt serving in America, commanded by Col Sausenio, under Gen Rochambeau. With the name he assumed the duties of an American citizen: in 1794 he purchased a large tract of land in the town of Butternuts, Otsego Co, then an almost unbroken forest, & with the late Judge Cooper was among the first settlers in that section of the state. He remained in Otsego Co till 1808, when he removed to Wilna, Jeff Co, & subsequently to Ogdensburg, where he remained until his death.

On Fri last, 2 young men, Alfred Cronan & Wm Thomas, engaged in the fanning mill factory of Burnet, Bornborough, & Co, in Chambersburg, took, by mistake, a quantitiy of cedar oil before going to dinner, which was mistaken for peppermint-bottles each standing together. Cronan lingered until Mon last, when he died. Thomas is yet alive, but very ill. -Whig

City Ord-Wash. 1-Act for relief of Osborn Turner: the sum of $150 to be paid to Turner, being the amount due as scavenger of the 5th & 6th wards for the years ending on Aug 31, 1837 & 1838. 2-Act for relief of Clement Woodward: for an alleged violation of the law relating to the erection of frame bldgs, the same is remitted, upon his paying the costs of prosecution.

Fatal rencounter in Vermillionville, parish of Lafayette, about 10 days since, between Mr Valery Beaux & Wm Reeves, which terminated in the death of Breaux by a stab in the lower part of the abdomen. Reward of $1,000 offered for the apprehension of Reeves.

Hse o/Reps: 1-Bills from the Senate, for relief of A G S Wight, for the relief of John H Sheppard; for relief of Jos Goggin; were read a 3rd time & passed. 2-Bills laid aside to be reported: *for the relief of*

Wm Cuddeback	Peter Hedrick	Sylvester Tiffany
Elijah Foochee	Erastus Pierson	Jas Smith
Eliz French	Michl Seitzinger	Wm Sloan
Jos Bailey	Wm Neel	Robt Whittle
Geo Morris	Asenath Campbell	Jos W Knipe
John Lathram	Peter A Myers	Levi M Roberts
Benj Mitchell	John Piper	Lyman N Cook
Reuben Murray	Job Wood	Wm Butterfield
Weathy Baker	Mary Hunter	Geo Hommill
Jas Boylan	John Keeler	Jacob Euler
Nathan Baldwin	Fielding Pratt	David Wilson
Sarah Oakley	Jas Fleming	Saml Brown
Jacob Adams	Saml M Asbury	Emanuel Srofe
Thruston Cornell	Neil Shannon	Isaac Boyd
Martha Strong	Elijah Blodget	Wm Bowman
Benj Price	Thos Collins	Benj McCulloch
Jas J Coffin	Jas Bailey	David A Baldwin
Conrad Widrig	Hiram Saul	John Allison
Jas Francher	Stephen Appleby	Levi Colmus
Thos Bennett	Danl W Goings	Wm Poole
John Lybrook	John H Lincoln	Josiah Strong
David Melen	Jared Winslow	Seneca Rider
Henry Bush	Nathl Davis	Peter W Short
Israel Parsons	Wm Hughes	Simeon Knight
Philip Hartman	Saml B Hugo	Robt Lucas
Matthew Wiley	Levi Johnston	John Brown
Wm York	Barton Frazier	Wilfred Knott
Isaac Austin	Myron Chapin	Wm Glover
John Black	Medad Cook	Jas Cummings
Helen Miller	Lyman Bristol	John E Wright
Stephen Olney	Chas Resley	Thos Wilson
Wm Andrews	Pamela Brown	Thos Latham
Christian Brougher		

Leonard Smith-with amendment providing payment be made to his heirs 3-Report & papers in the case of Sarah Herring be referred back to the Cmte on Invalid Pensions, with additional test. 4-Engrossed bills were read the 3rd time & passed: *relief of:*

Thos Atkinson	Eliz Davidson
Jos Wallace	Gen Duncan L Clinch
John H Genther	heirs of Michl Seitzinger

Heirs & reps of Robt Leckie & Jeremiah D Hayden, dec'd 4-Passed: relief of Ann Bloomfield, of John Davis to be restored to the pension roll, bill for relief of Mary

Tucker-postponed until Fri next. 5-Bill to refund a fine imposed on the late Matthew Lyon, under the sedition law, to his heirs & legal reps, coming up in its order, question on its engrossment.

TUE MAY 26, 1840
Mr Jos Cardinal will, this morning, marry the blooming widow of the late Mr Jas Chas Doyle, the banns having been published in the Roman Catholic Cathedral on Sun. Mrs Doyle's maiden name is Blache; & although she is only 27 years of age, she has buried 3 husbands, the last having died on Apr 1 last. -Montreal Herald

Senate: 1-Ptns presented & referred: from Sally Porter & Betsey Gay, in relation to a Revolutionary claim. 2-From Abraham Sinclair, relating to a land claim. 3-Documents in relation to the claims of the heirs of Agnes Gross. 4-From John B King, in relation to a Revolutionary claim. 5-Cmte on Naval Affairs: adverse report on the ptn of R B Mason. 6-Bill introduced for the relief of the legal reps of Nathl Pryor, dec'd. 7-Bill for relief of Jos Roby was taken up, & indefinitely postponed.

Appointments by the Pres: Capt John B Nicolson, to be a member of the Brd of Navy Commisioners from May 8, 1840. John J Young, to be Cmder in the Navy from Apr 15, 1840. Henry French to be Lt in the Navy from Apr 12, 1840.

Hse o/Reps: 1-Ptn of F W Bingham & other citizens of Cuyahoga Co, Ohio, praying that adequate protection may be given by Congress for the growth & mfgr of silk in the U S. 2-Ptn of Elisha Kellogg, praying to be placed on the roll of invalid pensions: referred to the Cmte on Invalid Pensions. 3-Memorial of Wm H Bruce, Darius Clark, Wm Sylvester, & others, praying an appropriation for the improvement of the navigation of the Neenah & Wisc rivers, & for the completion of the military road from Fort Howard to Fort Winebago. For same for R B Towslee, Rezin Bell, Chas Durkee, & others, citizens of Southport. 4-Memorial of Richd I Davis, Danl W Hubbard, & Lemuel Tyler, for the same purpose. 5-Ptn of Hiram Pearsons, Linus R Cady, S T Otis, & other citizens of Chicago, praying the construction of a harbor at Southport, in Wiskonsin. Ptn of Tarleton Jones, S H Porter, O B Dibble, & other citizens of Detroit, for the same purpose. 6-Ptn of Danl Campbell, J Chamberlin, N Strong & others, for a mail route from Fort Winnebago to Plover Portage. 7-Ptn of Wm B Slaughter, for leave to correct an entry made by mistake in the Land Ofc at Milwaukee. 8-Claim of Thos L Franks, for remuneration for property, taken by the U S troops at Green Bay, for the use of the army. 9-Ptn of Curtis B Brown, Rufus Parks, P C Schuyler, & others, in favor of a reduction in the price of the Milwaukee canal lands.

Mrd: on May 13, at St Augustine, East Fla, by the Rev Franklin Vail, Dr Henry A Stinnecke, Surgeon U S Army to Abigail, d/o the late Henry Boarman, of Montg Co, Pa.

Died: on May 25, in Wash City, in her 42nd year, after an illness of some months duration, Mrs Louisa Serena Weightman, consort of Gen Roger C Weightman. Her funeral is tomorrow, at 11 a m.

Died: on May 20, in Chas Co, Md, Col Francis W Hawkins, in his 76th year; among the most respectable inhabitants of the county in which he lived.

Died: on May 22, in Chas Co, Md, at his residence, Henry H Bean, sen, in his 87th year. The dec'd lived from the period of early manhood in the county & neighborhood in which he died. He entered in the defence of his country during her Revolutionary struggle, & continued in her service till the last blow was struck: he was discharged from her service [his aid being no longer needed] before the period of his enlistment had terminated. He died loved by his affectionate chldrn; died in the faith of the Redeemer, in the bosom of the church.

Land in St Mary's Co, Md, for sale: tract called *White Plains*, about 1,000 acs, more or less; adjoins the farm of Dr John Dulany, Clifton Factory, Great Mills, & bounding on the head waters of St Mary's river. Improved with a dwlg house & a tenement. Also, the watering place called the *Pavilion*, which is of great notoriety, on the Potomac river. Apply to my atty, Mr H M Morfit, Wash City, or on the premises. –Clement McWilliams, Clifton Factory P O, St Mary's Co, Md.

Orphans Court of Chas Co, Md: upon ptn, it is ordered that notice be given to Teresa Wathen to be & appear in this Court on the 4th Tue in Jun next, to show cause, if any, why letters of adm on the personal estate of Geo Boarman, late of Chas Co, dec'd, shall not be granted to Alexius Boarman, the ptnr therein mentioned.
–Aquilla Bateman, Reg/o wills for Chas Co, Md.

WED MAY 27, 1840
Co-partnership heretofore existing between the undersigned has this day been dissolved by mutual consent. Call & settle accounts. The business will hereafter be conducted by T J Fletcher. –Jas Fossett, Thos J Fletcher

Norfolk: U S ship *Delaware* 74, Capt Chas W Skinner, dropped down from the Navy Yard on Sat, to anchorage off the Naval Hospital: is employed as a receiving ship & school for naval apprentices.

Appointments by the Pres: Leigh Read, to be Mrshl of the Middle Dist of Fla, v J C Searcy, who declines that appointment. Jos B Browne, to be Mrshl of the U S for the Southern Dist of Fla, from Jun 8 next, when the term of service of the present incumbent will expire. Thos Gatewood, Naval Ofcr for the Dist of Norfolk & Portsmouth, Va, from May 6, 1840, when his late commission expired.

Norfolk: U S ship *Delaware 74*, Capt Chas W Skinner, dropped down from the Navy Yard on Sat, to anchorage off the Naval Hospital: is employed as a receiving ship & school for naval apprentices.

Senate: 1-Ptn from Prudence Barton, asking a pension. 2-Bill for relief of John Carter. 3-Cmte of Claims: bill from the Hse o/Reps for the relief of Duncan L Clinch, without amendment, & recommending its passage.

The N Y Courier publishs the substance of a letter received from Montg, Ala, which states that Mons Adrien, jr, who has been practising tricks of legerdemain in most of the principal cities, was recently shot, at Montgomery, by Dr McLeod, the husband of a lady who seemed to prefer Mons Adrien's society to that of her husband. The lady eloped, but was found on the steamboat & taken home. Adrien was pursued by the husband, the father of the lady & her uncle, & the husband shot him as he was attempting to cross a ferry about 12 miles from Montg. The letter adds that general commiseration was felt by the people at large for the fate of Adrien, from a conviction that he was innocent, but that the character of the parties implicated would prevent any serious inquiry into the subject.

Obit-died: on May 11, in Natchez, Mrs Anna D Haliday, w/o Mr Thos J Haliday, formerly of Wash, & one of the proprietors of the Free Trader. Her death was sudden. She had given birth to a child a short time previous to the dreadful storm; & was compelled, by the fall of her hse, to rush into the yard with her babe in her arms amidst the torrents of rain. She, of course, was very wet, yet, having been removed to the hse of her mother, which was still left standing, she did not seem sensible of any ill effects arising from this exposure, but was cheerful & apparently doing well up to the hr of her death.

For sale: real estate at & near the flourishing village of Ellicott's Mills, Md: on Jun 20: the 2 valuable Flour Mills, Saw, & Plaster Mill, Granite Quarries, & the remainder of the property advertised. For information: Benj H Ellicott, of Balt, or Nathl H Ellicott & Saml Ellicott, of Ellicott's Mills. –R Mickle, trustee

Wash City Affairs: May 26, 1840: votes for the Mayoralty of the City: Wm W Seaton: 475; John P Ingle: 330. R W Bates, 1st Ward; W H Gunnell & W Kirkwood, 2nd Ward; John C Harkness, 3rd Ward; John C McKelden, [Ward # not noted]; Jas Adams, 4th Ward; T R Riley, 5th Ward; N Young, 6th ward.
First Ward ticket: For Mayor: W W Seaton   For Alderman: Chas W Goldsborough
For Common Cncl: Edmund Hanly, Wm Wilson, Wm Easby
3rd Ward: announce Mr John H Goddard as a candidate for a seat in the Brd of Aldermen for Ward 3-oblige Many Voters. John W Maury is nominated as a candidate for re-election to a seat in Brd of Aldermen. Insert the names of Saml Bacon, Edw Dyer, & Jos H Bryan, as candidates for the Brd of Cmn Cncl-Many voters. J C Harkness Saml Bacon, & G C Grammer will be supported for the

Cnclmn at the ensuing election by Many Voters. Please announce Edw Dyer, Saml Bacon, & Dr Alex'r McD Davis as candidates for the Cmn Cncl at the coming election: Many Voters.

Nocturnal robberies: last Mon Mr Alexius Simms, who lives at the corner of F & 13th sts, had the contents of his money drawer emptied & carried away. Thieves attempted to rob the grocery store of Mr Wm Stewart in the same neighborhood. Attempt also at the grocery store of Mr Buist, but were alarmed by the continual barking of a dog, belonging to Mr Stewart who lives close by.

Wash Co, D C: Henry Gee, insolvent debtor, has applied to be discharged from imprisonment. Also, Lloyd Brown: ditto. -Wm Brent, clk

THU MAY 28, 1840
Ferdinand Pettrich has just completed a Mephistophiles, & the dying Tecumseh: these statues are in clay, & were made for exhibition only. At the end of 8 days they will be destroyed. Studio open for visiters: admittance 25 cents; chldrn half price.

Henry G Colemen, U S Consul for the port of Tobacco, died at there on Apr 23 last.

The undersigned have removed their stock of Dry Goods to their large warehse opposite the P O, Bridge st, Gtwn: large assortment on hand: liberal terms.
–P T Berry & Co

Senate: 1-Ptn from Nathl Niles, praying additional compensation for diplomatic services. 2-Ptn from Henry Goodyear & others, asking a grant of land in the Isl of Matacumba, on the coast of Fla, for the purpose of forming a settlement thereon.

Mrd: on May 25, by Rev Dr Bates, Chaplain to Congress, Gen Richd Dunlap, of Texas, to Mary Louisa, d/o the late T Winn.

Died: Apr 14, in Carthage, Smith Co, Tenn, Mrs Cath K, w/o Mr Jos W Allen, merchant of that place.

The People's Independent Candidate for Mayor: Jas Hoban-born with us, reared with us, & abiding with us, will be supported by us at the approaching election.
–The People

FRI MAY 29, 1840
Gen Jos M Street, died on May 5, on the Des Moines river. He was agent for the Sac & Fox Indians.

Accident: An engr for the B & O R R had both of his legs cut off on Tue, when near the Monocacy river, the cars were thrown from the track & the jar caused Mr Wm Lemmon to fall under the wheels, which instantly passed over him.

J C S Harrison, the eldest s/o Gen Harrison, became a defaulter to the Gov't as Receiver of Public Money at Vincennes. The manner in which he became involved exonerates his memory from any unworthy imputation. He was prevailed upon, by such assurances & evidences as any honorable man might confide in, to advance, for a late Indian Agent, in Indiana, some $5,500. He was led to believe that the agent had the authority to draw upon the Dept at Wash for the amount, &, if so, the Gov't would be accommodated by having the funds deposited at Wash rather than at Louisville. Of this sum, to which was added a large amount paid by young Harrison for high interest, he received from the agent only $1,500; & since his death his execs have secured to the estate of J C S Harrison 200 acs of land on White river as the sole indemnity for the advances. J C S died just after Gen Harrison returned from the public service abroad, in S America. He soon repaired to Wash, & urged Congress the propriety of granting some indulgence to the estate of J C S Harrison, for the debt, which, instead of being $25,000, does not exceed $6,000 or $7,000. J C Symmes Harrison, who had become a defaulter through the fault & misrepresentation of another high ofcr in whom the Gov't confided, mrd the only child of the heroic Pike, who fell in the arms of Victory at York, in Upr Canada. This chivalric Pike was the s/o Maj Zebulon Pike, of the Revolution, & of the ancestry of young Harrison let the eloquent speech of the gallant Col R M Johnson testify, as it as upon this occasion, he answered the question, 'Who is Genr'l Harrison?' High estimation of Harrison was held at Vincennes. Mr Elihu Stout, the editor of the Western Sun took an active part in the proceedings. The sense of Congress was finally obtained, by a resolution directing that the estate of J C S Harrison should be entitled to an indulgence for 18 years [10 of which have yet to run,] & that without interest. Gen Harrison insisted upon a lien being retianed by the Gov't upon the property of his son, & the provisions of that lien will be seen in the annexed law of Congress, approved by Andrew Jackson: An Act for the relief of Mrs Clarissa B Harrison.

John H Waters has removed from his old stand, to the hse lately occupied by Messrs Howison & Jackson, on Pa ave, between 12th & 13th sts: assortment of groceries, wines, & liquors. –J H W

Senate: 1-Cmte on Pensions: unfavorable report on the bill for the relief of John England. Also reported the bill for the relief of Jos Becker: recommended its passage. 2-Cmte on Naval Affairs: bill for relief of the heirs & legal reps of Melancthon W Bostwick, & the bill to regulate enlistments in the army & navy without amendment. 3-Mr Grundy presented a ptn from Saml Martin, of Tenn. 4-Cmte on Pvt Land Claims: hse bill for relief of Pierre Molaison. 5-Cmte on Pensions: unfavorable reports on the Hse bills for the relief of Phoebe Dickman, & of Cath Allen. 6-Unfavorable reports on the memorials of John Strickland & Lot Strickland.

SAT MAY 30, 1840
The Globe Hotel: recently added to the establishment, the house #64 Broadway, with a pvt entrance on Broadway, also a hall communicating with the Htl. –F Blancard, N Y-his establishment.

Wm D Ball, the High Sheriff of Balt City & Co, died at his residence in Balt City last night. He had been sick for several weeks. By his decease, Nicholas Tracy, [2nd on the return at the election last fall when Mr Ball was chosen,] becomes the Shrf. Mr Ball was a Van Buren man; Tracy is a Whig.

The Hon Francis Granger arrived in N Y yesterday from Wash, much enfeebled in body from severe & protracted illness. He is on his way to Canandaigua, & it is doubtful that he will be enabled to resume his seat in Congress the present session. –N Y Cmcl Adv of Thu.

Quebec Gaz: death by suicide: under tempo insanity, Gen Sir Wm Thornton, Col of the 85th Regt of Infty. Maj Gen Sir J F Fitzgerald is to fill the vacancy.

MON JUN 1, 1840
Western Mail: news of the death of Gen John Adair, of Ky, in his 83rd year: a soldier in the early Northwestern War, & commanded the troops at New Orleans in 1814-15: filled many civil ofcs, amongst which was that of Senator of the U S.

Lt M'Blair, when suspended from duty, did, indeed, earnestly request of the Dept an inquiry or investigation into his conduct: & it appears from a review of all the circumstances attending the recent difficulty, that he has only fulfilled his duty. All men whose characters may be suffering under unjust aspersions owe it to themselves, to the Society, to demand an examination as will lead to their exculpation.
-Republican

City Ord-Wash: 1-Act for relief of Wm B Wilson: fine imposed for an alleged violation, in relation to the enclosures of sts, be, & the same is remitted: provided he pay the cost of prosecution. 2-Act for the relief of Stanislaus Rigsby: fine imposed for a violation, in permitting a stallion, more than 16 months old, to run at large within the limites of the city, be, & the same is remitted, provided he pay the costs of proscution. 3-Act for the relief of Geo St Clair: Mayor is authorized to issue a license to Geo St Clair to keep a tavern & ordinary in the hse now occupied by him on the adjoining sq 329: provided he complies with the provisions of the ordinance relating to same, with the exception of the certificate of the Com'r of the Ward, & the said license shall commence from the time at which his last license expired.

The great case of the Cmnwlth, vs, Edw Prigg & others, for kidnapping, came up before the Supr Court at Harrisburg. Mr Nelson said the principles involved were of the deepest concern to all the slave states. It will come before the U S Supreme Court at Wash City, in Jul next.

The New Orleans Bee of May 21, announces the death, by paralysis, on May 20, of Jas B Anderson, ed of the New Orleans Sun.

Senate: 1-Ptn from J L Gibson, praying to be allowed a commission on certain disbursements made while acting purser. 2-Ptn from Richd Higgins, in relation to a land claim. 3-Cmte on Pension: bill for relief of Mary Snow. Also, an unfavorable report on the ptn of Ambrose Casey. Same cmte: a bill for relief of Mary Prettyman. 4-Cmte on Pvt Land Claims: asking to be discharged from further consideration of the Hse bill for the relief of Mary Sroufe, & that it is referred to the Cmte on Public Lands. 5-Papers of Richd B Mason reconsidered, & the papers referred back to the Cmte on Naval Affairs. 6-Bill for the relief of the legal reps of Philip Barbour was taken up. From a discussion of much length, it appeared that Philip Barbour was an ofcr in the French war of 1756; that he received a grant, as compensation for his services, of the lands now claimed, in 1767, under the broad seal of the British Gov't; that such grants had been confirmed by Congress; that the presentation of this claim was delayed by the death of Col Barbour, & by the death of his adm & solicitor, & still further delayed by the loss of the papers in the War Dept, in which dept they were recently found. 7-Question recurred on the engrossment of the bill for the relief of Gen Parker: Hse refused to lay the bill on the table. 8-Bill for relief of Benj Frye: passed. 9-Bill for relief of Andrew Lowe, assignee of Lowe, Taylor & Co, coming: engrossed. 10-Bill for the relief of John J Roane came up. 11-Bill for relief of John W Bond & Oliver Perrin: passed.

Orphans Court of Wash Co, D C. Letters of administration the personal estate of Thos Whalen, late of said county, dec'd. -Paul Kinchy, adm

Savannah, May 26. We learn from a passenger in the steamer *Genr'l Clinch*, Capt Brooks, from Black Creek, that on Sat, Mr Forbes' theatrical company, with others, were on their way from Picolata to St Augustine, a party of 2 wagons, when within 5 or 6 miles of the latter place, they were attacked by Indians, & Mr C Vase was killed. Two others are supposed to be missing.

Black Creek, E G, May 23. Extract from report to the editor of the Savannah Georgian: Lt Martin, 2nd Infty, le Fort Micanopy on May 19, with 3 men from his post, Wakahosta: fired upon by the Indians: he received 3 balls, one thru the lower part of the abdomen, one thru the arm, & one in his hand-one of his men & all the horses killed, the other 2 missing. Lt Sanderson, 7th Infty, with a party of 17 men went in pursuit of them. He fell in with the Indians, & he & 5 men were killed. Yesterday an express from Wakahosta to Micanpoy reported the post surrounded by Indians. Col Riley, with his command, has gone in pursuit. It was his command that picked up Lt Sanderson & his men. Supposed to be about 50 Indians. Supposed that Lt Martin would recover. Lt Sanderson had his fingers cut off & stuck in his mouth.

Mrd: on the 14th ult, by Rev Mr Matthews, Mr Richd N Barry to Mis Mgt Dawson, all of Wash City.

Mrd: on Tue last, by Rev T C Thornton, Mr Grandison Beall to Mrs Delila Lee.

Mrd: on Thu last, by Rev T C Thornton, Mr Thos J Jones to Miss Maria Hill, all of Wash City.

Mrd: on the 26th ult, by Rev J Kerr, Mr John E Turner, recently of Wash, to Miss Mary E Turner, of PG Co, Md.

Mrd: on Fri, in St Peter's Chr, by Rev Dr Henshaw, Perry E Brocchus, of Alexandria, D C, to Jane M Tinges, of Balt.

Died: on Thu last, in N Y, of consumption, Capt Julius A d'Lagnel, of the U S Ord Dept, & commandng the Ord Depot at Fort Columbus, aged 40 years.

Died: May 27, Mary Lucetta, aged 6 months, d/o Andrew & Mary Ann Carothers.

TUE JUN 2, 1840
N Y, May 31. Among the passengers in the ship *British Queen*, to sail tomorrow, are Mr Geo Combe, the phrenologist, Dr Macauley, of Balt, the Rev R Gurley, Sec of the American Colonization Soc, & M Delisle, French Ambassador from Mexico.

The Toronto, [U C] Transcript reports of a duel recently fought at Montreal, between Lt Col White, 7th Hussars, & Mr Grant, late of the 79th Regt. The Col fell from the fire of his opponent: cause of the quarrel had reference to the conduct of Col White towards a young lady related to Grant.

Great bargain: sale of a tract of land in Culpeper Co, near the Warrenton Spring, containing about 545 acs. It may be seen by applying to Wm McNish, at the Warrenton Spr, & the terms made known by application to Robt E Scott, at Warrenton, or to the subscriber, Robt E Lee, Oakwood, Va.

Trustee's sale: decree of PG Co Court, Court of Equity: case of Notley R Young & others, vs, Clementina Young & others, the undersigned, as trustees, will expose at Gregory's Tavern, in Piscataway, PG Co, Md, on Jul 30, the real estate of the late Dominick Young which he devised to his 4 sons Nicholas Young, Benj Young, Notley R Young, & Ignatius F Young, & to his grand-dght Sarah Ellen Clagett, lying in said town of Piscataway, now in possession of Clement Knott, & supposed to contain between 4 & 500 acs. –N C Stephen, D C Digges, trustees

Mrd: on May 26, by Rev Jas P Donelan, Mr Henry Shepherd to Miss Eliz White, both of Wash City.

Notice: By virtue of a commission issued out of Montg Co Court, for the dividing the real estate of which Thos B Offutt, late of said county, died seized & possessed: meeting on Aug 8 to discharge the duties assigned them in said commission. –Thos S Watkins, Burgess Willett, S T Stonestreet

Chas Co Court, in Chancery, Mar Term, 1840. Geo P Forrest & others, heirs of H H Chapman, vs, Fanny Chapman & others. Ordered that the sales made & reported by Geo P Forrest & Edw Chapman in this case be ratified. –Edmund Key –John Barnes, clk of C C Court [No dollar amount was given.]

Criminal Court-Wash: Judge Dunlop took his seat: grand jury: Thos Carbery, foreman

John W Maury	John Cox	W C D Murdock	Chas A Burnet
Jos Forrest	Wm Gunton		Ninian A Beall
John Boyle	Walter Smoot	Thos Munroe	Thos Fenwick
John F Cox	Benj K Morsell	John Mason, jr	John McClelland
Lewis Johnson	Lewis Carbery	Raphael Semmes	
Chas R Belt	Wm Hayman		
John Carter	Michl Shanks	Robt White	

Court of Inquiry, consisting of Brig Gen Wool, Col Garland, & Maj Andrews, now in session at Barnum's City Hotel, room 103, Balt. Cause of inquiry, is, that a cmte, purporting to be delegated by the Van Buren convention, have preferred charges against Maj Lendrum & Capt Dusenbury, of the U S Army, now upon the Balt station, of using influence & patronage of their ofcs in the purchase of supplies for the army, to the benefit of the opponents of the present administration, & to the injury & great wrong of the Democratic party. Letter to Pres Van Buren, signed by G B Wilson, T L Murphy, Saml Harker, R B A Tate, & others, requesting removal of those ofcrs forthwith from this station. Maj Lendrun now in Court with his cnsl Gen Wm H Marriott & Wm L Marshall, both of the V B party. Cmte assisted by W P Maulsby, as cnsl, also of the V B party. –Balt Patriot

Partnership under firm of Phillips, Hall, & Co, is this day-Jun 1, dissolved by mutual consent. Settle accounts with Hall & Brother who will continue the business. –G W Phillips, Saml Phillips, Baruch Hall

WED JUN 3, 1840
Sheriff Wm D Ball has not yet thrown off this mortal coil, but, on the contrary, is fast recovering. Balt Republican

Jabez Fuller was executed at White Plains on Fri last, for a murder committed about a year ago.

The 200th anniversary of the incorporation of the town of Quincy, Mass, was celebrated May 25.

On May 8, while on a hunting expedition near his school, in Miss, E Gales Wharton, s/o F Wharton, of New Orleans, was killed by the accidental discharge of a gun in the hands of his elder brother.

Geo Cathcart suspended himself out of the garret window of his house in Filbert st, near McAran's Garden, Phil. As he sprang out he exclaimed, "I am gone." His wife, hearing the noise, ran up stairs & cut the rope, but too late to save his life. He died a few hours afterwards.

Senate: 1-Mr Clay, of Ky, presented the memorial of Gen Jas C Reynolds, late postmaster at Reynoldsburg, Ohio. Mr Clay presented the ptn after other Senators had declined.

Mayor's Ofc, Jun 2, 1840 [Wash] Result of the election of Jun 1, 1840.
Aldermen:
Chas W Goldsborough
Wallace Kirkwood
John H Goddard
Cnclmn:
Edmund Hanly
Wm Easby
Wm Wilson
Lewis Johnson
W W Stewart
Wm Orme
Saml Bacon
Jos Bryan
John C Harkness
Peter Force, Mayor

Jas Carbery
Isaac Clarke
Jas Marshall

Wm J McDonald
Simon Bassett
John H Houston
Saml Byington
John L Maddox
Wm S Walker
Geo H Fulmer
Edw W Clarke
Jas Crandell

Died: on May 30, at Jas Cuthbert's Hotel, in his 79th year, Richd Eno, after a painful illness of 5 weeks.

Died: on May 18 last, at the residence of her mother, in Montg Co, Ind, Anne Scott, d/o Gustavus H & Eliz D Scott, after a painful illnes of 4 days.

Died: on Mon last, Edw, s/o John P & Susan H Ingle, aged 7 months.

Died: on the 29th ult, at Patten Hse, Staten Isl, of consumption, Mgt Ebbitt, in her 17th year.

THU JUN 4, 1840
Peru [Indiana] Gaz: departed this life on May 1, after a lingering illness, Francis Godfroy, Chief of the Miami Tribe of Indians, in his 53rd year: "Forest's Noblest Nobleman:"

Distressing case: Gen Jos W Winston, of Platte Co, disappeared on Mar 24 last: information leads to the conclusion that he drowned in the Missouri river. In Feb last, Gen Winston went to the Platte river with his 2nd son [grown] & a number of hands, for the purpose of improving the place; leaving his wife & the rest of his family with his eldest son, about 7 miles from where he was thus engaged. His wife & son hearing the Gen was indisposed, started to see him, but he was nowhere to be found. Gen Winston had lately removed to this state from Stokes Co, N C, where he was raised, & well known. He was the y/s/o Col Jos Winston, one of the heroes of King's Mountain, to whom, with Gov Shelby & Col Sevier, the state of N C presented swords in commemoration of that glorious victory which turned the scale of war in the south, & was the ground-work of the surrender of Lord Cornwallis. Gen J W Winston was in his 53rd year, left a family to mourn their loss.

Senate: 1-Ptn from Saml Norris & Fred'k Saugraire, asking to be relieved from the effect of certain errors committed at the Land Ofc at Fayettsville, Ark. 2-Memorial from Micajah T Williams, in relation to certain water privileges on the Milwaukee river. 3-Cmte on Foreign Relations: unfavorable report on the bill from the Hse o/Reps for the relief of Alex'r H Everett. 4-Cmte on Pensions: recommending indefinite postponement of the bill from the Hse for the relief of Wm A Cudderback. Also, same for Reuben Murray. Unfavorable reports on Hse bills for the relief of Sarah Oakley, Jos Bailey, & Jacob Adams, of Mass.

Stonecutters employed on the marble work for the new P O bldg, now in progress, have been compelled to suspend work thru aggression on the part of the contractors on said work: agreement was for $2.25 a day: on Jun 1, instead of complying with his agreement, he offered $1.75 to $2 per day, & in case of refusal, he wanted their services no longer; others he refused to pay at all. Cmte of Journeyman Stonecutters, of Wash City: John Milligan, Andrew Doig, Wm Johnston, Wm Dougherty, & John M Taggart.

Public notice to owners of delinquent lands in Va: Auditor's ofc, Richmond, May, 1840. All such lands which have been returned to this ofc for non-payment of taxes since 1831, will be exposed to public sale Oct next. –Jas E Heath, auditor of Va

Criminal Court-Wash: Jun 3, 1840. 1-Edw Thos Merton indicted & tried for stealing notes, the property of Lewis H Sands: verdict not guilty. 2-Lewis Goldsmith indicted & tried for rescuing Hanson Barnes, while under arrest by B A Thorn, cnstbl, by virtue of a warrant issued by C T Coote, against said Barnes, charging him with an assault & battery upon Mary Ann Hall. Also, assault & battery upon Benj A Thorn. Jury found him not guilty on either.

Valuable farm for sale: with a view of locating himself in the West, the subscriber offers his farm at pvt sale: near Davidsonville, in A A Co, Md: about 408 acs of land: frame dwlg. –T J Dorsett

Died: on the 30th ult, on his farm, on Seneca, Montg Co, Md, Wm Vinson, aged 88, a Whig of '76. A kind neighbor, & much respected by those who knew him well. As an agriculturist, untiring in his vocation, & few men were more successful.

FRI JUN 5, 1840
N Y Courier & Enquirer: History of a forger: Dr Wm H Eldridge was recently arrested in Phil on a charge of forgery: born in Woodbury, N J, in 1809: came to this city when a youth, employed as clk to a dry goods dealer. Oliver M Lowndes, late police magisrate, chiefly instrumental in procuring Eldridge's arrest. Leaving N Y, he went to Phil, & became a clerk in the store of Mr Wm O'Kie, chemist: remained a year or two, till he became enamored of a young lady, d/o one of the most respectable citizen of the place: about to marry her, he was arrested on a charge of robbing his employer: tried & convicted-sentenced to 1 year in the pen: same was commuted to that of confinement in the hse of refuge; the young lady eventually died of a broken heart. He apprenticed to a tailor who resided in the South, & with him left Phil. He was heard of about a 1½ years later in Balt: remained till 1830-returned to Phil: mrd a young lady named Carleton, & removed to Ohio: there 4 years, when he abandoned his wife & 4 chldrn & came to N Y. Became a friend & a visitor to Dr Mott: forged signatures over those on genuine checks in the hands of Dr Mott. In 1836, Dr Mott & his family, with Dr Eldridge, embarked for Europe: returned in 1838 with Dr Mott. Eldridge at the time of his arrest, was engaged to be mrd to a lady of the highest respectability in Phil & heiress to a large fortune. Tomorrow was the day which had been fixed for their marriage. [No date given.]

The two actors besides Mr Vose, killed by Indians near St Augustine, were Mr Lyne, & Mr Wegher, a clarinet player & a native of Berlin, Prussia. All the killed were scalped. Mr German, after running 3 miles, reached Fort Searle, hotly pursued the whole way by 2 Indians, who fired at him & missed.

Criminal Court-Wash, Jun 4, 1840. 1-Saml G McComb found guilty of an assault & battery upon Thos Plumsel about May 15, 1840. 2-Addison Brown found guilty of stealing, on Sep 1, 1838, property of Roswell Woodward. Also stole property of Hon B Thruston: a pair of silver sugar tongs, 2 shirts, & a pocket handkerchief. Trial in progress at the adjournment of the Court.

Liberty Town, [Md] May 18, 1840. Fred'k Herald of Sat-written by Dr John W Dorsey. I am no longer a supporter of the present Nat'l Admin: was among the original friends of Gen Jackson, gave him my zealous support at the election of 1836, acted in concert with his political friends, but I can act with them no longer. Gen Wm Henry Harrison, of Ohio, will receive my support. -J W Dorsey

Senate: 1-Ptn from Jas Allen & others, asking that the holding of the Court may not be removed from Jackson. 2-Memorial from Mary W Thompson, in relation to the claim for services of her late husband. 3-Cmte on Pensions: adverse report on the ptn of Jas Phelps. Also, on the claim of John Latham. 4-Cmte on Indian Affairs: bill for relief of legal reps of Nathan Pryor, dec'd, with an amendment. 5-Cmte on Pensions: referred the acts from the Hse o/Reps for the relief of Jacob Adams, & for the relief of Jos Bayley, reported the same, without amendment. 6-Bill reported for the relief of Col Robt Wainwright. 7-Cmte of Claims: bill from the Hse o/Reps for the relief of the heirs of Robt Fulton: unfavorable report. Mr Merrick adduced documents to show that the steamboat *Vesuvius* was pressed by the U S authorities for the defence of New Orleans, used in that service, & left aground, where it remained immovable about 40 days. Concurrent test went to show that the boat, during that time, called have earned at least $800 per day, & that it had done so subsequently in much less favorable times. Amount fixed on by the Sec of the Navy, & inserted in the bill, was $600 per day. The test also concurred in estimating the value of Fulton's superintendence of the construction of the steam battery at N Y at 10% upon its cost, & the use of the patent right at $100,000. Both items were made much less by the Sec of the Navy, & by the bill. Subject was laid over till tomorrow.

SAT JUN 6, 1840
Ground rents for sale: authorized by Chas A Williamson, actg for himself & the other heirs, & the excx & excs of the late David Williamson, of Balt, to sell all the ground rents belonging to the estate, secured upon property in Gtwn: bldgs substantial & occupied by the owners or tenants at good rents.
1-Rent of $45 per annum, on 30 feet front on High st, part of lot 13 in *Beatty & Hawkins'* add to Gtwn: excellent 2 story brick hse, occupied by H G Wilson, the owner.
2-Rent of $79.50, on 53 feet front, part of lot 22: improvements similar to those on the above: occupied by John Waters, owner.
3-Rent of $20, on 20 feet front, part of lot 13: with a similar hse, belonging to Henry Upperman.
4-Rent of $30, on 30 feet front, on part of said lot 13: with 2 story frame hse, belonging to P Ludeke.
5-Rent of $40, on 40 feet front, part of lot 93: with 2 two story brick hses, belonging to Mrs Bohrer.
6-Rent of $28, on 28 feet front, part of lots 127 & 128: with a new 2 story brick hse & store, belonging to Wm Hayman.
7-Rent of $27.50, on 25 feet front, other parts of the same lots: with a new 2 story hse & store, partly brick & partly frame, occupied by W M Walling, the owner.
8-Rent of $22, on 22 feet front, other parts of the same lots: with a 2 story brick hse belonging to the heirs of Dr Craig.
9-Rent of $40.50, on 36 feet 9 inches front, or therabouts, part of lots 127 & 128: with a new 2 story frame hse, belonging to the heirs of Matthew Dulany.

10-Rent of $51.70, on 47 feet front, part of the said lot 157: with two 3 story brick hses & stores, belonging to John A Wilson.
11-Rent of $19.80, on 18 feet front, other part of last named lot: with a 2 story brick hse, occupied by Mrs Stone.
12-Also, other part of lot 157, fronting 45 feet, with the frame tenements thereon, occupied by Mrs Crown.
13-Also, part of lot 19, fronting 25 feet.
All the lots upon High st, & in Beatty & Hawkins' add: rents payable annually on May 1. Apply at the ofc of the W Redin, in Gtwn. –Thos C Wright, auct

The Rev John Skinner, recently from Scotland, will preach in Dr Laurie's Chr tomorrow at 11 a m, & in the afternoon at 4½ o'clock.

Noticed in the Nat'l Intell of the 2nd, that S W Beall is represented as a defaulter to the amount of $10,620 on Jun 29, 1837: I beg leave to state that the amount now due the U S from Mr Beall is but about $6,000; the Gov't has ample security for that amount, & in addition thereto, I am myself responsible for the payment of the same; which facts can be ascertained on application at the ofc of the Sol of the Treas. Mr Beall has some unsettled claims against the U S, & whether these are allowed or not, the balance above will be paid the Gov't next Mar, or perhaps sooner. Cooperstown, N Y, May 8, 1840. -Henry Phinney [The paragraph below followed.]
+
Hse o/Reps, Wash, May 19, 1840. From a personal acquaintance of many years with Mr Henry Phinney, I hesitate not to state that he is a man of large pecuniary responsibility, & that his representations may be confidently relied on as being correct. Besides, I know that the Gov't has been secured for all Mr Beall's liabilities to more than four-fold the amount of his indebtedness. –Jno H Prentiss

At the late convention of the Prot Episcopal Church of Md, the Rev Dr Whittingham was appointed Bishop for this diocese, & has accepted the appointment.

The U S ship *Ontario*, 22 guns & 175 men, J D Williamson, Cmder, arrived at N Y from Pensacola, on Jun 2, via Havana & Key West, which latter place she left on May 19.

MON JUN 8, 1840
Valuable lot for sale: deed of trust made by Jas Friend, dec'd, to John Law, late of Wash City, dec'd, his heirs & assigns, the subscribers, heirs at law of the said John Law, will sell at public auct on Aug 7: lot 1 in sq 975, fronting on 11th st east. –Thos Law, Edmund Law -Edw Dyer, auct

Boston paper states that Mr Jas B Fellow, residing in Myrtle st, in Boston, suddenly disappeared on the last day of March, since which period nothing has been heard of him, there being nothing in his domestic or social relations that might seem to account for his absence.

Valuable lots at public auct: deed of trust made by Thos Foyles, dec'd, to John Law, late of Wash City, now dec'd, his heirs & assigns, the subscribers, heirs at law of the said John Law, will sell at public auct, on Aug 7 next: lot 24 in sq 882 with bldg thereon. Undivided half of lot 16 in sq 667; & lot opposite thereto, in sq east of sq 667. An undivided half of lot 1 in sq 706. An undivided half of lot 2 in sq 707.
–Thos Law, Edmund Law -Edw Dyer, auct

In pursuance of a decree of the Crct Court for D C, as a Court of equity for Wash Co, passed May 1, 1840, in the case of R Y Brent, surviving exec of Robt Brent, vs, Fleet Smith & others, the undersignd, trustees, will expose at public sale on Jun 20: lots 15, 16, & 17, in sq 533, on La ave: lots will be subdivided, if required to suit the purchaser. –R Y Brent, Jno A Smith, trust -E Dyer, auct

Richmond Whig: Wm Barrett Price, a respectable resident of Henrico Co, drowned on Tue in a creek about 2 miles from that city. He was thrown from his horse in attempting to ford the creek, which had been swollen with heavy rains.

The 15th Regt, under command of Lt Col Lord Wellesley, embarked at Montreal, on the 29th ult, for Quebec, en route for England. Many of the men belonging to the regt volunteered to remain in Canada to fill the vacancies caused by death & desertion in other regts. –N Y Com Adv

C & O Canal Co: cmte of 5: Clement Coxe, of Gtwn; Wm Gunton, of Wash; B Hooe, of Alexandria; Thos Carbery, of Wash; & John B Brooke, of Md; be appointed to examine into & report on the proceedings of the Pres & Dirs of the Co for the last 12 months, touching as well the construction of the canal as the management of the finances of the Co. Elected: Francis Thomas, Pres

Dirs:	Jas Swann	Wm Tyler
R P Dunlop	John McPherson	
Fred A Schley	Wm Lucas	

On the 22nd ult, at the Wilmington Convention, Ohio, 2 residents of New Petersburg, in that county, to wit, Philip Thurman & Eli Holman, were so seriously injured by the unexpected discharge of the cannon which they were loading, that both of them have since died.

Cincinnati Chron: Saml Welsh, sen, of Herveysburgh, Warren Co, committed suicide on the 20th ult, in a fit of insanity.

Mrd: on Jun 4, by Rev Mr Smith, Mr Jas E Given to Miss Isabella Dunn, both of Wash City.

Mrd: on Jun 4, at St John's Chr, by Rev Dr Hawley, Wm Selden, Treas of the U S, to Emily, d/o the late Nathl Chapman Hunter, of Va.

Mrd: on the 29th ult, at Lang Syne, St Matthew's Parish, S C, D J M'Cord to Miss Louisa Cheves, d/o the Hon Langdon Cheves.

Mrd: on Jun 2, at Catadoren, by Rev Mr Pinkney, Mr Jas Rawlings, of Montg Co, to Miss Eliz, d/o Wm Adams, of A A Co, Md.

Mrd: on the 21st ult, at Buffalo, N Y, by Rev Mr Hawks, Mr John Drake, merchant, of that city, to Mrs Harriet Lambert, formerly of Wash.

Died: on Sat last, Deborah Ann Moore, aged 19 months, y/c/o Silas Moore, of Wash City.

TUE JUN 9, 1840

Just received: oysters: will be sold low for cash. Apply to B O Shekell, east of the Centre Market, 7th st, in the hse formerly occupied by Thos Lloyd.

Servants wanted: female servant who can cook, wash, & iron well. Also, a good tempered girl to take care of a child. Slaves from the country would be preferred. –Wm P Elliot, Capitol Hill, near the railroad

Orphans Court of Wash Co, D C. Letters testamentary on the personal estate of Eliz Reeves, late of said county, dec'd. –John Hughes, Geo Gardiner, excs

Senate: 1-Cmte on the Judiciary: adverse reports on the bills from the Hse for the relief of John Roberts, Wm J Roberts, & Wm Lestrange. 2-Cmte on Patents: bill for relief of John W Faunce & Oliver W Perrin, with amendment. 3-Cmte on Pensions: adverse reports on Hse bills for the relief of the heirs of Michl Seitsinger & of Asa Bloomfield. 4-Bill for relief of the legal reps of P Barker, dec'd: pased. 5-Bill for relief of Gen Duncan L Clinch was considered in Cmte of the Whole, & ordered to be engrossed for a 3rd reading.

$15 reward for lost leather pocket-book: lost on Sabbbath, between my residence & Alexandria, D C. Return to me at my residence, 1st Ward. –Henry Walker, victualler

Extensive sale of grocs & liquors: subscriber intending to decline business for the present. -Anthony Addison -Edw Dyer, auct

Died: on Wed last, at Fredericksburg, in his 60th year, after a lingering illness, Carter L Stevenson, the senior member of the Fredericksburg Bar. He represented his county several years in the Hse of Dels, &, for the last 20 years has been Pres of the Branch of the Farmers' Bank of Va at Fredericksburg. -Arena

WED JUN 10, 1840

Madame Bihler has opened a Millinery & Fancy Goods store: curls done up at the shortest notice: Pa ave, between 9th & 10th sts.

Cabinet, Chair & Sofa manufactory: Edwin Green, at the old established manufactory, C & 10th sts.

Whig electoral ticket of Md is now complete as follows: David Hoffman, Western Shore

John L Kerr, Eastern Shore	Richd J Bowie, Montg Co
Thos A Spence, Worcester Co	Jacob A Preston, Harford Co
Theodore R Lockerman, Talbot Co	Jas M Coale, Fred'k Co
Geo Howard, A A Co	Wm T Wootton, PG Co
John P Kennedy, Balt City	

Mrd: on Jun 4, by Rev Mr Donelan, Mr Geo M Grubb, of Balt, to Caroline M Florida Mann, of Wash.

Died: on the 29th ult, in Phil, Lt John Weems, U S Navy. Amiable & generous qualities which caused him to be esteemed by all who knew him. –F

Orphans Court of Wash Co, D C: sale on Jun 13, by order of the Court, all the personal effects of Thos Whelan, late of Wash Co, dec'd. Terms cash. –P Kinchy, adm -E Dyer, auct

Senate: 1-Cmte on Pensions: adverse reports on the Hse bills for relief of Jas Deatly & David Morin. Reported an act for the relief of Robt Mitchell without amendment. 2-Bill for relief of Dennis Quinlivan: to be engrossed. 3-Cmte of Claims: bill from the Hse for the relief of the heirs of Robt Fulton: unfavorable report.

Ceremony of inducting into ofc the new Mayor, held at City Hall last Mon:
Members of the Common Cncl:

Edmund Hanly	Saml Bacon	John H Houston
Wm Easby	John C Harkness	Saml Byington
Wm Wilson	Jos Bryan	John L Maddox
Lewis Johnson	Jas Crandell	Wm S Walker
W W Stewart	Wm J McDonald	Geo H Fulmer
Wm Orme	Simeon Bassett	Edw W Clarke

In the Brd of Aldermen, all the members, new & old were present, viz:

John D Barclay	Wm Gunton	Nathl Brady
Chas W Goldsborough	John H Goddard	Isaac Clarke
Wm B Randolph	Wm Brent	Jas Marshall
Wallace Kirkwood	Jas Carbery	Marmaduke Dove

Wm W Seaton elected Mayor of Wash City for 2 years.

THU JUN 11, 1840
Senate: 1-Cmte of Claims: reported a bill for relief of Ephraim D Dickerson. 2-Cmte for D C: bill for the relief of the widow & heirs of Louis Grant Davidson. 3-Bills to be engrossed: relief of David McNair; of John Richey; of Francis Laventure;of Ebenezer Childs; of Linus Thompson. 4-Bills indefinitely postponed: relief of Alfred Westfall; of Jas H Ralston; of Jacob Hanks; of Saml Ferguson.

A farmer, Aaron Morton, a resident of Dela Co, Pa, committed suicide on Sat, by cutting his throat. His wife was a very respectable woman. –Penn Inq

Valuable real estate at public auct: on Jul 18, at the tavern of Richd Spates, in Poolesville, Montg Co, Md: my *Sugar Bottom Farm*-about 330 acs, on the C & O Canal. Divided from #1, by the main rd leading to Edwards' Ferry, is my *Hill Farm*, about 600 acs. Within a mile of this farm is a tenanted farm of about 250 acs, now occupied by Mr Jos Dawson. Also, 3 tenements in the neighborhood of the White grounds, about 150 to 250 acs, & occupied by Messrs Jos Leman, Robt Wade, & Robt Lee. –Geo W Peter, Darnestown, Montg Co, Md

Biography of Rev Heroes: containing the life of Brig Gen Wm Barton, & also of Capt Stephen Olney, by Mrs Williams, author of Religion at Home, Aristocracy, & Tales. For sale by W M Morrison, near Brown's Htl.

FRI JUN 12, 1840
Senate: 1-Cmte on Pensions: reported without amendment the act from the Hse o/Reps for the relief of Wm Andrews, & the act for the relief of Matthew Wiley; cmte of the opinion that the former ought to pass, & the latter ought to be indefinitely postponed. 2-Cmte on Pensions: bill for relief of Mary Hunter, recommending its rejection; bill for relief of Erastus Pierson, without amendment; bill for relief of the heirs of Leonard Smith, with sundry amendments. 3-Cmte on Pensions: without amendment-Hse bill for the relief of Thos Bennett, Jas Francher, & Phil Hartman; unfavorable reports on Hse bills for relief of Stephen Olney & Wealthy Barker. 4-Bills to be engrossed: relief of the legal reps of Henry Eckford, dec'd; relief of Reynell Coates & Walter R Johnson; relief of Chas L Fleischmann; relief of Wm P Rathbone.

Correspondence: Galveston, May 22, 1840. Sorry to inform you of the death of Capt Redd, of the army, & also that Col Wells was mortally wounded in a duel at San Antonio. It appears from verbal intelligence that on the approach of the Indians Capt Redd refused to fight, which brought forth some remarks from Col Wells, whereupon a challenge was given & accepted. They fought at the distance of 3 paces with pistols. Capt Redd was shot in the forehead, & died instantly. Col Wells was shot in the abdomen, & at that time, was still alive, but all hopes of his recovery were given up.

Potomac Pavilion, Piney Point, Md, will be open for visiters on Jun 20.
–Chester Bailey & Son

Appointments by the Pres:
1-Sullivan S Rawson, Collector of the Customs for the Dist of Passamaquoddy, Maine, v Saml A Morse, whose commission will expire on Jun 22, 1840. 2-H G Rogers to be Charge d'Affaires to Sardinia. 3-Wm Brown, Machias, Maine, to be Collector of the Customs, from Jul 5, 1840, when his present commission will expire. 4-Abraham B Fannin, Savannah, Ga, same, from Jul 10, 1840, do. 5-Miles Hotchkiss, Register of the Land Ofc at Kaskaskia, Ill, v John S Hacker, who declines the appointment. 6-Stenson H Anderson, Receiver of Public Moneys at Danville, Ill, v Saml McRoberts, resigned.

The Rev Robt Newton sailed from N Y on Mon in the packet ship *George Washington*, on his return to England.

Mrd: on Jun 2, Mr Lloyd Greene, of Mechanicsville, Montg Co, Md, to Miss Hannah Fawcett, of Colesville, Montg Co, Md.

Mrd: on Jun 4, at Downingsville, Caroline Co, Va, by Rev John P McGuire, Dr Andrew M Glassell to Miss Frances A, d/o Rufus Downing.

Criminal Court-Wash: 1-Robt Scott guilty of manslaughter in mortally stabbing one John Slim, free negro, at Gtwn, on Jun 1, 1837. Jury recommended the dfndnt to the mercy of the Court. 2-Ann Sheckells tried for keeping a hse of ill-fame in Wash City: found not guilty.

SAT JUN 13, 1840
For sale or rent in Gtwn: spacious residence on 3rd st, formerly owned & occupied by the late Danl Buzzard: hse is 3 stories high, with wing of 2 stories, & wood-hse underneath, attached; large yard. Apply to Wm Jewell, opposite the Union Bank, Bridge st, who will show the property & state the terms. -Wm W Corcoran, Wash

Com'rs apptted by Chas Co Court to valuable & divide the real estate of the late Gen Philip Stuart, dec'd, give notice that they will meet on Aug 12 next, at the late residence of Mr Richd H Stuart, called *Eutaw*, in said county, for the purpose of executing said commission according to law. –Francis C Green; Geo Dement; W W Hannon; Thos H Edelen; A F Beale, com'rs

Notice: the subscriber will apply to the corp authorities of Wash for a certificate of tax sale of north half of lot 5 in sq 700, sold by Geo Adams, collector, in Nov, 1837, in my name, & bought by Wm Easby, who transferred the same to me, & which is supposed to be lost. –Jos Radcliff

MON JUN 15, 1840
The Hon Abott Lawrence, the Rep in Congress from Boston, has recovered from his recent very dangerous sickness, as to have left Wash for his home. He was in Phil on Wed, & departed the next day for Boston.

On Thu last, the brick tobacco factory, on Church Hill, Richmond, Va, in the occupancy of Mr G W B Hale, was burned down, with much of the tobacco at the time in it.

Senate: Cmte on Naval Affairs: asked to be discharged from the further consideration of the claim of Cath Brinker. Same cmte made an adverse report on the bill for the relief of J J Coffee. 2-The Senate resumed the consideration of the motion to print 20,000 copies of the report of the Cmte on Military Affairs on the plan of Mr Poinsett for a standing army of 100,000 militia. 3-Cmte on Pensions: acts from the Hse o/Reps for the relief of Thos Wilson, for the relief of Asenath Campbell, & granting a pension to Martha Strong, without amendment, recomminding their indefinite postponement. Same cmte: favorable report on the claim of Chauncey Wright. Same cmte: adverse report on the following bills from the Hse o/Reps: for the relief of Fielding Pratt, of John Wood, of Peter Hedrick, of Geo Morris, of Ariel Shannon, of Levi Johson, of Sault B Hays. 4-Cmte on Pvt Land Claims: unfavorable report on the claim of Elihu Hall Bay.

Died: on Wed last, in Wilmington, Dela, Jas Price, Pres of the Union Bank of Dela. His activity, enterprise, talents, & experience, gave him an elevation & influence which few men attain & exercise. -Jrnl

Hse o/Reps: Mr Botts, of Va, asked leave to offer the following preamble & resolution: reference to the proceedings of a Naval Genr'l Court Mrtl, held May, 1839, on board the U S ship *Macedonian*, lying in Pensacola Bay, for the trial of Lt Geo Mann Hooe, of Va, U S Navy, on charges preferred against him by Cmder Uriah P Levy; following facts will appear, which call loudly for redress, to wit: on May 30, Jas Mitchel, the steward, a negro servant of the said Cmder Levy, ship *Vandalia*, was called to testify against Hooe; accused objected on the ground that he was a colored man; Court did not consider the objection a valid one. On May 30, Danl Waters, a negro cook, & pvt servant of Levy, was called before the Court. Accused pursued the same course with this witness that he decided to take with the other colored man. –Geo Mann Hooe, Lt U S Navy. Trial progressed, Jun 6, the Court entered up its judgment: Lt Geo M Hooe to be dismissed from the West India Squadron, after having been reprimanded in genr'l orders by the honorable Sec of the Navy. Approved-J K Paulding On the return of the Pres of the U S to the seat of Gov't, Lt Hooe addressed a remonstrance to the Pres, complaining of the irregularities of the Court. Response: the Pres could find nothing in the proceedings in the case of Lt Hooe which requires his interference. –M V B

Massacre of almost entire family: in Cromwell township, Huntingdon Co, on the 25th ult. Wm Brown was the father of the murdered family, which consisted of the parents & 6 chldrn; the eldest dght was mrd to Robt McConahy, who lived on his father-in-law's premises as a tenant. Brown worked in the neighborhood at carpentering, was a rough man, addicted to intemperance. McConahy conducted the farming operatons. McConahy ambushed & killed the family as they returned home or were in the field. McConahy's wife, d/o Mr Wm Brown, survives. McC was committed to Huntingdon jail to await his trial in Aug. –Repository

Va: at a Crct Supr Court of Law & Chancery, continued & held for Richmond Co, at the Court-house, on Apr 10, 1840. Jos W Chinn, exc of John Seward, dec'd, plntf, against, Thos B Seward, Almeda Seward, Jos Bailey, adm of Wm Seward, dec'd, Jos Seward, Jas Stewart & Martha his wife, Jas H Collier & Mary his wife, & Cath Seward, [or by whatever name she may be known,] Rebecca Finch, John Seward, & Paul Mitchell & Nancy his wife, [which said John, Paul, & Nancy, are out of this Cmnwlth,] Edwin Seward, Jas Rowell & Polly M his wife, Josiah Hollerran, adm of Jas Seward, dec'd, Wm H Berryman, adm of Jas Seward, dec'd, Wm H Berryman, adm of Sally Berryman his dec'd wife, Cornelius Smith, Geo N Hatch & Rebecca his wife, Nelson D Edwards, Benj Riggan & Matilda his wife, Jas D Edwards, Rebecca S Edwards, Thos N Edwards, & Mary Hunnicutt, dfndnts. On motion of Jos W Chinn, exc of John Seward, dec'd, it is ordered that notice be published requiring John Seward, s/o Britton Seward & Nancy Seward, who intermrd with Paul Mitchell, who are reputed to have removed from this state, or their descendants, if said persons be dead, to make their appearance, or assert their claims before John F B Jeffries, Com'r of this Court, on or before Oct 1 next, or they may be excluded from any benefit under the will of the said John Seward, dec'd. –Geo Saunders, clk of Court

A son of Mr John Haviland was severely wounded on Wed, at the Gymnasium in Walnut st, Phil, by the accidental discharge of a pistol. He is since dead.

Count Julian, a tragedy, by Geo H Calvert, of Balt, just published, in this day received for sale by: -F Taylor.

Furniture at auction, at the residence of the late Henry Warring, dec'd, on 2nd st, Gtwn, all the household & kitchen furniture. -Thos C Wright, auct

Notice: the subscriber will apply to the corp authorities of Wash for a certificate of tax sale of that part of lot 5 in sq 345, standing in the name of Mary Barron, sold for taxes Nov 4, 1837, by W W Billing, collector, & purchased by John Dix, which certificate was lost or mis-laid. –Richd G Briscoe, adm of John Dix, dec'd.

Milledgeville Recorder, Jun 3: Mon last, Convention called by the State Rights party: subject-Gen Wm Henry Harrison & John Tyler, for Pres & V P. Cmte:
Geo R Gilmer, of Oglethorpe   Col John W Campbell, of Muscogee
Gen Duncan L Clinch, of Camden   Maj Joel Crawford, of Hancock

Chas Dougherty, of Clark
Seaton Grantland, of Baldwin
Gen Andrew Miller, of Cass
Gen W W Ezzard, of De Kalb

C B Strong, of Bibb
John Whitehead, of Burke
Gen E Wimberly, of Twigg

Convention went into a ballot for a Congressional Tkt, which resulted in the choice of the following:

Richd W Habersham, of Habersham
Wm C Dawson, of Greene
Julius C Alford, of Troup
Eugenius A Nisbet, of Bibb
Lott Warren, of Sumter

Thos Butler King, of Glynn
Roger L Gamble, of Jefferson
Jas A Meriwether, of Putnam
Thos F Foster, of Muscogee
[Judge Berrien delivered an address.]

Georgia Journal: nomination of members of Congress by the Convention: Col Chappel, R W Toombs, Judge Law, & others, whose names were mentioned, declined a nomination, but, received votes.

W C Dawson-230
W T Colquit-9
E A Nisbet-229
M A Cooper-8
R W Habersham-229
E J Black-8
T B King-228
J N Williamson-7
J C Alford-227

W Law-7
Lott Warren-226
A H Stephens-7
R L Gamble-178
J A Meriwether-128
Col Thos F Foster-113
John Billups, 78
Dr Hamilton-75
Col Irwin-14

R A Toombs-12
Gen Vincent
B F Hardeman
A H Flewellen
D Newman
J S Calhoun
A H Chappel
Crawford

Jos Nock, late of Phil, Mfgr of the U S Mail Patent Locks: now permanently located himself in Wash City corner of G & 27th sts west, in Davidson's large stone warehse. He obtained permission of Mr Lindsley, hardware merchant, Pa ave, between 9th & 10th sts, to keep the locks for sale at his store. The work he has executed for this bank has given entire satisfaction & in my estimation he is an excellent Lockmkr. –J B Trevor, Cashier, Phil Bank, Mar 3, 1838.

TUE JUN 16, 1840
In Messrs Dixon's factory at Carlisle, on Tue week, one of the mechanics, a young man, was found strangled when the machinery caught hold of his handkerchief, so sudden & effectual had been the shock: he could not call out. -Argus

Pvt sale of land in Fairfax Co, Va: tract of about 230 acs, adjoins the lands of Philip Carper & Jas Walters. Also, a tract of 325 acs in said county, about 13 miles from Gtwn. Also, another tract of 330 acs, about 3 miles from Fairfax C H. Another adjoining tract of 200 acs. Also, the residence of the subscriber, know as *Ay Hill*, containing 200 acs, about 12 miles from Gtwn. Mr Alfred Moss, at Fairfax C H, or the subscriber at his residence, [*Ay Hill,*] will give information required.
–Geo W Hunter, jr

Sir Richd Phillips, formerly shrf of London & Middlesex, died on the 2nd inst, at Brighton, in his 73rd year: the proprietor of the Monthly Magazine, was also the author & publisher.

The subscribers, living on the old Gtwn rd, will accommodate a few boarders during the summer months. He also offers his farm for sale, containing 63 acs. Apply to me in the Centre Market, at my vegetable stand, #77. –Robt Hodgkin & Eliz F Hodgkin

Paul H Borland, Surveyor & Civil Engr, offers his services. Ofc: Pa ave, opposite Gadsby's.

Fire on Sat night, in the upper story of a frame hse at the corner of 10th st & La ave: Mr Thos Mitchell, in whose hse the fire originated, has had beds, bedding, clothing, & furniture destroyed to the amount of $250. Mrs Couch, who occupied the other hse, is only a small sufferer by the damage of removing & throwing out her furniture. Two frame bldgs belonging to Mr Jas Moore, jr, formerly of Wash City, but now residing near Zanesville, Ohio, had damages to the amount of $400 or $500. Mr Mitchell's chldrn were asleep at the time, but the firemen saved them from an untimely & horrid death.

Orphans Court of Wash Co, D C: insolvent debtor, Washington Maxwell, has applied to be discharged from imprisonment. -Wm Brent, clk

At Worcester, Mass, a few days since, Martin T Draper was convicted of perjury & sentenced to 5 years imprisonment in the State Prison.

Died: yesterday, after a short illness, Mr Nathan Moore, an old & respectable resident of Wash City, in his 69th year. Funeral this afternoon, at 4 p m, from his late residence, 20th st.

Military Inquisition: Official Paper: Hdqrtrs of the Army: Adj Gen Ofc: Wash, Jun 11, 1840. Gen Order #20. 1-Brd of ofcrs whereof Brvt Brig Gen J E Wool, Inspec Gen, is Pres: which convened at Balt, Md, May 25, 1840, for the purpose of investigating certain allegations made against Maj T W Lendrum, Cmsry of Sub, & Capt S B Dusenbury, Assist Q M, in relation to the manner in which they have performed their duties, reported the following opinions: Opinion in the case of Maj T W Lendrum: not the slightest foundation for the accusations made against Maj Lendrum; on the contrary, the board is of opinion that he has free from all party feeling, dischargd his duties conscientiously. In this opinion the board is cordially united. Same opinion for Capt S B Dusenbury. Board is dissolved. By order of Alex'r Macomb. Maj Gen Cmndng-in-Chf: L Thomas, Assist Adj Gen

A card of thanks to the firemen & other citizens of Wash who exerted themselves last Sun to save bldgs which were on fire in sq 382 in Wash City. –W Thompson, agent of Jas Moore, jr

Public aucts of household furniture, good stock, & farming implements: on Jun 19, at the residence of Jos Hughes, on Bladensburg rd. –Edw Dyer, auct

For sale: valuable property near the Poplar Springs, adjoins the town of Fredericksburg, & now in the occupancy of Mr Robt L Blackburn: about 27 acs, with a brick dwlg house. For terms of the sale: Mr John H Smith, of Wash City, or John Buck, of Fredericksburg, Va.

WED JUN 17, 1840

$10 reward for strayed or stolen, on May 31, from the commons of Wash City, a bay Chickasaw horse. Reward will be paid to any person who will deliver the above to the subscriber, living on F st, between 11th & 12th sts, in Wash City. –Jos Dove

Senate: 1-Memorial from Otho Hinton, asking compensation for services rendered under a contract made with the Postmaster Gen. 2-Mr Young obtained leave for Edw D Tippett to remove his memorial & papers presented at a previous Congress. 3-Cmte on Pvt Land Claims: discharged from the further consideration of the following ptns: of Joshua Kendely, in behalf of the reps of Don Francisco Gutierras de Arrago; of the heirs of Estevan Plauche; of Joshua Howard; of heirs of Jos Rolerdeau; of Thos Power; of Mgt Duvall; of Littleton Bailey; & of Ancon C Surlls. 4-The Senate again took up the unfavorable report of Cmte of Claims on the bill from the Hse o/Reps for relief of the heirs of Robt Fulton: resolution rejecting the bill was agreed to. Senate adjourned.

Hse o/Reps: 1-Cmte was referred the memorial of Wm Wright in relation to the settlement of the accounts of the Gov't with the Cmnwlth Bank of Boston: Hse refused to suspend the rule.

Sudden death of Capt Russell Glover, long known among our N Y Capts. Supposed he died from apoplexy, yesterday. He went to his rm to change, & not returning, his friends went to his rm & there found him dead.

Boston Journal: Mr Wm Cowen, from Natchitoches, La, aged about 20 years, only s/o a widowed mother, drowned in Charles river, Thu last. He had entered the law school at Cambridge a few months since.

Thos Parks, a cooper by trade, died very suddenly on the island opposite Gtwn, on Sun last. He was examined by a physician & found to have had a ruptured blood vessel. He has left a widowed mother to mourn his loss. He was formerly a resident of Balt. –Gtwn Adv

Marion [Ala] Herald states that Vincent Sanders recently shot himself in that place. He was the husband of the unfortunate lady who lately was found hung to a joist in the same house.

City Affairs: Wash-Crmnl Court, Jun 16, 1840. The Hon Kenneth Rayner, indicted by the Grand Jury for an assault & battery on the Hon Mr Montgomery, in the Capitol, came into Court, with several of his friends, & submitted to the indictment. Mr Philip Haas & the Hon Mr Proffit were examined as to the circumstances of the assault: Mr R met Mr M in the passage leading from the P O to the Hse o/Reps, & struck him with his hand; Mr M immediately seized Mr R by the breast & struck him with his cane. Mr R returned the blow with the large end of his sword-cane, & the sword flew out of the cane. Judgment has not yet been rendered by the Court.

Mrd: on Jun 2, by Rev Mr Hoff, John Marbury to Mrs Harriet H Corcoran, both of Gtwn.

Mrd: on Jun 11, by Rev Mr Edwards, Mr Aquilla Bowie, of Chas Co, Md, to Miss Mgt Ann Hammett, of Gtwn.

Undersigned, certify that the cartmen of Gtwn for many years been in the habit of forming a procession with their carts on or about May 1:

W Smoot
D Walker
R Woodward
S E Scott
Geo Waters
Geo Shoemaker
Saml Cropley
Judson Mitchell
E M Linthicum
Jas F Essex
O M Linthicum
P Warfield
John C Wilson
Jos Cogswell
Geo M Sothoron

Fort Augustine [Fla] News: correspondence between the cmte & Lt W K Hanson, 7th Infty, on the presentation of the sword: St Augustine, Aug 16, 1840: to Hanson: for your meritorious conduct at Fort Mellon on Aug 3, 1839, in capturing 48 Indians. Cmte: Chas Byrne, Benj A Putnam, Jos M Hernandez, Wh H Simmons, K A Gibbs. Reply: Ft #2, [E F] May 9, 1840 Accept, gentlemen, my thanks for the flattering manner in which you have conveyed the sentiments of those you represent.
W K Hanson, Lt U S A

The steamboat *Citizen*, while on a pleasure excursion round Staten Isl yesterday, when opposite Elizabethport, lost one of the bolts from her boiler. The noise alarmed the passengers, who made a rush for the stern boat, & Mr J F Warner, of this city, & Mr Benj F Disbrow, late of Westchester Co, were unfortunately drowned.
–N Y

THU JUN 18, 1840
Senate: 1-Ptn from Hezekiah L Thistle, stating that he has invented a mode of constructing wrought iron canon that has received the approbation of scientific persons, & desires the Gov't to have the benefit of the improvement.

Trustee's sale of real estate: decree of PG Co Court, in Equity: sale on Jul 10 next: about 200 acs, more or less, the real estate of which the late Richd Duvall died seized & possessed, which by his last will & test he devised in trust for his sons, Alex'r Duvall & Gabriel Duvall, described in his will as lying on the west side of Beet's Marsh or Branch, lying & being in PG Co, adjoining the estate on which the said dec'd resided, it being that part of the said land & real estate devised to the said Alex'r & Gabriel, that was conveyed to Alex'r by deed of partition of said land, executed by the devisees, bearing date of Aug 15, 1836. –C C Magruder, trustee, Upr Marlboro, Md.

All persons indebted to the late firm of Ricards, Gibbs, & Co, Wash City, will please make payments to John R Ricards or his authorized agent only, he alone, by arrangement, having the settlement of business of said firm. –John R Ricards
Note: I have placed the accounts of a number of persons due to the above named firm in the hands of Mr Wm Young, collector. –Jos H Bradley, Atty for J B Ricards

Sale by order of the Orphans Court: all the personal effects of Thos Dettrow, late of Wash Co, dec'd: horse, carts, gear, beds, furniture, tools, knives & forks.
–Edw Dyer, auct

The Hon Anson Brown, a Rep in Congress from Saratoga & Schenectady Dist, died this morning at his residence in Ballston. He passed thru this city to his home on Mon last, having left Wash a week ago on Sat, & has suffered much from indisposition for several months. –Troy Whig

Cincinnati, May 27, 1840. Melancholy effect of the tornado at Natchez: Timothy Flint passed thru here lately; he was one of those buried under the ruins of the hotel, from which, by a miracle, he escaped unhurt.

Col J W Brown, a prominent, &, until recently, an efficient supporter of Mr Van Buren, has boldly taken ground for Harrison & Reform. He is a native of Jefferson Co, & a nephew of the late Maj Gen Jacob Brown, one of the most distinguished ofcrs of the last war. –Alb Eve Jour

Cincinnati, May 26, 1840. Citizens of Cincinnati have examined the bust of Gen Wm H Harrison, by Mr Brackett, [a native of Ohio, but now a resident of N Y,] & consider it a work of art entitled to high commendation, the likeness being very striking.

John P Foote	J Burnet
C S Todd	David Gwynne

J C Wright	Othmiel Lookar, jr
N B Buford	Wm Smith
J Delafield, jr	B Drake
B Storer	N Longworth
John W Picket	John H Wood
Jo Graham	Saml B Findlay
John Locke	J C Culbertson
Albert Picket, sen	Wm Greene
Jesse Justin	E D Mansfield
Chas S Clarkson	Dan Drake
L Anderson	H E Spencer
Jos Pierce	N G Pendleton

Crct Court of Wash Co, D C: in Chancery. Matthew St Clair Clark & Wm H Randolph, surviving trustees of Elias B Caldwell, dec'd, vs, Agnes Wilson, John Wilson, Johnston Wilson, Mary Wilson, & Geo Wilson. Case: cmplnts sold & conveyed to David Wilson, since dec'd, who was the husband of Agnes Wilson & fr/o the other dfndnts, certain lands & tenements mentioned in the deed to said Wilson, which is filed as an exhibit; the same were conveyed to the cmplnts by David Wilson, by an indenture of mortgage dated Jan 13, 1836, to secure the residue of the purchase-money, amounting to $2,000 with interest; Agnes Wilson relinquished her right of dower in the manner prescribed by law; David Wilson gave his bond to the cmplnt in the penal sum of $4,000, conditioned for the payment of the $2,000 in 4 instalments of $500 each, on Jan 1, 1837, 38, 39, & 40; David Wilson died intestate, & administration has not been taken upon his estate. He failed in his lifetime to make the payments at the times before specified, & since his death his heirs, the dfndnts, have failed to make the said payments the sum of $2,000 with interest, is now due to the cmplnts. Object of the bill is to compel the dfndnts to pay the said $2,000, with lawful interest & all proper charges by a certain day, to be named by the Court. The bill avers that Geo Wilson resides beyond the jurisdiction of this Court, & has not been heard of for more than 12 years, & that Mary Wilson now lives in Scotland, & has always lived there; it is Jun 17, 1840, ordered that the cmplnts give notice to said absent dfndnts of the obj of this bill: absent dfndnts to appear by Nov next. -W Cranch, Chief Judge -Wm Brent, clk

Crct Court of Wash Co, D C: in Equity. Lewis Ross vs Geo D Gordon. Bill alleges that in 1838 cmplnt entered into a contract with the constituted authorities of the Cherokee nation east of the Miss river to furnish supplies to the emigrating people of that nation on their journey to the country ceded them to the West, under an arrangement for their removal, made with Gen Winfield Scott, on behalf of the U S Gov't; became necessary for the cmplnt to employ a number of agents to discharge the various duties; in Aug, 1838, cmplnt appointed, among others, the dfndnt Gordon under a verbal agreement, which was on Nov 10, 1838, reduced to writing, & signed by the parties. The emigration was to commence on Sep 1. Gordon applied for permission to employ Geo N Jeffrey to accompany him as clk, with the

understanding that he, Gordon, was to pay him for his services, & cmplnt was responsible for his travelling expenses. Cmplnt acceded to this request solely for the convenience of Gordon, but avers that he did not design to confer any authority on Jeffrey. Gordon, with Jeffrey, set out on the journey, & make the best possible terms for the subsistence of 6,000 persons & 3,000 horses. Cmplnt advanced to Gordon $5,000, to be expended in the purchase of sugar, coffee, & soap, at the Ohio & Miss rivers, so that the same might be issued to the several detachments as they should pass those points. About Nov 5, Gordon, returned to the agency, where cmplnt had been detained, & desired to dispose of his interest in the contract to cmplnt, alleging as his only motive that some disagreement had occurred between him & some of the agents of cmplnt, which rendered the employment disagreeable. Complnt having confidence in Gordon's integrity, lent & advanced $1,000, Gordon, as he supposed, returned to the discharge of his duties. Cmplnt avers that in consequence of a drought the Cherokees were halted at the commencement of the jrny, & the plan of route changed; the the number consisted of 12,000, & Gordon, having been instructed to contract for supplies for only half that number, cmplnt was compelled to appoint & despatch another agent to make arrangements for the remainder. He appointed Thos C Hindman. Cmplnt left the Cherokee agency early in Dec, & proceed to Nashville, by way of Columbia. At Nashville he found Gordon, who again proposed to sell his interest in the contract. He alleged that all had been done by him in making the contracts for supplies thru the whole route that called be done; that the contracts had been made on very advantageious terms, so as to secure large profits, & that he, Gordon, was anxious to relieve himself from any further agency in consequence of an important law suit with an Ins Co, which required his personal attendance at Cincinnati; & that he had also a misunderstanding with cmplnt's agent, Hindman. Cmplnt finally agreed to purchase his interest in the contract for $15,000. Gordon averred that the whole $5,000 originally advanced had been faithfull expended, & the supplies would arrive in time for the emgrants. Agreed that cmplnt should give his note to Gordon for $9,000, which, with the before $6,000, would amount to the $15,000 required by Gordon for his interest. Note for $9,000 was given: cmplnt charges that the agreement was entered into, in full confidence that all the contracts had been made in good faith, & the $5,000 which had been advanced to Gordon had been faithfully expended. Cmplnt charges that he was grossly imposed on by Gordon; that he was fraudulently persuaded to enter into the agreements, & to execute the note for $9,000 by the grossest misrepresentations & falsehoods.
Gordon has instituted several suits against him upon the note at Wheeling, Va, where cmplnt was arrested & discharged by a judge on common bail; at Wash, Pa, another writ was issued, which was not served; at Balt, cmplnt was arrested & held to bail upon an affidavit which cmplnt charges to be false. Bill states the Geo D Gordon is not a citizen of this District, but resides beyond the jurdisdiction of this Court. Ordered the cmplnt give notice to said dfndnt of the obj of this bill: same to appear on the first Mon in Nov next, then & there to answer the cmplnt's bill fully & truly, otherwise that the same will be taken pro confesso. –W Cranch, Chief Judge –Wm Brent, clk

The subscriber, who has been in the employ of Mr John Gadsby, the proprietor of the Nat'l Hotel, Wash City, for the last 7 years as a porter, gives notice to the public, that he has resigned, & left the employ of Mr Gadsby. –Martin Murphy

FRI JUN 19, 1840
Senate: 1-The subject of the claims of the heirs of Robt Fulton, for the present, was laid on the table.

To:Br Gen R Jones, Adj Gen, Wash. Headqrtrs, Army of the South: Fort King, May 30, 1840. Information of the Dept, Capt Rains' report: about his affair with the Indians on Apr 28, & Capt Bonneville's report of the destruction of the Indian town, on the 28th inst. An Indian village of 15 huts, concealed & surrounded by marshes & hammocks, & distant from here only 15 miles, was entirely destroyed, with a fine field of corn, & much Indian prop, valuable only, however, to themselves. Village appears it has existed some years. Capt B deserves great credit for the good conduct which he has exhibited on all occasions. The troops are constantly scouting in large bodies. Lt Col Riley's command is now on the Withlacoochee. Capts Bonneville & Kerr are also out with their commands in pursuit of some Indians. Lt Col Harney will shortly proceed south 70 or 80 miles. I shall proceed to withdraw an equal number of rglr troops from Middle Fla, to establish the line of posts as directed by the War Dept. –W K Armisead, Brig Gen Cmndng Army of the South.

Appointments by the Pres: Wm L Marcy, of N Y, & John Rowan, of Ky, to be Com'rs under the act of Congress to carry into effect the convention with the Mexican Republic of Apr 11, 1839. Alex'r Dimitry, of La, to be Sec to the said Com'rs.

Andrew Sieman threw himself down a precipe of 60 feet, above the wharf, at Alton, falling upon his head & was instantly killed. [No date-current item.]

Letter to Col D E Twiggs, Cmndng E D, wing of the South. Fort King, E F, May 29, 1840. Health still precarious: unable to make report until now: on Mar 24 last, 2 of the best men of my co were waylaid, &, assassin-like, shot down in sight of this post. At this place I put a small box as an engine of destruction, containing a bomb howitzer shell, some gunpowder, fragments of old iron, with a shirt of one of the above murdered men upon the top, so fixed that the removal of it would explode the whole, destroy the operator, & give the alarm of the approach of the enemy to this post. The machine went off at Tattoo, but no enemy was found. On the 28th following, with 16 men, I proceeded to the hammock again: men rushed past me, when, finding we were surrounded, each man to take his tree & give the enemy fair fight. As I passed Sgt Smith, my 1st Sgt, & a brave soldier, behind a tree, he observed, "Capt, I am killed," with the blood running from his mouth & nose; he was cool & collected, tho he had received 4 wounds, 3 of which were mortal each. Another of my men had been shot dead by the first fire, & another was wounded. While trying to rally my men, now reduced to 7 not wounded, while between my command & the Indians, I was shot thru the body; but this did not deter my efforts until I had stopped the retreat of my men. Cpl Bedford, by my side, fired & killed a distinguished Chief on our right flank. Three of the men carried me in their arms, one of these [named Taylor,] being wounded thru the shoulder, while, by my direction, 3 more brought up the rear as a guard. The Indians halted a while where their Chief was killed. We had a sgt & one man killed; myself, a cpl, & 3 pvts wounded. We killed 4 of the enemy; all our wounded were saved from the hand of the merciless savage. The Indians gathered their force, & filed towards the S W; there were 93 warrriors, 5 or 6 negroes, about 20 squaws, the latter carried away 4 dead men. Some Indians came in view of this fort, but were scattered by a few shell from a 5 ½ inch howitzer, 2nd Lt Scott in command. Your most obedient servant, G J Rains, Capt 7th Infty

Criminal Court-Wash, Jun, 1840. 1-This day the Hon Kenneth Rayner was sentenced to pay a fine of $50 for an assault & battery on the Hon W Montgomery in the Capitol. 2-Trial of the Granite Cutters indicted for a conspiracy, was brought to a close today. Verdict of guilty against all the descendants, viz: Alex'r Ledingham, Alvin Cole, Redman Burke, Geo Wex, & Redman Burke, jr. 3-Tried & convicted during the present term: Jas Diggs, free negro, [an old offender,] convicted of petit larceny: 2 years in the pen. Chas Green, free negro, [an old offender,] burglarized the dwlg-hse of Mr Seraphim Masi: 4 years in the pen. Addison Brown, grand larceny-the property of Mr Roswell Woodward, of Gtwn: 2 years in the pen. May Tyler, free negress, petit larceny: 2 months in the county jail. Letty Clark & Harriet Jones, free negresses, conspiracy in selling a free negress: 1 month in the county jail. Wm Tyler, convicted of selling liquor without license, & keeping a disorderly hse: fined $25, & give security of $200 for his good behavior for one year. Betsey Low, convicted of selling liquor without a license: fined $16.

Mr Wm Ritchie, of the firm of Paxton, Ritchie, & Co, of Phil, attempted to swim across the Ohio river & back, at Wheeling, a few days since, & was drowned, when on his return.

SAT JUN 20, 1840
Wash City property for sale: house & lot on Pa ave, 3rd & B sts: house yields an annual rent of $1,000, in stores & ofcs. Apply at my ofc on the premises: Chas Lee Jones.

Shannondale Springs, Jeff Co, Va: well-known watering place will be opened for the season on Jun 10. -T A Milton, Agent of Shannondale Springs Co

$50 reward for runaway negro Louis Cammell. I purchased Louis from the estate of Mrs Bowie, near Piscataway, in this county. He has a father & mother belonging to Mr Bezle, hatter, near Braddock. -John Pumphrey, Millwood, near Upr Marlboro, PG Co, Md.

Robt Manly, of Phil, is the mfgr of, & has for sale, at the furniture rooms of Boteler & Donn, nearly opposite Brown's Hotel, a superior lot of chairs, easy & invalid chairs, portable sofa & chair beds.

N Y: accident on the Boston & Worcester R R on Jun 17: a s/o Mr Saml Brooks, & a s/o Mr Ostinelli, were badly injured. Others were more or less wounded.

Died: yesterday, Alfred Newnan Balch, aged 19 years, only s/o Judge Alfred Balch, of Fla, after an illness of 10 days. Funeral from the hse of Mrs Craven, corner of G & 18th sts, this Sat at 5 p m.

Died: on Jun 12, in his 70th year, Danl Wheeler, a minister of the Society of Friends, formerly of Yorkshire, Eng, & late of Petersburg, Russia.

Died: on the 19th ult, at Geneva, Orleans Co, N Y, Capt Saml Angus, formerly of the U S Navy, aged 56 years. He was born at Phil, in 1784, & engaged in the service of his country at age 15, at a period when the ravages upon our commerce were most severe, & the prospects of the American Navy least encouraging.

Died: on May 29, at Wheeling, Va, after a short illness, Mrs Zilpha Perkins, consort of John Perkins, of Somerset, Parish of Madison, La. The best eulogy of this estimable lady will be the lasting regrets of a large circle of relatives & friends.

Died: on May 15, suddenly, in Bonne Co, Ky, in her 69th year, Mrs Ann James, consort of Elder Danl James, lately of Madison, Va, from which place she emigrated to Ky last fall. She was a pious Christian, a kind & loving companion, an affectionate mother, charitable to the poor, & bore an irreproachable character in all the various relations of life.

Dept of State: official, that Vinton Butler has been removed from the ofc of U S Atty for the western dist of Fla: on what grounds is not stated.

The U S ship *Lexington*, Capt John H Clack, 98 days from the Pacific [Valparaiso] & 45 days from Rio de Janeiro, arrived at Norfolk on Tue, & anchored off the Naval Hosp. Left at Callao, Feb 6, U S frig *Constitution*, Com Claxton; ofcrs & crew all well; about to sail for Valparaiso, via Talcahuana, from thence to the Sandwich Islands. The U S sloop *St Louis*, Cmder Forrest, had arrived upon the coast, & had sailed [conveying despatches] for Panama. The U S schn'r *Shark*, Lt Com Bigelow, had also arrived. The *Lexington* had been absent nearly 3 years, having sailed from Boston Aug 20, 1837, during which time, we learn, she has performed more actual sea service than any of our men-of-war. She has run over 56,000 miles, has been 516 days at sea, not having lost a man by accident or casualty.

For sale: schn'r *Waterloo*, 43 tons, now lying in the port of Gtwn. Apply for information at Mr Jos Libby's ofc. –L S Bennett

The steamboat *Patuxent* was leaving the wharf at Fair Haven on Thu last, a negro man was accidentally thrown overboard, & sank the third time before Capt M Weems plunged in the water & brought him up, & at the time the boat left he was in a fair way to recovery. –Sun

MON JUN 22, 1840
Mrd:on Jun 17th, by Rev Geo Adie, Robt W Gray & Miss Mary Eliz Bently, of Leesburg, Loudoun Co, Va.

Died: on Jun 15, at the White Sulphur Springs, Greenbrier Co, Va, Augustus A Calwell, a s/o the proprietor. He was a young man of elevated principles, highly esteemed by his friends & acquaintances.

Masonic: Cmte of arrangements anounce that the ceremony of laying the corner stone of the Fourth Presby Chr, on 9th st, will take place on Jun 24, at 11 a m. -J P Van Tyne, Chrmn of Cmte -Jas Lawrenson, Grand Sec

TUE JUN 23, 1840
Senate: 1-Cmte on Pensions, reported granting a pension to Molly Willey. 2-Cmte on Pensions: favorable reports on Hse bills granting pensions to Peter W Short, Israel Parsons, & Medad Cook. 3-Also, adverse reports on the bills granting pensions to Josiah Strong, Saml Brown, John Allison, Wm York, John Black, Thos Collins, John H Lincoln, Hiram Saul, Nathl Davis, Barton Hooper, & Isaac Justice. Same cmte reported Hse bill granting a pension to Sylvester Tiffany, without amendment. Also, made an adverse report on the ptn of John Davis. Also, on the Hse bills for the relief of Saml Asbury, Jas Bailey, Wm Sloan, & Levi M Roberts. 4-Cmte on Pvt Land Claims: bill for relief of Geo Tucker. Also, asked to be discharged from the ptn of the heirs at law of Edw McCabe, & that it be referred to the Cmte on Revolutionary Claims. 5-To be engrossed in Cmte of the Whole: bill for relief of the exc of Thos Cooper, dec'd. Joint resolution for the relief of Langtree & O'Sullivan.

$25 reward for runaway negro woman Anne Wood, age from 45 to 50, who left on Wed last: was raised by the late Mrs Digges, at *Millwood*, near this place, & purchased by me of the exec of the late D C Sim. Her husband belongs to R W West, at the Woodyard, & her mother resides in or near Wash City, where she has a dght, & another at Mr Tobias Nixdorff's in Balt. She chews tobacco & is addicted to drink. –H C Scott, Upr Marlborough, Md

Died: on Jun 15, at his residence, near Statesburg, S C, in his 72nd year, Col Thos Sumter, only s/o the late Gen Sumter, of Revolution memory, & father of the Hon J L Sumter, now a Mbr of Congress from that state. Col S was himself many years a Mbr of Congress, & subsequently Minister from the U S to the Court of Brazil.

Massachusetts: Whig Convention at Worcester, Mass nominated John Davis, U S Senator, as their candidate for Govn'r, & Mr Hull, the former Lt Govn'r, for that ofc. Number present was computed at 15,000. Following nominated as Electors of Pres & V P:

Isaac C Bates, of Northampton
Peleg Sprague, of Boston
Robt G Shaw, of Boston
Stephen C Phillips
Rufus Longley, of Haverhill
Sydney Willard, of Cambridge
Ira M Barton, of Worcester
Geo Grennell, of Greenfield
Thaddeus Pomeroy, Stockbridge
Saml Mixter, of N Braintree
Thos French, of Canton
Wilkes Wood, of Middleboro
Jos Tripp, of Fairhaven
John B Thomas, of Plymouth

Mrd: on Jun 18, at Phil, by Rev Henry J Morton, Chas Wallace Brooke to Eliz Tilghman, d/o Wm Rawle.

Died: on Jun 14, at his late residence in Madison Co, Va, Ebenezer Eliason, aged 68 years, after a long & protracted illness. He had been a useful & consistent member of the Meth Episc Chr for upwards of 50 years, & his influence & liberality will cause his loss to be deeply felt.

The gentleman who, thru mistake, took my umbrella [a blue French silk of the late style] from the store of Mr Edw Dyer, last week, will confer a favor by returning it & getting the one left in its place. -Robt W Dyer

WED JUN 24, 1840

Dog lost: $10 reward: a dun colored pointer, wearing a chain collar, with the name of Capt Canfield engraved on it. Return to me at the corner of 15th & H sts, Wash. –Geo Graham

Despatches received by the War Dept from Brig Gen Atkinson announce the peaceable removal of the whole body of the Winnebago Indians, about 1,700, of the bands of the Portage, from whom resistance was at one time apprehended. Gen A proceeds in person to attend to the final settlement of these Indians on the land allotted to them west of the Miss river. -Globe

The testimony of negroes in the recent trial of Lt Geo Mason Hooe, of the Navy, has very properly been brought before the Public, with feelings of stern indignation against the Court for admitting such testimony, & still more extraordinary conduct of the Pres of the U S in giving his sanction to it.

Died: on Jun 17, at the residence of his father, at North Bend, Dr Benj Harrison. He was in his 34th year. This intell will be a very great shock to the Gen as the Dr was in good health when he started to Fort Meigs. –Cinn Rep

Meeting of the Northern Liberties Fire Co at the school-rm of Mr John McLeod, today, at 8:30 p m. –Benj Evens, sec

The London Soc for promoting Christianity among the Jews: meeting on May 8 at Exeter Hall, London, Sr Thos Baring, bart M P occupied the chr, & on the platform were: Bishop of Ripon, the Rev Dr Marsh, the Rev Hugh Stowell, Sir Geo Rose, bart M P, & others. [Paper of Jun 22: The Jew barber was questioned & taken to prison, &, after the application of the bastinado, he confessed that the Rev Thomas had been beheaded in the hse of David Arari, a rich Jew, by 7 of his own faith of Damascus, adding that they cut the body into small pieces & it was thrown into the canal, after collecting all the blood in a large bottle for religious purposes. The Pashaw & the French cnsl, went immediately to the spot: they found in reality the Rev Thomas' body, all cut in small pieces. The French cnsl caused those remains of the poor victim to be put in a tin box, & buried with a grand procession in the Latin Chr.]

For rent: 2 story brick hse on 7th st, between E & F sts, recently occupied by Mrs Latimer. Key is with Mr John F Callan, corner below, on the same sq. –Trustees of the estate of Ed DeKrafft.

Senate: 1-Cmte on Pensions, made unfavorable reports on the following bills from the Hse: relief of Elijah Fouchee; of Hugh Davis; of Joles Collins; of Thruston Cornell; of Jas Smith: bill ordered to be engrossed yesterday were severally read a 3rd time & passed. 2-Bill for relief of the sureties of Archibald Snead, dec'd, ordered to be engrossed.

Hse o/Reps: 1-Cmte on the Judiciary, made a report, accompanied by a resolution, in the case of Jos Ramsey. 2-Mr Adams presented a work on political economy, by Danl Raymond, of Md, which was ordered to be placed in the Library of the Hse o/Reps.

THU JUN 25, 1840

U S mail line, daily to the south, via the Chesapeake Bay. –John C Moale, Pres Md & Va Steamboat Co, Balt, Md.

Henry F English, Atty at Law, Trenton, West Tenn. Will give prompt attention to collections in any part of the western District

By virtue of a writ of fieri facias, issued by B K Morsell, a J P for Wash Co, D C, public sale of all the right, title, & interest of Jas Standford in a schn'r, 2 barrels of herrings, 3 pieces of iron, seized & taken as the property of said Standford, & will be sold to satisfy a judgment due Danl Homans. –D S Waters, cnstbl

Stop the thief: stolen on Jun 21, while at his mother's near Master's Tavern, PG Co, Md, a bay mare. $5 reward for information or return of the said mare.
–Jas Thos Talbertt

FRI JUN 26, 1840
Gtwn, Jun 22, 1840. 1-Shortly before the negro cart procession was formed in Gtwn, I was present & heard the agreement between Jos N Fearson & Conrad Hogmire. Mr H would furnish the hard cider, Mr F would furnish the whiskey. –J W Dellawer 2-Gtwm. Kim 21. 1840. I certify that I had 2 carts in the negro procession, & the 2 small flags with the words: Hard Cider & Log-Cabin on them, were put on by one of the Administration party. –J H Knott 3-Gtwn, Jun 23, 1840. Heard the conversation which took place on May 2 last, relative to the procession of the cartmen. –Geo M Sothoron 4-Clk in Mr Hogmire's store: without his knowledge, consent, or privity, I took a board & inscribed on it the words Hard Cider. Being only 17 years of age, I did not consider there was any impropriety in preparing the board. –J S Wilson

Mr John North, age about 50 years, member of the Society of Friends, attended the meeting of the Friends, on 6th & Noble sts, on Tue: he addressed the congregation. His voice was somewhat different: he became feeble, fell back & fainted. He was carried to his residence & died immediately on arrival. –Phil Inq

Died: on Jun 24, Mrs Mary Wilson, relict of the late Mr Jos Wilson, a native of Ireland, & long a resident of this place. Funeral from her late residence, on F st, near 12th, at 4 p m, today.

Surgical operation for consumption of the lungs was recently performed in Phil upon Mr John Beitzel, of Kensington, on May 15 last, which promises entire success. Operation performed by Dr J P Bethell, in presence of Drs J E Taylor, J K Knorr, C Baker, G W Patterson, & T A Reilly. Incision made about 3 inches long: a gum elastic tube inserted into the cavity of the abcess, & pus drawn off by means of a pump. Cough subsided, respiration became easy.

Orphans Court of Wash Co, D C. Letters of administration on personal estate of Henry Ault, late of said county, dec'd. –Wallace Kirkwood, exc

Senate: 1-Cmte on Indian Affairs: reported Hse bill for the relief of Hiram Lassett, with an amendment. 2-Cmte on the Judiciary: asked to be discharged from the further consideration of the memorial of J F Sarchet. 3-Bill for relief of Augustus Davezac, Wm D Jones, & Nathl Niles. Bill for relief of Wm Hogan, adm of Michl Hogan, was taken up

Died: recently, at Steubenville, Ohio, of apoplexy, Mrs Betsey Tappan, w/o Benj Tappan, of the U S Senate.

SAT JUN 27, 1840
C Eckloff, Merchant Tailor, Pa ave, between 12th & 13th sts. [Ad]

Grocery & Wine store at private sale: wishing to decline his present business, will dispose of the stock: located on Pa ave, 4½ st. –Richd Thompson

Senate: 1-Cmte on Military Affairs: bill for relief of J & W Beeson & others. Same cmte, reported back the papers of Wallis Arthur & others, being claims for rations furnished, & the use of wagons for the Missouri volunteers acting against the Iowa Indians, & asked that they may be printed. 2-Cmte of Claims: bill for relief of J Mitchell & B F Fox, & asked to be discharged from the further consideration of the ptns of the heirs of Ebenezer W Ripley & of Matthew J Keith. 3-Memorial of Hiram H Lewis & Wm T Lewis, be referred to the Cmte of Claims.

$100 Reward for runaway negro man Chas Dyson, about 23 years old. –J Ed Keech, residence about 4 miles from Bryantown, Chas Co, Md.

American Sentinel of Wed announces the death of Judge Rossell, U S Dist Judge for N J, at his residence at Mt Holly on Sat.

Corp notice-Wash: Register's ofc, Jun 26, 1840. Appt'd ofcrs of the corp for year ending Jun 30, 1841.

Wm P Elliot, Surveyor
Richd Butt, Intendant of the Asylum
Henry H Lowe, Inspec of Tobacco
Saml S Briggs, Inspec of Fire apparatus
Peter M Pearson, Com'r of Wash Canal

Nicholas Callan, Gauger & Inspec: wards 1-2
Wm M McCauley, Sealer-Weights & Measures
Jacob Keliber, Inspec-Flour & Salted provisions

City Com'rs:
Saml Drury
John Sessford
H R Maryman

John Crier
Judson Richardson

Police Cnstbls:
Fielder B Posten
John Waters
Fielder Burch
Richd R Burr

David S Waters
H R Maryman
John Crier
Judson Richardson

Clk of the markets:
Wm Serrin
Wm Clarke
H B Robertson

Jas Johnson
Peter Little

Inspec & measurer of lumber:
David A Gardiner
Wm G Deale
Geo Collard

Benj Bean
John G Robinson

Wood corders & coal measurers:
Jas Gaither

Saml Kitman

Nathl Plantt   John B Ferguson
Richd Wimsatt
Measurers of grain, bean, shorts, & ship stuff:
Js Griffith   John B Ferguson
Superintendents of chimney sweepers:
Wm M Robinson   John E Keenan
Wm E Moran   Henry Awkward
Scavengers:
Thos Riggalls   Luke Richardson
Jas Hollidge   Sylvester Gray
Conrad Hess   Osbourn Turner
-C H Wiltberger, reg

MON JUN 29, 1840
N H Convention of Whig Dels from all parts of N H, held at Concord on Jun 17, Hon Ichabod Bartlett presided, & Enos Stevens as nominated candidate for Govn'r.
Candidates for Electors of Pres & V P:
Jos Healy, of Wash   Wm Bixby, Hillsborough
Geo W Nesmith, Franklin   Thos M Edwards, Cheshire
Jos Cilley, Rockingham   Amos A Brewster, Grafton & Cos
Andrw Pierce, Strafford
Resolutions adopted, Convention was addressed by Messrs Bartlett, of Portsmouth, Eastman, of Conway, Wilson, of Lynn, Mass, Wilson, of Keene, & Tyler, of Conn.

Boston Jrnl of Tue: accident on the Lowell R R last evening: Wm R Long, ticket-mstr at Lowell depot, age about 38 years, was returning from Newburyport on a visit to friends. Mrs Long was in the forward car, & Mr Long, with his son, took a seat upon the tender. He afterwards placed his son on the top of the forward car, & was in the act of placing himself by the side of his son, when the train reached the bridge & the back part of his head & neck came in contact with the bridge, threw him & killed him. He had formerly resided at Newburyport, where, as well as at Lowell, he was much esteemed respected. He has left a wife & 6 sons to lament this accident.

Printer's Festival: 400th year of the discovery of printing: festivall in Boston on Wed in Faneuil Hall: Chief Mrshl, Chas G Greene: Jos T Buckingham, Pres of the day: addresses by Robt C Winthrop, Mr Bancroft, Mr Grattan, the British Consul, Rev Dr Palfrey, Rev Prof Sears, Mr Prentiss, of Keene.

Wm Neff, was Chrmn of the Whig Meeting at Cincinnati, Jun, 1840.

Hse o/Reps: 1-Communication from the Hon Wm L Storrs, of Conn, resigning his seat as a Rep in Congress from Connecticut.

Sale of paintings took place in London recently: "The Good Shepherd," by Murillo, was purchased by Baron Rothschild for $14,798.70.

Laying of the corner stone of the Fourth Presby Chr Jun 24: services conducted by Rev John C Smith, pastor of the chr, assisted by Rev Messrs Webster & Colver, of the Meth Prot Chr, the Rev Mr Brooke, of the Meth Episc Chr, & Rev Mr McLain, of the Presby Chr. Chrmn of the bldg cmte approached the M W Grand Mstr, Robt Keyworth, & the stone was laid. R W Grand Treas John M St John held the box with valuable mementoes to be deposited in the stone; among them was a beautiful silver plate, the inscription read by M W Grand Sec, Jas Lawrenson. Jas King, R W Mstr of the Potomac Lodge, No 5, Gtwn, bearing the identical gavel with which Washington laid the corner-stone of the Capitol of the U S, which he received, exhibited the precious relic to the surrounding multidude. Deposited in the corner stone, on the part of the church, a parchment containing the names of the session & communicants of the church, the trustees, bldg cmte, architect & bldr, a copy of the pastor's sermon"Let us rise up & build" the confession of faith of the chr, & some coins of the U S

Appointments by the Pres: Robt H Kerr, Surveyor & Inspec of the Rev for the port of Pittsburg, Pa, v Aaron Hart, rsgnd. A B Morton, Register of the Land Ofc at Milwaukie, Wiskonsin, from Jul 5, 1840, when his present commission will expire. Receivers of Public Moneys: Seton Norris, at Indianapolis, Ind, from Jul 1, 1840, when his present commission will expire. Chas C Hascall, at Genesee, Mich, from Jul 5, 1840, do. Matthew Liefer, at Fayetteville, Ark, from Jul 10, 1840, do. Nimrod E Benson, at Montg Ala, from Jul 14, 1840, do. Rufus Parks, at Milwaukee, Wiskonsin, from Jul 5, 1840, do. Danl T Witter, of Wash, Ark, from Jul 10, 1840, do.

Mrd: on Jun 16, at New Haven Co, Col Victor Monroe, of St Louis, Mo, to Miss Mary T, eldest d/o Capt W Polk, of the U S Revenue service.

Died: on May 21, at the residence of Mr Thos W Hughlett, Northumberland Co, Va, in her 36th year, Mrs Eliza Henry, consort of Dr Edw H Henry, & d/o John Fitzhugh, of Pr Wm Co, Va.

Died: on Jun 28, Walter Lenox, only child of Thos & Lucy Wheeler, aged 21 months.

Salem Gaz: E H Derby had occasion to repair the stable connected with his dwlg-hse last week, took down the weathercock, which had been duty on the same estate for 1888 years, during which time the estate remained in the possession of the same family. The vane, which is of iron, is marked as follows: "W B*1651."

N Y Express: wealthy individuals who recently died without wills: Capt Glover, who left a large property. Saml Ward, personal estate amounts to $130,300, per the appraisers in the Surgeon's Ofc.

The dwlg of Mr Wm A Stevenson, 10 miles from Franklin, Tenn, with all its contents, was destroyed by fire some 10 days since. The family, except one son, saved themselves by leaping from the window. A boy about 10 or 11 years of age, perished in the flames.

Eutaw Hse, Balt & Eutaw sts, Balt, Md: Asahel Hussey, & F W Elder, late of the firm of B S Elder & Son, have associated themselves for the purpose of conducting the same.

TUE JUN 30, 1840
In the ninth century, the immortal Alfred sat on a three-legged stool, & swayed his sceptre o'er the English realm; but Mr Van Buren, in this our day, is not content with a seat of such homely & rude construction. He must have Turkish divans & French confortables: thousands of the people's dollars have been lavishly expended. Why was he so anxious to possess an elegant French bedstead? Does he desire to have the trimmings of a crown bed also? [Nine very interesting columns on this subject.]

Senate: 1-Cmte on Pensions: reported the bills from the Hse for the relief of Wm Butterfield, David Wilson, & John Brown, recommending their indefinite postponement. 2-Cmte on Pensions: same for granting a pension to Lyman N Cook; a pension to Robt White, a pension to Benj McCullough; relief of Jas Cummings: indefinite postponement. 3-Cmte on Pensions: reported a bill for the relief of John McClennehan. 4-Cmte of the Whole: to be engrossed: bill for relief of the heirs of Miguel Eslava; relief of the heirs of Danl Piatt, dec'd.

Geo W Smyth, late Surveyor, has been appointed com'r on the part of Texas, vice Memucan Hunt, the former com'r on the part of that Gov't. –New Orleans Bee

Letter from Harrisburg mentions the painful intell that the Hon Saml McKean, late U S Senator for Pa, attemped suicide at his residence, in McKean Co, by cutting his throat with a razor blade. Although he was alive when this information was written, it is added there was not the slightest prospect of his surviving many hiers.
–U S Gaz of yesterday

Mrd: on Jun 25, in St Andrew's Chr, Phil, by Rev John H Coleman, J Covington Burche, of Wash, to Ellen Jones Karrick, d/o the late Jos Karrick, of Balt.

Mrd: on Jun 23, at Delabrook Manor, St Mary's Co, Md, by Rev Mr Davis, Jas J Forbes, U S Navy, to Eliza Cath, eldest d/o Geo Thomas.

Mrd: on Jun 25, at Phil, Capt J J Abercrombie, U S Army, to Miss M A E Patterson, eldest d/o Gen Robt Patterson, of Phil.

Died: yesterday, Eleazer Early, Clk in the ofc of the Hse o/Reps, formerly of the state of Ga. Funeral from the hse of Mrs Sprigg, Capitol Hill, this morning, 30th inst, at 8 a m.

$5 reward for information about my horse that strayed or was stolen from my farm, near the toll-gate leading to Bladensburg, on Wed last. –Robt Isherwood

Valuable farm for sale: owned by the late Thos F Wilson: 261 acs: with a good frame dwlg. The farm is 5 miles from the canal, & adjoins the lands of Mrs M Wootton & the Hon Geo C Washington. Also, the hse in which the subscriber resides in Rockville: 2 story frame hse with a garden attached: was put up in 1837, & is very pleasantly situated. –Philip G Biays

$100 reward for runaway negro man Kiah, about 25, who eloped from Winchester, Va, [where he has been sent in company with one of the agents of the Western Lunatic hospital,] on Jun 12. –Jas A Cochran [Hagerstown Torchlight please copy, & send his account to the editor of the Staunton Spectator for settlement, or J A C.]

WED JUL 1, 1840
Notice: a stray sorrel horse came to the subscriber's on or about Jun 28. Owner will come forward, prove property, pay charges, & take him away. –Judson Richardson, L st south, near Navy Yard

Wash, Jun 30, 1840. The crew of the U S ship *Lexington* desirous of expressing their feelings towards Lt John P Gillis, subscribed $200 for the purchase of an epaulette & sword to present to him as an ofcr & gentleman, which he declined accepting; we now beg of him to accept our sincere thanks & good wishes for his kindness towards us on all occasions, & more particularly when performing the duties of our 1st Lt. Signed by all hands. [The names of those who signed was not given.]

Whig celebration at Bladensburg, on Jul 4: register with one of the following:
F Howard	Saml Bacon
Saml Stott	Chas W Boteler
Robt W Bates	Alex'r Shepard
Wallace Kirkwood	Wash Coffee-hse
Leonard Harbaugh	Nat'l Saloon, Pa av
John H Goddard	Wm Mockbee, Capitol Hill

The Hon Francis Granger, whose illness assumed an alarming aspect before he left Wash, after passing 2 weeks at Canandaigua, found himself sufficiently recovered to return to the seat of gov't. He very wisely, however took Saratoga Springs in his way back, where he will remain at the U S Hotel for a week. –Albany Evening Jrnl

The Pres of the U S has pardoned Chas Mitchell, convicted at the Apr term of the Crct Court of the U S for the Eastern Dist of Phil in 1834: forging U S Bank notes, & sentenced to 10 years imprisonment.

Died: on the 21st ult, in Jackson, Miss, after a lingering illness of pulmonary consumption, Mr Walter St Clair, formerly of Wash City.

Died: on the 29th ult, at the residence of his son, in Wash City, in his 80th year, Mr Robt Greenhow, an old & respected citizen of Richmond, Va.

Died: on May 30 last, at Cuba, where he had gone for his health, Chas F Sprague, eldest s/o the Hon Peleg Sprague, of Boston, aged 21 years.

Rev Nathl Thayer, of Lancaster, Mass, died suddenly at Rochester, N Y, of apoplexy, on Mon night. He arrived in the stage from the East but 2 hours before.

Philip Coyle was killed on Wed, at the junction of the Hudson & Mohawk R R, Albany. It is supposed he fell across the rails while intoxicated, & went to sleep there.

THU JUL 2, 1840
Continued from Tues paper: civil & diplomatic appropriation bill. Mr Chairman, in my opinion, it is time the people of the U S should know that their money goes to buy for their plain hard-handed democratic Pres knives, forks, & spoons of gold, that he may dine in the the style of the Monarchs of Europe. [Mr Waddy Thompson. No wonder. This, you know, is a gold & silver Administration.]
[6 cols of coverage in this paper.] Included: Gen Washington received no pay whatever for his services. He considered that he was in duty bound to relinquish to the people of the U S $200,000, the amount of his salary for 8 years services as Pres, in consideration of the rents & other expenditures incurred by the nation in maintaining his establishment while in their service.

Orphans Court of Wash Co, D C: sale at my auction store, on Jul 9: four wheeled carriage & harness; pr gray & 1 pairr bay matched horses; 2 negro boys, good coach drivers & fine managers of race & other horses. Part of the personal propertyof the late Jacob Dixon, dec'd. –Leonard Harbaugh, adm -E Dyer, auct

Died: on Jul 1, Mgt Hunter, w/o Col John W Hunter. Her funeral is at his house in C st, at 11 a m today.

FRI JUL 3, 1840
Duly elected mgrs of the St Vincent's Orphan Asylum, on Jun 18:
Mrs Newman	Mrs Stubbs	Mrs A Hill
Mrs Orme	Mrs Hughes	Mrs C Hill
Mrs Talbot	Mrs Huntt	Mrs Blade

Mrd: on Jul 2, by Rev Mr Thornton, Mr Wm H Winters, formerly of Balt, to Miss Martha A Downer, of this place.

Mrd: on Tue, at Alexandria, by Rev C B Dana, Reuben Johnston, jr, of that place, to Mary Cath, d/o C F Le Grand, of La.

Mrd: on Jun 23, at St Vincent's Chr, Madison, N J, by Rev Dr Newell, Geo W Riggs, jr, to Janet M C, d/o the late Thos Shedden, of Glasgow.

Mrd: on Mon, by Rev T C Thornton, Mr Isaac Mitchell to Mrs Mary Ann Jackson.

Mrd: on the 9th ult, Henry C Neal to Miss Susan E, only d/o the late Edmund Maddox, all of St Mary's Co, Md.

Mrd: Jun 25, at Fred'k Co, Md, Wm Carlton, Reg of that city, to Miss Mary P Niell, of Phil.

Died: Jul 2, at Bladensburg, after a long & painful illness, Thos Ferral, long & extensively known as a merchant, & respected as an honorable & honest man. His funeral is from his late residence today, at 4 p m.

Died: on Jul 2, after a short but painful illness, Grafton Dulany, y/s/o John & Mary E Addison, aged 10 months.

Died: Jun 27, at Hackensack, N J, Rev Jas V C Romeyn, in his 75th year, & for more than 30 years the pastor of the United Reformed Dutch Chrs of Schraelenbergh & Hackensack, in N J, & having borne the ministerial ofc for more than half a century.

Another old soldier gone: on the 18th ult, in Fauquier Co, Va, David Wickliff, aged 86 years. He was a soldier in the American Revolution, & was wounded at the memorial battle of Brandywine.

Eagle Hotel for sale: pursuant to a deed of trust made on Sep 3, 1839, by Mgt Johnson & others: the leasehold tenements, improvements, & appurtenances laying on north side of Main st in borough of Norfolk, between the property of Jas Mitchell & Miles King: terms of years yet to come & unexpired therein: being the same tenements leased to J Johnson, dec'd, by Walter Heron & the widow & heirs of Frank Smith, dec'd, as by their deed of lease, duly of record, will fully appear.
–John N Tazewell, trustee -Chas Johnson & others

Appointments by the Pres: Fred'k Kappel, to be U S Cnsl at Pesth, in Hungary. John B Hogan, to be Coll of Customs at Mobile, Ala, reappointed from Jul 1, 1840. Wm B Snell, Surveyor & Inspec of the Rev for the ports of Warren & Barrington, R I, v Wm Turner, whose commission expired Jun 21, 1840.

Mr Peter J Kellerman, tuner of piano fortes, Star Hotel, 9th st: a German, lately arrived from Paris: tuning $2. He had the greatest proof of what he could perform by the certificate he lost by shipwreck at Capt Sable, but he hopes to remain here long enough to make satisfactory proof of what he can do in that line. For his qualifications he begs leave to refer to Mr Wagler.

Orphans Court of Wash Co, D C: Benj K Morsell, the adm of Sarah McDowell, reports that no other payment has been made by him since his first account, & that he is ready to distribute the balance in his hands amongst her creditors: on 3rd Tue in this month. –Ed N Roach, reg/o wills

Wash Corp: 1-Mayor nominated Wm Douglass for Measurer & Inspec of Lumber, & John Hilton for Wood Corder & Coal Measurer; nominations were considered & confirmed. 2-Ptn from Edwin G Miller: referred to the Cmte of Claims. 3-Ptn from Mary Kealy & others: referred to the Cmte on Improvements. 4-Communication from Robt Y Brent in relation to a site for a public fish-wharf: read & laid on the table. 5-Ptn from W W Cox & others: praying the graduating & paving an alley in sq 374. 6-Ptn of Josiah Essex & others: praying for the grading & gravelling of I st, from 6th to 7th st. 7-Ptn of Harvey Cruttenden & others: praying that the curb-stone be set in sqs 344 & 345. 8-Ptn of D W Middleton & others: praying the improvement of the gravel footway on 3rd st, between C & D sts: referred to the Cmte on Improvements. 9-Cmte of Claims: asked to be discharged from further consideration for the relief of Morris Myers: indefinitely postponed. 10-Resolved: that the Mayor be, & he is hereby authorized to loan the full-length portrait of Gen Washington, now in the old Cncl Chamber, to the Met Lyceum Soc for the uses named in their ptn: provided he have sufficient assurance of its being safely returned.

SAT JUL 4, 1840
For rent: 2 story frame house on 20th st west: 7 rooms: besides a kitchen. To a punctual tenant the rent will be moderate. Inquire of Mrs Auld, Pa ave. Possession given immediately.

Senate: 1-Ptn of Wilfred Knott, of D C, praying a pension: referred to the Cmte on Pensions. Bills considered in Cmte of the Whole, to be engrossed for a 3rd reading: relief of Hugh Steward; relief of Jas Herron; relief of Benj Mitchell & Benj F Fox. 2-Bill for the relief of Don Carlos Dehault Delassus, late Spanish Lt Govn'r of the fort & dist of Baton Rouge, in West Fla: indefinitely postponed. 3-Ordered to a 3rd reading: act for the relief of Capt John Downes.

The following ticket will be supported by the Whigs of Chas Co, Md, at the ensuing Oct election: For the Hse of Dels: Gen John Matthews, John D Bowling, Geo Brent. For the Levy Court: Francis E Dunnington, Hugh Cox, Minchin Lloyd, Geo R Spalding, Ignatius F Garner, Theodore Mudd, H H Hawkins. –Many Voters

The Character of Jefferson, as exhibited in his own writings, by Theodore Dwight, 1 vol, just published, is for sale by F Taylor.

The Hon Wm R King was yesterday elected Pres pro tempore of the Senate, the V P of the U S having left Wash City.

Holtzman's Mansion Hse, St Paul & Fayette sts, Balt: free from the fumes of alcohol & everything that is unpleasant attending its use: either for meals, or pleasant abode. –Jno T Holtzman, Balt, Md.

MON JUL 6, 1840
W B Cooper, of Sussex Co, has been nominated for Govn'r, Geo B Rodney, of Newcastle, for Rep to Cong, & Benj Caulk, Peter F Causey, & Dr H F Hall, for Electors of Pres for the state of Dela.

Univ of Md: faculty of Physic will commence on Sep 1 next, & will continue until Mar 1 following. Profs N Potter, R W Hall, S G Baker, W E A Aikin, W N Baker, N R Smith. –Wm E A Aikin, dean

Missouri: the Whigs of Missouri have determined to run as candidates for Congress Edw M Samuel, of Clay Co, & Geo C Sibley, of St Chas. Mr Sibley is one of the old pioneers of the country: one of the patriarchs of the west, the personal friend of Gen Harrison, a true-hearted Whig. –St Louis Bltn

Texas: John H Walton has been elected Mayor of Houston.

Houston, Jun 11, 1840. The wound Col Wells received some time since, from a pistol ball, in the duel he fought at Bexar with Capt Redd, of the Army, has proved fatal. He died at San Antonio a few days since, regretted by all who knew him; for he was a brave, chivalrous, & gallant ofcr, always ready for the service of his country in the hour of danger.

New Orleans: on Jun 25, Mr Breakey & his wife were proceeding to the lake on Bayou rd in a carriage, when the horse suddenly becam unmanageable & jumped into the Bayou. Mr B succeeded in saving his wife, to whom a plank was passed from the shore; but unfortunately he sunk & was drowned, before similar assistance could be extended to him. His body was found & conveyed to his residence.

Sale of handsome furniture at the residence of Mr Aaron Vail, in Pres' Sq, on Jul 13, at 10 a m. Latest from the best workmen in N Y & Phil.] -Edw Dyer, auct

Wanted: a healthy woman, with a fresh breast of milk, to nurse an infant a few weeks old. Apply to T B Dashiell, Treas Dept, or West st, Gtwn.

Died: on Jun 28, Henry Coombs, s/o Thos Johns, aged 10 months & 14 days.

Died: on Jul 4, Octavia, y/d/o Jos & Octavia Bryan, aged 3 months.

TUE JUL 7, 1840
Senate: 1-Memorial of Nye Hall, late Assist Inspec Gen of the U S Army, asking arrears of pension. 2-Cmte on Commerce, reported Hse bill for relief of Gilbert A Smith & Nathan Stark, with amendments. 3-Hse bill for the relief of Robt Milnor, late gauger at the custom-hse in Phil, without amendment.

Trustee's sale: decree of the Court of Appeals for Western Shore of Md, passed in the case of Thos H Luckett vs Valentine P Luckett, Eliz Clapham, Eliza Thompson, Jas B Murray, Peter Augustus Jay, Eliza Ratcliffe, & others: sale at the Court-house in Rockville, land in Montg Co, being part of 3 tracts of land called *Conjurer's Disappointment, Gleanings, & Discord*, which was devised to Valentine P Luckett by his father, subsequently sold to Saml Clapham, & is now in the possession of the heirs of the late Judge Mason. On ratification of the sale & payment of the purchase money, the trustee is authorized to convey the property to the purchaser in fee simple, free & clear, & discharged from the claim of the said dfndnts, & persons claiming under them. –Somerville Pinkney, trust

Orphans Court of Wash Co, D C. Letters of administration, as prayed for on the estate of Chas S Ridgely, be granted to Jas H Caustin, unless cause to the contrary be shown on or before the 4th Tue of Jul. –Nathl P Causin –Edw N Roach, reg/o wills

Trustee's sale of valuable improved property: on Jul 11: deed of trust from the late Thos Chagnier, dated Oct 3, 1838, duly recorded, all that part of lot 6 in original division of the sq 458, known in the subdivision of the heirs of Wm Whetcroft, & recorded in the book kept by the Surveyor of Wash City for that purpose, as lot 4; together with the bldgs. –Benj Burnes, trustee –Edw Dyer, auct

WED JUL 8, 1840
St Geo Hotel, 61 Broadway, N Y: comfort & luxury at reasonable terms.
–A Hinckley, proprietor

$50 reward for runaway negro boy Elias, about 16 years of age. –John Eversfield

Appt'd by the Pres: Jos P Junkins, Collector of the Customs at York, Maine, from Jul 1, 1840, v Mark Dennet, resigned.

At Phil on the 4th, friends of the Fed Administration met in Indep Sq: Col John Dennis, a Revolutionary soldier, presided. Speeches by Messrs Grundy & Brown, of the U S Senate, & other members of their party in Phil.

Died: on Jun 14, at Mason Hall, Orange Co, N C, Mr Chas A Richards, of Winthrop, Maine.

Died: on Jul 2, at Alexandria, in her 54th year, Sarah, w/o Anthony P Gover, & d/o the late Elisha Janney, formerly of Alexandria.

Died: on the 29th ult, in Amwell township, N J, after a protracted illness, Mrs Emily Hull, w/o Rev David Hull, & d/o the late David Rittenhouse, of Pa, leaving a husband & 2 small chldrn.

Valuable real estate for sale in Chesterfield Co & city of Richmond, Va: by virtue of 2 decrees of the Crct Supr Court of Law & Chancery for Henrico Co & Richmond city: pronounced on the 6th & 8th of Feb, 1840, in a suit in Chancery therein depending, styled Cosby's guardian against Cosby et als, Com'r will offer for sale: land in Chesterfield Co: 908¾ acs: part of the *Falls Plantation* which was purchased by Saml Cosby of Chas Brown, Jesse Snead, & Efford B Bently, trustees of A L Wooldridge & wife, G V Clarke & wife, & Henry Clarke & wife, by deed of record in the ofc of the county Court of Chesterfield. A parcel of ground in Richmond, east side of Locust st, north corner of a lot sold by Jno G Gamble to the trustees of the Jewish Synagogue. A parcel of ground adjoining the above. A parcel of ground on the east side of Mayo or Locust st, between the Unitarian chr lot & the property of Wm Sinton & wife. A parcel of ground on 18th st. A parcel of ground on D or Cary st, being part of lot 375 described in a deed of record in the ofc of the Hustings Court of Richmond, from Chevalie & wife to John Heth, as then lately occupied by G L Sampson. A parcel of ground on F st, being the same lot purchased by Saml Cosby of Wm Smith, by deed of bargain & sale of record in the ofc of the Clk of the Court of Hustings for Richmond, & which was purchased by the said Wm Smith of Thos Rutherford & wife, by deed of record in the same ofc. –Jos Mayo, Com'r
-Templeman & Dickinson, aucts

Senate: 1-Cmte on Pensions: unfavorable reports on Hse bills for the relief of Wm Lomax, of Nathan Baldwin, & of Jas Boylan. 2-Bill for relief of Jas H Clark was considered in Cmte of the Whole, & amended as to allow Clark $160.94: ordered to be engrossed. 3-Senate proceeded to consider Hse bill for the relief of Sylvester Phelps, & the heirs & legal reps of Chas Landon, dec'd.

THU JUL 9, 1840
Senate: 1-Cmte on Pensions: favorable report for relief of Chas Risley & of Wm Neel. Same cmte: relief of Jas Winslow & of Gideon Sheldon. Same cmte: unfavorable reports on Hse bills for relief of Robt Frazier & of Helen Miler, of N Y.

Died: on May 12, on board the ship *Oneco*, from New Orleans to Havre, Benj T Wright, aged 30 years Jul 22 next, s/o the editor of the Cincinnati Gaz. Mr Wright had been urged to try the effect of a foreign climate for his health: that he did not reach, the wide ocean has become his tomb.

Boarding in Gtwn: hse on sq above the Presby Chr, on Bridge st. –Mrs Stanford

Whilst engaged as one of the artillerists, in giving the Nat'l Salute, on Jul 4, Mr John Dudley, of this place, was dreadfully wounded by the accidental discharge of a cannon. Much sympathy is excited thorughout our community for the misfortune which has befallen Mr Dudley & his family. –Gaz

Subscriber has a vacant room suitable for a single gentleman, or for a small family, which he wished to rent. -Louis Galabrun, F st, between 11th & 12th sts.

FRI JUL 10, 1840

New line of stage between the East & West: over the Northwestern Trnpk Rd, from Winchester to Parkersburg & Marietta, thru in 48 hours: distance-235 miles, & fare only $14.00. Proprietors: M Kuykendall, John Lewis, Jesse Hildebrand

To tavern keepers & house keepers of Wash City: I have taken the corner store & cellar on 10th st, Pa ave, for the purpose of bottling Porter, Ale & Cider, selected from the choicest establishments in Phil. You may rely on all orders being executed at the shortest notice. Emply bottles bought. –Jas Palmer

J P Ingle resigned his ofc as Clk of the C & O Canal Co, & Thos Turner, of Gtwn, was appointed to succeed him yesterday. The ofc of the company is to be removed to Fred'k City on Aug 1 next.

Balt, Jul 8-trial of Jefferson Griffith, alias John Alexander, indicted for the murder of Thos H Laughlin on May 4 last: verdict of acquittal was rendered. –American

Fire last week at Clintonville, Essex Co, N J, destroyed the stores of Messrs Blinn & Parker, & of Messrs Hathway, Heller, Clifford & Durand, & W Mears. A widow, Mrs Laurence, perished in the flames. Loss of property is estimated at $20,000.

Died: on the 24th ult, in Franklin Co, Pa, John Jones, sen, a soldier of the Revolution, aged 110 years & 6 months, having been born at Worcester, Eng, on Dec 24, 1729.

Died: on Jun 20, at his residence, in Kirkland, Oneida Co, N Y, Thos Godsell, another soldier of the Revolution, aged 95 years.

Died: on Jul 4, at Phil, Wm Needles, late of Talbot Co, Md, in his 79th year.

Appointment by the Pres: Benj B French, to be a J P for Wash Co, D C.

SAT JUL 11, 1840

House for rent: 2 story brick hse on Md ave, near 4½ st. Attached to the hse is a good stable for 4 or 5 horses. Apply to S J Todd, or A Coyles.

Pleasure excursion: the steamer *Columbia*, will proceed down the Potomac on Jul 14, leaving Foulkes' & Lambell's wharf at 7, & returning there about 11: a band of music for cotillion parties will be on board; no supper will be provided. Passage .50, or for one gentleman & 2 ladies $1. Passengers will be pleased to furnish themselves with change. –Geo Guyther, Capt

Montg Co Court: Thos B Dawson & Mary E Dawson, ptn to divide lands. Ordered, this 7th day of Jul, 1840, that the sale made by Levi Veirs, Geo Byrd, & Saml Darby, a majority of the com'rs to divide the real estate of Wm Dawson, dec'd, be ratified & confirmed. Report states the amount of sale to be $2,673.91. –T H Wilkinson -B Selby, clk

Elder R C Leachman, of Va, is to preach at the Shiloh Bapt Chr, in Wash City, next Sabbath.

Administrator's sale: order of Orphans' Court: sale on Tue next, all the personal property of the late Henry Ault, dec'd: clothing, books, silver spoons, & gold watches. –Wallace Kirkwood, admin -John A Blake, auct

MON JUL 13, 1840
Mrd: on Jul 7, by Rev R T Berr, Edmund H Brooke to Miss Emily, d/o Robt Getty, of Gtwn, D C.

Died: on Jul 1, at the dwlg of her son-in-law, Mr Follansbee, on Capitol Hill, Mrs Milcha Kissuck, in her 71st year, after a long & painful illness.

South Bloomfield, Jun 26, 1840. We, the undersigned, citizens of So Bloomfield, Pickaway Co, Ohio, learn with regret that our fellow citizen John W Bear has been slandered in the vilest manner by the press: he has lived amongst us for more than 3 years, a poor but honest blacksmith, & that he is just what he profess to be, John W Bear: has no family, never known by any other name; not a defaulter.

Nathan Denny	Anthony Shaff
Hugh O'Mara	John Adel
A S Williams	Isaac Homes
F W Kellogg	A Newman
I R Hill	Jos Enochs
J Dennis	John Cochran
Wm Morgan	B F Gand, M D
Jacob Gessler	J G Thompson- M D
A Dennis	
A C Styles	

I fully corroborate their statements. –W B Riall

Hse o/Reps: 1-Cmte on Revolutionary Pensons: reported the following bills: relief of David Sherar, of Pa; of Desire Merriam, of N Y; of Jos Hewins, of Mass. Mr Davis asked the cmte be discharged from the ptn of David McMullin, & that he be referred to the Cmte on Invalid Pensions. Adverse report on the application of Betty Warner 2-Cmte appointed on the memorial of sundry inhabitants of Coventry & Hebron, praying aid from Congress to erect a monument to the memory of Capt Nathan Hale, reported a joint resolution appropriating $1,000 for that purpose: read twice, & committed.

Charleston, S C, Jul 6. A small sail boat *Rosalie*, belonging to H E Vincent, jr, on board of which were Mr T R Horsey, a s/o his named Chas, about 10 years of age, & Mr Henry Humphries, when about to leave the wharf at Morris Island, on a fishing excursion, on Sat, was capsized: all persons in the boat were drowned: the bodies of Mr Horsey & Mr Humphries, were recovered. Mr Horsey has left a wife & 10 chldrn. -Patriot

Horatio Roberts, of Clinton, Alleghany Co, Pa, was killed on the 20th ult, by the discharge of a gun in the hands of Mr Vail: at the house of Dr Morgan, between whom & some relatives of the same name there had been much bad feeling, & on the evening alluded to the door's house was stoned by a mob. To frighten them off, a percussion cap was placed on the nipple of the gun & exploded, no one supposing it to be loaded till Mr R fell, mortally wounded. Mr Vail has been arrested on a charge of murder.

Appointments by the Pres: Deputy Postmasters:

Henry W Tilley, Gtwn, D C
Geo Schley, Savannah, Ga
Fred'k Lims, Macon, Ga
Robt Davis, Concord, N H
John Rigney, Fred'k, Md
Alvin Hunt, Watertown, N Y
Henry F Baker, Winchester, Va
John S Roberts, Springfield, Ill
John R Childs, Jackson, Miss
Geo F Baltzell., Appalachicola, Fla
Ephraim Mills, Burlington, Vt
John Schley, Columbus, Ga
Jonathan J Coddington, N Y, N Y
Saml Cushman, Portsmouth, N H
Asa Green, Brattleboro, Vt
Nathl Greene, Boston, Mass
Simeon Bailey, New Bedofrd, Mass
Jos Couch, Newburyport, Mass
Thos Shepherd, Northampton, Mass
Robt R Carr, Newport, R I

Edw J Mallett, Providence, R I
Gideon Welles, Hartford, Conn
Albert Lester, Canandaigua, N Y
Godfrey J Grosvener, Geneva, N Y
Ebenezer Mack, Ithaca, N Y
Hezekiah W Scovell, Lockport, N Y
Jonas Earll, jr, Syracuse, N Y
Jacob Van Benthuysen, Pughkeepsie, N Y
Isaac McConiche, Troy, N Y
Augustien G Daney, Utica, N Y
Jas Peacock, Harrisburg, Pa
Mary Dickson, Lancaster, Pa
Jas Page, Phil, Pa
Nicholas G Williamson, Wilmington, Dela
Eleazer P Kendrick, Chilicothe, Ohio
Bela Latham, Columbus, Ohio
Sheldon McKnight, Detroit, Mich
Danl Bryan, Alexandria, D C

John D Murrell, Lynchburg, Va
Thos Shore, Petersburg, Va
John McRae, Fayetteville, N C
Thos G Scott, Raleigh, N C
Alfred Huger, Charleston, S C
Benj Rawls, Columbia, S C
Neil Blue, Montg, Ala
Marcus B Winchester, Memphis, Tenn
Robt Armstrong, Nashville, Tenn
Jos Ficklin, Lexington, Ky
John Scott, Vincennes, Ind

John Cain, Indianapolis, Ind
Wm H Jones, New Haven Co
Pruden Alling, Newark, N J
Smith Jackson, Erie, Pa
Wm Burke, Cincinnati, Ohio
Reuben T Thom, Fredericksburg, Va
Thos Watson, St Lousi, Mo
Woodson Wren, Natchez, Miss
J K Morehead, Pittsburg, Pa
Geo Rathbun, Auburn, N Y
Eliphalet Case, Lowell, Mass

Meeting on Jul 7, 1840, organized by appointing the Mayor Edgar Snowden, chrmn, & A C Cazenove & Jos Eaches, secs. Appt'd to prepare resolutions: Mr Brent having declined serving for want of time, John Grubb was substituted in his place. Robt H Miller, chrmn of the cmte. Cmte to carry into effect the unanimously expressed desire that the town & county of Alexandria be RETROCEDED to the State of Va as soon as practicable. Cmte: Chrmn: Edgar Snowden

John Roberts	Wm H Irwin	Thos Semmes
A C Cazenove	Robt Jamieson	Turner Dixon
Presley Jacobs	Jas Vansant	L B Taylor
R H Miller	Wm Veitch	
Jas Green	Henry Daingerfield	

$20 reward for stolen or strayed: 2 bay horses, Jun 21st, from the commons in Gtwn. –Henry Kengla

Writ of fieri facias issued by B K Morsell, a J P for Wash Co: sale on Jul 18, for cash, the property of Wm Poston, to be sold to satisfy a judgment due the Mayor, Brd of Aldermen, & Brd of Cmn Cncl of Wash City. –R R Burr, cnstbl [10 pitchers, box of segars, water bucket, 10 plate stove, cotton awning, 17 decanters & contents, nine waiters, two pine tables, & 17 glass tumblers.]

Elliot Cresson, of Phil, who has labored so long for the advancement of African colonization, just returned from an extensive tour thru the south & southwestern portions of our country, where he has been to collect funds & to arouse the spirits in that section, in behalf of this noble scheme of benevolence.

TUE JUL 14, 1840
Senate: 1-Cmte on Revolutionary Claims: reported a bill for the relief of the heirs of Ezra Chapman, dec'd. 2-Cmte of Claims: unfavorable reports upon the claims of Hiram H & W J Lewis.

Died: on the 26th ult, at Huntsville, Ala, the Hon Wm Smith, aged 76 years. Greater part of his life was spent in S C, whence he removed to Ala 7 or 8 years ago: was a State Leg, a Judge of the Superior Court of Law, & a U S Senator.

$100 reward for runaway negro man Dennis Burgess: has a sister living in Balt: probably lurking in the vicinity of Balt, Md. –Mordecai Plummer, Friendship, Md

WED JUL 15, 1840

Mrd: on Jul 11, by Rev Mr Brown, Geo W McLean, of N Y, to Miss Rebecca J McCormick, d/o Jas McCormick, jr, of Wash City.

Mysterious disappearance accounted for: Benj Smith, book-keeper in the Pa Bank of Phil disappeared, last May, & as his accounts were believed to be all right, it was feared he had wandered off in a state of insanity. By the Phil North American of Sat: B Smith proves to be an adroit swindler, having left the city thru fear of exposure from a mistake which he made in the bank the day before his departure. He was a stock speculator, & of his course of villany, which has continued for 8 years, is supposed to have originated in this prolific mine.. The amounts he took from the teller's drawer in the bank is variously estimated. It is believed to be $100,000, but the ofcrs of the bank have secured the institution to a considerable extent by finding real estate & other security belonging to him.

Hse o/Reps: 1-Cmte on Revolutionary Pensions: reported a bill for relief of John Morgan, & for relief of Esther Parrot. Same cmte: unfavorable report in the cases of Abel Harrock, Benj Cox, Cath Cobb, Lucy Whitmore, Martha Conly, & Esther Honeywell: ordered to lie on the table. 2-Cmte on Revolutionary Pensions: *unfavorable report* on cases of:

Solomon Jarors	Patrick Horn
Thos Fulton	Phineas Allen
Eliz Nutter	Cath Snider
Francis Chandler	Wm Keller
Mgt Penn	Tirzah Hunt
Lydia Rogers	Robt Brownfield
Mgt M'Caw	Mellon Potter
Mary Harrison	Cath Hayward
Sally Sanders	John Phillips
Rhody Polk	Wm Steele
Jane Johnson	Polly Wigginton
Martha Lemon	Phineas Bell
Janetta McClure	Eliz Pratt
Mary Biggs	Saml Phillips
Eliz Christler	Lydia Wentworth
Mgt Smith	Jeremiah Cady
Lucy Catlett	Benj Cox
John Carey	JohnP Becker

Arenth Chapman	Philip Sutton
Lettis Pond	Jeremiah Needham
Nancy G Van Rensselaer	Danl Ingalls
Wm Tevis	Eliz Pierce
Hannah Leighton	Wid/o Stephen Pierce
Simon Early	Lors Smith
Christiana Hawkins	Sarah T Field
Mary Kilbourn	Nathl Bradley
Chas Tutter	Wm Gillilan
David Tucker	Ethan A Allen
chldrn of Jos Plumb	John Fisher
Penelope Plunkett	Jonathan Rogers
Danl Story	Peter Houck
Wm Slick	Jos Wilkinson
Jeremiah Needham	David Tucker
Chldrn of Mary Addoms	chldrn of Mary Addoms
Aaron Bennet	Clayton & Mitchell
Hannah Strong	reps of Wm Kemplin

Ordered to lie on the table, & be printed. 3-Cmte on Revolutionary Pensions: ptn of Reuben Roberts, be recommitted to the cmte, with additional test now presented. 4-Cmte on Revolutionary Pensions: bill for relief of Jos Parker, a bill for relief of Leah Mundy, & a bill for relief of Benj Chapman: committed to the Cmte of the Whole Hse tomorrow. 5-Cmte on Revolutionary Pensions: reported a bill for the relief of John Hagie: committed to a Cmte of the Whole Hse. 6-Cmte on Invalid Pensions: bill granting a pension to Seth Willey, & a bill granting a pension to Wm H Wilson: committed to a Cmte of the Whole. 7-Cmte on Invalid Pensions: unfavorable reports in the cases of Henry Overly, Aaron Adams, Theophilus Sumerly, Saml Spalding, Wm A Houston, & Linza Thomas: ordered to lie on the table. 8-Same cmte: relief of John McCloud: committed to the Cmte of the Whole. 9-Same cmte: relief of John S Billings: committed to the Cmte of the Whole. 10-Same cmte: bill or relief of John Flood: same. 11-Same cmte, unfavorable report in the cases of Amanda A Dade, Pugh Cannon, Danl W Church, B H Manliet, Jesse Oldham, John Johnson, Wm Perry, Leonard Wardwell, Madison Collins, & Sylvester Nash: to lie on the table. 12-Cmte on Invalid Pensions: discharged from the ptns of Aaron Mellon & Titus Everhart, & leave given them to withdraw their ptns. 13-Cmte on Invalid Pensions: discharged from further consideration of the cases of John Russell, Jos Ellery, Henry Eberly, Seth Morton, Patrick Kennon, John C Farrel: to lie on the table. 14-Select Cmte on the memorial of the heirs of Jas Rumsey, dec'd, reported a bill for the relief of the said heirs: committed to the Cmte of the Whole. 15-Cmte of Ways & Means: unfavorable reports on the cases of John G Ford, D W Haley, & others, sureties of Alfred W McDaniel & David Watkinson & Co: ordered to lie on the table. 16-Cmte of Claims: reported a bill for the relief of Geo Randall & others. And a bill for the relief of Presley Scott. Both committed to a Cmte of the Whole Hse. 17-Cmte of Claims: bill for the relief of Jas S Calhoun, accompanied by a report. 18-Same cmte:

unfavorable report on the case of Robt McGuire: laid on the table. Adverse report on the cases of

Geo A Winslow
John G Bibb
John Wilson
Wm McKnaught
Thos J Stone
Saml Carter
Allen H Powell
Rufus K Love
Wm Fleming
W C Ewing
Isaac Carmack
John Brown
Adam Hall
Arthur R Owens
Turner Chamblin
Reps of Elbert Anderson & Co
Saml U Varian-adm of David D Varian

Jos M Shepard
Alfred Sandy
John P Baldwin
Jos Croskey & others
Saml D Enoch
J & M Hamblin
Wm G Sanders
Wm Cooley
Alex'r Watson
Thos W Coker
Vincent J Strickland
Wm Fleming
Spartan Allen
Isaac S Middleton

19-Cmte of Claims: reported back to the Hse Senate bill entitled "An Act for the relief of John Richey," with recommendation it be rejected: bill was then committed to a Cmte of the Whole Hse. 20-Cmte of Claims: bill for relief of Saml Mackay, committed to a Cmte of the Whole Hse. 21-Leave was granted Alex'r Watson to withdraw the papers with his ptn. 22-Cnte of Claims: bill for relief of John M Brodhead: committed. Unfavorable report on the case of Ephraim L Gilbert: to lie on the table. Same for case of Alex'r W Sanders. 23-Dr John Gray: leave granted to withdraw his papers.

Senate: 1-Cmte on Naval Affairs: discharged from the consideration of the ptns of Thos Goin, of Timothy Winn, of Polly Clough, & of John Judge. 2-Cmte of Military Affairs: moved that this cmte be discharged from further consideration of the memorials of Gen Edmund P Gaines & others, in relation to the military defences of the country. 3-Mr Underwood spoke for 2 hours in relation to the Fla war; in vindication of Gen Jesup, & especially in vindication of that part of his conduct which related to the capture of Seminoles under a white flag-a circumstance, Mr U insisted, which was justifiable in itself, & which one day will be explained to the entire satisfaction of the country.

Wash Corp: 1-Cmte of Claims: bill for relief of Andrew Rothwell, Jos Radcliff, & Wm E Howard: passed. Same cmte: without amendment the bill for relief of John Peake: passed. 2-Ptn of Edw Simms & others, praying that a culvert or drain may be opened thru sq C into the canal: referred to the Cmte on Improvements. 3-Same cmte: ptn of Geo Crandell & others, on act authorizing the alley in sq 403 to be graduated & paved with stone: passed. 4-Same cmte: ptn of Josiah Essex & others, for grading & gravelling I st north from east side of 6th to & 7th st: passed. 5-Ptn of D

W Middleton & others: for repairing the gravel footwalk on 3rd st: passed. 6-Ptn of Harvey Cruttenden & others: to cause the curbstone to be set on 11th st. 7-Same cmte: ptn of Wm W Cox & others: graduating & paving with stone the alley in sq 374: passed. 8-Cmte of Claims: to whom the ptn was referred, reported a bill for relief of Jos M Munding: laid on the table. 9-The Pres presented a communication from Gen Templeman, requesting the return of the portrait of Lafayette, now in the Cncl Chamber, & purchased by him from Alex'r Simpson, the owner: resolved that it be returned to Mr Templeman.

THU JUL 16, 1840
Celebration of Jul 4th arrangements: White Sulphur Springs, Greenbrier Co, Va: on Jul 3-on motion of Dr Moorman, [resident physician of the Springs,] Jas W Williams, of Harford, Md, called to the chr: Thos McKean appointed V P; Dr J W Geyer, of Fred'k, Md, sec. Motion by Maj C H Smith, U S A for a cmte to devise measures for carrying into effect the object of the meeting. Cmte: Maj Smith, Hon T H Perkins, of Boston, Peter A Browne, of Phil, J L Jernegan, of Indiana, & C S Early, of New Orleans. Cmte reported that Rev Dr Coit, of S C, to open the exercises: P A Browne, to read the Declaration of Independence.

Orphans Court of Wash Co: case of Benj Beall, adm of Edw Wyer, dec'd, the adm has appointed the 4th Tue in Jul for settlement of said estate. –Ed N Roach, reg/o wills

One cent reward & no charges: for runaway bound white girl, Sarah Ann Dunnington, between 13 & 14 years of age. Persons are forewarned from harboring said girl at the peril of the law. –Wm Uttermuhle

Francis A Dickens, having undertaken to prosecute claims before the Com'rs under the Convention between the U S & Mexico, offers his services as agent at Wash. Ofc on Pa ave, residence on 13th st, between Pa ave & F st. He has associated with him the Hon Cornelius P Van Ness, formerly Govn'r of Vt, & late Envoy Extra & Minister Pleni of the U S in Spain.

Delaware lotteries for Jul, 1840. Jas Phalen & Co, mgrs, Pa ave, near 4½ st, Wash City.

Executive Jrnl of the Senate, vol 1, p 284, following record: I nominate Geo Washington, of Mt Vernon, to be Lt-Gen & Cmder-in Chief of all the armies raised, or to be raised, in the U S. –John Adams. U S, Jul 2d, 1798. The father of this country was twice appointed to the ofc by the same John Adams.

Senate: 1-Bills from the Hse indefinitely postponed: bills for relief of:
Cath Allen	Eliz French
Phebe Dickson	John Genther
John Keeler	Wm A Cuddeback

Sarah Oakley	Wm Sloan
Reuben Murray	Levi R Roberts
Jacob Adams	Thos Collins
Jos Bailey	Hiram Saul
John Lathram	John K Lincoln
Jas Phelps	Nathl Davis
Conrad Widrig	Barton Hooper
Eliz Case	Isaac Justice
Jas Deatley	Saml Brown
Lamech Bland-adm	Lt John Allison
Ann Bloomfield	Jabez Collins
Benj Mitchell	Hugh Davis
David Mallen	Elijah Foochee
Mary Hunter	Thruston Cornell
Stephen Olney	Jas Smith
Wealthy Barker	Robt Whittel
Matthew Wiley	Lyman N Cook
Jas J Coffin	Benj McCulloch
Peter Headrick	John Lybrook
Jos Wood	Christian Brougher
Fielding Pratt	John Piper
Saml B Hugo	Jas Cummings
Levi Johnston	John Brown
Neil Shannon	David Wilson
Martha Strong	Isaac Austen
Asenath Campbell	Elijah Blodget
Thos Wilson	Helen Miller
Wm Poole	Wm Dean
Myor Chapin	Stephen Appleby
Jos W Knipe	Isaac Boyd
Simon Knight	Robt Frazier
Robt Lucas	Jas Fleming
Wilfred Knott	Wm Glover
John Davis	Chas Risley
Sam M Asbury	Michl Seitsinger-heirs
Jas Bailey	John Lindsey-heirs

2-Bills ordered to a 3rd reading & passed: bills for relief of:

Wm Rand	Philip Hartman
Jacob Becker	Thos Bennett
Mary Snow	Jas Francher
Mary Prettyman	Wm Andrews
Eliz Davidson	Chauncey Rice
Mgt Jamison	Seneca Rider
Erastus Pierce	Sylvester Tiffany
Leonard Smith	Medad Cook

Peter W Short
Wm Bowan
Jared Winslow
Danl W Going
Ichabod Beardsley

Peter A Myers
Israel Parsons
Lyman Bristol
John McClanahan
Gideon Shelden

3-Bill for the relief of Gen Hernandez was considered, & ordered to a 3rd reading.

FRI JUL 17, 1840

Boston Mercantile Jrnl, Jul 14: died-B B Thatcher, of this city, at age 31 years: well known in this country & in Europe for his scientific & literary attainments: educated to the profession of the law: at one time editor of this paper: attacked in Gr Britain with a chronic affection of the stomach, & on his return to this country he suffered much from ill health.

Ladies Companion periodical: $2,000 prize to Mrs Ann L Stephens, for the tale "Mary Derwent."

Charleston, S C, Jul 13. Died: on Fri last, unexpectedly with an apoplectic fit, & the next day a corpse, the Hon Jas R Pringle: Pres of our State Senate in 1819, received the appointment of Collector of the Customs from Pres Monroe, & upwards of 20 years discharged his duties with fidelity: served as Intendant [or Mayor] of the city. –Courier

Mgrs of the Jefferson Library: in existence in Wash City for 12 years: soliciting cmte will soon call on the citizens for donations. Cmte: John T McCarty, Geo Dewees, John S Bogan

$10 reward for strayed bay mare: brought from Loudoun Co, Va, about 4 months since, & purchased by the subscriber from Victor Beyer, of D C. Information given to Mr Geo Lipscomb, of Wash City, or the undersigned, will be thankfully received. –John T Bevans, living at the Lodge, PG Co, Md.

Lts Pendergrast, Du Pont, Misroon, & Godon, who were sent home by Cmdor Hull in consequence of some misunderstanding on points of etiquette, have been ordered by the Navy Dept to return to the Mediterranean for duty on board the ship *Ohio*. –A & N Chron

Mrd: on Jun 23, by Rev Mr Childs, Mr Saml Dent, lately of Miss, to Miss Matilda Grey, d/o Robt Grey, of Chas Co, Md.

Mrd: on Jul 14, by Rev T C Thornton, Mr Wm C Bauberger to Miss Hannah Stephenson, all of Wash City.

Died: in Marblehead, Mass, Lt John E Prentiss, of the U S Navy, aged 47 years. [No date-current item.]

Died: on Jul 11, at his residence in Wash City, after an illness of only 7 days, Saml B Lowe, in his 56th year. He was kind & gave devoted care, both temporal & spiritual, to a large & interesting family: born & died a member of the Church: within the last years, taken from him, the partner of his bosom & a beloved son, just entered upon the stage of manhood. He was attacked with the fatal disease on Jul 5: received the sacraments of his holy Church, resigned his soul to the mercy of his God. May He rest in peace.

Died: on Jul 16, in this county, Mr John Store, aged 92 years: a native of Ire, emigrated to this country 24 years ago, losing his wife on the passage out, & having ever since resided in Wash City & neighborhood.

Died: on Jul 13, in Gtwn, Maria Blake, d/o Wm A & Glorvina Gordon, aged 6 years.

Appointments by the Pres: P Mdshpmn Wm Leigh, to be a Lt in the Navy from May 30, 1840. P Mid Saml Larkin, jr, to be Lt in the Navy, from Jul 1, 1840. Elias Kane, to be Navy Agent for the Navy in Wash City, for the Navy Dept, for 4 years from Jul 14, 1840, when his former commission expired. Benj D Heriot, to be Navy Agent for the post of Charleston, S C, for 4 years from Oct 4, 1840, when his present commission will expire.

Cabinet makers wanted: shop on 9th st, between E & F sts. –Peter Callan [Printers' furniture made to order; funerals attended to with despatch.]

Agatheridan Soc of the Nashville Univ, on Jul 1, preamble offered by Mr R P Atkinson adopted: we have been apprized of the death of Mr Alfred Newnan Balch, formerly an active & much beloved member of this Soc. We console the afflicted parent, relatives & friends. –E H Foster, jr, Pres

N Y Jul 15. From Africa: the U S brig *Dolphin*, Lt Sell, which has been some time on the coast of Africa, returned last evening. The last African port at which she touched was Monrovia, which she left on May 23. The *Dolphin* left Sierre Loone, in early May, the brig *Eliza Davidson*, Hanna, of Balt. She was captured by a Brit man-of-war off Sherbro, sent to Sierra Leone, & condemned as a Spanish slaver. On her way home the *Dolphin* touched at St Pierro's, island of Martinique, from when she sailed on the 1st inst.

City Ord-Wash: 1-Act for relief of John Peake: fine for keeping a dog without a license, same remitted: provided he pay the costs of prosecution. 2-Act of relief of Andrew Rothwell, Jos Radcliff, & Wm E Howard: to pay each $100 for extra services rendered by them in preparing the tax & genr'l assessment bks for 1839, payable out of the genr'l fund. Approved, Jul 15, 1840.

For rent: 2 story brick house of the late Mr T Arbuckle, on 13th st, above G st, just below the residence of Mr S Davidson King, where the key is left. Possession immediately.

SAT JUL 18, 1840
Wm P Bender still has his Drug Store for sale: wishing to leave the city because of ill health. Store is at the corner of 6th st & Pa ave.

Jas H Causten, Genr'l Agent, tenders his services to those having claims against the Mexican Gov't under the late treaty with the U S. Letters to his address, at Wash City, will receive prompt attention.

Training stable: Wm Holmead has engaged the services of Pleasant H Rowlett, of Va, to train at the Wash Race Course for the ensuing fall meeting. Terms moderate.

Valuable bldg lots for sale: lot 1 & part of lot 2 sq 252, corner of Md ave & 10th st, adj the residence of Lewis H Machen. Also, part of lot 3 in sq 268, near the Long Bridge. Apply to E Dyer, auct.

Persons who have subscribed to the raffle for the Flower Piece, painted by the celebrated Dutch Artist, John Van Huysum, call at the room of Mr Franquinet, artist, in north wing of the Capitol, on or before Jul 18, & pay the amount of the subscription, as the raffle will be between 5 & 6 p m, Jul 18.

For Boston: the regular packet brig *Columibia*, Seth Ryder, jr, master, will sail on Jul 18. For freight apply to Wm Fowle & Son, Alexandria.

MON JUL 20, 1840
Senate: 1-Bills considered in Cmte of the Whole, ordered to be laid on the table: relief of Eliza Causin, dght & heir of John H Stone, dec'd. 2-Bills for relief of Jas McCrory; relief of the heirs of Fred'k Seigle; relief of the legal reps of John Jordan, dec'd, late a Capt in the Continental line of Artllery artificers: laid on the table. 3-Ptn of John Ross, in behalf of certain Indian warriors, & praying pensions for them. Mr Davis obtained leave for Mr Ross to withdraw the papers presented.

Europe: 1-Attempt was made to assassinate the Queen & Prince Albert on Jul 11, as they rode together in the streets of London, by a man named Oxford, who fired 2 pistols at them in quick succesion, both of them, however, missed. Oxford was arrested but refused to give reason for his conduct. 2-The death of the King of Prussia is confirmed. 3-The Emperor of Russia is making a tour in Europe. 4-Paganini, the celebrated violinist, is dead. 5-Courvoisier, the valet of Lord Wm Russell, was found guilty of his lordship's murder & afterwards made a full confession of the fact.

The U S schn'r *Flying Fish* [of the exploring expedition] was at the Bay of Islands on Mar 25: suffered much from ice. Only 3 men were on duty when she reached the bay. Her ofcrs are Lt R F Pinckney-Cmndnt, Geo T Sinclair-Mstr, Wm May-P Mid, Geo W Harrison-do.

We have before us an admirable likeness of the Hon J J Crittenden, Senator from Ky, just executed by Mr Chas Fenderich, of Wash City. It is unnecessary to point out his professional merits.

Nashville [Tenn] Whig, of Jul 8: Edw W Dale, the Cashier of the Branch Bank of Tenn at Columbia, committed suicide yesterday, at his own house, by cutting his throat with a razor.

Died: on Jul 9, in Chas Co, Md, in her 73rd year, Mrs Marion Campbell, relict of the late Hon John Campbell, for many years a Rep in Congress from that district.

Died: on Wed last, at Albany, N Y, Mr Robt Packard, age 66 years. He was the oldest practical printer in Albany, & for many years superintended the business of printing for the state, under the firm of Packard & Van Benthuysen. –Ev'g Jrnl

Died: on Jul 17, Cornelia Speak, d/o Wm & Cordelia Holmead, aged 17 months & 2 weeks.

Appointments by the Pres: Receivers Genr'l-
Stephen Allen, at N Y C, N Y   Jos Johnson, at Charleston, S C
Isaac Hill, at Boston, Mass   Geo Penn, St Louis, Mo.
Land Ofcrs:
John B Larwill, Reg of Land Ofc at Bucyrus, Ohio, vic John Caldwell-commission expired Jul 5, 1840.
John Caldwell, Receiver of Public Moneys Bucyrus, Ohio, vice Jos H Larwill, resigned.
Parker Dudley, do, at Palmyra, Mo, vice Abraham Bird, removed.
Henry Deas, Col of the Customs at Charleston, S C, vice Jas R Pringle, resigned.

On Jul 6, 1840, information was laid before a J P for Wash City, that Alex'r Duncan, a Mbr of Congress from Ohio, who, it is said, voted for the law, had, on the Fri previous, passed as currency to a citizen of Wash a note of less denomination than $5, & the note was produced & exhibited to the justice, & he issued a warrant for the apprehension of Duncan. The next day, the warrant not having been served, the justice recalled it, & has since refused to issue it on the ground that, as a Mbr of Congress is privileged from arrest, except in cases of treason, felony, & breach of the peace, Duncan was not liable to arrest. It is time for us to think of a remedy for a great evil.

Navy Dept, Jul 16, 180. Board recently convened at the Naval Asylum, Phil for the exam of Midshipmen: following passed in an order of rank asssigned them by the Board, viz:

1-Isaac N Brown
2-R Delancy Izard
3-Napoleon Collins
4-John L Worden
5-Wm L Blanton
6-Benj S Gannt
7-Henry A Wise
8-Callender St G Noland
9-Jennings F Marrast
10-Edw C Anderson
11-Reed Warden

12-Wm H Macomb
13-Stephens Tranchard
14-Wilson R McKinney
15-A Harrell
16-A H Jenkins
17-Saml J Shipley
18-John J Guthrie
19-Mayo C Watkins
20-Melancthon B Woolsey
21-Robt Poinsett Loved

Mdshpmn Robt M Bowland passed in seamanship, but was rejected in navigation & math.
Mdshpmn P C Van Wyck was prevented from appearing before the Brd by sickness.
Mdshpmn Jas Riddle, reported himself, but declined an exam.

Miss Braschard's Seminary, corner of E & 9th sts, Wash: exam on Jul 14. Classes under the charge of Miss Hewitt, Miss Whitney, Miss Reed, & Miss Solms. Awards given to:

Miss Augusta Mechlin
Miss Matilda Wallace
Miss Mary Jesup
Miss Jane Wilkes
Miss Sarah Lovell
Miss Frances Houghton
Miss Hannah Bridge
Miss Mary Cross
Miss Cath Hawley
Miss Sarah Gardner
Miss Sarah Hogan
Miss Jane Thornton
Miss Louisa Reardon
Mid Edmonia Jones
Miss Eliz Hobbie
Miss Matilda Semmes
Miss Josephine Linton
Miss Sarah Prout
Miss Mildred Coles
Miss Isabell Walker

Miss Fanny Jones, of Wash
Miss Mary Brawner
Miss Lucinda Bean
Miss Caroline Seaton-Washington
Miss Helen Coles
Miss Cecilia Hooe
Miss Marion Fletcher
Miss Mary Howle
Miss Charlotte Webb
Miss Sarah E Morsell, of Wash
Miss Frances E Houghton, of Chilcothe, Ohio
Miss Adeline Ripley, of Augusta, Maine
Miss Frances Williams, of Berryville, Va
Miss Hannah N Bridge-present 3 months

The View of the Capitol: drawn by Mr W A Pratt, Mural Architect, & lithographed by the celebrated Fenderick, for sale at the Stationers Hall-Mr Fisher.

The Naval Genr'l Court Martial, at Phil, on May 4 last, for the trial of Cmdor Elliott, found him guilty of the 1st, 3rd, 5th, & 8th charges preferred against him: sentenced him to be suspended for 4 years, with a suspension of pay for the first 2 years. Sentence approved by the Sec of the Navy; but so much of it as deprived Cmdor Elliot of his pay has been remitted by the Pres. –Globe

TUE JUL 21, 1840
Senate: 1-Cmte on Commerce: bill for the relief of the owners & crew of the schn'r *Buffalo* was indefinitely postponed.

Cincinnati, Jun, 1840: to the Whig Cmte of 76 of D C: I forward you a genuine Buckeye Log Cabin, in minature, which I beg you will place upon your table while doing for the good our country's cause. It was constructed for me by Mr Wm H Roser, from Norfolk, Va, now a resident of this city, & a staunch Whig. Fellow-citizen, S MacDonald

Wythe Journal: protest: we are not associated with a party who surrport the present Fed Admin in its gross & profligate waste of the People's money. Expunge our names from any list associated with the present admin. –Henry Earhart, Matthias Tartar, Michl Lambert, Weyman Lambert, Wm Lambert

Danvers, Jul 2, 1840. Letter to Danl Shattuck, Chrmn of the Cmte of Arrangements at Concord. The most interesting remembrance of the events of Apr 19, 1775, when, with my musket in hand, at the head of my brave minute men from Danvers, I met the enemy on their way from Concord, near the borders of Lexington. If my life is spared, I will add another to the ballots in favor of true Whig principles the present year by voting for Harrison & Tyler. The infirmities of more than 91 years now remind me of the hazard of undertaking a jrny of more than 50 miles. My wishes will be with you on the coming 4th of Jul at Concord. –Gideon Foster

Friends of Harrison & Reform in the counties of Va & Md: Cmte of Invitation: Thos Griggs, Henry Berry, Andrew Hunter, W C Worthington, W B Thompson

Dr Joshua Bates, the Chaplain of the Hse o/Reps, narrowly escaped being drowned about a week ago in Boston harbor. In stepping on board the steamboat, the foot plank slipped, & he was precipitated 12 feet into the water, between the pier & paddles of the boat. Being an excellent swimmer, he sustained himself until he was rescued by a boat which brought him safe to land.

For sale: tract of land in Fairfax Co, Va, containing 200 acs. For particulars inquire at the law ofc of Swann & Swann, between 14th & 15th sts, Wash City. –Edw Swann, atty for proprietor.

Orphans Court of Wash Co, D C: insolvent debtor, Joshua Benner, has applied to be discharged from imprisonment. –Wm Brent, clk

Having determined to remove to the west, I have this day transferred to Middleton & Beall my stock in trade, with all notes & bk accounts, who alone are authorized to collect the same. My creditors will please present their claims against me to those gentlemen. –Wm Mockbee

Died: on Jul 15, at Cincinnati, Ohio, Jos S Benham: one of the oldest, & for many years one of the most distinguished advocates at the Cincinnati Bar. About a year since he removed to New Orleans, & had already obtained a successful position in his practice at that place. With his family he was journeying north to pass the summer, & while visiting with his old friends in Cincinnati, became ill & died. He will long be remembered. –Cincinnati Gaz

Died: on Jul 17, in Wash City, Mrs Matilda Young, in her 53rd year, consort of the late Richd Young, after a long & painful illness.

Died: on Jul 5, in St Louis, Mo, Frances, aged 18 months, only d/o Mr I Smith Homans, formerly of Wash City.

Died: on Jul 3, at Farmerville, Seneca Co, N Y, in his 26th year, Mr Noyes C Barber, merchant of the firm of Chester Barber, & s/o Hon Noyes Barber, of Groton, Conn.

WED JUL 22, 1840
List of Acts passed at the First Session of the 26th Congress, which closed yesterday.
1-Act for relief of:

Richd Booker & others	Medad Cook
Thos W Taylor	Lyman Bristol
Gamaliel E Smith	Sylvester Tiffany
Wm Wickham	Wm Bowman
Geo Willis	Seneca Rider
Nathan Levy	Ebenezer Lobdell
Sutton Stephens	Oliver Welch
Jacob Becker	Mary Perkins
Capt John Downes	Cornelius Tiers
Jas L Cochran	Wm Marbury, of La
Jas Brewer, of Ohio	Jos Cochran
Jas Francher	A G S Wight
Erastus Pierson	John H Jacocks
Peter A Myers	Peter Warner, of Ind
Danl W Going	John W Monette
Jared Winslow	Thos Bennett
Gideon Sheldon	Hyacinth Sassel
Gen Duncan L Clinch	Wm Andrews, of N Y

John H Sheppard, adm of Abiel Wood
Robt Milnor & John Thompson
Gilbert A Smith & Nathan Stark
Alvarez Fish & legal reps of Thos P Eskridge
John W France & Oliver Perrin
Chldrn of Stephen Johnston, dec'd
John L Bowman & Enoch J Noyes

Peter W Short, of Woodstock, N Y
Legal reps of Wm Williams, sen, dec'd
Meigs D Benjamin & Co
John T Addoms, exc of John Addoms
Ichabod Berdsley, of N Y
Eliz Davidson, wid/o John Davidson

2-Relief of heirs & legal reps of John Grimball, sen, dec'd. 3-Relief of Boggs & Thompson, Robert & Thos Hutchinson, & others. 4-Relief of the widow & heirs at law of the late Lewis Grant Davidson, dec'd. 5-Relief of Pierre Molaisen, wid/o Pierre Richom, Alex Comean, Alice L Foley, wid/o John Foley, & Francis Martin, of La. 6-Relief of sureties & heirs & reps of Melancton W Bostwick, dec'd, & for other purposes. 7-Relief of Thos Latham, & for other purposes. Also, of Masterton & Smith, & for other purposes. 8-Act to authorize Jas Alexander to relinquish certain land, & to locate other land in lieu thereof. 9-Refund of fund imposed on the late Matthew Lyon, under the sedition law, to his legal heirs & legal reps. 10-Act confirming the claim of Augustine Lacoste to a certain land tract of land therein named. 11-Pension to Chauncey Rice. 12-Pension to Israel Parsons. 13-Pension to Philip Hartman, of Va. 14-Resolution authorizing the Pres of the U S to accept certain presents from the Imaum of Muscat, & the Emperor of Morocco. 15-Act for relief of Chastelain & Ponvert: [in this bill are contained the following:]
Payment of an award in favor of the owners of the steamboats *Stasca & Dayton*
Payment of balance due for supplies furnished to the Creek Indians
Payment of the expenses of a division of the lands of the Brotherton Indians
Payment of the accounts of Henry Lucas & A P King, of Ala
Payment of an account of Hart & Bosworth, & John Hart
Payment of an account of John H Craddock, of Ala
Payment of Mitchell & Fox for labor at branch mint at New Orleans
Payment of Chas Gordon for maps
Payment of Auguste Davezac, late Charge d'Affairs of the U S at Hague.
Payment of Wm D Jones for diplomatic services
Payment of Nathl Niles, Charge d'Affairs to Sardinia
Payment of Clarke & Force for Diplomatic History
Paying Capt Snodgrass' Co of vols

$30 reward for runaway negro woman Susan Wright, about 40: has some relations who live in Wash City. –John A Pye

Ex-Govn'r Hiram G Runnells, & Pres of the Miss Union Bank, & Volney E Howard, ex-editor of the Mississippian, the Admin state paper, fought a duel a few days since. Runnells escaped unhurt. Howard was dangerously wounded in the breast, the ball having entered at a point near the right lobe, & made its exit 12 inches on the opposite side. The distance was 12 paces-each one fire. Mr Howard mrd at Wash City, Miss Gooch, the poetess, about 2 years since. –Mobile paper

Letter dated Exeter, Jul 6, 1840. Subject: Maj Miller was very sick at the time the army moved from Fort Harrison, with a bilious intermittent fever, which rendered it utterly impossible for him to march with the army. He was left with a small party, mostly invalids, in command of the fort. In 1813, I served with the gallant old 4th. During the campaign I messed with Major, afterwards Col Snelling, [who commanded a company at Tippecnoé, & who was, a short time before the surrender of Hull, breveted for his good conduct in the battle of Brownstown, where Gen Miller commanded,] & frequently heard him give an account of the Tippecanoe fight. I do not believe there was another man in the country that could have saved the army from the scalping knife. –P Chadwick

Meeting of the Northern Liberties Fire Co: at the school room of Mr John McLeod, this evening, at 8:30. -Benj Evens, sec

$5 reward for return of strayed or stolen sorrel mare. –John Williamson, 5th & I sts, Wash City.

THU JUL 23, 1840
Orphans Court of Wash Co, D C. Letters of administration on personal estate of Jas L Anthony, late of said county, dec'd. –A Binney Anthony, Theodore Fowler, M D, adms. Payments to A Binney Anthony, 12th st, above E.

Hse o/Reps: Rg: Martin Van Buren's *official organ* denounces Gen Harrison as a *"coward,"* a *"granny"*, & a *"petticoat hero."* 1-Ofcrs-11. who fought under Gen Harrison at the battle of Tippecanoe paid him this tribute: Should our country again require our services to oppose a civilized or a savage foe, we should march under Gen H with the most perfect confidence of victory & fame.

Joel Cook	Joshiah Sneeling
R B Burton	O G Burton
Nathan Adams	C Fuller
A Hawkins	G Gooding
H Burchstead	J D Foster
Hosea Blood	

2-Col Davies was killed at the battle of Tippecanoe, Aug 24, 1811.
3-The undersigned, a portion of the surviving members of the Petersburg [Va] Volunteers, now residing in Petersburg. One day of the several sorties, May 5, 1813, we as frequently saw him coolly & deliberately encouraging his ofcrs & men to do their duty. We cannot forbear acknowledging a debt of gratitude of long standing, & yet due to Gen H, for his kind & personal attention to those of our company who were wounded in the engagement on May 5, at Fort Meigs, & for his general deportment towards our crops during our term of service. Jos Scott, John H Smith, Jos Mason, Wm R Chieves, Jas Page, Wm P Burton, R Clements. 4-Cmte of ofcrs who had served nearest Gen H in the Northwestern army, during the late war: Col John B Alexander, a brave & gallant ofcr, head of the cmte. With him were Gen Jos

Markle, Maj Reeves, Col Daily, & Dr McGheehan, all gentlemen of admitted gallantry, intelligence, & high character. They served as ofcrs in the Northwestern army, under Gen H, in the campaign of 1812-13. In command, he was composed yet vigilant. 5-Following general, field, & staff ofcrs of the Nortwestern Army gave their testimonial in writing, in which they express their surprise & regret that charges as improper in form as in substance have been made against Gen H.

Lewis Cass, Brig Gen U S Army
Saml Wells, Col 17th Regt U S Army
Thos D Owings, Col 28th Regt U S Infty
Geo Paull, Col 17th Regt U S Army
J C Bartlett, Col Q M Gen
Jas V Ball, Lt Col
Ropert Morrison, Lt Col
Geo Todd, Maj 19th Regt, U S Infty

Wm Tringg, Maj 28th Regt, U S Infty
Jas Smiley, Maj, 28th Regt, U S Infty
Rd Graham, Maj 17th Regt, U S Infty
L Hukill, Maj & Assist Inspec Gen
Geo Crogham, Maj 17th Regt, U S Infty
Ed Wood, Maj Engrs

6-Fort Meigs, Apr 18, 1813. Sir, the confidence we have entertained of your Excellency as our Genr'l & Cmnder-in-Chief of the Northwestern Army.

David Nelson, Maj
Thos Lingham, Maj
E Cassetts, Surg
John Junkins
J Baracman

Wm Harper
Jas Bonner
Wm Johnson
Thos Jack
Joshua Logan, Adj

7-After their term of service, we are happy in assuring you our fullest confidence, & that of our respective commands, in the measures you have taken.

Edw W Tupper, Brig Gen
Simon Perkins, Brig Gen
Chas Miller, Col
John Andrews, Lt Col
Wm Rayen, Col
Robt Spafford, Lt Col 2nd Regt Ohio quota

N Beasley, Maj
Jas Galloway, Maj
Solomon Bentley, Maj
Geo Darrow, Maj
W W Co_greave, Maj
Jacob Frederick, Maj

8-Maj Willock, of Pittsburg, has borne witness to the bravery & courgage of Gen H. 9-John D Davis, of Pittsburgh, testifes that he was an eyewitness to the services of Gen H on the field of battle. 10-Mr John W Lynch, of Pittsburgh, testifies the same. 11-Mr Pollock, of Muskingum Co, Ohio, in a recent debate in the Hse o/Reps of that state, speaking relative to the battle of Fort Meigs, said: I was in that battle: I saw a cannon ball strike within 2 feet of Gen H during that fight. I was there. Gen H was a brave, prudent & fearless genr'l. 12-Langdon Cheves: on the battle of the Thames: the victory of Harrison-put an end to the war in the Uppermost Canada. 13-Robt Orr, Maj-some years after the termination of the war, had the honor of a seat on this floor. 14-Gen H possessed the confidence & approbation of every U S Pres, from Washington down to the election of Gen Jackson.

In 1791-age 19 years, appointed by Washington an ensign in our army.
1792-promoted to the rank of Lt
1795-made a Capt & placed in command of Fort Washington.

1797-appointed by Pres Adams Sec of the Northwestern Terr, & ex officio Lt Govn'r.
1798-chosen a Del to Congress
1801-appointed Govn'r of Ind, & in the same year, Pres Jefferson appointed him sole com'r for treating with the Indians.
1803 & 06-re-appointed Govn'r by Pres Jefferson.
1809-appointed by Pres Madison, Govn'r of Ind.
1814-appointed by Madison one of the com'rs to treat with the Indians, & in the same year, with his colleagues, Gov Shelby & Gen Cass, concluded the celebrated treaty of Greenville.
1815-again appointed such com'r, with Gen McArthur & Mr Graham, & negotiated a treaty at Detroit
1816-elected a member of Congress
Jan, 1818-introduced a resolution in honor of Kosciusko, & supported it in one of the most feeling & classical, & eloquent speeches ever delivered in the Hse o/Reps.
1819-elected a member of the Ohio State.
1824-elected Senator in Congress, & was appointed, in 1825, Chrmn of the Military Cmte, v Gen Jackson, who had resigned.
1827-appointed Minister to Columbia, & in 1829 wrote his immortal letter to Bolivar, the deliverer of So America.
15-Judge Chinn, of La, who now enjoys the honor of a seat on this floor, tells of the time when he was a boy, in Gen H's army, but being young & unused to the hardships of sldr's life, was having difficulty in keeping up with the march of the troops, & had fallen into the rear, & in danger of being left by the way; Gen H passed him on horseback, & seeing his jaded condition, immediately dismounted, lifted him into the saddle, & walking himself on foot, thus rescued him from the savage scalping-knife. 16-Rev Poe, a Meth crct rider, came to the door of Gen H's abode, late in the evening, upon a feeble & jaded horse, which he had ridden for hundreds of miles, & sought a nite's lodging. He was welcomed with open-hearted hospitality, & when about to depart in the morning, to his great surprise, he found his own saddle & saddle-bags on the back of a fresh & far better steed, provided by Gen H: unknown that his horse had died in the stable. 17-Gen H's residence at North Bend: a plain, old fashioned house, erected some 40 years ago, a part of which is actually built of hewed logs, weatherboarded-the other part is frame work, 2 stories high, painted many years ago white. Furniture is all of old fashioned make, in use perhaps for 40 years. At dinner a large pitcher was set on the table, & when asked to have my glass filled from it, I could not help smiling to find it to be hard cider.
18-Cmte on Expenditures on Public Bldgs: members who examined the vouchers & that upwards of $18,000 of these were for furniture for the Pres' hse made by the Pres & his agents, when there was no cmte of Congress in existence. –Edw Stanly, John W Allen, of Ohio; Chas Naylor
19-Gen Tipton, late of the U S Senate, from Ind, who had served as an ensign in the battle of Tippecanoe, testifies in the regard to Gen H's courage: I think him as brave a man as ever lived.

20-Mr Will, of Ross Co, Ohio, in relation to the battle of the Miami Rapids, was a soldier under Wayne: first met Gen H when he was the aid of Gen Wayne: he was a brave man & a better ofcr I never saw. 21-Jos Loranger, a citizen of Monroe, Mich, was with Gen H at Fort Meigs: I was near him when Gen Proctor demanded the surrender of the Fort, & I heard Gen H say that he would never surrender: the flag of our country waved in triumph over the fort.

Troy Whig: at Schaghticoke, Rensselaer Co, N Y, on Jul 14, John Knickerbacker, s/o Col Wm Knickerbacker, swung his scythe over his shoulder, & with the motion of walking, it entered the calf of his right left, severing one of the arteries, & caused his death in less than an hour.

Mr John Dudley, of Alexandria, who was wounded by the accidental discharge of a cannon on Jul 4 last, died from his wounds on Fri last, & was buried on Sun, a large concourse of citizens following his remains to the grave.

The Southern papers announce the death of Lt Alex C Maury, of the Navy, of congestive fever, on the 23rd ult, in Sumpter Co, Ala.

The Cmte on D C, of which I was a member, was unable in the 8 months session of the Hse o/Reps, to get a single request granted, or a single request or measure emanating from that cmte for a decent hearing or respectful consideration. To the people of Gtwn, I prepared a favorable report on their memorial for retrocession to Md, but I was unable to have a day set apart for considering Dist business.
-Wm Cost Johnson, Wash, Jul 22, 1840.

Appointments by the Pres: 1-Edw Jas Glasgow to be Cnsl of the U S for the port of Guaymas, in the Republic of Mexico. 2-Wm H Haywood, jr, to be U S Atty for the dist of N C. 3-LW Smith to be U S Atty for the Southern Dist of Fla. 4-Robt Butler to be Surveyor of the public lands for the Terr of Fla, for 4 years from Jun 11, 1840, when his former commission expired. 5-Henry L Pinckney, Collector of the Customs at Charleston, S C, v Henry Deas, who declined the appointment.

Mrd: Jul 21, by Rev Dr Laurie, Fred'k A Tschiffely, of Wash, to Eliz A W Berry, of Montg Co, Md.

Died: on Jun 29 last, at Lovettsville, Va, suddenly, after a lingering disease of the heart, Mr John Booth, aged 52 years.

Died: Fri last, at Bedford Springs, in his 33rd year, Capt Washington Hood, of U S Topog Engr Corps.

Orphans Court of Wash Co, D C. Letters of administration de bonis non, with will annexed, on the personal estate of John Leonard, late of said county, dec'd. -W A Bradley, adm d b n with w a

Montpelier Watchman publishes that the undersigned, have heretofore been supporters of the adm of Van Buren, will give now give their support to Wm H Harrison. [Northfield, Jul 4, 1840, all reside there except 1.]

Isaac Kinsman	Rufus Woodbury	Asahel Blake
Parley Tyler	Geo Stanton	Asahel Blake, jr
Simon Engleston	Philander Carpenter	John Bacon, jr
Lyman Houghton	Ichabod Hatch	John Leonard
Wm W Knapp	John Plastridge	Wm Noyes
Wash Morse	Wm Parker	David Colemen-Berlin
Saml W Woodbury	Orace, Emerson	
Rufus Woodbury, jr	Chas F Blake	

Republican Free Press: inhabitants of Colchester, heretofore supporters of Martin Van Buren, now give their support to Wm H Harrison: [Colchester, Jul 14, 1840.]

Chancey Wheeler	Heman Washburn	Elias Lord
Enoch Burbank	Peter Aland	Mark Norris
Jas A Parsons	G W Norton	Asel Harris
Wm Hakins	Wm W Wardwell	Stephen Gale
Reuben Whicher, jr	J S Munson	

$5 reward for return of strayed or stolen small bay gelding. –Wm Keefe, Coachmaker, near 7 Bldgs.

FRI JUL 24, 1840
The whole cmte bolted: the entire Van Buren Vigilance Cmte at Belmont, Ohio, rallied under the patriotic flag of Harrison &Reform:

Wm James	Thos Proe	John Boulfont
Jas McFadden	D Rosebrough	Wm Brammhall
Jas Mitchell	Dorson Finch	M Harrison
John Pollock	David Mercer	Eli Marlow

Gtwn: on Jul 22, Mr Robt Ould, sen, while sitting in coversation with his son at his residence, suddenly fell from his chair & immediately expired. He has for many years been a resident of Gtwn, a highly respectable & useful citizen, having been engaged for many years as the Preceptor of the Lancasterian Free School, his death will be sensibly felt in the community. -Advocate

Columbia [Tenn] Observer of the 10th, contains 2 letters left by the late Edw W Dale, the first dated 4 days before he commtted suicide, & the last on Mon: suicide was committed on Tue. Private pecuniary difficulties appear to have led to this shocking catastrophy. He writes he knew nothing of the robbery of the bank in 1839. I have done some good to my fellow man, but I have also done a great deal of harm, though unintentionally. Sorry to leave his family but he has nothing to live for. -E W Dale

Widow Reuben Young, of Hampden, about 3 miles from Bangor, Maine, with her 2 dghts, on Wed, drowned while bathing in the river. Girls were 18 & 20 years old: They were found by their 16 year old sister.

Mr Z Farrell, of Waltham,Mass, suddenly met his death on Fri week, by the accidental discharge of a pistol in his own hands. He had just returned from a residence of 2 years in the west. He saw the pistol on the mantel, & remarked to his sister that it should't be there. In removing it, he looked into the muzzle, the pistol went off, the ball penetrated his forehead to the brain, causing death within the next hr. Mr Fox was about 30 years of age, an only son.

Orphans Court of Chas Co, Md. Letters testamentary on personal estate of Notly Luckett, late of said county, dec'd. –Alexius Lancaster, Port Tobacco, Md, Exc of Notly Lucket, dec'd.

Phil Co, Jul 10, 1840. The Democratic citizens of Phil Co, purpose holding a Harvest Home Celebration at the Hunting Park, Old York Rd, 4 miles from Phil, on Jul 23: to mingle with the real inhabitants of the Log Cabin & the humble dwlg. –A L Roumbport, W F Bockius, Jos Deal, John Felton, Mathias Hass, Jos Greenough, T Cummiskey. Letter from W W Chapman, of Iowa: dated-Wash City, Jul 2, 1840. Regarding-accepting an invitation to the above meeting. In the last 6 years he has witnessed the wilderness, until then inhabited only by savages & wild beasts of the forest, suddenly converted into meadows & cultivated fields.

Gathering Fri last, the Old Dominion Tippecanoe Club formed & headed by its V P, Maj Hugh M Patton, [in the absence from indisposition, of the Pres, T B Barton,] proceeded to the residence of Mr J S Wellford, paid their respect to Hon Mr Preston; then to the residence of Gen Botts, & paid similar honor to the Hon Mr Wise. Other distinguished guests-the Hon Mr Hoffman, Mr B W Leigh, & Gov Barbour, presented to the Club, received with cheers, & made brief addresses. Col Hugh Mercer, Hon Ogden Hoffman, of N Y; Hon Henry A Wise; John S Pendleton; Mr Cropper, Delegate from Accomac Co; were present & some gave addresses.

Stray cow & calf strayed from the residence of the subscriber on the 23rd: liberal reward to any person delivering them or information where he can find them. –Peter Callan, F & 7th sts

History of the Fed Gov't for fifty years, from Mar, 1789, to Mar, 1839, by Alden Bradford, L L D editor of the Mass State Papers. Just received for sale by F Taylor, immediately east of Gadsbys.

For rent: 2 story brick dwlg on Md ave, east of the residence of Col R M Johnson. Possession given immediately. Apply to Mrs Eliz Thompson, on the premises.

Appointments by the Pres:
Mahlon Dickerson to be U S Judge for the Dist of N J, v Wm Russell, dec'd.
Jas T Archer to be U S Atty for the West Dist of Fla, v Vinton Butler.
Ramom Leon Sanches to be U S Cnsl for the port of Carthagena, in Republic of New Granada.
John J Barley to be U S Cnsl for port of Genoa, in the kingdom of Sardinia, v Robt Campbell, dec'd.
Robt Henry Clements to be a J P for Wash Co, D C.
Richmond Dennis, Register of the Land Ofc at Greensburg, La, v H P Womack, resigned.
Custom-Hse ofcrs: Robt White, Coll, Gtwn, D C, v Thos Turner, resigned.
Robt M Cornelison, Assist Coll for the dist of N Y, to reside at Jersey City, v John J Plumps, appointed during the recess of the Senate.
Jas H Battie, Surveyor, City Point, Va, v Edw Pescud, dec'd.
A H Wildes, Coll, Ipswich, Mass, v Timothy Souther, rsng'd.
David C Judson, Coll, Oswegatchie, N Y, v Smith Stilwell, resigned, to take effect Oct 1, 1840.

For rent: 2 story brick dwlg on Md ave, east of the residence of Col R M Johnson. Possession given immediately. Apply to Mrs Eliz Thompson, on the premises.

Crct Court of Wash Co, D C, Jun 16, 1840. U S vs Kenneth Rayner: indictment for assault & battery. Philip Haas sworn: he was present at the affray which occurred between Mr Rayner, the traverser, & Mr Wm Montgomery, in the Capitol, on May 30. The Hon Geo H Proffit was then sworn on behalf of the dfndnt. Mr Richd S Coxe observed that he had nothing further to lay before the court, on behalf of the dfndnt, except a publication in the Globe. [K Rayner writes: I regret the necessity which compels me to trouble the Public further with this matter, & regret still more the necessity which compelled me, in the first instance, to lay my hands on such a wretch. Wash City, Jul 20, 1840.]

On Wed last, fire broke out in a stable belonging to Dr Bradley, & late in the occupancy of Mr G Kendirck, hack-driver: carelessly set on fire by a person with a lighted candle.

Wash Corp: 1-Ptn from Geo Stewart was referred to the Cmte of Claims. 2-Ptn of John McLeod, praying that the Columbian Academy may be exempt from taxation: referred to the Cmte on Public Schools. 3-Bill for relief of Jos M Munding was taken up, read the 3rd time, & passed. 4-Cmte on Improvements: ptn of Jas Owner & others: rg curbstones: passed.

SAT JUL 25, 1840
Elihu Burritt, the blacksmith of Worcester, Mass, has learned some 50 languages. He still labors daily at his vocation, & pursues his studies with unremitting diligence.

Col J C Odell, a highly respectalbe citizen of Pettis Co, Mo, was murdered on the 3rd inst, by a man by the name of Davis L Owen. Reward of $400 has been offered for the apprehension of Owen.

Died: on Jul 23, Mrs Ann Clephane, aged 38, w/o Mr Jas Clephane, leaving a disconsolate husband & 6 chldrn to lament their bereavement. Her funeral is at 4 p m, this evening.

Negroes wanted: 25 to 30, of both sexes, highest cash prices will be paid.
–Jilson Dove

Mrs Edw J Coale, of Balt, will receive into her family a limited number of chldrn whose parents desire to avail themselves of the advantages offered by the Day Schools of Balt City.

Robt Ould, sen died suddenly at his residence in Gtwn, on Wed. He came into the house from his usual duties, & complained to his son of being very unwell. His physician was sent for; in a few mins arrived, & found him in great agony. He expired in his son's arms. Mr Ould was a pupil & assoc of Jos Lancaster, the founder of the system of education which still bears his name. Mr Ould, with his brother, came to this country in 1811, on a special invitation from some distinguished gentlemen in our District, for the purpose of conducting Lancaster free schools.

MON JUL 27, 1840
Arabian horses at public auct: on Aug 4, in front of my auction store: they were presented by the Imaum of Muscat to the Pres of the U S. Can be seen at the Capitol this morning. –Edw Dyer, auct

The Cunard & Ocean Steam Navigation banqueted in the Pavilion erected for the occasion, in Boston, on Tue. Mr Saml Cunard, the projector, & the Capt, the pioneer of the Liverpool, Halifax, & Boston Line, were present. Mr Grattan was among the guests, & made a brilliant speech. Mr Webster is said to have exceeded himself. Judge Story delivered a powerful address. "The Hon Saml Cunard-the only man who has dared to beat the Queen."

Natchitoches Herald: Capt McCrea, of the U S Army, is alive & doing well, having recovered from the amputation of his leg.

On Thu, on the Falls Rd, about a mile & a half from Balt, the 4 & 6 years old sons of Mr Tansey, a quarryman at Mr Scott's stone quarry, went into an outbldg in which there was some gunpowder, & applied fire to a keg of powder. One of the chldrn was so burnt & mangled as to die almost instantly, & the injuries of the other are so extensive as to forbid the expectation of recovery.

The late Gen Santander, the distinguished Colombian soldier & statesman, died a few weeks since at Bogota, of a severe liver cmplnt: deeply regretted by his countrymen.

Mrd: on Jul 23, in Wash City, by Rev Elias Harrison, the Hon Jos Fornance, of Pa, to Miss Anne B, y/d/o the late Capt John McKnight, of Alexandria, D C.

Died: The last of the Md Line & another Revolutionary hero gone! Departed this life on Tue, at his farm Walnut Grove, in A A Co, Md, Col Gassaway Watkins, in his 85th year.

Died: at New Haven, Conn, Philip Clyme, long well known under the cognomination of Old Clyme, at the advanced age of 96. [No date-current item.]

Died: on Jul 25, Richd Thos, s/o Jas H & Cath Chezum, aged 2 years & 16 days.

$100 reward for runaway negro man Frank: left the residence of Mrs Eliz Gardiner, near Piscataway, PG Co, Md, on Jul 1. He has an uncle living in Wash City. Above reward for the apprehension of said runaway, provided he is returned to me near Bryantown, Chas Co, Md, or secured in any jail so that I get him again. –Jos E Simms, adm de bonis non of Thos C Reeves, dec'd.

Woodstock, [Combaree, S C] Jul 20, 1840. Thunderstorm on the 17th hit the hse that 20 negroes had taken refuge: 2 were severely shocked, 5 stunned, & 9 were killed on the spot. They belonged to the Hon Henry Middleton.

TUE JUL 28, 1840
$200 reward for runaway negroes Peter Carey, about 30, & Moses Fox, about 25, both belonging to Mrs L L Turner, of Alexandria, D C. Peter may have a fur hat manufactured by A Ruff, of Balt. No doubt will direct their course for Canada. Information of the above servants may be directed to E I Lee, Shepherdstown, or to the subscribers. –Jas Brown, L C Cordell, Charlestown, Jeff Co, Va

Locomotive engine for sale: lately finished & ready for delivery. Please address Wm A Jackson, Pres of Fredericksburg U Mfgr Co, Fredericksburg, Va.

Fish, Fish, just received & for sale: near the Steamboat wharves. –R H Lambell

$50 reward for runaway negro Wm: at first sight he would be taken for a white man. Ran away on Jul 21. –Thos W Gardiner, near Chaptico, St Mary's Co, Md

The Army-Genr'l Order. Headqrtrs of the Army: Order #38: Adj Gen Ofc, Wash, Jul 21, 1840.
Corps of Engrs:
2nd Lt Isaac J Stevens to 1st Lt Jul 1, 1840.

Cadet Paul O Hebert, to be 2nd Lt Jul 1, 1840.
Ord Dept:
1st Lt John Williamson, to be Capt May 22, 1840, v d'Lagnel, dec'd.
2st Lt Peter V Hagner, to 1st Lt May 22, 1840, v Williamson, promoted.
Cadet Chas P Kingsbury, to 2nd Lt Jul 1, 1840.
Cadet John McNutt, to be brvt 2nd Lt Jul 1, 1840.
1st Regt of Dragoons:
Cadet Richd S Ewell, to be brvt 2nd Lt Jul 1, 1840.
Cadet John W T Gardiner, to be brvt 2nd Lt Jul 1, 1840
Cadet Wm G Torrey, to be brvt 2nd Lt Jul 1, 1840.
2nd Regt of Dragoons:
1st Lt Alex S Macomb, to be Capt Feb 18, 1840, v Dade, dismissed
1st Lt Croghan Ker, to be Capt May 8, 1840, v Winder, dec'd.
2nd Lt H W Merrill, to be 1st Lt Feb 18, 1840, v Macomb, promoted
2dt Lt Owen P Ranson, to 1st Lt Feb 18, 1840, v Ker, promoted.
Cadet Fowler Hamilton; Cadet Oscar F Winship; Cadet Reuben P Campbell: to 2nd Lt Jul 1, 1840.
Cadet Wm Robertson; Cadet Wm Steele; Cadet Danl G Rogers: to brvt 2nd Lt Jul 1, 1840.
1st Regt of Artl:
Cadet Jas G Martin to 2nd Lt Jul 1, 1840.
2nd Regt of Artl: Cadet Wm Hays to 2nd Lt Jul 1, 1840.
3rd Regt of Artl: 2nd Lt Jas L Rankin to 1st Lt, Apr 1, 1840, v Board, resigned.
Cadets to be 2nd Lts Jul 1, 1840: Wm P Jones, Wm Gilliam, Wm T Sherman, Wm H Churchill, Stewart Van Vliet, Geo H Thomas, Horace B Field.
4th Regt of Artl: Cadets to 2nd Lts Jul 1, 1840:
John P McCown, Francis N Clark, Geo W Getty, Theophile d'Oremieulx, Job R H Lancaster.
Step. D Carpenter to be brvt 2nd Lt, Jul 1, 1840.
2nd Regt of Infty: Cadet Bryant P Tilden, jr, to be 2nd Lt, Jul 1, 1840.
Cadet Jas N Caldwell, to be brvt 2nd Lt, Jul 1, 1840. Cadet John D Bacon, ditto.
3rd Regt of Infty: 2nd Lt Lewis S Craig to 1st Lt, Jun 1, 1840, v Martin, resigned.
Cadet Burhrod R Johnson to 2nd Lt, Jul 1, 1840
Cadet Henry D Wallen, to brvt 2nd Lt, Jul 1, 1840
4th Regt of Infty:
2nd Lt Wm G Grandin to 1st Lt, Apr 1, 1840, v Hooper, resigned.
Cadet Thaddeus Higgins to 2nd Lt, Jul 1, 1840. Cadet Oliver L Shepherd to brvt 2nd Lt, Jul 1, 1840
5th Regt of Infty:
1st Lt Jas L Thompson to be Capt, Mar 1, 1840, v Low, resigned.
2nd Lt Danl H McPhail to 1st Lt, Mar 1, 1840, v Thompson, promoted
Cadet Henry Whiting to 2nd Lt, Jul 1, 1840.
Cadet Pinkney Lugenbeel, to brvt 2nd Lt, Jul 1, 1840. Cadet Thos Jordan, ditto.
6th Regt of Infty:
Cadet Robt P Maclay, to brvt 2nd Lt, Jul 1, 1840. Cadet Douglas S Irwin, ditto.

7th Regt of Infty:
Cadet Chas H Humber, to 2nd Lt, Jul 1, 1840. Cadet Henry Wardwell, to brvt 2nd Lt, Jul 1, 1840.
8th Regt of Infty:
Cadet Jos L Folsom, to brvt 2nd Lt, Jul 1, 1840. Cadet Wm B Johns, ditto.
Medical Dept:
Assist Surgeon Geo F Turner, to be Surg, Jan 1, 1840.
Thos C Madison, of Fla, to be Assist Surg, Feb 27, 1840.
Alfred W Kennedy, of Ky, to be Assist Surg, Jun 15, 1840.
Wm H Van Buren, of Pa, to be Assist Surg, Jun 15, 1840.
Jos K Barnes, of Pa, to be Assist Surg, Jun 15, 1840.
John Robertson, of Dela, to be Assist Surg, Jun 15, 1840.
Levi H Holden, of R I, to be Assist Surg, Jun 15, 1840.
John S Griffin, of Ky, to be Assist Surg, Jun 18, 1840.
Transfer: 2nd Lt Thos L Ringgold, of the 4th Regt of Artl, transferred to the Ord Dept, & will stand on the list next below 2nd Lt Callender.
Casualties: resignations:
Capt Gideon Lowe, 5th Infty, Feb 29, 1840.
1st Lt Buckner Board, 3rd Artl, Mar 31, 1840.
1st Lt Wilmot Ma_in, 3rd Infty, May 31, 1840.
1st Lt John L Hooper, 4th Infty, Mar 31, 1840.
2nd Lt J T Metcalf, Ord, May 31, 1840.
2nd Lt Wm H Korn, 1st Infty, Mar 15, 1840
2nd Lt E W Hardenbergh, 2nd Infty, May 31, 1840.
Assist Surgeon Robt Archer, Feb 29, 1840.
Assist Surgeon Geo R Clark, Jun 17, 1840.
Assist Surgeon R McSherry, jr, Apr 30, 1840.
Deaths:
Capt J A d'Lagnel, Ord, at N Y, May 21, 1840.
Capt Ed S Winder, 2nd Dragoons, Eastern Shore, Md, Mar 7, 1840.
Capt Washington Hood, Corps of Topog Engrs, Bedford, Pa, Jul 17, 1840.
2nd Lt Jas S Sanderson, 7th Infty, 8 miles from Fort Micanopy, Fla, May 19, 1840.
[Sanderson: Killed in action by the Indians in Fla.]
Dismissed:
Capt T Dade, 2nd Dragoons, Feb 17, 1840.
1st Lt W Hardin, 2nd Dragoons, Feb 17, 1840.
By order of Alex'r Macomb, Maj Gen Cmndng-in-Chf: R Jones, Adj Gen
After order: Jul 22, 1840.
Corps of Topog Engrs:
1st Lt Howard Stansbury, to be Capt Jul 18, 1840, v Hood, dec'd.
2nd Lt Lorenzo Sitgreaves to be 1st Lt Jul 18, 1840, v Stansbury, promoted.
Brvt 2nd Lt Geo Thom to be 2nd Lt Jul 18, 1840, v Sitgreaves, promoted.
-R Jones, Adj Gen

WED JUL 29, 1840
Meeting of the citizens of Wash on Jul 27: On motion of Mr Jos H Bradley, Wm W Seaton, Mayor of the city, was called to the chr, & Walter Lenox appointed sec. Resolution by Mr Saml Harrison Smith: appoint cmte as Delegates to a Convention to assemble in Wash City in Aug, that the citizens of Alexandria & Gtwn be invited to appoint a list of Delegates to attend said Convention. Cmte:

Florroardo Howard	John H Goddard	Thos R Riley
John A Blake	Danl Homans	Dr Alex'r McWilliams

Cmte recommended the following citizens to be appointed Dels to the Convention:

Saml Harrison Smith	Walter Jones	Danl Carroll, of Dud'n
Benj O Tayloe	Jos H Bradley	Thos Blagden
Wm Easby	John C Harkness	John W Martin
Alex'r McIntire	Jacob A Bender	Griffith Coombs
Thos Munroe	John C McKelden	Thos R Riley
Jno McClelland	Dr Fred'k May	Noble Young
Anthony Preston	Henry J Brent	Jas Marshall
Wm H Gunnell	Gen Watterston	Dr Alex McWilliams
Wallace Kirkwood	John Kedgely	Robt Clarke
Wm M McCauley	W McGill	Robt Coombs

Mrd: at Framingham, Mass, Philip D Edmonds, of Lowell to Miss Susan Harriet Willis. Also, Thos S Edmonds, of Lowell, to Miss Harriet Susan Willis. The bridegrooms were twin brothers & the brides twin sisters. [No date-current item.]

Died: on Jul 23, at Crawford House, in Portsmouth, suddenly, John L Ball, late a Lt in the U S Navy. The dec'd entered the service of his country in 1822.

Ofc of Potomac Ins Co: meeting for election of Dirs: on Aug 3 next.
–Wm J Goszler, sec

Protection Ins Co: Seth Hyatt, agent-Wash City. –J M Goodwin, sec, Hartford, Conn

Any person or persons found trespassing on the subscriber's farm on the Beaver dam, PG Co, Md, with dog, or gun, or otherwise, will be dealt with according to law.
–Wm Hodge

S S Prentiss, of Miss, arrived at St Louis on the 16th inst, & was waited on by some Whigs, & asked to deliver an address. He consented: citizens turned out en masse: such a display of eloquence, ready wit, sarcastic talents, & power of ridicule, we never before saw combined in any one man. He spoke 3¼ hrs: deathless silence pervaded the dense multitude, except when they gave vent to their uncontrollable feelings in bursts of applause.

To let: 2 new brick bldgs in Northern Liberties, I st, btwn 6th & 7th sts.
–J C McKelden, baker, 7th st

Phil Jul 27. Capt John Barr, of this city, was lost overboard from the ship *United States*, of this port, on Jul 21, just outside the Capes. He formerly commanded the ship *Momtezuma*. The *U S* is owned by Mr Barton. Capt Barr has a wife & chldrn residing in this city. -Lodge

The ship *Illinois* took a very fair portion of passengers this morning. On board were Gen Winfield Scott, Col Bankhead & staff, a large number of ladies, & the band of the 2nd Regt. –Com Adv

Farmers' & Mechanics' Bank of Gtwn, Jul 27. John Kurtz, Pres

American & French Restaurant: just received, by way of the Baldwin train, a large Green Turtle, which he will have dressed when sufficient orders shall be received from the amateurs of Green Turtle Soup, as otherwise it would spoil by the inclemency of the hot weather. –J Boulanger

Wash Corp: 1-Ptn of Z Hazel, praying remission of a fine: referred to the Cmte of Claims. 2-Same cmte was referred the ptn of Harriet Johnson, asked to be discharged from its further consideration.

Appointment by the Pres: John Gardner, Register of the Land Ofc at Winamac, Ind, v Edw A Hannegan, resigned.

In passing thru Middleburg, Loudon Co, Va, a few days ago, the Rev Robt Cadden stated to me that on Christmas eve, about 1815, Gen Harrison arrived in Wmsport, Wash Co, Md, & stopped at Towson's Tavern. The Rev Jas Reed, now in Balt, had made arrangements to form a procession to march to the church, singing an anthem in celebration of the nativity of the Saviour of the world. They passed by the house where Gen H was sleeping. The next morning, a gentleman saluted the Gen, saying he was very sorry that his rest was disturbed this morning by the singing of a parcel of enthusiasts. The Gen replied, "I assure you, sir, my rest was not disturbed, for I thought it was the most heavenly music I ever heard. –John C Green, Brucetown, Fred'k Co, Va, Jul 13, 1840.

THU JUL 30, 1840
Strayed or stolen from my stable on Sun last, a dark bay work horse. $20 for the conviction of the thief-as the door was forced, it may be possible it was stolen. –Thos Burch, a mile west of Bladensburg, PG Co, Md.

Promotions & appointments by the Pres:
Passed Midshipman Henry S Stellwagen to be Lt in the Navy from Jul 2, 1840.
Passed Midshipman Jas L Henderson to be a Lt in the Navy from Jul 6, 1840.
Christopher C Rice, of N Y, to be a Purser in the Navy from Oct 17, 1839.
John B Rittenhouse, of Ala, to be a Purser in the Navy from Jul 21, 1840.
Thos Gadsden, of S C, to be a Purser in the Navy from Jul 21, 1840.

At the late session of the U S Crct Court, at Columbus, Ohio, Justice McLean persiding, Lt Matthew F Maury, of the U S Navy, recovered $2,300 damages, & costs, of the proprietors of the line of coaches on the Nat'l road between Lancaster & Wheeling, for injury sustained by him by the upsetting of a stage, in Oct last, near Somerset. In another case, before the same Court, McKenney vs Neil & others, it was shown satisfactorily to the Court & jury that Messrs Neil, Moore & Co, were very extensively concercerned as stage-coach proprietors, & generally give entire satisfaction to the Public. In this case the driver was incapable of taking charge of the horses. Verdict of damage for the plntf: $5,325.

Appointment by the Pres: Thos James, Receiver of Public Moneys for the dist of lands subject to sale at Danville, Ill, v Stenson H Anderson, who declined the appointment.

Prof Thompson, of Marion College, Mo, formerly of Mass, committed suicide recently in a stage of partial derangement, & was found dead in the woods with a pistol in his hand.

Annual commencement of Gtwn Coll, D C: on Jul 28. Degree of A M conferred on Pemberton P Morris, of Pa, Joshua A Ritchie, of D C, & Nicholas Stonestreet, of Md.

Degree of A B conferred on the following students:

John E Devlin, N Y	T Robt Jenkins, Md	Wm H Lewis, Tenn
W H C Whiting, Miss	Henry Jos Lang, Ga	
Jos B Rindge, Maine	John A Kennedy, N Y	

Students who received silver medals or premiums: [Includes the above named students.]

Hugh Caperton, Va	Alex'r A Simmes, Md
John H O'Neill, Md	Wm E Bird, Ga
Wm S Walker, Miss	Virgil H Walker, Ga
Geo B Clark, D C	Jas M Wilcox, Pa
Thos J Semmes, D C	Wm B Cross, D C
Jos Johnson, La	Alfred Cuthbert, Ga
Saml Lilly, Pa	John M Whiting, La
Wm J Paulding, N Y	Wm M Gardner, Ga
Oscar B Queen, D C	Jos H Stonestreet, Md
Benj Young, Md	Jasper S Whiting, La
Florence J O'Sullivan, Pa	Walter Smith, D C
Walter S Cox, D C	Henry A R Simmons, N Y
Wm M Bradford, Ga	Thos B Phinizy, Ga
John C Thompson, Ga	Jos L Brent, D C
Wm A Colton, Pa	John L May, Ala
Wm P Brooke, Md	Edw C Brent, D C
John L Kirkpatrick, Ga	John T Semmes, Ga

Hugh Caperton, Va	Robt R Aylmer, Va
Sheridan Miles, Md	Wm H Mills, Fla
Robt B Watkins, Va	Robt B Watkins, Va
Michl Wallace, Va	Prosper Landry, La
Henry C Watkins, Va	Talcott Eliason, D C
Walter Warren, Ga	Patrick F Drain, D C
Theodore J Talbot, D C	Edw H Holliday, Ga
Saml Lilly, Pa	Raphael P Neale, Md
Alex H Cross, D C	Justin McCarthy, Cuba
John M Adler, D C	John Wilcox, Pa
Robt M Lusher, S C	John Nevins, D C
Thos B Kenny, Va	Valery Londry, La
Chas R Queen, D C	Robt Kenny, Va
Robt E Luckett, Ga	Robt M Cox, D C
John Wilcox, Pa	John Warren, Fla
Dean Barnes, Pa	Thos R Reordan, Va
John W Archer, Va	John D Twigg, Ga
Adonis Petit, La	Henry B Thompson, Ga
Wm A Colton, Pa	Richd T Merrick, Md
Theodore J Tabot-D C	Thos B Kenny, Va
Wm D McSherry, Va	Manuel Garcia y Abello-Spain
Jos Johnson, La	John Soler y Morell, Cuba
Wm M Bradford, Ga	Emilio Muruago, Spain
Jas Waring, Md	Francisco Garcia y Porto- Spain
Edw Owen, Pa	John McPherson B Lovell- Ga
Wm Marbury, D C	Eugene Cummiskey, Pa
Alex'r M Campau, Mich	Walter S Cox, D C
Luther W Walker, Ga	Virginius B Billisoly, of Va
Peter P Brady, D C	Bartholomew Accinelly, Va
Geo J Marshall, Va	Lycurgus C Valdenar, Md

For sale; farm of about 150 acs on the so side of the Eastern Branch of the Potomac, adjoining the farm of G W Young, known as Upper Gisboro: with brick dwlg house. -Edw Dyer, auct

Orphans Court of Wash Co, D C. Letters of administration the personal estate of Saml F Lowe, late of said county, dec'd. -Geo W Lowe, adm

Hagerstown, Jul 26-the block of bldgs called Hager's Row, in this place, has been burned to the ground. The ofcs of the Torch Light, Herald of Freedon, & Our Flag, were located in said bldgs. Stewart's bookstore & bindery destroyed; Kealhofer's saddler's shop & material on hand a total loss; Ainsworth's hatter's shop, with many of its contents, destroyed; barber's shop & contents destroyed.

FRI JUL 31, 1840
John Varden informs his patrons that after Aug 1, the Museum will be closed until the end of the month for the purpose of refttting & remodeling the rm. [–J V]

House wanted, suitable for the accommodation of a moderate sized family: leave a note describing the premises, situation, terms, & address, at the residence of J M Hepburn, Gtwn.

F Pettrich invites the Public to visit his Studio on Aug 1, where will then be exhibited, for that day only, the first & small model of the Equestrian Statue, hereafter to be executed in colossal size for the city of Phil. No charge for admittance.

The venerable Geo Reed, for the past 31 years a terror to the evil doers in Boston, as a cnstbl, & prior to that a deputy sheriff in Kennebec Co, in the then Dist of Maine, died on Wed, at the age of 72, by his own account, & 82 by the calculations of others who have known him for nearly a century. He was born in the house north to the Federal st Theatre, Boston, of German parents. For 20 years he was the most celebrated rogue catcher in the U S. As a husband, father, & grandfather, he was an example which the best in the community might look up to with benefit. After marrying & settling down in the world by themselves, his chldrn, one by one, died, leaving families, which he gathered under his own roof, & supported, & looked after them. He has probably left some property, perhaps from $2,000 to $3,000.
–Boston Patriot

Mr Jos Gannett, of East Bridgewater, Mass, committed suicide on Jul 20 by hanging himself in a barn. He was a mfgr to some extent, but had become reduced to poverty. He had made several attempts before but was discovered before life was extinct.

Died: on Jul 27, at the residence of his grandfather, Chas Bohn, Balt Co, in his 19th year, Chas B Cross, only s/o Truman Cross, of Balt.

Died: on Jun 7, at Vernon, Oneida Co, N Y, in his 83rd year, Col Lawrence Schoolcraft, a soldier of the Revolution. He rendered active service under Gen Washington's movements on Canada, was at the siege of Fort Stanwix under Gen Gansevoort, & volunteered in the sortie on the British under St Leger & Johnson. After having served the period of his enlistment in the regular army, he returned to his native county, Albany, & as an ofcr of the militia remained in service, in that & the county of Schoharie, during the remainder of the war. He introduced the art & mfgr of glass: with his son, Henry R Schoolcraft, of Mich, established several works in his native state, & in N H & Vt.

Orphans Court of Wash Co, D C. Letters of administration the personal estate of Lt Chas S Ridgley, late of the U S Navy dec'd. –Jas H Causten, adm

J B Morgan has moved on C st, between 8th & 9th sts, to the house formerly occupied by Capt Blake as an auction store, & will be happy to continue to serve his old customers, & all others who may favor him with theirs. Those indebted will be good enough to have their accounts closed as early as possible.

SAT AUG 1, 1840
Laws of the U S passed at the first session of the 26th Congress: 1-Act for relief of Chastelain & Ponvert, & for other purposes: Collector of the Port of N Y is to deduct from the account of a bond given by them, for duties on merchandise imported in the schn'r *Gen Jackson*, Hawes mstr, from Neuvitas, in the island of Cuba, such duties as may have been charged on that portion which was not landed in the U S, having been destroyed by fire in the harbor of N Y. 2-Award made by the accountng ofcrs of the Treas in favor of the owners of the steamboats *Stanca & Dayton*, for services rendered under an agreement with Maj Chas Thomas, Q M, for the transportation of supplies, & laborers, for the use of the works at Fort Smith, Ark, in 1838, $13,350. 3-Payment of an account of Henry Lucas & A P King, of Ala, for the loss & injury sustained by them by the impressment of their teams & wagons into the service of the U S by D H Baldwin, Q M Gen of the Fla militia, in 1836, a sum not to exceed $6,050. 4-Payment of an account of Hart & Bosworth, merchants of Irwinton, Ala, & of John Hart, merchant of the same place, for stores, arms & ammunitions, taken for the use of the troops in the service of the U S by the order of Gen Wm Irwin, commandnt of the 5th Div of the Ala militia, during the Creek campaign of May, 1836, a sum not to exceed $2,311.90. 5-Payment of an account of John H Craddock, of Ala, for property of his destroyed by the order of Col J T Lane, an ofcr in the service of the U S, in Sep, 1836, the sum of $164.63. 6-Payment of a balance due to John Mitchell & Benj F Fox, contractors for the erection of the Branch Mint at New Orleans, as admitted by & recommended from the accountg ofcrs of the Treas, a sum not to exceed $8,588.55. 7-Payment of Chas Gordon, agreeably to the certificate of the Cmte on Public Lands, for services rendered by him in making maps, $2,100. 8-To Pay Auguste Davezac, late Charge d'Affaires of the U S at the Hague, $989.08, being the balance due to him as actg Charge d'Affaires between May 24 & Oct 15, 1831, after deducting therefrom the pay of Sec of Leg during that period, which he has already received. 9-That $11,360.95, be paid to Wm D Jones, in full for diplomatic services rendered to the U S at the Gov't of Mexico, from Dec 28, 1836, to Jul 1, 1839. 10-Nathl Niles to be paid the same outfit, salary, & allowances as tho he had been regularly commissioned as a Charge d'Affaires to Sardinia, from Jun 7, 1837, until Jun 18, 1839, being the termination of his special mission to Sardinia, during which time he negotiated the subsisting treaty between the U S & the King of Sardinia, deducting therefrom the amount of the salary & the contingent expenses which he has already received during the same period as special agent to Austria & Sardinia. 11-The sum of $20,000, in part payment for the expenses incurred by Matthew St Clair Clarke & Peter Force, & for work done by

them, in publishng the 2nd & 3rd vols of the Documentary History of the American Revolution, & for collecting materials for publishng said history. Sum shall not be considered as giving any sanction whatever, by Congress, to any contract alleged to have been entered into between the said Clarke & Force & Edw Livingston, the late Sec of State, under the act of Mar 2, 1833, providing for the publication of said history. 12-Sum of $1,126.57 be appropriated to defray the expenses of calling into service Capt Snodgrass' company of Alabama volunteers to serve as a guard in accompanying a part of emigrating Cherokees from Bellante to Waterloo, in Ala.

Tavern for sale in the village of Port Tobacco, Chas Co, Md, on Aug 20, being Court day, a house & lot in said village, formerly occupied by Capt Brown, & at present by W Shackelford, as a tavern. –Thos H Marshall

The new market in Ward 4 will be opened on Mon, & several butchers will be in attendance with supplies of meat. –H B Merryman, Com'r 4th ward

Died: on Jul 27, at Piney Point, Mary Eliz, d/o Capt A R Hetzel, of the U S Army, aged 10 months.

Died: Jul 19, at the residence of Col Thos Turner, in Granville Co, N C, in her 72nd year, Mrs Courtney Ingles, wid/o the late Col John Ingles, formerly of Wake Co.

MON AUG 3, 1840

Three of the sons of Rev Saml Lotspeich, in Cooke Co, Tenn, near Newport, on Jun 25, were struck by lightning, when they took shelter by a large sycamore tree. Elbert & Hyman, the youngest, were killed.

Mrd: on the Jul 30th, by Rev G G Brooke, Mr Wm T Jones to Miss Cecilia Taylor, all of Wash.

Gen Geo Talcott, of the Ord Dept, encouraged the use of a pair of good substantial cast iron cylinder bellows. They work well, giving a regular steady blast, & supply wind.

To all persons who may be concerned: from & after Jul 8 last, the partnership existing between myself & Jas Mazeen was dissolved, as I am prepared to prove. –John M Keeton, house carpenter

Bacon! Bacon! Bacon! Just received & for sale by Jas Robertson, Gtwn, near the Market.

For rent: a 3 story brick house on 10th st, near Pa ave: premises formerly occupied as a tavern & boarding-house: contains 18 excellent rooms. Apply on the premises- Ann McGunnigle.

TUE AUG 4, 1840

Alligator Line for Mobile, Ala: via the Ga R R cars to Greensboro, thence by stages to Macon, Perry, Pindartown, & Bainbridge, thence by steamers *Leroy & Charleston* to Iola, via Chattahoechie, thence by R R to St Jos', thence per steamers *Champion & Kingston*, via Pensacola, to Mobile. The staging upon the Alligator Line being reduced to 210 miles, much less than by any other route. Leave Augusta every Tue, Thu, & Sat, & assured to arrive in Mobile in 4 days. For seats apply at the ofc at the U S Hotel, Augusta, Ga, to Geo M Dent, agent

Situation of Principal of Brookville Academy being about to become vacant by the resignation of Mr E J Hall, the Trustees will receive applications to fill the vacancy. Salary, the proceeds of tuition, averaging from $800 to $1,000 per annum; the brdghse free of rent, except enough to insure & keep it in repair; & whatever profits may be made by boarders. -Wm B Magruder, Pres't: Brookville, Montg Co, Md.

Crct Court of Wash Co, D C: Mar 31, 1840: case of the ptn of the heirs of Jos Borrows, dec'd. Order passed in this case on Apr 22, 1839, has not been published as therein directed: ordered that the report of the com'rs in this case be ratified, unless cause to the contrary be shown. -Wm Brent, clk

Obit- died: on Aug 1, in his 16th year, Virginius Spence, y/s/o Fleet Smith, after a painful & lingering illness of several weeks. He leaves his bereaved parents, & brother, & sister.

Died: on Jun 26, at her residence, *Woodlawn*, in Pr Wm Co, Va, Mrs Mary Tyler, consort of John W Tyler, in her 40th year, after an illness of 5 days. She leaves a disconsolate husband & family of chldrn. For years she has been in communion with the Episc Chr, a member of Christ, a child of God.

Died: on May 21, at Waterview, in her 36th year, Mrs Eliza Henry, consort of Dr Edw H Henry, & d/o John Fitzhugh, of Pr Wm Co, Va. She was a consistent & devout member of the Meth Episc Chr: from religious instruction she received from her parents. She leaves her husband & 3 small chldrn.

Died: on Aug 1, at Beltsville, PG Co, Md, Mr Frederic W Allen, elder brother of the editor & proprietor of the Madisonian, aged 29 years: native of Pittsfield, Mass, & had resided in Md 2 years.

Died: on Jul 28, Mary Christina, infant d/o Stanislaus & Mary P Murray, aged 7 months & 5 days.

Wash Co, D C: insolvent debtor, W C Kramp, has applied to be discharged from imprisonment. -Wm Brent, clk

Warrenton, Aug 1. The only s/o Jos C Wilson, of Balt, formerly of this county, was drowned in a well on the 27th inst, whilst on a visit to his grandmother, in this county. The child lost its life by the hand of a negro girl belonging to Mr Wilson. She confessed that she had inviegled the child to the well to see a bird's nest-& pushed him in. He was about 8 years old, & an only son. The wretch who has entailed all this misery, & her husband, have both been committed to jail, to wait the judgment of the law. –Times

Liberal reward for strayed cow: John Coburn, 17th st & Pa ave, near War Ofc.

$50 reward for runaway negro man Harrison. Said negro belongs to Mr Cumberland George, of Culpeper Co. Deliver to us at Charlottesville, Va. –Phillips & Word

WED AUG 5, 1840
Wm M'L Cripps has on hand & continues to make all kinds of furniture: stand, 11th st, near Pa ave. He is now making those fashionable German Low Bedsteads. Funerals attended to promptly.

John Young, age 74, of Niagara, who was returning from Montreal home with his wife, threw himself overboard from the steamer *Great Britain*, on Lake Ontario, while in a state of derangement, & was drowned. He had been some time sick: was one of the most wealthy & long-est'd merchants in Upr Canada, of high mercantile standing, & a very exemplary man.

Mrd: on Jul 29, by Rev Mr Matthews, Mr Simeon Bronson to Miss Mgt Rixter, both of Wash City.

Mrd: on Apr 29 last, in Pulaski Co, Ark, by Rev Wm W Stevens, Chas H Wagner to Amelia Ann Osbourn, of Wash City.

Died: on Jul 17, in Newbern, N C, in his 58th year, John W Guion, Cashier of the Merchants' Bank of Newbern, a highly respectable & worthy citizen.

Died: on the 21st ult, in Easton, Pa, after a short illness, Mr Solomon Grotz, Printer, in his 25th year.

Died: on the 20th ult, at Stroudsburg, Pa, Mr John A Carter, Printer, in his 31st year. His death was occasioned by wounds received on Jul 4, by the unexpected explosion of a cannon which he was in the act of loading.

Died: on Jul 27, in St Mary's Co, Md, Colbert Good, in his 29th year, after a few hours of intense suffering, leaving an affectionate wife & 2 small chldrn, with many near & dear relatives.

Wash Corp: 1-Ptn of Jasper Duflon: referred to the Cmte on Claims. 2-Ptn of W P Ferguson & others: referred to the Cmte on Improvements. 3-Ptn of Richd Butts & others, praying for the opening of an alley in sq 404: referred to the Cmte on Improvements.

Extensive sale of excellent household furniture: on Aug 5, at the residence of Mrs Mary Ronckendorff, on Pa ave, between 3rd & 4½ sts. -Ed Dyer, auct

THU AUG 6, 1840
On Tue last, an attempt was made to set fire to the new & handsome Tinner's Shop & Stove Factory lately erected by Mr Clement Woodward, on D st, between 10th & 11th sts, in Wash City: happily it was aborted. The Mayor, W W Seaton, offers $200 reward for information which shall lead to the discovery & conviction of the perpetrator.

Cash for negroes: from 40 to 50 servants, such as farm hands & hse servants. Call on me at my establishment on 7th st. -W H Williams

For sale: a nearly new valuable machine for getting out wheat: now at *Delacarlia*, late the residence of Clement Smith, dec'd, & will be shown by Wm B Thompson, now residing there. -Walter Smith

FRI AUG 7, 1840
Jas Lewis, a citizen of Petersburg, Va, committed suicide on Sat night, by cutting his throat with a carving knife. He was laboring under a fit of insanity produced by excessive drinking.

Official: Navy Dept, Jul 10, 1840. Naval Gen Court Martial convened at the Navy Yard, Phil, on May 4 last, for the trial of Cmdor Jesse D Elliott: Court composed of ofcrs:

Cmdor Jacob Jones, Pres	Capt Foxhall A Parker
Cmdor Lewis Warrington	Capt David Conner
Cmdor John Downes	Capt John D Sloat
Cmdor E P Kennedy	Capt Geo W Storer
Capt Chas W Morgan	John M Read, Phil, Judge Adv

Upon this oppressive & cruel order being communicated to Dr Thos J Boyd by Lt Boerum, Dr Boyd went into the cabin of Capt Elliott, & then & there remonstrated personally to the said Capt Jesse D Elliott against the removal of P Mid Chas C Barton from the ship *Constitution* to the schn'r *Shark*, & afterwards, on the same day, remonstrated against such removal by letter addressed to the said Capt E, which letter was delivered to him, the said Capt E, before the removal of the said P Mid Barton, which paragraph is not proved. The Court is of opinion that the 3rd specification of the first charge is not proved; & the Court is of the opinion the first charge is fully proved, & does accordingly adjudge the accused guilty of the same. The Court is of the opinion that the 1st & 2nd specifications of the 2nd charge are not

proved, & does accordingly adjudge the accused not guilty of the 2nd charge. The Court does therefore sentence & adjudge the said Capt Jesse D Elliott to be suspended for the term of 4 years from this date, & that his pay & emoluments, be suspended during the first 2 years of his suspension. Approved, Jul 6, 1840. –J K Paulding [Article is 3 cols: Oppression & cruelty, & conduct unbecoming an ofcr. This is specification #1: For that he, the said Jesse D Elliot, being in command of the naval forces of the U S in the Mediterranen Sea, did, on Nov 30, 1835, oppressively & cruelly order Chas C Barton, a P Mid in the U S Navy, who was severely wounded in his right leg, & who was then on board the U S ship *Constituion*, under the medical charge of Dr Thos J Boyd, Surgeon of the Fleet, for the said wound, to be removed from the *Constitution*, then lying in the harbor of Smyrna, to the U S schn'r *Shark*, against the expressed objections & remonstrances of Dr Boyd, & did cruelly cause Barton to be removed, causing him great & excruciating pain, & endangered not only the leg, but also the life of him, the said Barton. Spec #2: Barton wounded in the right leg by a ball, which passed through the tibia, fracturing it transversely, & splintering it into fragments, was operated on by Dr Boyd, who extracted the ball.] The finding & sentence of the Court has been approved by the Sec of the Navy. Suspension of pay & emoluments has been remitted by the Pres of the U S.
–M Van Buren

Died: on the 22nd ult, at *Oatland*, Montg Co, Md, Mrs Mgt C Bowie, relict of Warrington Bowie, formerly of Gtwn, D C, in her 67th year.

Valuable land for sale known as the *Manor*, in PG Co, Md: tracts contain from 5,000 to 6,000 acs. Apply to John Calvert, living on part of said tract. Or to-Chas B Calvert.

$5 reward for runaway indented colored boy Wm Roach, about 17. He has worked at the butcher's business & attended with me at my stall in the Centre Market.
–John Bohlayer

SAT AUG 8, 1840
Book of Shipwrecks & Narratives of Maritime Discoveries & Interesting Voyages, & Naval Adventures, from the time of Columbus to the present day, 1 octavo vol of 492 pages, filled with engravings, & full bound in leather. Price.75. –F Taylor

Sealed proposals will be received for improving C st; likewise for the construction of a wooden bridge over the run on 2nd st. –Wm Cooper, jr, com'r-Ward 3
-Benj E Gettings, W W Lowe, Assist Com'rs.

Wm Linkins who has applied for the benefit of the act is not Wm Linkins, Butcher.

Rev Courtland Van Rensselaer, of Burlington, N J, was elected pastor of the 2nd Presby Church of Wash, at a meeting held on Jul 22nd.

Hagerstown, Md: on Aug 5, a duel was fought, within 2 miles of Hancock, in Morgan Co, Va, between Wm Price, of Hagerstown, & Hon Francis Thomas, of Fred'k. One fire was exchanged without effect. The challenge was then suspended, & an explanation, satisfactory to both parties, took place. -Torch-Light

Death of one of the brave sldrs of the Revolutionary war: was brought to us by our venerable townsman, Mr Jacob Gideon, his fellow soldier, who was himself in every battle in which Everhart was engaged. Nat'l Intell. We learn through the Hagerstown Herald, that Sergeant Lawrence Everhart died on Sun last, at his residence near Middletown, Fred'k Co, Md, in his 85th year. He belonged to Col Wm Washington's troop of cavalry, & on one or two occasions saved the life of his commander. A friend says he was born in Fred'k Co, on *Carroll's Manor*, about 16 miles from the place where he died. He enlisted in the Continental Army early in 1776: was in the battles of Germantown & Brandywine in the north, & in the battle of Guilford Court Hse, Camden, Monk's corner, & the Cowpens, in the south.

As the train of cars was coming from Harper's Ferry last night, one of the firemen, Mr Jas Briggs, fell between the engine & tender, & one of his legs was so horribly mashed as to render amputation immediately. Prof N R Smith operated upon the limb.

Mr Jos Smith, of Shepherdstown, Va, committed suicide by hanging himself in the basement of his dwlg on Sun last. The event has filled his friends & acquaintances with surprise, as Mr S was a gentleman of easy circumstances, an upright & moral character. However, since the death of his wife, to whom he was ardently attached, he has been subject to fits of melancholy.

MON AUG 10, 1840

Mrd: on Thu last, by Rev Mr Ryland, Mr Chas E Mitchell to Miss Mary Jane, only d/o the late Capt Michl Bulley, all of Wash City.

Died: Aug 9, in Wash City, Mrs Mary Ann Carothers, aged 34 years, after a lingering disease of several months, leaving a husband & 4 chldrn. Her funeral is from her late residence on F st, today at 4 p m.

Died: on Aug 9, Victoria Rowena, infant d/o Richd L & Martha Spalding, aged 9 months. Her funeral is today at half past 3.

It appears that Capt Elliot is sentenced to 4 years leisure, with full pay. Mr Wall's bill was to authorize the Sec of the Navy to put an ofcr on furlough & half pay at his discretion, & that was not deemed a power to punish; so that it is the additional half pay which makes the punishment. According to this logic, Barton might be recompensed for his suffering by allowing him 4 years service & no pay. –Q E D

The Jonesborough Whig of the 22nd inst notices the death of Susan Gaines, sister of Gen Gaines, in Kingsport, at an advanced age; Dr E R Dulaney, of Blountville; Adam Shipley & 3 of his chldrn in the vicinity of Jonesborough; Wm Crawford, aged 15, & Capt John Hoes, all of Jonesborough.

The 8 year old s/o Mrs Stanford, brdg house keeper on Bridge st, Gtwn, was drowned in the Canal, at the Wash st bridge, on Thu last. His elder brother stated that he had left him about dusk sitting on the wall of the canal. Parents cannot be too strict in forbidding their chldrn from playing near the canal.

Dissolution of the partnership existing under the firm of Anderson & Espey: by mutual consent. Settlement by R P Anderson, by whom the business will be conducted. –R P Anderson, John Espey

TUE AUG 11, 1840
Fresh Ruta Baga Seed at Saml Redfern's Grocery, corner of 19th & Pa ave.

Public sale of valuable land: by powers vested in him by the last will & test of Mary Ann O'Neale, late of Montg Co, Md, dec'd, Wm Chiswell, exc of M A O'Neale, dec'd, will sell, at the Hotel of Jas Black, in Cumberland, Aug 29: 6 lots of ground that front on the C & O R R. 21 lots, from 8 to 40 acs, adjoins the lands of Mr Geo Thistle. Prop known as *Bell's Island*, in the Potomac river, about 40 acs. Portion of the second part of *The Brothers*-156 acs, on the west side of Evitt's crk. Tract called *The Surprise*, 183 acs, on the east side of Evitt's crk. Titles are indisputable. Plats can be seen in the possession of Jas Smith, at Cumberland. –Wm Chiswell, Cumberland

Charlottesville Academy, by A Duke & P Powers. Exercises will be resumed on the first Mon in Sep. Address the above, c/o Alex Garrett, Charlottesville, N H. References: Govn'r Gilmer & the Profs of the Univ. –P Powers

$20 reward for the recovery of my horse, which was stolen from my farm near Benedict by a certain Edwin B Harwood, on Aug 2. Harwood is about 6 feet high, sandy hair, dark eyes, rather a good-looking fellow: raised in PG Co, Md. –Jno W Lamar, Benedict, Chas Co, Md.

By deed of trust, made by Geo W Dashiell, sale-Sep 10, all right, title, & interest of Geo W Dashiell in: lot 2 of the subdivision of lots 1 & 2 in square 490, & part of lot 25 in same square, with houses & bldgs thereon, subject, nevertheless, to a deed made to Wiltberger & Selden in favor of B Pollard. –W W King, trustee

Died: on Aug 1, at Red Bank, N J, Anna Maria, d/o Capt S Eastman, U S A.

Died: on Aug 10, at the residence of John L Brightwell, Owen Brightwell, only s/o Owen H & Eliza Bestor, aged 20 months.

Mrs Dyson's Seminary for Young Ladies, corner of G & 9th sts, will resume on Sep 1 next.

WED AUG 12, 1840
Female Institute, Columbia, Maury Co, Tenn: wanted by Sep 1, 2 ladies skilled in music, & a 3rd to take charge of the higher Eng Classes. To each a salary of $500 in addition to board & washing. No travelling expenses paid. Refer, if by letter post paid, to Rev Dr Colton, Gamlber, Ohio, the Rev Dr Seaberry, N Y, the Rev Mr Hooker, Phil. –F G Smith, rector

Jos Beach, Postmaster of Ridgeville, Madison Co, N Y, instead of soliciting dollars for Mr Kendall, has boldly declined that work. Letter to the ex-Pmstr Gen-Hon Amos Kendall: a candidate for re-election to the Presidency is asking the suffrages of our people, & at the same time is unwilling to admit that during the almost 4 years of his admin the public Treas has been plundered by more than a hundred hands. Under Mr Van Buren's adm laws have been violated with impunity; moral obligations scoffed at & discarded; knavery walks the streets with the bold face of honesty; even the high public functionaries who scoff at & disregard the authority of the highest judicial tribunal in the country, obtain sympathy & forgiveness. Yours, for Harrison, Tyler, & Reform, Jos Beach, P M, Ridgeville.

Tue on board the ship *Erie*, Capt Titus, when ascending the Detroit river, about 3 miles from Maiden, the steam chimney burst: Wm Dely, fireman, badley scalded: Chas Hamborlin, do; Edw Erwin, deck hand, dangerously; Timothy Buckley, do, do. Andrew Looney, a resident of Fort Gratiot, badly scalded. Jas Corey, of Buffalo, deck passenger, has a family here, also badly scalded-died. The ship *Great Western*, Capt Walker, coming down, met the Erie soon after the accident, & took her in tow. Mr Baby, Sheriff of the Western Dist, Upr Canada, sitting on the deck with his niece, heard the explosion, & attempted to throw her overboard. A person nearby caught her by the arm, & Baby, in the ecstacy of his fear, jumped overboard himself. He sunk before assistance called be rendered him. –Com Adv

Thos Rich is the sec of the Franklin Fire Co: meeting on Wed. [Wash & Gtwn area.]

Mrd: on Aug 6, by Rev Mr Bean, Mr Levi Scott to Miss Mary Davis, all of Wash City.

Died: in Gtwn, D C, at the residence of his father, Mr Jas Remington, printer, in his 26th year. Funeral this evening at half past 5 p m. [No date-current item.]

Died: on Aug 2, in Northumberland, Pa, in her 30th year, Mrs M J Woods, w/o Mr C Woods, & d/o the late Rev Robt Little, after a long & painful illness.

I hereby forewarn all persons against paying any account due to Payne & Iddins, & against paying, purchasing, or receiving in any way any notes made payable to Payne & Iddins, to said Iddins, or any other person, without my special permission.
–Thos Payne

For rent: the Union Hotel in Gtwn, D C: recently rebuilt: 50 to 60 lodging rooms.
–W S Nicholls, John Kurtz, E M Linthicum

THU AUG 13, 1840
N Y, Aug 11. The appearance of a letter from Bronk Van Buren in the Kinderhook [V B] paper, announcing that he was the author of an effigy clad in a petticoat, which was showed to insult the Whigs of Kinderhook in their celebration of Jul 4, attracts attention, from the fact that Bronk Van Buren is the nephew of Mr Pres Van Buren.

Recent meeting of the Columbian Horticultural Soc: Col Henry Naylor; Master Perkins; John Agg; Joshua Peirce; J F Callan; Mrs Seaton: exhibited their vegetables or flowers.

FRI AUG 14, 1840
Missouri election for Govn'r: Gen John B Clark, [Whig,]-1079 votes. M M Marmaduke, [Loco] 581 votes.

Maj Wm Fay, editor of the Rutland Herald, died at Rutland, Vt, on the 31st ult, in his 60th year. He had been for nearly 40 years a faithful laborer in the political vineyard. He was an apprentice with the late Judge Buell.

Master Geo S Robinson, an interesting boy aged 13 years, was instanly killed at Norfolk on Sat last while looking at the operation of heaving down a schn'r. The mast of the vessel broke about midway up from the deck, & the spar & rigging fell directly on him.

Henry Cahmann McNeill, s/o Maj Wm G McNeill, of N Y C, died, while bathing with some companions in the Conn river, at Springfield, when venturing out too far, he suddenly disappeared. His body has been recovered. He had been educated at the school of Messrs Pougnet & Brothers, in N Y, & was on a visit at his uncle's, Lt Whitler's, at Springfield, when this fatal event took place.
–N Y Cour

Fatal affray between Mr F W Quackenboss & Jas H Hunter, of Yazoo City, on the 20th ult, resulted in the death of Hunter, he being shot thru the head. Mr Q gave himself up: unanimous acquittal by the magistrates composing the Court.

Mr & Mrs Michard propose opening on Sep 1, a Female Seminary in the First Ward, Wash City.

Appointed by the Pres: Philip Schuyler, of N Y, to be U S Cnsl for the port of Liverpool, v Frances B Ogden, resigned: his commission to take effect from Oct 15 next.

Mrd: on Aug 11, at Jackson Hill, by Rev Mr Thornton, Danl Gold, of Delhi, N Y, an assist clerk in the Hse o/Reps, to Miss Mary Ann Kendall, d/o the late Postmaster Genr'l.

Mrd: on Aug 6, by Rev T C Thornton, Mr Jos Goodyear to Miss Eleatha Meade.

Mrd: on Aug 11, by Rev T C Thornton, Mr Thompson H Saunders to Miss Ann C Davis, both of Loudoun Co, Va.

Mrd: on Tue last, in Wash City, by Rev Mr Smith, Mr Joshiah Goodrich to Miss Harrriet Elliott, all of this place.

Died: on Aug 8, in Gtwn, D C, after a long & painful illness, Miss Eliz Swann, in her 19th year.

List of defaulters under the present administration: the Gov't, under Martin Van Buren, has lost nearly one-half as much as was lost under all the previous administrations for 48 years!

Saml Swartwout, N Y	$1,225,705.69
Wm M Price, N Y	$75,000.00
A S Thurston, Key West, Fla	$2,822.14
Geo W Owen, Mobile, Ala	$11,173.49
Israel P Canby, Crawfordsville, Ind	$39,013.31
Abner McCarty, Ind, Ind	$1,338.92
B F Edwards, Edwardsville, Ill	$2,315.76
W L D Ewing, Vandalia, Ill	$16,754.29
John Hays, Jackson, Miss	$1,386.16
Willis M Green, Palmyra, Mo	$2,312.12
B S Chambers, Little Rock, Ark	$1,146.28
David L Tod, Opelousas, La	$27,230.57
B R Rogers, Opelousas, La	$6,624.37
Maurice Cannon, New Orleans	$1,259.28
A W McDaniel, Wash, Miss	$6,000.00
John H Owen, St Stephen's, Ala	$30,611.97
Geo B Crutcher, Choctaw, Miss	$6,061.40
Geo B Cameron, Choctaw, Miss	$39,059.64
S W Dickens, Choctaw, Miss	$11,831.91
S W Dickens, Choctaw, Miss	$898.53
Wiley P Harris, Columbus	$109,178.08
Wm Taylor, Cahawba, Ala	$23,116.18
U G Mitchell, Cahawba, Ala	$54,626.55

J W Stephenson, Galena, Ill	$3,294.04
Littlebury Hawkins, Helena, Ark	$100,000.00
S W Beall, Green Bay	$10,620.19
Jos Friend, Washita, La	$2,541.91
Wm H Allen, St Augustine	$1,997.50
Gordon D Boyd, Columbus, Miss	$50,937.29
R H Sterling, Chocchuma, Miss	$10,733.70
Paris Childers, Greensbrug, La	$12,449.76
Wm Linn, Vandalia, Ill	$55,962.06
Saml T Scott, Jackson, Miss	$12,550.47
Jas T Pollock, Crawfordsville, Ind	$14,891.98
Morgan Neville, Cincinnati, Ohio	$13,781.19
M J Allen, Tallahassee, Fla	$26,621.57
Robt T Brown, Springfield, Mo	$3,600.00

On Mon last an inquest was held in view of the body of a free nego named Thos McDowner, who was found dead that day in his dwlg, near the Baptist Meeting-hse, near 4½ st. Dec'd came to his death by a spasmodic affection of the bowels: the unfortunate man had been addicted to intemperance.

$5 reward for strayed cow: -John Pettibone

For sale low, near the corner of Mr Nourse's Exchange Ofc, 13th st, Misses Corsets, & Braces for both sexes; also linen drilling French corsets at $2 & $2.50; also gentlemen's shoulder braces at $2.00

Wash Corp: 1-Ptn from E Lindsley & others, for the construction of a reservoir in the third ward: referred to a cmte consisting of Messrs Randolph, Clarke, & Marshall. 2-Ptn of D O'Donnoghue & others, for making an appropriation for enlarging the passage to the water thru the run which crosses G st north, between 4th & 5th sts: laid on the table. 3-Cmte of Claims: asking to be discharged from the further consideration of the ptn of Harriet Johnson was taken up, & agreed to.

Cash for negroes: for the Louisiana market: can be found at the Steamboat Hotel, formerly kept by Thos Lloyd, & now by B O Shekell, on 7th st, opposite the Centre Market. –Jas H Birch

SAT AUG 15, 1840
Iowa lands: description of the U S lands in Iowa, full & complete of every section, 1 vol-just published. For sale by F Taylor.

Died: on Wed, Mrs Mary Daery, in her 20th year.

Died: on Aug 11, at Claysville, Montg Co, Md, Mrs Ann Redman, consort of Josiah Winn Redman, in her 49th year. She died as she had lived, a devoted Christian.

Small farm for sale: a tract of land in Montg Co, Md, 138½ acs: with convenient stone spring-house on the premises: about 8 miles from Wash City.
–Cath E A Reynoldson

MON AUG 17, 1840
We learn from the Poughkeepsie that Maj Hatch, keeper of one of the principal hotels in that place, was killed by lightning on Wed. No other person was seriously injured.

My school will be re-opened on Aug 17, in that commodious room over the Western market, for the instruction of youth. –John M Allison

N Y Whig Convention: from the Albany Evening Journal: Utica, Aug 12, 1840. Speeches were made by the Hon N P Tallmadge, the Hon Mr Stanly, of N C, Hiram Ketchum, of N Y, Alfred Kelley, of Ohio, a s/o Danl Webster, of Ill, & the Rev Mr Southard, of N Y. Tippecanoe songs were sung by Mr Hoxie, of N Y, & Mr Covert, of Albany. Peter R Livingston presided: Govn'r Seward & Lt Govn'r Bradish were nominated by resolution for re-elected. The Hon Jas Burt, of Orange, a venerable soldier, statesman, & patriot, who was a Jeffersonian elector for Pres in 1800, & Gen Peter B Porter, of Erie, who fought with a lion's heart & courage at Chippewa & Fort Erie, were nominated by acclamation for Senatorial electors. Following electoral ticket was nominated:

Abraham T Rose	Elbridge G Mesick
John T Harrison	Isaac Ogden
John L Lawrence	Saml Balcom
Jos Tucker	Peter Pratt
J Phillips Phoenix	Jacob Livingston
Richd S Williams	John J Knox
Pierce Van Cortland	John Williams
Barte White	B Davis Nozen
Nathl Dubois	John J Speed
Peter G Sharp	Danl Hibbard
Elisha Jenkins	Grattan H Wheeler
Hervey Watson	Albert Crane
Archibald M'Intyre	Chas Bradish
Griffith P Griffith	John Wheeler
Earl Stimpson	Gideon Lee
Josiah Hand	Davis Hurd
Keyes P Cool	Phineas L Tracy
Jonathan Wallace	Wm Garbutt
H P Voorhies	Henry R Seymour
Thos Buck	Phile Orton

Patriot, Jun 20, 1840. We, the undersigned citizens of Posey township, Switzerland Co, Ia, supporters of Martin Van Buren, do declare that we cannot, as Democratic Republicans, support the administration any longer; therefore have made up our minds to support Harrison & Tyler:

farmers:

Wm Nott	R R Hutcherson
Benj Stogdale	Jos Bonnell
Chas Beaty	Jas Wade
John Wilson	Jesse Turner
Michl Long	Jeremiah Kinney
Chas Van Boren	Vincent Rudd
Madison Chase	Standford Rudd
W Johns	Erastus Rudd
Jas Chase	John W Cochran
Robt Seymour	Aaron M Cochan
Seth Samson	

Laborers: 3

David Shave	John Taylor, jr
Lazarus Yocum	

Mechanic: 1
Wm Clark

Portland [Maine] Adv: were supporters of the administration, now supporters of Gen Wm H Harrison: [Entirely mistaken in Martin Van Buren, as far as related to his democracy, honesty, or capability.]
We are all laborers, farmers, & mechanics:

Jos Barton	Mark Trafton
Danl Woodman	Geo Farmsworth
Wm L Wheeler	Warren Preble
Danl M Barker	Henry Preble
Jas D Littlefield	Jos Woodman
Wm Trafton	

[All of Norridgewock, Aug 3, 1840.]

Died: on Thu last, S D Langtree, infant s/o J L & Ann Anderson, aged 11 months.

Groceries at auction on Aug 19, at the store of Edw Chapman, on Bridge st: sale of his remaining stock. -T C Wright, auct

Albany Lumber: D E Thomas, ofc head of Union dock, on the Falls, below Pratt st bridge, Balt.

$10 reward for strayed mare: also a large sorrel horse. Give information to me or to Wallace Kirkwood, Wash. -Correll Brooks, corner of 12th & D sts, Wash City.

$10 for a stolen lean Roan Horse, saddle & bridle: stolen from the Campmeeting near Horse Head, PG Co, Md, on Aug 11. –Edw Bean, near Horse Head

TUE AUG 18, 1840
Wash Co, D C: this is to certify that John Peake, of said county, brought before me a buffalo cow that was trespassing on his enclosure: lives on Greenleaf's Point. –Edw Mattingly, J P

Gen J W Pegram having accepted the ofc of Cashier of the Bank of Va, has addressed a letter to the Chrmn of the State Central Cmte, B W Leigh, requesting some other name be substituted for his on the Whig Electoral Tkt.

Richd, Va, Aug. Wm Meeker, about 23 years of age, shot himself on Sun, at the house of Mr J P Hodgden, his relation, of this city. He died in a few minutes; was a carpenter by trade. –Compiler

Alex'r Ray has opened an agency ofc for the purpose of prosecuting claims against the Gen Gov't, & before Congress. From a long & intimate acquaintance with the transaction of business with the ofcrs of Gov't, he feels assured of being able to give satisfaction. Reference may be made to Maj Gen Macomb, Col J J Abert, Chief of the Topog Engrs, & Richd S Coxe. -A R

Boston, Aug 14. Richd R Wiley, age 19 years, with a friend, while climbing cliffs at Little Nahant, had a large mass of rock fall upon him, wounding him dreadfully. He died yesterday. -Jrnl

The Prince of Canino, Lucien Bonaparte, died at Viterbe, on Jun 29, at age 66. He was the 2nd brother of Napoleon, & born in 1775: exiled from Corsica in 1793: was Minister of the Interior after the French Revolution: then ambassador to Spain. Quarrelling with Napoleon about his 2nd marriage, he separated himself from politics. He was taken prisoner by the English off the coast of Malta, & fixed his residence at Ludlow. At the peace of 1814 he went to Rome, but returned to Paris on Napoleon's escape from Elba. After the final overthrow of his brother he retired to Italy, where he passed his remaining days.

Havana, Jul 23. On Jul 22nd, 5 pirates were shot on the Mole: Francis Dennis alias Davis Francis Laores, John D Armas, Juan Romero, natives of Canary Isls; Augustin Lopez alias San Martin, native of Portugal; Lorenzo Fernanez, native of Porto Rico; convicted of the crime of piracy by the Marine Court, sentence approved by his Excell the Govn'r of the Isl. These culprits were published in the Bulletin at the time as having captured the English brig *Vernon*, on her voyage from Falmouth, Jamaica, to Halifax, & who murdered Capt Cunningham & several sailors, plundered the cargo, & burned the vessle. The sentence was that the head of David should be cut off & placed at the highest point of Cape Antonio, the scene of the piracy. Heads of the others were to be taken off & placed about the harbor of Havana.

John Terhune wishes to obtain a situation as teacher in some pvt family at the south. He is a graduate of Nassau Hall, Princeton, N J, from whose Professors he brings recommendations. He would prefer the family of a lawyer, as he intends to pursue lgl studies. –J T, Atsion, Burlington Co, N J

Mrd: on Aug 9, at Spartanburg, S C, by Rev Mr Landrum, Hosea J Dean, Atty at Law, of the former place, to Mary, only d/o Mr Edw Owen, of Wash City.

Died: on Aug 12, at his late residence in Essex Co, Va, Robt S Garnett, Collector of the port of Tappahannock, after a long & distressing illness.

Died: on Aug 6, at the Nat'l Hotel, in the city of St Louis, Capt Wm Day, of the U S Army.

Died: on Aug 6, in Frankfort, Ky, Mrs Sarah Ann Harris, d/o the late Achilles Sneed, & consort of Lt Wm S Harris, of the U S Navy, in her 34th year.

WED AUG 19, 1840

Wash Corp: 1-Memorial from Jos Stephenson & others: referred to the Cmte on Improvements. 2-Memorial from Levi Pumphrey & others, against the passage of the bill to regulate the weighing of hay, straw, & fodder: referred to the cmte on that subj. 3-Ptns of M Shanks & others, concerning the present graduation & conveyance of water on 9th st, near N Y ave; also of Jas Towles & J S Wilson, on same subject; referred. 4-Ptn of Geo Crandell & others, praying for curb stone & a footway in front of sq 404. 5-Police Magistrate for the 4th Ward to be designated, vice W Brent, resigned.
4-Duly elected Trustees of the Public Schools:

Rev Wm Matthews	G H Fulmer
Rev Wm Hawley	Richd Barry
Jas Larned	Jas Carbery
John D Barclay	Jas Marshall
Wm Lloyd	Rev A T McCormick
W B Magruder	Thos Blagden
John W Maury	Rev G G Brook

Mrd: on Aug 6, by Rev Dr Wilson, Lt Geo Minor, of the U S Navy, to Miss Ann Eliza Chew, of Fredericksburg.

Mrd: on Aug 11, by Rev Mr Bean, Lt Wm L Young, U S M, of N C, to Miss Ann E, eldest d/o Marmaduke Dove, of Wash City.

Died: on Aug 18, suddenly, Mrs Matilda Koones, relict of David Koones. Funeral today at 5 p m.

Died: on Aug 16, Benj Duncan, late High Sheriff of the city & county of Phil, in his 50th year.

Mr Adam Barnes, jr, a resident of Freedom Dist, Carroll Co, Md, while on his way home from New Windsor, on Sat last, was thrown from his horse, by which accident his skull was so badly fractured the he was deprived of all sensibility. Having a friend with him, he was removed to the hse of Mr Jacob Ecker, where he died on Sun, failing to restore consciousness. He has left a wife & several chldrn, numerous relations & friends, to mourn his untimely end. -Carrollonian

THU AUG 20, 1840
Josiah J Crosby & J S Jones, Attys & Cnslrs at Law, Montg Co, Texas. [Aug 18 ad.]

Scioto Gaz: Lower Sandusky, Aug 27, 1813. Extract of a letter from Maj Croghan. Gen Harrison's conduct: his character as a military man is too well established to need my approbation or support.

Mrd: on Aug 4, at the residence of Robt Ralston, near Phil, by Rt Rev H U Onderdonk, C Cazenove Gardner, of Savannah, to Maria Ridgely, d/o the late Dr John Syng Dorsey.

Died: on Aug 9, at Easton, Md, Wm H Hayward.

Died: on the 25th ult, at Cairo, Ill, of congestive fever, Col Anthony Olney, the Active Com'r & Principal Engineer of the works & improvements of the Cairo City & Canal Co. An irreparable loss to that company.

Died: on Jul 23, at *Belle Forest*, the residence of his step-son, Gen Lawrence T Dade, in Daviess Co, Ky, Capt Wm Dade,late of Orange Co, Va, aged 80 years.

Died: on Aug 4, at St Louis, Mo, of a short but severe illness, Capt Jas Robinson, aged 66 years, a native of England, & formerly a resident of Alexandria, D C.

Died: on Aug 7, at Mt Salubria, PG Co, Md, Mrs Mary Frances Bayne, consort of John H Bayne, M D, in her 32nd year. She has left a devoted husband & 2 chldrn.

Personal rencounter, [political cause] occurred at Summerville, Tenn, a few days ago, between L H Coe & P T Scruggs, the former the Van Buren candidate for elector in Dist 13, & a member of the Summerville Bar. Coe shot Scruggs in the abdomen: wound extremely dangerous. --Louisville Jrnl

Geo W Trueheart, Atty at Law, Charlottesville, Va. [Ad]

$100 reward for runaway negro boy Allen, about 21 or 22 years of age. --John A Pye, Chas Co, Md, near Port Tobacco.

Exercises will be resumed in my Academy on Aug 29. —Wm R Abbott, Gtwn

Handsome, airy apts in Wash City, Elliot's Row, on Pa ave: apply to Mrs Mount.

Whig Central Cmte of Vigilance of Fauquier to meet at Warrenton, Va, on the 4th Mon of Aug. Invited are: B W Leigh, Gov Barbour, Wm C Rives, the Hon Jas Garland, Jas Lyons, John M Patton, Hon Henry A Wise, & Gen Walter Jones: & all our fellow citizens. Cmte of arrangements: R E Scott, Saml Chilton, Tho T Withers, Richds Payne, John P Phillips & John Walden.

FRI AUG 21, 1840

Life of Alex'r Hamilton, by his son. The 2nd volunteer is just received by F Taylor, where 1st volunteer can be supplied. Located immediately east of Gadsby's.

Died: on Aug 18, Mr Richd Cole, in his 51st year. He was a native of Phil, but has been a resident of Wash City for the last 30 years.

Extract of a letter from Hon Erastus Root to Mr J Whiting, will show on which side the olde Jeffersonian Democrats are now to be found. Of the 12 individuals now living, who as electors & members of the Leg voted for Mr Jeff for Pres in 1800, 11 now support Harrison & 1 Van Buren. Delhi, Aug 1, 1840: names of the electors who now survive: Jas Burt, of Orange; Pierre Van Cortlandt, of Westchester; & John Woodworth, then of Rensselaer, now of Albany.

Army Register, to Oct 1814. Extracts from records: Genr'l Staff, Rank, Dist, Stations:

Henry Dearborn	Maj Gen 27 Jan, 1812	Dist 1	
Thos Pinckeny	Maj, Gen	27 Mar	Dist 6
Jas Wilkinson	Maj Gen	2 Mar, 1813	blank
Morgan Lewis	Maj Gen	2 Mar, 1813	Dist 3
Geo Izard	Maj Gen	24 Jan, 1814	Dist 9-1st Div
Jacob Brown	Maj Ben	24 Jan	Dist 9-2nd Div
Andrew Jackson	Maj Gen 1 May, 1807	Dist 7	

One cent & a horse cake reward: for runaway apprentices to the bread making business, namely Geo M Wise & John Leaden. Both about 15 years old. — Christopher Hager

SAT AUG 22, 1840

Teacher wanted: trustees of Wash Academy wish to engage a gentleman to take charge of the school, as Principal, for the next year. Address to: Henry Taylor, Oak Grove, Westmoreland, Va.

Caution: forewarn all persons from trading or receiving in any way 2 notes drawn by me in favor of Saml McPherson & endorsed by my father, Jas Williams, dated Jun 6, 1840; one for 6 months, the other for 12 months, from date-each for $100. I am determined not to pay either, unless compelled by law, owing to a deception having been practiced in a purchase for which they were given as a consideration, which can be substantiated in a Court of justice. –Jas A Williams, Mail Contractor, Wash.

Wash Co, D C: I certify that Kinlaugh Deneale brought before me, a J P for the county, on Aug 21, 1840, a stray trespassing on his enclosure, a small white horse. – Will Hebb [Owner to prove property, pay charges, & taker him away. –K Deneale, near Congress Burial Ground.]

Montg Co Court, Court of Equity: Christopher W *Landsdale, vs, Eliz Holtzman, Edw Wilburn & Jane J his wife, Thos N Holtzman & Marcellus Holtzman. Object of bill is to obtain a deed of conveyance of lands sold by Eliz Holtzman to the plntf. Geo Holtzman purchased of Wm Needham a tract of land in said county, in Md, called *Tranquebar*; Geo Holtzman requested the said Needham to convey the same to John Holtzman in trust for the sole use of said Eliz, with power to sell the tract of land, & that, upon request of Eliz, in writing, to the said John, he was to convey the same to the purchaser. Eliz did sell, after the death of her husband, Geo Holtzman, the said land to Christopher W *Lansdale; that between the time of sale & payment of the purchase money the said John Holtzman, trustee, died, leaving a widow, Jane J Holtzman, who has since intermrd with Edw Wilburn, & 2 infant chldrn, Thos N Holtzman, & Marcellus Holtzman, all of whom are made dfndnts; they being non-residents of this state, & pray an order of publication. Dfndnts to appear in Court by the 2nd Mon in Nov next. –T H Wilkinson -Brice Selby, clk Montg Co Court. [*2 spellings of Landsdale: Lansdale.]

Orphans Court of Chas Co, Md. Letters of administration de bonis non on personal estate of Thos C Reeves, late of Chas Co, D C. -Jos E Simms, adm de bonis non

The Rev Joshua N Danforth will preach in the 2nd Presby Church tomorrow: service at 11 o'clock.

The Rev Eliphalet Bosworth will preach in Dr Laurie's Church tomorrow at 11 a m.

MON AUG 24, 1840
The Danville Rifle of the 15th says: the Hon S H Anderson died, at his residence, near Lancaster, Garrard Co, Ky, on Aug 11: ill for several months & suffered greatly. In Aug last he was elected to Congress from this Dist, & able to attend to the duties of his ofc but a short time.

Daily Evening Gaz: title of a new paper, the first number of which appeared at Balt on Thu: is edited by Wm Ogden Niles, assisted by E P Roberts.

Key West, Aug, 1840. Letter to the Courier: Aug 7, number of Indians landed on Indian Key, about 100 to 150: they went aboard the wrecking sloop *Vevilia*. In Indian Key, the house owned & occupied by Mr Chas Howe, Inspec of Customs was destroyed. Mr Houseman & wife, & Mr Howe, wife & 5 chldrn escaped to Tea-Table Key. Dr Perrine, wife, & 3 chldrn, were in their house: Dr Perrine went to talk to the Indians in Spanish, but it is supposed they then shot him, for he was not again seen. The others in the family escaped. Mr John Motte, mstr of the wrecking sloop *Key West*, with his wife, & 2 chldrn, & his mother, secreted themselves in the privy, but they were found & Mr Motte & his wife were shot, the mother escaped: they then dashed out the brains of the 2 infants against the rocks & left them with the corpses of the parents. The house of Dr Perrine was burnt, his body must have been consumed in it. The 12 year old bro/o Mrs E Smith hid with a carpenter named Blocks; the latter was saved but much burnt; the lad perished in the flames. Mr Otis, a carpenter, was wounded by a rifle ball: he is doing well. Mr Howe's family, & the rest of the unfortunate sufferers, are on board the wrecking schn'r *Sylph*, at Indian Key. Detachment of Marines, under command of Lt Sloan, in the U S schn'r *Wave*, for Cape Romano, to join the expedition of boats in the everglades, under command of Lt Com McLaughlin-hearing of the attack, pushed towards the scene of action, with a barge, in which was mounted a gun, which they discharged on approaching the place; it recoiled & went overboard. The Dr was obliged to haul off when the Indians came in the water firing.

Worcester Co [Md] Banner: Zedekiah Williams, of Salisbury, in that county, put an end to his life on Thu last by jumping into the Chesapeake Bay, on his way from Balt to Salisbury. Pecuniary difficulties are said to have caused this rash act. Mr W was an upright man & an attentive ofcr; for some time had discharged the duties of deputy shrf with great satisfaction.

Mr John Smith, of Tyrone township, Fayette Co, Pa, died on Aug 15, aged about 31 years. He was stung on the back of the neck by bumblebees while engaged in making hay, & died of lock-jaw about 3 days later.

Mrd: on Aug 20, by Rev J P Donelan, Mr Enoch King to Miss Maria Pauline Pritchard, both of Wash City.

Died: on Aug 20, at Balt, Wm A Tyson, in his 36th year.

Died: on Aug 2, at her residence in Northampton Co, Va, Mrs Harriet B Parker, relict of the late John A Parker, in her 56th year.

Died: on Aug 18, at Albany, Henry Nixon, Pres of the Bank of N America.

Died: on Aug 9, at Belleville, Ill, J R Cannon, editor & proprietor of the Great Western, published in that place.

Died: on Aug 18, at Newbridge, N J, Wm W Weller, aged about 91 years, formerly of London, & for many years a resident of N Y.

Died: on Jun 12, at Mt Hope, Yazoo Co, Miss, aged 56 years, 1 month & 12 days, Mrs Rebecca Chew, w/o Wm L Chew, & 4th d/o the late Frisby Freeland, formerly of Calvert Co, Md. She leaves her husband, chldrn, & grandchldrn.

Died: on Aug 20, Minerva Teresea, d/o Peter & Rowena Callan, aged 1 year & 7 months.

Notice: this is to forewarn all persons from crediting my account, as I am determined to pay no debt contracted after this date. –J T Elwood

For rent: dwlg house & lot on Capitol Hill, on part of lot 3 in sq 730, on Pa ave, for some time past occupied by Mr Hamilton. Possession on Sep 4 next.
–S Frazier, near the Mansion House

THU AUG 25, 1840
Peter D Vroom, Philemon Dickerson, Wm R Cooper, Danl B Ryall, & Jos Kille are entitled to occupy, as members of Hse o/Reps, five contested seats from N J. Others in the running: T Jones Yorke, Chas C Stratton, Wm Halsted, J P B Mawell: John B Ayerigg-1: Philemon Dickerson-3 votes..

For sale: a saddle pony: can be seen at O Connolly's new Livery Stable, 8th st.

Mrd: on Aug 20, at Wash, by Rev Mr Matthew, Mr Wm H Wimsatt, formerly of Wash, to Miss Mary Helen Massey, of Alexandria, D C.

Mrd: on Aug 19, at Hobart, Delaware Co, N Y, by Rev F Harrington, Wm Hunt, of Bromsgrove, Worcestershire, Eng, to Sarah Arabella, 2nd d/o Dr Calvin Howard, of the former place.

Proposals will be received for 500 cords of pine wood. -Elias Kane, Navy Agent, Navy Yard.

Archibald & Wm Thompson, Cabinet makers, have removed 3 doors west of Mr Butler's tavern.

$5 reward for strayed buffalo cow. She left the commons, near the Eastern Tollgage, on Aug 16. –Jas Maguire, residence near the Navy Yard, Wash.

Sale of household furniture at auction: on Aug 25, at the house lately occupied by Mr Keller, on F st. -John A Blake, auct

New cash shoe store, on Pa ave, opposite Brown's htl. Bargains may be accepted. Terms cash. —Jos Cogswell

Splendid chance for Capitalists: pvt sale, my plantation, in PG Co, Md, upwards of 700 acs: with a splendid mansion: lies in centre of *Forest of PG*. —Robt Bowie, near Good Luck P O, PG Co, Md.

For sale: a choice of Green House Plants: will be sold at the residence of Chas F Mercer, Aldie, Loudoun Co, Va. —Theodore S Garnett, agent

WED AUG 26, 1840

On Aug 14, John Westwood, s/o Mr Newton Vowler, residing near Warrenton, Va, was accidentally caught by the wheels of a thrashing machine, tearing up his leg in such a manner as to effect his death in about 12 hours. He was just enereing his 14th year, & was a boy of sprightly disposition & much beloved by his family & schoolmates.

$2 reward for strayed or stolen dark brindled dog with a leather collar. —Jos Bryan, residence corner of N Y ave & 10th st.

Wash City: Aug 17: named Trustees of the Public Schools:

Rev Wm Matthews	Thos Blagden
Rev Wm Hawley	Geo H Fulmer
Jas Larned	Rev A T McCormick
John D Barclay	Rev G G Brook
Wm Lloyd	Richd Barry
Wm B Magruder	Jas Carbery
John W Maury	Jas Marshall
—C H Wiltberger, reg	

Afflicting calamity: from the Albany Eveining Jrnl Extra: Sat, Aug 22. Just as the steamboats were departing for N Y, & when hundreds of people were crossing the bridge over the canal basin, the draw broke, & 70 to 80 people, horses, & carts, were precipitated into water from 20 feet to 12 feet. Dead bodies recovered: Jas Hinman, cnstbl of this city; Mr Driscoll, Merchant, of Palmyra; Chas Lyons, Tobacco Pedlar, of this city; a 14 year old s/o Jacob Henderer, of Columbia st;a 16 year old s/o Sybrant Kettle, of this city; Roderick Davidson, 16 years, employed in this ofc;a_____ Groesbeck, a boy belonging to the boat Mohawk;a Mr Cavener, an insane man from Westmoreland, Oheida Co, under the charge of Mr Stevens & Orin I Fuller, of Rome, on his way to Hudson. Cavener & Fuller were lost, & Stevens was saved. Lost: Jas Van Buren, of German Flatts, a canal driver; Saml Fisher, lamp-lighter, of this city; Francis Rogee, laborer, of this city; _____ Wood, a boy about 14 years, of this city; Thos McDowell, of this city; Wm L Morey, of Vt; _____ Jones, of this city; H L Hoffman, of Fultonville; Smith Matthews, of Troy. Capt Jacobs, of the boat *Col Little-John*, was saved. Jas Henry, bookseller, saved himself.

Mr Carr, of the Pearl st Hse, was slightly injured, but saved himself. Saml H Ransom, a young man, saved himself & an old man. Thos Greene, of the firm of Rathbone, Chapin, & Greene, swam out. Mr Wilson, of Juliet, Ill, s/o J Q Wilson, of this city, swam out. Col Morgan, of a canal-boat, saved himself. Danl Gavit, engraver, swam out. Several cartmen saved themselves & horses: David Terry, John W Butler, Chas Rock, John Stackpole, & Peter Simonds. Among the hats recovered was one with a letter addressed to Jonathan Hart. Our medical men, among whom we noticed, Drs Coggswell, Armsby, Van Olinda, M'Naughton, Hinkley, & Staata, were prompt & untiring in their efforts to restore life. Praiseworthy efforts to save lives & recover bodies were Col Groesbeck, Robt L Kearney, John McCardle, Edw Brinkerhoff, S M Fish, J E Gavit, David Terry, jr, Elijah Brainard, & several othrs whose names do not occur to us.

THU AUG 27, 1840
Trustees' sale of valuable real estate: virtue of a decree of the High Court of Chancery of Md: sale at *Rose Mount*, late the residence of Gov Jos Kent, dec'd, all the real estate of which he died seized: about 1,000 acs in PG Co, Md, adj the lands of Gov Sprigg, Jos H Wilson, & B Berry, jr: with a dwlg house. The widow's dower has ben laid off by com'rs for that purpose appointed by the Chancellor's decree, & so much of said land will be sold subject to the widow's dower; the residue of the estate will be sold free from the widow's dower. –Thos G Pratt, Jas Kent, trustees

Liverpool Mail: death of the Earl of Durham: for if ever a husband was doated on by an amiable & affectionate wife, it was John Geo Lambton, Earl of Durham. Lambton: Earl of Durham, Viscount Lambton, & Baron Durham, of the city of Durham, in the peerage of the United Kingdom, was born Apr 12, 1792, & mrd, first, Jan 1, 1812, Miss Harriet Cholmondeley, who died in May, 1815. He mrd 2nd, Lady Louisa Eliz Grey, eldest d/o the Earl & Countess Grey. His lordship had issue by his first marriage, 3 dghts, all of whom are dead; & by his 2nd wife, 5 chldrn, 2 sons & 3 dghts. His 2nd son, Geo Fred'k Viscount Lambton, [the Hon Chas Wm, his eldest son, having died at age 13] succeeds to the family honors.

Board of Visiters at West Point of Jun 25, 1840, to the Hon J R Poinsett, Sec of War, & signed by Jacob Medary, jr, of Ohio, H King, of Mo, Jas Hagan, of Miss, & Leigh Read, of Fla. Passage from the report: *the inaptitude of many of the graduates of West Point for military life is strikingly illustrated by the resignation of 117 ofcrs of the regular army during the 1st year of the Seminole war, & the annual resignation since of about 30, or $3/4^{ths}$ of the number added yearly by the Academy.* An old soldier remarks that many of the 117, of 1837, were not graduates from the Academy. Of the 2 Cols, neither was from West Point, & not one of the five staff ofcrs was from the Academy. My purpose is to advocate the continuance of the Military Academy: if the people of this country desire to abolish it, let it be done.

The undersigned have this day associated with them Geo W Adams & Jos G McPherson, under firm of Adams, McPherson & Co, for the transaction of the dry goods business, at their old stand, Pa ave, between 8th & 9th sts. -A W & J E Turner

FRI AUG 28, 1840

Newport, Jul 9, 1840: letter to Dr Usher Parsons from Asher Robbins: subject- administration party questions the military talents of Gen Harrison in the late war with Great Britain; as you were in the battles of Lake Erie, & were an intimate friend of Cmdor Perry, & must have known the concert & co-operation between him & Gen Harrison. Request you to make a statement in writing, to the public. -Asher Robbins +
Providence, Jul 14, 1840. Reply to the above: I feel no reluctance in stating what I know of Gen Harrison's services whilst with Cmdor Perry, & of his popularity in the army he commanded. In Jan, 1813, Gen Winchester's small army was captured at the river Raisin, & as they were returning home, on parole, from Fort George to Ky, they passed the barracks at Black Rock, where I was stationed as a medical ofcr of the Navy: ofcrs & troops informed of the estimation in which Gens Harrison & Winchester were held in the west. The fleet under Cmdor Perry, was created at the recommendation of Gen H. On Aug 19, a review on the deck of the ship *Lawrence* stood Gen H with his Chief ofcrs in full military dress: rest of the day was employed in planning the future operations of the fleet. On Sep 10, the enemy appeared: result of the day was sent to the Gen with these words: "Dear Gen, we have met the enemy, & they are ours-two ships, two brigs, one sloop, & one schn'r." -Usher Parsons

St Louis, Aug 19. The 8th Regt, Col North, now stationed at Jeff Barracks, below this city, received orders to repair to Prairie Du Chien: due to the conduct of the Winnebago Indians. A short time ago they were removed by Gen Atkinson to the west side of the Miss: when the troops left, they returned. They have had but little time to recover from the fatigues of the north, in removing these same Indians. -Republican

Geo Phillips was arrested at Balt on Tue by ofcrs Basil James & Jesse Sumwalt, charged with having robbed the mail for the west from Balt between that city & Hagerstown. Phillips was examined by Joshua Vansant, Postmaster, before Justice Wright, & committed for further exam.

Mrd: on Thu last, in the Borough of Pottsville, by Rev Mr McCool, Mr Wm Provins to Miss Jane Bond, both of Port Clinton, & all for Harrison. –Miner's Jrnl

Died: on Aug 27, at the residence of Mr Wm H Edes, Green st, Gtwn, Mr Jas C Dunn, after a few weeks illness, leaving an aged mother & 5 chldrn to lament his departure. Funeral today at 4 p m, at the residence of Mr Edes.

Died: on Aug 23, Richmond Johnson, the 2nd & only s/o Edmund & Eliz Ann Coolidge, aged 2 years & 20 days.

Died: on Aug 25, Marian Eliz, d/o Valentine & Ellen Harbaugh, aged 1 year & 23 days.

Died: last Fri, in Alexandria, Chas Osgood, y/s/o Elisheba & Harrison Bradley, aged 3 years & 5 months.

Died: on Aug 4, at St Stephen's, Ala, Theophilus S Wilkinson, grandson of the late Hon & Rev Harry Toulmin, formerly of England, & grandson of the late Gen Jas Wilkinson, of the U S Army. The subject was a distinguished graduate of West Point, remaining some years in the army, where he was conspicuous for his lofty bearing & high sense of virtue.

Appointment by the Pres: Geo Adams to be a J P for Wash Co, D C.

City Ord-Wash: Act for relief of Jos M Munding, by judgment of Vincent King, for an alleged violation in the erection of wooden bldgs, be, & the same is hereby remitted: provided, he shall pay the costs of prosecution.

City News: Inquest was held by T Woodward on Sun last over the body of John Barry, who was found dead in his bed in his brdg house, on F, near 10th st, in Wash City. He was a stone-cutter by trade, & had for some time been employed at the Patent Ofc bldg: he worked as usual on Sat: verdict-death by rupture of a blood-vessel in the lungs.

Mr Walter Berry, of Gtwn, was dangerously injured by a fall from a horse on Sat last, a few miles from town: his bridle bit broke, & he was thrown against a stone by the road side, which literally scalped his forehead, threw his shoulder out of place, & broke his arm between the elbow & shoulder. He is now considered out of danger. -Advocate

Wash Corp: 1-Ptn of Wm Prather, praying the remission of a fine: referred to the Cmte of Claims. 2-Cmte of Claims: asked to be discharged from further consideration of the ptn of Geo Johnson.

Lost cow came to my place of residence east of the new jail, where the owner is requested to call, prove property, pay charges, & take her away. –Martin Loxman

Wash Co, D C: insolvent debtors, Adam Belzarus, John W H Browning & Danl Gallagher, have applied to be discharged from imprisonment. -Wm Brent, clk

SAT AUG 29, 1840
Mrd: on Aug 18, by Rev Tippet, Egbert Heisler, formerly of Dela, to Mary Jane, d/o Cornelius Dushane, of Balt.

Mrd: on Aug 27, in Wash City, by Rev Geo G Brook, Mr John Thomas to Miss Eliza Taylor, all of Wash City.

The Northampton Courier says that Boswell Stevens, of N Wilbraham, was killed at the depot there on Wed of last week, when endeavoring to climb on one of the bars of the freight train, & fell beneath the car, & was crushed to death. He has left a wife & 5 chldrn. No blame to the conductor.

Maine: nominees thus far for 8 members of Congress:

Whigs	Locofocos
Danl Goodenow	Nathan Clifford
Benj Randall	Albert Smith
Geo Evans	Jos Sewall
Zadoc Long	N S Littlefield
S A Kingsberry	Alfred Marshall
Jos C Noyes	Hannibal Hamlin
John Hubbard	

John Fairfield, the present Govn'r, is a candidate for re-election, & is opposed by Edw Kent.

$15 reward for brindled cow, missing from the premises since Aug 2. –J S Henshaw

Mrd: on Aug 18, Col Jas W Walker to Miss Ann Eliza, y/d/o the late Ebenezer Eliason, all of Madison Co, Va.

Died: on Aug 19, at Prospect Hill, Chas Co, Md, Columbia, in her 13th year, the y/d/o Mr Chas Fletcher, of the Genr'l Land Ofc.

MON AUG 31, 1840

Huntington [Pa] Jrnl. On Mon of last week, while moving a small bldg formerly occupied as an ofc by J G Miles, Saml Read, 15, s/o Thos Read, of our town, fell under the axle & his leg was almost torn off at the knee. He lived but a few short hours.

Gen Harrison's resignation, in May, 1814, on his military staff learning his determination to resign his commission, & of the blessings imparted by him to a frontier where there had been no peace for 20 years, they say: although your country has a right to claim your assistance in her struggles, & you are bound to afford it upon honorable principales, & your retirement may deprive her of her greatest chieftain, yet, under existing circumstances, we cannot but approve your determination.

Died: on Aug 22, in PG Co, Md, Mrs Louisa D Dement, consort of Chas F Dement, in her 39th year.

Macon, Ga, Aug 11. On Tue last, as Mr Douglass Honeycutt, of this county, was returning home from town, whither he had come to attend the Supr Court then in session as a juror, when about 2 miles from town his horse stumbles & threw him. His head struck a stump, fracturing his skull: he lived til next morning. Mr H was an honest & hard-working man, & a large family laments his loss.

Died: on Aug 9, in consequence of injuries received by a fall thru the hatchway of the store, in Poydras st, New Orleans, Mr Jas Greenleaf, jr, aged about 40 years, a native of Bristol, R I, but for many years a resident of that city. On his first voyage from Balt to New Orleans, in 1822, he was captured by pirates off the coast of Cuba, severely wounded on the head with a cutlass, several days in prison with cruel treatment, but succeeded in making his escape with the mate of their own vessel. After rowing for 2 days & nights on the briny deep, without provisions or water, succeeded in reaching the coast, near Matanzas, from whence a U S vessel was despatched, who finding themselves in hot pursuit, run the vessel on shore, & many escaped in the woods. In this engagement, Lt Allen of the U S Navy, lost his life. He has encountered death in almost every form. He has left an orphan son, age about 6 years old.

In Pa: The Hon Chas Ogle has been unanimously nominated as a candidate for re-election to Congress in the dist composed of Bedford, Somerset, & Cambria Cos. Dr W A Irvine, of Warren Co, nominated as a candidate for Congress in the 25th dist, composed of the counties of Crawford, Erie, Warren, & Venango. In Dela Co, John Edwards nominated for re-election, & in Lancaster Co, Jeremiah Brown nominated as a candidate. The 2 companies, with Chester, send 3 Reps.

Capitol Hill Seminary for Young Ladies: 3rd term of the 7th year will comence on Sep 1. Trustees:

Rev A T McCormick	John P Ingle
Jas Adams	Dr Fred'k May
Rev H H Bean	Wm J McDonald
Capt Marmaduke Dove	Dr Thos Sewall
Col C K Gardner	John Underwood

Teachers: O N Stoddard, A M, Principal; Mrs E W Stoddard, Ast.

Died: on Aug 10, near Crawfordsville, Ind, Miss Isabella C Tyler, 2nd d/o Chas Tyler, formerly of Wash City. Her numerous friends in this place will deeply sympathize with her family. –C C B

Valuable farm for sale: about 3 miles from Rockville: 497 acs of improved land, with a good 2 story brick dwlg house. Title is unquestionable. –Lemuel Clements, Montg Co, Md

C Strahan informs that his school will resume on Aug 24.

Female Institute, Columbia, Maury Co, Tenn. Teacher skilled in music wanted by Sep 1. Refer to Rev Dr Colton, Gambier, Ohio, Rev Dr Seaberry, N Y, or Rev Mr Hooker, Phil. –F G Smith, Rector

Alexandria Boarding School, D C: will resume on Sep 1. Information from the following gentlemen, all of whom have had students in the Institution during the term that has just closed, & most of them for several years:

G B Lamar, Savannah, Ga	Hon John Bell, Tenn
Malechi Haughton, Edenton, N C	Hon Walter Coles, Pittsylvania Co, Va
Hon John Henderson, U S Senator	Hon Geo W Crabb, Ala
from Miss	–Benj Hallowell, Principal &
Isaiah D Hart, Jacksonville, Fla	Proprietor: Alexandria, D C
Saml A Roberts, Galveston, Texas	

Rich Neck for sale: tract on the head waters of Toteskey Crk, Richmond Co, Va: 1,303 acs. Refer to Thos Brown, near Westmoreland Court-house, Va, & to John F B Jeffries, Warsaw, Va, the latter gentleman will show the land. Also, a small farm, of 140 acs, adjoining the one on which the subscriber resides, in Fairfax Co, Va, near Gtwn, D C. Also, a farm for rent, 150 acs, 8 miles from Gtwn. I have for rent or lease an excellent Tavern-stand & drove-yard, where the Prospect Hill, Va, P O & relay of the mail coach horses are kept. For particulars to the 3 last mentioned, apply to Gen R Jones, Wash City, or to the subscriber, near Prospect Hill, Va.
–Thos Ap C Jones

Trust sale: deed of trust from Benj Blackford & Thos T Blackford & wife, to the undersigned, dated Sep 7, 1839, & recorded in the ofc of the Courts of Shenandoah & Page Cos: all the lands attached to & including *Caroline Furnace*, in Shenandoah Co, part of some of the tracts running into Page Co: altogether, 3,254 acs.
–Wm J Roberts, Hugh M Patton, trustees, Fredericksburg, Va

TUE SEP 1, 1840

Mr & Mrs Streeter's Boarding School for Young Ladies, Saratoga, near Cortland st, Balt: institution established by Wm Hamilton, in 1831: school commences on the 1st Mon in Sep. Referred by the following gentlemen, most of whom have had dghts under their charge during the past year:

Rev Dr Johns	Chas R Carroll
John Glenn	Chas F Mayer
John B Morris	Hugh W Evans
C C Jamison	J I Donaldson
Edw Hinkley	Wm McConkey

$5 reward for strayed cows, one with a piece of her tail bit off by the dogs; the other with large horns. -Thos Hendal, mgr for Jno A Smith, residence at the Navy Yard bridge, on the south side.

Wash Co, D C: this is to certify that Washington Simms, a colord man, brought before me as an estray, a bay gelding. Given under my hand & seal Aug 31, 1840. –Jas Marshall, J P

Notice: teacher wanted to take charge of the Union School near Dawsonville, Montg Co, Md. Letters address to Col Robt T Dade, Jos C White, or Nathan S White, for information.

The late Dr Perrine, formerly U S Cnsl at Campeachy, & lately killed at Indian Key by the Indians,] was a remarkable man: science is robbed of a bright ornament, & social life of the firm friend & kind parent. –St Aug News

Died: on Aug 29, at Glen Ross, Rev Jas B Noblit, Rector of Berlin & Snow Hill Parishes, Eastern Shore of Md, in his 27th year. He died triumphant in the Christian faith.

$200 reward for runaways, negro man & woman: Dick, about 50, & Cynthia, about 19 years, who is pregnant with her 2nd child. At the same time a large sorrel horse was stolen. –Conway Spilman, Robt Huffman, Jeffersonton, Culpeper Co, Va.

David Bronson who was nominated as a candidate for Congress in the Kennebec & Somerset district of Maine, declines the nomination. The Whigs will now show undivided support of the Hon Geo Evans.

WED SEP 2, 1840
The N Y Evening Star & the N Y Times have been united, & will be hereafter published as one paper.

Cow lost: strayed from the subscriber, on Aug 8: liberal reward for her delivery to me, or information that will lead to her recovery. –Chas H Lane, corner of 3rd & C sts; or Lane & Tucker, Pa ave.

Wash Corp: 1-Cmte on Police, on the ptn of Jas Hollidge, reported a bill entitled an act prohibitng the enclosure of sts & aves, & for other purposes. 2-Cmte of Claims: asked to be discharged from further consideration of the ptn of Z Hazel.

Mrd: on Aug 27, by Rev Mr Donelan, Mr Richd I Jones, of Wash City, to Miss Eliz Ann Burch, d/o Thos Burch, of PG Co, Md.

Died: Sep 1, Clement Wm, oldest child of Eleazer & Mgt C Brown, aged 14 months. Funeral from 18th st, this afternoon, at 3½ o'clock.

Died: on Sat last, Va, d/o Urias & Eliz Hunt, aged 2 months & 24 days.

Died: on Aug 30, Jos A L Tate, o/c/o Jas & Marion Tate, aged 15 months.

Died: on Aug 29, Wm Augustus, infant s/o Wm & Jane A Walker, aged 13 months & 20 days.

THU SEP 3, 1840
Died: yesterday, Mr John Hitz, a native of Switzerland, but long a respectable citizen of this country, after a protracted & painful illness, aged 68 years. Funeral from his late residence, *Christina Thal*, near Wash City, on Sep 4, at 3 p m.

Died: on Aug 26, in Chas Co, Md, at the residence of his father, Saml John Edgar Amery, after a long & painful illness, aged 28 years.

Died: on Sep 1, in Gtwn, D C, Mrs Rosella, consort of Saml T McPherson, in her 28th year, formerly of Balt, after a long & painful illness. May she rest in peace.

Centreville, Aug 18, 1840. Latest from Savannah papers. The Indians have done a good deal of mischief on the Suwanee, & it is thought they have again come into the Okefenokee. Last Fri they killed Jos Howell's wife & 2 chldrn, & Danl Green's wife, & shot his dght thru the shoulder. Jos Howell & Geo Johns got in here today. They followed them several miles & found 11 dwlgs burnt. They all are forted in at old Bill Cone's & Capt Sanderlain's. Absalom Cossey's chldrn, 6 in number, were killed last Wed, on the South prong of the St Mary's, supposed by the same party. Thos Wright is burn out. –Stephen McCall to Geo Long. 2nd letter: Centreville, Aug 23, 1840: the Indians have killed Thos Davis & 2 of his chldrn, & John Patrick's wife. They gathered at Arch Hogan's, & burnt Davis' place & Miney's. Capt Tracy is trying to raise 50 men for 30 days, under an order from Gen C FLoyd. I shall at once take my family away from here. –Stephen McCall to Geo Long

Letter from Puerto Cabello, dated the 14th ult, mentions the death of J G A Williamson, our Charge d'Afaires at Caraccas. He died on the 7th, of dysentery, after an illness of only a few days.

Trustee's sale: decree of Fred'k Co Court, Court of Equity: sale on Oct 3 next: of *Cotocton Furnace*, in Fred'k Co, Md, being part of the real estate of John Brien, dec'd: about 6,000 acs. Also, the one undivided half part of the *Antietam Iron Works*, that was owned by John Brien, sen, at his death. They have connected with them about 15,000 acs of land. –John McPherson, trustee

FRI SEP 4, 1840
Wash & Alexandria Boat: the steamboat *Jos Johnson* will leave Wash at 10 & 2 a m: at 4 & 6 p m: will leave Alexandria at 9 & 11 a m: at 3 & 5 p m. She will also make a daily morning trip between Alex & Gtwn. –Ignatius Allen, Capt

Mr Michl Rumble, of Westmoreland Co, Pa, was suddenly killed on the 22nd ult, whilst engaged in thrashing out grain, by the bursting of the cylinder of his machine. Death was instant.

Reminiscences of the last 65 years, commencing with the battle of Lexington; also, Sketches of his Own Life & Times: by E S Thomas, formerly editor of the Charleston City Gaz, & lately of the Cincinati Daily Evening Post: in 2 volumes.
–Balt Patriot

City News: on Tue night, a stable occupied by Mr Castateel, in the Eastern part of this city, near the Baptist Church, was totally consumed by fire.

Franklin Fire Co: cmte appointed to investigate the attempt to set fire to the premises of Mr Clement Woodward, on Aug 4, 1840: Mr Duncanson & Mr J E Given-sec. Mr Given resigned his post due to a death in his family, & Mr Geo M Davis was appointed to the place. Mr C Fraler examined. Mr Hamilton examined-do you know if Mr Stewart hauled shavings here or not?-I heard his son say so. Mr Pulling, Mr Burr, Mr Blake, Mr Powell, Mr Lyons, Mr Holliday, Mr Harbaugh, Mr Cunningham, Mr Farquhar, Mr Buckingham, & Mr McGarr, were examined. Witness list: Barney Manly, Jas O'Neale, ____ Hutchins, Seabright, Stubbins, & Franks. Testimony closed.

Appointments by the Pres: Saml Crawford, Receiver of Public Moneys at Kaskaskia, Ill, vice Edw Humphreys, dec'd. Elijah H Gordy, do, at St Stephen's, Ala, vice T J Wilkinson, dec'd. J A Parker, Coll at Tappahannock, Va, vice Robt S Garnett, dec'd. Ebenezer H Stacy, Surveyor at Gloucester, Mass, vice John M Moriarty, resigned.

Mrd: on Sep 1, by Rev Mr Brooke, Mr Thos Wilson to Miss Ann E Speiden, all of Wash City.

Died: on Sep 2, John E Leatherbury, only s/o the late Wm A Leatherbury, aged 8 years, 10 months & 9 days. His funeral will be from his mother's residence, D & 12th sts, today, at 3 p m.

Died: yesterday, in Wash City, Mrs Emily Goddard, w/o Saml B Goddard. Funeral at 10 a m from his residence on 20th st west.

Died: on Sep 1, at Rockville, Md, Eugene J, infant s/o T L & G A Moody.

To let & possession given Oct 1, a 2 story brick hse, now occupied by Mr Chas Keller. Inquire of Geo Lambright, corner of 9th & I sts.

Notice: the public are forewarned not to receive any notes of mine in favor of Edw Garrau, as I am determined not to pay the same. Given under my hand Sep 3, 1840. –J D Lafontaine

Meeting of the Historical Dept & Nat'l Instit for the Promotion of Science will be held at the rooms of the Institution on Sep 4, at 8 p m. –Pishey Thompson, sec

SAT SEP 5, 1840
$20 reward for my stolen setter dog: last seen on Mon last. –Henry May, Capitol Hill

Collector's ofc, City Hall, Sep 1, 1840: Wash City property to be sold for taxes.

Adams, Mgt: 1838-39
Anderson, Saml B: 1836 thru 1839
Bates, Ann: 1837 thru 39
Bean, Benj: 1836 thru 39
Bryan, Caroline C & Eliz A S: 1838-39
Ball, Wm H: 1838-39
Brent, Danl: 1837 thru 39
Boyer, Jacob: 1836 thru 39
Breckenridge, John: 1837 thru 39
Bailey, John-heirs: 1838-39
Boone, J B: 1838-39
Coote, Clement T: 1836 thru 39
Carroll, Danl: 1837 thru 39
Cooper, Isaac: 1836 thru 39
Davidson, John-heirs: 1837 thru 39
Digges, Wm: 1837 thru 39
Campbell, Geo W: 1838-39
Davis, Gideon-heirs: 1837thru 39
Dunlop, Jas: 1836 thru 39
Dick, Robt: 1837 thru 39
Dulaney, S A: 1837 thru 39
Frye, Jas: 1836 thru 39
Forrest, Julius-heirs: 1936 thru 39
Fowler, Saml: 1838-39
Grammer, G C: 1836 thru 39
Gratiot Chas: 1838-39
Guest, Jonathan: 1837 thru 39
Gorman, John B: 1837 thru 39
Greenleaf & Eliot: 1836 thru 39
Gelston, Hugh: 1837 thru 39
Hall, David A: 1836 thru 39
Howison, Henry: 1036, 1838 thru 39

Herrity, Jas: 1836 thru 39
Hamilton, Saml-heirs: 1837 thru 39
Hazle, Zachariah: 1836 thru 39
Holmead, Anthony: 1836 thru 39
Jones, Walter, & Bank of Wash: 1837 thru 39
Kavanaugh, Patrick: 1836 thru 39
Kerr, Robt E: 1838-39
Keane, Stephen: 1838-39
King, Henry: 1836 thru 39
Kemp, Mary: 1837 thru 39
Keyworth, Robt: 1837 thru 39
Lynch, John: 1836 thru 39
Longacre, J B: 1837 thru 39
McGunigle, Ann: 1837 thru 39
Miller, Geo & Henry: 1838-39
McNerhany, John-heirs: 1838-39
Milburn, Mgt: 1838-39
McGlue, Owen-heirs: 1836 thru 39
Middleton, Arthur: 1837 thru 39
McCall, Benj F: 1837 thru 39
McDuell, John: 1837-39
Orr, Benj G-heirs: 1836 thru 39
O'Neale, Wm-heirs: 1836 thru 39
Palmer, Innis B: 1836 thru 39
Phillips, Overton C: 1838-39
Peake, Dr H: 1837-39
Peltz, John-heirs: 1838-39
Parsons, Jos B-heirs: 1836 thru 39
Peter, David-heirs: 1836 thru 39
Rodbird, Absalom-heirs: 1836 thru 39
Rodbird, Ebenezer: 1836 thru 39
Roberts, John: 1837 thru 39

Ramsey, Wm W: 1837 thru 39
Sands, Comfort: 1836 thru 39
Stuart, John A: 1838-39
Sweet, Parker H: 1836 thru 39
Slade, Henry C: 1837 thru 39
Scott, Susan Ann: 1837 thru 39
Smith, Thos: 1837 thru 39
Swann, Thos-heirs: 1837 thru 39
Simpson, Tobias-heirs: 1836 thru 39
Tucker, Eliz: 1838-39
Thomas, Hope: 1837 thru 39
Thomas, Jos & Jas: 1837 thru 39
Thomas, Thos T-heirs: 1837 thru 39
Tayloe, John-heirs: 1837 thru 39
Tucker, John-heirs: 1837 thru 39
Van Coble, Aaron & Co: 1837 thru 39
Venable, Eliz: 1836 thru 39
-A Rothwell, collector

Van Ness, John P: 1836 thru 39
Walter, A B: 1838-39
Williams, David: 1838-39
Wood, Ferdinand F-heirs: 1837 thru 39
Wells, John, jr: 1837 thru 39
Walker, John: 1838-39
Wilson, John A, & others: 1837 thru 39
Watson, Jas W: 1836 thru 39
Wood, Mary Ann E: 1838-39
Wilson, Jas & Thos: 1837 thru 39
Withers, John & Geo Johnson: 1836 thru 39
Wilson, Jos: 1837 thru 39
Whalen, Nicholas: 1836 thru 39

May 27, 1839: a naval genr'l Court-martial convened, under a precept of the Sec of the Navy, on board the U S ship *Macedonian*, in the bay of Pensacola, for the trial of Geo Mason Hooe, of Va, a Lt in the U S Navy, on charges preferred against him by Cmder Uriah P Levy. Court continued in session till Jun 5, 1839, when they found the accused guilty of: 1-Treating with contempt his superior ofcr in the execution of his duty. 2-Disobedience of orders. The accused, serving on board the ship *Vandalia*, on Jan 3, 1839, directed Wm O'Brien, a Marine, to receive 12 lashes, contrary to the internal rules. The accused, serving on board the ship *Vandalia* as 2nd Lt, on Dec 16, 1838, ordered Danl Waters, the Cmder's cook, to be flogged. The accused directed John Dennis, a seaman, to be flogged with 18 lashes, in direct violation. On 2 several days the accused whipped Calvin Morgan, a boy, between 12 & 13 years of age, in further violation. The Court doth sentence the said Lt Geo M Hooe to be dismissed from the West India Squad; after having been reprimanded to genr'l orders by the Hon Sec of the Navy.

Wm Bradford Shubrick, Pres
L Rousseau
Beverly Kennon
Benj Page
H Paulding

Wm E McKenney
J P Wilson
Thos M Blount, Judge Adv
Approved, J K Paulding

MORE: yet the Pres thinks it right that the Lt should be reprimanded & dismissed from the squad, & also thinks it right that the Cmdor should be rewarded for oppression, cruelty, scandalous conduct, illegal infliction of punishment, unofficer-like conduct, & embezzlement, by a gratuity from the Public Treas of $15,000 or $20,000. Inconsistency so glaring connot be without a motive.

Meeting of St Patrick's Total Abstinence Assoc: on Sep 6, at the rm of the Wash Lyceum, on C st. All in favor of following the example of Rev Theodold Mathieu, the apostle of temperance in Ireland. –Geo Savage

Died: on Aug 2, at Oak Spring, Caroline Co, in her 82nd year, after a brief illness, Mrs Christian Bankhead, relict of the late Jas Bankhead, of Port Royal, Va, & the mother of Col Bankhead, of the U S Army.

Died: on Aug 28, at her residence, in Hempstead, L I, Mrs Marion Eckford, wid/o the late Henry Eckford, aged 65 years.

Wheeling Times: Sep 1-died: yesterday, at Steubenville, Lt Jos C Vance, of this city. He was travelling from this city to New London, on Fri last, with his father-in-law, S Sprigg, when the horses ran off & were precipitated with the carriage down a steep bank, about 3 miles beyond Steubenville. Mr V was taken up insensible & continued so until he died. He was the s/o ex-Govn'r Vance, of Ohio, had resided here for many years. His death will be felt by a large circle of acquaintances & friends.

Rev Theodore Gallaudet will preach in Dr Laurie's Chr tomorrow at 11 a m. Rev Mr Sparrow, agent for the Assembly's Brd of Education, will preach there at 4:30 p m.

$20 reward for my stolen setter dog: last seen on Mon. –Henry May, Capitol Hill

The undersigned takes this method of informing all concerned that he will visit Wash City, on or before Dec 20 next, for the purpose of making arrangements to prove up his heirship to the estate of the late Bilaby Portens & sister, of London. Also, to investigate his title to a portion of military lands on Green river, Ky; after which he will depart for London. –Albert Ball [Address him at St Louis, Mo, before his departure.]

Committed to the jail of Fred'k Co, on Jul 29 last, negro man Thos Rankin, about 27. He says he is free & from Wash City. Owner, if any, is requested to come forward & have him released; he will otherwise be discharged according to law.
–Henry Houck, Sheriff of Fred'k Co, Md

MON SEP 7, 1840
At Phillipsburg, Lower Canada, on Sep 1, Lt Farquhar, of Col Dyer's corps of volunteers, was shot dead [assassinated] by Capt McAdam, of the same corps. The murderer was secured by the police.

Died: on Sep 2, at Cumberland, Md, in his 81st year, Wm McMahon, father of John V L McMahon, of Balt. Mr M was a native of Ire, but came to this country at a very early age. A man of the most warm zeal as a Christian, & respected by all who knew him. The repeated ofcs of high trust with which he has been honored by the people of his county will attest the fact of his irreproachable integrity.

Official statement it appears that Gen Harrison is not in any sense a defaulter to the Gov't. In the statute-book for the act of Mar 2, 1831, referred to in the Sec's letter, we find: An act for the relief of Mrs Clarissa B Harrison: Treas to allow the reps of J C S Harrison, late Receiver of Public Money at Vincennes, credit of $1,500 for bringing up the books of Nathl Ewing, his predecessor; $2,015.04, paid out under a deed of trust from the Bank of Vincennes, with commissions on the same, amounting to $35.51; & to settle the account of the late Receiver, arising from the discharge of his official duty. Sec of the Treas to allow to the legal reps & heirs of said Receiver the period of 18 years to pay the amount which shall be found due from said Receiver, without int: by taking a lien on the estate of said Receiver. –Andrew Stevenson, Speaker of Hse o/Reps. –Saml Smith, Pres protem of the Senate. Approved Mar 3, 1831. -Andrew Jackson In the ptn of Clarissa B Harrison, wid/o the late J C S Harrison: at the time of his death he was endeavoring to sell his real property to repay the sum of which he had thus been defrauded to the U S. If the whole property left by her husband is disposed of at a public sale, it will not be sufficien to pay the debt, leaving herself & 6 orphan chldrn without the means of support. To his dght, & only child, Gen Pike left no inheritance but his claims upon that country which he had so long, so faithfully, & sucessfully served, & in whose cause he at length expired, in the arms of victory. [He fell at the battle of York, in Upr Canada, during the late war: leaving only his sword & a few books.] –Clarissa B Harrison, Boone Co, Dec 9, 1830. [Cmte on Public Lands: On Jun 30, 1830, it appears he was indebted to the Gov't for $12,803.63, entitled to a credit of $1,500, paid for clk hire in making out th accounts of his predecessor in ofc; he was entitled to a credit of $2,015.04, paid for the defence & repairs of property of the U S, for which he was one of the trustees; & that he ought to be credited the sum of $1,989.50, for expenses incurred in transporting the public moneys to the place appointed for their deposite.] AND-on Apr 2, 1828, an act was passed by Congress for the relief of Mrs Brown, wid/o the late Maj Gen Brown: to pay her a sum equal to the pay & emoluments & allowances of her late husband from the time of his death until Dec 31 next. After the death of Cmdor Perry, an act was passed by Congress, on Mar 2, 1821, making provision for the support of his family: an annuity of $400 given to his wife, & $150 to each of his 4 chldrn during their minority.

Mrs R Howard, opposite Mr Fuller's City Hotel, can accommodate 2 or 3 gentlemen with board.

Appointments by the Pres: Montgomery Blair, of Miss, to be U S Atty for the Dist of Mo. Christian F Gobrecht, of Pa, to be Engraver of the U S Mint at Phil, v Wm Kneass, dec'd.

John H Smoot has removed from the corner of Bridge & High sts to the store-room nearly opposite, on the south side of Bridge st, lately occupied by Mr Richd Osbourn, where he will keep fashionable Dry Goods.

Fire on Sat last destroyed a stable & carriage-hse occupied by Mr Albert Parris, hackdriver, situated in the rear of the Six Bldgs, in Ward 1. Six valuable horses & 2 hackney-carriages were destroyed.

Mrd: on Sep 1, by Rev Mr Matthews, Mr Patrick Lyddane, of Wash City, to Miss Ann Lyddane, of Montg Co, Md.

TUE SEP 8, 1840
Pa College: in the new college edifice, in Filbert st, above 11th, Phil. Saml Geo Morton, M D: Geo McClellan, M D; Wm Rush, M D; Saml Colhoun, M D; Saml McClellan, M D; Walter R Johnson, A M. Students are admitted to the practice of the Pa & Blockley Hospitals on the same terms as the other students of the city. −S Colhoun, Dean, 15, south 7th st.

Portland Adv: on Tue, in that harbor, 5 young ladies drowned: The boat *Banner*, belonging to the City, left the wharf: a white squall struck the top of the sail of the *Banner*, & the boat capsized. Lost were: Frances Ingraham, d/o widow Ingraham. Adeline Thurston, d/o Mr Saml Thurston, calker. Julia Ann Milliken, d/o Capt Millikin, of the barque *Oceola*. Caroline & Eliz Ilsley, dghts of Mr Nathan Ilsley. The young ladies were between the ages of 11 years & 18 years.

Elisha Stone, of Stafford Co, exhibited in Fredericksburg, on Sat last, a watermelon raised by himself: weighed 71 pounds when pulled from the vine: round the middle: 3 feet & 6½ inches: length-4 feet & 7 inches.

Died: on Sep 7, after a distressing illness, of consumption, at the residence of her sister, Mrs Mary A Connor, Miss Ann Fowler, in her 18th year. Funeral this evening at 4 p m. [The Winchester & Cumberland papers will please copy the above.]

Prospectus of the Ladies' Academy of the Visitation, in Gtwn, D C: located on the hghts of Gtwn, D C: under whose superintendence & care the studies are conducted by members of the religious order founded in 1610 by St Frances de Sales, & first governed by St Jane Frances Fremiot de Chantal.

Com'rs appointed by Chas Co Court to value & divide the real estate of the late Gen Philip Stuart, dec'd, give notice that they will, on Nov 13 next, meet at the late residence of Mr Bernard H Stuart, dec'd, called *Eutaw*, in Chas Co, Md, for the purpose of executing said commission. −A F Beall, Thos H Edelin, Sylvester F Gardener, Thos B Berry, Wm Beall

Classical Institute: corner of H & 9th sts, Wash. J E Norris has recently taken Mr John Phillips, A B, as an Assistant. School opened on Thu last. Recommended by Thos C Thornton. −J E Norris

WED SEP 9, 1840
Newnansville, Aug 13: Mr Saml Smart, about 23 years of age, & a native of Miss, & for the last 8 years a resident of this county, was killed by the Indians, while with Mr Jas Lanier, in their field at Fort Tarver guarding their negroes, who were gathering fodder. Mr Lanier was severely wounded, but made his escape.

St Mary's, Ga, Aug 24, 1840. Mr Jas Howell, formerly of Camden Co, one of the sufferers, found his wife & one child butchered by the Indians. About 10 days since, they made an attack upon the family of Mr Courey, who was absent from home at the time. In the evening when he returned, he found his dwlg in smoking ruins, & his wife, with 6 small chldrn, laying about his field, shot down in attempting to escape, & their bodies horribly mutilated. He lived on Brandy branch, [I think,] one of the head waters of St Mary's river, in Fla. Mr Howell was able to save 3 of his chldrn as they ran from the Indians. Mrs Green & 1 of her chldrn were killed- information derived from a settler who was with Miss Chanty Green on horseback, whom he had rescued. On the 19th, while Mrs Patrick was preparing a bed for her little chldrn, she was fired at thru the window, by the Indians, & fell dead on the bed in front of her father. Mr Thos Davis, of our county, & 2 of his chldrn, were killed. Mr Patrick rushed for the picket, bearing the dead body of his dght. The Indians were driven off by men in the fort. Mr A Jernakin killed one. The Indians crossed into Camden Co, burnt the places of Davis, a Mr Mincey's, & several others.

$1 reward for runaway indented apprentice to the bricklaying business, Thos Gates, aged about 18 years. Reward for his apprehension & return to me. –Thos Lewis, 7th st, near Patriotic Bank

St Louis Republican: a murder was committed on the 17th ult near Van Buren, Iowa Terr, on the person of John L Davis, by his brother-in-law, John B Turner, who shot his victim with a rifle. Turner escaped.

Mrs Graeff has opened a school for small chldrn near the corner of 6th & D sts.

The splendid mansion on the Hudson, 4 miles above Harlem, built 2 years since by R E Thompson, was burned on Fri. It was one of the most beautiful bldgs on the banks of the river.

Gen Hinds died on Aug 23, at his residence in Jeff Co, Miss: rupture of a blood vessel. Gen Hinds was with Gen Jackson at the battle of New Orleans: & during the whole of the last war rendered his country much valuable service.

Mrd: on Sep 2, at N Y, by Rev Dr Milnor, J S MacDonell, of Cornwall, U C, barrister-at-law, to Christine, d/o the Hon Geo A Waggaman, of La.

Died: on Sep 2, Levin Killmon, after a long & painful illness of about 10 years standing, for many years a master of a vessel out of the port of Balt, Md.

Died: Aug 27, at Greenwich, Conn, Rev Isaac Lewis, D D, in 95th year of his age, & in 72nd of his ministry.

Died: on Sep 1, in Talbot Co, Md, after a lingering illness, Mrs Eliz Hindman, in her 90th year, respected & beloved by all who had the pleasure of her acquaintance.

THU SEP 10, 1840

The brig *Florence*, of & for N Y, Saml Rose, mstr, sailed from Rotterdam Jun 30, with a crew of 8 persons & 79 passengers. On Aug 9, they were assailed with gales, & the brig struck the rocks: she filled, & fell on her side. Capt Rose commanded all to remain by the wreck. Mr Wm Robbs, of Springfield, Mass, a devoted sailor, was dashed against the rocks, a mangled corpse. 30 of the 79 passengers were saved: many by Capt Rose & Mr Schofield, chief mate.

The murder of Thos Dougherty, Judge of the Co Court of St Louis Co, in Jun, 1838, & over which there has ever since been hanging the deepest mystery, has been cleared by the letter dated Texas, signed by a Dr Hughes, in which he confesses the murder of the Judge: his revenge for an injury he suffered over 10 years ago. Hughes was engaged in counterfeiting, & sentenced to imprisonment in the Ky Penitentiary. -Missouri Repiblican

Died: yesterday, Henrietta Slater, aged 55 years, of fever. Funeral at 3 p m, today, from the residence of Jos Little, on D st, adjoining Dyer's auction store.

Died: on Tue, Oliver, infant s/o Mr Chas Fletcher, a clk in the Gen Land Ofc, aged 6 months.

Died: on Sep 2, at *Howard Grove*, the residence of the family of the late Jos Howard, on South river, [where she had been for a few weeks on a visit,] after a few days illness, of congestive fever, Margaret Cath, y/d/o Dr Chas G Worthington, of Elk Ridge, Anne Arundel Co, Md, in her 12th year.

Cmte of arrangements for the Harrison rally in Old Allegany, in Cumberland, Md, on Sep 22:

Thos Shriver	Michl Wilson
Saml Athy	Geo W Haller
Danl Wineow	U R Lowdermilk
Wm Lynn	R V Hook
Thos Rizer	John Pickell
H G Grieves	Jos Shumate
John Gephart	J J Johnson
Jas H Hoblitzell	Geo Mattingly
H B Pigman	Saml Eckles
Thos A Healy	Wm Saylor

Abraham Russell	J M McCleary
Wm R M'Culley	Thos Reid
Matthias Rizer	Harrison D Black
Jonathan Butler	Henry Hudson
Aza Twigg	Henry B Osborn
Gustavus Beall	Wm Cappeller
Jacob Rizer	Fred'k Shipley
John M Maguire	Robt V Craggs
Patrick Crowley	Wm L Lamar
Danl Cresap	Danl Folck
Benj Davis	R Worthington
Alex'r King	Isaac Rice
Geo C Perry	Jesse Hinkle
J W Magruder	Jos Shriver
Saml Charles	Saml P Smith
Jacob Bargdoll	Jos Schuck
Alpheus H Gross	Geo Stubblefield

FRI SEP 11, 1840
The Frankfort Commonwealth gives the following as the Whig Electoral Ticket: on the part of the state: Richd A Buckner, Jas T Morehead.
<u>Congressional Dists:</u>

R Patterson	W H Field
I Hart	W W Southgate
J W Irwin	R H Memefee
C G Wintersmith	M P Marshall
B Y Chosley	A Beatty
J Harlan	D Breck
T W Riley	

Portsmouth [Ohio] Tribune, Sep 4. We have supported Van Buren, & now oppose him:

Wm M'Cauley	Geo Dudley
W G Piles	Geo Chad
E Wallace	W H Taylor
John Brant	Geo W Graves
Henry Thomas	Wm Shelpman
David Glaze	John Parkins
Geo Glaze	Wm Burrell
David Mustard	Cornelius Shelpman-aged 78
Castleman Streat	

<u>From the same paper-add our names to the straight-out Harrisonians:</u>

Jos Williamson	Geo Calvert
Thos Williamson	John Freeman
Jacob Cox	Perry Martin

Levi Moore			B F Lemon
John Browse			Isaac Cade
Wms Holt			Lloyd S Hogan

Louisville, Ky, Sep 3. On Tue evening with a party of pleasure on board, & by accident, our barge club was run over by the Louisville & Jeffersonville steam ferry boat. The barge was capsized, & Miss Ainsley, the d/o our fellow citizen, Mr Hugh Ainsley, was drowned. Her body has not yet been found. -Gaz

On Thu week, Mr Benj Dolterer, of Tinicum township, Bucks Co, Pa, while thrashing with a horse power machine, got his right hand into the cylinder, whreby it was so much lacerated that amputation at the elbow was necessary. Dr Jas Martin performed the operation, & the patient is doing well. A similar accident happened in Springfield, on the day after, to Mr Jacob Mann, whose right hand was also lost. Dr Bodder amputated the hand above the wrist. Mr Mann is recovering.

Mrd: on Thu, in Alexandria, by Rev Geo G Cookman, Mr John Geo Adams, of Wash City, to Miss Elvira Frances, 2nd d/o Harrison Bradley, of the former place.

City News-Wash. Columbian Horticultural Soc:
Robt Barnard, Pres. V Ps:		John F Callan, Treas
J A Smith				Madison Cutts, Corr Sec
A McWilliams				Wm Thompson, Rec Sec
R Dick					A Suter, Librarain
A Suter					H Stone, Draughtsman
G Watterston
Dr T P Jones, Lecturer on Horticultural Chemistry
[Soc makes note of the death of Dr Perrine, late one of our members.]
Cmte on holding an Exhibition of the Soc this fall:
Dr McWilliams				Mr Buist
Mr Suter				Mr John Douglas
Dr Gunnell
Flowers exhibited by: Mrs Wm Thos Carroll; Mrs Suter; Mr Buist.
Fruits by Mr Wm Cooper, of PG Co, Md. Also, by Mr Watterson.

Administrator's sale of valuable farm: *Greenfield*, the residence of the late Anna Roszel: about 600 acs: sale on Oct 29 next: subject to a lease of 2 years from Mar 1 next, at $400 per annum. Land lies on the waters of Secolin, in Loudoun Co, 4 miles so of Leesburg, Va: good brick bldg with a good brick kitchen adjoining: several out hses: brick merchant & grist Mill, with a miller's hse. With a little expense this might be made one of the best grazing plantations in the country. -Stephen G Roszel, adm, with w a

Colored girl burnt to death: Mary Simms, aged about 12 years, employed in watching some cooking operations in her father's house, near the Capitol Hill, on Sun last.

Morton McMichael adopted as the Whig Candidate for Congress in the 3rd Congress Dist of Pa, vice Chas Naylor, who felt himself obliged by delicate health & the calls of his private affairs to decline.

SAT SEP 12, 1840

Madame Dorman will open her French & Eng Boarding Schools & Day Schools on Sep 1 next, for young ladies: F st, between 12th & 13th sts, Wash City.

Lost: a pair of fine gold spectacles, in a red Morocco case, somewhere between the Upr Bridge, Rock Crk, & the Glass-hse. Liberal reward. Leave with either Mr Eckle, in Gtwn, or Jas Galt, Wash City.

B Storer & Wm Key Bond have connected themselves as partners in the practice of law. They will attend the Courts held in Hamilton Co, Ohio, & the Crct & Dist Courts of the U S at Columbus. –Sep 1, 1840, Cincinnati, Ohio

Extensive sale of very handsome furniture: on Sep 23, at the 3 story brick hse on Pa ave, recently occupied by the late Spanish Minister, Mr Calderon. -Edw Dyer, auct

$200 reward for runaway negro man Jacob Shaw, aged 35: has a free brother in Wash City by the name of Sandy Shaw. –Thos Berry, PG Co, Md, opposite Alexandria

Orphans Court of PG Co, Md. Ordered that Eliz Ferrall & Dennis W Ferrall, excs of Thos Ferrall, late of said county, dec'd, give notice to dec'd creditors. –Phil Chew, Reg [Said notice followed: letters testamentary on the personal estate of Thos Ferrall, dec'd. –Eliz Ferrall, DennisW Ferrall, excs of the dec'd.]

Orphans Court of Wash Co, D C. Letters of adm, as prayed for on the estate of Martha Cotter, late of Harper's Ferry, Va, dec'd, be granted to John F Callan, unless cause to the contrary be shown on or before the first Tue of Oct next. –Nathl P Causin. -Ed N Roach, reg/o wills

Mrd: on Sep 8, by Rev Mr McLean, W D Wallach, of Matagorda, Texas, to Mgt Chapman, eldest d/o Mr Augustin Newton, of Wash City.

Mrd: on Sep 9, at Mt Vernon Pl, Balt, the residence of the father, by Rev Dr Wyatt, Isabella M, only d/o Granville S Oldfield, to John S Wright, of Rio de Janeiro.

Mrd: on Sep 1, at Hancock Barracks, Maine, by Rev C C Beaman, Lt Jos A Haskin, 1st Regt U S Artl, to Miss Rebecca Eustis Sprague, d/o Assist Surgeon L Sprague, U S Army.

Mrd: on Sep 9, in Clark Co, Va, by Rev Wm G H Jones, Maj Richd Bennett, of Wash City, to Miss Mgt Funsten, d/o the late Oliver Funsten.

Balt, Sep 10: daring robbery at the Eutaw Hse, of a leather wallet with checks & bills, the property of Mr Wm N McVeigh: including one to the order of W N & J H McVeigh, drawn by the Farmers' & Planters' Bank of Balt on the Mechanics' Bank of N Y. reward of $100. –Patriot [Sep 14 paper: wallet & money found under the carpet in the room of the negro servant who waited on Mr McV. He was arrested on suspicion of the theft. –Patriot]

Appalachicola, Aug 29. On Sun last our city lost Mr Chas Ross, a pilot; Mrs Sabia Roane, w/o Mr Wm P Roane; Mrs Susan Lewis, a widow, & her only child, a boy about 5 years of age. Here were the wife but a few days ago a bride, the strong man, high in health, & the lone widow & orphan, all united in one common destiny. They set our in a pilot boat as passengers, but the boat being old & leaky, it sunk, & they were all drowned. –Adv

Robt C Clarke, Barber & Hair-dresser continues to operate at his old stand on Pa ave. [Local ad.]

Trustee's sale: decree of Chas Co Court, Court of Equity: sale on Oct 9 next: 450 acs, more or less: the late residence of Wm P Compton, known as the *Retreat*: with a framed dwlg. Property is of the estate of Barnes Compton, an infant under the guardianship of the subscriber, & will be sold on long credit. -Jno Barnes, trustee: Port Tobacco, Md.

MON SEP 14, 1840
Letter dated: Northern Liberties, Aug 19, 1840, to Hon Chas Naylor: subject-his declining the nomination as a candidate for Congress. Signed:

Elihu D Tarr	F Suplee	Danl Clark	J Mussleman
Thos Robinson	Jacob Rice	H C Pratt	

Mr Chas Naylor's reply: dated Phil, Sep 1, 1840: declines because of feeble health, [to say nothing of the situation of his affairs.] –Chas Naylor

Subscriber wishes to sell his farm: 146 acs, more or less, on Oxon run, adjoining the farm of Mr Washington Berry: indisputable title. –Geo W Talburtt

Wanted: a situation by a respectable middle-aged woman, either as laundress or hsekeeper, in respectable family. Inquire at Mr Lewellen's, near Squire Drury's ofc, near the West Market.

Tavern for rent: the 3 story brick tavern on 9th st, between D & E sts, occupied as same for a number of years. Apply to Edw Dyer, auct, or to Geo W Talburtt

Dissolution of the copartnership under the firm of J B Wingerd & Co, on Aug 5, by mutual consent. −J B Wingerd, Henry Bradley, John T Catlett. J B Wingerd & Chas Bradley have entered into a copartnership, under firm of Wingerd & Bradley, in the dry goods business at the old stand.

To the citizens of Balt: the undersinged have this morning, for the first time, been apprized that F H Knapp, Pres of the Balt Savings Instit, has named us as the assignees of the funds & assets of that instit. We inform that we decline the trust, & have nothing to do with the settlement, or in any capacity. −S C Leakin, Wm E Coal, Chas H Pitts

Earthenware, china, & glass, for sale: Thos Pursell, opposite Brown's Hotel, Pa ave, Wash City.

Died: on Sep 11, at his residence in Wash City, Abraham Howard Quincy, in his 74th year. Funeral this day at 2 p m. The Hon Heads of Depts & other ofcrs of the Gov't are invited to attend. Masonic notice: of the death of our venerable Bro, R W Resident Rep of the M W Grand Lodge of the state of N Y, who expired on Sep 11, at the advanced age of 73 years. −Jas Larrenson, Gr Sec: D O Hare, Sec

Fourth anniversary celebration, Sep 12, celebrated by a public parade & members firing at a target for a silver cup. Best shot was found to have been made by Mr J B Philips. Capt France presented the cup to him. Inscription engraved on the silver cup: "Presented to the Washington Light Infantry by Captain France. Won at target firing on the 4th Anniv of the Corps, Sep 12, 1840, by J B Phillips."

TUE SEP 15, 1840
On Sep 1, Mrs Huie, w/o Jas B Huie, of Louisville, Ky, was so much injured when thrown from her carriage, as to cause her death the next night-Sep 2.

Mr Reynolds P Starke,of Trenton, Ky, was shot dead from an ambuscade near that place on Aug 26. Assailant unknown.

Mrd: on Sep 8, in Fauquier Co, Va, by Rev Mr Horrindon, Mr Adam L Rose, of Wash, to Miss Jane Reid, of the former place.

Died: on Sep 13, Robertson George, infant s/o Lydia & Flodoardo Howard. Funeral today at 11 a m, from the residence of his father.

Notice: There will be a Barbecue given at Mr Capron's Spring, in Vansville dist, PG Co, Md, on Sep 19, to which the Electoral Candidates for the State, are invited.

By writ of fieri facias, issued by B K Morsell, a J P for Wash Co, D C, I shall expose for public sale, on Sep 22, at the Centre Market-hse, for cash, one negro boy, Richd, about 10 years of age, seized & taken in execution as the property of Wm Turner, & will be sold to satisfy a judgment due Thos MacGill. -Horatio R Maryman, cnstbl

WED SEP 16, 1840
Mrd: on Sep 14, by Rev Mr Thornton, Mr Danl Smith to Miss Matilda B Croggon, all of Wash City.

Mrd: on Sep 15, in St John's Chr, Wash, by Rev Wm Hawley, John J McLaughlin, of the U S Navy, to Salvadora, d/o the late Richd W Meade, of Phil.

Mrd: on Sep 15, at the residence of J J Sayers, in Alexandria, by Rev Mr Harrison, Wm Henry Brawner, of Chas Co, Md, to Miss Mary Cath, y/d/o the late Francis Speake, of the same county & state.

Died: on Sep 6, at his residence in Zanesville, Ohio, in his 38th year, Dr John Adams Turner, a native of Fauquier Co, Va, & for several years past a highly esteemed citizen of Zanesville.

Died: Sep 11, at Gtwn, Saml Howell, only child of Alex H & Anna Dodge, aged 8 months & 20 days.

Capt Thos Oxhard, who, during the late war, was capt of the privateer *True Blooded Yankee* but who for many years past had resided at Marseilles, died in that city on Jul 17, &, pursuant to his dying request, was wrapped in an American flag for a winding sheet.

Mrs Milligan, recently arrived from Ire, was instantly killed at Cleveland, a few days since, by a ball discharged from a rifle by a lad who was shooting at a mark: the ball passed thru the target board & struck Mrs M on the head.

John E Scheel, late of Va, offers his services to the citizens of Wash as an instructor on the piano. Apply at Mrs Sengstack's, D st, between 12th & 13th sts.

$5 reward for a bundle of paper with notes, lost between the market & my stable.
–Fred'k Golding

J H Ritter, Surgeon Dentist: ofc between 9th 10th sts, on Pa ave. Teeth set from one to a whole block.

Wanted: a woman to attend on a lady & infant to New Orleans next month. Apply to Mrs Clement Smith, in First st, Gtwn, at the corner house lately occupied by Mr Ralph Semmes.

THU SEP 17, 1840
Attys: 1-V D Barry, Bolivar: J T Leath, Memphis: Tenn. 2-Jas Downer, Louisville, Ky. 3-Josiah J Crosby & J S Jones, Montg Co, Texas. [Taken from their ads.]

The Hon John Quincy Adams, accompanied by his son, & Nathl Curtis, of Roxbury, Mass, are at present on a visit to the British Province of Nova Scotia.

Mr Corwin, candidate for Govn'r of Ohio, is now lying sick in or near Gambier, Ohio. His illness will prevent his fulfilling some very important appointments. –Wheeling Times, Sep 12

Long Old Fields, Md, Sep 12, 1840. Public barbecue on Sep 24 given by the Whigs: candidates of both parties are expected to be present. –W B Brooke, F M Bowie, Tho W Clagett, Allen P Bowie, Rd W Bowie

Phil papers: notice of death of E J Bancker, on Mon. He was injured from a fall from his horse & carried to his father's hse, but medical aid was unavailing, & he died during the night.

App'td by the Pres: Gabriel Montamat, to Deputy Post Master at New Orleans, La, v Wm McQueen, resigned.

Letter to the Post Master at Balt, from an agent of the Post Ofc Depts, dated at Columbus, Ohio, Sep 10, 1840, states that the individual who robbed the U S mail east of Springfield, Ohio, on Mar 10 last, has been arrested, & $16,000 of the money recovered. Chas Bostwick, the driver of the mail stage, turns out to be the robber.

Allegany Academy, Cumberland, Md: exam took place on Jul 30 & 31. Classical Dept under Rev L H Johns, Principal of the Academy. Eng dept under c/o Thos F White. Brd of Trustees: B S Pigman, Pres. Jon W Magruder, Jas Smith, John Gephart. Visiters: G A Thruston, S M Semmes, Rev S H M'Donald, Th L Patterson, Geo W Devecmon

Orphans Court of Montg Co, Md. Letters testamentary on personal estate of Benj S Forrest, late of said county, dec'd. Claims to be presented on or before Aug 25, 1841. –Anna Maria S Forrest, admx

Farm for sale: on which he now resides: near Leonardtown, St Mary's Co, Md: 696 acs, binds upon the Potomac river upwards of half a mile, which affords an abundance of sea-ore, which is considered a valuable manure & used at this time for the improvement of land: :farm is divided into 4 fields of 100 acs ea: brick dwlg, ice hse, & tobacco hses: remainder in timber & woods. –Edw Plater, near Leonardtown

Died: Thu last, at his residence in Clarke Co, Va, Judge Richd E Parker, of the Va Court of Appeals.

From Texas: 1-Galveston Daily Courier of Aug 29-arrival of a sloop from Campeachy with Cmdor Rebeau, of the Fed Mexican Navy on board. Rebeau reports that Urrea had been driven out of the city of Mexico, but was fortifying himself outside to make a determined resistance 2-Col Burleson has resigned his command of the 1st Regt of Infty, & W G Cooke appointed his successor. Capt Howard promoted to Maj, & expected to proceed against the Camanches immediately. Gen Huston pursued the Indians, after his engagement with them on Plumb crk, till his horses tired, & was compelled to abandon the pursuit. He returned to Austin, & has been very ill since his return.

Subscribers who have been receiving the Pilot & Transcript will please leave their names & places of residence at the Log Cabin Print Establishment of H R Robinson, on Pa ave, next to the Billiard Saloon, so they will receive the Pilot regularly. –P W Toy, agent for Wash & Gtwn

Orphans Court of Wash Co, D C. The case of Ezekiel Young, adm of Alfred Young, dec'd: first Tue in Oct next set for settlement of said estate. –Ed N Roach, reg/o wills

Obit-died: on Sep 5, at the *Glebe*, the residence of his father, in Westmorealnd Co, Va, Dr John Ford Chandler, in his 25th year. In the bosom of his cherished family circle he was loved with no bounds.

FRI SEP 18, 1840
The Hon Martin Chittenden, formerly Mbr of Congress, & afterwards Govn'r of Vt, died on Sep 5 at Williston, Vt. He had a week previous to his death returned from Ill, sick of the prevalent fever.

I will sell at public auct, on Oct 31, a small farm of about 250 acs: in the nieghborhood of Good Luck, PG Co, Md: possession on Jan 1, 1841. Refer to Chas Duvall, near the premises. –Horace Rideout

Dancing Academy: Mr F C Labbe will re-open Oct 6, at his dwlg house, Pa ave; & at Gtwn, on Oct 5.

Five days from England: the remains of the Earl of Durham were interred at Tyne, attended by a vast concourse of people.

Died: on Aug 25, at Macomb, McDonough Co, Ill, John Pickrell, infant s/o John M & Angelina Walker, aged 6 months & 4 days.

Mrd: Sep 16, by Rev J C Smith, Saml J Cramer, of Fred'k, Va, to Eliz C, d/o John Mountz, of Gtwn.

Mrd: on Sep 15, at Abingdon, Harford Co, Md, by Rev Mr Prettyman, Mr Wm Nourse, of Wash, to Miss Isabella L Bond, 4th d/o Thos W Bond, of Balt.

Splendid hats: standard fashion for the season. Wm B Todd, 6 doors west of Brown's Htl.

Charlotte Hall School: duties under the direction of Dr Chas Kraitsir; assistants Chas A F Shaw, in math, & Mr Wm C Barnes, in the classical dept. –Jos F Shaw, Brd of Trustees

SAT SEP 19, 1840
Thos M Wilson intends to open school on Sep 21, on D, near 6th & 7th. Mr W hopes, from his experience in teaching, & a strict attention to the duties of his school, to give satisfaction to all who may favor him with their patronage.

Died: on Aug 19 last, at the residence of his grandfather, Wm Locke Chew, near Benton, Yazoo Co, Miss, Geo Biscoe, s/o Frisby F & Angelica Chew, aged nearly 3 years, a most interesting child.

For sale: 2 story dwlg house on 6th st, near E, now occupied by Mr J J Greenough. Also, a hse on E st, between 11th & 12th, now occupied by Mrs Morgan as a grocery & dwlg. Title to both is indisputable. -Reuben Johnston, Alexandria

Whereas my wife, Mary A Head, has, without cause, deserted my bed & board, this is to warn the public not to credit her on my account. –Geo M Head

Sale of good household furniture: on Sep 21, at the residence of Mrs Canedy, on Pa ave: all her household & kitchen furniture. -Edw Dyer, auct

Teachers wanted for female school in Warrenton, Va. For info:
John Walden
B Ward
W H Gaines
Baldwin Day
Wm F Phillips
Erasmus Helon
Thos P Knox
John P Philips

Full blooded mare at auction: named Sal Hornet, was left at the farm of John W Brown, who resides at the White Hse, on the Wash & Balt Trnpk, by Mr Thos Chaney, on Apr 12 last, to be kept there at livery, at $10 per month; no part of the debt due hath been paid. –John W Brown

MON SEP 21, 1840
Mrd: on Tue last, by Rev T C Thornton, Mr Wm Baldwin to Mrs Mary Sibley.

Bladensburg Academy is under superintendence of Mr M R Shyne.
–Alex Keech, Pres Brd of Trust

Balt, Sep 19. W R T Chaplain, who had been staying at Barnum's Hotel on Wed, left for Phil on Thu. Yesterday he was mrd to Miss Murdock, of Phil, & they arrived here in the steamboat line, & took apts in the City Hotel. After dining, he fell down in a fit, & in a short time expired. He was a native of Cambridge, Md, & a resident of Miss. –Sun

Balt, Sep 18. Mr Fred'k H Knapp, the projector & Pres of the Balt Savings Instit, was brought to this city yesterday by deputy high cnstbl Jeffers, who effected his arrest in Albany. He was conducted before Justice Gorsuch, &, in default of bail in the sum of $1,000 for his appearance to answer the charge of conspiracy & fraud at the regular term of the Court, was committed to jail. -American

Died: on Sep 12, at his residence in Phil, aged about 76 years, Mr Benj King, formerly for many years Mstr Blacksmith in the Wash Navy Yard. He was a native of the Isle of Man, but had resided in this country more than 40 years, a great part of the time in this city; where he was esteemed by the public authorities & by all who knew him as an honest & kind-hearted man, & for his pre-eminent skill in his profession.

From France: M Sanson, the public executioner, who died the other day, was remarkable for the horrible task he had to perform in 1793, when, in virtue of his ofc, he had to bind the hands of Louis XVI, & then place the monarch's head under the guillotine. He was the 3rd of his name who had filled the same functions, & he has a son & a grandson. He was fond of the arts & spent most of his evenings playing the piano. Of the 2 men who assisted him on Jan 21, 1793, one died on Jan 21, 1795, precisely 2 years afterwards, & the other was killed in the streets of Paris on Mar 21, 1794.

TUE SEP 22, 1840

Wash Univ of Balt: faculty-J H Miller, M D; Saml K Jennings, M D; W W Handy, M D; John C S Monkus, M D; Edw Foreman, M D; W R Handy, M D; John R W Dunbar, M D-Dean.

M Pageot, brother-in-law of M Serrurier, passes from Wash, where he has been Sec of Leg, to Madrid, as 1st Sec of the Embassy. He is replaced [at Wash] by M Chartry-Lafosse, s/o the Col of that name.

Convention at Hagerstown, Md, Sep 16: Wm Price, of Wash Co, Pres. V Ps:
S D Warfield, of Fred'k Co   John Braddock, of Montg Co
Alpheus Beall, of Allegany Co   David Hoffman, of Balt City
Secs: Wm D Bell, of Wash Co: Dr J E Snodgrass, of Balt City.
Addresses by: Mr Coale; Mr Cooper, of Pa; Mr Bradford,of Balt; Mr Laird, of Gtwn; Mr Orten, of Ind; Mr Bowie; Mr Wm Cort Johnson, of Fred'k.

Strawberry plants for sale: $2.50 per hundred, at my garden, on the old county rd, half way between Gtwn & Alexandria. —Anth R Fraser, stall #94, Centre Market

Evening school will commence in my Academy, on 14th st, near Pa ave, on Sep 28. —Henry Hardy

Univ of Va: J A G Davis, is Chairman of the faculty.

Tippecanoe Club #1 of Va: Jas Lyons, Pres.

A young lady of Sandwich, U C, Miss Amelia Marcott, aged about 16 years, on Sep 6, was seized with a cramp while at the dinner table, & died in a few minutes. During her illness, her bro was despatched on horseback to do an errand; the horse took fright, & threw the boy, causing his death.

For rent: 2 story brick dwlg on 14th st. Apply to Mrs S Craven, Pa ave, between 12 & 13th sts.

Mrd: on Sep 8, at Easton, Pa, by Rev John Vandeveer, the Hon Jos F Randolph, of New Brunswick, Mbr of Congress for N J, to Sarah Ann, d/o John Cooper, M D, of Easton, Pa.

Died: on Sep 20, in Wash City, Mrs Emily Ferguson, consort of Mr John W Ferguson, aged 27 years. Funeral from her residence near the Navy Yard, today at half past 1 p m.

Died: Sep 20, after a severe illness of 24 hours, Mrs Mary Kibby, aged 23 years, w/o Mr Alex'r Kibby.

Died: on Sep 13, at his residence in Wash City, Thos Welsh, a native of Ire.

Died: at the residence of her father, in Chas Co, Md, after an illness of more than 8 weeks, Amelia, eldest d/o Thos O & Ann Bean, in her 19th year. About 12 months since she returned, after an absence of some years at school, to her parents' house to dispense & enjoy around the domestic altar the tender pleasures of filial & parental love. [No date-current item.]

Died: on Sat, at Balt, John McFadon, aged 82 years.

Died: on Sep 17, at Balt, Geo Adam, s/o Geo B Cranston, aged 15 months & 13 days.

Died: on the 20th ult, at Picolata, East Fla, John Gross, in his 26th year, of the 2nd Regt U S Dragoons. He was a native of Hanover, Pa, & for many years a resident of Balt, Md.

Died: on Sep 19, at Balt, Chas A Walker, in his 20th year, y/s/o Col S D Walker.

Died: on Sep 6, at Charleston, S C, with the prevailing fever, after an illness of 3 days, Capt Benj F Spencer, for many years a resident of Alexandria, but for the last few years a resident of Charleston.

Died: on Sep 13, in Raleigh, after a short illness, aged 63 years, Beverly Daniel, Adj Gen of the State, & late Mrshl of the U S for the Dist of N C, an ofc which he honorable filled for more than 30 years.

Died: on Sep 13, at Tulip Hill, PG Co, Md, in his 39th year, Henry L Coombs; a valuable member of society, leaving his wife & chldrn & his father, & numerous relatives & associates. [Globe, Alexandria, Marlboro, Annapolis, Balt, N Y, & Port Gibson, Miss, papers will please insert the above.]

Auction sale of horses, cows, & farming utensils: at the distillery & dairy of the late Mr John Hitz, dec'd, about 2 miles north of City Hall. –Wm Hayman, trustee -Thos C Wright, auct

WED SEP 23, 1840

Our fellow townsman, Wm M Morrison, has just published A Word in Season, or Review of the Political Life & Opinions of Martin Van Buren.

Phil, Sep 18. Last evening, Caroline Yeager, with her sister & mother, stepped into the grocery store of Mr Thompson Black, at the corner of 10th & Chestnut sts, & felt faint. She had just seated, when she fainted & before medical assistance called arrive, she expired. She was 19 years of age, & the d/o a respectable butcher of Spring Garden. She had for some time been afflicted with an affection of the heart, the ultimate cause of her death. –Phil Gaz

Wash Corp: 1-Ptn from G W Kendrick: referred to the Cmte of Claims. 2-Cmte of Claims: unfavorable report on the ptn of Wm Prather, & asked to be discharged from further consideration of the same: report was ordered to lie on the table. 3-Memorial of John Gadsby & others: agreed to. 4-Ptn of Saml Smoot & others, praying the construction of a flag footway across K st, at 27th: referred to the Cmte on Improvements.

Died: on Sep 22, in Gtwn, D C, Henry Foxall McKenney, in his 22nd year. Funeral from the residence of his father in Dunbarton st, today, at 4 p m.

THU SEP 24, 1840

New fall dry goods received at the old stand corner of 8th st, opposite Centre Market. –Riley & Perry

Rockville Academy: by recent arrangements, the long tried services of Mr John Neely, the Principal of the Classical dept, are retained; therefore the expected vacancy will not occur. Mr Jos Braddock, Princ of the Math & Eng depts, ia a competent & faithful teacher. Order of the Brd, John Mines, Pres.

On Sep 6, Lt W K Hanson, 7th Infty, discovering numberous signs around his post at Wacahoote, proceeded with 30 men in search of the trail. He had not advanced far before he received a heavy fire from the enemy: one of his men was killed & 4 wounded, whom he succeeded in taking back to the garrison. There were over 100 Indians.

Lt Wm A T Maddox, U S Marine Corps, who arrived in this city on Sep 20, from Phil, with a detachment of U S Marines, repaired to his mother's residence, & on opening the door to abserve the weather, he was precipitated to the ground, breaking his right arm & sustaining other injury. Had not the night been extremely dark, he would have discovered his mistake, the porch having been removed during his absence. Medical aid was resorted to, & the Lt is doing well.

Mr R Hay, Surgeon of Glasgow, has performed the operation of piercing the mememberanes of the brain of a child, 8 months old, for hydrocephalus, or water in the head. No less than 25 fluid ozs of water were extracted. The child, a girl, is doing well. –Glasgow paper

Mrd: on Sep 20, in Alexandria, by Rev Geo G Cookman, Mr Geo Waters, formerly of London, Eng, to Mrs Susan Calvert, of the same place.

Died: on Sep 21, Herbert, s/o S D & Mary Juana Langtree, aged nearly 9 months.

Died: on Sep 21, Thomas, aged 3 years, 7 months & 17 days, 2nd s/o David & Elisha Barry, of Wash Co, D C.

Boots & Shoes: store opposite Brown's Hotel, Pa ave. –Andrew Hoover [Local ad.]

The Hon Abbot Lawrence has resigned his seat in Congress on account of his health. Letter to Philip Marett, Chrmn Co Convention. From the Boston Atlas, Sep 21.

FRI SEP 25, 1840
From the Southern Churchman: Pocahontas. *A Legend: with Historical & Traditionary Notes*: by Mrs M M Webster, Phil, Herman Hooker, publisher: 1840. A fair volume of poetry, with the title-Pocahontas, a Legend. Interest increased when found she was a native of Va, & lineal descendant of the *Forest Queen*.

Drawing of: Map of the disputed territory, reduced from the original of Messrs Featherstonhaugh & Mudge: British Com'rs 1839. [Quebec, Canada, U S, Lawrence river, Dist of Gaspe, New Brunswick.]

Wash Co, D C: on Sep 23, 1840, John Miller, the s/o Isaac S Miller, of said county, brought before me, a J P of said county, 2 stray cows. –Edw Mattingly, J P [Miller lives on Greenleaf's Point.]

SAT SEP 26, 1840
Sale of steamboats: at the Balt Exchange, on Thu: R M Hall, made the following sales: steamboat *Jewess*, $15,250; boat *Pocahontas*, $8,000; boat *Columbus*, $8,100; boat *South Carolina*, $15,000; 2/3rds of the boat *Patrick Henry*, $6,000. These boats, we believe, all belonged to the Balt & Norfolk line, which has lately been discontinued.

B O Lowndes, Bladensburg, has a few Ewe Lambs of the Southdown & Bakewell breed, which he wishes to dispose of.

Sale of very handsome furniture, on Sep 28, at the residence of Mr Powell, on 3rd st, next adjoining Mrs Pittman's brdg hse. –Edw Dyer, auct

Robt W Haywood, appointed Adj Gen of the state of N C, v Beverly Daniel, dec'd.

Wheeling, Sep 22. Govn'r John Tyler arrived in this city last evening, weak from recent attack of bilious fever, did however, eloquently, address the Mechanic's Assoc.

Loudoun & Fairfax land for sale: my tract near Goose Crk, 9 miles from Leesburg: farm having been in the hands of tenants for some years. I have also, a tract of about 400 acs in Fairfax Co, adjoining *Mt Vernon*, in an uminproved state. Information from Algernon S Tebbs, of Leesburg, or to:-Julia A Wilson.

Wash Co, D C: I certify that Jas McKnight brought before me, as an estray, a sorrel mare colt, last spring's foal. He thinks it followed his carryall on Sep 21, from near Beltsville. –Jas Marshall, J P

MON SEP 28, 1840
Orphans Court of Wash Co, D C. Wm S Nicholls, adm de bonis non, of Jas Kincaid, of said county, dec'd: final settlement on the 2nd Tue in Apr, 1841. –Ed N Roach, reg/o wills

Dayton Convention, Sep 10, 1840: speech by Gen Harrison: convention organized by calling to the chr ex-Govn'r Metcalf, of Ky, & appointing 19 V Ps, among whom were Preston W Farrar, of La; Maj A Miller, of Miss; Govn'r Bigger, of Ind; ex-Govn'r Vance, of Ohio, & W Snethen, of La, Sec.

Mrd: on Sep 24, by Rev Mr Davis, Mr Benj H Duvall to Miss Lydia Ann Birth.

Eng, French, & Spanish Academy: Mr & Mrs Santangelo have taken the 3 story hse east of 6th st, between E & F sts, & will open on the first Mon of Oct next, a Day School for young ladies. Mr S, an inhaitant during 17 years of the U S, in which he became in 1829 a naturalized citizen; was formerly a professor of languages in Columbia College of N Y.

TUE SEP 29, 1840

For rent: fashionable hses in Franklin Row, #5: possession can be given immediately. Inquire of R France, Pa ave, or on the premises.

Valuable property at pvt sale: my residence at Mt Pleasant, Fred'k Co, Md, 5½ miles northeast of Fred'k City: hse is large & convenient, meat hse, stables, & carriage hse. As I wish to turn my attention to farming, I will sell the property low, & make the payment accommodating. –Henry Simms

Wm H Thumlert, having a few leisure hours in the day, would devote them to posting books, making off accounts, & copying. He can be found a all times at his brother's store, [Jas E Thumlett,] near the steamboat wharf, or information left at his father's shop, opposite Brown's Hotel will meet with prompt attention.
–Wm H Thumlert

Subscriber will receive, in a few days, 2 more Vienna Pianos, purchased for the purpose of keeping up his small assortment. One may be safey pronounced the best instrument ever sold in the District The other, in the good ship *Vesper*, not yet opened. Call at the piano ware-rm on H st. –F A Wagler

Preston's Pure Concentrated Extract of Lemon: for flavoring. For sale by Chas Stott.

The Yeoman, a paper issued weekly, published at Richmond, Va, by Mr J S Gallaher, since Jan.

WED SEP 30, 1840

Loudoun Whig Festival: appointed ofcrs of the festival: Sydnor Bailey, Pres.
V Ps: R H Henderson	John Simpson
S M Edwards	Abner Gibson
C C McIntyre	Ludwell Luckett
David Shawen	Nathl Oden
Wm Slater	John J Coleman
Thos Hough	John Wornell
Jno Conrad	Gen Asa Rogers, Chief Mrshl

Public sale on Oct 3: furniture & sundry items, seized & taken as the property of Jos Letourno, by order of distress for hse rent, in arrear due to the Bank of the Metropolis. –H B Robertson, blf

Bladensburg, Sep 21-inquest over the body of a stranger found on the trnpk rd leading from Wash to Balt, whose name is supposed to be Edw Martin; paper found in his possession being a Navy pension certificate, entitling a person of that name, a disabled seaman of the U S Navy, to $3 per month, payable on Jul 1, & Jan 1, semi-annually, during his life, or the continuance of such disability, at the Mechanics' Bank of N Y.

A pvt in the Phil Wash Blues, Malcolm Connelly, while escorting the Reading Vols into the city with his company on Tue last, fell, from fatigue & sickness, in North 3rd st, & expired on Sat last.

Dr Nathl Emmons died at Franklin, Mass, on Wed last, in his 96th year: was the oldest clergyman, probably in the U S, & previous to his death he was the oldest surviving graduate of Yale College. He was settled in 1773 as Pastor of the Chr in Franklin, in which ofc he remained 54 years, & then resigned his pastoral charge, but continued to reside in that town till his death. –Boston Transcript

Fatal affray: man killed in the public sts: Allen Watts & Richd Collier, quarrelled at Sauter's tavern: also there was Henry Tucker, shoemaker, who resided in Gtwn. Watt's was seen to give Henry Tucker 3 or 4 stabs with a pkt knife, & in less than 2 mins, he fell dead. Watts was seized & taken before Judge Drury, & committed for trial at the ensuing Crmnl Court on charge of wilfully murdering Tucker.

Died: on Sep 26, in Wash City, Mrs Ann Smith, in her 52nd year, after enduring a long & painful suffering of 5 years, with most Christian-like resignation.

Died: on Fri, at Alexandria, Reuben Johnston, sr, age 73 years & 8 months.

Died: on Sep 18, at Phil, Prof C S Rafinesque, for many years a resident of that city, & the author of several scientific & literary works.

Died: on Sep 23, Emily Geo, aged 11 months & 16 days, y/d/o Ellenor & Wm Cammack.

New Fall Goods: Tucker & Son-the newest for overcoats, Diamond Beaver. Store near Gadsby's Htl.

Order of distrain from Jas Adams, exc of Thos Law, to me directed: sale on Oct 6 of furniture & sundry items, [same were listed,] seized & taken as the property of Saml P Lowe, dec'd; & will be sold to satisfy ground rent due the estate of Thos Law, dec'd. Sale at the late residence of S P Lowe, dec'd, on N J ave. –Horation M Maryman, blf

THU OCT 1, 1840
Household furniture at auction: on Oct 5, at the 3 story hse on F st, between 12th & 13th, occupied by Miss Henderson as a brdg hse. -Edw Dyer, auct

Sep. 1839, Ofcrs of the Customs at N Y:
Jessie Hoyt, Coll: $4,400
Deputy Coll: $1,500
J T Ferguson
John J Mumford
Geo Davis
Cashier: Talman J Waters: $3,000
Assist Cashier: J R Bleecker: $1,500
Aud: John A Flemin: $3,000
Appraisers-
Jeromus Johnson: $2,000
A B Mead: $2,000
A B Vanderpool: $2,000
J Lounsberry: $1,500
Clks:
R M Mitchell: $1,250
J L Tiffany: $1,250
S H Eakin: $1,050
A N Philips: $1,050

C P Clinch
G A Wasson
Sidney Wetmore
Assist Auditor: W P Holl: $1,500
John W Hunter: $1,250

B J Messerole: $1,500
J Prall: $1,500
P Thomas: $1,500

Leon'd A Bleecker: $1,050
Nath Olcott: $1,050
Wm Lang: $1,050
D Sullivan: $1,050

$1,000:
C Duryee
R C Overton
Isaac Bluxome
J Leonard
W J McMaster
T V Mumford
Chas A Gardiner
D Bonnet
D Stansbury
John R Hinchman
Leonard Wyant
M S Swartwout
Jas B Thruston

Wm C Dayton
G A Brown
Elias D Ogden
Wm A Spies
Edw Bleecker
J E Chadeayne
Chas J Chipp
Wm A Cox
H M Graham
Munson Gray
Jas H Greenfield
John D Herttell
John R S Hugget

D Kohleast
Danl Monroe
E H Nichols
Wm Prall
Edgar Tripler
Geo C Tyler
Jas N Jones
Francis Vosburg
Adrian Van Riper
Geo M Wetmore
Chas W Johnson

$900:
J A Bogart
Saml Cadle
R S Newby
J B Wood
Wm Dempsey
G S Brisbin
W C Gray

H W Christie
P V Remsen
G W Rose
G D Overton
G L Oothout
E H Plume
W Fream

C Gill
P A Young
D R Strachan
C Radcliff
C J Cannon
E L Matthews
H Doane

J H Roe
$800:
J C Delmar
J L S Grandin
E Hyde
E G Livingston
J C Niebuhr
P K Ogden
D S Grandin
$600:
R V Newby
$500:
Chas H Innes
$400:
G W Blake
$300:
W M Haff
$250:
J P Haff, messenger
$200:
John H Dunn
Inspectors: -$1095:
Henry Abell
Rowland P Allen
Robt Adams
Abra'm Ackerman
Henry C Atwood
John Bleecker
Jas D Bisset
John R Browne
Wm J Brown
Jacob Burdette
John Black
Wm Benjamin
Thos Brownell
Dennis Brink
Geo H Biddle
Barnabas Bates
Wm Boggs
Jefferson Brown
Adam Blacklidge
Wm Berbe
Pascal Bertine
Alex'r Bidwell
Saml W Coe

S Paret
W B Fremain
F Bruce
W W Fream
T H Dennison
C M Tucker
C W Baker
W A Pearson

G D Cooper

Wm C Connor

W Elder- messenger

Wm Cairnes
Amos Coles
Henry Cheavans
Barnet Cole
John Colvill
Jos Clark
Peter Cutant
John Connor
John Cox
Wm Currie
Abra'm W Cooper
Jacob J Cohen
Thos Chatterton
Pat'k Caffry
L K Campbell
John Commerford
Thos Caslin
John De Camp
Abra'm Davids
Jos Dreyfouse
Nat'n Chamberlain
T J Davis
Moran Dugan

Thos Shankland

H Ulshoeffer
Thos J Gillilan
Saml Lupton
Fred'k Schwanck
F C Niebuhr-
messenger
Abra Vanderpool

Abra'm Dally, jr
Jeremiah Dodge
Edmund Driggs
Chas Denike
Thos S Day
Darius Darling
A G Dixon
J O Dissoway
Nathl Deveau
John J Earle
Jos Ellis
R J Everett
Anthony B Ellison
Richd Fining
Saml B Fleming
Chas D Field
Job Funnan
Henry Fanning
Peter Field
David Feeks
F B Fitch
Peter Fairchild
John H Frederick

Joshua Fleet	Saml Lloyd	Geo Rocard
David Gardner	John Little	Wm H Randall
W H P Graham	Richd Lewis	N C Robertson
Peter Gordon	Thos H Lyell	Saml D Rouse
Thos M Gahogan	P P Livingston	Jas K Roe
Chas Green	Jas Ladd	Wm Shute
Edmund Gross	Jos Y Miller	Chas Stuart
Nathl H Green	Alex'r Ming	Wm Smith
Fred'k Groshon	Leroy McEvers	Dennis Striker
D Henderson, jr	Henry Libernau	Henry Raymond
Edw Hitchcock	Geo S Messerve	Asa H Swift
Elias Hicks	Abra'm A Leggett	Henry Storms
Wm Honay	John Morrris, jr	Jas Smyth
Ward B Howard	John McGloin	Henry F Sands
D R Hitchcock	Abra'm Messerole	C V Schermerhorne
Andrew Hutton	Henry McCaddin	Andrew Sure
Wm D Hughes	John McKibbin	Thos S Stevens
Geo Howard	Wm B Mott	Danl Sparks
John H Hunt	Jos Marsh	John Salmon
Edwin A Hopkins	Geo McCready	Egbert G Sweet
Thos Hope	Wm McLaughlin	Jas Smith
Addison Hill	Geo W Matsell	Levi D Slane
Chas Hunter	John McGrath	Pater Tappan
Thos Hall	Montg Moses	Peter Taylor
Archibald Hays	Jas McMillan	Jas T Thompson
Thos Howard	John Marston	Andrew Tombs
David Holly	John J Manning	Thos Trenon
Isaac A Isaacs	Wm Marshall, jr	Wm Thorne
Geo Inness	D McGrath	Jas Thorne
Edgar Irving	Donald McDonald	Griffin Tompkins
Andrew Jackson	Chas McDermott	O H Tompkins
Obadiah Jackson	Pat'k McCafferty	John Townsend
Thos Jenkins	Wm C Neilson	Thos W Titus
Wm D Jones	S C Nicoll	John J Tracey
Henry Kevser	Gideon Ostrander, jr	Richd Tyson
Robt E Kelly	Jas M Oakley	Saml Utter
Geo H Kellinger	Corn's W Oakley	John Townsend, jr
John C Keeler	Morris Oakeley	John Van Dyk
Wm Lee	John W Ogsburg	B M Van Beuren
Amos Leeds	Robt Phillips	J L Van Boskerck
Geo W Lent	Napli Phillips	C Van Antwerp
John M Lester	Abra K Patterson	T B Vermilyea
H G Lewis	Alex V Phister	John W Vethake
Jos Lyon	Hump Ricketson	John Van Dine
Wm Lupton	John Pierce	Wm Welling

Benj Wood
Everasdus Warner
Isaac Wood
Wm J Wiswall
John W Wheeler
Barnum Whipple: $912.50
Night Inspectors: -$638.75:
Wm Angevine
Wm Boardman
Thos Bloomer
Francis Boss
Bernard Conway
Peter F Cisco
Jas Carpenter
Michl Christal
Saml Doxey
Philip Doyle
L Dunkley
Wm W Fisher
Thos J Foote
John F Gantz
Barnabas Gillespie
Philip Gibson
Geo G Glazier
Geo Gordon
Richd Harcourt
Leonard D House
Peter Hull

W W Wells
M R Walsh
J W Westervelt
J R Waldron
Thos Wiswal

Richd Harrold
J E Hatfield
Stephen A Kent
Christian Kramer
Nathl Ladd
Lawrence Langton
Jas O Ludlow
Robt Lawrence
John McMahon
Chas Magness
Boltis Moor, jr
Jas Moncrief
Parker Muren
John Neafie
John McPherson
John Priestly
Alfred Palmer
Fred'k Roome
Thos Standerwick
Wm Speight
Chas K Smith

Asa W Weldran
Danl Winans
Wm Seymour

Michl Smith
Enoch Soper
Jacob B Mesereau
J Tyson
John H Tupsler
A J F Tombs
Philip Tabele
P G Turish
Jas Van Tassel
John Vandervoort
A Van Orden, jr
John E Wood
Saml Wood
Wm Wason
Wm Whitley
Zophan Wood
Wm Woodhull
Amos Warring
Jas G Yates
G B Wooldridge

Weighers:
Alex Bleecker: $1,548.56
Jeremiah Brower: $2,897.64
Wm E Cruger: $1,134.40
E H De Camp: $1,796.05
Robt Dumont: $3,870.15
John Franklin: $2,254.21
Thos Hazard: $1,264.42
Step B Hoffman: $2,596.82
Thos Kirk: $1,996.00
Gaugers:
Benj Fuller: $3,088.44
Thos W Garniss: $1,150.13
A C Houghton: $2,332.51
Thos Morris: $1,068.62
Alex Ming, jr: $2,288.43
Elias Nexsen, jr: $2,118.65

Lewis Loutrel: $2,560.02
Chas Mills: $2,516.77
John W Oakley: $1,866.69
John M Pattison: $3,132.50
David Poore: $2,156.77
Geo Sibell: $3,463.06
John Sickles: $2,036.82
Jas Westervelt: $2,317.99

Wm Ryer, jr: $2,723.42
Henry E Riell: $2,625.12
John Tuomy: $2,343.08
Edw C Thruston: $1,936.60
A J Walker: $3,059.09
T P Walworth: $1,960.50

Measurers:
John Alwaise: $2,013.54
Jacob D Clute: $1,911.74
Wm Durell: $1,780.72
J W Forbes: $1,712.83
Edmund Fitch: $1,683.97
W M Hitchcock: $1,734.18
Wm Hagodon: $1,836.49
Jos Hopkins: $1,618.31
G W McPherson: $1,820.88
Geo Nixon: $1,553.11
Lemuel Pittman: $1,925.64
J J B Rowan: $1,738.32
J W Richardson: $1,677.03
Henry C Sperry: $1,664.44
Alfred G Stevens: $1,110.56
John M Thorne: $1,829.92
J B Vanderpool: $1,779.47
Jacob M Vreeland: $1,829.40
E J McCarthy: $753.63
Garrit T Bratt: $47.49
Robt Gourlay: $1,767.00

Deputy Ins of Rev or Marker:
G H Richards: $1,637.00
Marcus Sears: $1,285.65

Allan M Sniffen: $1,829.65

Asst Coll:
John J Plume: $1,000.00
Surveyor: Hiram Perry: $150.00
Surveyor: Ely Moore: $2,900.00
Dpty Surveyor: S Brewster: $1,500.00
Chief Clk: Andrew A Jones: $1,150.00
2nd Clk: E H Sears: $1,150.00
3rd Clk: Chas F Lineback: $850.00

4th Clk: Wm Froment: $1,000.00
5th Clk: Jas W Carpenter: $700.00
Messenger & Porter: R Davenport: $600.00
Naval Ofcr: Wm S Coe: $3,000.00
Dpty Naval Ofcr: Geo W Coe: $1,500.00

Clerks:
Elias B Dayon: $1,200

$1,050.00:
John Cockle	Samson M Isaacks	Wade Hough
M H Van Dyck	Geo W Gantz	Abijah Ingraham
Saml Van Wyck	Saml H Moore	

$900.00:
| Joshua S Bowne | Francis D Swords | Timothy F Cooke |
| John V Largee | Wm C Thompson | Jos Crosthwaite |

Clks:
Jeremiah Green: $600.00   John H Robins: $375.00
Richd Kidney, jr: $600.00   W B Rhodes, Por'r: $300.00

The sums of the weighers, gaugers, measurers, & markers are here put down agreeably to the returns of those ofcrs for the fees on the cargoes of vessels which arrived during the year; but each ofcr of his class receives an equal division of the aggregate amount of fees of that class.

Hon S S Prentiss, of Miss, arrived in New Orleans on Sat, in the ship *Auburn*, from N Y, & left yesterday for Vicksburg: intends to be at Whig State Convention & Barbecue at Baton Rouge Sep 21.

Notice to fishermen: I would rent for one or lease for 4 years 2 good herring & shad fisheries; on one is a shed, for curing fish, & a good hse for a fisherman. –Jas B Pye, Pomonkey P O, Chas Co, Md

FRI OCT 2, 1840
Valuable real estate adjoining the city of Raleigh for sale: by order of the Convention of the Protestant Episcopal Church, that valuable property known as the Episc School, with land attached: about 160 acs. –Geo W Mordecai, agent

A J Young, Merchant Tailor, informs his patrons that he has associated with him in business, Phineas J Steer, his former foreman & cutter, & the business hereafter will be Young & Steer.

Mrd: on Thu last, by Rev Mr Deluol, Mr Richd Nalley, of Wash, to Miss Mary Ann Keenan, of Clairmont Pl, near Balt.

Mrd: on Sep 28, by Rev Mr Smith, Mr John T Mitchell to Miss Sarah A Kerr, y/d/o the late Wm Kerr, jr, all of Wash.

Died: on the 20th ult, at his residence in Woodville, PG Co, Md, Austin L Miles, of a protracted & painful illness. By his death a young widow is bereft of a beloved husband; brothers & sisters weep for the loss of a devoted brother; & a numerous circle of connexions & acquaintances deplore the loss of a most estimable friend.

Coach Mgfr: Main st, near Md ave bridge. -John M Young [Local ad.]

SAT OCT 3, 1840
Sale of household furniture on Oct 8: at the residence of Col Hunter, on C st. -Edw Dyer, auct

The Hon Danl Webster arrived in Wash City yesterday, accompanied by his son, Danl F Webster, on his way to the Richmond Convention, scheduled for Mon

The Misses Wood inform the public that they have removed their School to the session-room of Trinity Chr, on the City Hall Sq.

$10 reward for runaway indented apprentice to the Baking business, Jos A Blagrow, age 19. –A Noerr, corner 11th & E sts

MON OCT 5, 1840
New Albany, Ind: on Sep 7, Jas M Perry, one of the most respectable citizens of Vandalia, Ill, was found murdered in the streets of that city. No clew to the author of the bloody deed. –Gaz

Mr J P White's class for instruction in Vocal Music on Pestalozzian system, will meet at the Meth Prot Chr, on 9th st, Mon & Thu evenings.

Bridegroom killed: Mercer [Pa] Luminary: a few evenings since, Mr John Douglass, of New Bedford, in Mercer Co, was mrd to the d/o Mr Hyde of Vernon, Ohio, & on the following day, his brother-in-law asked Mr D to look at a young horse he had purchased. His wife came out & said she could ride it. The horse took fright & kicked him on the back & took off with his hand caught in the halter. At full speed the horse reached the fence & the side of the young man struck the panel, fracturing his head. He lingered until Sat, when he expired.

Wash Corp: 1-Ptn of John Purdens: referred to the Cmte of Claims. Same for ptn of S Briggs. 2-Ptn of Jas Towles: referred to the Cmte on Improvements. 3- Communication from Jas E Thumlert, remonstrating against an obstruction by a wooden bldg near the intersection of 11th & Water sts: referred to the Cmte on Police. 4-Geo Johnson has leave to withdraw his ptns & papers, presented at the last Cncl.

Partnership between Wm B Todd & Robt J Roche is dissolved by mutual consent. Roche will continue the business at the old stand: Hats & Capes. –Wm B Todd, R J Roche

Mrd: on the 23rd ult, at Friends Meeting, Balt, Caleb S Hallowell, of Alexandria, to Ann Reese, d/o Thos L Reese, of Balt.

Mrd: on Sep 22, at Balt, by Rev Mr Frey, Mr Jos Newman to Miss Johanna Burke.

Mrd: on Sep 15, at the residence of Wm D Hart, Albemarle Co, Va, by Rev Jos H Baxter, the Rev John R Ross to Miss Eliz E Young.

Mrd: on Sep 30, at Annapolis, by Rev Mr McIlheny, Jas G Berrit, of Carroll Co, Md, to Miss Julia W, only d/o the late John W Bordley, of the former place.

Died: yesterday, on *Greenleaf's Point*, Lucy Lavinia, y/d/o David & Mary Ann Wilson, aged 18 months.

Died: on Oct 2, in Wash City, Mrs Mgt M Achman, aged 71 years.

Died: on Sep 30, at the residence of Chas King, Gtwn, Miss Nelea Waples, after a long protracted & painful illness.

Valuable lot on Pa ave for sale: under a deed of trust from Matthias Jeffers, dated Dec 5, 1833, for the whole of lot 10 in Reservation #10, with all bldgs: lot is on north side of Pa ave. –Thos Carbery, trustee of M Jeffers. –Edw Dyer, auct

Caution: all persons attending the sale advertised above are requested to take notice that I hold the property described under a lease not yet expired; that the stable on said lot belongs to me, with a right to remove it at the end of the term. I shall continue to hold my lease, notwithstanding any sale by the trustee. –Nace Adams

TUE OCT 6, 1840
Convention at the Cumberland Gap on Sep 10, was organized by the election of Hon John White, of Ky, as Pres, & Alfred Taylor & Wm Lowry, of Tenn, Martin Beaty & Frank Ballinger, of Ky, & John Campbell & John D Sharp, of Va, as V Ps. Connally F Trigg, of Va, & Thos W Humes, of Tenn, & Silas Woodson, of Ky, appointed Secs. Hon John J Crittenden introduced the Convention; Hon John Bell, of Tenn, succeeded him, altho seriously indisposed. Gen Leslie Combs was next. Addresses by Wyndham Robertson, of Va, Mr Anderson & Mr Center, Pres electors in Tenn. -Ky Commonwealth

Trustee's sale of improved property: deed of trust to me, dated Nov 20, 1839, & of record amongst the land records for Wash Co, D C: public auct of lot 23, as subdivision of lot 5 in sq 462, fronting on 7th st, with a good & comfortable frame dwlg. –Saml Byington, trustee -E Dyer, auct

Boarding: Mrs Sryock has taken the hse lately occupied by Mrs Canady, west of the Globe ofc.

Obit: departed this life recently at Phil, in the 19th year of his age, Stephen Dandridge Tucker, s/o the Hon Henry St Geo Tucker, Pres of the Court of Appeals. His heart-riven parents & relatives, pray they may be enabled to justify the ways of Providence. –S T, Warrenton, Va, Sep 25, 1840

Died: on Oct 3, in Wash City, Elias Kane, Navy Agent, in his 69th year. He was a long time a merchant of distinction in N Y, & for some years past Navy Agent in Wash City. As a husband, father, friend, & neighbor he was most affectionately regarded, & will be long remembered.

Died: on Oct 4, Robt I Taylor, in his 63rd year. Funeral from his late residence, in Alexandria, this morning at half past 11 o'clock.

Died: on Aug 27 last, at Passy, [nr Paris, in France,] Mrs Ann M Lee, wid/o the late Maj Henry Lee, of Va. Long illness had reduced her to a state of remarkable debility, but her last moments were tranquil & apparently without pain. The last ofcs were performed for her by an Episc Clergyman & American friends.

Died: Oct 4, Mrs Ellen Thumlert, in her 53rd year. Funeral this morning at 11 a m.

Died: on Sun week, at Norfolk, on board the U S ship *Delaware*, Edw Goggins, s/o Mrs Julia Goggins, of Wash, aged 13 years. He came to his death by a fall through the hatchway of the ship.

Died: on Sep 29, in Wash City, Miss Maria Benfield, after being severely afflicted for upwards of 10 years.

Died: on Sep 22, in Balt, Miss Caroline Norbeck, formerly of Wash, aged 24 years.

Died: on Sep 23, in the hse of Prof Rogers, at the Univ of Va, Dr Geo W Boyd, formerly Curator of the Lyceum of Natural History in N Y, & lately one of the Assists in the Geological Srvy of Va. His amiable deportment & modest worth, & his generous devotion to his relatives, will be long remembered. –Va Advoc

Two female teachers wanted: in the Female Academy at Oxford, Granville Co, N C. Address: Benj Sumner, Arcadia, N C.

Lewistown Republican: Govn'r Porter has signed the death warrant of Robt McConachy, the wretch who, for the sake of a few dollars, murdered the whole of the Brown family, 6 in number. He is to be executed on Nov 6. No sympathy can be felt for such a fiend.

Eleven hundred dollars were realized at the Bunker Hill Monument benefit given by Fanny Elssler at the Tremont Theatre on Thu.

WED OCT 7, 1840
For rent: 2 desirable & well furnished rooms: 18th & I sts. Apply to occupant within. –Mrs D Walker

Mrd: on Oct 4, by Rev Mr Davis, Mr Richd Kelly to Miss Eliza E Turner, all of Wash City.

Mrd: on Oct 6, by Rev O B Brown, Mr Jas W Shields to Mrs Mary Given, both of Wash City.

Sale: excellent household furniture: on Oct 12, at Polk Boarding-hse on Pa ave. -E Dyer, auct

For rent & possession given immediately: large 2 story brick hse on sq 925, recently occupied by Col Wm Doughty, & a little north of Col A Henderson's residence. –Geo Adams, agent

Clairmont Nursery, near Balt: fruit trees, & roses. Orders left with J F Callan, Wash, will meet with prompt attention. –Robt Sinclair, sr

Glen Asile for sale of rent: farm contains 100 acs: dwlg is spacious & in good order: located in Fairfax Co, near Falls' Chr, in Va. For terms apply to J C Generes, the subscriber.

THU OCT 8, 1840

Undersigned will make every effort to make the great mail route not only the most safe, expeditious, & comfortable, but to continue in it these advantages in the highest degree. Moncure Robinson, Pres Richmond, Fredericksburg, & Pot R R Co. Jos H Coates, Pres Richmond & Petersburg R R Co. Henry D Bird, Pres Petersburg & Roanoke R R Co. -Richmond, Va, Oct 5, 1840

Died: yesterday, Mr John Abbot, aged 71 years, a highly respectable citizen of Gtwn: native of Albany, & was formerly engaged in commerce in St Domingo, whence he escaped, with the loss of his property, during the massacre at that place. He accompanied the Administration as one of its ofcrs when the seat of Gov't was moved from Phil to Wash City, & up to the time of his last sickness continued faithfully to discharge his duties as a clk in the 3rd Aud's ofc. Funeral on Thu at 4 p m, from his late residence.

Died: on Aug 31, at Fort Gibson, Ark, of consumption, Mrs Eliz Larned, aged 22 years & 1 month, w/o Lt C H Larned, 4th Regt U S Infty.

FRI OCT 9, 1840

Miss Ashwood informs that she has opened a handsome assortment of ribbons, plaid silks, & flowers. Pa ave, between 10th & 11th sts.

A letter from Yazoo City, Sep 15, states that Mr Henry H Pease, formerly of N Y, was accidentally killed near the former place, on Sep 14. He was riding in a barouche with a friend: the horses took fright & darted, throwing the gentlemen some 36 feet. Mr Pease fell upon his back & neck, & was killed almost instantly. His companion, Mr Geo B Dixon, escaped with some slight bruises & internal hurts. Mr Pease was 36 years of age, & s/o John B Pease, of Utica. His body was interred at Yazoo on Sep 15, with military honors.

From Texas: Dates of the 19th ult have been received at New Orleans from Galveston, & of the 9th from Austin. We notice the death of Col Karnes, a meritorious ofcr in the Texian army. His fame stood very high as an Indian fighter & pioneer. Gen Felix Huston had recovered from sickness. Col W G Cook appointed to command of the 1st Regt of Infty, v Col Burleson, resigned. Decided improvement in the health of Pres Lamar, who had been ailing for sometime. In Galveston they are about erecting an Episc Chr. Inhabitants had returned to Linnville, & were busily engaged in repairing the injuries done by the savage enemy. The loss in bldgs & other property estimated at $100,000. Advices received that an army of Mexican Centralists, 1,000 strong, had crossed the Rio Grande: probably in pursuit of the Federalists. Indians have fled into the mountains. -Bulletin

Died: on Oct 1, at *Blenheim*, his late residence, near Bladensburg, PG Co, Md, Richd Tasker Lowndes, in his 77th year, after a long & severe illness. He was forced into retirement early in life by ill health.

Alexandria Gaz: Tribute of respect: death of Robt L Taylor, a member of the Common Cncl, & for many years Pres of that body. Members will wear the usual badge of mourning for 30 days & will attend his funeral.

On Mon, a young gentleman, Mr Paul, residing in the western part of Balt City, out gunning with a friend in a boat, on the Patapasco, was killed by the accidental discharge of his friend's gun. His body was brought to the residence of his bereaved parents on the same evening.

Wash City Affairs: meeting of the residents of that part of the city called the *Island*, was held at corner of Md ave & 10th sts: Mr Wm Loyd called to the Chr, & Wm Cooper, jr, sec. Mr W W Stewart offered resolutions: cmte appointed to ascertain assistance from several Fire Ins Cos: Messrs W A Bradley, H W Queen, & W W Stewart. Cmte to prepare a Constitution & By-laws for the Co: Messrs J W Martin, J Drummond, W M Morrison, Jas E Thumlert, & W Cooper, jr. Meeting adjourned.

Wash Corp: By ballots, Mr Barclay, & Mr McDonald, appointed tellers: the following named were declared to be duly designated:

Saml Drury	Wm Hebb
Jos Forrest	R H Clements
C H W Wharton	Nat Brady
Vincent King	Isaac Clarke
B K Morsell	Jas Marshall
Wm Thompson	Marmaduke Dove

The Mayor nominated for the Brd of Appeals: John Gadsby, Geo Crandall, & Thos Blagden: considered & confirmed.

Health Report: ofc of the Brd of Health, Wash, Oct 6, 1840. 51 deaths-Harvey Lindsley, Pres

Notice: I have withdrawn myself from business as a butcher in Wash City, in consequence of my embarrassments, & the want of means to carry it on, & on Oct 2, sold & transferred to Henry Walker my good wishes & my stands in the markets. I also inform, that I have engaged my personal service to the said Henry Walker to aid him in his business. –John Walker Followed by:
The subscriber, having arrived at the age of maturity, will now transact business in his own name, having also purchased from John Walker his stalls in the different markets. –Henry Walker, victualler

SAT OCT 10, 1840
St Mary's Hall, Green Banks, Burlington, N J. Rev R J Germain, chaplain, principal teacher, & head of the faculty.

John Evans was executed for the murder of John C Ritter, at Sandusky, Ohio, on Wed week. The gallows were erected on the common back of town, & witnessed by a large assembly of people. He said drunkenness & infidelity had brought him to his miserable situation. He was born in Newfoundland in 1811, & his father & mother died when he was young: he had apprenticed to a farm in Bedford, Mass, in whose service, in a drunken fit, he fell from a wagon, & his leg had to be amputated above the knee. He was bound to a tailor at Plymouth, from whom he ran away & went to Lowell, but had to fly for wounding a man's head with a stone; worked in various parts of the U S.

Meeting of the Old Sldrs of the Rev at Faneuil Hall: from the Balt American. The patriarch of R I, Asher Robbins, spoke.

Died: on the 21st ult, at the residence of Gov Call, at Tallahassee, Middle Fla, Lt Col John Green, of the 6th Infty, U S Army. He entered the service in 1812, as a subaltern of the 22nd Infty; was app't Adj of his regt by its Col, [now Brig Gen Hugh Brady, of the Army.] Served on the Niagara frontier, in the campaign of 1814, during which period he was promoted to a captaincy: was retained on the peace establishment of 1815, & after 18 years service as a Capt in the 3rd Reft of Infty, was promoted in 1833, to Majority of the 5th, & in 1838 he was promoted to be Lt Col of the 6th Infty, of which he was in command at the period of his death.

MON OCT 12, 1840
Chas B Fish, the Principal Engr of the C & O Canal, has been removed from ofc by the Pres & Dirs of that Co. He is one of the ablest & most experienced engineers in the country. We presume, this removal was made purely from party considerations.
–Alexandria Gaz

Military movements: N Y, Oct 8. On Oct 1st, 213 recruits, for 1st Regt of Infty, embarked on the ship *Leopard*, for Tampa Bay, Fla: Capt Pegram commandng: Lt Reynolds, Lancaster, Caldwell, & Carpenter, attached to the command. They all belong to the 1st Regt of Infty. On Oct 3, 239 recruits for the 6th Regt of Infty, embarked on the ship *Moslem*, also bound for Tampa Bay. Capt Hoffman, of the 6th Infty, in command; with Lt Monroe, Lovell, Armistead, McClay, & Irwin, of the same regt, attached to the command. On Oct 6, a 3rd detachment of 143 recruits, for the 2nd Regt of Infty, left Govn'rs Isl, on the ship *John Cumming*, for Savannah, & thence to St Augustine. Lt Penrose, 2nd Infty, in command. Ofcrs with him: Lts Tilden & Bacon, of 2nd Infty; Lt Johnson, 3rd Infty; Lts Sherman & Field, 3rd Artl. Com Ad

Promise, in the name of the Whigs of Md, that the victory recently achieved will be followed by one still more signal & triumphant on the first Mon in Nov next. We are you obedient servants,

N F Williams, Chrmn	A G Cole	Thos Y Walsh
Saml Harden	Chas H Pitts	Asa Needham
Jas Harwood	Geo W Krebs	Geo M Gill
Hugh Birckhead	Jas L Ridgely	Wm Chestnut
Wm H Gatchell	Jas Frazier	John P Kennedy
Jas Grieves	Neilson Poe	Sam McClellan
Geo R Richardson	Gus W Lurman	Wm R Jones

H F O Thrun informs that he intends giving an American & German Ball on Oct 12, at the Masonic Hall. Ample refreshments will be provided for the ladies. Tickets will be $1.50.

Fossett's Log Cabin Hse: on 6th st, between Pa ave & C st: open to the public: choice wines, liquors & ale. –Henry J Fossett

Night School: for artisans, apprenticces & young men: Wash Academy: E st, between 13th & 14th sts. -J Fill, princ

France: the Royal College is scarcely rivalled in France, in dignity & extent of the bldgs: erected between 1766 & 1770, by the Queen of Louis *1$\underline{5}$, d/o Stanislaus of Poland, as a convent for the regular canonesses of the order of St Augustin. In 1790 it was converted into a military infirmary, & continued such until 1804. [*Written over on the paper-looks like 15.]

Whig Marshal in the Convention of the 5th, was our worthy townsman, Thos Green, son-in-law of our venerable contempo, the editor of the Enquirer. Mr Green is descended from the Greens of Culpeper, game Whig stock in '76 & '98, & not less so in 1840.

THU OCT 13, 1840
Mrd: on Oct 8, Mr Robt M Combs to Miss Cath C Forrest.

Died: on the 22nd ult, at Ormond Estate, in the Parish of St Chas, German Coast, La, Mr Saml McCutchon, in his 68th year, formerly of Phil, but for the last 30 years a resident of La.

Died: Oct 4, in Jeff Co, Va, Maj H L Opie: for a long time a respected member of the Senate of Va.

Died: on the 5th ult, at his mother's plantation, Yazoo Co, Miss, Benj Grayson Lindsay, Atty & Cnslr at Law, aged 24 years.

Died: on Oct 11, at the residence of her mother, after a few days' severe illness, Mrs Sarah, McCallion, of this place.

Order of Chas Co Court, the com'r will expose to public sale at Perry's Store, in Nanjemoy, Chas Co, Md, on Nov 6, a large & valuable estate belonging to the heirs of the late John Stermott, of said county, & estimated to contain upwards of 400 acs. Farm is near the Potomac river: good dwlg house. –Jos Brummett, Francis E Dunnington, Wm L Coby, Richd B Posey.

WED OCT 14, 1840
The U S sloop of war *Levant*, Jos Smoot, Cmder, arrived in Hampton Roads on Wed last from N Y, whence she sailed on Oct 3.

Mr Jacob *Reese*, of Tamaqua, was killed on the 2nd inst by the accidental explosion of a keg of powder while at work in the coal mines near Pottsville. He was in his 54th year, & worthy member of society. He has left a large family.

The Havre packet ship *Rhone*, which sailed from N Y on Fri, carried out $240,000 in specie. The ship *Great Western* took less than $100,000.

Died: Oct 3, in his 23rd year, John Francis, eldest s/o Maj John Mercer, of Cedar Park, A A Co, Md.

Columbia Artl annual meeting, held at the Perserverance Engine-hse, on Oct 12, on motion, Lt C Buckingham took the chr, Cpl I Beers, sec. Mr Stanley resolved, that a cmte of 5 be appointed to receive the names of new members. Appt'd: Cpl I Beers, Thos Stanly, Jacob Kleiber, Gabriel Barnhill, & Jacob A Bender, who reported 43 new members. –Jos Etter, sec

<u>Jefferson College, Pa: commencement took place on Sep 24. Degree of A B was conferred on the following members of the senior class:</u>

J P Anderson, Ky	Danl L Hughes, Cape May
Geo E Austen, Somerset Co, Md	David Hughes, Cape May
Saml F Boyd, Seneca Co, O	Parker Jacob, Lewistown, Pa
Hugh A Brown, Logansport, Ind	Saml Mehaffey, Zanesville, Ohio
Jas C Carson, Hagerstown, Md	David W McConough, Wash, Pa
Alfred W Carter, Cincinnati	Solomon McNair, Bucks Co, Pa
Saml L Coulter, Co, Pa	Geo Miller, Massillon, Ohio
Robt W Dougherty, Somerset Co, Md	Jas W Miller, Erie
Archibald B Earle, Clark Co, Va	John T Moore, Port Gibson, Miss
Geo Earl, Centreville, Md	N G Parke, York Co, Pa
John Haldiman, Harrisburg	W A Passavant, Zelionople, Pa
D S Hatch, Vt	Robt Patterson, Pittsburg
Jos M Hayes, Erie	W H Reed Woodstown, N Y
Jas C Herron, Wash Co, Va	Robt A Ross, Concord, N H

Robt Steele, Newville, Pa   G A Wensel, Germany
Jas Wason, Hancock, Md   Henry A White, Somerset Co, Md

Degree of M A conferred on the following Alumni of the College, having completed the course of professional studies:

Jas W Buchanan	Jos W Fowler	Cyrus Dickson
John T Bucher	J R Franklin	Wm Eaton
Jonathan K Cooper	Wm Gass	T Buchanan Hall
E Criswell	T Grier	Geo Hill
W M Galbraith	J K Henderson	B D Jackson
Robt Gracy	B W Huntington	Thos W Kerr
Jas Grier	John J Marbury	Harrison P Laird
R S Holmes	Jas Mason	John Y Lind
M D Johnson	John R McFee	Walter M Lourie
Wm Lawrence	H McLean	Griffith Owen
John W Murray	F A Muhlenburg	John Patrick
Jas McGinnis	Wm Ramsey	John Pentzes
E Peale	Cyrus C Riggs	Saml Pettigrew
Chas Ramsay	C W Russel	Geo W Purnell
W H Riley	Th M Stevenson	Wilson Scott
L Stright	F A Thomas	Philip M Semple
D W Schwartz	W W Wise	Jos Smith
Jas Walker	H B Pitman	Kensey J Stewart
L Yarnall	Irvin Carson	Saml Templeton
H F Bowen	Wm G Barnett	John Tod
Jas Cameron	Newton Braken	David Wilson
Philip Condit	J T Buchanan	A D Wilson
S Cooper	Jas Campbell	
Edmund S Doty	Alex W Campbell	

The annual Address was delivered by Dr Robt Brackenridge, of Balt. Jefferson College is located in Canonsburg, a small village removed from the temptations of the cities & large towns. College expenses, including tuition, brdg, & fuel, from $100 to $120 per annum.

Mr E McCardle, long experienced in keeping a brdg house, has the commodious 3 story brick hse on E st, between 6th & 7th sts, next door of Col Seaton's, comfortably fitted up for citizens & clerks.

Meeting of the Columbia Artl on this Wed, in the Lyceum room over Mr Buckingham's shop, on C st. –Jos Etter, sec

THU OCT 15, 1840
$15 for runaway negro Charity Ann Young, about 19. –Jas G Cadle, near Piscataway, Md.

On Oct 2, Wm Wallace, mate of the steamer *Gen Harrison*, a resident of Cincinnati, was accidentally killed by falling into the hold of the steamer while she was at one of the wharves at New Orleans.

Died: on Oct 5, after a long & painful illness, Mrs Cassy Anna Gray, in her 70th year, long a resident of Montg Co, Md.

Eligible Situation for sale: Richd Cropley, the younger, having assigned & conveyed, by indenture dated Sep 16, 1840, recorded in the Clk's ofc in Wash Co, D C, all his estate, real & personal, unto Saml John Barnard & Robt Barnard, & also the debts due & owing to the late firm of Geo & Richd Cropley, of which he is the surviving partner, in trust to sell. For sale: property on High st, Gtwn, being the dwlg-hse, store, bakery, & premises, as heretofore owned & occupied by Geo & Richd Cropley, & lately by said Richd Cropley, & also all the inventory, used in carrying on the business of Baker & Confectioner; the same being in good repair.
–Saml John Barnard, Rob Barnard, trustees

Jas W Seymour, a journeyman printer, a native of Newark, N J, last week fell from the 4th to the 2nd story of Piercy & Reed's printing ofc, in N Y, & received such injury as to occasion his death on Sat.

FRI OCT 16, 1840
An account of the late gallant affair between 35 men under Lt W K Hanson, 7th U S Infty, & a superior force of Indians. He is the same ofcr who so promptly captured 47 Indians last summer at Fort Mellon, on his learning the treacherous conduct of their comrades to Lt Col Harney at Caloosahatchie. Lt Turner was proceeding from Fort Walker to Waka-hoo-tee, & found a large body of Indians in the open woods. It is supposed that it was not the intention of the Indians to kill Lt Turner. Their object was to massacre the command of Lt Hanson. Capt E S Hawkins heard the firing at Waka-hoo-tee, but when he arrived with a detachment of men, at the battle ground, firing had ceased, & the Indians had gone.

From N Y: Maj Gen Sir Jas Macdonnell is now the Cmder of the British troops in Upr Canada. The colored sldrs at Chippewa who insulted Dr Page, of Va, & his family, have been arrested. When the union is proclaimed, Sir Geo Arthur goes home.

Mrd: on Oct 15, by Rev Mr Marbury, Mr Wash Simmons, of Fredericksburg, Va, to Miss Louisa G Brown, of Gtwn, D C.

Mrd: on Tue last, by Rev Mr Bean, Geo M Dove, M D, to Miss Sarah A Bean, all of Wash City.

Mrd: on Oct 14, at Trinity Chr, by Rev Mr Stringfellow, Lewis Edwards, formerly of the War Dept, to Mary Ellison, d/o the late Maj Abraham Broom.

Died: on Oct 12, at the residence of his son-in-law, R E Duvall, in Gtwn, D C, David Frame, sen, formerly of Brook Meadow Farm, Montg Co, Md.

Died: on Oct 10, after a short but severe illness, Mrs Amelia Townshend, w/o Capt Elijah Townshend, of the schn'r *Chas Pitman*, of Phil.

Died: on the 3rd ult, at Red Sulphur Springs, in Monroe Co, Va, Miss Lucy Ann Colston, of Berkeley Co, in her 40th year.

Died: on the 30th ult, Mr John Chamblin, of Loudoun Co, Va.

Died: on Oct 3, at his residence in Smithfield, of typhus fever, Thos Timberlake, in his 40th year.

Died: on Oct 9, off North Point, Chesapeake Bay, on board of the ship *Seaman*, for Tampa Bay, Fla, Miss Emily Ogden, of Unadilla, N Y, only d/o the late Henry Ogden, in her 21st year.

Died: suddenly, in Wash City, with cramp in the stomach, Mrs Jenet Eliza Cooley, w/o David Cooley, aged 31 years. Printers in Mich, Ind, N Y, & Mass, are requested to insert the above.

$50 reward for runaway negro man John, about 20 years of age: at the junction of Fredericksburg & Louisa R R, on Oct 10: purchased of Mr W H Cassady, near Leesburg, Va. –Wm H Williams [The Genius of Liberty, Leesburg, will please copy the above 7 times & charge W H W.]

Wash Co, D C: Wm Robbins, Thos B Hopkins, & Danl Pierce, insolvent debtors, have applied to be discharged from imprisonment. –Wm Brent, clk

SAT OCT 17, 1840
Conn: Wm W Boardman nonimated by the Whigs to fill the vacancy in Congress occasioned by the resignation of Hon Wm L Storrs.

Valuable land for sale: all the real estate the late Benj S Forrest died seized of: tract called *Needwood*, on Rock crk-166½ acs, being the tract on which the mill was, the dam & race yet in tolerable order. Another tract near Rockville, called *Haymond's Addition*-260 acs: with bldgs. Also, a tract of about 80 acs south side of Wash trnpk. Also a tract on north side of same, 80 acs. Another adjoining the lands of Mr Brice Selby, 1½ miles from Rockville, containing 10 acs. If not sold at pvt sale, will be offered for public sale on Nov 12 next, at Hay's tavern, Rockville. –Anna Maria S Forrest

Dissolution, by mutual consent, the copartnership of Essex & Lazenby. Those indebted or who have claims to the late firm will please call on Josiah Essex, who will continue the business at the old stand. -Josiah Essex, D L Lazenby

$600 reward for runaway negro man named Garrison Russle, sometimes calling himself Clemence Russle: about 30 years of age: belongs to Thos Hall, PG Co, Md, near *Good Luck* P O. Also, a negro man named Bill Hammond, about 21: belongs to Osborn Cross, near Good Luck. Also, a negro man named Jos Gaiter, about 35: belongs to John Perkins, PG Co, near Good Luck P O. They went off together without provocation, & supposed have made their way to Pa. -Thos Hall, Osborn Cross, John Perkins

The Rev Jas McVean will, by Divine permission, preach in Dr Laurie's Chr tomorrow at 11 a m.

MON OCT 19, 1840

The Whigs of Montg Co, Md, will give a Barbecue, at Rockville, on Oct 22, to which the voters of Md & adjoining states, & citizens of D C, are invited. -Geo C Washingon, Thos T Wheeler, Horace Willson, Elisha J Hall, Robt Y Brent, cmte: Rockville, Montg Co, Md

For sale: barouche & harness, household furniture, by order of the Orphans Court of Wash Co, D C, on Oct 21, the personal effects of the late Eleazer Early dec'd. -Edw Dyer, auct

$50 reward for runaway negro man Wm, alias Wm Jackson: about 21. -John G Lane, Falmouth, Va

Election for members of the next Congress, as far as heard from, compared with the representative in the present Congress:

Present:	Next Congress:
L Paynter	Chas Brown
John Sergeant	John Sergeant
G W Toland	**G W Toland
Chas Naylor	Chas J Ingersoll
	Jeremiah Brown
Edw Davies	
Francis James	Francis James
John Edwards	John Edwards
Jos Fornance	Jos Fornance
John Davis	Robt Ramsay
D D Wagener	J Westbrook
Peter Newhard	Peter Newhard
Geo M Keim	Geo M Keim
Wm Simonton	Wm Simonton

Jas Gerry	Jas Gerry
Jas Cooper	Jas Cooper
Wm S Ramsey	Wm S Ramsey
Geo McCulloh	Jas Irvin
David Petrikin	B A Bidlack
Robt H Hammond	John Snyder
Saml W Morris	*Davis Dimock
Chas Ogle	Chas Ogle
A G Marchand	*A G Marchand
Enos Hook	Enos Hook
Isaac Leet	Jos Lawrence
Richd Biddle	Wm W Irwin
Wm Beatty	*Wm Jack
Thos Henry	Thos Henry
John Galbraith	*Arnold Plumer

In the 22nd district H M Brackenridge [W] is elected to supply the vacancy in the present Congress, vice the resignation of Mr Biddle. [Oct 26 paper: *these names have been inserted. They were not included in the Oct 19 paper.] [**Corr in Oct 29 paper: this was Henry & should be G W.]

Columbian Horticultural Soc: Resolved-thanks of the Soc to Mr Varden, for the liberal offer made by him of the use of his hall, for the purposes of exhibition. A piece of plate of the value of $15, with a suitable inscription, be presented to Mr Wm Buist, for the large contributions made by him to the late Fall Exhibition. That a vase, of usual form adopted by the Soc, be presented to Miss Mgt Meade, for the handsome contributions made by her to the late Exhibition, & her tasteful arrangement of cut flowers. A handsome premium be presented to Miss Price & Miss Smith, for same. That there be presented to the gardeners of Mr Blagden, Mr Fox, Mr Naylor, Mrs Nicholls, Mrs Seaton, Mr J A Smith, & Mr Wiltberger, each a premium of value of $2.50, for their exhibitions. That there be presented to Alex'r Newell & John Smith, orphan apprentices to Wm Buist, each, some appropriate book on horticulture, as a testimonial of the Society for the flowers.

Fatal occurrence on Pa ave last Fri night. As Mr Warren Masters, age about 30 years, who lived in Spalding's dist, PG Co, Md, was returning home with 2 or 3 other citizens of that county, who had spent the day with him at the races, the former, suddenly put his horse into a gallop, & fronting the Capitol, the rider & horse were thrown down, & Mr Masters dreadfully injured. He was conveyed to the tavern of Mr Patrick Moran. Prof May was immediately sent for, & found he had his thigh broken & serious injuries about the head. Mr Masters died on Sat morning. He has left a wife & 4 chldrn. Inquest revealed that Mr M had been drinking, & was not quite sober at the time of the accident. It is remarkable that one of our citizens, a messenger attached to the Capitol, met with his death by being thrown out of his carryall, about a year ago, near or at the fatal spot. Another person also narrowly escaped being killed, racing his horse along Pa ave.

On Oct 9, committed by Justices Gettys & Stull, Benj Dorsey, charged, on the oath of Wm Cushen, of A A Co, Md, with stealing one brown horse, the property of the said Wm Cushen. The prisoner was arrested in Gtwn by A K Arnold, cnstbl & will remain in the Wash Co prison until demanded by the authorities of Md.

Surrender of Yorktown, Oct 19, 1781: [3½ cols-taken from the Custis Recollections & Pvt memoirs of the Life & Character of Washington.] Chevalier de Barras, the commander of the French Naval forces at R I, announced to Gen Washington that Count de Grasse would sail from the West Indies, with a powerful fleet & 3,000 troops, on Aug 3, expected in the Chesapeake about Sep 1. The Count preferred the Chesapeake to the bay of N Y: this induced Washington, while continuing to threaten Sir Henry Clinton, to strike at Cornwallis in Va. The 3,000 veteran troops were under Marquis de St Simon. Washington with Count de Rochambeau, arrived at Wmsburg, the head-qrtrs of Lafayette, on Sep 14. The ship *Ville de Paris*, a magnificent vessel of 110 guns & 1,300 men, was a present from the city of Paris to the French King. Lafayette had family connections with the family of De Noailles. On Sep 5 Adm Graves, with 19 sail of line, appeared off the Capes of Va. Count de Grasse put to sea with 24 ships: engagement ensued; no results on either side. A red hot shot from the French, set fire to the British frig *Charon*, which was consumed, with 3 transports. One detachment was under Lt Col Hamilton, long the favorite of the Cmder-in-Chief: the French under the Baron de Viomenil. Lt Col Laurens, aid-de-camp to the Cmder-in-Chief appeared at the head of 2 companies. Maj Fish hailed him with :Why, Laurens, what brought you here?" the hero replied, " I had nothing to do at headqrtrs, & so came here to see what you all were about." He made Maj Campbell, the British commandnt, a prisoner of war. [Others named: Col Cobb; Col Lamb; Dr Craik; Gen Nelson; Col Cochran. The Col was born to the grave in the arms of the sldrs.] On the 19th, the British army laid down its arms. Cornwallis did not appear at the ceremony, but sent his sword by Gen O'Hara. On the day of the surrender, Washington rode his favorite & splendid charger, Nelson, a light sorrell 16 hands high: this charger died at *Mt Vernon* many years after the Revolution, at a very advanced age. When the Chief ceased to mount him, he was never rode, but grazed in a paddock in summer, & was well cared for in the winter. Col Tarleton, alone of all the British ofcrs of rank, was left out in the invitations to head-qrtrs. He was particularly obnoxious to the Americans from his conduct in the south. Washington's step-son, who was with him at Cambridge, & was the first among the first of his aids in the dawn of the Revolution, sickened while in the trenches before Yorktown, of camp-fever, which would be mortal. He wanted to behold the surrender & was supported to the ground, witnessed the spectacle, & was then removed to Eltham, 30 miles from camp. Washington arrived a little while before he expired. After he died, Washington embraced the bereaved wife & mother. From this moment I adopt his 2 youngest chldrn as my own. He remounted & returned to camp. Oct 19, 1781 was indeed the crowning glory of the Revolutionary war.

Mrd: on Oct 15, at College Hill, D C, by Rev Dr Chapin, Thos W Sydnor, of Richmond, Va, to Sarah L M, d/o Rev Dr Chapin.

17th Anniversary of Howard Institute of Wash City:
Peter W Gallaudet appointed chrmn   Wm Nourse, sec.

Ofcrs elected for the ensuing year:
Wm W Seaton, Pres	Jas Adams, Treas
Archibald Henderson, 1st V P	John P Ingle, Acc't
Jas L Edwards, 2nd V P	Wm Nourse, Sec

Mgrs:
Geo Gilliss	Wm Brent
John McClelland	Geo Adams
John Nourse	Wm J McDonald
Flodoardo Howard	Simeon Bassett
Michl Nourse	Saml Byington
P W Gallaudet	Alex Shepherd
N B Van Zandt	Griffith Coombe
Anthony Preston	Thos Blagden
Seth J Todd	Geo Adams
J W Maury	Wm E Howard
Geo Wood	Peter M Pearson
Abner H Young	Marmaduke Dove
Jno P Ingle	

Hse & lot at public auction: 2 story frame bldg on east half of lot 29 in sq 563, usually called *English Hill*, & is a comfortable small tenement. –Edw Dyer, auct

Died: on Oct 15, in Wash City, Isaac Rockwell, infant s/o Wm Henry & Sarah Ann Prentiss, aged 8 months & 26 days.

Island Fire Co, composed of citizens of wards 2, 3, & 5, in that part of Wash City termed the Island. Jos Radcliff, called to the chr: Wm Cooper, jr, appointed Sec.

Ofcrs elected:
Wm Lloyd, Pres	Jno W Martin, Capt of Engrs
F A Doniphan, V P	Noah Drummond, Capt of Hosemen
Wm Cooper, jr, Sec	Peter Hepburn, Capt of Propertymen
W W Stewart, Treas	

Appt'd to solicite donations for the use of the company:
W W Stewart	H K Lambell
John R Queen	N Drummond
F A Doniphan	

House & lot at public auction: 2 story frame bldg on east half of lot 29 in sq 563, usually called *English Hill*, & is a comfortable small tenement. –Edw Dyer, auct

TUE OCT 20, 1840
Mr Wm S Ramsey, of Carlisle, Pa, put an end to his existence on Sun at Barnum's Hotel, in Balt, by shooting himself in the right eye. He was a member of the present, & recently elected to the next Congress, from the 13th Congress Dist of Pa. – American [Oct 21 paper: The dec'd was recognized by the Hon Mr Jenifer, of Md, who sent for the Hon Messrs Carroll & Howard. Inquest was held by Seth Pollard. He came to Wash in the train of cars on Sat last; returned to Balt in the evening train. Whilst here, he purchased a pistol at one of the variety stores of Wash City, with percussion caps for it, & procured some bullets to be molded. –Nat'l Intell]

Sir Geo Arthur will continue to exercise the ofc of Lt Govn'r until the official act of Lord Sydenham proclaims the union of the provinces. It is intmated he remains at the advice of his medical advisors.

Gtwn property at pvt sale: commodious brick dwlg-hse, the property of the heirs of the late Dr Geo Clarke, corner of Gay & Wash sts: with brick stable. The whole is enclosed by a brick & stone wall.

News from Europe: Marshal Macdonald, Duke de Tarente, died 3 days ago at his country seat, the Chateau de Courcelles, near Gien, in the Loiret. He was descended from a Scotch family who came into France with the Stuarts, was born at Sancerre, in the Cher, 1765, & was in his 75th year.

Died: on Wed last, in Raleigh, N C, after a lingering illness, Mrs Eliz, the amiable consort of His Excell Edw B Dudley, Govn'r of N C.

Died: on Oct 5, at his residence in Surry Co, Maj Jos Williams, in his 65th year. He had a useful & active life, a character for sterling integrity.

Died: on Oct 12, in Pitt Co, in his 83rd year, Dr Robt Williams, a Surgeon in the Revolutionary army. He was a member of the Convention, which met at Hillsborough, to assent to the adoption of the U S Constitution. He was repeatedly a Rep in the Leg from Pitt Co. Also, a Delegate in the Convention, called in 1835.

Died: on Oct 2, in Mobile, Ala, Mstr Wm Kelly, in his 18th year, s/o Wm & Isabella Kelly, of Balt. He came to his death by drowning.

Died: on the 30th ult, at sea, Wm B, s/o Capt J M Hill, U S A, aged 1 year & 4 months.

Genr'l Agency in Wash: having been more than a qrtr of a century the Chief Clk of the ofc of the Hse o/Reps of the Congress of the U S, I offer my services as agent or atty to all persons who have business to transact at Wash, with the Gov't, or with individuals or companies. –Saml Burche

WED OCT 21, 1840
Library of Congress will be closed on Nov 24. –John S Meehan, Librarian

For rent: 2 frame hses on F st, near Bradley's wharf. Apply to E Brook.

Thos Semmes elected by the Cmn Cncl, Atty of the Corp of Alexandria, v Robt I Taylor, dec'd.

The Treas of the Bunker Hill Monument Assoc acknowledges the receipt of $10,000 as a donation from Amos Lawrence. He is a brother in blood & spirit of the late distinguished Rep from Boston.

On Sep 22, at Clarence Hse, St James' Palace, after a long & painful illness, departed this life, her Royal Highness the Princess Augusta Sophia, aunt to her Most Gracious Majesty, to the great grief of all the Royal family. She was in her 72nd year, having been born on Nov 8, 1768: the 6th child & 2nd d/o Geo III & Queen Charlotte.

Plymouth Rock, Mass: the w/o Mr Jas Raymond, of Ponds, in this town, came to her death on Sun last, when in examining the lock of a gun, he snapped it, killing her. She was 19 years of age.

Mrd: on Oct 16, by Rev O B Brown, Mr Wm S Burch, of Wash City, to Miss Frances Almira, eldest d/o Capt Abraham Cocke, of Annandale, Fairfax Co, Va, formerly of Westchester Co, N Y.

Died: on Oct 16, in Chester, N H, aged 73 years, Hon Danl French: lawyer & formerly Atty Gen of N H: appointed Post Master at Chester in 1807, held the ofc until a few weeks before his death, when he resigned. He has left a wife & large family of chldrn. He was father of Benj B French, of Wash City.

Wash Corp.: 1-Ptn of Geo Seitz: referred to the Cmte of Claims. 2-Bill for relief of Geo W Kendrick: passed. 3-Ptns of W A Randall & of M Worthington, praying remission of fines: referred to the Cmte of Claims. Brd adjourned.

Edw Maynard, Dentist, has returned to town, & resumed his practice on 3rd st.

THU OCT 22, 1840
Supposed to have strayed on the premises of Mrs Sanderson, across the Eastern Branch Bridge, a small cow. Owner will please call & prove property, pay charges, & take her away.

Carpetings & Rugs at cost: Gtwn, oppo P O. –Morton & Mackall

For rent: the west house in the fine block of bldgs erected by Count de Menou, in sq 250: house adjoins the residence of the Spanish Minister, & has been much improved. Apply to Jas Larned or to Richd Smith.

Mrd: on Oct 12, at Upperville, Va, by Rev Mr Slaughter, Col Alfred Rust to Miss Jane Eliza, d/o the late Hendley Boggess.

Mrd: on Oct 20, by Rev Mr Bulfinch, R B Allyr, of Belfast, Me, to Rebecca P Upton, d/o Saml Upton, of Wash City.

Boston & N Y Coal Co: meeting at Fountain Inn, Light st, Balt City, Nov 2. –Thos W Storrow, sec

Register's Ofc, Wash, Oct 20, 1840. Notice to all tavern & shopkeepers, retailers of wines & liquors, dry goods, hardware, med, perfumery, watches, & jewelry, boots & shoes, hats; also, to owners of hackney carriages & billiard tables, keepers of porter-hses & confectionaries, that their license will expire on Nov 2, & said licenses must be renewed at this ofc within 10 days after that time. –C H Wiltberger, Reg

Died: on Oct 9, at Hampton, Livingston Co, N Y, after an illness of 4 days, Duncan, y/s/o the last Robt Fitzhugh, in his 6th year.

FRI OCT 23, 1840
Brookeville Academy, Montg Co, Md: Mr E J Meany, Princ: W B Magruder, Pres.

Accounts from Greece mention the death of the much respected Gottingen Prof, Carl Ottfried Muller, at Athens: attacked with a fever which carried him away in a few days. His funeral was celebrated with great pomp. He was one of the 7 professors who refused to break the oath he had taken to observe the Constitution of 1833.

Wm Pearce, of Boston, one of the few remaining survivors of the celebrated Tea Party, died in that city on Sat last, aged 96 years.

By writ of fieri facias, issued by C T Coote, a J P for Wash Co, D C: sale of all the right, title, claim, & interest of Ellen Gray to an undivided half part of lot 16 in sq 455, in Wash City; with improvements thereon, seized & taken as the property of Ellen Gray, & will be sold to satisfy an execution in favor of John West. –Wm Wallis, cnstbl

Mrd: on Oct 21, by Rev O B Brown, Mr C I R Thorpe, of Balt, to Jane Susannah, eldest d/o the late Thos Dunn, of Wash City.

Died: on Oct 6, at Winchester, Va, Amanda M Buchanan, after a painful & lingering disease-consumption. Her mother & friends have sustained an irreparable loss.

Life-boats are being introduced into the ships of the Navy. U S brig *Consort*, sloop of war *Boston*, & revenue cutter *Wolcott*, have recently been furnished with boats of Francis' construction.

SAT OCT 24, 1840
Upr Marlboro, Md: trial of Jas Bridewell, for murder, near Bladensburg, in PG Co, on Jul 4, 1825, commenced in our Co Court on Tue last: jury returned a verdict of guilty of murder in the 2nd degree. [He has been confined in the county jail 5 or 6 months.] Sentenced: 8 years & 8 months in the pen.

Yesterday while the Whigs of Wash City were firing a salute in honor of the late Whig victory in Ohio, Mr Jas Williams, late jailer, who was attending the cannon, was engaged in ramming down a cartridge, the cannon suddenly went off, blowing away 3 fingers of the left hand, breaking the left arm in 2 places, & also breaking the right arm of Mr Williams. Amputation of Mr Williams' left arm was deemed necessary, & that operation was performed yesterday evening.

Trustee's sale: decree of Chas Co Equity Court: sale in Port Tobacco, on Nov 10: all the real estate of Gustavus A Adams, dec'd: *Troop's Rendezvous, St Thomas, Barnes' Purchase:* containing 425 acs, by estimation. This estate will be sold subject to the life estate of Miss Rachel Adams in 105 acs, which has been allotted to her by the com'rs. --Peter W Crain, trustee

Tomorrow, Oct 25, Mr Henry Dodge will be publicly ordained to the word of the Gospel ministery. Exercises will commence at 11 a m in the Baptist Chr, on 10th st.

MON OCT 26, 1840
Troops for Fla: 222 recruits for the 7th Infty, under the command of Lt J Van Horne, 3rd Infty, embarked at N Y on Mon, on board the ship *Gen Parkhill*, for Pilatka, Fla, via Savannah. Lt Stephens, 3rd Infty, Lts Sherwood & Humber, 7th Infty, & Lt Lugenbeel, 8th Infty, were attached to the command.

Whig Meeting in Gtwn: on Oct 28, in the 2nd story of the Tobacco Warehse: band of music. Boys will not be admitted unless under the immediate charge of their parents. Cmte to prepare the house for the meeting:

Geo Shoemaker	Wm J Goszler	Dr Wm Plater
Saml Cropley	Levi Davis	P W Magruder
Jos Libby	Mathias Duffy	

Appt'd cmte of reception:

Col John I Stull	Wm Land	G C Bomford
Gen W Smith	W S Ringgold	Saml Clarke
Saml Whitall	C C Fulton	Wm Hayman
Wm S Nicholls	John Waters	E Cammack
D English, jr	Wm Plater	Francis Lutz
C E Eckel	Wm Noyes	Raphael Semmes

Judson Mitchell	Col John Carter	Jesse Lipscomb
L Morton	John Kurtz	P T Berry
Dr Lauck	Wm Grindage	Ignatius Clarke
Col Wm Robinson	Thos Brown	Bennet Sewell
S E Scott	Wm H Edes	E M Linthicum
John Pickrell	Dr J Riley	Caleb Bentley
Richd Davis	John Wilson	P W Magruder
Lewis Carbery	F Dodge, sr	Evan Lyons
J G Smoot	Paul Stevens	Jenkin Thomas
Wm J Goszler	Jeremiah Orme	Geo Mahoney
Wm Jewell	Wm Shanks	Edw S Wright
Chas Myers	Dr Hez Magruder	John Rose
Jos Nicholson	John Marbury	J L Kidwell
Dr P Warfield	Dr Wm Sothoron	

Henry Addison, Pres of the Gtwn Whig Assoc. V Ps: John Myers, O M Linthicum. E S Wright, sec

Whigs of the Central Cmte of Md: N F Williams, chrmn.

Geo R Richardson	Neilson Poe	Jas Frazier
Wm H Gatchell	Geo M Gill	Hugh Birckhead
Jas Grieves	Jas Harwood	Jas L Ridgely
Saml Harden	Wm Chesnut	Gustav W Lurman
Geo W Krebs	John P Kennedy	Wm R Jones
Asa Needham	Saml McClellan	T Yates Walsh
Chas H Pitts	A G Cole	

TUE OCT 27, 1840
Lewis Co, N Y: Van Buren seceders: John W Martin, First Judge of the co & P M at Martinsburgh; Gen Geo D Ruggles,a former Jackson member of the Assembly. & other leading Democrats.

Pilatka, Fa, Oct 17. Gen Armistead has suspended active operations for the present, in consequence of an agreement between him & the Seminole Chief to hold a talk on Oct 20. No one here has any confidence in him or his treaties.

Election Fraud. A foul conspiracy exploded, & the conspirators caught in their own net. Deposition of Mr Jas B Glentworth, of N Y C, being duly sworn, saith that within the last 30 days, at different times & places, in N Y C, he has been applied to by Jonathan D Stevenson, Benj F Butler, U S D A, Jesse Hoyt, Coll, & John W Edmonds, to make statements that should implicate Govn'r Seward & the leading friends of the Govn'r in N Y, in charge of having countenanced frauds at the election in N Y C in 1838. J B G, sworn Oct 23, 1840. Jos P Pirsson, com'r of deeds. [Depo is ½ a col.] Deposition of Jona D Stevenson: N Y C & CO. Jonathan D Sevenson, of N Y C, being duly sworn, dothe depose & say that he is well acquanted with Jas B Glentworth, of N Y C, tobacco inspec for part of N Y; deponent wanted to know if said Glentworth would be continued in the said ofc, or re-appointed in the event of the success of Govn'r Seward. [Others named in the depo which is 2 cols: R M Blatchford; Simeon Draper; Jas Bowen; R C Wetmore; Moses H Grinnell; Robt Swartwout; Chas Gill-Phil; Mr Bridges; Mr Dorrance; Jas Young-police ofcr; Robt Miller-capt of the watch; Mr Swift-Mayor of Phil; Henry W Havens-of N Y; Noah Cook; Wm C Lawrence; J Nathan; Robt Looney-Phil; Geo W Rhawn; Armstrong J Flomerfelt-sailmkr; Bela Badger; Geo Riston; Saunders; Thornton; Mr Jarvis; John Swint; Benj Bowne; C Hill; Mr Jeffers-High Cnstbl of Balt; Hon Sol Hillen, jr; Mr Vansant-P M at Balt; Isaac L Varian; Stephen Allen; John W Edmonds; Benj Butler.] Sworn Oct 22, 1840, before me, Robt H Morris, Recorder of N Y C. –J D Stevenson This was followed by denial statements: N Y, Oct 23, 1840: M H Grinnell; R M Blatchford; Jas Bowen; S Draper, jr; R C Wetmore; Wm A Lawrence; Jonathan Nathan. Statements by John Swift; G W Rhawns; John Saunders; Bela Badger; Robt Miller; Jas Thornton; Armstrong I Flomerfeldt; Andrew McClain; John Taylor; Chas Strine; Wm Young; Solomon B Walker; Francis C N Walton; Thos W Wallace; Chas M Graff; Wm Hunter

Yorktown Convention came off on Oct 19: Henry A Wise was Pres: Mr Sergeant, of Pa, addressed the people. Every thing went on in the finest style.

WED OCT 28, 1840
Hon John S Spence, Senator in Congress from Md, died at his residence in Worcester Co on Thu last.

Millington Bank. The Kent News of Sat states that on Tue last J C H Ellis, the Pres of this swindling institution, was committed to the jail of that town. He is charged with having been concerned with Weed, Adams, & others, to cheat & defraud the Public. They were concerned in the management of the Commercial Bank of Millington. –Balt Amer

Boston, Oct 24. Cmdor John Downes has been released from the command of the East India Squad, if 2 ships can be called a squad, due to ill health, & he will be succeeded by Capt Thos Ap Catesby Jones. Cmdor John D Sloat ordered to the command of the Navy Sta at Portsmouth, v Cmdor Crane, who retires on leave of absence.

Trustee's sale of valuable property: deed of trust from Chas Horace Upton & wife, dated Jun 6, 1838, recorded in the land records of Wash Co, D C, in liber W B #70, folios 53 thru 56: sale of part of sq 74, on Pa ave, with a 3 story brick tenement. –J H H Smith, trust -Edw Dyer, auct

Mrd: on Oct 24, by Rev Mr Bulfinch, Mr Normand M Porter, merchant of Charlston, S C, to Miss Priscilla Clark, of Wash City.

Wash: Grand Jury, Oct 26: Judge Dunlop.

Peter Force, foreman	Otho M Linthicum	John W Maury
Jos Forrest	B K Morsell	Geo W Young
John F Cox	John Mason, jr	Henry McPherson
John Boyle	Ninian Beall	John Pickrell
Lewis Johnson	Thos Blagden	John Lutz
Geo B Magruder	Joshua Peirce	Chas A Burnet
Chas R Belt	Jehiel Brooks	
Robt White	Edw Simms	
Michl Shanks	John Cox	

Mrd: on Oct 22, in Alleghany Co, Md, by Rev Mr Petrikin, Robt MacLeod, Civil Engr, formerly of Wash City, to Miss Cordelia F, d/o Enos Childs, of Montg Co, Md.

Died: on Oct 3, at Rose Hill, Montg Co, Md, Eliza, w/o Rev John Mines, in her 56th year. A blood vessel ruptured & in less than 5 minutes life was extinct.

The opening of St Matthew's Church, recently erected in the 1st Ward of Wash City, is to take place on Nov 1, All Saints Day. [Nov 2 paper: Dedication of the new Catholic Chr yesterday: the ArchBishop of Balt, in full pontificals, attended by a number of clergymen, commenced the solemnities. Sermon by Rev Dr Moriarty, of Phil. Probably 3,000 persons in the body of the chr.]

On Oct 16, I disposed of my interest in the Auct & Commission business, Wash City, to Mr Wm Marshall, who has taken the store lately occupied by me on Pa ave, between 9th & 10th sts. –John A Blake

THU OCT 29, 1840
Biog of Gen Harrison is stated that at the confernce held between him & Tecumsthe in 1810, a Methodist preacher by the name of Winans behaved with great gallantry in seizing a musket & standing in defence of the ladies, when an instant attack was anticipated from the savages. Mr Levi C Harris, of Raymond, Miss, sent a letter to the Rev Wm Winans, of the same state, requesting to know if he were the clergyman alluded to. His reply was that he was, & traveled as a Meth itinerant preacher on the crct which embraced the town of Vincennes, the place of Gen, then Govn'r, Harrison's residence. I was, as I often did, enjoying the hospitality of the Govn'r. The cncl was held in his yard, not more than 50 feet from his door. The Indians in the party were from 60 to 70. I was standing at the back of Gen Gibson, Sec of the Terr, who had been some 20 years a prisoner among the Shawnee Indians, & I heard him tell Lt Jennings, "Have your men ready-there is danger." About the same instant the Govn'r rose & bade the interpreter tell Tecumsthe that "the cncl was dissolved, for he would sit no longer with such a scoundrel." Of the patriotism of Gen Harrison, the history of the west, for nearly 50 years, is the impartial record.

Edw Owen & Evan Evans have taken into partnership of E Owen & Co, John S Owen. The firm will be known as Owen, Evans, & Co. Merchant Tailors on Pa ave, near Fuller's Htl.

Clothes, cashmeres, & vestings: for sale as low as the lowest. –Jas B Clarke, #2 8th st, Wash City.

Phil, Oct 27. The Grand Jury yesterday presented Wm O Kline, Clk of the Crmnl Sessions, for misdeameanor in ofc, in reference to naturalization papers unauthorizedly issued by him previous to the late election. Let our friends in the country be on guard against false papers issued by Courts of this county

Letter to Hon Levi Woodbury, Sec of the Treas, from Wm Hendricks, Madison, Aug 31, 1836. Subject: I am gratified in learning that Col John Spencer's, Receiver at Fort Wayne, deposites have been made to your satisfaction. He is reputed to be an honest & honorable man. It would to some extent produce excitement if he were removed, for he has many warm & influential friends, both at Fort Wayne & in Dearborn Co, from which he removed to his present residence. Better let it be. –Wm Hendricks, then a Senator in Congress from Ind.

Two female teachers wanted in the Female Academy at Oxford, Granville Co, N C: liberal salaries. -Benj Sumner, Arcadia, N C

Jas Boteler, guilty of having murdered Jas Bridewell, near Bladensburg, Md, on Jul 4, 1825, was sentenced by Judge Stephen to 8 years in the pen. *You have caused the widowhood of his affectionate partner, & a premature orphanage to 2 infant chldrn, the early pledges of their mutual love.*

Died: on Oct 28, Mrs Permelia Whitney, of a painful lingering disease of 12 to 15 years duration. Funeral at 2 p m today, from her late residence, north side of E st, to a burying ground in Gtwn.

FRI OCT 30, 1840
Mrd: on Oct 26, in Wash City, by Rev W McLain, Robt C Gardiner, of New Orleans, La, to Louisa M Browne, of Lexington, Va.

Mercer potatoes for sale: from the state of Maine: will be sold from the vessel. –J H Thecker, Water st, Gtwn.

Wash City-Crmnl Court, Oct 29, 1840. 1-Trial of Henry T Newton, John Tilley, & Wm Lucas, under indictment charging them with unlawfully & wickedly conspired, combined, on Apr 1, 1840, to cheat, defraud, & swindle Walter Reeves of $28, by enticing him, while intoxicated, to play with them at cards, in Gtwn. Verdict: guilty. 2-Oct 28, 1840: Patrick Collins, alias John Collins, free negro, was tried & found guilty of stealing a coat of the value of $5, the property of Walter Devaughn.

Wash Co, D C: insolvent debtor, Wm Hickman, colored, has applied to be discharged from imprisonment. -Wm Brent, clk

SAT OCT 31, 1840
Cmder John H Aulick, for some time past on duty at the Wash Navy Yard, having been ordered to sea, in command of the sloop of war *Yorktown*, Cmder C K Stribling succeeds him at the Navy Yard.

Mrd: on Thursday, by Rev Mr Davis, Mr Jas Wollard to Miss Mary Murphy, all of Wash City.

Died: on Aug 29 last, near Pine Bluff, Ark, at the residence of her father, Gerard N Causin, Mrs Eliza Dickinson, consort of Judge Dickinson: cut down in the prime-time of life.

Dr Chas H Lieberman has located in Wash City: Med, Operative Surgeon & Obstetrics. Grad of the Univ of Berlin, under Profs Dieffenbach V Griffin & Strohmeyer, & practised for some time with success on the Continent of Europe. Ofc: n e corner of 12th & E sts.

MON NOV 2, 1840
Daily to the south: via the Chesapeake Bay & the Portsmouth & Roanoke R R: fast & superior steamboats *Georgia*, *Jewess*, *South Carolina*: Capt Jas Coffey, Capt Jas Holmer, Capt Thos Suttona, respectively. -John C Moale, agent Balt Steam Packet Co, Balt.

Wash & Alexandria Boat: the steamboat *Phenix*-regular trips between Wash & Alexandria. -John Wilson, Capt

Forgery. Cincinnati, Oct 27, 1840: letter from Wm H Harrison to the editor of the Republican. Letter directed to me, dated Sep 21, & signed by Arthur Tappan, J Leavett, & H Dresser, & an answer to that letter, purporting to be signed by me, Oct 2, 1840, in this city. I have never in my life received a letter from the above. It was opened this day in front of Mr E P Langdon, the Dpty P M. -Wm H Harrison

Augusta Chron: the Hon Richd H Wilde, of Ga, who has been for some time residing in Europe, having accomplished the object of his visit, is about to return to Ga.

Riviere du Loup, Oct 20. The whole of the American exploring party, with Prof Renwick, are now at Lake Temiscouata. Capt Hawkshaw, R E & Mr Harvey, s/o Sir John Harvey, have just started in company with Lt Broughton, R E, one of the Com'rs; they are going to Quebec for a day or two. Mr Featherstonhaugh remains here, & joins Lt Broughton at Riviere Ouelle, which they have to explore, & then they close their labors for the winter.

Capt Easby, of this city, has succeeded in raising the hulk of the old frig *New York*, which has been sunk in the Potomac for a number of years, & has removed it to his ship yard.

St Augustine News of the 17th ult: we learn that Brig Gen Atkinson was stricken with paralysis, & there is little probability of his ever being able again to take the field.

Lost, going to, or returning from the fire on M ave, near 4½ st, on Oct 28, a brass cap of the axle of one of the hose carriages of the Union Fire Co. The Cap has the maker's name, Geo Jeffries, Phil, engraved thereon. Suitable reward for the finder. Leave at the Engine house, H & 19th sts. –Edm Hanly, Pres Union Fire Co

Frauds in Dela. A slip from Wilmington states that the collector at Mill Creek Hundred, Wm C Pierson, [democrat] has been arrested & held to bail in sum of $500 on account of : "adding names to his duplicate & giving tax receipts, whereby illegal votes were given in Brandywine & Mill Creek Hundreds at the late election."

Boston Atlas says that Mr Webster is quite ill at his farm in Franklin, N H. It is altogether probable that the state of his health will not allow him to visit other places before the election.

Robt Keyworth offers to the Public an assortment of lamps to burn the camphine & other chemical oils. Apply to R K, Pa ave, Wash.

New Grammar School: in the Conference rm of the Meth Prot Chr, on 9th st, between E & F st, on Nov 16. This enterprise is to assist the Chr of which he is Pastor, in an effort to relieve itself from an oppressive debt. –W Webster, Paster of the M P C

Boarding at Mrs Hough's, on 6th st, between E & F sts, Wash City.

Mrd: on the 29th ult, at Gtwn, by the Rev Mr Reese, Mr Chas Edmonston, of Wash, to Miss Ann Henrietta Barneclo, of Gtwn.

Criminal Court-Wash City. Fri, the trial of Alex'r Ledingham, against whom the Grand Jury had found a bill presenting him for violating the person of a girl named Maria Foote, who is only 14 years of age, & totally blind since she was 3 days old. Prisoner about 25, his wife with him, & a little boy about 4 years of age, s/o Ledingham. Maria's mother was a witness & her father was seated beside the D A. The jury returned a sealed verdict, which, we presume, will be made known this morning. [Nov 3 paper: Criminal Court-Wash City. Nov 2-verdict of not guilty as indicted; his Hon Judge Dunlop ordered Ledingham to be discharged, the D A having intimated his intention of entering a *nolle prosequi* on the other indictment. The prisoner then walked out of the Court room with his wife, who remained at his side during the whole trial.]

The splendid chandelier lately suspended in the Hall of the Hse o/Reps was lighted last Wed: it was manfactured to the order of the Hse o/Reps, by Messrs H N Hooper & Co, of Boston: $4,000.

Notice: Should Thos Harris, if living, or his heirs, if dead, desire now to sell lot 8 in sq 217, north of the new Catholic Chr in Wash City, which has been sold for taxes, & irredeemable after the early part of next month, [unless there are heirs-minors entitling the same to redemption in the residue of 20 years, under certain expenses,] fair consideration will be paid by the person to whom authoried application was made some months back, upon calling immediately upon A McCready, at Newton & Gadsby's Htl.

A drove of horses from the lakes just arrived & for sale at the stable of Walker & Kimball in Wash.

TUE NOV 3, 1840
The Hon Jas F Simmons elected a Senator in the U S Congress from R I, v Hon Nehemiah R Knight, whose term of service expires next Mar.

Letter to a gentleman in Wash City from his friend in Alexandria, La, dated Oct 7, announces the decease of Richd Winn. He died on Oct 5, after a short illness of 7 days. He was a public benefactor.

Criminal Court-Wash City: Patrick Collins, convicted of stealing a coat, the property of Walter Devaughn: 18 months in the pen. Nicholas Walkins, about 16, convicted of stealing a silver watch, the property of Conrad Hogmire: 1 month in the county jail & pay a fine of $1.00

A late number of the Wiskonsin Enq says that Messrs W Alford & P W Thomas, of New Balt, in that Terr, have met with complete success in their experiments in smelting copper ore. Neither had any experience in the business of smelting, & the result is deemed a matter of great consequence to that Territory, which abounds in rich copper ore.

Died: on the 31st ult, at Brooklyn, N Y, Lt T L C Watkins, of the U S Marines.

The firm existing under the name of Hilbus & Ricker is this day dissolved by mutual consent. Present bills for or against the said firm to Mr Ricker for settlement. –Jos Hilbus, Fred'k Ricker

WED NOV 4, 1840
Orphans Court of Wash Co, D C: ordered that letters of administration be granted to John Foote, on the estate of John Barry, late of said county, dec'd, unless cause be shown to the contrary. –Nathl P Causin -Ed N Roach, reg/o wills

N Y American: a grandson of the late Sir Philip Francis, & his widow, Lady Francis, are preparing a life of that statesmen, in which the identity of the author of Junius' Letters will unquestionably be established. The box with the secret of the authorship of Junius, found 12 years ago, now re-discovered by the grandson of Sir Philip Francis. History: in Oct, 1827, Lord Nugent, & the Duke of Buckingham, the grandson of Mr Geo Grenville, were examining the library of the latter, which had descended to the Duke, they lit upon a parcel which contained 3 letters. This parcel was shown to Lord Grenville, the bro/o G Grenville, who at once recognized it. Lord Grenville has been dead some 2 or 3 years. John Horne Tooke was the author of Junius's Letters. –J F

Fairview for rent: pleasant residence on *Fairview Hill*, near the centre of sq 513, fronting on M st, now occupied by Lund Washington, sen: will be for rent on Jan 1 next, when Mr Washington's lease will expire. Hse has 9 rooms & a cellar, & about 3 acs of land. Inquire of Jas A Kennedy, City P O.

Orphans Court of Wash Co, D C. Letters of administration on estate of John L Ball, late a Lt in the U S Army, dec'd, be granted to Jas H Causten, unless cause to the contrary be shown. –Nathl P Causin, Judge Orphans' Crt -Ed N Roach, reg/o wills

Orphans Court of Wash Co, D C: ordered by the Court that the admx of Thos Sheckel sell at auction the whole of his personal estate, first giving notice for 3 days in some public newspaper, for all sums of & under, $10 cash; & for all sums above $10, a credit of 60 days, taking notes, with approved endorsers, to secure the payment of the same, with interest from day of sale. –Nathl P Causin
-Ed N Roach, reg/o wills

Mrd: on the 29th ult, by Rev John Davis, Mr Richd Barnhouse to Miss Frances Ann Dulen, all of Wash City.

Mrd: on Nov 1, by Rev Mr Hawley, Mr Lazaro Beinvenida, of Italy, to Susan Colston, of Wash City.

Died: on Mon, after a lingering indisposition, Mr Wm W Edwards, of Wash City. His funeral will be from the house of his father, Jas L Edwards, F & 19th sts, this morning, at 10 a m.

Died: on Sep 26, in Columbus, Ga, Ann J, aged 19 years, w/o Robt L Moore, formerly of Wash City.

By the steamer *Forester*, which arrived at Savannah yesterday week from Fla, we learn that the schn'r *Henry Barger*, Capt Case, of N Y, from Balt, bound to Pilatka, with Gov't stores, was wrecked on St John's Bar on Mon, 19th ult. Part of the cargo, sails, & rigging saved. The vessel was a loss.

THU NOV 5, 1840
In the last Presby Advocate, the Rev Richd Lee gives an account of the death of Mrs Mary Woods, w/o Dr Wm Woods, & d/o the late Wm Semple, who died near Lawrenceville, Oct 11, 1840, her chldrn at her bedside. "Your dying mother requests you to give yourself away to Jesus Christ."

Knoxville, Tenn, Oct 27. John W Sassean, Deputy P M at Morristown, Jeff Co, aged about 18 years, has been apprehended on a charge of embezzling the lost money, & on Sat brought for trial, but it was postponed to the next term of the Court. -Times

Superior Balt Hams: for sale at reduced prices, to close sale, by G Cassard & Son, 67 Calvert st, Balt.

New Grocery Store: corner of 7th & I sts, Wash City. --D Lingan Lazenby

$200 reward for runaway negro man Ben Gross, about 37 years of age: left on Oct 24, near Petersville, Fred'k Co, Md. His mother is a free woman, lives in Fred'k, where he has a brother living. --Jas L Hawkins

The Prussian Minister of Worship & Public Instruction having represented to the King that the 2 Catholic churches in Berlin were insufficient for the wants of the Catholic population, which amounts to 12,000, his Majesty has ordered a 3rd church to be erected at the expense of the state.

Having removed from the store formerly occupied by him between 10th & 11th sts, to the new one between 12th & 13th sts, so side Pa ave: now prepared to execute all orders: silver plate manufactured of the newest & most fashionable patterns & jewelry repaired. --J W Gaither, silversmith & jeweller

France: sentences of the Court of Peers on Prince Louis Napoleon & his fellow prisoners: Prince Louis Napoleon, perpetual imprisonment in a fortress; Count Montholon, 20 years detention; Voisin, 10 do; Mesonan, 15 ditto; Parquin, 20 ditto; Beuffet Montaubon, 5 ditto, Forestier, 10 ditto. 2nd Rank: Bataille, 5 years detention; Aladenize, transportation for life; Laborde, 2 years detention; Desjardins, acquitted; Galvani, ditto; De Lambert, ditto; Bure, ditto.

FRI NOV 6, 1840
Paris, Oct 7, 1840: you will have learnt that the old King Wm, of Holland, was to abdicate this day in favor of his son the Prince of Orange, who will ascend the throne as Wm II. The latter is brother-in-law of the Emperor of Russia & the King of Prussia, who have, each, about the same number of years.

Capitol Hill Academy, a Select School for boys, will open in the commodious chamber of the Columbia Engine-hse, on Mon next, at 9 a m. --Chas H Cragin, A M

The late Prof Bonnycastle, Univ of Va: the disease under which he had long suffered terminated fatally on Oct 31. A meeting of the Faculty followed with resolutions offered by Prof Tucker: sympathy to his bereaved wife & chldrn: wear crape round the left arm for 2 months. –J A G Davis, Chrmn of the Faculty. -Wm Wertenbaker, Sec of the Faculty

Nine days from England: 1-Another attempt to assassinate Louis Phillippe was made on Oct 15 by a nam named Darmes, age 43 years, a native of Marseilles. He fired at the King as he was passing along the quay of the Tuilleries on his way to St Cloud. No one was injured: the assassin was arrested. 2-The Marquis of Camden died at his seat, The Wilderness, in Kent, on Oct 8, in his 81st year. 3-The Queen was expected to take up her residence at Buckingham Palace, for her accouchement, about Nov 1. Her Majesty, was mrd, it may be remembered, on Feb 10. [Paper of Nov 9: Darmes said that the carbine he fired was loaded with 5 bullets & 8 buck-shots: this in all probability preserved the lives of the King, Queen, & Madame Adelaide. A footman, Grus, was struck on the right leg-wound not serious.]

Boarding Hse: Mrs Waggaman, on E st, near the Med College, is prepared to accommodate a few genteel brdrs on moderate terms.

Great Bargains: Red & white ash coal, broken & screened. –B M Deringer, wharf-Jeff st, Gtwn.

Wash Corp: 1-Cmte of Claims: asked to be discharged from further consideration o f the ptn of Jasper Duffore: discharged accordingly. Same for the ptn of Edwin G Miller. 2-Ptn of Geo Johnson: presented to the Cmte of Claims. 3-Brd of Cmn Cncl, authorizing the removal of the frame bldg in Water & 11th sts, occupied by Geo St Clair, was taken up, twice read, & ordered to lie on the table. Ptn from F B Poston & others: rg the location of a flag footway to be made in Ward #1: laid on the table. 4-Cmte of Claims: relief of Jonathan Scolfield, reported the same without amendment. 5-Relief of Geo W Kendrick was taken up: passed. 6-Cmte of Claims: asked to be discharged from further consideration of the ptn of Zachariah Hazle: report was agreed to.

Valuable property for sale: deed of trust executed to the subscribers by the Catawha Iron Works Co, of record in the Co Court of Botetourt, Va: sale on Dec 17 next, at the Furnace Iron Works Co Catawha creek, 9 miles from Fincastle, in said county: sale of all the lands: 1,200 acs on which the said Furnace are situated; another tract between 7,000 & 10,000 acs, made up of several tracts formerly owned by David Ross, & which were conveyed by the same David Ross' exec & heirs to the Catawba Iron Works Co. On the tract is also a valuable grist mill, saw mill, & several good dwlg houses. The title of the above property is believed to be good. –Wm B Archer, Alex P Eskridge, trustees

Valuable fisheries & lands in Va for sale at public auct: deed of trust, executed by John Mason, jr, & Cath his wife, on Aug 17, 1835,: sale at the tavern of Mr Geo P Wise, in Alexandria, D C, on Nov 26: land called *Dogue* or *Dogue's Neck*, in Fairfax Co, Va: line established between the late Geo Mason, of *Gunston*, dec'd, & the late Wm Mason, of *Lexington*, both of said county of Fairfax-described in the will of the late Geo Mason, of Lexington, [the f/o the said Geo & Wm,] about 2 to 3 acs; dividing line marked by a stake drove in the ground, where was planted a stone marked IM GM WM by the side of the rd leading from Lexington, line being one of the trees described in the aforesaid will as near old Crawford's grave yard, & for a corner in said dividing line, at which place corners with the tract herein descirbed a tract of land conveyed by said Wm Mason, late of Lexington, dec'd, to his brother, the late Geo Mason, of *Gunston*, dec'd, as also a tract of land sold by said Wm, of Lex, to Wm Mason, of Mattawoman. To a planted stone marked I & W, near the head of a lane called *Graham's lane*, thru woods to a field of the plantation formerly called *Nace's plantation;* up the river Potomac: at the mouth of the Great marsh, line thru the marsh to the beginning, supposed to contain 1,450 acs of land, be the same more or less; being the same tract of land heretofore conveyed by Wm Mason, late of Lexington, dec'd, to a certain John Mason, by deed dated Nov 9, 1818. Some of the fisheries are known as the *High Point Fisheries.* –Rd Smith, trustee [Only a line that included a *name* or *date* was extracted: not in sequence. Refer to total article for exact boundaries.]

The Queen of Portugal gave birth to a dght on Oct 4, after a very long, violent & critical labor; her life was considered in danger for some time, but her Majesty struggled thru it. The child lived only long enough to be baptized.

Mrd: on Nov 3, by Rev J Van Horseigh, Edw Duvall to Miss Mary Gates, all of Wash City.

Notice: the public are cautioned against Saml Cooper, who acted as agent for my property at the corner of 12th & D sts, as he refuses to come to a settlement with me of nearly a year's rent. I therefore apprize the public, that he is no more agent for me. I have appointed Mr Danl Hampton my agent. –Danl W Keiler, of Dayton, Ohio

Wash Corp: 1-Act for relief of Geo W Kendrick: fine imposed for an alleged violation of the act in relation to the erection of wooden bldgs, be, & the same is hereby, remitted: provided, he pay the costs of prosecution. Approved, Nov 5, 1840.

Boarding: single persons or families: at Mrs McCardle's, opposite the New Gen Post Ofc, on E st, between 7th & 8th sts.

SAT NOV 7, 1840
The Rev John E Norris will, by Divine permission, preach in Dr Laurie's Chr tomorrow, 11 a m.

Columbia Typog Soc will meet at 7 p m this evening, in the Hall of the Perserverance Fire Company. -W J Delano, sec

Mrd: on Oct 27, at Fayetteville, N C, by Rev Simeon Colton, Jas C Hepburn, M D, of Milton, Pa, to Miss Clara Maria, d/o Harvey Leete, of the former place.

Mrd: on Tue last, in Balt, by Rev Mr Schriever, Mr Jos Van Reswick to Miss Marion, y/d/o Mr Amon Woodward, all of Wash City.

Died: on Thu, after a short illness, Miss Ellen Schneeman, eldest d/o Mrs H Ulrich. Funeral from the residence of her mother, on Nov 8, to start at 3 p m precisely, for the Eastern Branch burying ground. [Nov 11 paper: obit-died in Wash, Nov 5: short illness was not alarming.]

Died: yesterday, in Wash City, John J Thruston, aged 27 years. Funeral from the residence of his father, Judge Thruston, this day, at 12 o'clock.

Died: on the 12th ult, in Sussex Co, Va, Dr Richd D Field, s/o Dr Geo Field, of said county, aged 21. His sister, Mrs Lucy Ann Eppes, w/o Victor M Eppes, died on Sep 1, in her 19th year of age.

Died: on the 26th ult, Chas Krause Wagler, formerly Prof of Music, in his 26th year.

Died: on the 30th ult, at his residence near Upr Marlboro, PG Co, Md, Alex'r H Boteler, aged about 60 years. He had suffered much from a lingering & painful indisposition. Few men enjoyed in a greater degree the confidence of the community in which he lived for more than half a century. -Gaz

The Vicksburg Whig of the 15th ult, states that John R Chiles, P M at Jackson, Miss, has been removed, & Howell Hobbs appointed in his place.

MON NOV 9, 1840
Courrier Belge: His Majesty is in his 69th year, having been born on Aug 24, 1772: mrd on Oct 1, 1791, a Princess of Prussia. The Prince of Orange, now about to ascend the throne, is in his 48th year, having been born on Dec 6, 1792.

A card from John P Donelan: subject the dedication of St Matthew's Chr, in Wash City: gratitude to Rev Dr Moriarty, of Phil; to Dr Ryder, Pres of Gtwn Coll; Rev Dr Matthews, of St Patrick's Chr; Messrs Buckinghm, Mathias Duffey, Carusi, McLeod, Slattery, Hendly, Drury, & the Hon Mayor of Wash City. Thanks also to Mr Franquinet who loaned his paintings to add to the interest of the lectures at Carusi's saloon. He merits, indeed, the warmest thanks of all concerned. [Separtate article signed X: *the new Catholic Church in this city can lay claim neither to architectural beauty or taste.*]

Copy in the paper of an annexed translation from the pen of our townsman, Jas Hoban, being a specimen of the style of Ludwig Uhler, the Campbell of German poets. Title: *The Herdsmen of the Height*. [Five verses.]

On Tue last, while the ofcrs at West Point were practising riding, Lt S J Bransford was thrown from his horse & so badly hurt that he died in a few hours.

Trustee's sale: decree of Chas Co Equity Court: sale at the Court Hse in Port Tobacco, all the right, title, interest, & claims, in law & equity, of Geo Mason, John Tucker, & the late Thos Martin, & their heirs, in fishing landing called *Rum Point*, with all the land, about 50 acs, & hses. Bldgs are excellent & of brick. Also, a tract of land adjoining the town of Benedict: with several good houses. All property was conveyed by Tucker, in trust, to Martin, & title is deemed clear. –W B Stone, trustee, Port Tobacco, Md.

Flour, window-glass, vinegar, & mercer potatoes. For sale at the *cheap store* opposite Brown's Htl. -W H Tenney

TUE NOV 10, 1840
Trustee's sale of valuable real estate: decree of Chas Co Court, [Md]-Court of Equity: sale of all the real estate on which the late Walter Latimer resided: about 760 acs, which has been divided into 2 lots; one of which is the widow's dower, & laid off by the com'rs, & contains 187 acs, & will be sold subject to her life estate in the same. The other lot contains about 570 acs, & will be sold free of any incumberance. Notice to the creditors of said Walter Latimer, to file their claims, with vouchers, with the Aud of Chas Co Court, on or before Mar 20, 1841. –Peter W Crain, trustee, Port Tobacco, Md.

Naval: the N Y Sun of Fri says, Cmder John C Long yesterday assumed the command of the sloop of war *Boston*, v Cmder Stringham, detached. The U S sloop of war *Concord*, Cmder Boeram, fittout out at Boston for the West India station, will be sent to the Brazils instead.

A traveler, recently from Mexico, reports that Gen Urrea had joined the Fed army under Canales, near Mier, on the Rio Grande. He will be a valuable accession to the Federalists in that qrtr. –N O Bltn

Fort Brooke, Tampa Bay, E Fla, Oct 22, 1840. Pvt correspondence: all of the 6th Regt are here, 8 companies of the 8th, & 4 of the first. The 3rd Regt is expected daily. Rumor says the 8th will leave Fort King on the 1st proximo. We have 4 or 5 women, & 2 chldrn prisoners, taken in Middle Fla last spring, & 4 warriors, taken by Capt Beall while I was absent from the Ferry. Tigertail, with 11 warriors, is in camp about 17 miles from this post.

Died: on the 30th ult, at *Parnham's Retreat*, near Newport, Chas Co, Md, Ann D P Goodwin, only d/o the Rev Henry B & Susan A Goodwin, aged 4 years & 9 months.

Died: on Oct 31, in N Y C, of congestive fever, Andrew McD Jackson, Purser in the U S Navy, leaving a widow & 2 orphan sons to bewail their affliction. The dec'd, accompained by his distressed widow, arrived in N Y to join the sloop of war *Boston* bound to the East Indies. In a few days after he was attacked by fever, which terminated fatally. –R T P

For rent: 2 story brick hse-13th & Md ave. The pavement is continuous to the Centre Market by 7th & 12th sts. –Rosina Chesire, 7th st near D st

WED NOV 11, 1840
Boston: Bunker Hill Monument, says Boston Courier: contracts for completing the monument were signed yesterday by the contractor, Mr Jas S Savage, on the one part, & the the Pres of the Monument Assoc on the other. It is specified that the monument shall be completed agreeably to the orginal design by Oct 1, 1843, for $43,000. Mr S will commence operations at the quarry immediately.

On Mon week the faculty of the Univ of Va chose Dr Jos Togno, Tutor of Italian & French, & Mr Paul Dioda, Tutor of Spanish & German languages in that institution.

Steamboat explosion: steamboat *Le Roy* exploded her boiler on the 25th ult, near Appalachicola, by which the following were killed:
Danl Rowlett, passenger   Pressly Hicks, fireman
Wash Smith, mstr   John Waller, fireman
John Ashton, engr   Henry Carter, steward, a free mulatto
The boat was owned by the mail contractors on the great southern route, Messrs Hopkins & Stockton.

Dr Palmer, of Pittsfield, Mass, who was injured a short time since by accidentally inhaling concentrated sulphuric acid, has since died.

The Russian order of St Andrews, which has just been conferred by the Emperor Nicholas on the Baron Brunow, was instituted by Peter the Great, in 1698, & dedicated to the Apostle, to whom tradition attributes the introduction of Christianity into Muscovy. It ranks very high among Russian orders, & is only bestowed on men of the first consequence. –Globe

Mrd: on Nov 5, by Rev T B Sargent, Mr Wm Winn, s/o the late Timothy Winn, Purser of the U S Navy, to Miss Gough Carroll, d/o the Hon Jas Carroll, of Balt.

Died: on Nov 8, in Gtwn, D C, after a long & painful illness, Richd Hall, in his 37th year, leaving a large number of friends & relations to mourn his loss.

Died: on Oct 27, in St Louis, in her 5th year, Ross, y/d/o Richd Wright, late of Wash.

On Fri last, a fire was found in the bldg between 9th & 10th sts, on the margin of the Wash Canal, & occupied by Mr S W Handy as a hat manufactory. Suspicion having fallen upon John Smith, a journeyman hatter lately in the employment of Mr H, & had been discharged that evening, who made threats against Mr H. Smith was arrested by T C Wilson, cnstbl, & taken before Justice Morsell, & committed for trial at the Crmnl Court now in session.

Venetian blinds made & repaired: Pa ave, between 11th & 12th sts.
–Wm Noell, venetian blind maker.

THU NOV 12, 1840
$5 reward for pale red buffalo cow, that strayed from my residence in Wash.
–Isaac Hill-apply at the woodyard of King & Hill, Marsh Market, Wash.

Died: on Nov 7, at his residence, in Chester Co, Pa, Col Caleb North, in his 88th year. He was at one time High Sheriff of the City & County of Phil, & was, at his death, the Pres of the Pa Soc of Cincinnati. He retired a few years since to his farm in Chester Co, the same neighborhood in which he raised a company & went out as Capt in the Army of the Revolution; was distiguished by his bravery & prudence, & pronounced to the rank of Lt Col, which rank he held at the close of the war. In all duites of life, whether as a father, a husband, a Christian, or a friend, his conduct has been most exemplary. He descended to the tomb surrounded by chldrn & friends, without an enemy in the world, one of the best of men, & the last of the field ofcrs of the Pa line of the Army of the Rev. –U S Gaz

Prince Jerome of Montfort, the s/o Jerome Bonaparte, now resides in Wirtemberg.

FRI NOV 13, 1840
Edgefield Court Hse was the scene on Fri last, of a bloody & disgraceful outrage, which resulted in the death of an amiable young man, Thos Bird. Difficulty between Col Lewis Wigfall & Preston Brooks, of Edgefield: during a tempo absence of Preston Brooks, his father, Col Whitfield Brooks, answered a publication of Wigfall. Result was a challenge from Wigfall, which was declined by Col B. Col Carrol & Thos Bird volunteered to call on Wigfall & request him to wait until Preston Brooks came home, as he was the proper person to protect his father. Wigfall stood on the Court Hse steps to defend a paper he had put up, armed with a pair of dueling pistols. Bird intimated his intention of tearing down the paper, when pistols were drawn by both him & Wigfall, & both fired without effect. Bird drew a 2nd pistol, again without effect. Wigfall then returned his fire, the ball lodging in his left breast. He lingered until Sun in great agony, when his spirit took its flight. –Columbia [S C] Chron

Wash Co, D C: insolvent debtor, Miley Travers, has applied to be discharged from imprisonment. -Wm Brent, clk

"Memoir of the Life of the Rev Wm White", D D Bishop of the Protestant Episcopal Church in Pa, by Bird Wilson, D D, is for sale. -W M Morrison, 4 doors west of Brown's Htl.

Prepared to play music for assembies & parties during the approaching season. Instructions given on the flute, clarionet, & key bugle. -F Schenig, I & 18th sts

Brooke's Universal Gaz: cheap, last edition, 1840, large actavo, 830 closely printed pages, with 200 engravings, containing a Commercial Dictionary, with much other valuable matter. For sale by F Taylor, $2.75.

Colt's patent fire-arms: just received one of Colt's Patent Revolving Rifles, of superior finish, in a fine mahogany case, at $100, also 2 cases of pistols at $30 each, manufactory prices. At the Old Snuff, Tobacco, & Fancy Store, 4 doors east of the City P O. -Lewis Johnson

Trustee's sale of vacant lot: deed of trust from Geo W Way, dated May 21, 1833: recorded among the land records for Wash Co, the subscriber, as trustee, will offer lot 6 in sq 439, fronting on 8th st west. -E J Middleton, trustee

Mrd: on Nov 10, by Rev Dr Hawley, Mr J H Waters, of Wash, to Miss Mary E Jackson, d/o Thos Jackson, of Gtwn.

Mrd: on Mon last, at Norfolk, Va, by Rev M Parks, Mr Geo Krafft, of Wash City, to Mrs Wilhelmina Myres, of the former place.

SAT NOV 14, 1840
Cmte of Arrangements: to plan & superintend public celebrations.

Wash:	Gtwn:	Alexandria:
Walter Jones, chrmn		Chas E Eckel
Henry Addison		Benj Kinsey
Jas Irwin		Richd S Coxe
Wm L Brent		Geo Crandell
Lewis Carbery		Jos H Bradley
Stephen Shinn		Geo Watterston
Wm Easby		

Died: on Oct 29, in Phil, Dr Saml J Cramer, Clk of Jeff Co, Va, in his 62nd year, a native of Ire [whence he emigrated about 40 years ago] & highly esteemed as an accomplished gentleman, & a most expemplary one in all his domestic & social relations.

For sale: a sq of ground near the Eastern Branch, enclosed with a post & rail fence, containing about 3½ acs: with a new stable, small 1 story brick house; & there is now being erected a brick 2 story house, 36 x 16 feet, 2 rooms on each floor. Apply to Jas Young, Capt Hill.

The following 10 Whig members of Congress are elected in Mass:
Leverett Saltonstall   Wm B Calhoun
Caleb Cushing   Wm S Hastings
Levi Lincoln   John Q Adams
Osmyn Baker   Robt C Winthrop
Geo N Briggs   Barker Bursell

Sale on Nov 17, of handsome & fashionable furniture: at the residence of Col Chas Downing, on 6th st, between E & F, all his furniture. The house is for rent, & possession immediately after sale. –Edw Dyer, auct

Destructive fire at Gtwn: on Wed night: the bakery of Messrs Thos Brown & Co almost entirely consumed: shingled roof of the house on the north side of the canal, belonging to F S Key, & tenanted by Mr Gideon Pierce, several times caught fire, & repeatedly extinguished by the fire engines & apparatus, which were worked with great skill: same for the new & extensive brick mill, lately erected by Mr Thos J Davis, in Water st. A respectable citizen states that the Navy Yard Fire Co arrived, with their apparatus, at the fire in Gtwn, in 25 minutes: the distance is at least 4 miles.

MON NOV 16, 1840
Died at Stoke, Mr Wm Doyle late a superannuated boatswain of her Majesty's Navy, aged 84: the last, we believe, who sailed round the world with Capt Cook. He entered the Navy when very young, & in 1776 sailed from this port with the redoubted navigator, in the ship *Resolution*, attended by Capt Clerke, in the ship *Discovery*, & was coxswain of the ship at Owyhee, Sandwich Islands, when Capt Cook was killed, on Feb 14, 1776. He was boatswain of the ship *Blanche* in that desperate fight with the ship *Pique*, in the West Indies, when her commander Capt Faulkner, lost his life, & his brave 1st Lt, now Adm Watkins, swam with his sword in his mouth to board the enemy. He also served in the ship *Atlas*, in which ship he lost the sight of his right eye, & afterwards in the ship *Magnificent*, where the other was injured. He was wrecked in the Crocodile, & saved the lives of several persons at Salcombe Sands, where he was 8 hours in the water, & succeeded in saving the lives of Lady Berkeley & her 3 chldrn. He served in the ship *Bienfaisant*, & was pensioned from her in 1800 on account of his blindness. After using every effort to regain his sight, he was advised to try the air of the west: accordingly came to this place, & remained till the time of his death. He was boatswain in the ship which took the celebrated scholar, Sir W Jones, to India in 1783, by whom the dec'd was taken much notice of. –Devonport Telegraph

Provision Store: corner of 7th near the bridge: sale of fresh beef. –David Weaver

Large beets were last week exhibited to the Cmte of the Horticultural Soc of Wash City, raised by Benj Carr, of Montg Co, Md, weighing 8 lbs, & were 23 inches in circumference; & a white sugar beet, by Wm Ball, of Wash City, weighing 15½ lbs, & 3 feet in length.

This long & painfull investigation is at last concluded, & the Court decided this morning that Mad. D'Hautville shall have the guardianship of the child. [See paper of Nov 20.]

TUE NOV 17, 1840
It is intended on Nov 26 to remove the remains of Gen Mercer, of Va, who was mortally wounded at the battle of Princeton, from Christ Chr burial ground to Laurel Hill Cemetery, near Phil. This removal has been undertaken by the St Andrew's Soc, who, at considerable expense, have procured a monument to be erected on the spot.

John Van Buren, who is elected to Congress in Ulster & Sullivan Cos in N Y, is not the President's son who bears the same name. The latter lives in Albany. –Boston Atlas

Bridgeton Chron: we are informed that Clark Henderson, brother of the Senator from Miss, died at Cape May, N J, on Nov 2. He was taken with an apopletic fit. The servant called a physician, but Mr H had breathed his last.

Orphans Court of Wash Co, D C. Letters of administration on personal estate of John H Grimes, late of said county, dec'd. –J F Callan, adm

Destructive fire in Natchez recently: among the suffers–D H Mobley, store & dry goods, $18,000, ins $5,000. Saml Cotton, bks & papers saved, $4,500. P N Falconer, agent for Hawes & Robinson, $4,000. Precise, $3,000. Hawkes, $2,500. Estimate of P F Merrick, $2,000. Rhodes, $1,000. H O'Neil, $2,000. D David, $3,000. Dominique, $2,000. F Randolph, $8,000. A Pew, $1,500.

Robt McConaghy was executed in Huntingdon, Pa, on Nov 6. He declared his innocence, the rope broke, & the cord then was doubled. He confessed his guilt this time, & was hung.

Died: on Nov 14, Lt Col Chas R Broom, U S M C, in his 46th year, having been a member of the Corps upwards of 27 years. His funeral was attended to the Congress burying ground on Sun by his numerous friends. Military honors were performed by the Wash Light Infty, under command of Capt R France.

Wanted: a young man qualified to take charge of a school in Nanjemoy, Chas Co, Md. Will open in Jan. –Bennet Dyson

WED NOV 18, 1840
We learn by pvt letter from Charlottesville, that Prof Davis, of the Univ of Va, died on Nov 14 of a wound inflicted on Nov 12 by the hands of an assassin. He leaves a bereaved & heart-stricken family.

Gen John Armstrong, now in his 84th year, & in full possession of his uncommon faculties, is in N Y, on a visit to his son-in-law, W B Astor. His object is to revise the proof-sheets of the concluding volume, now about to appear, of his *History of the Last War*. –N Y American

Died: on the 23rd ult, at the residence of Maj Nicholas Peay, in Little Rock, Ark, Miss Jane D Tastet, formerly of Wash City. Some 2 years ago, prompted by motives unknown, she left the scenes of her childhood to seek a home among strangers in this distant land. –Ark Gaz

Wash Corp: 1-Ptn from John H Reily & others: referred to the Cmte on Improvements. 2-Ptn from Lewis Carusi: same. 3-Communication from Jacob Kleiber, asking an increase of compensation as messenger in the Mayor & Reg's Ofcs: referred to the Cmte of Ways & Means. 4-Ptn from P Kay, praying permission to continue the sale of certain articles in his stall in the Centre Market, with recommendation from sundry persons to the same effect: referred to the Cmte of Ways & Means. 5-Motion for relief of N A Randall was taken up, read the third time, & passed. The Board adjourned.

THU NOV 19, 1840
Tampa, Nov 3, 1840. I have pleasure in announcing the arrival last night of the Western Deputation of Seminole Indians under the charge of Capt John Page, of the U S Army. It consists of the 2 principal Chiefs, Hola-toochee & Nolore Ohola, 12 other Indians, & 2 interpreters. Capt Armistead, Capt Page, & the Deputation march this morning to Fort King, [100 miles] when Tiger-tail & other hostile chiefs are to meet in cncl. [Annexed letter addressed to the editor of the Army & Navy Chron.]

For sale: small farm, in Montg Co, Md, about 3 miles from Beltsville, containing 100 acs, more or less: & a small log dwlg-house. Title indisputable. Apply at W H Stewart's Furniture Rooms, corner of E & 11th sts.

Wm T Gentry, of Heard Co, was convicted before the U S Crct Court in this place last week for robbing the mail, & sentenced to imprisonment in the pen, at hard labor, for 7 years. Wm Jordan, a lad, was also convicted of embezzling letters from the mail, in Lee Co, & sentenced to 10 years imprisonment, at hard labor. – Milledgeville Recorder

I have just received, & for sale: glades butter, raisins, sperm candles, hemp mats, family shad, herring, new live geese feathers, & buckwheat. –Wm Dove, Pa ave between 12th & 13th sts.

Suitable reward for strayed setter dog, having but one eye. –John F Webb, opposite Gadsby's Hotel.

Wanted: Va Continental & State Line Warants. For sale: Corp 6% stock. Corp 5% stock. Inquire of John F Webb, broker

For rent: 2 story brick dwlg-hse on D, near the corner of 13½ st. Possession immediately, upon application to C Eckloff, Pa ave.

Chas U Stobie writes of Dr Lieberman correcting his cross-eyed, [squinting,] which he had since his 9th year. Operation was performed in 2 minutes, in presence of Messrs Chas Fenderich, Wm Buist, & others. Anyone desirous of seeing me will be welcome at my residence at Mr Buist's. Dr L's ofc is on the corner of 12th & E sts. –C U S

FRI NOV 20, 1840
[See paper of Nov 16.] In the ptn upon which the writ was issued, Mr D'Hautville set forth that he was a citizen of the Canton de Vaud, in Switzerland, & that he was mrd in the Chr of Montreus, in said canton, & according to law, on Aug 22, 1837, to Ellen Sears, whose father was then a citizen of Mass, in the U S. That in the early part of 1838, his wife, with his consent, came to Boston, on a tempo visit, & has since, without any just cause known to the partner, refused to return to him, or has been prevented from so doing; & that on Sep 27 following she gave birth to the child whose custody he now claims. Mr D'Hautvile adds that he arrived in the U S in Jul, 1839, & has ever since been engaged in a fruitless attempt to recover his wife & child, the latter of whom has been restrained of its liberty by its mother & her parents, & detained by them in this country against his consent & permission. Mr & Mrs Sears said the child was not in their custory, which they did not claim, & never had claimed. That the child & mother, [their dght,] for some time, had been living with them for their comfort & protection. Mrs D'Haurville is compelled to continue separation from him, for a variety of circumstancs, all based upon an alleged total failure of her husband to realize the expectations of sympathy & affection which he had excited previous to obtaining her consent of marriage, & his conduct towards herself & her mother was inexpressibly wretched.

Criminal Court-Wash: Nov 18, 1840. The whole day was consumed in the trial of John Thompson & Mary Story, who were indicted for an assault & battery on Jun 23, 1840, on John Dewdney, for resisting him in the execution of his ofc as cnstbl Jury returned a verdict of guilty. Cnsl intimated for a new trial. Nov 19-trial for murder. Allen Watts is charged with wilfully murdering Henry Tucker, in Wash City, on Sep 30, 1840: trial will be resumed. [Nov 21 paper: Watts was acquitted.]

Norfolk, Nov 17. The U S frig *Macedonian*, bearing the broad pendant of Com Jesse Wilkinson, was towed down to Hampton Roads on Sunday by the U S steamer *Poinsett*, Lt Com Lynch. Ofcrs of the *Macedonian*: Lts John Rudd, F A Neville, R L Page, R W Brent, J C Walsh, & J W Cooke, [actg]

Purser, E T Dunn   Cmdor's Sec, Thos Miller
Surg, M Morgan   Prof of Math, J McDuffie
Marine ofcr, Lt R C Caldwell   Cmdor's Clk, W Cooper

Midshipmen: H A Clemson, J N Morris, M W Ripley, V R Morgan, J R Duer, J S Kinnard, J M B Clitz, J M Wainwright, J N Briceland, J B Creighton, H K Davenport, Chas Bertody, J L Nelson, Saml Marcy, D Ochiletteree

For rent, the brick house on 11th st, near the canal. It is well calculated for a blacksmith or carpenter's shop. It was formerly occupied as a foundry. –W Kirkwood, adm of H Ault's estate.

Mrd: Nov 12, by Rev Mr Van Horseigh, Mr Michl Downey to Miss Mary Barnes, all of this District

Mrd: Nov 15, by Rev Mr Donelan, Mr Wm F Seymour, of Gtwn, to Miss Mary Cath Smith, of Wash.

Died: on Nov 1, at Charlottesville, Va, Mrs Eliz Garland, aged 74 years, the mother/o the Hon Rice Garland, of La.

Died: on Nov 15, Mrs Lucretia Minor, eldest d/o Smith Minor, of Laurel Hill, Fairfax Co, Va. This young lady belonged to a class of beings who without the formalities of any wordly assoc, may well be designated as Sisters of Charity, as she spent her time in attending to the sick & afflicted neighbors.

Died: on Nov 15, at the residence of Rev R Keith, Theological Seminary, Chas Hopkins, infant s/o Rev Danl N Emerson, recently of Northboro, Mass.

SAT NOV 21, 1840
Cabinet, Chair, & Sofa Manufactory, corner of C & 10th sts: Edwin Green has a large stock for sale.

Mrd: on Nov 12, at Willow Brooke, in PG Co, Md, by Rev Mr Mackenheimer, Thos Duckett to Mrs Cath Clarke, d/o the late Wm Bowie.

Died: on Nov 5, at Gtwn, Mrs Maria E Reiss, consort of Benj Reiss, in her 24th year.

Valuable land for sale in Albemarle Co, Va: on Dec 9, 2,000 acs of my *Bienheim* estate: bldgs are dwlg house, barn, & stable. Land will be shown by J Ross, jr, or Mr Saunders. –Jas Ross, Fredericksburg, Va

$200 reward for runaway negro man Wm Brooks-Bill, age about 24 or 26 years. He has relations in the neighborhood of the Messrs Hilleary, near Bladensburg, & at Plumb Point. –Henry Hilleary, Upr Marlboro, Md

Rev G G Cookman will preach at Wesley Chapel Sta on Sabbath next at half past 6. Rev Courtland Van Renssealer, Pastor elect of the 2nd Presby Chr, will preach at the Medical Hall tomorrow at 11.

MON NOV 23, 1840
Meeting of the Law Class of the Univ of Va, on Nov 16, Mr Gales Seaton, of Wash City, was called to the chr, & Mr B D Howard, of Miss, appointed sec. Resolution offered by Mr W P Bayley, of Accomac Co, Va. Rg: sudden death of John A G Davis. Prof Tucker states that he was shot down before his own door sill, in wantonness of ruffian malice, with no means of self defence. Students met on Nov 13: cmte appointed to draught a suitable preamble: Messrs Caskie, Withers, White, Clay, Jones, Gray, Barksdale, Howard, Miller, & Humphreys. –T W Preston, chrmn/Jas J Jones, sec [Paper of Dec 2: A native of Va, & was born, the writer believes, in Middlesex, whence he moved to Albemarle Co, & there mrd the amiable lady who, with a numerous family, lives to mourn his loss.]

Francis B Ogden, of N Y, appointed by the Pres, to be U S Cnsl for the port of Bristol, Gr Britain.

Hat! Hats! Hats! Complete assortment. –R J Roche, east of Gadsby's

Stray cow came to my residence, commonly called the *Spring Tavern*, on the Bladensburg rd. Owner will please come forward, pay charges, & take her away. –Saml S Suit

Cow lost: strayed from the subscriber, on Nov 16: liberal reward. –Jos Bryan, 10th & N Y ave.

Died: on Nov 10, suddenly, Mrs S C Gibson, w/o Dr Wm Gibson, Prof of Surgeon in the Univ of Pa, & d/o Saml Hollingswroth, of Balt.

Died: on Nov 21, in her 22nd year, Louisa, w/o Wm W Corcoran. Funeral from the residence of her father, Cmdor Morris, in Gtwn, this afternoon, at 3½ o'clock.

TUE NOV 24, 1840
Among the rumors from the continent of Europe is one that the Emperor of Austria was about to resign his throne to his brother Chas Jos, now 38 years of age.

Notice of the death of Lord Holland is mentioned in the London Exam of Oct 25.

Whig vets-Editor. 1-I make reference to Mr John Westwood, a worthy citizen of Balt, who is 92 years old: was a Whig in '76, a whig in '98, & evinced his adhesion to Democ Whip principles in 1840 by voting for Gen Wm H Harrison for President. –A Young Whig 2-In the town of Barrington, Isaac Waldron, age 94 attended the polls & deposited his ballot: Col W has attended every annual meeting in his native town for the last 73 years, without a single exception. He voted for Harrison. –Portsmouth Gaz. 3-Among the voters in this town is Ezra Green, now in his 96th year, voting for Harrison. –N H Enq. 4-Capt M'Neill, of Hardy Co, between 70 & 80 years of age for many years bed-ridden with chronic rheumatism had himself taken out of bed & carried to the polls, 4 or 5 miles distant, to vote for Gen Harrison: incurring great bodily pain. –Nat Intell

Van Buren, on the Ark, Oct 8, 1840. John Ross, the Cherokee chief, reached Van Buren, Oct 7: Cherokees alarmed for his safety, sent on a deputation to look for him, & he was met by a party previous to his arrival at V B, where a still larger band of his nation awaited to escort him to the cncl ground. John Howard Paine, who accompanies the Cherokee chiefs in their country, proceeded alone on foot, in advance of the wagon.

The steamer *Persian* collapsed a flue on Nov 27, at Napoleon, killing on the spot, David Green, 1st engr; John Williams, 2nd mate; Oscar Brown, fireman, & 2 chldrn, deck passengers; scalding 32 others, 7 of whom have since died, viz: Washington Marks, fireman, John Cover, 2nd cook, John O'Brien, deck passenger, & four persons in one family whose names are unknown. Missing: Saml Hammers, Union Co, Ill; __ Fields, Tenn; & 2 others, names unknown. Those badly scalded:

Rev H Roach, Graves Co, Ky	John C Campbell, Rodney, Miss
Jas Haughton, Tenn	Wm T Evans, Graves Co, Ky
Geo Smith, Tenn	B Farrel, Hickman Co, Ky
John Berry, Ire	Johana Carrol, Jacksonville, Ill
D Berry, Ire	Ann O'Bright, Yorkshire, Eng
___ Berry, Ire	Wm Bowen, Hickman Co, Ky
Jacob Burk, Germany	N C Thompson, Carroll Co, Ten
Oliver J Lloyd, Yorkshire, Eng	Wm Meggwater, Cincinnati
Monroe Hazlett, Mo	Peter McDonald, Dist of Col
Wm Narcissi, Cincinnati	Bartholomew McKilten
Nicholas O'Neal, New Orleans	Jas Grammer, Union Co, Ill
Jacob Snyder, Union Co, Ill	Chas O'Neal, Ire, slightly

The boat *Maid of Orleans* went alongside the *Persian* on Nov 9: every attention is bestowed on the sufferers by Capt Goslee & ofcrs of the boat.

Mrd: Nov 23, by Rev W McLain, Geo W Milan to Mary E J Lee, of Fairfax Co, Va.

Died: on the 5th ult, near Hawesville, Ky, Mrs Susan A Hawes, w/o the Hon A G Hawes, of Ky.

Died: on Oct 21, in Gtwn, D C, Capt Robt Goodwin, aged 42, a native of Alexandria, but for the last 20 years a resident of Gtwn, D C.

Tax sale on Feb 27, 1841, at the ofc of the Clk of the Corp of Gtwn, the following:
Jas Claggett-heirs: north part of #17, old Gtwn, fronting on n side of Prospect st: 1840: tax: $3.57
Lots 28 & 29, Peter Beatty, Threlkeld, & Deakin's add: 1840: tax: 76½
Mary Sands: lot 23, Beatty & Hawkins' add: 1840: tax: $4.08
Thos G Waters: part of lot 117, Threlkeld's add, on Third st: 1840: .51 Same lot: 1839: .75
Alex'r Hanson-heirs: lot 264, Beatty & Hawkin's add: 1839: $1.02
Ditto-same lot, valued for assessment of 1835: 1839: $3.00
Eliz Weems: part of lots 5 thru 8, Holmead's add, on so side of Bridge st: 1840: $2.04
Chas Carroll-heirs: lots 215 thru 218, Beall's add: 1840: $4.08
Jacob Carter, jr: pt of lots 163 & 164, Beatty & Hawkin's add: 1840: .77
Same parts of lots: 1839: $1.12½
Thos B Williams: n e part of lot 39, old Gtwn, on Dock la: [no year specified] $2.29½
Geo Clarke-heirs: lot 207, Beall's add, on West st & Green st: 1840: $2.29½
Lot 208: 1840: $1.78½ -Wm Jewell, coll of the Corp of Gtwn: Nov, 1840.

$5 reward for strayed or stolen black mare. Deliver to Mr Pumphrey's stable, where the above reward will be paid. –Benj Spelman

Died: at San Antonio, Texas, Mr Jos C Hill, of Wash, in his 24th year. [No date-current item.]

Mrs Ann E Bronaugh has taken a hse lately in the occupancy of Jas Young, on N J ave, prepared to accommodate 8 or 10 members of Congress without families, or 4 or 5 members with families.

Ofcrs of the Nat'l Institute for the Promotion of Science: located at the seat of the Genr'l Gov't: Hon Joel R Poinsett, Sec of War, & Hon Jas K Paulding, Sec of Navy, dirs; John John Quincy Adams, Col J J Abert, Col Jos G Totten, A McWilliams, M D, & A O Dayton, cnclrs; Wm J Stone, treas; F Markoe, jr, corr sec; Pishey Thompson, rec sec. There are already 84 resident, 3 honorary, & 91 corr members.

Tavern Stand & Farm for sale: east of Romney, Va: contains 400 acs. Also, for sale, another farm on *Tear Coat*: 367 acs, 2 miles from the first tract. I wish to remove to the Western country, I will sell on reasonable terms. The Augusta & Shenandoah rds intersect at the Tavern-hse. –Saml Park

Fashionable corsets: Mrs Truman executes all orders with neatness & punctuality, at her residence, on west side of 6th st, near the corner of I st.

Public sale, order of the Orphans Court of PG Co, Md: sale on Dec 18, at the residence of Alex'r H Boteler, dec'd: all the personal estate: 30 or 35 negroes, men, women, & chldrn; crop of tobacco in the houses; barrels of corn; horses, cattle, sheep, hogs-about 50; crop of grain; household & kitchen furniture of every description. –Sophia Hodgkin, Thos Hodgkin, adms

WED NOV 25, 1840
Fashionable millinery: Mrs Finley, store on so side of Pa ave, between 9th & 10th sts.

$50 reward: my trunk was cut off from behind my carriage on Mon: a peculiar one, being made in China: contains my apparel, & some of the female apparel was marked Mgt Contee, or with the initials M C. Apply at Maj T P Andrews', near the War Ofc. –John Contee

Among the passengers by the ship *British Queen*, arrived at N Y from London, we notice: Mr Hodgson, of Wash, from a mission to Berlin; Majs Baker & Wade, Capts Huger & Mordecai, of the S Army; & Prof Bartlett, of West Point. These ofcrs of the Army were sent to Europe last spring by the War Dept as a commission to visit & report upon the military establishments of Europe: understood to have been in Eng, France, Prussia, Denmark, Sweden, & Russia. Their reception by the Emperor Nicholas is represented to have been particularly flattering. The day after their arrival in St Petersburg, he invited them to assist at a grand review of the Imperial guards at Czarskeselo, where they remained as guests for several days.

The Harrisburg Reporter contains a table of all the votes cast for each Electoral ticket at the late Presidential Election in Pa:

Harrison tkt:	Van Buren tkt:
J A Shulze	Jas Clark
Jos Ritner	Geo A Leiper
Levis Passmore	Geo W Smick
J P Wetherill	Benj Mifflin
Thos P Cope	Fred'k Stoever
Jon Gillingham	Wm H Smith
Amos Ellmaker	John F Steinman
Ab R McIlvain	John Dowlin
John K Zelim	Henry Myers
Robt Stinson	Danl Jacoby
Wm S Hendrie	Jesse Johnson
J J Ross	Jacob Able
Peter Filbert	Geo Christman
Wm Adams	Wm Schoeuer
John Harper	Henry Dehugg
Wm McIlvaine	Henry Logan
John Dickson	Fred'k Smith

John McKeehan	Chas McClure
John Reed	Jacob M Gemmil
A B Wilson	G M Hellenback
N Middleswarth	Leonard Pfouts
Geo Walker	John Horton, jr
B Connelly	Wm Philson
Jos Markle	John Morrison
J G Fordyce	Wesley Frost
T T McKennan	Benj Anderson
Harmar Denny	Wm Wilkins
Jos Buffington	A K Wright
Henry Black	John Findley
John Dick	Stephen Barlow
The highest Harrison elector has 144,023	The lowest on the Harrison ticket has: 143,990
The highest V Buren elector has 143,784	The lowest on the V Buren ticket has: 143,663
Harrison majority: 239	Harrison majority 327

Mrs Preuss can accommodate several members with or without their families, on Missouri ave, between 4½ & 6th sts, near Newton's & Brown's Htls.

$20 reward: on Mon last, a large piece of granite was thrown by some villanous assassin in at my front parlor window, with the obvious design of injuring myself or some of my family. Above reward will be paid, on conviction, for the apprehension of the villain, or for such information as will lead to his detection & conviction.
–Jas Owner, jr, near the R R depot

St Louis Bulletin: the jury, in the case of Wm P Darnes, indicted for the murder of the proprietor of the St Louis Argus, brought in a verdict of manslaughter in the fourth degree.

Criminal Court-Wash: Nov 21. 1-Jas Simms indicted for stealing, on Aug 3, a gold watch of the value of $200, & a gold chain, value $70, the property of Julia Simms. Jury found him guilty. 2-Bernard Martin & John Keating indicted & tried for a riot & assault & battery on Conrad Hess, scavenger of Ward 3 of Wash City, on Sep 22, 1840. Verdict was guilty for both dfndnts.

An attempt was made last Sat to set fire to the dwlg of Maj Nicholson, in Ward 4 of Wash City. Suspicion falls upon 2 negroes, Chas Hopp & Henry Howard: arrested & committed for trial. Howard was found concealed under a quantity of hay in a stable at the Navy Yard.

Wash Corp: Ptn from Ann McGunnigle, praying remission of a fine: referred to the Cmte of Claims.

THU NOV 26, 1840
Trustee's sale of valuable property: deed of trust from Richd Wright to the subscriber, dated Jan 28, 1832, recorded in Liber W B #41, folios 147 thru 151, of the land records of Wash Co, D C: sale on Nov 30, all the west half of lot 2 in sq 320 in Wash City, with 3 story brick dwlg. It fronts on F st, between 11th & 12th sts, & now occupied as a brdg hse by Mr Galabran. –Clement Cox, trust -Edw Dyer, auct

Trustee's sale of lot: deed of trust dated Oct 18, 1838, from the late John Dix & Aleth Dix, in my favor: sale of lot 8 in sq 325, with bldgs, to the same belonging. –Jas Hoban, trustee -E Dyer, auct

Promotions & appointments in the U S Army since the publication of Genr'l Orders, Jul 21, 1840.
1st Regt of Dragoons:
Brvt 2nd Lt Richd S Ewell to 2nd Lt, Nov 1, 1840, v Gaither, resigned.
2nd Regt of Artl:
2nd Lt Wm B Blair to 1st Lt, Nov 4, 1840, v Bransford, dec'd.
4th Regt of Artl:
2nd Lt Thos Williams to 1st Lt, Oct 5, 1840, v Tufts, dec'd.
1st Regt of Infty:
1st Lt Geo H Pegram to Capt, Aug 5, 1840, v Day, dec'd.
2nd Lt Ferdinand Coxe to 1st Lt, Aug 5, v Pegram, prmt'd.
Brvt 2nd Lt Jas N Caldwell, 2nd Inf, to be 2nd Lt, Aug 5, 1840, v Coxe, prmt'd.
Brvt 2nd Lt Stephen D Carpenter, to be 2nd Lt, oct 12, 1840, v Paine, resigned.
2nd Regt of Infty:
Brvt Maj Jos Plympton, Capt 5th Infty, to be Maj Sep 22, 1840, v Loomis, prmt'd.
3rd Regt of Infty:
2nd Lt Jas M Smith, to 1st Lt, Oct 2, 1840, v Blanchard, resigned.
Brvt 2nd Lt Oliver L Shepherd, 4th Infty, to 2nd Lt, Oct 2, 1840, v Smith, prmt'd.
Brvt 2nd Lt Jos L Folsom, 8th Infty, to 2nd Lt, Nov 18, 1840, v Peyton, dropped.
Brvt 2nd Lt Wm B Johns, 8th Infty, to 2nd Lt, Nov 18, 1840, v Lindenberger, dropped.
4th Regt of Infty:
2nd Lt Robt M Cochrane, to 1st Lt, Oct 4, 1840, v Grandin, resigned.
Brvt 2nd Lt Henry D Wallen, 3rd Infty, to 2nd Lt, Oct 4, 1840, v Cochrane, prmt'd.
5th Regt of Infty:
1st Lt Caleb Sibley, to Capt, Sep 22, 1840, v Plympton, prmt'd.
2nd Lt Carter L Stevenson to 1st Lt, Sep 22, 1840, v Sibley, prmt'd.
Brvt 2nd Lt Pinkney Lugenbeel to 2nd Lt, Sep 22, 1840, v Stevenson, prmt'd.
6th Regt of Infty:
Maj Gustavus Loomis, 2nd Infty, to Lt Col Sep 22, 1840, v Green, dec'd.
8th Regt of Infty:
1st Lt Jas M Hill to Capt, Sep 28, 1840, v Bonnell, dec'd.

1st Lt Henry McKavett to Capt, Oct 1, 1840, v Phillips, resigned.
2nd Lt Geo Lincoln to 1st Lt, Sep 28, 1840, v Hill, prmt'd.
2nd Lt W C Brown to 1st Lt, Oct 1, 1840, v McKavett, prmt'd.
Brvt 2nd Lt Henry Wardwell, 7th Infty, to 2nd Lt, Sep 28, 1840, v Lincoln, prmt'd.
Brvt 2nd Lt Robt P Maclay, 6th Infty, to 2nd Lt, Oct 1, 1840, v Browne, prmt'd.
Med Dept:
Richd F Simpson, of Va, to be Assist Surg, Aug 1, 1840.
Wm E Fullwood, of Ga, to be Assist Surgeon Oct 1, 1840.
Re-appointment:
W H T Walker, late 1st Lt 6th Infty, to be 1st Lt in same regt, to take place next below Lt Todd, & to rank from Feb 1, 1838, the orginal date of his commission.
Resignations:
Capt J A Phillips, 8th Infty, Sep 30, 1840.
1st Lt A G Blanchard, 3rd Infty, Oct 1, 1840.
1st Lt J C Fletcher, 6th Infty, Nov 10, 1840.
1st Lt W G Grandin, 4th Infty, Oct 3, 1840.
2nd Lt E A Paine, 1st Infty, Oct 11, 1840.
2nd Lt E B Gaither, 1st Drag, Oct 31, 1840.
Assist Surgeon M C Leavenworth, Sep 30, 1840.
Assist Surgeon Saml Forry, Oct 31 1840.
Assist Surgeon Elias Hughes, Jul 31, 1840.
Rev Jasper Adams, Chaplain, Nov 15, 1840.
Deaths:
Lt Col John Green, 6th Infty at Tallahassee, Fla, Sep 21, 1840.
Capt Wm Day, 1st Infty, at St Louis, Mo, Aug 4, 1840.
Capt Jos Bonnell, 8th Infty, at Phil, Pa, Sep 27, 1840.
1st Lt D H Tufts, 4th Artl, at Detroit, Mich, Oct 4, 1840.
1st Lt S J Bransford, 2nd Artl, at West Point, N Y, Nov 3,1 1840.
Memo: the name of Wm Smith, a Capt of the Corps of Engrs, having been changed by the Leg of the state of N Y to Wm Davidson Fraser, he will hereafter be known & recognized accordingly.

Valuable property in Gtwn for sale at auct: on Dec 10: now occupied by Mr Jas Thomas as a bookstore: property is at the corner opposite the Farmers' & Mechanics' Bank, fronting 24 feet on Bridge st & 120 feet on Congress st, two of the most frequented sts in Gtwn. Sale in front of Mrs Lang's tavern: possession given 3 months after the day of sale. –Thos C Wright, auct

Pensacola, Nov 27. The mail steamboat *Leroy*, plying between Chattahoochee & Iola, collapsed her flue on Sun last, near Blountstown: capt killed, & a passenger supposed to be Mr Danl Rowlett, of Appalachicola. Information from Mr Willis Auston, a passenger. Capt Tupper, a passenger in an oppo berth, was knocked out, then came to. There was no water in the boilers. –St Jos' Times

Orphans Court of Wash Co, D C. Letters of administration the personal estate of Wm W Edwards, late of said county, dec'd. -J L Edwards, adm

Manager wanted to take charge of a small farm. Inquire of Mr F Lowndes, Bridge st, Gtwn.

Govn'r of Va: proclamation: duly elected Electors for & on behalf of the state of Va, to vote for a Pres & V P of the U S.

Richd Logan, Halifax	J D Halyburton, New Kent
Jas Jones, Nottoway	Jas Hooe, Pulaski
Arthur Smith, Isle of Wight	Thos J Randolph, Albemarle
John Cargill, Sussex	Waller Holladay, Spottsylvania
M Jones, Gloucester	Benj Brown, Cabell
Chas Yancey, Buckingham	Inman Horner, Fauquier
John Hindman, Brooke	Jas Gibson, Hampshire
John Gibson, Pr Wm	Wm Byars, Wash
Archibald Stuart, Patrick	Jacob D Williamson, Rockingham
M Jones, Gloucester	Wm Taylor, Rockbridge
M A Harris, Page	Wm R Baskerville, Mecklenburg
Austin Brockenbrough, Essex	Augustus A Chapman, Monroe

Given under my hand at Richmond, Nov 22, 1840. -Thos W Gilmer, Govn'r of Va

Miss H A White has just returned from the north with the latest fashions for bonnets, caps, dresses, cloaks, & mantillas: stand to be opened today on Pa ave, next door to D Claggett's.

Died: Nov 19, at Boston, Jos Coolidge, aged 67 years, a truly estimable, faithful, & public spirited citizen.

Died: on Nov 24, Mrs Eliz Gale Handy, in her 75th year. Funeral at 10 a m today, from her late residence, at corner of 6th & La ave.

Died: on Aug 18, at San Jose del Parral, State of Chihuabua, Republic of Mexico, of fever, Dr Oliver Rice, a native of the state of Maine. This small tribute of respect is from one to whom his virtues were known, & to whom he was an elder brother.
–C W D

FRI NOV 27, 1840
M Eichorn has been appointed Minister of Public Instruction by the King of Prussia. [Foreign news.]

Rev Henry B Bascom, D D Prof of Moral Science & Belles letters in the Augusta Coll of Ky, has been elected to the Pres of the Coll of La, at Jackson.

Notice given that application has this day been made by me for leave to keep a Ferry across the river Potomac, & the order has been passed. –Wm Easby [Nov 26, 1840: Wash Co, D C, Crct Court.]

The pvt fortune of King Wm I of Holland, who just abdicated, is said to be 168,000,000s of francs.

$20 reward for pocketbook lost, containing $200, & plain gold ring, broken. I had it out last in Mr Ford's shoe store, whence I walked to Mr Alex'r Shepherd's ofc, on 7th st, near the canal; at this place I entered a hack & rode to the steamboat wharf, when I missed my pocketbook as I got aboard the steamboat. Whoever will deliver it & the contents to the editor of this paper or to myself shall be entitled to the above reward. –Uzziel Nalley

N Y Nov 23-Mr Wm Marmicke, a native of Bordeaux, France, who resided at 6 Courtlandt st, shot himself with a pistol. He wrote a letter to Mr J Heydecker, who resides in Hanover st, that he called no longer bear up against a painful disease, which had almost maddened him, & he was determined to commit suicide. His personal effects included $650, & he asked Mr H to have his body sent to Havre to Bordeaux by the steamboat. He had been in this country some years, & came to this city from the south a few months back. –Jour Com

Mrd: on Nov 11, at St Jas Chr, Accomac Co, Va, by Rt Rev Bishop Meade, the Rev Benj M Miller, Rector of St Paul's Chr, Norfolk, to Ann D, eldest d/o the late Col Thos Bayly, of the former place.

Mrd: on Nov 24, in Gtwn, by Rev R T Berry, Mr Geo French to Miss Sarah Drusilla, eldest d/o the late Jos Van Lear, of Wash Co, Md.

Died: on Nov 24, at Balt, after a short illness, Geo Winchester, a member of the Bar of Balt City.

Crct Court of Wash Co, D C: in Chancery: Nov Term, 1840. The Pres & Dirs of the Bank of the Metropolis, cmplnts, vs, Philip & Mary Smith, Jas McNerhaney et al, heirs a law of John McNerhaney, Robt E Kerr et al, heirs at law of Alex'r Kerr, dfndnts. Trustee, Geo Thomas, having made his report: ratify same: sold lot D in sq 380, to Alex'r Provost, for $4,025; trustee has paid out of the purchase money the debt due to the cmpnlnt, $2,599.78, & the expenses of the sale amounting to $16.87: Nov 25, 1840. -Wm Brent, clk [Coxe & Carlisle, solicitors.]

SAT NOV 28, 1840
Wm Wallace & Fred'k Evans were on Mon delivered into the custody of Jonas L Sibley, U S Mrshl for Mass, by Mr Anthony, Mrshl of R I, having been arrested on charge of stealing drafts & money from letters obtained from the Boston, Providence & Phil post ofcs.

St Stephen's, Ala, Nov 15-explosion of the steamer *Express*, the steamboat *Odd Fellow* a short distance ahead rendered assistance. Sufferers: drowned: Moses Netherton, bargeman; Wm Johnson, deck hand, Wm Bosworth, deck hand. Dead: John Langdon, fireman, John, [French boy,] cabin boy. Badly injured: Jas Sweeny, 2nd Engr, W M Bagby, 2nd pilot, Luke McGuire, passenger. Injured: Capt J C McGuire; Edwin Anderson, mate; E K Weaver, steward; deck hand, name unknown.

The exhumation of the remains of Brig Gen Hugh Mercer, preparatory to reinterment, with due solemnities, at Laurel Cemetery, took place at Phil on Tue. Gen Mercer received his death wounds on Jan 3, 1777, & died on the 19th of the same month. His remains were interred, a few days after, in Christ Churchyard in presence of a vast assemblage of people. The place of interment was pointed out by ex-Sheriff Jacob Strembeck, who was present at the burial. The disinterment took place in presence of Dr Mitchell, Mr Ramage, & other members of the St Andrew's Soc of Phil. The skull was found to be uninjured by any wound, &, with the other bones, was in a good state of preservation.

We learn from visiters that Nathl P Howard, of Richmond, Prof of Law in the Univ, to supply the vacancy occasioned by the death of Prof Davis. The appointment is tempo. -Whig

Wm Thaw elected Cashier of the Mechanics' Bank of Phil, in the room of J B Mitchell, late Cashier, now Pres.

The schn'r *Love*, Capt Godfrey, on Nov 14, fell in with the wreck of the schn'r *Butterfly*, Capt Kemstry, from N Y, bound to Curacoa, & took from her John Bramels, seaman, of Phil, the only survivor out of seven. The *Butterfly* left N Y on Nov 5 & capsized Nov 6. The capt, a seaman, & the steward were washed off & drowned on Nov 12; next day, Mr Franklin, mate, died in Brammel's arms. The same night J Cannion got delirious, & washed overboard; next day, the 14th, the *Love* took Bramels off, who has nearly lost the use of his legs & foot, being very much bruised. The *Butterfly* was owned by Messrs Jos Koulke & Son, of N Y.

Solemnities in Phil with the reinterment of the remains of Gen Hugh Mercer took place on Thu. The chr was in Wash Sq: coffin was covered with a flag & borne by a number of Pa vols, at the very battle in which Gen M lost his life. Religious exercises performed by Rev Albert Barnes: address by Wm B Reed: Govn'r Porter, of Pa, & Govn'r Gilmer, of Va, among those present. Mr Reed alluded to the early life of Gen M, who was born in the north of Scotland. He began his public life as a surgeon's mate in the ranks of the chivalric army that rallied round the standard of Prince Chas Edw, & fought under his banner, until the fatal field of Culloden drove him into exile. About a year later, the youthful Mercer came to this country & took up residence in Pa. –Penn Inq

Geo W Trueheart, Atty at Law, Charlottesville, Va. [Ad.]

Mr Reed Smith, of Athens Co, Ohio, was suddenly killed on Nov 11, by the accidental discharge of a rifle gun, in the hse, in the midst of his family.

Orphans Court of PG Co, Md. Ordered by the Court that Sophia Hodgkin & Thos Hodgkin, adms of Alex H Boteler, late of PG Co, Md, dec'd, give notice to dec'ds creditors. –Phil Chew, reg [Said notice followed: letters of adm on personal estate of Alex H Boteler, dec'd. –Sophia Hodgkin & Thos Hodgkin]

Died: on Nov 26, Sarah Barcroft, w/o John Barcroft, of the G P O Dept. Funeral on Sun next, at 3 p m, from his residence on 18th st, near the Friends' meeting-hse.

Died: on Tue night, Nov 2, at 20 minutes past 9, Benj Franklin, 4th s/o Wm H & Susan Perkins, aged 4 years & 2 months. [See below.]

Also-Died: on Fri morning, Nov 27, at 20 minutes before 2 o'clock, Ann Eliz, only d/o Wm H & Susan Perkins, aged 22 months. Her funeral will take place this day, Nov 28, at 12 o'clock. [See above.]

MON NOV 30, 1840
Chas McClure, [V B,] elected Rep to Congress from the Cumberland Dist in Pa, v Wm S Ramsey, dec'd.

The mill of Sylvanus Holbrook, of Northbridge, Mass, was burnt on Nov 13, used for the mfgr of cotton & wool, was formerly the property of the Northbridge Mfgr Co. Loss estimated to be about $20,000.

Norfolk, Nov 26. 2 seamen, late of the schn'r *Wm J Watson*, of & for Phil, from St John's river, E Fla, arrived Tue last, & report the schn'r was cast away on Boddy's isl on Nov 16. The 2nd mate [brother-in-law of the capt] & one of the crew were lost. The capt & remainder of the crew & 2 passengers were left on the island. -Beacon

Sackett's Harbor Journal: Col John Gotham, a wealthy farmer of Watertown, & his Irish laborer in his employ, were found drowned, their bodies floated ashore on Navy Point.

Mr Henry Kelder, a respectable citizen of Rochester, Ulster Co, N Y, lost his life on Nov 2, by falling backward from a fence & breaking his neck. He was about 35, & has left a large family of small chldrn.

A short time since the 300th anniv of the foundation of the Order of Jesuits was celebrated by the Pope at the chr of that order in Rome. The ceremony was accompanied with great solemnity.

Mrd: on Nov 26, by Rev W H Odenheimer, the Hon Henry A Wise, of Va, to Sarah, d/o the Hon John Sergeant.

Mrd: on Nov 17, in Franklin Co, by Rev Jas Leftwich, the Hon Wm L Goggin, of Bedford, Va, to Miss Eliz Cook, d/o the late Saml Cook, of Franklin Co.

Mrd: on Nov 25, in St Michl's Chr, Trenton, N J, by Rev Mr Starr, Richd Eberle, M D of Cincinnati, to Miss Theodosia W Higbee, d/o Chas Higbee, of Trenton.

Mrd: on Nov 26, by Rt Rev H U Onderdonk, Alonzo Potter, D D of the Union Coll, to Sarah, d/o Robt Benedict, of N Y.

Two fires in this city last Sat, the one a stable, on Capt Hill, belonging to Mr John P Ingle, the other a frame bldg, near the R R depot, occupied by Mr J Etter as a printing ofc. Bldgs were totally consumed.

TUE DEC 1, 1840

Dr Edw Field, of Waterbury, Conn, committed suicide on the 17th ult, while in a state of tempo derangement. He was a skilled physician, & had been for many years in extensive practice.

Mrd: on Nov 26, at Lancaster, Pa, by Rev Mr Boarman, Mr Horatio N Easby, of Wash City, to Miss Eliz Barton, of Lancaster.

Died: yesterday, after a lingering illness, Mr Thos Bowen, aged 75 years. Funeral today at 3 p m, from the residence of Mr Carroll, opposite the Patriotic Bank.

Died: on Sun last, at Meridian Hill, near Wash, Philip Lansdale, in his 50th year. His remains will be removed for interment in the Family Cemetery in PG Co, Md.

Died: on Thu last, in Frankfort, Ky, after a lingering illness, Jas G Dana, Reporter of the Decisions of the Court of Appeals.

Montg Co Court [Md] sitting as a Court of Equity, Nov Term, 1840. Wm Brandenbrug, vs, Thos A Duley. Object of this suit is to procure a decree for a sale of mortgaged premises in said county, which were, on Jul 17, 1835, mortgaged by dfndnt, Thos A Duley, to cmplnt. On Jul 17, 1735, Duley conveyed real estate, described in the bill unto Wm Brandenburg, by way of mortgage to secure the payment of a bond for $600 with interest, which was due on Jun 26, 1838. Bill admits 2 payments, each of $100 made by Thos A Duley, but said mortgaged premises is charged with & liable to be sold for the payment of the residue: & Duley resides out of Md. Same to appear on or before Mar 12 next, to show why a decree ought not to pass. –Thos B Dorsey, J H Wilkinson, Nich Brewer. Brice Selby, Clk Montg Co Court

The picture painted by order of Congress, for the Rotundo of the Capitol, by Mr J C Chapman, was yesterday opened to the public view, in the niche designated for it in the Rotundo. Of 3 niches, or sq compartments, in the wall of the circular hall in the centre of the Capitol, there are 8. Four are occupied by Mr Trumbull's celebrated Nat'l Paintings; Mr Chapman's is the 5th in the series; the remaining 3 being in the hands of other artists. The subject of this painting, is the <u>Baptism of Pocahontas</u>. When the existence of the Colony was at stake, a firmness of spirit prompted her to traverse the midnight forest alone, & brave the indignation of her kindred, to give advice & warning. Name & history of Pocahontas interwoven with the very existence of the first permanent Christian community of this great Confederation. On a Sabbath morning, the church bells echoed about Jamestown, to witness this converted heathen girl, Pocahontas, d/o Powhatan, *"the first Christian ever of her Nation,"* turning from her idols to God. The sgts took their stations, & the Indians gathered, as Rolfe supported his destined bride to the rude baptismal font, hewn from an oak of her native forest. Nantequaus, her favorite brother, stood nearest to her of her kindred; an elder sister, with her Indian boy, in front, while her uncle, Opehankanough, shrunk back, & probably even brooded over the deep laid plan of massacre which he so fearfully executed years after, when Pocahontas had gone to Heaven. The artist has been governed by the best authorities as to facts & details. The interior of the church may appear strange. It was adopted from one now in existence, built about the time of that of Jamestown, & the description of an actual resident of Jamestown at the period, Wm Stratchy, suggested. The pulpit with its cloth embroidered with the Arms of Va & the initial of King James, the martial character of Sir Thos Dale, & the regulation of the Colony that obliged the Colonist to wear their arms even to Church. The Govn'r went forth attended with his Consailers, Captaines & other ofcrs, & a guard of Holberdiers to the number of 50 in his Lordships liverie, with his Standard Bearer & Page-the younger sons & cousins of nobility, the vine dresser, the mechanic, the naked limbs & costumes of the savages, are a matter of history which the artist has only followed with the best of his ability.

Meeting of the Tobacco Planters of Chas Co, Md, held at Port Tobacco, on Nov 24, John Barnes, called to the chr, assisted by J B Wills & J Ferguson. Edw J Hamilton & Henry C Bruce appointed secs. The Hon Danl Jenifer adessed the meeting: followed by Hon Wm D Merrick. Regarding: call to meet in Wash City on Dec 18, & 25 Delegates be appointed from each election district in the county, to attend said convention. Delegates appointed:

Danl Jenifer	Minchin Lloyd	C F Green
Wm D Merrick	Zach Lloyd	Thos Berry
John T Stoddert	Alex Lancaster	Francis Neale
Nath Harris	Val Miles	Henry Neale
John Hughes	John Briscoe	Jas T Neale
C T Lancaster	W H Smoot	Wm Nevitt
Geo Dent	R Diggs	Chandler F Shaw
Francis Diggs	John Diggs	Richd Barnes

Geo Barnes	John G Chapman	John F Gardiner
Walter A Haislip	Pearson Chapman	T F Gardiner
Wm Queen	Chas Wills	Thos E Gardiner
O Gibbons	Francis Thompson	Thos J Gardiner
Jos Young	Walter Mitchell	Robt Gray
Jas Brawner	Jas Johnson	Wm B Stone
Gustavus R Brown	John J Jenkins	Walter M Miller
Wm F Rennoe	Peter W Crain	Jas D Freeman
Philip Marshall	John Spalding	Edmond Perry
Thos H Marshall	Hez Brawner	John Lawson
Edw Sanders	Geo Dement	Jas D Carpenter
Townly Robey	Richd Dement	Jas B Brent
Edw Miles	A F Beal	Jos Brummett
Wm Thompson	Chas A Pye	John Hamilton
Alex Mathews	Jas B Pye	Peter Wood
Wm Mathews	Henry S Hawkins	Aquilla Turner
Henry Bowling	B S Gardiner	A Middleton
John D Bowling	Josias Hawkins	Allison Roberts
F E Dunnington	Josias H Hawkins	Francis Robey
John Hammersly	Hawkins Jameston	Wm F Robey
John Fendall	Henry L Mudd	Jas Hollis
Benj Peun	Wm A Mudd	Hugh Cox
Wilson Compton	Saml C Moran	John Matchett
Thos O Bean	Alex Bowling	Thos Perry
John Matthews	Francis Bowling	R Burgess

Wash Museum: proprietor desirous of gratifying the public, has engaged the great magician, Monsieur De Coursey, for a few nights, beginning on Nov 30. Open 9 a m to 9 p m.

Died: on Fri week, in Fayetteville, N C, Wm Nott, aged 52, of the hse of Nott & Starr, merchants. Mr Nott was a native of Middletown, Conn, but has resided in Fayetteville about 25 years, where he maintained a high character in all the relations of life.

Died: the 18th ult, at his seat in the immediate vicinity of Raleigh, in his 73rd year, after a severe illness of about 10 days, Capt Theophilus Hunter, one of the most substantial planters of Wake Co, N C.

Madame Bihler informs she has just received, at her Ladies' Ornamental Hair Dressing & Fancy Store, on Pa ave, between 9th & 10th sts, a handsome assortment of goods in her line: wigs, half wigs, frizettes, bandeaux, braids, plaits, curls, & ringlets.

Public Lands: compilation of facts concerning valuations & sales of Public Domain: includes Ill, Mo, Ohio, Ala, Miss, & Ind. [1½ cols.]

Dr Edw Field, of Waterbury, Conn, committed suicide on the 17th ult, while in a state of tempo derangement. He was a skilled physician, & had been for many years in extensive practice.

WED DEC 2, 1840
An American gentleman residing at Paris informs us that the learned David B Warden, of that city, formerly U S Cnsl at the French Court, has collected all the works relating to North & So America which he called find in both hemispheres, & in all languages.

Miss Mgt Ingersoll, in her 18th year, d/o John Ingersoll, jr, of German Flats, N Y, was killed a few days since by her head coming in contact with a bridge over the canal at Medina, while riding in a canal boat.

Boston Transcript of Sat: Richd Child, an estimable citizen, who resided at Hollis & Wash sts, in great depression, cut his throat & died this morning.

The mother of Mr Benj F Horde, of Evansville, Ia, his sister, & 2 chldrn, were recently drowned in the Bonpas river, Wabash Co, Ill. The river was swollen, & the driver of the vehicle missed the path.

Died: on the 25th ult, at Easton, Md, Thos Jas Bullitt, in his 78th year.

The Wiskonsin Enq says that Messrs W Alfred & P W Thomas, of New Balt, in that Terr, have been very successful in smelting copper ore.

Public sale: as administrator of Portia Hodgson, I shall sell, at public auct, on Dec 3, all the household & kitchen furniture of the dec'd: also several handsome clocks, silver ware, piano forte, new carriage & horses. Sale will take place at her late residence on Oronoko st, Alexandria, at 10 a m. Also, on Dec 8, at the tavern of Saml Catis, in Fairfax Co, I shall sell several valuable household servants, particularly a first rate dining-room servant & chamber maid. –John Wornal, adm

Criminal Court-Wash. 1-Judy Jasper, free negress, convicted of stealing sundry waring apparel, the property of Patrick Robbins: 2 years in the pen. 2-Jas Simms, convicted of stealing a gold watch & chain, the property of Julia Simms: 2 years in the pen. 3-Henry Wootten, free negro, convicted of stealing a calf, property of John Mason, jr: 2 years in the pen. 4-John Allinger, convicted of stealing foreign coins of the value of $16, property of Michl Tolhouse: 2 years in the pen. 5-Isaac Beddo, free negro, an old offender, convicted on 2 indictments of stealing a coat, property of Dr Lacy: 3 years in the pen for both offences. 6-John Smith, convicted of setting fire to the hat factory of S W Handy: 3 years in the pen. 7-Jos Fletcher alias Joe Greasy, convicted of stealing a beef hide & kine skin, the property of John Hoover: fined $4.50, & 3 months in the county jail. 8-Wm Gibbs, free negro, convicted of stealing

12 lbs of butter, the property of Mr Knight, butter-dealer, Gtwn: fined $3, & 2 months in the county jail. 9-Thos Hoban, convicted of an assault in attempting to steal a pocket book, containing $15, from the person of John H Clarvoe: 3 months in the county jail. 10-C Magruder, free negro, convicted of stealing a wagon wheel, the property of John Dove: fined $4, & 2 months in the county jail. 11-Mary Ann Clements, convicted of stealing sundry chairs, the property of Zephaniah Jones: fine $1, & 1 month in the county jail. 12-Jas Morris, free negro, convicted of stealing 4 breastpins of the value of $3, the property of A Schneider: fined $3, & 1 month in the county jail. 13-Geo T Hall & Henry T Newton, convicted of a conspiracy to defraud Walter Rives, while playing at cards: fine $20 each. 14-Saml Casson, convicted of an assault by setting a savage dog on a colored boy hired to R S Patterson: fine $5. 15-John Frank, convicted of a violent & aggravated assault on the person of Susan Moore; also convicted of another violent assault on the person of Eliz Hazlett: fine $50, & 1 month in the county jail for the first offence, & a fine of $50 for the second offence. 16-Bernard Martin & John Keaton, convicted of an aggravated assault & battery on the person of Conrad Hess, scavenger of the 3rd Ward. John Keaton was sentenced to a fine of $25, he having already been 2 months in prison, for want of bail. Bernard Martin, who was out on bail, did not make his appearance: his recognisance was consequently forfeited.

Wash Corp: 1-Cmte of Claims: reported a bill authorizing a license to Jas Riordan as vender of lottery tkts for 6 months. 2-The resignation of R H Clements as police magistrate for Ward 4: read & laid on the table. 3-Ptn from Richd France & others: lottery ticket venders: referred to the Cmte of Claims. 4-Cmte of Claims: relief of N A Randall: passed. 5-Select Cmte: to examine the claim of M C Ewing, a bill for his relief: laid on the table.

At the Univ of Va, on Sat, the 14th ult, John A G Davis, Prof of Law, died, in his 39th year, of a shot received nearly 2 days before, from a pistol, by the hands of a disguised student, whom Prof Davis had just endeavored to arrest & discover. The offender is in custody of the Law; our present concern is with the lamented dead. Thank heaven the parricide was not of the Law-class, or Va-born. Prof Davis left a widow & 7 chldrn. About 6 years ago he embraced Christianity, becoming a member of the Episc Chr.

The unhappy youth, who is considered to have perpetrated the act-the killing of Prof Davis, is described as a stripling, weighing scarcely over 100 lbs & about 17years of age. His trial will take place on the 2nd inst.

Mrs Susan L Hewitt, having fixed up in handsome style that large & commodious hse on north side of Pa ave, at 3rd st, is prepared for boarders, & to receive a mess of Members of Congress this season.

New Boarding Hse: Miss Chisholm has taken the large brick house lately occupied by Col Brent, on 9th near E st, for the accommodation of boarders.

Mrs J Little, Dress & Habit Mkr: on D, between, 10th & 11th sts.

THU DEC 3, 1840
The P M at Rochester offers a reward of $50 for the apprehension of John Herrington, charged with having robbed the mail on the packet *Orleans*, between that city & Buffalo.

Table Diapers: rich damask table diapers, napkins, huckaback diapers, & towelling, of ever description, received at the store of Wingerd & Bradley.

Little Rock, Ark: Nov 11. Companies A, C, G, & I, of the 3rd U S Infty, arrived in town on Fri last, & immediately embarked for New Orleans on board the steamboat *Corvette* & 2 keels. Event which occurred, was the murder of a man named Osborn, by a comrade; both belonging to Co I. The number comprising these 4 cos is 352 rank & file. Ofcrs accompanying the btln: Maj H Wilson, Capts J B Clark & L N Morris, Lts J M Smith, S D Dobbins, & G B Field, A C A & A A Q M, & Dr Griffin, Assist Surgeon U S A. –Gaz [Admin]

Richmond Compiler of Sat: Rev Z Meade died on Fri, after a protracted & painful illness. He had not long been a citizen of Richmond, but was endeared to all who knew him.

Balt, Dec 2: 1-We are informed by a gentleman, last evening from Whitemarsh, the seat of David Ridgely, about 11 miles from this city, on the Phil road, that the elegant mansion on the estate was entirely destroyed by fire on Mon last, & a great portion of the valuable furniture was consumed in the flames. 2-Last night the steam engine factory of Mr Jenkin Lloyd, on East Falls ave, near Pratt st, was discovered to be on fire & completely enveloped in flames. -American

For sale: at the tavern of Wm Nelson, half a mile from Little Falls Bridge, 200 acs of land, adjoining the property of Reed & McLehany.

Orphans Court of Chas Co, Md: order to sell at public sale, on Dec 30, 1840, at the late residence of Mrs Eliz Reeves, dec'd, near Beantown, all the personal estate of the late Thos C Reeves, consisting of 34 or 35 negroes. –Jos E Simms, adm de bonis non

Tippecanoe Club of Wash, cmte to report a time to plan the reception of Wm H Harrison, upon his arrival in Wash City. Cmte:

Walter Lenox	J W Martin	Jas F Haliday
John T Towers	Geo S Gideon	Chas H James
R H Stewart	L Harbaugh	Thos Allen
D Homans	John H Goddard	R W Bales

For rent: 2 frame dwlgs on so F st, each, 8 rooms, with a basement.
–E Brooke, near Todd's Ice-hse.

Died: on Mon, at Alexandria, in his 43rd year, Mr Saml Messersmith, a native of Balt, but for many years a respectable merchant of that place.

Died: on Oct 12, at the residence of Thos Martin, PG Co, Md, Miss Susan Jane Wall, in her 29th year.

Died: on the 25th ult, at Stockbridge, Mass, Mr Jas Davidson, aged 86. He was in the American Revolutionary army with the rank of Maj.

Governess wanted to teach Eng & Music: competency to teach will be required.
–Robt Ghiselin, near Nottingham, PG Co, Md.

FRI DEC 4, 1840
Wash Corp ofcrs:
Wm W Seaton, Mayor   Coll of Taxes: Andrew Rothwell
Reg: Chas H Wiltberger   Surveyor: Wm P Eliot
1st Clk: Jos Radcliff   Atty: John H Bradley
2nd Clk: Wm E Howard   Messenger: Jacob Kleiber

Brd of Aldermen:
C H Goldsborough	Wm Gunton	Nathl Brady
John D Barclay	John H Goddard	Isaac Clarke
Wm B Randolph	Wm Brent	Marmaduke Dove
Wallace Kirkwood	Jas Carbery	Jas Marshall

Sec, Brd of Aldermen: E J Middleton
Sec, Brd of Cmn Cncl: Richd Barry

Brd of Cmn Cncl:
Edmund Hanly	John C Harkness	Saml Byington
Wm Wilson	Saml Bacon	John L Maddox
Wm Easby	Jos Bryan	Wm F Walker
Lewis Johnson	John H Houston	Edw W Clark
Wm W Sewart	Simeon Bassett	Geo H Fulmer
Wm Orme	Wm J McDonald	Jas Crandell

Brd of Health:
Dr Wm B Magruder	Dr Harvey Lindsly	Thos Blagden
John D Barclay	Geo C Grammer	John B Ferguson
Dr H J F Condict	Dr John Frederick May	Dr Noble Young
Jas Larned	John P Ingle	Marmaduke Dove

Police Magistrates:
Saml Drury	B K Morsell	Isaac Clarke
Jos Forest	Wm Thompson	Jas Marshall
Ch H W Wharton	Wm Hebb	
Vincent King	Nathl Brady	

Police Cnstbls:
F B Poston	R R Burr	H R Maryman
John Waters	David S Waters	John Cryer
Fielder Burch	H B Robertson	Judson Richardson

Com'rs:
Saml Drury	Wm Cooper, jr	John Cryer
John Sessford	H R Maryman	Judson Richardson

Inspec of Tobacco: Henry H Lowe
Sealer-Weights & Meas: Wm M McCauley
Com'r of the Canal: Peter M Pearson
Inspec of Flour & salted provisions: Jacob Kleiber
Inspec of Fire Apparatus: Saml Briggs

Com'rs of the Centre Market:
Wm B Randolph	Jesse Brown	Saml Bacon

Clerks of the Markets:
Wm Serrin	H B Robertson	Peter Little
Wm Clarke	Jas Johnson	

Inspecs & Meas of Lumber:
D A Gardiner	Geo Collard	John G Robinson
Wm G Deale	Benj Bean	Wm Douglass

Wood Corders & Coal Meas:
Jas Gaither	Nathl Plantt	J B Ferguson
Saml Kilman	Richd Wimsatt	John Hilton

Assessors:
Saml Drury	John Sessford	Geo Adams

Board of Appeals:
John Gadsby	Geo Crandell	Thos Blagden

Guardians of the Poor:
Danl H Haskel	Henry J Stone	Dr A McWilliams
John McClellan	John B Ferguson	Rich Butt-intendent
Leonard Harbaugh	Noble Young	

Superintendents of Sweeps:
Wm M Robinson	John Krenan	Henry Awkward
Wm E Moran	John L Martin	

Scavengers:
Thos Riggalls	Conrad Hess	Sylvester Gray
Luke Richardson	Osburn Turner	
Jas Hollidge	Jas Hollidge	

Com'rs of West Burial Ground:
French S Evans	Jacob A Bender
Lewis Johnson	John Douglass-sexton

Com'r of East Burial Ground:
Mat Wright	John P Ingle

Trustees of Schools:
Rev Wm Matthews	Rev Wm Hawley	Jas Larned

John D Barclay	Rev A T McCormick	Richd Barry
Wm Lloyd	G G Brooke	Jas Carbery
Wm B Magruder	Thos Blagden	Jas Marshall
John W Maury	G H Fulmer	

Teachers:

Joshua L Henshaw	Hugh McCormick	

Com'rs of the Wash Canal:

Thos Carbery	Jas Young	Jas Adams-clk
John Sessford	C T Coote	
Jacob Gideon, jr	Matthew Wright	

Somerville, N J: Dec 1. David Polhemus, about 20 years of age, s/o Peter Polhemus, of Hillsborough, was killed on Fri last, near Boundbrook, when a large wagon passed over his body. He attempted to jump out when he had proceeded as far as he wished to go. A brother of the dec'd met his death in the same manner. He was named after his unfortunate brother. -Messenger

Crct Court of Wash Co, D C: in Chancery: Nov Term, 1840. Anthony Preston & Rosina Cheshire, vs, the heirs-at-law of Archibald Cheshire. Ratify sale by J B H Smith, trustee: Lucy A Laskey was the highest bidder & purchaser of pt of lot 1 in sq 267, for the sum of $505; Wm Wilson purchased the northern half of lot 16 in sq 267 with improvements, for $260; Dearborn Johnson purchased the southern half of lot 16 in sq 267, with improvements, for $260; Wm Evans purchased lot 2 in sq 267, for $437.25; & that Lucy A Laskey has paid all the purchase money; the other purchasers have fully complied with the terms of the sale. -Wm Brent, clk

Sig Raphael Thiay, leader of the Marine Band, informs he has made arrangements, & will be prepared to attend any parties this winter that may require his services. Orders may be sent to him through the P O, at Wash.

Orphans Court of Wash Co, D C. Letters of administration on personal estate of Wm Holland, late of said county, dec'd. –Jas Williams, adm

City Ord-Wash: Act for relief of N A Randall: the fine imposed for an alleged violation of the laws relating to free negroes, be, & the same is hereby, remitted: provided he pay the costs of prosecution. -Approved, Dec 3, 1840

Farm for sale or exchange in part: farm in the confines of Loudoun & Pr Wm Cos, Va, upwards of 400 acs; with a house suitable for a tenant, & out houses. –Will Hebb, Wash

SAT DEC 5, 1840
Col G W Phillips, of the parish of Assumption, La, met with an untimely end, a few days since, by the bursting of the boiler of his sugar house.

The eldest d/o J B Guthrie, of Pittsburgh, Pa, lost her life when her clothes caught fire, on Sat last.

Reading papers state that on Thu last, the d/o of Maj Muhlenburg, age between 2 or 3 years, of that borough, fell into a bucket of boiling water, & died on Sat, after lingering in dreadful torment.

The will of the late Miss Jane Innes, spinster, formerly of Picardy-pl, Edinburg, but late of Stow, in North Briton, has just been proved in the Prerogative Court of the ArchBishop of Canterbury, in Dr's Commons, by Geo Scott & John Thompson, the excs. The dec'd was possessed of upwards of L800,000 in funds, & property in different parts of Scotland, in the amount of L1,200,000, making together the enormous sum of 2 million: to be divided amongst all her relations who can be found, without respect to the nearest kindred. About 5 years since, the testratrix became entitled to L500,000, upon the death of her brother, he having died intestate, & she being his only next of kin. Miss Innes, nearly 80, fell & broke her leg, which accident ultimately caused her death. The supposed wealthiest spinster in the world [Miss Burdett Coutts] was not entitled to that appellation until the present time.
–London paper

Mrd: on the 27th ult, by Rev Mr Stringfellow, Mr Columbus Drew, of Wash City, to Miss Marietta H Robertson, of Richmond, Va.

Mrd: on Dec 3, in Wash City, by Rev Thos Thornton, Alfred Lindsay, of Alexandria, D C, to Willa Ann, d/o the late Capt Wm B Dyer.

Died: on Tue last, at Brooklyn, N Y, in his 67th year, the Hon Peter W Radcliff.

Died: on the 23rd ult, in Montg Co, Md, Mrs Eliz Davis, relict of Thos Davis, in her 69th year.
She leaves her chldrn & relatives to mourn her loss.

Died: on the 26th ult, at the residence of his father, Geo D Page, s/o J L Page, of Fairfax Co, Va, formerly of Salem, Mass. This youth was an ardent lover of nature, & delighted in the cultivation of music & flowers. *"Whom the Gods love die young."*

MON DEC 7, 1840
The U S store-ship *Relief*, Lt J S Nicholas, sailed from N Y on Wed for the Pacific Ocean, with stores for the U S squad there.

Wm M'Queen, late P M of New Orleans, absconded some days ago for Texas, carrying with him 12 negroes, in defraud of his creditors & his securities. One of the securities of Mr M'Queen, John L Lewis, sent 2 ofcrs after him with a writ: unable to catch up with M'Queen.

Boarding: 1-Mrs Harbaugh: 7th st. 2-P Brady: N J ave. 3-John Pettibone: Pa ave & 9th st. 4-Mrs Miller: Mo ave between 4½ & 6th sts. 5-E McCardle: E st between & 7th & 8th sts. 6-Mrs Preuss: Mo ave, between 4½ & 6th sts. 7-Mrs Anne E Bronaugh: N J ave. 8-Mrs Susan L Hewitt: Pa ave & 3rd st. 9-Mrs Ramsay: Pa ave & E st. 10-Mrs R Howard: oppo Fuller's Htl. 11-A R Dowson: Capitol Hill. 12: Mrs A Cochran: on F between 13th & 14th st. 13-Mr M Taylor: Boyle's row, E st. 14-Mrs Mount: Pa ave near 4½ st. 15-Miss Chisholm: 9th & E st. 16-Mrs Mary C Bronaugh: in Gen Duff Green's row. 17-Mr Houston: E Capitol st. 18-Mrs Dashiell: C st, next dr to Dr Sewall. 19-Mrs Hough: 6th st between E & F sts. 20-Mrs K Turner has taken & newly fitted out the house formerly occupied by Mrs Page, where she is prepared to accommodate Members with their families; also transient & yearly boarders. 21-Mrs Wimsatt: Pa ave near 4½ st.

Died: on the 2nd ult, at Fort Winnebago, Lt Saml Whitehorn, of the 5th Regt Infty U S A.

On Thu last on Mr Addison's farm, 5 miles from the Capitol, Mr Walter Meehan, s/o John S Meehan, Librarian to Congress, gunning along with another young gentleman, the former, after firing his piece, was in the act of reloading, when his powder-flash suddenly exploded in his right hand, blowing off 2 or 3 fingers. Dr Addison rendered assistance. Mr Meehan was conveyed to the residence of Dr Hall, who found that amputation was necessary, & the operation was immediatly performed by Dr Hall. Mr Meehan is at present doing well in the hands of his surgical & medical attendants.

TUE DEC 8, 1840
Leslie Combs has resumed the practice of Law: Lexington, Ken.

Meeting of Tobacco Planters of Anne Arundel Co, Md, convened at Butler's tavern, on Nov 28, 1840: John Thomas, chrmn; Richd Estep, sec. Cmte: John Mercer, Cephas Simmons, Wm O'Hara, John G Rogers, & David M Brogden. Appt'd Delegates to the Convention to be held at Wash on Dec 15:

John Thomas	Jas Owens, jr
Jos G Harrison	Chas Hodges
Thos J Lawrence	Jas S Owens
Benj Carr	Thos Owens
Nathan Childs	Rinaldo Pindell
Cephas Simmons	Thos J Richardson
Robt Garner	Jas Cheston
Thos J Hall	John Mercer
Richd Estep	Sprigg Harwood
Jas Kent	Saml H Hamilton
Wm C Lyles	Geo Gale
Philip Pindell	Jos Bucey

Wm O'Hara	Wm Harwood
Richd Sellman	Saml A Claggett
Alfred Sellman	Martin Fenwick
Francis Bird	Chas Steuart
John Iglehart	Wm Ghiselin
Thos J Dorsett	Henry Owens
Geo T Ditty	Saml Owens
Wm Brogden	Alex'r Murray
David M Brogden	Wm H Peake
Geo H Steuart	Chas Steele
Richd S Steuart	B W Marriott
Jas H Watkins	John F Wilson
Jas Davidson	Isaac Jones
Thos Davidson	John W Iglehart
John S Sellman	David Griffith
Robt W Kent	Alex'r Franklin
Solomon G Chaney	John C Weems
Edw Harvey	Jacob Bird

Norfolk, Dec 5: imposing sight. Lying at the anchorage off Town Point, abreast of the Naval Hosp: U S ship *Delaware*, of 74 guns, Capt Skinner, bearing the broad pennant of Cmdor Shubrick; sloop of war *Levant*, Cmder Smoot, of the West India squad; sloop of war *Yorktown*, Cmder Aulick; sloop of war *Dale*, Cmder Gantt, destined for the Pacific; steamer *Poinsett*, Lt Com Lynch. A fleet of small coasters add to the scene, with a sharp northeaster in the distance. -Beacon

Tubingen, Wurtemburg: new printing establishment, lately opened by Theodore Helgerad: all the compositors & pressmen, 196 in number, 11 of the former being women, are deaf & dumb, & educated at his cost for the employment in which they are engaged. The King has conferred a large gold medal on Helgerad, of the order of civil merit, for this great reclamation from the social & moral waste.

Tue last, John B Slaughter, charged with the murder of Jos Pledge, was convicted of murder in the 2nd degree, & sentenced to 18 years in the pen. –Petersburg Intell

Valuable farm for sale: 3½ miles from Wash City, formerly the property of Maj T P Andrews: 115 acs: with comfortable dwlg house, & tobacco house. Property well known in Wash City & Md. –Wm G Sanders

Mrd: on Dec 3, by Rev J T Johnston, Wm P Johnston, M D, of Savannah, Ga, to Mary E Hooe, d/o Bernard Hooe, of Alexandria, D C.

Died: on Sun, after a short but painful illness, Miss Bridget Rodgers.

Died: on Dec 4, in Gtwn, Mrs Eliz Wall, consort of Mr Jesse H D Wall, in her 45th year.

Died: on Nov 4, at Wm & Mary College, in his 22nd year, Battaile J Goulden, s/o Mr John Goulden, of Caroline Co, Va. He endeared himself by is manly, virtuous, & amiable deportment.

Died: the 5th inst, Mrs Nancy Craven, relict of the late John Craven, in her 87th year. For nearly 70 years she was a member of the Baptist Chr, & an ornament to her Christian profession. She died in perfect peace. Funeral this morning, at 11 a m, from the residence of her dght-in-law, Mrs S Craven, G & 18th sts.

Meeting of the Nat'l Instit for the Promotion of Science: at 7 p m. —A O Dayton, sec

Farm on which I reside is for sale: 800 acs, in Calvert Co, Md: with comfortable dwlg house, kitchen, servants' hses, & granary. I desire to remove to Balt.
—Thos J Hellen, St Leonard's P O until Dec 20: after that time to Annapolis.

For rent: small farm ¼ mile beyond Tenallytown, recently occupied by Mr David Shoemaker: 100 acs. Apply to Walter Smith, Gtwn.

WED DEC 9, 1840
Madison & Wm B Nelson, Attys at Law: Westminster, Carroll Co, Md. [Ad]

Dr G M Dove has taken an ofc on 8th st, opposite the Marine Garrison, & offers his professional services.

Troy, Ohio, Dec 3. Mr J J Crampton, of our town, a hatter by occupation, on Sat, lost his life by the accidental discharge of a shot-gun. He was in the act of blowing into the muzzle of the gun when from some cause the piece went off producing instant death. He has left a widow & 1 or 2 small chldrn to mourn his untimely death. -Times

Montg, Nov Term, 1840. Hilleary L Offutt, ptn to divide lands. Ordered the report made by Com'rs appointed by this Court to divide the real estate of Thos B Offutt be ratified. —T H Wilkinson -H Selby, clk

Wash Corp: 1-Ptn of Jonathan Guest: referred to the Cmte of Claims. 2-Ptn from Geo Bell: do. 3-Ptn from Simon Canter: do. Brd adjourned.

Dedication of the Armory of the Wash Light Infty: Cmder, Capt France: for the last 3 months, the company succeeded in renting the large & commodious room on C st, formerly occupied by the Soc of Odd Fellows as their lodge. This room has been fitted up & is now the Armory of the Wash Light Infty. It was opened on Mon in the presence of the Mayor of Wash, Capt Blake, & others.

Meeting of Tobacco Planters, in Bedford Co, Va: at the Eagle Tavern, at Bedford C H, on Nov 23, 1840. Object of the meeting was explained by John O Leftwich- approve the organization of a Convention of Tobacco Planters, at Wash City, in May last. Cmte: Robt Campbell, Saml Hobson, Benj A Donald, Wm C Leftwich, Roderick McDaniel, John O Leftwich, Hon John M Botts, Hon Jas Garland, & Hon Wm L Goggin. –Jas Jopling, chrmn -Wm Harris, sec

Columbia Artl to meet at 6½ p m, this evening at the usual place. Uniformed members are to attend in their uniforms. –V Harbaugh, sec

J V N Throop has removed his engraving ofc to Missouri ave, between 4½ & 6th sts.

Wines & Grocs: I Mudd, so side of Pa ave, between 4½ & 6th sts. [Ad]

THU DEC 10, 1840
Furnished rms for rent: Jas Williams: on 4½ st, between Pa ave & C st.

Boarding: Mrs D Galvin, on C st, between 4½ & 3rd st.

The new Episc Chapel, in Queen Anne Parish, PG Co, Md, will be consecratd on Dec 13, by the Rt Rev Bishop Whittingham, D D, who will at the same time administer the holy apostolic rite of confirmation. On the following day the Bishop will officiate at St Barnabas, known by the name of the Brick Church.

Stray cows trespassing on premises at the Congress Burying Ground. Owner to prove property, pay charges, & take them away. –Jas Little, keeper of Congress Burying Ground. Test: Wm Hebb, J P

L Kervand would be happy to accommodate a mess of gentlemen with brd & lodging at his hse, 7 Bldgs, Pa ave. Stable for carriages & horses. –L K

Boarding: Mrs Holdsworth, on C st, just back of Gadsby's Htl.

After so long a retirement from the turmoils of political life, to re-enter upon them at my years would probably be to sacrifice my happiness. Letter by Hon Wm Gaston, of N C, to John Gray Bynum: dated Newbern, Oct 31, 1840. Regarding: to put in nomination for appointment of Senator in Congress.

Cows wanted: persons having dry cows to dispose of may hear of a purchaser by calling at O Sheckles' Hotel, on 7th st.

For sale: 3 fine Jennets & a young Jack. Apply to the Hon Wm M McCarty, of the Hse o/Reps, for those wishing to purchase such animals.

FRI DEC 11, 1840

Ark frontier: Govn'r Yell, of Ark, speaks of the exposed condition of the frontier from the Indians placed there by the Genr'l Gov't. This subject claims the early attention of Congress.

The Hon Joel Holleman has resigned his seat in Congress as Rep of the 1st Congress Dist of Va; assigning as his reason that he can no longer represent the feelings & wishes of a majority of his constituents.

Eight years ago the first mail west of Ann Arbor, Mich, was taken to Jackson on foot, by Mr R Thompson, in his vest pocket, & consisted of 1 letter. This year the business of the P O will exceed $2,000. The same year the mail route was established, the contents of the P O, at Marshal, Mich, were deposited in a cigar box, which was usually kept in a Connecticut clock. –Detroit Daily Adv

Trustee's sale: decree of PG Co Court, Court of Equity, made in the case of Dennis Ferral & Eliz Ferral, vs, Thos Ferral, Rebecca Ferral, & others: sale at the tavern of Thos Baldwin, in Bladensburg, Md, on Dec 22: frame dwlg now occupied by the undersigned. Also, the frame dwlg now in the possession of Mr N McGregor, in the heart of Bladensburg, fronts on the principal st. Also, the frame dwlg now occupied by Mr W Tutle. Also, a large frame granary: 2 tracts of land called *Grove Hunt & Plummer's Pasture*, together, about 218 acs, now in the possession of Mr John Harvey. These tracts lie contiguous to each other. Also, 2 tracts called *Fairfax Beall & Second Thought*, about 166 acs, on the road leading to Upr Marlboro, now in the possession of Mr John Pumphrey. –Eliz Ferrall, trustee, Bladensburg, Md

Wm Cheeks, residing at the corner of Race & Bache sts, while in the hotel of Mrs Duncan, 180 Market st, Phil, on Sun, fell down & immediately expired.

B Storer & Wm Key Bond have connected themselves as partners in the practice of the law. They will attend all the Courts held in Hamilton Co, Ohio, & Crct & Dist Courts of the U S at Columbus.

Classical Academy, 10th & Walnut sts, Phil: tuition & brd-$320 per annum. –M L Hurlbert

On Tue, at the R R depot at Newark, N J, Mr Ichabod Condict, a highly respectable merchant of Orange, on his way to N Y, fell dead on the floor, in the ticket ofc, in an apoplectic fit.

At New Brunswick, N J, Mr Abraham Suydam, Pres of the Farmers & Mechanics' Bank at New Brunswick, disappeared on Thu last: reward of $100 for discovery of his body, on the supposition that he may have been murdered. His accounts with the bank are said to be all in order. It is alleged on good authority that Mr S was seen on that same day in N Y. –N Y American

Mrd: on Dec 3, at Eastern Hill, D C, by Rev Mr Van Horseigh, John M Brown, of PG Co, to Sarah Ann, eldest d/o Maj Ignatius M_nning. [Could be Manning-letter was not complete.]

Mrd: on Dec 6, at the Monumental Chr, Richmond, by Rt Rev Bishop Moore, John Contee, of Md, to Mary L, d/o Chas D Brodie, of Mobile, Ala.

Mrd: on Tue last, by Rev Mr Stringfellow, Mr C C Berry, of PG Co, Md, to Miss Ann R Butts, of Berlin, Md.

Died: on Dec 4, very suddenly, Adam S E Dungan, of Cashtown, Adams Co, Pa. He was on his return from Balt in a carriage with his wife, when about 14 miles below Gettysburg was seized with apoplexy, & died immediately.

Died: on Dec 3, in Livingston Co, Ky, aged 80 years, Maj Wm Wells, a soldier of the Revolution.

Died: on Dec 2, at the residence of his son-in-law, Dr Jos L McWilliams, St Mary's Co, Md, after an illness of 5 days, Mr Jeremiah Alvey, in his 77th year. [Ky papers will please copy.]

For rent: a neat & comfortable 2 story brick dwlg, on north side of G st, between 12th & 13th sts west. Apply to Jos Wimsatt.

Public sale: deed of trust from Francis Lowndes & others, dated Jul 21, 1840, to the subscriber: sale at the auct rm of Thos C Wright, Bridge st, Gtwn, on Jan 14: all that part of a piece of land in Wash Co, D C, lying north of the public rd leading from the Little Falls rd as it now runs thru said land towards Tenallytown, it being part of the land conveyed to Mgt C Stewart & Helen L Stewart, by Henry W Smith & Mary Smith, his wife, on May 23, 1828, containing 27 acs, more or less, as will appear by the said deed & the deed to said Francis Lowndes. –W Redin, trustee

SAT DEC 12, 1840
Whig Electoral Dinner: at Swann & Iglehart's Hotel, on Dec 1. Cmte of arrangements: John Johnson, Pres: Jos H Nicholson, Richd W Gill, & Thos S Alexander, V Ps. Appropriate airs were played by Roundtree's excellent band. Volunteer toasts: Gen J N Watkins; Washington G Tuck; Jas L Ridgley, of Balt; Dr Preston, of the Electoral College; Z Collins Lee; Wm McNier; Geo G Brewer; Thos Karney; Wm H Gatchell, of Balt; John S Skinner; Geo McNier; Hugh W Evans, of Balt; H Capron; Geo C Washington; Z C Lee; John P Kennedy; S Teackle Wallis; R R Goodwin; Dr S Collins, of Balt; Wm H Hall; John Bozman Kerr; Richd Swann; & C H Pitts.

Ohio State Jrnl, Dec 4. On Wed last, being the day on which the Electors for Ohio assembled to fulfill the high ofc of recording her vote for Tippecanoe & Tyler too, Columbus city was in celebration. Dinner at Col Olmstead's Nat'l Hotel at 9 p m: toasts to Gen Wm Henry Harrison: like his predecessor, Granny Washington, *First in peace, first in war, first in the hearts of his countrymen.* Toasts were also given by N H Swayne & Micajah T Williams.

NY: Whig Electoral Dinner at Stanwix Hall, on Dec 2: Hon John C Spencer presided, assisted by Lewis Benedict & S De Witt Bloodgood. Whig State Central Cmte: John Townsend, Saml Stevens, Jas Horner, Sanford Cobb, Robt Thompson, & John Taylor. Toasts by: [About 300 present.]

Gen Van Cortlandt
Archibald McIntyre
G C Verplanck
Peter G Sharpe
Gideon Lee
Col J Watson Webb
P G Sharpe
Thurlow Weed
Col J J Speed
Jas Horner
Mr P L Tracy
Col Robt H Pruyn
Gen N Dubois
Gen R King
Henry P Voorhees
Gen Earl Stimson
Col H A Livingston
Hon F A Tallmadge
Judge Ogden, of Dela
Col S S Benedict
Willis Hall
Cashier Jas Taylor
Thos L Greene
Lewis Joy
Henry G Wheaton
Gen John F Townsend
A M Goodrich
Jacob Acker, of N Y
Cyrus T Francis
N W Roberts
Col Littlejohn
Henry Green
O M Tomlinson
John Q Wilson
C L Austin, of Vt
E W Skinner
A B Dickinson
Col Thaddeus Joy
Lewis Benedict, jr
W H Moore
R Dorlan
Wm Greene
Jesse Buel
Saml N Payn
Horace Much
F W Huxford
Thos Fitzpatrick
Jas T Stevenson
Wm McCaskey
I Sayles
Benj C True
J S Van Rensselaer
Herman Seward
C Loveridge
Geo W Carpenter
Nelson Scovel
Mr T Huntington
Philip W Groot
Thos James
Joshua A Spencer, of Utica;
Friend Humphrey, of the Senate
Chas P Kirkland, of Utica
Geo W Kellogg, of Troy
Geo Brainard, of Albany
Hon Ambrose Spencer, late Chief Justice

Gen Harrison, we understand, is expected to leave home for Va the latter part of this month. He will spend Jan with his friends in the Old Dominion, & repair to Wash in Feb, to be ready on Mar 4 to enter upon the duties of the important ofc to which the people have elevated him. –Maysville Eagle

On Nov 13, John Leignher, aged 30, was executed at Augusta, Ind: killed his friend, John Farley, with whom he had been drinking.

The paper mill of Messrs J & S Roberts, Waltham, Mass, was entirely consumed by fire on Dec 5.

Mrd: on Dec 6, by Rev Mr Matthews, Mr John Ellis, sen, to Mrs Ann M Fagan, both of Wash City.

Mrd: on Dec 5, at Annapolis, by Rev Dr Humphreys, Lt Henry S Burton, 3rd Regt U S Artl, to Miss Eliz F, d/o the late Dr Saml Smith, U S A.

Mrd: on Mon, at Norfolk, by Rev Mr Parks, Dr Geo W Codwise, of the U S Navy, to Mrs Va E Byrd, of that Borough.

Died: at the residence of his uncle, Mr Thos Havenner, on C st, Mr Thos Smith, printer. Funeral on Sun at 2 p m. [No date-current item.]

Died: on Dec 8, in his 26th year, Mr John Weaver, a native of Manchester, Eng, but lately of Phil.

For rent: a parlor & 3 chambers, with breakfast & tea, if desired. Inquire of Mrs Sarah Shields, 5th st, next to Trinity Chr.

Mrs Dawes has 3 furnished rooms, a parlor & 2 chambers, to let: breakfast & supper will be provided if desired. Residence on Pa ave, 2 doors east of Mr Purdy's.

MON DEC 14, 1840
Mr Grundy, Senator from Tenn, is prevented from coming on to Wash by severe illness.

The Pres of the U S Elect, we learn, was at Frankfort on the day of the meeting of the Ky Electoral College, & dined in company with the Electors at Gov Letcher's.

Letter from Havanna, published in the New Orleans Commercial Bltn, dated Nov 20: "F P Blair, of the Wash Globe, is here, on account of the health of his dght."

Col Geo F Strother, a member of the St Louis Bar, died in that city on Nov 28: he was formerly a Rep in Congress from Va.

Mr Jacob Fowler, about 22 years of age, left the schn'r *Deposit*, lying at Bartlett's Cove, Newbury, Mass, on Sat, in a small boat to visit his friends at Salisbury. In the morning his boat was found locked in ice, & the body of Fowler was entirely lifeless & frozen stiff.

Miss E J Baynes, miniature painter: residence on F st, near the Navy Yard, oppo Gen Hunter's, where specimens of her painting may be seen.

Wilmington, Dec 11. Court of Appeals of Dela ,at Dover, trying the important cause of the Excs of Jas A Bayard, dec'd, vs, the Excs of Allan McLane, dec'd. An appeal from the Court of Chancery of New Castle Co. Robt Frame & Reverdy Johnson, the Hon John M Clayton for the Messrs Bayard; & Jas Rogers, Gen Walter Jones, & Hon John Sergeant for Mr McLane. We learn that Chief Justice Bayard, being a party concerned, & the Hon John J Milligan, being connected by affinity with one of the parties, will not sit in the cause. The absence of these judges leaving the Court without a quorum, the Govn'r, has appointed the Hon Geo B Rodney judge *ad litem*, for the trial. This cause was argued 2 years ago; but in consequence of the death of Judge Black, the Court was unable to deliver an opinion. It will now be argued *de novo*. -Jrnl

Wash Co, D C: I hereby certify that Overton Prather, of said county, brought before me 2 milch cows as strays trespassing on his enclosures. –Nathl Brady, J P [Owners to come forward, prove property, pay charges, & take them away. –Overton Prather]

Mrd: on Dec 8, by Rev Geo I Wood, John A M Duncanson, of the Treas Dept, to Miss Martha Duncan, d/o the late John N Moulder, of Wash City.

Mrd: on Nov 25, at St Louis, Mo, Jos Corlay, of St Louis, to Donna Maria Del Refugio Antonina Mucia Isidora Johanna Bernarda De Jesu Solares Covian, of New Mexico.

Died: on Dec 11, Mrs Anne Joncherez, in her 67th year, relict of the late Alex L Joncherez, of Gtwn, D C. For many months the sufferings of the dec'd were such as to call forth the heartfelt sympathies of her afflicted family & friends. She bore them with Christian patience & fortitude.

Wash Co, D C: insolvent debtors, John A B Leonard & Geo Marbury, has applied to be discharged from imprisonment. -Wm Brent, clk

The Trustees of School Dist 7, Chas Co, Md, wish to employ a teacher for the ensuing year. He will be rquired to teach English education. Salary $350 to $400: brd can be obtained on reasonable terms in the neighborhood. –W Mitchell, Pres of the Board, Port Tobacco, Md.

Orphans Court of Wash Co, D C. Letters of administration the personal estate of Geo M Stepper, late of said county, dec'd. –Mary E Stepper, admx

TUE DEC 15, 1840
Senate: 1-Ptn from Origen Batchelder, of N Y, praying that a brd may be appointed for settlement of all difficulties without recourse to arms. 2-Ptn from Rufus & Chas Lane, owners of a vessel wrecked while employed in the cod fishery, asking that the fishing bounty may be allowed them. 3-Ptn from the wid/o Dr Perrine, of Fla, stating the losses she had sustained in the death of her husband & the destruction of his property by the Indians. 4-Bill introduced for the relief of Avery, Saltmarsh & Co. 5-Bills introduced for the relief of Saml White, Mgt Barnes, Danl Waller, Geo W Paschal, Jas Smith-of Ark, Wm Jones, & Joab Seely.

Edw Swann, Atty for the proprietor, will sell a valuable tract of land in Alexandria Co, about 4 miles from the town of Alexandria: contains 160 acs. Apply at my residence in the Six Bldgs: Edw Swann.

Meeting at Albemarle, Va, Dec 8: Wm H Meriweather, chrmn; Wm W Dawson, sec. Delegates to attend the Tobacco Convention to be held in Wash City, on Dec 15:

Wm C Rives	Thos J Randolph	Tucker Coles	Jas Garland
Jas Barbour	David Anderson	Dr John Gantt	Wm P Farish
Wm Garth	Dr Mann Page	John D Moon	
Richd Duke		Nathl Goolsby	
		Danl Scott	

Thos H Bowen, Merchant Tailor: Pa ave, one door east of Brown's Hotel.

The gentleman elected to the Hse of Commons of N C from Orange, v Wm A Graham, is Col Jas Graham, & not John Graham, as published.

Gen Waddy Thompson escaped injury by the accident on the r r near Petersburg, when he was knocked senseless by the shock, & fell longitudinally between the rails, *precisely in the only spot, on the whole length of the road,* where one of the transverse sleepers had been removed. His head fell so close to the rail, that the flange of the wheels, passing over it, pressed it into the mud. Had the ground been frozen, his head would have been crushed. [No date-current item.]

New Orleans Picayune: F A Weed, Pres of the Bank of Millington, his brother, Wm Weed, & another person, were arrested in that city on Dec 2 by virtue of an affidavit made before Recorder Baldwin by Mr Ambrose A White, of Balt, stating that F A Weed fraudulently obtained the presidency of the bank, & then passed off & exchanged to a very large amount the bills of the bank which were worthless, for the bills of other banks that were solvent. His property of $20,000 has been attached at the suit of Mr Jas Jameson. –Balt American

Naval: the U S ship *Yorktown*, Cmder Aulick, & the ship *Dale*, Cmder Gantt, were towed down to Hampton Roads, & will sail with the first fair wind for the Pacific station.

Mrd: on Nov 24, by Rev Abbe Baupre, Henry J Heard to Miss Sophia Eastin, d/o Judge Ransom Eastin, both of St Martinsville, La.

Mrd: on Dec 3, in St Mary's Co, Md, Aloysius E Fenwick to Miss Charlotte, the eldest d/o the late Benedict Spalding, of that county.

Mrd: on Dec 3, in St Mary's Co, Md, John T H Sothoron to Mrs Mgt Hodges, all of that county.

Died: on Dec 3, in Newport, Chas Co, Md, suddenly, Thos Amery, in his 61st year.

Died: on Dec 2, suddenly, of apoplexy, Miss Jane Llewellen Key, d/o Judge Key, of PG Co, Md.

Died: Dec 5, at her residence, at Stafford Co, Va, Mrs Sarah F Taliaferro, in her 46th year. She has left 10 chldrn & a wide circle of relations & friends to lament her loss.

Died: on Oct 5, at Cincinnati, Ohio, at the residence of her brother, Miss Louisa Zebold, of consumption, y/d/o Mr Peter Zebold, formerly of Wash City.

Frederic Clitch will soon open his new store, on Pa ave, between 9th & 10th sts: a variety of articles suitable for presents for the approaching holydays.

WED DEC 16, 1840
Gen Harrison reached his home at the North Bend on Dec 10, in excellent health, from his business & social visit to Ky.

Charleston Mercury: the health of Hon R B Rhett has prevented him from being present at the opening session of Congress. He is still detained at his country residence in Ashepoo.

Col Wm Hughlett chosen Pres of the Branch of the Farmers' Bank of Md, in Easton, Md, v Thos J Bullitt, dec'd.

Mr Jas H Looker has retired from the Cincinnati Republican, a paper with which he has been connected for 20 years-Mr J B Russell takes his place.

Chas Gautier, Gardener & Florist: a Frenchman, young, & lately mrd, has been in this country 2 years, offers his services for a fair compensation, & is willing to go to any part of the country that is not sickly. He was taught his art in the best school of France. Please address at Gtwn, D C, box #47. -C G

Died: on Nov 27, in Marietta, Ohio, Col Ichabod Nye, in his 78th year. His remains were attended to the grave by many relatives, & a large concourse of citizens. He was one of the oldest citizens in Ohio, & believed, resided longer in the state, as head of a family, longer than any other person living within it at the time of his decease. He was born in Tolland, Conn, on Dec 21, 1762: removed when a youth to Hampshire Co, & served in the latter years of the Revolution, in the Northern Army, when still a young man. He mrd Minerva, a d/o Gen Benj Tupper, of Chesterfied, Mass, & with him & his family, Col Cushing, Maj Goodale, & Maj Coburn, [all since dec'd,] & their several families, he removed to the then N W Terr in 1788; emigrating in company by land, about Aug 10 of that year, from the Monongahela, followed by the families above named, who arrived at Marietta on Aug 19, 1788, having traveled by water. Ohio is now a powerful state with a million & a half people. –Gaz

Senate: 1-Ptn from W W Chew, praying an allowance for services as Charge near the Court of St Petersburg, in Russia. 2-Ptn from R B Clements & Needham A Bryan, asking remuneration for losses sustained in consequence of a violation of contract on the part of the U S. 3-Ptn from Chas Howe, praying indemnity for property destroyed by the Seminole Indians, at Indian Key. 4-Ptn from B L Halleck & others, members of the Leg of Ark, asking the establishment of a certain mail route. 5-Ptn from Edmund Ruffin, praying equalization of postage rates on newspapers & periodicals. 6-Cmte on Public Lands: relief of Wm Jones. 7-Cmte of Claims: bill for relief of Geo Pasteh, without amendment. 8-Bill for the relief of the heirs of John De Trennile. 9-Bills for the relief of the legal reps of Wm Sandford, dec'd; for the relief of Robt White; & relief of the reps of Stephen Morris, dec'd. 10-Bill introduced for the relief of the legal reps of Col Francis Vigo. [This bill passed the Senate last sesson, but was not taken up in the Hse.]

Hse o/Reps: Election of the Chaplain: Mr Craig nominated the Rev Levi R Reese: Mr Hand the Rev Joshua Bates-Chaplain of the last session; Mr Taliaferro the Rev Thos C Braxton, of Va; Mr Barnard the Rev Joshua N Danforth, of this Dist; Mr Williams, of Conn, the Rev Peter H Shaw; Mr N Jones the Rev O B Brown. Braxton-76 votes; Bates-61; Reese-30; Danforth-14; Shaw-4; Brown-1. No majority. Hse o/Reps proceeded to a 2nd vote: Braxton-101 votes; Bates-53 votes; Reese-16.

Robbery of the Wash Museum: Mr Varden, the worthy proprietor, was robbed of silver coins, deposited in the Museum as curiosities, value of $70, & $4 in money, which were taken from his desk.

On Sat last, negro Chas, belonging to Mr T N Wilson, of Montg Co, Md, was driving his master's wagon, on 7th st, near the Alms Hse, the horses suddenly took fright, & in jumping out, he was killed.

Pocahontas painting: by Chapman: Her face is not so beautiful as it is represented to have been in life; the sister of P is seated on the floor, with her child clinging to her: Opechankanough scowls at the ceremony: the foreshortening of one of his feet is admirable: Rolfe, the husband of P stands behind her, but in no very graceful attitude; minister has one hand in the font, & the other extended in the attitude of prayer; Sir Thos Dale, in the martial costume of the age, stands on the right of the officiating clergyman, Whitaker, & his standard-bearer & page near him. When but 13, P performed an act that will cover her name with eternal honor; & her humanity, courage, & devotion in the cause of the first settlers of Va, during her short life, were, for one so young, almost without parallel. She was born about 1594-95, saved the life of Capt Smith, on whose body she cast herself when about to be killed by order of her father, in 1607, & was baptised & died in 1616, at age 21 or 22 years. Her name was originally Matoaka, which signifies a streamlet between 2 hills. She was called among her Indian friends the Snow-Feather, as was also her mother, from their remakrable gracefulness & swiftness of ft, & was christened by the named of Rebecca. The baptism of P took place prior to her marriage with Rolfe & her departure from her native country. It is thought this ceremony was performed in the rude chr which had been erected at Jamestown, the ruins of which still remain. She was the first Christian convert among the Indian tribes of N A. [Another description of the painting can be found in the Dec 1 paper.]

Died: on Dec 15, in Gtwn, Mr Thos Spurling, formerly a resident of Va, after a short but painful illness of 3 days, in his 66th year. Funeral on Dec 16 at 3 p m, from the residence of Mr Jas Robertson, near the corner of Potomac & Bridge sts.

Notice: I forewarn all persons from trusting my wife, Sarah Steward, on my account, as I am determined to pay no debts of her contracting, as she left my bed & board without any just cause whatever. –Geo W Steward

Yesterday an inquest was held over the body of Jos Mozeen, an inmate of the Alms Hse. Verdict: he died in a fit caused by habitual intemperance.

Wash Corp: 1-Mayor nominates Edw Miller as Super of Chimney Sweeps for Ward 2, v Wm E Moran, resigned: nomination was confirmed. 2-Ptn from Geo Hercus: referred to the Cmte of Claims. 3-Cmte of Claims: bill for relief of Geo Seitz: passed. 4-Cmte of Claims: bill for relief of Geo Bell: passed. 5-Cmte of Claims: asked to be discharged from further consideration of the ptn of Ann McGunnigle. 6-Communication from the Mayor, enclosing letters from Th C Wilson & V Harbaugh, claiming compensation for the discovery & arrest of a person recently convicted as an incendairy: referred to a Select Cmte, & Messrs Houston, Johnston, & Bacon were appointed the cmte.

Furnished apts to let: in the neighborhood of the Foundry Chr & Pres' Hse. Inquire of N Mullikin, 2nd hse east of the Lancasterian School, on G st, or at the Ord ofc.

THU DEC 17, 1840

Senate: 1-Ptn & papers on file, with additional papers of Zadock Smith: referred to the Cmte of Claims. 2-Ptn from Richd Patten, asking remuneration for charts furnished for the use of the Navy. 3-Papers of Richd Harris & Nimrod Farrow referred to the Cmte of Claims. 4-Papers of Hannah Leighton were referred to the Cmte on Pensions. 5-Ptn of Albin Mitchell, in behalf of the heirs of Madame De Lusser, were referred to the Cmte on Pvt Land Claims. 6-Ptn of John J D'Wolf, of Bristol, R I, praying compensation for services as Cnsl for the Port of Sydney, Cape Breton, in 1838: referred to the Cmte on Foreign Affairs. 7-Ptn of Thos Cook, John G Howe, & others: referred to the Cmte on Mfgrs. 8-Memorials of Robt Johnson & others, of Simon Dodge & others, of N G Rutgers & others, of Nicholas Brown & others: for a harbor on Block Island. 9-Memorial of Elisha Dyer & others: for removal of obstructions in Patuxent Harbor. 10-Same for Jas Rhodes & others. 11-Ptns of Asa Armington, Susan Rogers, Ephraim Bowen, Benj Fry, Elisha Dillingham, Robt Eldred, David Bartlett, for relief respectively. 12-Mr P J Wagner, of N Y, presented the ptn of Wm J Stilwell, praying for a pension for inventing in 1796 the Centre Board, or Slip Keel, now in common use in river & coasting vessels. 13-Ptn of Rufus Henry, of N Y C, who was an artificer in the service during the late war with Great Britain, praying to be placed on the list of invalid pensioners. 14-Ptn of Ruth Taylor, wid/o Saml Taylor, a Revolutionary pensioner; & Dorothy Woleben, wid/o Abraham Woleben, a Revolutionary pensioner, praying the benefits of the act of Jul, 1830. 15-Memorial of Capt Eldridge, praying the return of duties overcharged: referred to the Cmte on Commerce. 16-Ptn of Robt T Norris, for compensation for injuries received while in employ of the U S: referred to the Cmte on Commerce. 17-Ptn of Seth Driggs, praying for the interference of the Gov't in relation to a claim on the Colombian Gov't: referred to the Cmte on Foreign Affairs. 18-Memorial of Jas M Duffield & 460 others, praying for a general bankrupt bill: referred to the Cmte on the Judiciary. Ptn of Saml Lyon; Wm S M Coffin, & many others, of N Y, for the same. 19-Ptn of John Spear, of Mercer Co, Pa, a soldier for 3 years in the Indian war, under Gen Wayne, now poor & infirm, unable to support himself, praying Congress for a pension: referred to the Cmte on Invalid Pensions. 20-Ptn of Saml Carley,of Beaver Co, a soldier in the Revolutionary war, praying for a pension: referred to the Cmte on Revolutionary Pensions. 21-Ptn of Josiah Westlake, a soldier in the late war, praying to have a portion of a pension which was improperly withheld from him restored: referred to the Cmte on Invalid Pensions. 22-Ptn of Thos Hall, a soldier of the Revolution, praying to be placed on the pension list: referred to the Cmte on Revolutionary Pensions. 23-Ptn of Henry Holbrook, of Somerset Co, Md, asking to be allowed for certain timber furnished the Gov't at the Navy yard in Phil. 24-Memorial of John Prock: referred to the Cmte on the P O & Post Roads. 25-Mr C H Williams, of Tenn, presented the ptn of Hugh Wallace Wormely, asking for a pension: referred to the Cmte on Invalid Pensions. 26-Ptn of Jeremiah Fields, praying the correction of an erroneous land entry: referred to the Cmte on Public Lands. 27-Ptn of John H Murphy & Thos McKebbin, praying relief in the case of a mail contract: referred to the Cmte on the P O & Post Roads. 28-Ptn of R C Paine & others, praying an appropriation for a harbor at Racine, Wiskonsin.

29-Ptn of Garret Vliet, for compensation for services rendered as a Surveyor. 30-Ptn of Saml Ryan, for compensation for services rendered in the Indian Dept. 31-Bill introduced by Mr Fulton: for the relief of Peter A Dixon. 32-Bill for relief of Benj Murphy & for the relief of Robt T Banks. 33-Bill to refund to Noah Miller & others part of the proceeds of the British sloop *Mary* & cargo, captured by them, & libelled & sold for the benefit of the U S. 34-Bill for the relief of Chas M Keller & Henry Stone. 35-Cmte of Claims: to inquire into allowing to Jas H Relf compensation for his services in removing intruders from the military reservation attached to Fort Leavenworth.

Wash Hse, #223, Chestnut st, next door to the Masonic Hall, Phil: H J Hartwell, proprietor. New & splendid house is open, fitted up in the most fashionable style.

Sat, John J Allen, of Botetourt, was elected a Judge of the Court of Appeals of Va.

Whigs of Luzerne Co, Pa: resolved, that in John Sergeant, the oldest member of the Hse from Pa: we recognise one of the purest & ablest statesmen this Commonwealth has ever produced: in Congress for near 20 years: Whig party selected him, in 1832, to run as V P on the ticket with Mr Clay.

N Y papers confirm: the body of Abraham Suydam, who had been missing for some days, was found buried about 4 feet deep in the cellar: believed he was murdered by Peter Robinson, carpenter by trade, & had purchased the lot & received money for bldg the house on credit from Mr S, who was undoubtedly induced to come to the house of Robinson under promise of paying off his obligations. Robinson, his wife, & brother are secured. There is not the least shadow of a doubt of Robinson's guilt.

Phil: on Dec 15, John Foster, employed on the Columbia R R, was killed by the locomotive & train of cars passing over him, when he did not observe them coming. He was 55 years of age, & has left a wife & 9 chldrn.

The inclemency of the weather should remind all of the sufferings of the poor. The Soc presents its 22nd report. Western Dorcas Soc: Sarah R Porter, sec.

FRI DEC 18, 1840
Recently arrived in Wash City: Maj Gen Winfield Scott, U S A, [via Norfolk,] & Hon H A Muhlenberg, late Minister of the U S to Austria.

Municipal Court at Boston: a few days ago, John McCord was convicted of sending a challenge to fight a duel, & sentenced to the House of Corrections for 6 months.

Harrisburg, Pa: on Sat last, Mr J H Hickok attempted to jump on the cars of the Cumberland Valley train for Carlisle, his foot slipped, & he fell on the rails, the train went over both legs. Amputation of both legs below the knees was necessary. – Telegraph

Poem pronounced before the Ciceronian Club of Tuscaloosa, Ala, by Alex'r B Meek, & published in the Southern Ladies' Book for Sep last. [Extract was in the paper.] Followed by this note: the distinguished Revolutionary vet, whose character & deeds J P Kennedy beautifuly delineated in his historic novel, died at his residence, near Tuscaloosa, on Apr 28, 1838. His proper name was Jas Robinson, & not Galbraith, as stated by Mr Kennedy. Galbraith was the name of an uncle of Horse-Shoe, who himself distinguished in the Revolution. Jas Robinson himself told Mr Kennedy the story in 1819, in S C. Horse-Shoe Robinson was born in Va, near Petersburg, in 1759: removed to S C, at very early age: joined the army of the Revolution, when but 16, & continued until the close of the war. He was made a prisoner at the capture of Charleston-escaped: was never wounded: after the war he resided in S C, on a section of land given him by the state, until about 1820, when he removed to his recent residence in Ala. At the time of his death he was in his 79th year of his age, in full possession of all his mental energies. A short time previous, his wife died, in her 75th year. Both were members of the Bapt Chr, & highly esteemed.

Senate: 1-Bill for relief of the heirs of Francis Newman; of Gregoire Sarpy; of the heirs of Miguel Eslava; of Sebastian Butcher; of Thos P Lopez; of Jos Bogy; of the heirs of Jos Thompson; of the heirs of Pierre Bonhomme; bill confirming the title of Geo Tucker to a certain land tract. 2-Cmte on Pensions: bill to authorize the payment of invalid pensions in certain cases. A bill granting a pension to Lemuel White; & also to David Waller. A bill for relief of Mgt. Barnes. 3-Cmte on Revolutionary Claims: bill for relif of Eliza Causin & other heirs of John H Stone, dec'd. 4-Cmte of Claims to inquire into paying Wm Cunningham, of N C, for services rendered to the U S as wagon-mstr when the Gov't was preparing to remove the Cherokee Indians. 5-Cmte of Claims: to inquire into paying John G Bibb for a horse & property lost in the Fla war. 6-Cmte on Invalid Pensions: to inquire into placing the name of Saml Neely on the list of invalid pensioners.

Hse o/Reps: 1-Ptn of Conrad Herts, a soldier of the Revolution, asking an addition to his pension. 2-Ptn of Wm Annelaly, praying an extension of his patent for a new & improved mode of bldg boats & ships. 3-Pending at former sessions: ptns of Nancy Tompkins & of Eliz Mayes, for pensions. 4-Ptn of Sally C Wenwood & Eliza S Wenwood, dghts/o Godfrey Wenwood, praying for compensation for the services of their father in the detection of the treasonable correspondence of Dr Church, Dir Gen of the hospital of the U S in 1775. 5-Ptns of Esther Carter for Revolutionary claims; of Sarah J Pratt for pension; of Anna Swinnerten for pension; of Francis Bush & others, of Chelmsford, Mass, for a genr'l bankrupt law; of Jonathan Morse & others, of Methuen, for the same object.

Mrd: on Dec 8 at Mrs Gen Pike's, in Boon Co, Ky, by Rev Wm Whittaker, John Hunt to Miss Zebulino A P Harrison, grand-dght of Gen Wm H Harrison.

Died: on Dec 10, in Augusta, Ga, Mrs Eliz W Twiggs, w/o Col David E Twiggs, & d/o Col W Hunter, of Wash City, in her 31st year.

Died: on Dec 14, at the residence of D'Arcy A French, near the Navy Yard, in her 40th year, Mrs Mary Madden, a native of county of Galway, Ire. Her only relative in this country is an orphan son of about 12 years of age, but she had in Wash City many sincere friends to whom she was endeared by her amiable qualities, & who deeply lament the loss of so esteemed a friend. –F

Died: on Dec 3, at Detroit, Lewis Cass, s/o Lt Col John Garland, U S A.

Public sale: decree of the Crct Court of Wash Co, D C: on ptn of Francis Kirby's heirs, they will, on Dec 22, expose for sale the title & estate of the heirs of the said Francis Kirby in & to part of lot 24 in sq 728 in Wash City, on A st. Also, all the undivided right & estate [being an undivided 3/4th, of the late Francis Kirby, of, in, & to part of a tract of land called *Blue Plains*, containing 5 acs, more or less, with a valuable fishery & improvements annexed. Also to public sale the estate & title of Eliz Herbert, formerly Kirby, [being the remaining undivided 4th] of, in, & to the last described parcel of ground. Thus the whole of the above last described piece of ground will be sold, if preferred, together. Title to all the property will be shown by Messrs Brent & Brent, at their ofc, in the City Hall. The sale will be clear of dower. -Zachariah Walker, Geo W Young, C B Hamilton

Duel prevented-Balt, Dec 16. Information on Mon night, Justice Gorsuch received information on Mon that Mr Wm H Stump & Mr John W Williams, were in this city, & a challenge had passed from the latter to the former, to meet, to dispose of a long standing difference between them, by an appeal to arms. Warrant issued for their arrest: both required to $2,000 bail. –American

The N Y Courier anounces the suicide of Mr Wm H Jefferd, a promising respectable young merchant, a member of the firm of Burns, Hays & Co, of that city. He was a native of Maine, about 30 years of age, & had resided at the Mansion House for some months past, where his death occurred.

To Jos T Hall & Lucy his wife; Caroline D Alves; Stewart C Bruce & Helen his wife; Chas Raikes & Justina his wife; Wm G Alves & Magdalen Alves-chldrn & heirs of Wm Alves & Sarah his wife. The ptn of John Alves & Dunvan Alves, 2 of the heirs of Wm & Sarah, the Crct Court of Wash Co, D C, did, on Nov 27, 1840, appoint the undersigned com'rs to divide the real estate of the said Wm & Sarah, lying in D C, if the same will admit of division without loss to the parties interested therein, & to make return of our doings in the matter to said Court: on the 3rd Mon in Apr, 1841, we shall execute the duty required of us; shall meet on lot 2 in sq 186, in Wash City, being the premises referred to in the commission. –M St Clair Clarke, Benj O Tayloe, Jonathan Seaver, John Coburn, Jas Larned, com'rs -D A Hall, atty

Wash City news: A colored girl, Harriet Mason, who had for some time lived in the hse of a free-colored man, Ignatius Adams, near the R R depot came to her death yesterday, by cruelty & inhuman treatment. T Woodward, the coroner held an inquest. Excessive inhuman treatment by Mary Ann Adams, w/o Ignatius Adams, was inflicted on the dec'd, for a long time. Mrs Adams is in custody. Butler, a negro boy, was accidentally shot on Sun last with a pistol by another boy, near the African Meeting-hse, Gtwn. Dr Bohrer probed the wound, but found the ball to have gone too deep to be extracted: below the shoulder blade. Not known if fatal or not. –Advocate

SAT DEC 19, 1840
Mrd: on Dec 15, in Wash City, by Rev Mr Davis, Mr John W Hodgson to Mrs Sarah Ellen Baron, all of Wash City.

Mrd: on Dec 8, in Pr Wm Co, Va, by Rev Mr Towles, Wm H Roy, of Matthews Co, to Euphan Washington Macrae.

Mrd: Dec 10, at the residence of her father, Orange Co, Va, by Rev John Cole, the Hon Richd H Field, of Culpeper Co, Va, to Miss Philippa Barbour, d/o Judge P P Barbour.

Mrd: on Nov 13 last, in St Louis, Mo, at the residence of Dr Smith, Dr Hamlet Neale, of that city, to Miss Elza Okill Newman, eldest d/o Dr Robt Newman, of Romney, Va.

Died: on Dec 10, Mrs Rebecca Cohen, in her 80th year. She was a resident of Charleston, S C, the greater part of her life, where she reared a numerous family, & was the relict of Mr Gershom Cohen, a soldier of the Revolution.

Trustee's sale: decree of St Mary's Co Court, [Md] Court of Equity, in the case of Henry A Ford & L J Ford against Thos J Stone & wife & others: sale in Leonardtown, St Mary's Co, on Jan 12, the tract called *Gilmet's Hills*, or part of same, containing about 120 acs. Land is located on Britain's Bay: improvements are ordinary. –Benj G Harris, trustee

On Dec 11 a trial for seduction was held at Worcester, Mass, in which the plntf was Mr Levi Pollard, who sued for the lost services & character of his dght, & Seth Maynard was the dfndnt. Mr Pollard is an aged man & father of a large family, all of highly respectable character. Mr Maynard is a mrd man, the father of 3 chldrn. Verdict of $4,000 for the plntf. Above is from a letter published in the Boston Mail.

Julius Knop informs he has a few hours left for taking pupils on the German flute. His residence is at the hotel of Chas Rosenthal, Pa ave, between 12th & 13th sts, or in the orchestra of the Nat'l Theatre.

Jas Iliff, a Harrison Pres Elector of N J, died suddenly at his residence in Sussex Co, on Dec 10.

Indian Key massacre: attack was made in Aug last, by a band of Seminole Indians- Dr Henry Perrine, a gentleman of distinguished education, who had temporarily settled there for the purpose of introducing the culture of tropical plants, into the Territory of Fla, fell victim to Indian ferocity. Dr P had intended to locate on a township near Cape Fla; but due to the war he was not allowed to carry his designs into execution. The township was granted to him in 1838, by Congress. A band of savages landed on the island, desolated it, & assassinated a portion of its inhabitants. A concise account of the affair by a dght of Dr Perrine, who was a witness of the bloody transaction, is in our hands: on Aug 7, awakened by the Indian war-whoop: father was lying in the hammock to watch Sarah who had been ill for some weeks: got up while the Indians were firing at the chamber windows: ran to get Henry: ran to a trap-door that led to the cellar which we used for bathing, [as the tides filled it twice a day.] Father went back: mother told him he had no caps in his rifle: heard the Indians break into the hse of Mr Howe-opposite ours: father came & closed the trap dr & pulled a heavy chest over it, thinking, no doubt, he should be saved, & by doing this, he might save us. At daybreak they returned-my father evidently had retreated to the cupola-they killed him like demons & broke everything they called lay their hands upon. We passed thru the crawl & got out, heading for a launch at Houseman's wharf: taken up by the schn'r *Medium*. Mr Howe, wife, & 5 chldrn, Capt Houseman & wife, & Capt Oris had reached the vessel before us. Fri & Sat we were on the transport, & every attention & service was rendered to us by the capt & ofcrs McCreary & Murray, of the Naval Depot. On Sat, the U S schn'r *Flirt* arrived, & Capt McLaughlin offered us the use of his pvt state room: on Sat we took the steamer *Santee* for passage for St Augustine, under the protection of Dr Edw Worrell, of the army. –Hester M S Perrine, Aug 20, 1840.]

Jonathan Chapman was re-elected Mayor of the city of Boston, by a Whig majority of 2,608 votes over his opponent, being double his former majority.

MON DEC 21, 1840
Alexandria: on Dec 17, the 2 story brick hse on Water st, owned & occupied by Mr Geo Brown, carpenter, of this place, fell with a tremendous crash, burying & destroying almost everything in the interior in the ruins. Mr Brown was engaged in digging a cellar, & the walls caved in. Providentially, the family were all out of the hse, except one of the chldrn, who was extricated without being seriously injured. The laborers in the cellar has just quit their dangerous position. -Gaz

Lt S G Aston, of the U S Navy. who was on board the barque *Ronaldson*, from Marseilles, died at sea on Oct 12, of consumption.

Mr Luman Reed, of Buffalo, who was reported to have been killed at Toronto, has returned from a trip to Canada to read his own epitaph.

The Hon Nathl Garrow, our esteemed citizen, has not died, but is rapidly recovering from a severe attack of disease. –Cayuga Patriot

There is a man living in Greenfield township, Gallia Co, Ohio, Jas Rice, who was 116 years old on Apr 24 last, & yet bids fair to add some years to the days of his earthly pilgrimage.

Furnished rooms to rent: inquire of Mary G Handy, at the corner of 6th & La ave.

Died: on Dec 19, in Wash City, Miss N Sexsmith, after a long & painful illness. Funeral this afternoon at 2 p m, from the residence of her father on Pa ave.

Died: on Dec 17, Mrs Mary A Upperman, relict of the late Geo Upperman, aged 63 years. She was a native of Winchester, Va, but had resided in Gtwn a period of 45 years.

For rent: 2 two-story hses on D st, near N J ave. Inquire of Jas Fry, Capitol Hill. -Ambrose White, next door to D Claggett's, Pa ave.

Notice: stray dark brown cow came to my plantation about Aug 1: prove property, pay charges, & take her away. –John Eversfield, Bladensburg

Having learned that Ignatius Adams, hack driver, husband of the colored woman who was committed to prison for cruel treatment of Harriet Mason, was likely to be injured in his business, I take the liberty of stating that he never had been seen to treat the dec'd with cruelty. I make this statement, as foreman of the Coroner's jury, of my own free accord, without any consultation with my brother jurors.
–W Thompson

TUE DEC 22, 1840
Hse o/Reps: 1-*Resolved:* Clk of this Hse to report by what authority the sum of $1,1850.50 was paid to Chas J Ingersoll, for his expenses in taking testimony, in the contested election with Chas Naylor, pending the last session of Congress, & out of what fund such amount was paid, as reported in Doc #7 to this Hse. 1-A-Reply: I beg leave to report that, on Jul 20 last, a paper was handed the Accounting Clk of this ofc, containing a list of the witnesses in the contested case of Naylor & Ingersoll, with the number of days each witness had been in attendance. On the face of this paper is an order signed J Johnson, Chrmn of Acct's, that the witnesses above named be paid $2 per diem. I paid Mr Ingersoll $1,128 for 564 days: at the beginning of the session, Mr I returned the receipts of the individuals paid, & $41.50 in money, stating that that amount had been overpaid. –Hugh A Garland 1-B: Subj-What authority that E Bulkley was paid $500; Bayse Newcomb paid $416, & Geo Lowry paid $104: all for services in taking depositions in the case of the contested election. 2-Ptn of John Hicks, praying to be placed on the list of invalid pensioners. 3-Ptn of

David Melvill, of Newport, R I, adm of Benj Fry, dec'd, for certain allowances to be credited to said Fry. 4-Ptn of Lt Stephen Cornell, of the rev cutter service, for pay as Lt in the U S naval service while serving in that capacity in Fla; which was pending at the last session, & again referred to the Cmte on Naval Affairs. 5-Ptn of Betsy Beebe, for the same relief which is provided in every other case of the widows of those who have been wounded in the service of the country. 6-Ptn of Danl Penharlow, praying to be placed on the pension roll for wounds received while in the service of the U S during the late war. 7-Memorial of Saml B Gaston, of N Y, & others, praying for the passage of a bankrupt law. 8-On motion of Mr Williams, of Conn, it was resolved: the ptn of Eunice Clark, praying to be allowed the arrearages of a pension of which her late husband was deprived by being wrongfully stricken from the pension roll, be now referred to the Cmte on Revolutionary Pensions. 9-Ptn of the heirs of Mary Addoms & papers: referred to the Cmte on Revolutionary Claims. 10-Ptn & papers of Jos S Thomas: referred to the Cmte of Claims. 11-Ptn & papers of Amable Mority: referred to the Cmte of Revolutionary Claims. 12-Ptn & papers of the chldrn of Jos Plumb & Mary Addoms be recommitted to the Cmte on Revolutionary Pensions. 13-Ptn of John Wilson: referred to the Cmte on Invalid Pensions. 14-Referred: addition papers in the case of Levi M Roberts. 15-Cmte on Invalid Pensions: the papers in the cases of Danl Chase & Jos Veazie: both introduced. 16-Papers in the cases of Mrs Jemima Bisbee, wid/o Elisha Bisbee, & of Ebenezer Johnson: referred to the Cmte on Revolutionary Pensions. 17-Case of Beriah Wright; case of widow Lydia Hoard: referred to the Cmte on Invalid Pensions. 18-Post Master Gen to inform the Hse whether Ralph Jackson is a contractor for carrying the mail in Ill; who are his sureties, or who is responsible to the Dept for any failure on his part to fulfill his contract. 19-Ptn of Mgt C Meade, widow & excx of Richd W Meade, praying for the adjustment of the claims of her dec'd husband. 20-Ptn of John B Fulkes, praying a pension for the services of his father in the Revolutionary war. 21-Mr Underwood presented 5 ptns, to wit: from Henriettta Hope & others, ladies of Balt; from Emily G Fulton & others, ladies of Balt; from John Coates & others, of Chillicothe, Ohio; from Seth Lockwood & others, of N Y; from Capt Geo Guyther & others, passengers on board the steamboat *Columiba*, praying Congress to act upon the bills reported by the select cmte at the last session to prevent steamboat disasters. Letter by Dr J P Vanyne stated the number of steamboat disasters which occurred within the last 10 years: able to obtain information concerning was 185: lives lost-1,733; wounded-739: of these, there were killed on the Miss & its tributaries, 991, & wounded 260; on sea & tide-water, deaths from the same causes 368, wounded 94; on the lakes, deaths from the same causes 85, wounded 4.

Silk net reticules, black & fancy colored silk; also a variety of bead reticules, at his new Snuff, Tobacco, & Fancy Store, #11, east of Gadsby's Htl. –J P McKean, successor to Lewis Johnson. [Webster: reticule is a small bag carried by women as a workbag or pocket.]

Wm Emmert, Confectioner: is at his old stand on Bridge st, Gtwn. Will have an assortment of cakes, & a pyramid cake which will weigh 150 pounds.

Fruit, butter, raisins, & vinegar: for sale: W H Tenney, opposite Brown's Htl.

Senate: 1-Bill for relief of Jas Smith, of Ark. 2-Cmte of Claims: relief of Gad Humphreys; of Malachi Hagan; of Clements, Bryan, & Co; of John Moore; of John J Bulow. Same cmte asked to be discharged from the further consideration of the ptn of Jas Williams, & that it be referred to the Cmte on the Judiciary. 3-Cmte on Commerce: bill for relief of John Miller & others. 4-Cmte for D C: relief of Jno Carter. 5-Bill introduced for the relief of Jabella Hill, widow, & Saml Hill, Jno Hill, & Elijah Hill, heirs of Saml Hill, dec'd. 6-Bill authorizing the issuing of a patent to Jos Campau, for a tract of land in Mich. 7-Bill for relief of the legal reps of Thos Cooper, dec'd. 8-Bill allowing rations to Brig Gen Wool & Col Geo Croghan. 9-Bill for relief of Mgt Jamison, wid/o Saml Jamison. 10-Bills for relief of Wm Rand; of John McClanahan; of John S Billings; of Saml Crapin; of Tyler Spafford; of Saml Allen; of Mary Neal, wid/o Saml Neal; of Mary Snow, wid/o Jonas Snow; of John McLeod. 11-Bill for relief of Madame de Lusser & her legal reps. 12-Bill confirming the claim of Jean Baptiste Lecompte to a tract of land in La. 13-Bill for relief of Therese Marlette, wid/o Gaspard Feile. 14-Relief of the lgl heirs of Wm Conway. 15-Relief of John Compton, assignee of G Flaujac. 16-Relief of John Baptiste Comeau; of Pierre Babin; of Juan Belgar; of Jean Baptiste Grainger; of Geo de Passeau, of La; of Chas Morgan, of La. 17-Relief of Thos L Winthrop & others, dirs of an assoc called the New Eng Miss Land Co. 18-Bill for relief of Jos E Nourse. 19-Bill for relief of Geo W Paschal; & of Wm Jones.

Com'r Notice: Va-at a Crct Supr Court of Law & Chancery held for Augusta Co, at the Court-house, Nov 21, 1840. Walter Davis, trustee for the creditors of Lewis Wayland, plntf, vs, Abraham Wayland & others, defndts. Represented to the Court that no sale was made in pursuance of the order of Nov, 1837, & the period has arrived at which the trust deed is closeable by its terms & all the property subject to sale, it is ordered that the trustee, Walter Davis, advertise the time & place of the sale for at least 4 weeks in the Staunton Spec, proceed to sell at public auction, all the personal property now remaining subject to said trust. This cause is referred to Mstr Com'r Saml Clarke, who is to take an account of the liabilities of said trust fund to creditors, as well those who are parties to the suit as all others. –N C Kinney, County Clk Above are hereby notified. –Saml Clarke, Mstr Com'r

Nashville, Tenn, Dec 11. Hon Felix Grundy has been confined to his home in this city, from indisposition, for 6 to 8 weeks past. His case is understood today to be a very critical one. –Whig

WED DEC 23, 1840
History of West Point & the U S Military Academy, by Roswell Park, A M, just received by F Taylor.

Orphans Court of Wash Co, D C. Letters of administration on personal estate of Geo M Stepper, late of said county, dec'd. -Mary M Stepper, admx

Wanted: specie-checks & drafts; canal scrip & land scrip, by Chas J Nourse, corner 13th st &Pa ave. For sale as above: a few thousand dollars of land scrip.

Wash Co, D C: insolvent debtor, G Warren Dashiell, has applied to be discharged from imprisonment. -Wm Brent, clk

Genr'l meeting of the stockholders in the Farmers' & Mechanics' Bank of Gtwn, on Dec 28, at 10 a m. -John Kurtz, pres

Senate: 1-Ptn from Henry Simpson, asking remuneration for services performed under instructions from the Sec of the Treas. 2-Report on Pvt Land Claims: bill to confirm to Geo Tucker, his heirs or assigns, a certain tract of land in Ala. Bill confirming the claim of the heirs of Jos Thompson. Bill for relief of Thos R Copes. Bill to authorize the issuing of a patent to the heirs of Francis Rivaud. Bill for relief of Gregoire W Sarpy; & for relief of Joslyn Bogy. 3-Cmte of Claims: bill for relief of Walter Loomis & Abel Gay; for relief of Philip Weademan. 4-Cmte on Public Lands: bill for relief of Francis Laventure, Eb Childs, & Linas Thompson. 5-Bill introduced for the relief of the heirs of Capt John Williams. Also a bill for relief of the heirs of Nathl Pryor.

Just received: 30 baskets of Champagne, Harrison brand, a superior article, & will be sold low for cash, or to punctual customers. -T F Semmes, corner 7th st & Pa ave

Portsmouth [Va] Times of Dec 16. Atrocious murders perpetrated by a miscreant in Southampton Co on Mon. An aged Quaker, of the name of Scott, residing near Jerusalem, his sister, also aged, a little girl, about 9 years old, named Pretlow, a negro woman, & her child, were butchered to further the design of robbery. One negro girl escaped to tell the story & identify the assassin.

Va Star of Dec 16: murder in Dinwiddie Co on Sun last, by Jeremiah Conway, on the person of Edw Lewis, about 18 years of age, who, at the time resided with Conway's family. Conway has been committed to the jail of Dinwiddie Co, where he awaits his trial.

Crct Court of Wash Co, D C: Nov Term, 1840: in Chancery. Darius Clagett, cmplnt, vs, B K Morsell, adm, Wm McDonald & Geo McDonald, infant chldrn of Sarah McDonald, dec'd. Ratify sale by trustee, on May 9, 1840, to Allison Nailor, all that part of lot of ground 5 in sq 229, & premises, in Wash City, beginning for the same 82' from the corner of 15th st. -Wm Brent, clk

For sale: 1,000 pounds of Seine Twine, manufactured by Moses Shepherd, Balt. –Walter Smoot, Water st, Gtwn

Fatal stage accident last week near Frostburg, Md: a man named Franck, a drover, was killed when he attempted to leap out, when the horses took fright: the vehicle was upset upon him

Orphans Court of Wash Co, D C: on the application of Jas Robertson, of said county, it is ordered that letters of administration on personal estate of Thos Spurling, late of said county, dec'd, be granted to the said Jas Robertson, unless good cause be shown to the contrary. –Nathl P Causen -Ed N Roach, reg/o wills

Louisville, on Dec 15: Wm Stephens, from Springfield, Mass, about 35, was killed while attending the machinery in the paper mill belonging to J Eliot & Co near 10th st. –Public Adv

Hse o/Reps: 1-Cmte on Revolutionary Claims: reported adversely on the case of Vincent Voss: laid on the table. 2-Same cmte reported a bill for the payment of the 7 years half pay due to the heirs of Lt Jonathan Dye: committed for tomorrow. 3-Cmte on Revolutionary Pensions: bill for relief of Jas Dealty; & bill for relief of Danl Strong: both committed for tomorrow. Same cmte reported against the cases of Mgt & Mary Daring: laid on the table. Same for the ptn of John Grigsby.

Wash Corp: 1-Brd of Common Cncl: authorizing the removal of the frame bldg in Water & 11 sts, occupied by Geo St Clair: was taken up. 2-Ptn of Thos Nicholls: referred to the Cmte of Claims. 3-Ptn from Miss V Monier, lessee of the Nat'l Theatre, praying certain modifications in the laws respecting the tax on theatrical amusements: laid on the table. 4-Bill for relief of Geo Seitz; & for the relief of Geo Bell: severally taken up: referred to the Cmte of Claims. 5-Cmte of Claims: asked to be discharged from its further consideration of the ptn of C E Upperman.

Wash City Ordinance: that all acts relating to hackney carriages now existing, same are made applicable to the modern vehicles called cabs. –Edm Hanly, Pres Brd of Cmn Cncl -Ch W Goldsborough, Pres of Brd of Aldrmn Approved, Dec 22, 1840. –W W Seaton, Mayor

THU DEC 24, 1840
Columbia Trnpk Rd: election for pres & 4 dirs on 1st Mon in Jan. –Wm Gunton, pres

Cheap confectionary: & toys & dolls for sale. -W H Palmer, Bridge st, Gtwn.

Divine services will be held in the new Catholic Chr, St Matthew's, corner of 15th & H sts, on Christmas Day. High mass at 5 a m & at 11 a m. –J P Donelan, Pastor

Explosion: entire bldg demolished on Mon, in the paper mfgr of Mr Gabriel Moore, dist of Kinsington, between Edw & Lydia sts. Enoch Garside & John Grant, engrs, in the bldg at the time, were dreadfully scalded & injured by the bldg falling upon them. Mr Grant had one or both legs broken-condition is serious. Mr Moore had his head fractured. –Phil Gaz

Senate: 1-Ptn from John Ward & others, asking to be allowed to import free of duty iron to build 2 steamboats for the purpose of navigating the Red river. 2-Ptn from the wid/o Barton Blizard. 3-Ptn from Dr Saml White. 4-Cmte of Claims: bill for the relief of Danl Steinrod; of Jas M Morgan; of Francis Gehan; of Jas H Relfe. Same cmte ask to be discharged from further consideration of the claim of the adm of Geo Simpson, & it be referred to the Cmte on Finance. 4-Cmte on Indian Affairs: bill for relief of Jubal B Hancock. 5-Cmte on Patents & Patent Ofc: bill for relief of Chas Keller & Henry M Stone. 6-Bills introduced: relief of the legal reps of Aaron Vail, late U S Cnsl at L'Orient. Bill for the allowance of invalid pensions to certain Cherokee warriors, under the treaty of 1835. 7-Bill for the relief of Elisa Causin, dght & heir of John H Hand, dec'd, was postponed until the 1st Mon in Jan. 8-Bill for the relief of Hannah Laighton was taken up: 29 yeas & 13 nays.

Hse o/Reps: 1-Cmte on Revolutionary Pensions: to inquire into granting a pension to John Everly, of Giles Co, Tenn, for his Revolutionary services. 2-Papers on file in favor of the claim of the heirs of Jacob Thomas be referred to the Cmte on Pvt Land Claims. 3-Ptn of Messrs Burr & Smith, of Warren, R I, praying for the refunding of certain duties paid on oil reshipped coastwise: referred to the Cmte of Ways & Means. 4-Cmte on Public Lands: reported a bill for the relief of Jeremiah Field: committed. 5-Cmte of Claims: reported bills for the relief of Chauncey Calhoun, of Wm P Rathbone, of Garret Vleit, of Nicholas Hedges, of Jas Cox, of Ebenezer A Lester, of John Haw, & of John Wilkinson's heirs at law. 6-Cmte of Claims: reported bills for the relief of Benj C Roberts, of Sylvester Phelps & of Chas Langdon, or their heirs: twice read & committed. 7-Cmte on Revolutionary Claims: to inquire into reporting a bill for the relief of the heirs & legal reps of Capt Jno Smith, dec'd, late of Cumberland Co, Pa, whose ptn & papers were mislaid & lost by said cmte at a former session of Congress, after it had been determined to report in favor of his claim as an ofcr of the Revolution army.

FRI DEC 25, 1840
Senate: 1-Ptn from J S Nevins, praying compensation for his services as clk to the commander of the So Sea Surveying & Exploring Exped. 2-Ptn from the heirs of Robt Fulton. 3-Cmte on the Judiciary: bill for the relief of Thos Haskins & Ralph Haskins. 4-Bill for relief of the legal reps of Thos Cooper, dec'd, with an amendment. 5-Bill for the relief of the heirs of Francis Newman. 6-Ptn of Geo Whitman to be referred to the Cmte of Claims. 7-Claim of Jere Hinans to be referred to the Cmte on Indian Affairs. 8-Cmte on Naval Affairs: asked to be discharged from further consideration of the ptn of John Pritchard. 9-Cmte on the Judiciary: adverse report on the claim of Jas Williams, which was ordered to be printed. 10-

Cmte on Indian Affairs: bill for relief of John C Reynolds. 11-Cmte on Public Lands-reported the following bills: relief of Madame de Lusser & her legal reps; of Jean Baptiste Lecompte to a tract of land in La; relief of the reps of Therese Malette, wid/o Gaspard Feole; relief of the legal heirs of Wm Conway; relief of John Compton, assignee of G Flanjac; relief of John Baptiste Comeau; of Pierre Babin; of Juan Belgar; of Jean Baptiste Grainger; of Geo de Passeau, of La; of Chas Morgan, of La. 12-Bill introduced: relief of Jno M Strader.

Hse o/Reps: 1-Bill for relief of Geo W Paschal: referred to the Cmte of Claims. 2-Bills read: relief of Jas Smith, of Ark: referred to the Cmte on Pvt Land Claims. Same for the relief of Wm Jones, of Ala.

Appt'd by the Pres: Wm Thompson & B K Morsell, to be J Ps for Wash Co, D C.

Mrs Ann advertises in the St Louis Bltn for information of her husband, who had preceded her to Iowa Terr. The ad conveys the awful intell that their 7 chldrn were scalded to death on board the steamboat *Persian*, & herself considerably injured.

Mrd: on Dec 22, in Gtwn, D C, by Rev R T Berry, Geo McCeney, of A A Co, Md, to Miss Harriet A B Patterson, of Gtwn, D C.

Mrd: on Dec 8, by Rev John Neale, Chas Morgan, of Texas, to Miss Mary, d/o the late Lewis Bridewell, of Stafford Co, Va.

Mrd: on Dec 1, at Snowhill, Md, at the hse of Gordon Handy, by Rev Isaac W K Handy, Mr Chas N Handy to Miss Eliz R Handy, d/o the late Richd Handy, of Somerset Co, Md.

Mrd: on Dec 17, by Rev J B Jeter, Mr Robt H Maury to Miss Sarah Ann, d/o R C Wortham, all of Richmond, Va.

Died: on Dec 23, at his residence, on Capitol Hill, Mr John Johnson, formerly a messenger at the Capitol. Funeral today at 2 p m.

Died: on Dec 19, after a lingering illness, Mr Benedict Adams, in his 55th year.

Died: on Dec 16, at Middletown, R I, Hon Christopher Ellery, aged 72 years, who had, during his life, filled different public ofcs of high trust, amongst which for a time was that of Senator of the U S.

Died: on Tue last, at Norfolk, Va, Henry Woodis, Cashier of the Farmers' Bank of Va in Norfolk, precisely at the completion of the 49th year of his age. He was a native of Newburyport, Mass, but was removed to Norfolk with his parents in childhood. In private life, he was distinguished for his benevolence, kindness, & suavity of manners.

Died: on Dec 16, at the Episc Theological Sem, near Alexandria, Mrs Eliz S Keith, wid/o the Rev Ruel Keith, D D.

To the honorable: the Judges of the Montg Co Court sitting as a Court of Equity: the ptn of Wm O Chappell & Henrietta Bennett, of said county, represents that Wm Bennett departed this life in Oct, 1839, & letters of adm were committed to your ptnrs, by the Orphans' Court of Montg Co, on the personal estate of Wm Bennet. Wm Bennet in his lifetime exhibited his bill of cmplnt in Montg Co Court, Court of Equity, against Chas B Ross & Otho Sprigg, adms of Thos Sprigg, in Dec 1830; that the dfndnts appeared to said suit by John Cook, their solicitor & the case was continued until Oct, 1839, when Wm Bennett died. Your ptnrs state that the said case has abated. Your ptnrs pray that the said case may be revived, & that your ptnrs may be admitted to appear & prosecute the said case, & in duty bound they will ever pray. –Alex Kilgour, Sol for ptnrs. FOLLOWED: ordered that the ptnrs, admitted as parties to the suit, in place of the said Wm Bennett; said ptnrs are to give notice to the dfndnts of such admission, by causing a copy of the within ptn & this order be published in the Nat'l Intell for 3 successive weeks before Feb 1 next. –Thos B Dorsey, T H Wilkinson, Nichs Brewer. True copy: Brice Selby, clk

The steamboat *Cherokee* blew up when just about to leave the landing at Louisburg, on the Ark river, killing 16 or 18 passengers, some of the cabin, & some of the crew, amongst them the Capt, C Harris. Maj Armstrong & ladies, [his dght, niece, & Col Rector's dght,] who were passengers on board, miraculously escaped unhurt. [Letter from New Orleans dated Dec 13.]

Orphans Court of Chas Co, Md: letters of adm on personal estate of Jos Bailey, late of said county, dec'd. –Jane Bailey, admx: John A Bailey, adm

Wash news: Mr Banks has sold out his Cabs to Messrs Walker & Kimmell, but they are to remain under his genr'l supervision & conrol.

$100 reward for runaway negro Saml Sprigg, about 28 years old. –D Crauford, jr: Long Old Fields P O, PG Co, Md.

MON DEC 28, 1840
Brooklyn, N Y, Dec 18, 1840. Invitation to Hon Henry Clay, to a dinner in his honor: signed-Benj D Silliman, David A Bokee, Rollin Sanford. [Clay had to reply in the negative.]

Savannah, Dec 23. More recruits for Fla: detachment of 110 recruits belonging to the 2nd Regt U S Infty, arrived in town yesterday, in the ship *Liverpool* from N Y, on their way to Fla. Ofcrs with the detachment: Capt Dimmick, 1st Artl, commandng. Capt McKenzie, 2nd Artl. Lt Penrose, 2nd Infty, lady & 2 chldrn. Lt Foote, 7th Infty.

Bedford, [Pa] Inq: states that a Frenchman, Jonas Charles, drowned himself last week, about 10 miles from that place. He paid his passage from Phil to Pittsburg: was well clad, about 28 to 28 years of age. His baggage is at the stage ofc in Bedford.

Fred'k Md, Dec 26. Wm Carlton, Reg of the Corp of Fred'k, a young man much esteemed, was running with the Reel belonging to the Young Men' Eng Co, on Tue, on the occasion of an alarm of fire. When nearly opposite Mr Marshall's ofc, he fell & expired instantaneously, as is supposed, from the breaking of a blood vessel. Mr Carlton had not been long mrd, & leaves a disconsolate wife.
-Herald

Yesterday's mail furnished the list of names of persons killed & wounded by the explosion of the boiler of the steamboat *Cherokee*, at Louisburg, on the Arkansas river, mentioned in our last paper.

Killed: Mr Osgood, of New Orleans
Mr Pittman, of Louisburg
Capt Wyman, of steamer *Lady Morgan*
Mr Smith, of Louisville
Senior Forsyth, of La
Mr Miles, of Van Buren
Mr Cook, of Ark

Thos Fanning, [boy,] of Ark
Budd, watchmen
S Gibson, hand
Mr Hobson, of Steubenville, Ohio
R L Hubbard, of Conn
Mr Kensy
2 brothers, names unknown

Wounded-dangerously:
Capt C Harris
Louis Clauten, engr
Martin Williams, mate
Mr Clyde, passenger, N Y

Mr Perry, passenger
Frederic, German, deck-hand
Campbell, fireman
Wm, cabin boy

London Morning Herald, Dec 4. The frig *Belle Poule*, commanded by the Prince de Joinville, has arrived at Cherbourg from St Helena, with the remains of the Emperor Napoleon. [This is followed by the report of his Royal Highness to the Minister of Marine: with details of the above. -F D'Orleans]

New-Family Grocery store: on 7th st, above I st. -Jas E Given

Wash Co, D C: I certify that John H Clarvoe brought before me a stray taken up by Robt Bader, on Dec 23, in Wash City, a large dark bay horse. -Clemt T Coote, J P [Owner to prove property, pay charges, & take him away. -Jno H Clarvoe, near Centre Market-hse.]

Middledgeville, Dec 22. Announce the death of Jefferson J Lamar, on Dec 15, at his residence, in Stewart Co, from a wound he received at the hands of John Reynolds, about Oct 1 last. We know of no one whose death will be more regretted. -Jrnl

Died: on Dec 27, in Wash City, Mr Remigius Burch, after a long & painfull illness: aged 53 years.

Died: on Dec 24, Josephine Johnson, d/o Solomon & Ellen Hubbard, aged 2 years & 2 months.

Died: on Dec 24, Mrs Mary Gibbons, consort of Mr John Gibbons, in her 61st year.

TUE DEC 29, 1840
Valuable drug establishment in Balt for sale: for some time past conducted by themselves, & formerly by Messrs C & D & S Keener: profitably conducted for upwards of 25 years: business conducted in a 4 story fire-proof warehse, in the central part of Balt city. –J B Fitzgerald & Co, Balt, Md

In Chancery, Dec 3, 1840. Benj Willett, vs, John Penn & Lucy Penn & others. Case: Robey Penn, in 1800, sold & conveyed a tract of land called *Addition to Rags'Adventure*, in Montg Co, Md, to Chas Penn, in fee; that Chas Penn, on Jan 1, 1801, sold the same to Zaccheus Penn, which was fully paid, & gave bond of conveyance to said Z Penn, soon after which Z Penn died, having first made by will, & thereby divided said land to his sister, Eliz Penn; Eliz, in 1802, sold the land to John House, of Mont Co, Md, & assigned to him the said bond of conveyance; that in 1817, the land was sold under a decree of Montg Co Court, as a Court of equity, to the cmplnt, Benj Willett, jr, who fully paid for the same. The bond of conveyance was placed in the hands of a solicitor in 1816 or 1817, by Edw House, the trustee, which bond has been lost. That Chas Penn has since died, leaving John & Lucy Penn his heirs-at-law; that Zaccheus Penn died without chldrn, leaving the following bros & sisters, to wit, Caleb Penn, John W Penn, Chas Penn, jr, Benj Penn, Robey Penn, & Sarah, the w/o Greenbury Beet, & Eliz, w/o Fielder Palmer. The said Caleb has since died, leaving Wm G Penn, of Montg Co, Md, & Sarah Dowden, w/o Wm Dowden, of Fred'k Co, Md, Eliz, w/o Jas K Archbold, of Harrison Co, Va, his heirs-at-law. John W Penn has also since died, leaving Joshua A Penn, of Fred'k Co, Md, & Ellen Penn, of Va, his heirs-at-law. Benney Penn has also since died, leaving Caleb R Penn, of Montg Co, Rezin Penn, Chas H Penn, Greenbury V Penn, Mary Ellen, w/o J Brown, Nancy, w/o L Anderson, & Ann Penn, all of Ohio, & 2 other chldrn, whose names are unknown, The said Robey emigrated to N Y, & died, leaving sundry heirs whose names are unknown. Eliz Parker hath died without chldrn. John House hath also died, leaving Richd, John, Nathl, Reuben House, & Mrs Davis, & Mrs Brown, of Montg Co, Md. The bill prays that the dfndnts, John & Lucy, may be decreed to convey the aforesaid piece of land to the cmplnt, & for other relief. All who have claims or interest to appear in this Court on or before May 3 next. –Ramsay Waters, reg c c

The Pres' House will be opened, as usual, for the reception of visitors on Jan 1, between 12 & 3 p m.

Senate: 1-Ptn from the exc of David Gelston, praying the allowance of certain items in the settlement of said Gelston's account. 2-Ptn from Ross Williams & other citizens, praying the enactment of a bankrupt law. 3-Ptn from Thos Huslic, praying remuneration for lost time in consequence of the suspension of the work on the U S Arsenal at Fayetteville, N C. 4-Ptn from Col Robt D Wainwright, of the Marine Corps, praying an increase of pension. 5-Ptn from Geo Taylor, praying indemnity for losses by French Spoliations prior to 1800. 6-Ptn of Jos Vidal was referred to the Cmte on Pvt Land Claims. 7-Bills engrossed: pension to Lemuel White; relief of Mgt Barnes, wid/o Elijah Barnes; pension to David Waller; relief of the legal reps of Rich T Banks, of Ark; adjust & pay to Benj Murphy, of Ark, the value of his corn, cattle, & hogs, taken by the Cherokee Indians in Dec, 1828. 8-Also, engrossed: relief of Jacob Seely; of Saml Collins, of Jos Basset; & of Wm P Rathbone. Senate adjourned.

Died: on Sat, in Wash City, Mary Eliz, aged 6 years, d/o Chas & Lucy A Lemon, of Boston.

Mrd: on Dec 24, by Rev Mr Thornton, Mr John Henry Gibbs, of Wash City, to Miss Frances Eliz Lakin, of Warrenton, Fauquier Co, Va.

Mrd: at Meg-Willie, near Charlestown, Jeff Co, Va, by Rev A Jones, Mr Robt G McPherson, of Fred'k Co, Md, to Miss Millissent F, d/o Wm T Washington. [No date-current item.]

Mrd: on Nov 26, in Rockbridge Co, Va, by Rev Horatio Thompson, the Rev Saml Davies Campbell, lately of Brandon, Miss, to Miss Jane Eliza Orbinson, d/o Thos Orbinson, dec'd, formerly of Gtwn, D C.

The undersigned having been appointed Com'rs by Montg Co Court to divide the real estate of John Waters, dec'd, among the reps of the said dec'd, do hereby give notice to all concerned that they will meet on the premises on Feb 27, to carry said commission into effect. –Hy Harding: John Jones, of A: W O Chappell, com'rs

Cleveland, Ohio: on Dec 16, Jabez Wright, of Huron, one of the old, most useful citizens of the Lake country, lost his life. His body was found in the lake opposite the village of Huron on the 17th, & it appears a fence near the brow of the bank gave way & by some means he was precipitated some 12 or 15 feet. The fall caused his death. The death of Judge Wright is not only a severe affliction to his family, but a public calamity. A large circle of friends & relatives mourn his death. -Herald

Anthony Hasbrouck, of Fallsburgh, Sullivan Co, N Y, [who was the candidate for Congress in 1838,] was inhumanly murdered a few days since by a neighbor & connexion of his, Mr Hardenbergh. The criminal was arrested & committed. Hardenbergh went to Mr Hasbrouck's hse, & shot him in front of his wife. It is said that Hasbrouck had lately commenced an ejection suit against him. -Times

Died: on Sun last, Christiana, eldest d/o the late Fred'k Keller, in her 21st year. Her funeral is on Wed next, at 3 p m, from the residence of her mother.

Hagerstown, Md, Dec 24. On Mon last an aged & respectable woman, Mrs Murphy, who has been a resident of our town for a number of years, while engaged in drawing water from a well, slipped upon some ice on the boards, & was precipated headlong into the well. The alarm was given by her niece, who was a witness to the scene, but the body was not recovered until about an hour after the catrastrophe. The dec'd was upwards of 70 years. -Torchlight

Hse o/Reps: 1-Ptn of John B Glover & others, of N Y, for a bankrupt law: referred to the Cmte on the Judiciary. 2-Bill for relief of Hannah Leighton: referred to the Cmte on Revolutionary Pensions.

Strayed on Nov 25, a sorrel horse. The horse was purchased a short time since of Saml Suit, & well known in the District Reasonable reward. –Christopher O'Neale, near the Navy Yard gate.

Notice: Wheras I did, in conjunction with my sisters, Polly Timberlake, Eliz Timberlake, & Martha Timberlake, execute to Robt B Gaines a power of atty, dated Nov 14, 1839, authorizing him to draw, sell, transfer certain military land warrants issued to the heirs of Capt Benj Timberlake; & whereas the siad Robt B Gaines has, by vitue of said power, drawn from the Reg's Ofc of Va 2 warrants, viz: #8,732 for 2,666¾ acs, & #8,733, for 1,333¼ acs; now be it known, that I do, for myself & my sisters, revoke the said power of atty, & all authority therein given to the said Robt B Gaines, except in regard to the warrant #8,733 for 1,333¼ acs. My object is to take from the control of Gaines the other warrant, #8,732, for 2,666¾ acs.
–Henry Timberlake

Public sale: order of the Orphans' Court of PG Co, Md: sale at Bladensburg, the residence of the late Thos Ferral, on Jan 19 next, part of the personal propertyof the said Ferral: horses, cows, hogs, farming utensils, & saddles. –Dennis W Ferral, Eliz Ferral, exc & excx of Thos Ferral

Found on Tue last, in Ward #1, a Fustian Overcoat, which the owner can have, by paying charges, on application to Forrester Young.

WED DEC 30, 1840
W Lankford will continue open with additional supplies of Fancy Goods, until Thu next, to which he invites their attention, as bargains will be given. –W L, next door to Mr D Clagett's.

All indebted to the subscribers are requested to settle their account on or before the year 1841. -Wm & Geo Stettinius

Mrd: Dec 27, by Rev Mr Smith, Jacob Colclazer to Eliz Crawford, all of Wash City.

Senate: 1-Announcement of the death of Felix Grundy, of Tenn. The dec'd, at the time of his death, was not a member of this Hse, but he was once a member of it, the lapse of nearly 30 years. His public career commenced more than 40 years ago, in the convention for revising the Constitution of Ky: he was then but 21 years of age. Elected one of the judges of the Supr Court of Ky in 1806. Served in the Leg of Tenn, beginning in 1819: had moved there in the winter of 1807-08. To her, who has been the wife of his bosom from youth to old age-from the days of his poverty to those of wealth & fame, whom we so lately saw watching by his side, with such conjugal affection & such Christian hope, what to her must be his loss. What to his chldrn. The Hse will wear crape for 30 days.

Criminal Court-Wash. Grand Jury: Thos Carbery, foreman

Jos Forrest	Benj K Morsell
Lewis Carbery	Jehiel Brooks
John Boyle	Geo Parker
John F Cox	G C Grammer
Wm Hayman	Chas A Burnett
Thos Munroe	Chas R Belt
Wm Gunton	John W Maury
Abner C Pearce	Thos Fenwick
John Cox	Raphael Semmes
Wm D C Murdock	Geo Thomas

Mrs Kinney, whose trial attracted so much attention in Boston, has been acquitted of the murder of her husband.

Wash Corp-Dec 28, 1840: Wm S Walker resigns his seat as a member of the Brd of Common Cncl.

Estray horse came to my hse on Dec 13, a handsome sorrel horse. He was owned by me for some years, & was exchanged by my son on Nov 14 to a stranger in Wash who had a drove of horses for sale. Owner will please come & take him away.
–John Dulin, Lowhill, Fairfax Co, Va

M Slattery will dispose of all his school furniture, & give immediate possession to the school room, to any gentleman who is well qualified to take charge of it. The school has numbered from 40 to 50 boys for the last 2½ years he has had charge of it. –M S

THU DEC 31, 1840

Mrd: on Dec 22, at Mattaponi, PG Co, Md, by Rev Mr Kerr, Osborn Sprigg to Miss Caroline L Bowie, d/o R W Bowie, all of PG Co, Md.

Died: on Oct 11 last, at sea, Lt Gurdon C Ashton, of the U S Navy.

Died: on Sat last, after a lingering illness, Capt Abraham L Sands, of Manhassett, L I, formerly of the U S Army, aged 57 years.

Senate: 1-Ptn from J K Rogers, praying payment of certain requisitions held by him. 2-Ptn from the heirs of Silas Deane. 3-Ptn from Jas Williams, for property destroyed by the Fla Indians. 4-Ptn from John Landis, asking Congress to purchase his picture. 5-Cmte on Pvt Land Claims: bill for relief of Miguel Estava, with an amendment. 6-Same cmte: bill for relief of Madam De Lusser. 7-Cmte of Claim: bill for relief of Jos Paxton. 8-Cmte on Public Lands: bill for relief of Henry Wilson. 9-Cmte on the P O & Post Roads: bill for relief of Francis A Harrison. 10-Also, a bill for relief of Colen Bishop. 11-Cmte on Indian Affairs: bill for relief of Guerdon S Hubbard, Robt A McKenzie, & others. 12-Bill introduced: for relief of Saml Norris & Fred Saugrain.

Hon Felix Grundy died at Nashville, Tenn, on Dec 19. He was born in 1777, in Berkeley Co, in the Old Dominion, that mother of patriots. His father emigrated to Ky in 1780. At an early period he was left an orphan, guided & cherished by a mother on whom misfortune had cast its deepest shadows. He was educated at the Academy of Bardstown, Ky, then under the super of Dr Priestly: studied law with Geo Nicholas. His remains were interred in the city burying ground, on Dec 20: funeral sermon was delivered in the Presby Chr, of which Mr G was a member, by Rev John T Edgar. Masonic honors conducted by Rev J T Wheat, Rector of the Episc Chr.

Richmond: on Dec 28, Wm Sinan, machinist, who resided near Louisa Court-house, was run over & killed by the train of cars going to Fredericksburg, not far from Taylorsville. He was employed in his trade in Powhatan, & was on his way to visit his family. -Compiler

A

Abbot, 44, 313
Abbott, 147, 148, 149, 267
Abell, 36, 43, 305
Abell's Chance, 35
Abell's Lot, 35
Abell's Scuffle, 36
Abello, 248
Abercrombie, 209
Aberdeen, 37
Abert, 264, 352
Able, 353
Aborn, 143
Abrams, 136
Accinelly, 248
Achman, 310
Ackein, 26
Acker, 377
Ackerman, 305
Actland, 54, 62
Actlard, 62
Adair, 176
Adams, 18, 26, 30, 34, 41, 46, 51, 69, 74, 86, 114, 119, 131, 136, 152, 160, 170, 173, 181, 183, 186, 189, 204, 222, 224, 225, 234, 236, 273, 274, 276, 281, 289, 293, 294, 303, 305, 311, 312, 324, 328, 330, 345, 352, 353, 356, 368, 369, 388, 390, 396
Addison, 60, 126, 186, 212, 329, 344, 371
Addition, 36
Addition to Hope Enlarged, 97
Addition to Partnership, 39
Addition to Rags'Adventure, 399
Addoms, 69, 94, 100, 134, 158, 222, 233, 391
Adel, 218
Adelphia Mills, 134
Adie, 202
Adkins, 50
Adler, 248
Adrain, 165
Adrien, 173
Ager, 104
Agg, 259
Aikin, 214
Ainsley, 289
Ainsworth, 248
Aisquith, 35
Aladenize, 337
Aland, 238
Alcock, 78
Alcorn, 64
Alert, 167
Alexander, 33, 66, 73, 108, 111, 119, 130, 134, 150, 159, 217, 233, 234, 376
Alford, 192, 335
Alfred, 364
Allan, 74, 138, 139, 167
Allen, 7, 16, 18, 19, 27, 32, 43, 60, 63, 69, 74, 75, 91, 103, 117, 119, 120, 126, 127, 133, 140, 167, 174, 175, 183, 221, 222, 223, 224, 229, 236, 252, 261, 279, 305, 330, 366, 385
Alling, 220
Allinger, 364
Allison, 11, 75, 107, 147, 148, 149, 156, 170, 202, 225, 262, 363
Ally, 165
Allyr, 327
Almy, 41
Alsop, 59
Alston, 26, 39, 146
Alvarez, 54
Alves, 387
Alvey, 38, 376
Alvord, 7
Alwaise, 308
Alwood, 78
Ambler, 47, 74
Amery, 279, 381
Ames, 87
Amy, 75

Anderson, 10, 30, 36, 95, 114, 134, 177, 189, 197, 223, 230, 247, 257, 263, 268, 281, 311, 317, 354, 359, 380, 399
Andraole, 93
Andrews, 20, 74, 78, 82, 86, 162, 170, 179, 188, 225, 232, 235, 353, 372
Anelli, 73
Angell, 122
Angevine, 307
Angus, 201
Aniba, 84
Ann, 396
Annelaly, 386
Anster, 26
Anthony, 84, 234, 358
Antietam Iron Works, 279
Antoine, 19
Appleby, 75, 170, 225
Appleton, 13, 118
Arabia, 39
Arari, 204
Arbuckle, 228
Archbold, 399
Archer, 240, 244, 248, 338
Armas, 264
Armington, 384
Armisead, 199
Armistead, 110, 132, 141, 315, 329, 347
Armor, 43
Armsby, 272
Armstead, 32
Armstrong, 10, 35, 79, 109, 110, 220, 347, 397
Arnan, 69
Arnold, 106, 323
Arnot, 88
Arrago, 194
Artault, 157
Arthur, 5, 206, 319, 325
Arthur's Seat Enlarged, 53
Artman, 75
Asbury, 75, 170, 202, 225
Ashby, 90, 141, 159

Ashcom, 36
Ashton, 27, 342, 403
Ashwood, 313
Askins, 11, 75
Aspden, 92
Aston, 389
Astor, 347
Atcherson, 47
Atherton, 75
Athy, 287
Atkins, 67
Atkinson, 73, 167, 170, 203, 227, 273, 334
Atwell, 30
Atwood, 305
Auland, 69
Auld, 89, 159, 213
Aulick, 101, 114, 333, 372, 381
Ault, 148, 149, 151, 205, 218, 349
Austen, 225, 317
Austin, 74, 98, 133, 147, 170, 377
Auston, 356
Averill, 102
Avery, 49, 123, 158, 380
Awkward, 207, 368
Ay Hill, 192
Aycrigg, 165
Ayerigg, 270
Aylmer, 248

B

Babbitt, 33
Babcock, 157
Babin, 59, 392, 396
Babock, 20
Baby, 258
Bach, 166
Bache, 25
Bachelor's Comfort, 36
Bachelor's Hopewell, 35
Bachelor's Rest, 36, 39
Bacon, 90, 126, 147, 148, 149, 151, 173, 180, 187, 210, 238, 243, 315, 367, 368, 383

Baden, 67, 78
Badeolet, 11
Bader, 398
Badger, 160, 169, 330
Badle, 60
Bagby, 359
Bailey, 69, 74, 75, 78, 100, 108, 134, 170, 181, 189, 191, 194, 202, 219, 225, 281, 302, 397
Bainbridge, 47
Baker, 40, 63, 69, 74, 82, 114, 147, 170, 205, 214, 219, 305, 345, 353
Balch, 33, 85, 106, 201, 227
Balcom, 262
Balding, 50
Baldwin, 7, 14, 49, 74, 75, 78, 114, 170, 216, 223, 250, 296, 375, 380
Bales, 366
Ball, 16, 31, 118, 165, 176, 179, 235, 245, 281, 283, 336, 346
Ballagh, 11
Ballard, 14, 69, 168
Ballinger, 311
Ballou, 20
Baltzell, 219
Bancker, 294
Bancroft, 142, 207
Bankhead, 246, 283
Banks, 385, 397
Bannon, 133
Baptist's Hope, 37
Baracman, 235
Barbaugh, 72
Barber, 4, 38, 80, 88, 232
Barber's Enclosure, 39
Barbour, 2, 14, 177, 239, 267, 380, 388
Barclay, 11, 65, 187, 265, 271, 314, 367, 369
Barcroft, 130, 360
Bardin, 135
Bargdoll, 288
Baring, 204
bark *Brontes*, 20
Barker, 5, 6, 160, 186, 188, 225, 263

Barksdale, 350
Barland, 162
Barlett, 102
Barley, 240
Barlow, 162, 354
Barnard, 15, 80, 81, 123, 155, 289, 319, 382
Barneclo, 334
Barnes, 7, 43, 47, 56, 64, 107, 114, 120, 130, 160, 179, 181, 244, 248, 266, 291, 296, 349, 359, 362, 363, 380, 386, 400
Barnes' Purchase, 328
Barnett, 318
Barney, 72, 90, 92
Barnhill, 317
Barnhouse, 336
Barnum, 131
Baron, 388
barque *Mary*, 17
barque *Oceola*, 285
barque *Ronaldson*, 389
Barr, 246
Barras, 323
Barret, 149
Barrett, 149
Barron, 191
Barry, 101, 116, 128, 147, 150, 157, 178, 265, 271, 274, 294, 300, 335, 367, 369
Bartholet, 133
Bartlett, 41, 108, 207, 235, 353, 384
Barton, 41, 86, 114, 173, 188, 203, 239, 246, 254, 263, 361
Bascom, 357
Basford Berry Gleaning, 38
Baskerville, 357
Basset, 2, 133, 400
Bassett, 77, 180, 187, 324, 367
Bassford, 140
Bataille, 337
Batchelder, 87, 380
Bateman, 172

Bates, 10, 11, 16, 69, 78, 94, 100, 123, 126, 127, 134, 173, 174, 203, 210, 231, 281, 305, 382
Batin, 2
Battie, 240
Bauberger, 226
Baupre, 381
Baxter, 7, 51, 310
Bay, 190
Bayard, 159, 379
Bayley, 119, 183, 350
Baylis, 33
Bayliss, 95
Bayly, 358
Bayne, 13, 101, 148, 150, 266
Baynes, 379
Beach, 32, 258
Beal, 363
Beale, 27, 30, 110, 189
Beall, 32, 84, 114, 139, 144, 149, 178, 179, 184, 224, 232, 261, 285, 288, 297, 331, 341
Bealle, 107
Beaman, 291
Beamish, 42
Bean, 46, 132, 148, 172, 206, 230, 258, 264, 265, 276, 281, 298, 319, 363, 368
Bear, 218
Beard, 59, 69
Beardsley, 127, 226
Bearsley, 74
Beasely, 86
Beasley, 235
Beatty, 10, 76, 288, 322
Beatty & Hawkins', 183
Beaty, 263, 311
Beaux, 169
Beaver Dam, 36, 37
Beaver-dam, 37
Beck, 97, 146
Becker, 74, 175, 221, 225, 232
Beckett, 111
Beckford, 87
Beddo, 364

Bedford, 118, 200
Bee, 113
Beebe, 391
Beecher, 12, 24
Beeler, 64
Beers, 143, 148, 317
Beeson, 206
Beet, 399
Beinvenida, 336
Beitzel, 205
Belgar, 2, 64, 392, 396
Bell, 119, 138, 149, 157, 171, 221, 277, 297, 311, 373, 383, 394
Bell Park, 138
Bell's, 257
Belle Forest, 266
Bellevue, 162
Belt, 7, 8, 89, 138, 179, 331, 402
Belzarus, 274
Bemiz, 159
Bender, 60, 151, 228, 245, 317, 368
Benedict, 102, 361, 377
Benfield, 312
Benham, 112, 232
Benjamin, 42, 69, 94, 100, 113, 134, 233, 305
Benner, 232
Bennet, 25, 222
Bennett, 34, 36, 65, 74, 132, 153, 170, 188, 201, 225, 232, 291, 397
Benson, 4, 208
Bent, 78, 114
Bentley, 7, 86, 235, 329
Bently, 202, 216
Benton, 67, 160
Berbe, 305
Berdsley, 233
Berkeley, 345
Berkley, 99
Berlin, 238
Bernard, 67, 157
Berr, 218
Berrien, 192
Berrit, 310

Berry, 7, 9, 60, 80, 107, 114, 130, 162, 174, 231, 237, 272, 274, 285, 290, 291, 329, 351, 358, 362, 376, 396
Berryman, 191
Bertine, 305
Bertody, 349
Berwick, 39
Best, 78
Best Land, 39
Best's Marsh, 138
Bestor, 257
Bethel, 137
Bethell, 205
Betts, 36, 113
Bevans, 226
Beverly, 38, 39
Beyer, 27, 226
Bezle, 200
Bibb, 223, 386
Bicker, 168
Biddle, 121, 132, 166, 305, 322
Bidlack, 322
Bidwell, 305
Bienheim, 349
Bigelow, 201
Bigger, 301
Biggs, 50, 221
Bihler, 187, 363
Billing, 191
Billings, 2, 133, 222, 392
Billisoly, 248
Billmyer, 14
Billups, 192
Bingham, 53, 171
Binns, 124
Birch, 261
Birchard, 23, 90
Birckhead, 119, 316, 329
Bird, 229, 247, 313, 343, 372
Birdsall, 44
Birth, 301
Bisbee, 391
Biscoe, 296
Bisham, 44
Bishop, 48, 69, 101, 133, 344, 403

Bispham, 59, 81, 85
Bissell, 11, 69
Bisset, 305
Bixby, 207
Blache, 171
Black, 74, 131, 170, 192, 202, 257, 288, 305, 354, 379
Blackbock, 54
Blackburn, 194
Blackford, 277
Blackistone, 36
Blackland, 38
Blacklidge, 305
Blade, 211
Blagden, 52, 80, 146, 245, 265, 271, 314, 322, 324, 331, 367, 368, 369
Blagrow, 309
Blair, 58, 284, 355, 378
Blake, 5, 18, 20, 31, 64, 67, 111, 127, 218, 238, 245, 250, 270, 280, 305, 331, 373
Blakesale, 30
Blakiston, 157
Blakistone, 38
Blancard, 176
Blanchard, 73, 355, 356
Bland, 3, 225
Blandin, 78
Blanton, 230
Blasinger, 64
Blatchford, 330
Bleecker, 90, 169, 304, 305, 307
Blenheim, 314
Blight, 22, 61
Blinn, 217
Blizard, 395
Blocks, 269
Blocksom, 114
Blodget, 75, 170, 225
Blodgett, 75
Blood, 86, 234
Bloodgood, 77, 92, 377
Bloom, 2, 64
Bloomer, 307
Bloomfield, 74, 170, 186, 225

Blougher, 65
Blount, 282
Blue, 220
Blue Plains, 387
Bluxome, 304
Blythe, 93
Board, 243, 244
Boardman, 307, 320
Boarman, 56, 107, 114, 171, 172, 361
boat *Banner*, 285
boat *Col Little-John*, 271
boat *Columbus*, 301
boat *Maid of Orleans*, 351
boat *Pocahontas*, 301
boat *Rosalie*, 219
boat *Victoria*, 169
boat *Patrick Henry*, 301
Bock, 75
Bocker, 167
Bockius, 239
Bodder, 289
Bodisco, 117
Bodley, 140
Boeram, 341
Boerum, 254
Bogan, 104, 226
Bogart, 304
Boggess, 327
Boggs, 42, 69, 94, 100, 133, 233, 305
Bogy, 2, 64, 386, 393
Bohlayer, 255
Bohlem, 78
Bohlen, 92
Bohn, 249
Bohrer, 121, 183, 388
Bokee, 397
Boker, 161
Boland, 66
Bomford, 40, 53, 109, 328
Bonaparte, 15, 264, 343
Bond, 177, 273, 290, 296, 375
Bone, 57
Bonhomme, 133, 386
Bonhommie, 79
Bonnell, 263, 355, 356

Bonner, 235
Bonnet, 304
Bonneville, 199
Bonnycastle, 338
Booker, 69, 94, 100, 110, 133, 232
Boon, 44, 52
Boone, 144, 281
Bootes, 126
Booth, 30, 36, 38, 237
Booth's Endeavor, 36
Borden, 68, 75, 83
Bordley, 310
Borland, 52, 193
Borremans, 147
Borrows, 126, 149, 252
Boss, 307
Bostwick, 74, 167, 175, 233, 294
Boswell, 124
Bosworth, 22, 103, 233, 250, 268, 359
Boteler, 18, 60, 93, 126, 201, 210,
    332, 340, 353, 360
Botler, 132
Botton, 37
Botts, 190, 239, 374
Boulanger, 147, 246
Boulfont, 238
Bowan, 23, 226
Bowen, 126, 151, 318, 330, 351, 361,
    380, 384
Bowes, 36, 41
Bowie, 32, 110, 119, 140, 187, 195,
    200, 255, 271, 294, 297, 403
Bowier, 50
Bowin, 53
Bowland, 230
Bowles, 29
Bowling, 38, 107, 114, 213, 363
Bowly, 53
Bowman, 6, 73, 75, 108, 115, 170,
    232, 233
Bowne, 308, 330
Boyce, 50
Boyd, 28, 33, 42, 52, 65, 75, 101, 139,
    162, 170, 225, 254, 255, 261, 312,
    317

Boyer, 281
Boylan, 74, 170, 216
Boyle, 7, 80, 104, 179, 331, 402
Brace, 2
Brackenridge, 318, 322
Bracket, 20
Brackett, 196
Bradburn, 36
Braddock, 297, 300
Bradford, 21, 22, 118, 239, 247, 248, 297
Bradish, 79, 262
Bradley, 7, 47, 59, 60, 82, 113, 126, 127, 143, 150, 196, 222, 237, 240, 245, 289, 292, 314, 344, 366, 367
Brady, 47, 187, 248, 314, 315, 367, 371, 379
Brainard, 272, 377
Braken, 318
Bramels, 359
Brammhall, 238
Branch & Chas' Victory, 37
Brandenbrug, 361
Brandenburg, 134, 361
Bransford, 341, 355, 356
Brant, 5, 6, 288
Brantley, 80
Braschard, 230
Brashear, 24
Brashears, 132
Bratt, 308
Brawner, 107, 230, 293, 363
Braxton, 33, 382
Bray, 142
Breakey, 214
Breck, 288
Breckenridge, 91, 281
Breedin, 114
Breedlove, 32
Breese, 110
Brent, 60, 114, 126, 143, 185, 187, 213, 220, 245, 247, 265, 281, 321, 324, 344, 349, 363, 365, 367, 387
Brent, clk, 8, 59
Brereton, 149

Brevoort, 166
Brewer, 36, 38, 65, 73, 108, 119, 134, 232, 361, 376, 397
Brewster, 22, 207, 308
Brian, 90
Briceland, 349
Brick Kilns, 36
Bridewell, 328, 332, 396
Bridge, 230
Bridges, 73, 330
Brien, 279
Briers, 162
brig *Colorado*, 4
brig *Columibia*, 228
brig *Consort*, 328
brig *Dolphin*, 227
brig *Dundee*, 42
brig *Eliza Davidson*, 227
brig *Escambia*, 105, 110
brig *Florence*, 287
brig *Francis*, 160
brig *Genr'l Scott*, 26
brig *Illinois*, 163
brig *Northumberland*, 81
brig of war *Bonita*, 153
brig of war *Pickering*, 106
brig *Otho*, 137
brig *Phenix*, 42
brig *Susan Mary*, 155
brig *Vernon*, 264
brig *Virginia*, 4
brig *Warrior*, 41
brig *Wm Penn*, 124
Briggs, 59, 75, 206, 256, 310, 345, 368
Brigham, 61, 88
Bright, 11
Brightwell, 149, 150, 257
Brink, 305
Brinker, 190
Brinkerhoff, 272
Brisbin, 304
Brisbois, 87
Briscoe, 39, 107, 148, 149, 191, 362
Bristol, 75, 170

Britton, 69
Broad, 75
Broad Neck, 37
Broadhead, 102
Brocchus, 178
Brockenbrough, 357
Brocket, 158
Brodhead, 223
Brodie, 376
Brogden, 371, 372
Bronaugh, 117, 352, 371
Bronson, 85, 253, 278
Brook, 265, 271, 275, 326
Brooke, 14, 75, 91, 100, 111, 132, 140, 144, 147, 154, 185, 203, 208, 218, 247, 251, 280, 294, 349, 367, 369
Brooking, 156
Brooks, 4, 7, 30, 46, 76, 110, 147, 158, 177, 201, 263, 331, 343, 350, 402
Broom, 319, 346
Brothers, 257
Brotherton Indians, 233
Brougham, 15
Brougher, 74, 170, 225
Broughton, 333
Brower, 75, 307
Brown, 5, 18, 19, 20, 21, 22, 36, 40, 41, 46, 53, 64, 74, 75, 78, 84, 85, 100, 102, 103, 107, 116, 120, 133, 140, 146, 147, 148, 157, 159, 170, 171, 174, 182, 189, 191, 196, 200, 202, 209, 215, 216, 221, 223, 225, 230, 242, 251, 261, 267, 276, 277, 278, 284, 296, 304, 305, 312, 317, 319, 321, 326, 327, 329, 345, 351, 354, 356, 357, 363, 368, 376, 382, 384, 389, 399
Browne, 108, 120, 172, 224, 305, 332, 356
Brownell, 78, 305
Brownfield, 221
Browning, 76, 148, 274
Brownwell, 6

Browse, 289
Bruce, 88, 107, 114, 128, 133, 171, 305, 362, 387
Brummett, 107, 317, 363
Brundage, 88
Brunet, 62, 104
Brunow, 342
Brush, 22
Bruton, 5
Bryan, 60, 85, 120, 136, 173, 180, 187, 215, 219, 271, 281, 350, 367, 382, 392
Bryant, 5, 6, 8, 136
Bryden, 69
Bucey, 371
Buchanan, 28, 157, 318, 327
Bucher, 318
Buck, 91, 111, 118, 194, 262
Buckingham, 207, 280, 317, 318, 336
Buckinghm, 340
Buckland Mill, 120
Buckler, 93
Buckley, 78, 258
Buckner, 288
Budd, 398
Buel, 377
Buell, 259
Buffington, 354
Buford, 197
Buist, 28, 174, 289, 322, 348
Bulfinch, 122, 327, 330
Bulkley, 105, 390
Bull, 127
Bullard, 4, 20
Bulley, 256
Bullitt, 364, 381
Bulow, 15, 392
Bumley, 73
Buncombe, 65
Burbank, 5, 238
Burch, 13, 126, 148, 149, 150, 151, 206, 246, 278, 326, 368, 399
Burche, 160, 209, 325
Burchstead, 86, 234
Burdett's Neck, 35

Burdette, 305
Burdine, 149
Bure, 337
Burger, 72
Burgess, 45, 75, 114, 221, 363
Burgs, 93
Burk, 66, 351
Burke, 23, 135, 156, 200, 220, 310
Burleigh, 87
Burleson, 29, 125, 295, 313
Burnes, 215
Burnet, 179, 196, 331
Burnett, 7, 16, 80, 117, 134, 402
Burney, 124
Burns, 60, 387
Burr, 92, 100, 149, 206, 220, 280, 368, 395
Burrell, 288
Burrill, 158
Burritt, 240
Burrough's Gift, 39
Burrows, 68
Bursell, 345
Burt, 262, 267
Burton, 86, 91, 234, 378
Burts, 12
Burwell, 59
Bury, 46
Bush, 57, 124, 170, 386
Bushnell, 114
Bussey, 161
Butcher, 2, 64, 386
Butler, 16, 58, 68, 127, 135, 148, 201, 237, 240, 270, 272, 288, 329, 330, 371, 388
Butt, 30, 206, 368
Butterfield, 75, 170, 209
Butts, 44, 254, 376
Buyarde, 13
Buzzard, 189
By the Mill, 35
Byars, 357
Byers, 163
Byington, 69, 180, 187, 311, 324, 367
Bynum, 374

Byrd, 26, 218, 378
Byrne, 126, 195
Bytewood, 155

C

C & O Canal, 61, 66, 185, 188, 217, 315
Cadden, 99, 246
Caddo Indians, 9, 76
Cade, 289
Cadle, 304, 318
Cadwallader, 48, 61
Cady, 171, 221
Caffry, 305
Cain, 122, 220
Cairnes, 305
Calderon, 290
Caldwell, 24, 46, 47, 96, 125, 197, 229, 243, 315, 349, 355
Caleby, 43
Calhoun, 47, 69, 94, 100, 192, 222, 345, 395
Calkins, 88
Call, 95, 166, 315
Callan, 87, 148, 149, 150, 151, 204, 206, 227, 239, 259, 270, 289, 290, 312, 346
Callender, 5, 74, 244
Calvert, 10, 145, 191, 255, 288, 300
Calvert's Hope, 167
Calwell, 202
Camanches, 295
Cambreleng, 159
Cameron, 260, 318
Cammack, 70, 90, 106, 147, 148, 150, 151, 303, 328
Cammell, 200
Camp, 28, 32
Campan, 2
Campau, 59, 79, 248, 392
Campbell, 5, 46, 60, 74, 75, 112, 117, 126, 151, 170, 171, 190, 191, 225, 229, 240, 243, 281, 305, 311, 318, 323, 351, 374, 398, 400

Canady, 311
Canby, 139, 260
Canedy, 296
Canfield, 203
Cannion, 359
Cannon, 10, 79, 139, 161, 222, 260, 269, 304
Canter, 373
Cantley, 94
Caperton, 247, 248
Cappeller, 288
Capron, 97, 292, 376
Caradeur, 17
Carbery, 7, 60, 84, 101, 111, 143, 179, 180, 185, 187, 265, 271, 310, 329, 344, 367, 369, 402
Cardinal, 171
Cards, 112
Carey, 221, 242
Cargell, 125
Cargill, 357
Carleton, 103, 182
Carley, 44, 384
Carlisle, 126, 358
Carlos, 74
Carlton, 212, 398
Carmack, 223
Carmichael, 81
Caroline Furnace, 277
Carothers, 149, 150, 151, 163, 178, 256
Carpenter, 36, 88, 238, 243, 307, 308, 315, 355, 363, 377
Carper, 192
Carr, 31, 219, 272, 346, 371
Carreras, 23
Carrico, 39
Carrington, 77
Carrol, 351
Carroll, 103, 111, 245, 277, 281, 289, 325, 342, 352, 361
Carroll's Gift, 39
Carroll's Manor, 256
Carseley, 39
Carson, 48, 104, 114, 125, 317, 318

Carter, 7, 17, 33, 60, 95, 115, 157, 173, 179, 223, 253, 317, 329, 342, 352, 386, 392
Cartmell, 114
Cartwright, 39
Carusi, 72, 97, 104, 340, 347
Carver, 20, 60
Cary, 157
Case, 74, 145, 220, 225, 336
Casenove, 97
Casey, 50, 177
Caskie, 350
Caslin, 305
Cass, 23, 86, 235, 236, 387
Cassady, 320
Cassard, 337
Cassetts, 235
Cassidy, 114
Cassin, 143
Casson, 365
Castanis, 45
Castateel, 280
Castel, 93
Catharine's Isl, 38
Cathcart, 180
Catis, 364
Catlett, 29, 50, 75, 126, 221, 292
Catling, 142
Catron, 80
Catson, 14
Caulk, 214
Causey, 214
Causin, 10, 17, 27, 70, 90, 155, 215, 228, 290, 333, 335, 386, 395
Causten, 27, 228, 250, 336
Caustin, 215
Cavedo, 54
Cavener, 271
Cawood's Expense, 39
Cawood's Inheritance, 38, 39
Cayce, 125
Cazenave, 151
Cazenove, 220
Cemmerling, 156
Cennacher, 157

Center, 311
Chabert, 92
Chace, 157
Chad, 288
Chadeayne, 304
Chadwick, 234
Chagnier, 215
Chain bridge, 52
Chain Bridge, 84
Chalmers, 64, 105
Chamberlain, 105, 305
Chamberlin, 171
Chambers, 103, 129, 139, 260
Chamblin, 223, 320
Champlain, 108
Champlin, 73, 108
Chandler, 41, 51, 117, 221, 295
Chaney, 296, 372
Chapin, 41, 75, 170, 225, 272, 324
Chaplain, 297
Chapman, 46, 83, 107, 114, 156, 179, 220, 222, 239, 263, 290, 357, 362, 363, 383, 389
Chappel, 88, 192
Chappell, 75, 397, 400
Chaptico Manor, 38
Charles, 288, 398
Charleton, 63
Charlotte Hall, 39
Chartry-Lafosse, 297
Chas' Chance, 36, 37
Chas' Srvy & Rolly, 37
Chase, 127, 136, 263, 391
Chaseldine, 38
Chastelain, 69, 94, 100, 120, 233, 250
Chasterlain, 17
Chatterton, 305
Chauncey, 28
Cheavans, 305
Cheavens, 99
Cheeks, 375
Cherokee, 10, 29, 88, 197, 198, 351, 386, 395
Cherokee Indians, 386, 400
Cherokee nation, 10

Cherokees, 10, 64, 122, 198, 251, 351
Cheseldine, 38
Cheshire, 52, 152, 369
Chesire, 342
Chesnut, 119, 329
Chester, 63
Chestnut, 316
Cheston, 371
Chevalie, 216
Chevalier, 19
Cheves, 78, 186, 235
Chew, 134, 265, 270, 290, 296, 360, 382
Chezum, 242
Chieves, 234
Child, 18, 102, 364
Childers, 139, 261
Childs, 21, 39, 47, 65, 96, 126, 133, 188, 219, 226, 331, 371, 393
Chiles, 340
Chilton, 267
Chinn, 191, 236
Chipp, 304
Chisholm, 365, 371
Chism, 146
Chisom, 39
Chiswell, 257
Chittenden, 295
Choctaw, 3
Cholmondeley, 272
Chosley, 288
Chrismond, 107
Christ, 78
Christal, 307
Christer, 50
Christian, 23
Christie, 304
Christina Thal, 279
Christler, 221
Christman, 353
Christophe, 46
Christy, 45
Chuard, 92
Church, 2, 18, 20, 222, 386
Churchil, 112

Churchill, 26, 141, 157, 243
Cilley, 207
Cipriant, 78
Cisco, 307
Cissell, 140
Cissell's, 37
Cissell's Venture, 37
Clack, 4, 201
Clagett, 3, 121, 143, 178, 294, 393, 401
Claggett, 352, 357, 372, 390
Claiborne, 162
Clair, 41
Clapham, 215
Clark, 24, 32, 42, 50, 72, 94, 114, 115, 119, 149, 158, 171, 197, 200, 216, 243, 244, 247, 259, 263, 291, 305, 330, 353, 366, 367, 391
Clarke, 7, 25, 36, 50, 55, 67, 120, 126, 129, 147, 148, 149, 150, 156, 180, 187, 206, 216, 233, 245, 250, 261, 291, 314, 325, 328, 329, 332, 349, 352, 367, 368, 387, 392
Clarkson, 197
Clarvoe, 1, 13, 148, 365, 398
Clauten, 398
Claxton, 13, 81, 97, 100, 126, 201
Clay, 64, 81, 160, 180, 350, 385, 397
Claypoole, 2
Clayton, 47, 128, 222, 379
Cleland, 33
Clemens, 26
Clements, 38, 85, 90, 120, 126, 148, 152, 234, 240, 276, 314, 365, 382, 392
Clemson, 349
Clephane, 241
Clerke, 345
Clifford, 217, 275
Clinch, 32, 47, 134, 170, 173, 186, 191, 232, 304
Cline, 4
Clinton, 32, 61, 323
Clitch, 7, 381
Clitz, 349

Clough, 22, 83, 223
Cloutman, 46
Clute, 308
Clyde, 398
Clyme, 242
Co_greave, 235
Coal, 292
Coale, 187, 241, 297
Coates, 47, 65, 90, 188, 313, 391
Cobb, 133, 221, 323, 377
Coburn, 253, 382, 387
Coby, 317
Cochran, 2, 59, 73, 91, 97, 108, 119, 134, 167, 210, 218, 232, 263, 323, 371
Cochrane, 355
Cocke, 11, 326
Cockle, 3, 308
Cockrell, 77
Coddington, 219
Codwise, 378
Coe, 266, 305, 308
Coffee, 111, 190, 210
Coffey, 333
Coffin, 74, 170, 225, 384
Coggswell, 272
Cogswell, 195, 271
Cohen, 73, 305, 388
Coit, 224
Coker, 223
Colclazer, 402
Cole, 29, 33, 35, 73, 118, 119, 200, 267, 305, 316, 329, 388
Coleman, 209, 302
Colemen, 11, 174, 238
Coles, 1, 230, 277, 305, 380
Coley, 137
Colgate, 42
Colhoun, 285
Collard, 206, 368
Colley, 103, 120
Collier, 26, 191, 303
Collinard, 78
Collingsworth, 140

Collins, 2, 16, 24, 47, 51, 74, 75, 88, 146, 151, 167, 170, 202, 204, 222, 225, 230, 332, 335, 376, 400
Collman, 78
Collmus, 75
Colly, 75
Colman, 153
Colmus, 170
Colquit, 192
Colquitt, 67
Colston, 166, 320, 336
Colt, 59, 344
Coltman, 31, 150
Colton, 247, 248, 258, 277, 340
Columbus, 255
Colver, 49, 208
Colvill, 305
Colyer, 7
Comanche Indians, 135
Comb, 101
Combe, 13, 178
Combs, 148, 149, 311, 316, 371
Comean, 233
Comeau, 133, 392, 396
Comeon, 74
Commerford, 305
Commons, 13
Compton, 32, 38, 77, 133, 140, 291, 363, 392, 396
Comstock, 18, 20
Condict, 367, 375
Condit, 318
Cone, 279
Congdon, 127
Conjurer's Disappointment, 215
Conly, 51, 221
Connelly, 303, 354
Conner, 129, 147, 254
Connolly, 270
Connor, 11, 23, 111, 167, 285, 305
Conrad, 114, 302
Constantinople, 39
Contee, 53, 89, 353, 376
Converse, 15, 46, 123
Conway, 2, 59, 307, 392, 393, 396

Cook, 16, 28, 43, 48, 75, 86, 102, 170, 202, 209, 225, 232, 234, 313, 330, 345, 361, 384, 397, 398
Cooke, 14, 24, 27, 32, 125, 295, 308, 349
Cookendorfer, 148, 151
Cookman, 2, 3, 28, 30, 32, 33, 45, 51, 52, 62, 64, 70, 77, 85, 87, 99, 289, 300, 350
Cool, 262
Cooledge, 41, 142
Cooley, 223, 320
Coolidge, 273, 357
Coomb, 80
Coombe, 68, 149, 324
Coombs, 127, 214, 245, 299
Coon, 88
Cooper, 36, 51, 71, 76, 133, 137, 150, 160, 169, 192, 202, 214, 255, 270, 281, 289, 297, 298, 305, 314, 318, 322, 324, 339, 349, 368, 392, 395
Coote, 101, 181, 281, 327, 369, 398
Cope, 353
Copes, 123, 133, 393
Corbett, 136
Corcoran, 119, 189, 195, 350
Cordell, 242
Cordis, 53
Cordova, 70
Corey, 20, 258
Corlay, 379
Corley, 18
Cornbury, 94
Corneau, 79
Cornelison, 240
Cornell, 41, 74, 170, 204, 225, 391
Cornwall, 148
Cornwallis, 115, 122, 145, 181, 323
Cort, 69
corvette *Lexington*, 4
Corwin, 294
Coryell, 58
Cosby, 216
Cosely, 18
Cossey, 279

Costigan, 147, 149, 150
Cotg, 86
Cotheal, 42
Cotocton Furnace, 279
Coton, 133
Cotter, 290
Cotton, 346
Cottrel, 74
Cottrell, 88
Couch, 193, 219
Coulter, 317
Count de Menou, 327
Counts, 152
Courey, 286
Coursey, 363
Courtitenden, 60
Courvoisier, 228
Cousin, 118
Coutts, 370
Coventry, 219
Cover, 351
Covert, 262
Coves, 53
Covian, 379
Cowan, 25
Cowen, 194
Cowgill, 74
Cowles, 125
Cox, 7, 21, 69, 80, 89, 94, 100, 107, 110, 114, 118, 134, 143, 179, 213, 221, 224, 247, 248, 288, 304, 305, 331, 355, 363, 395, 402
Coxe, 60, 67, 87, 143, 185, 240, 264, 344, 355, 358
Coxen's Rest, 37
Coyle, 73, 126, 147, 211
Coyles, 217
Crabb, 277
Crackburn's Purchase, 36
Craddock, 233, 250
Craggs, 288
Cragie, 129
Cragin, 337
Craig, 15, 18, 20, 32, 83, 183, 243, 382

Craik, 323
Crain, 114, 154, 167, 328, 341, 363
Cramer, 123, 295, 344
Cramp, 57
Crampton, 373
Cranch, 144, 197
Crandall, 89, 314
Crandell, 60, 180, 187, 223, 265, 344, 367, 368
Crane, 129, 132, 262, 330
Cranston, 298
Crapin, 44, 124, 392
Craton, 36
Crauford, 397
Craven, 137, 201, 298, 373
Crawford, 23, 44, 95, 168, 191, 192, 257, 280, 339, 402
Craycroft, 78
Creamer, 111
Creason, 25
Creek Indians, 233
Creighton, 349
Crenshaw, 65
Creny, 54
Cresap, 288
Cresson, 220
Criddle, 166
Crier, 206
Cringem, 78
Cripps, 107, 253
Criswell, 318
Crittenden, 67, 229, 311
Crocker, 110
Crockett, 4, 82
Croft, 74
Croggon, 293
Crogham, 235
Croghan, 124, 266, 392
Cronan, 169
Crooks, 123, 137, 164
Cropley, 80, 195, 319, 328
Cropper, 239
Crosby, 127, 266, 294
Croskey, 50, 223
Cross, 166, 230, 247, 248, 249, 321

Crossfield, 126
Crossgrove, 159
Crossman, 78
Crosthwaite, 308
Crowley, 288
Crowly, 18
Crown, 69, 184
Crowninshield, 32
Cruger, 307
Cruit, 147, 148, 149
Crutcher, 139, 260
Cruttenden, 50, 213, 224
Cryer, 152, 368
Cubberly, 47
Cubieres, 118
Cuddeback, 74, 170, 224
Cudderback, 181
Culbertson, 197
Culbreth, 58
Culvert, 3
Cumanche Indians, 125
Cumming, 91, 166
Cummings, 5, 6, 75, 82, 120, 170, 209, 225
Cummins, 78
Cummiskey, 239, 248
Cunard, 241
Cunningham, 32, 46, 75, 101, 124, 264, 280, 386
Curloch, 43
Currie, 305
Currier, 20, 167
Curry-glass, 38
Curtis, 155, 294
Curver, 60
Cushen, 323
Cushing, 125, 345, 382
Cushman, 219
Custis, 95, 104, 105, 323
Cutant, 305
Cuthbert, 148, 180, 247
Cutler, 6, 137
Cutts, 60, 289

D

D'Hautville, 346, 348
d'Lagnel, 178, 243, 244
D'Orleans, 398
D'Wolf, 384
Dabadie, 25
Dabney, 95, 115, 119, 153
Dade, 222, 243, 244, 266, 278
Daery, 11, 261
Daggett, 154
Daingefield, 60
Daingerfield, 158, 220
Dal_arn, 91
Dale, 229, 238, 362, 383
Dalliner, 46
Dally, 305
Dalton, 103
Daly, 147, 148, 149
Dalzell, 68
Dameron, 139
Dana, 146, 159, 212, 361
Danbury, 37
Dancey, 112
Daney, 219
Danford, 90
Danforth, 33, 146, 268, 382
Dangerfield, 23
Daniel, 31, 71, 82, 117, 139, 160, 299, 301
Darby, 218
Darcy, 165
Daring, 75, 394
Darling, 42, 305
Darmes, 338
Darnel, 51
Darnes, 354
Darrow, 86, 235
Darvis, 68
Dashiell, 69, 214, 257, 371, 393
Dashiells, 118
Datcher, 98
Davenport, 35, 92, 112, 124, 308, 349
Davezac, 205, 233, 250
David, 17

Davids, 305
Davidson, 49, 74, 78, 167, 170, 188, 192, 225, 233, 271, 281, 367, 372
Davies, 9, 234, 321
Davis, 3, 13, 16, 20, 31, 36, 39, 47, 64, 74, 75, 77, 83, 84, 99, 101, 107, 110, 126, 128, 132, 134, 147, 156, 157, 167, 169, 170, 171, 174, 202, 203, 204, 209, 219, 225, 228, 235, 258, 260, 262, 279, 280, 281, 286, 288, 298, 301, 304, 305, 312, 321, 328, 329, 333, 336, 338, 345, 347, 350, 359, 365, 370, 388, 392, 399
Davs, 74
Dawes, 97, 378
Dawson, 86, 178, 188, 192, 218, 380
Day, 15, 29, 265, 296, 305, 355, 356
Dayon, 308
Dayton, 78, 304, 352, 373
De Camp, 305, 307
De Geerston, 19
De Gerstner, 124
de Grasse, 323
de Kalb, 116
De Lusser, 67, 384, 403
De Passan, 65
de Rochambeau, 323
De Selding, 35
De Silver, 164
De Treville, 24
De Vilers, 169
Deach, 41
Deacon, 66
Deal, 239
Deale, 206, 368
Dealty, 74, 394
Dean, 44, 75, 120, 225, 265, 297
Deane, 403
Dearborn, 5, 124, 153, 267
Dearbought, 39
Deas, 229, 237
Deatley, 167, 225
Deatly, 187
Decatur, 59, 110
Decker, 74

Deckman, 167
Defrees, 40
DeHart, 121
Dehugg, 353
DeKrafft, 204
Delabrooke, 36, 37
Delabrooke Manor, 36
Delacarlia, 254
Delafield, 197
Delamotta, 136
Delano, 57, 340
Delassaus, 99
Delassus, 213
Delaware 74, 172
Delesdernier, 75
Delespine, 67
Delisle, 178
Dell, 23
Dellawer, 205
Delord, 69, 100, 108, 119, 134
Deluol, 309
Dely, 258
Dement, 107, 189, 275, 363
Demotte, 92
Dempsey, 304
Deneale, 68, 268
Denham, 23, 31, 126
Denike, 305
Dennet, 215
Dennis, 48, 215, 240, 264, 282
Dennison, 305
Denny, 89, 218, 354
Dent, 114, 131, 226, 252, 362
Dent's Venture, 39
Depford, 35
Derby, 208
Deringer, 338
Derkheim, 32
Derwent, 226
Desjardins, 337
Detter, 159
Dettrow, 196
Devalengin, 80
Devaraigne, 92
Devaughn, 332, 335

Deveau, 305
Devecmon, 294
Devereux, 104, 160
Devlin, 247
Dew, 127
Dewdney, 348
Dewees, 226
Dewey, 41
Dewing, 78
Dexter, 148
Dibble, 171
Dick, 67, 281, 289, 354
Dickens, 224, 260
Dickerson, 76, 188, 240, 270
Dickinson, 216, 333, 377
Dickman, 74, 85, 175
Dickson, 139, 219, 224, 318, 353
Diell, 23
Dielman, 14
Digges, 97, 107, 126, 152, 178, 202, 281
Diggs, 200, 362
Dillard, 47
Dillenger, 126
Dillingham, 41, 74, 384
Dimitry, 22, 199
Dimmick, 397
Dimock, 322
Dioda, 342
Disbrow, 102, 195
Discord, 215
Dissoway, 305
Ditty, 372
Dix, 191, 355
Dixon, 69, 130, 140, 192, 211, 220, 305, 313, 385
Dixon's Lot, 30
Doak, 44
Doane, 304
Dobbins, 88, 168, 366
Dobbyn, 8
Dock, 37
Dodd, 34
Dodge, 7, 32, 293, 305, 328, 329, 384
Doe Park, 36

Doe Park with Add, 38
Doe Park with Addition, 36
Dogue, 339
Dogue's Neck, 339
Doherty, 77
Doig, 181
Dolterer, 289
Domingues, 50
Dominique, 346
Donald, 374
Donaldson, 277
Donalson, 95
Donaphin, 167
Donelan, 33, 63, 103, 178, 187, 269, 278, 340, 349, 394
Donellan, 11
Donephain, 32
Doniphan, 324
Donn, 201
Donnell, 33, 125
Donnelly, 22, 33
Donoho, 147
Donohoe, 148
Donohoo, 149, 150, 151
Donoyer, 133
Dooley, 122
Dorlan, 377
Dorman, 290
Dornenburg, 160
Dorr, 85
Dorrance, 330
Dorsett, 182, 372
Dorsey, 3, 10, 36, 99, 161, 165, 166, 182, 266, 323, 361, 397
Doty, 318
Dough, 3
Dougherty, 36, 64, 165, 181, 192, 287, 317
Doughty, 58, 312
Douglas, 124, 289
Douglass, 10, 32, 58, 93, 148, 213, 310, 368
'Dougless, 7
Doutherty, 88

Dove, 11, 101, 126, 187, 194, 241, 265, 276, 314, 319, 324, 348, 365, 367, 373
Dover, 103
Dow, 18, 20, 160
Dowden, 399
Dowlin, 353
Dowling, 148, 149, 151
Downer, 212, 294
Downes, 51, 69, 94, 100, 113, 213, 232, 254, 330
Downey, 45, 349
Downham, 36
Downing, 189, 345
Dowson, 371
Doxey, 307
Doyle, 171, 307, 345
Drain, 248
Drake, 60, 156, 186, 197
Draper, 193, 330
Drayden's Hills, 37
Dresser, 333
Drew, 61, 149, 151, 370
Dreyfouse, 305
Driggs, 144, 305, 384
Drummond, 314, 324
Drury, 31, 36, 206, 291, 303, 314, 340, 367, 368
Dryadocking, 37
Dryden, 39
Du Flon, 152
Du Pont, 226
Dubison, 57
Dubois, 142, 262, 377
Ducachet, 125
Ducatel, 33
Duckett, 349
Duckworth, 148, 150
Duddington, 143
Dudley, 62, 217, 237, 288, 325
Duer, 31, 78, 126, 349
Duffey, 340
Duffield, 162, 384
Duffore, 338
Duffy, 67, 80, 328

Duflon, 82, 254
Dugan, 305
Duke, 380
Duke de Tarente, 325
Duke of Nemours, 156
Duke of Wellington, 79
Dulaney, 257, 281
Dulany, 172, 183
Dulen, 336
Duley, 361
Dulin, 402
Dumas, 43
Dumont, 307
Dun, 80
Dunawin, 153
Dunbar, 75, 297
Duncan, 9, 54, 64, 162, 229, 266, 375
Duncanson, 280, 379
Duncombe, 157
Dundas, 9, 122
Dungan, 376
Dunham, 34, 105, 135
Dunkley, 307
Dunlap, 2, 112, 162, 174
Dunlop, 7, 59, 179, 185, 281, 331, 334
Dunn, 15, 18, 185, 273, 305, 327, 349
Dunnington, 107, 125, 213, 224, 317, 363
Durand, 78, 217
Durant, 17, 157
Durell, 308
Durkee, 125, 171
Duryee, 304
Dusenbury, 179, 193
Dushane, 54, 274
Dutilh, 92
Duval, 31, 133
Duvall, 32, 53, 113, 135, 138, 194, 196, 295, 301, 320, 339
Duveyrier, 14
Dwight, 214
Dye, 73, 167, 394
Dyer, 21, 27, 52, 78, 107, 121, 127, 147, 148, 173, 174, 203, 283, 287, 292, 301, 370, 384

Dyhrenforth, 92
Dyson, 206, 258, 347

E

Eaches, 220
Eakin, 304
Earhart, 231
Earl, 317
Earl of Bellamont, 94
Earl of Durham, 272, 295
Earle, 305, 317
Earll, 219
Early, 210, 222, 224, 321
Easby, 60, 99, 173, 180, 187, 189, 245, 334, 344, 358, 361, 367
East Gift, 38
Eastham, 32
Eastin, 155, 381
Eastman, 5, 207, 257
Easton, 59
Eaton, 22, 88, 140, 318
Ebbitt, 180
Eberbach, 148
Eberle, 361
Eberly, 222
Eckel, 328, 344
Eckell, 60
Ecker, 266
Eckford, 28, 65, 188, 283
Eckle, 290
Eckles, 287
Eckloff, 148, 149, 150, 205, 348
Ecleston, 137
Eddy, 14, 123
Edelen, 39, 167, 189
Edelin, 285
Edes, 27, 118, 273, 329
Edgar, 403
Edinborough, 36, 38
Edinborough with Add, 38
Edmonds, 65, 245, 329, 330
Edmondson, 48, 75
Edmonston, 334
Edmundson, 126

Edson, 29, 110
Edw'd Discovery, 39
Edwards, 71, 72, 90, 99, 101, 188, 191, 195, 207, 260, 276, 302, 319, 321, 324, 336, 357
Egan, 91
Egg, 29
Eichorn, 357
Eiglehart, 32
Elder, 15, 130, 209, 305
Eldred, 384
Eldridge, 40, 100, 182, 384
Eliason, 104, 203, 248, 275
Elibert, 24
Eligible Situation, 319
Eliot, 281, 367, 394
Ellege, 64
Ellery, 158, 222, 396
Ellicott, 23, 173
Elliot, 22, 52, 59, 126, 186, 206, 256
Elliott, 73, 129, 132, 153, 165, 231, 254, 260
Ellis, 101, 119, 150, 165, 305, 330, 378
Ellison, 305
Ellmaker, 353
Ellsworth, 84
Ellwood, 112, 126
Elmendorf, 4
Elmore, 141
Elssler, 156, 312
Elwood, 270
Ely, 42
Elzuardi, 50
Emack, 76, 91, 106, 136, 149, 150, 151
Emerson, 238, 349
Emmert, 392
Emmons, 303
Emperor Nicholas, 342, 353
Emperor of Austria, 350
Emperor of Morocco, 233
Emperor of Russia, 228, 337
Enclosure, 37
Enclosure with Addition, 39

England, 74, 167, 175
Engler, 84
Engleston, 238
English, 110, 204, 328
English Hill, 324
Ennis, 100, 104, 148, 149, 150
Enniscothy, 1
Eno, 148, 180
Enoch, 223
Enochs, 218
Epperson, 73
Eppes, 340
Ericsson, 157
Erie, 168
Erwin, 98, 258
Esclava, 27, 57
Eskridge, 59, 73, 108, 233, 338
Eslava, 130, 209, 386
Espey, 257
Essex, 126, 195, 213, 223, 321
Estava, 403
Estep, 371
Estes, 167
Estko, 109
Etcheson, 45
Ethel, 74
Etter, 126, 146, 317, 318, 361
Eubanks, 6
Euler, 75, 170
Eutaw, 189, 285
Evans, 19, 46, 50, 52, 64, 68, 90, 103, 128, 130, 133, 134, 136, 275, 277, 278, 315, 332, 351, 358, 368, 369, 376
Evens, 204
Everett, 21, 74, 167, 181, 305
Everhart, 222, 256
Everly, 395
Eversfield, 215, 390
Evin, 98
Ewell, 243, 355
Ewing, 68, 139, 223, 260, 284, 365
Expedition, 22, 47, 97
Ezell, 32, 105
Ezzard, 192

F

Fagan, 148, 378
Faile, 78
Fairchild, 305
Fairfax Beall, 375
Fairfield, 275
Fairview Hill, 336
Falconer, 346
Falconet, 121
Fallen, 74
Falls Plantation, 216
Fane, 32
Fannin, 189
Fanning, 22, 40, 41, 49, 98, 305, 398
Farish, 159, 380
Farley, 378
Farmsworth, 263
Farnham, 104
Farnsworth, 69, 96, 108
Farquhar, 136, 280, 283
Farrar, 148, 161, 165, 301
Farre, 77
Farrel, 222, 351
Farrell, 239
Farrington, 43
Farrow, 384
Farthing's Fortune, 36, 38
Farthing's Fortune & Additon, 38
Fassett, 41
Faulkner, 345
Faunce, 186
Fauntleroy, 62
Favier, 148
Fawcett, 189
Faxon, 75
Fay, 259
Fearing, 157
Fearson, 205
Featherstonhaugh, 300, 333
Feeks, 305
Fehrman, 78
Feile, 392
Fellow, 184
Fellows, 40

Felt, 20, 84
Felton, 239
Fenasye, 98
Fendall, 60, 70, 363
Fenderich, 229, 348
Fenderick, 230
Fenn, 62
Fenwick, 36, 179, 372, 381, 402
Feole, 396
Ferguson, 7, 9, 34, 65, 66, 85, 93, 107, 114, 152, 165, 188, 207, 254, 298, 304, 362, 367, 368
Fergusson, 107
Fernandes, 39
Fernanez, 264
Ferney Hills, 36
Ferral, 212, 375, 401
Ferrall, 104, 114, 290, 375
Ferriole, 158
Ferris, 30, 158
Fessenden, 108
Feuchtwanger, 22
Ficklin, 220
Field, 222, 243, 288, 305, 315, 340, 361, 364, 366, 388, 395
Fields, 351, 384
Filbert, 353
Filebrown, 135
Filesola, 70
Fill, 316
Fillebrown, 69, 94, 100, 104
Fillman, 103
Fillmore, 69
Finch, 191, 238
Findlay, 3, 54, 197
Findley, 54, 354
Fining, 305
Finley, 70, 353
Finn, 18, 20
First Vacancy, 36
Fischer, 129
Fish, 17, 59, 233, 272, 315, 323
Fisher, 42, 46, 61, 144, 222, 230, 271, 307
Fishers, 125

Fisk, 2, 72, 73, 104, 108
Fitch, 102, 305, 308
Fitzgerald, 16, 92, 148, 149, 150, 157, 176, 399
Fitzhugh, 17, 40, 89, 208, 252, 327
Fitzpatrick, 54, 95, 148, 377
Flack, 33
Flagg, 58, 112
Flanjac, 396
Flaujac, 133, 392
Fleet, 306
Fleischmann, 67, 188
Flemin, 304
Fleming, 75, 170, 223, 225, 305
Flemming, 81
Fletcher, 78, 94, 148, 172, 230, 275, 287, 356, 364
Flewellen, 192
Flint, 157, 196
Floeher, 47
Flomerfeldt, 330
Flomerfelt, 330
Flood, 90, 222
Flood's Qrtr, 37
Flower of the Forest, 35
FLoyd, 279
Folck, 288
Foley, 74, 233
Follansbee, 73, 218
Follen, 18, 20, 21, 25
Folsom, 244, 355
Fonda, 49
Foochee, 170, 225
Fooches, 74
Foote, 154, 196, 307, 334, 335, 397
Forbes, 42, 67, 69, 70, 92, 95, 135, 159, 177, 209, 308
Force, 80, 127, 180, 250, 331
Ford, 36, 47, 75, 110, 126, 222, 358, 388
Ford's Security, 37
Fordham, 19
Fordyce, 354
Foreman, 297
Forest, 367

Forest Land, 38
Forest of PG, 271
Forest Queen, 300
Forestier, 337
Formby, 39
Fornance, 242, 321
Forney, 46
Forrest, 3, 7, 80, 129, 132, 147, 179, 201, 281, 294, 314, 316, 320, 331, 402
Forrester, 110
Forry, 50, 79, 356
Forsyth, 5, 6, 140, 398
Fort Augustine, 195
Fort Brooke, 341
Fort Columbus, 178
Fort Erie, 262
Fort George, 273
Fort Gibson, 20, 313
Fort Gratiot, 258
Fort Harrison, 234
Fort Howard, 171
Fort Jesup, 20
Fort King, 145, 199, 341, 347
Fort Leavenworth, 385
Fort Meigs, 34, 86, 203, 234, 235, 237
Fort Mellon, 143, 195, 319
Fort Micanopy, 177, 244
Fort Searle, 182
Fort Smith, 10, 250
Fort Stanwix, 249
Fort Tarver, 286
Fort Towson, 3, 163
Fort Walker, 319
Fort Washington, 86, 143, 235
Fort Washington Point, 143
Fort Wayne, 6, 14, 101, 332
Fort Winebago, 171
Fort Winnebago, 171, 371
Fortress Monroe, 103
Fossett, 148, 172, 316
Foster, 6, 20, 86, 168, 192, 227, 231, 234, 385
Fouchee, 204
Foulke, 146

Foulkes, 218
Four Square, 36
Fowke, 141
Fowle, 228
Fowler, 18, 20, 74, 80, 234, 281, 285, 318, 379
Fox, 49, 127, 206, 213, 233, 242, 250, 322
Fox Indians, 64, 87, 133, 174
Foy, 26, 28, 53, 104, 133, 148, 149, 150
Foyles, 185
Fraler, 280
Frame, 320, 379
France, 24, 121, 127, 148, 149, 150, 151, 233, 292, 302, 346, 365, 373
Francher, 74, 170, 188, 225, 232
Francis, 55, 85, 328, 336, 377
Franck, 394
Francois, 127
Frank, 365
Franklin, 8, 60, 126, 169, 307, 318, 359, 372
Franks, 171, 280
Franquinet, 228, 340
Fraser, 163, 298, 356
Frauds, 334
Frayley, 67
Frazer, 93
Frazier, 69, 75, 119, 140, 170, 216, 225, 270, 316, 329
Fream, 304, 305
Frederic, 398
Frederick, 86, 235, 305
Freeland, 93, 270
Freeman, 6, 14, 74, 75, 78, 107, 114, 135, 168, 288, 363
Freeman's Lodge, 39
Freemen, 130
Frelinghuysen, 4
Fremain, 305
Fremiot, 285
French, 74, 106, 135, 155, 170, 171, 203, 217, 224, 326, 358, 387
French King, 323

Frere, 148
Frevail, 25
Frey, 310
Freylinghuysen, 165
Friend, 139, 184, 261
Friend's Discovery with add, 35
Friendship Enlarged, 89
frig *Alliance*, 116
frig *Belle Poule*, 398
frig *Brandywine*, 66
frig *Charon*, 323
frig *Constitution*, 52, 81, 201
frig *Macedonian*, 349
frig *New York*, 334
frig *U S*, 82
Froment, 308
Frost, 128, 354
Fry, 73, 167, 384, 390, 391
Frye, 177, 281
Fugitt, 31
Fulkes, 391
Fuller, 86, 88, 116, 148, 179, 234, 271, 284, 307, 332, 371
Fullwood, 356
Fulmer, 180, 187, 265, 271, 367, 369
Fulton, 22, 51, 61, 79, 98, 138, 141, 160, 183, 187, 194, 199, 221, 328, 385, 391, 395
Fulton Grove plantation, 82
Funnan, 305
Funsten, 291
Furniss, 157
Furtney, 31

G

Gaddes, 117
Gadsby, 104, 116, 150, 161, 193, 199, 299, 303, 314, 368
Gadsbys, 239
Gadsden, 113, 246
Gahogan, 306
Gaines, 79, 88, 223, 257, 296, 401
Gaiter, 321
Gaither, 45, 206, 337, 355, 356, 368

Galabran, 76, 355
Galabrun, 217
Galbraith, 318, 322, 386
Gale, 69, 238, 371
Gales, 25, 160
Gallagher, 9, 274
Gallaher, 302
Gallaudet, 283, 324
Gallitzin, 166
Galloway, 86, 235
Gallup, 118
Galt, 58, 290
Galvani, 337
Galvin, 374
Galway, 62
Gamage, 136
Gamble, 192, 216
Games, 80
Gammen, 92
Gand, 218
Gannett, 249
Gannt, 230
Gansevoort, 249
Gantt, 372, 380, 381
Gantz, 307, 308
Garbutt, 262
Garcia, 95
Garde, 98
Gardener, 285
Gardiner, 39, 99, 107, 114, 137, 186, 206, 242, 243, 304, 332, 363, 368
Gardner, 68, 230, 246, 247, 266, 276, 306
Gardner's Chance, 37
Garland, 5, 6, 73, 76, 123, 179, 267, 349, 374, 380, 387, 390
Garner, 1, 213, 371
Garner's Lot, 38
Garnett, 265, 271, 280
Garniss, 307
Garrabranta, 165
Garrabrantz, 152
Garrau, 281
Garrick, 124
Garrow, 1, 390

Garside, 395
Garth, 380
Garvean, 17
Gass, 318
Gassaway, 15, 76
Gaston, 374, 391
Gatchell, 119, 316, 329, 376
Gates, 116, 141, 286, 339
Gatewood, 98, 172
Gattrell, 40, 72
Gautier, 381
Gavean, 17
Gavelle, 78
Gavin, 61
Gavit, 272
Gay, 171, 393
Gaynard's Lot, 36
Gedney, 19, 29, 82
Gee, 19, 43, 174
Geer, 103
Gehan, 395
Gehon, 65
Gelston, 281, 400
Gemmil, 354
Generes, 313
Genther, 74, 167, 170, 224
Gentry, 133, 347
Geo III, 326
George, 253
Gephart, 287, 294
Gerard, 23
Germain, 137, 315
German, 182
Gerry, 322
Gessler, 218
Getling, 68
Gettings, 255
Getty, 218, 243
Gettys, 323
Geyer, 224
Ghiselin, 367, 372
Gibbons, 363, 399
Gibbs, 13, 112, 158, 195, 196, 364, 400
Giberson, 18, 72

Gibney, 121
Gibson, 13, 71, 177, 302, 307, 331, 350, 357, 398
Gideon, 7, 60, 126, 145, 256, 369
Gilbert, 107, 126, 223
Gilchrist, 67, 145
Giles, 92
Gill, 28, 47, 119, 304, 316, 329, 330, 376
Gillespie, 156, 307
Gillet, 162
Gilliam, 243
Gillilan, 222, 305
Gillingham, 353
Gillis, 210
Gilliss, 324
Gilman, 41, 112
Gilmer, 119, 191, 257, 357, 359
Gilmet's Hills, 388
Gilpin, 20, 23, 118, 154
Girault, 33
Girod, 100
Gist, 75
Gitt, 46
Gittings, 126
Given, 31, 67, 126, 185, 280, 312, 398
Giveny, 149
Givin, 52
Gladd, 110
Gladney, 64
Glasgow, 237
Glassell, 189
Glaze, 288
Glazier, 307
Gleanings, 215
Glebe, 138, 295
Glebe mansion, 23
Glemar, 163
Glen Asile, 313
Glenard, 78
Glenn, 277
Glentworth, 7, 329
Glover, 42, 75, 170, 194, 208, 225, 401
Gluck, 54

Gluick, 82
Glymont, 31
Gobrecht, 284
Gobright, 10
Godbold, 14
Goddard, 69, 149, 173, 180, 187, 210, 245, 280, 366, 367
Godfrey, 17, 148, 359
Godfroy, 181
Godon, 226
Godsell, 217
Goggin, 170, 361, 374
Goggins, 312
Goin, 104, 223
Going, 226, 232
Goings, 75, 170
Gold, 260
Golding, 71, 96, 134, 293
Goldsberry's Acre, 38
Goldsberry's Race, 36
Goldsbery, 75
Goldsborough, 68, 119, 173, 180, 187, 367, 394
Goldsmith, 40, 102, 124, 149, 181
Gooch, 233
Good, 253
Good Luck, 36, 39, 53, 97, 132, 271, 295, 321
Good Lucks, 39
Goodale, 382
Goodell, 143
Goodenow, 275
Goodhue, 42, 164
Gooding, 86, 149, 234
Goodman, 78
Goodno, 74
Good-penny-worth, 39
Goodrich, 126, 260, 377
Goodwin, 98, 245, 342, 352, 376
Goodyear, 137, 174, 260
Goolsby, 380
Gordon, 17, 20, 24, 135, 197, 227, 233, 250, 306, 307
Gordy, 280
Gore, 13
Gorman, 71, 151, 281
Gorsuch, 297, 387
Goseler, 2
Gosher, 156
Goslee, 351
Gossage, 27
Goszler, 245, 328, 329
Gotham, 360
Gottheil, 4
Gough's Level, 36
Gouin, 118
Gould, 11, 17, 118
Goulden, 373
Gourlay, 308
Gracy, 318
Graden, 37, 38
Graeff, 286
Graff, 330
Grafton, 100
Graham, 16, 46, 86, 90, 158, 197, 203, 235, 236, 304, 306, 380
Graham's lane, 339
Grainger, 392, 396
Grammer, 72, 173, 281, 351, 367, 402
Grandin, 243, 305, 355, 356
Granger, 176, 210
Grant, 134, 178, 395
Grantland, 192
Grass-Water, 126
Gratiot, 67, 80, 112, 281
Grattan, 207, 241
Graves, 37, 46, 288, 323
Gray, 58, 74, 107, 114, 126, 157, 202, 207, 223, 304, 319, 327, 350, 363, 368
Grayson, 316
Greaves, 28, 52, 105, 106
Gree, 110
Green, 7, 18, 19, 20, 69, 82, 85, 90, 99, 102, 107, 110, 114, 117, 138, 139, 151, 187, 189, 200, 219, 220, 246, 260, 279, 286, 306, 308, 315, 316, 351, 355, 356, 362, 377
Green Hills, 36, 37
Green Meadows, 38

Greene, 62, 116, 162, 189, 192, 197, 207, 219, 272, 377
Greenfield, 70, 142, 203, 289, 304
Greenhow, 211
Greening, 135
Greenleaf, 276, 281
Greenleaf's Point, 264, 301, 310
Greenough, 239, 296
Greenway, 29
Greenwell, 35, 37
Gregg, 3, 157
Gregory, 48, 73, 167, 178
Gremball, 108
Grennell, 88, 203
Grenville, 336
Grey, 226, 272
Grieg, 92
Grier, 318
Grieves, 119, 287, 316, 329
Griffin, 16, 88, 244, 333, 366
Griffith, 45, 207, 217, 262, 372
Griffiths, 54, 158
Grigg, 28
Griggs, 231
Grignon, 30
Grigsby, 394
Grimball, 73, 134, 233
Grimes, 346
Grimm, 83
Grindage, 329
Grinnell, 330
Griswold, 49, 158
Groesbeck, 271, 272
Groom, 57, 64
Groot, 377
Groshon, 306
Gross, 171, 288, 298, 306, 337
Grossard, 126
Grosvener, 219
Grosvenor, 145
Grotz, 253
Grove Hunt, 375
Grubb, 120, 187, 220
Grumne, 110
Grund, 152

Grundy, 175, 215, 378, 392, 402, 403
Grus, 338
Guest, 156, 281, 373
Guion, 253
Guire, 92
Gulion, 82
Gunnell, 58, 173, 245, 289
Gunnison, 24
Guns, 117
Gunston, 339
Gunton, 7, 26, 140, 179, 185, 187, 367, 394, 402
Gurley, 178
Guther, 146
Guthrie, 230, 370
Guttachlick, 15
Guttschlick, 149
Guyther, 57, 116, 218, 391
Gwathmey, 90
Gwynne, 496

H

Haas, 48, 54, 74, 82, 195, 240
Habersham, 192
Hacker, 128, 189
Hacket, 87
Hacket's Thicket, 38
Hackley, 54
Hadley, 70
Haff, 305
Hagan, 15, 272, 392
Hagar, 126
Hagden's Discovery, 39
Hagedorn, 123
Hager, 267
Hagie, 222
Hagner, 10, 243
Hagodon, 308
Haile, 32
Haislip, 363
Hakins, 238
Haldiman, 317
Hale, 32, 42, 74, 190, 219
Haley, 222

Haliday, 107, 173, 366
Hall, 1, 11, 19, 43, 44, 58, 60, 75, 85, 88, 111, 145, 149, 157, 165, 179, 181, 214, 215, 223, 252, 281, 301, 306, 318, 321, 342, 365, 371, 376, 377, 387
Hallard, 17
Halleck, 382
Haller, 6, 287
Halliday, 126
Halloway, 58
Hallowell, 60, 277, 310
Halsey, 74
Halsted, 165, 270
Haly, 130
Halyburton, 357
Hamblin, 95, 223
Hamborlin, 258
Hamburgh, 95
Hamill, 88
Hamilton, 31, 33, 35, 51, 54, 57, 58, 62, 75, 97, 107, 110, 114, 133, 136, 167, 192, 243, 267, 270, 277, 280, 281, 323, 362, 363, 371, 387
Hamlin, 69, 91, 275
Hammers, 351
Hammersly, 363
Hammet, 37
Hammett, 35, 195
Hammold, 6
Hammond, 115, 127, 321, 322
Hampstead, 38
Hampton, 51, 115, 124, 152, 339
Hanchett, 24
Hancock, 7, 19, 59, 63, 117, 133, 149, 395
Hand, 262, 382, 395
Handley, 104
Handy, 65, 297, 343, 357, 364, 390, 396
Hank, 9, 99
Hanks, 34, 188
Hanly, 57, 64, 173, 180, 187, 334, 367, 394
Hanna, 227

Hannegan, 246
Hannon, 189
Hanover, 36, 38
Hansberger, 99
Hansell, 28, 88
Hanson, 6, 26, 99, 114, 128, 143, 195, 300, 319, 352
Haraden, 16
Harbaugh, 28, 60, 126, 147, 151, 152, 210, 211, 274, 280, 366, 368, 371, 374, 383
Harcourt, 307
Hard, 88
Hard Bargain, 36
Hard Fortune, 37
Hardee, 5
Hardeman, 192
Harden, 20, 316, 329
Hardenbergh, 244, 400
Hardening, 22
Hard-fortune, 37
Hardin, 121, 244
Harding, 20, 400
Hardship's Addition, 37
Hardtimes, 38
Hardy, 298
Hare, 126, 292
Hargis, 69
Harker, 179
Harkness, 126, 173, 180, 187, 245, 367
Harkney, 163
Harlan, 54, 288
Harman, 116, 157
Harmon, 44
Harm-watch-harm-ketch, 38
Harnden, 20
Harney, 199, 319
Harper, 235, 353
Harper's Ferry, 256, 290
Harrell, 230
Harrington, 10, 75, 149, 270
Harris, 68, 85, 101, 102, 114, 133, 139, 164, 238, 260, 265, 331, 335, 357, 362, 374, 384, 388, 397, 398

Harrison, 1, 11, 16, 34, 39, 40, 60, 67, 69, 71, 73, 79, 86, 87, 93, 98, 99, 111, 114, 133, 142, 152, 168, 175, 182, 191, 196, 203, 214, 221, 229, 231, 234, 235, 238, 242, 246, 253, 258, 262, 263, 266, 267, 273, 275, 284, 287, 293, 301, 331, 333, 351, 353, 354, 366, 371, 377, 378, 381, 386, 389, 403
Harrock, 221
Harrold, 307
Harrow, 1
Harry, 10
Hart, 32, 208, 233, 250, 272, 277, 288, 310
Hartman, 74, 170, 188, 225, 233
Hartshorne, 165
Hartstene, 105
Hartwell, 385
Harvey, 74, 78, 112, 151, 155, 157, 333, 372, 375
Harwood, 119, 257, 316, 329, 371, 372
Hasbro, 135
Hasbrouck, 400
Hascall, 208
Hasey, 75
Haskel, 368
Haskell, 127, 152
Haskin, 291
Haskins, 110, 133, 395
Hason, 143
Hass, 239
Hassler, 101, 125
Hastings, 88, 105, 120, 345
Hatch, 14, 112, 191, 238, 262, 317
Hatfield, 43, 307
Hathaway, 69
Hathway, 217
Hatlett, 127
Hatton, 22
Haughton, 277, 351
Haughwout, 52
Haull, 122
Hausten, 122

Havener, 126
Havenner, 126, 378
Havens, 330
Haviland, 24, 75, 191
Haw, 395
Hawes, 250, 346, 351
Hawkes, 40
Hawkins, 41, 44, 70, 86, 96, 107, 114, 139, 154, 172, 213, 222, 234, 261, 319, 337, 363
Hawks, 186
Hawkshaw, 333
Hawley, 29, 96, 98, 130, 146, 152, 185, 230, 265, 271, 293, 336, 344, 368
Hay, 78, 85, 300, 320
Hayden, 36, 38, 73, 106, 167, 170
Hayes, 46, 99, 317
Hayfield, 154
Hayman, 7, 60, 179, 183, 299, 328, 402
Haymond's Addition, 320
Hayne, 57, 110, 121, 124, 128
Hays, 75, 139, 190, 243, 260, 306, 387
Haysham, 47
Hayward, 221, 266
Haywood, 108, 165, 237, 301
Hazard, 42, 307
Hazel, 246, 278
Hazell, 149, 150
Hazen, 115
Hazle, 281, 338
Hazlett, 351, 365
Head, 99, 107, 133, 296
Headrick, 225
Healy, 207, 287
Heard, 381
Heard's Friendship, 37
Heath, 133, 181
Heaton, 69
Hebb, 22, 47, 101, 128, 268, 314, 367, 369, 374
Hebert, 243
Hebron, 219
Hedge, 61

Hedges, 69, 94, 100, 134, 395
Hedric, 74
Hedrick, 170, 190
Heisler, 274
Helgerad, 372
Hellen, 35, 106, 126, 373
Hellenback, 354
Heller, 217
Helon, 296
Hemmingway, 157
Hemphill, 68
Hempstead, 18
Hemsted, 21
Henckley, 22
Hendal, 277
Henderer, 271
Henderson, 46, 69, 112, 137, 246, 277, 302, 304, 306, 312, 318, 324, 346
Hendley, 14
Hendly, 340
Hendricks, 332
Hendrie, 353
Henry, 12, 16, 18, 20, 21, 28, 208, 252, 271, 322, 384
Henry & Elizabeth, 45
Henry & Elizabeth Enlarged, 45
Henshaw, 29, 60, 178, 275, 369
Hepburn, 126, 150, 157, 249, 324, 340
Herald, 118
Herbele, 121
Herbert, 387
Hercus, 383
Hercuss, 150
Heriot, 227
Herkimer, 104
Hernandez, 28, 69, 195, 226
Herndon, 110
Herold, 101
Heron, 212
Herring, 118, 170
Herrington, 366
Herrity, 281
Herron, 97, 103, 141, 213, 317
Herts, 386
Herttell, 304

Herz, 71
Hess, 149, 159, 207, 354, 365, 368
Heth, 156, 216
Hetzel, 5, 251
Hewins, 108, 219
Hewitt, 162, 230, 365, 371
Heydecker, 358
Heyser, 33
Hibbard, 262
Hick, 46
Hickey, 24, 132
Hickman, 75, 333
Hickok, 385
Hickory Hills, 38
Hickory Thicket, 38
Hicks, 306, 342, 390
Hidden, 144
Higbee, 28, 123, 361
Higginbotham, 125
Higgins, 177, 243
High Point Fisheries, 339
Hilbus, 31, 335
Hildebrand, 217
Hilden, 76
Hildreth, 11
Hill, 31, 49, 57, 87, 122, 127, 137, 143, 152, 178, 211, 218, 229, 306, 318, 325, 330, 343, 352, 355, 356, 392
Hill Farm, 188
Hilleary, 350
Hillen, 330
Hilliard, 16, 18, 20, 21, 165
Hills, 102, 151
Hilton, 65, 213, 368
Himea, 88
Hinans, 395
Hinchman, 304
Hinckley, 215
Hinde, 61
Hindman, 198, 287, 357
Hinds, 286
Hines, 10
Hinkle, 288
Hinkley, 272, 277

432

Hinly, 145
Hinman, 271
Hinton, 194
Hitchcock, 154, 159, 306, 308
Hite, 114
Hitz, 279, 299
Hoard, 83, 391
Hoban, 104, 149, 151, 174, 341, 355, 365
Hobart, 21
Hobbie, 230
Hobbs, 111, 340
Hoblitzell, 287
Hobson, 155, 374, 398
Hodgden, 264
Hodge, 245
Hodges, 13, 66, 156, 371, 381
Hodgkin, 193, 353, 360
Hodgson, 353, 364, 388
Hoes, 257
Hoff, 42, 50, 69, 195
Hoffman, 157, 187, 239, 271, 297, 307, 315
Hog Island, 38
Hogan, 79, 205, 212, 230, 279, 289
Hogge, 157
Hogmire, 132, 162, 205, 335
Hoisey, 157
Hola-toochee, 347
Holbrook, 360, 384
Holden, 244
Holder, 69
Holdsworth, 374
Holford, 157
Holiday, 126
Holl, 304
Holladay, 357
Holland, 157, 350, 369
Holledge, 128
Holleman, 375
Hollerran, 191
Holliday, 248, 280
Hollidge, 207, 278, 368
Hollinger, 81, 94
Hollingswroth, 350

Hollis, 363
Holly, 306
Holman, 185
Holmead, 55, 228, 229, 281
Holmer, 333
Holmes, 27, 40, 63, 71, 141, 144, 157, 318
Holt, 289
Holtzman, 214, 268
Homans, 97, 100, 149, 150, 204, 232, 245, 366
Homer, 78
Homes, 218
Homiller, 117
Hommel, 75
Hommill, 170
Honay, 306
Honey Creek, 35
Honeycutt, 276
Honeywell, 221
Hood, 96, 119, 125, 147, 237, 244
Hooe, 185, 190, 203, 230, 282, 357, 372
Hook, 287, 322
Hooker, 258, 277, 300
Hoole, 157
Hooper, 110, 202, 225, 243, 244, 335
Hoover, 16, 83, 126, 144, 147, 148, 150, 151, 300, 364
Hope, 39, 157, 306, 391
Hopewell, 37, 38
Hopewell's, 37
Hopewell's Dance, 35
Hopewell's Delight, 35
Hopkins, 155, 306, 308, 320, 342
Hopp, 354
Hopper, 30, 137
Hopton Park, 36, 38
Horde, 364
Horn, 221
Hornbeck, 75
Hornby, 92
Horner, 88, 357, 377
Horrindon, 292
Horse-Shoe, 386

Horsey, 118, 219
Horton, 354
Hose, 40
Hosper, 75
Hotchkiss, 128, 189
Houck, 222, 283
Hough, 302, 308, 334, 371
Houghton, 230, 238, 307
House, 307, 399
Houseman, 50, 95, 269, 389
Housman, 137
Houston, 180, 187, 222, 367, 371, 383
How, 63
Howard, 9, 20, 37, 41, 42, 81, 102, 122, 125, 126, 127, 135, 158, 187, 194, 210, 223, 227, 233, 245, 270, 284, 292, 295, 306, 324, 325, 350, 354, 359, 367, 371
Howard Grove, 287
Howe, 12, 69, 94, 100, 134, 269, 382, 384, 389
Howel, 41
Howell, 18, 21, 78, 279, 286, 293
Howes, 22
Howison, 31, 93, 148, 160, 175, 281
Howland, 102
Howle, 151, 230
Howze, 128
Hoxie, 262
Hoyt, 2, 20, 304, 329
Hubband, 87
Hubbard, 171, 275, 398, 399, 403
Hudson, 288
Huffman, 278
Huger, 220, 353
Hugget, 304
Huggins, 61
Hughes, 4, 9, 63, 72, 75, 104, 107, 114, 115, 157, 165, 170, 186, 194, 211, 287, 306, 317, 356, 362
Hughlett, 208, 381
Hugo, 170, 225
Huie, 292
Hukill, 235
Hulcomb, 18

Hulcumb, 21
Hull, 66, 88, 105, 122, 145, 203, 216, 226, 234, 307
Humber, 244, 328
Humes, 311
Humphrey, 377
Humphreys, 15, 280, 350, 378, 392
Humphries, 156, 219
Hunnicutt, 191
Hunt, 1, 3, 5, 41, 42, 156, 209, 219, 221, 270, 278, 386
Hunter, 48, 69, 75, 166, 168, 170, 185, 188, 192, 211, 225, 231, 259, 304, 306, 309, 330, 363, 379
Huntington, 318, 377
Hunton, 162
Huntt, 211
Hurd, 262
Hurlbert, 375
Hurlburt, 16
Hurlbut, 105
Hurst, 78
Huslic, 400
Hussey, 209
Huston, 158, 295, 313
Hutcherson, 263
Hutchins, 280
Hutchinson, 42, 43, 69, 94, 100, 233
Hutchmion, 74
Hutton, 28, 306
Huxford, 377
Huyler, 90
Hyat, 148
Hyatt, 60, 98, 127, 149, 151, 245
Hyde, 146, 149, 305, 310

I

Iddings, 68
Iddins, 259
Iglehart, 372, 376
Iken, 29
Iliff, 389
Ilsley, 285
Imaum of Muscat, 241

Inch, 148, 150
Industry, 38
Ingalls, 222
Ingelby, 78
Ingersoll, 25, 58, 321, 364, 390
Ingle, 147, 173, 180, 217, 276, 324, 361, 367, 368
Ingles, 251
Ingolls, 14
Ingraham, 102, 285, 308
Ingsbeth, 38, 39
Inman, 15
Innes, 305, 370
Inness, 306
Iowa Indians, 206
Iowa lands, 261
Iredell, 160
Ireland, 63
Ironsides, 119, 120
Irvin, 322
Irvine, 51, 276
Irving, 95, 306
Irwin, 60, 192, 220, 243, 250, 288, 315, 322, 344
Isaacks, 308
Isaacs, 60, 162, 306
Ishamel's Right, 35
Isherwood, 210
Ishmael's Right, 35
Island, 314
Israel, 99
Ives, 78
Izard, 230, 267

J

Jack, 235, 322
Jackson, 3, 4, 27, 50, 66, 79, 83, 87, 88, 96, 98, 104, 105, 116, 129, 133, 156, 157, 160, 165, 168, 175, 182, 183, 212, 220, 235, 236, 242, 267, 284, 286, 306, 318, 321, 342, 344, 391
Jacob, 317
Jacobs, 16, 87, 108, 220, 271
Jacoby, 353
Jacocks, 69, 232
Jacox, 1
Jacquelin, 11, 69, 100
Jacquellin, 94
James, 34, 89, 97, 106, 121, 137, 146, 147, 148, 149, 201, 238, 247, 273, 321, 366, 377
Jameson, 107, 380
Jameston, 363
Jamieson, 220
Jamison, 56, 225, 277, 392
Janes, 46
Janney, 216
Jarboe, 37, 150, 160
Jarors, 221
Jarvis, 21, 50, 53, 118, 330
Jas' Additon, 37
Jasper, 364
Jaubert, 118
Jay, 215
Jefferd, 387
Jeffers, 297, 310, 330
Jefferson, 34, 71, 86, 109, 160, 168, 214, 236
Jeffey, 11
Jeffrey, 197
Jeffries, 191, 277, 334
Jellison, 69, 100
Jencks, 102
Jenifer, 107, 114, 160, 325, 362
Jenkins, 11, 81, 84, 107, 114, 122, 230, 247, 262, 306, 363
Jenkinson, 75
Jenks, 133
Jennings, 6, 134, 297, 331
Jennison, 27, 71
Jenny, 40
Jernakin, 286
Jernegan, 224
Jesuits, 360
Jesup, 223, 230
Jeter, 396
Jewell, 60, 189, 329, 352
Jewett, 58

John's Dread, 35
John's Ramble, 35
Johns, 117, 214, 244, 263, 277, 279, 294, 355
Johnson, 16, 18, 21, 23, 28, 37, 43, 47, 51, 53, 55, 63, 65, 67, 68, 70, 75, 80, 82, 88, 89, 90, 96, 97, 103, 104, 107, 117, 124, 128, 134, 136, 146, 149, 157, 160, 166, 175, 179, 180, 187, 188, 206, 212, 221, 222, 229, 235, 237, 239, 240, 243, 246, 247, 248, 249, 261, 273, 274, 282, 285, 287, 297, 304, 310, 315, 318, 331, 338, 344, 353, 359, 363, 367, 368, 369, 376, 379, 384, 390, 391, 396, 399
Johnston, 63, 74, 89, 105, 122, 167, 170, 181, 212, 225, 233, 296, 303, 372, 383
Johson, 190
Jolly, 49, 58
Joncherez, 379
Jones, 5, 6, 7, 19, 26, 41, 45, 49, 51, 58, 60, 64, 67, 69, 70, 74, 77, 88, 108, 117, 118, 119, 122, 124, 126, 129, 130, 134, 138, 147, 148, 151, 167, 168, 171, 178, 199, 200, 205, 209, 217, 220, 230, 233, 243, 244, 245, 250, 251, 254, 266, 267, 271, 277, 278, 281, 289, 291, 294, 304, 306, 308, 316, 329, 330, 344, 345, 350, 357, 365, 372, 379, 380, 382, 392, 396, 400
Jopling, 374
Jordan, 75, 104, 111, 115, 124, 228, 243, 347
Joshua's Addition, 39
Joshua's Plains, 36
Joy, 37, 110, 377
Joyce, 104, 149
Judge, 71, 223
Judson, 19, 25, 240
Junius, 336
Junkins, 215, 235
Justice, 75, 202, 225
Justin, 197

K

Kalorama, 53
Kammiski, 125
Kane, 101, 227, 270, 311
Kappel, 212
Karnes, 313
Karney, 376
Karrick, 209
Karsner, 113
Kauffman, 88
Kavanaugh, 281
Kaweeksley, 157
Kay, 347
Kealhofer, 248
Kealy, 213
Kean, 114
Keane, 281
Kearney, 82, 123, 272
Kearsley, 33
Keating, 354
Keaton, 365
Kedgely, 245
Keech, 39, 206, 296
Keeche's Folly, 39
Keefe, 238
Keeler, 75, 170, 224, 306
Keenan, 207, 309
Keene, 28
Keener, 399
Keeton, 159, 162, 251
Keiler, 339
Keim, 25, 160, 321
Keirle, 18, 20, 21
Keith, 134, 164, 206, 349, 397
Keithley, 150
Kelder, 360
Keliber, 206
Kellar, 46
Keller, 19, 77, 123, 134, 221, 270, 280, 385, 395, 401
Kellerman, 213
Kelley, 69, 76, 104, 128, 262
Kellinger, 306
Kellogg, 171, 218, 377

Kelly, 57, 125, 306, 312, 325
Kelsey, 43
Kelso, 82
Kemble, 53
Kemp, 281
Kemplin, 47, 222
Kemstry, 359
Kendall, 91, 120, 143, 151, 159, 258, 260
Kendely, 194
Kendig, 87
Kendirck, 240
Kendrick, 155, 219, 299, 326, 338, 339
Kengla, 220
Kennard, 78
Kennedy, 18, 24, 33, 55, 65, 90, 96, 98, 119, 132, 138, 157, 187, 244, 247, 254, 316, 329, 336, 376, 386
Kenney, 75
Kennock, 39
Kennon, 81, 95, 222, 282
Kenny, 248
Kensett, 149
Kensy, 398
Kent, 112, 272, 275, 307, 371, 372
Kenton, 169
Ker, 78, 243
Kern, 63
Kerney, 17
Kerr, 15, 67, 153, 178, 187, 199, 208, 281, 309, 318, 358, 376, 403
Kervand, 147, 148, 150, 151, 374
Kesciusko, 87
Kessler, 116
Ketchum, 43, 262
Kettle, 271
Kevser, 306
Key, 35, 79, 81, 109, 117, 130, 139, 160, 179, 345, 381
Keyworth, 208, 281, 334
Kibbe, 61
Kibbey, 51
Kibby, 298
Kidney, 308

Kidwell, 329
Kilbourn, 88, 222
Kilgour, 39, 397
Kilgour's Addition, 39
Kilhour, 40
Killburn, 35
Kille, 76, 270
Killenger, 44
Killmon, 286
Kilman, 368
Kimball, 20, 335
Kimmell, 397
Kimmey, 13
Kincaid, 301
Kinchey, 91
Kinchy, 9, 93, 148, 150, 177, 187
Kinderhook, 259
King, 40, 41, 43, 59, 66, 69, 92, 103, 133, 148, 151, 160, 171, 192, 208, 212, 214, 228, 233, 250, 257, 269, 272, 274, 281, 288, 297, 310, 314, 343, 367, 377
King James, 362
King of Prussia, 228, 337, 357
King of Sardinia, 250
King Wm, 337
Kingsberry, 275
Kingsbury, 243
Kingsley, 44
Kinnard, 349
Kinney, 263, 392, 402
Kinsey, 344
Kinsman, 238
Kinzey, 60
Kirby, 19, 387
Kirby's Choice, 36
Kirk, 307
Kirkby, 156
Kirkland, 137, 141, 377
Kirkpatrick, 247
Kirkwood, 31, 126, 173, 180, 187, 205, 210, 218, 245, 263, 349, 367
Kissuck, 218
Kitman, 206
Kittle, 49

Kleiber, 317, 347, 367, 368
Klimkiewicz, 160
Klimkiewiez, 109
Kline, 332
Knapp, 88, 238, 292, 297
Kneass, 284
Kneller, 126
Knephly, 74
Knickerbacker, 237
Knight, 40, 48, 75, 92, 169, 170, 225, 335, 365
Knipe, 75, 170, 225
Knop, 388
Knorr, 205
Knott, 75, 170, 178, 205, 213, 225
Knotting, 36
Knowles, 19, 123
Knox, 262, 296
Kohleast, 304
Kohler, 42
Koones, 265
Korn, 244
Kortwright, 85
Kosciusko, 28, 236
Koulke, 359
Kowalewski, 57
Krafft, 147, 148, 149, 151, 344
Kraitair, 160
Kraitisr, 22
Kraitsir, 296
Kramer, 307
Kramp, 252
Krebs, 119, 149, 316, 329
Krenan, 368
Kunklee, 52
Kurtz, 16, 246, 259, 329, 393
Kuykendall, 217

L

L'Enfant, 130
Labbe, 295
Laborde, 337
Labranche, 90
Lacon, 11, 69, 94, 100, 123, 134

Lacoste, 74, 167, 233
Lacy, 55, 165, 364
Ladd, 306, 307
Lafayette, 115, 116, 118, 224, 323
Lafon, 72
Lafontaine, 281
Laighton, 2, 395
Laing, 157
Laird, 297, 318
Lakin, 400
Lamar, 257, 277, 288, 313, 398
Lamb, 31, 145, 323
Lambell, 128, 146, 218, 242, 324
Lambert, 85, 108, 137, 169, 186, 231, 337
Lambright, 64, 280
Lambton, 272
Lamore, 75
Lancaster, 52, 56, 107, 114, 239, 241, 243, 362
Lancaster's Discovery, 38
Land, 328
Landing Neck, 38
Landis, 403
Landon, 94, 100, 216
Landrum, 265
Landry, 248
Landsdale, 268
Lane, 57, 126, 156, 250, 278, 321, 380
Laney, 99
Lang, 7, 126, 247, 304, 356
Langborne, 74
Langdon, 4, 69, 160, 333, 359, 395
Langlois, 17
Langton, 307
Langtree, 119, 123, 202, 263, 300
Langtry, 122, 133
Lanham, 53
Lanier, 286
Lankford, 401
Lanning, 165
Lansdale, 68, 268, 361
Lansdall, 132
Lansing, 5
Lantz, 24

Laores, 264
Lapice, 162
Laporte, 126
Lapsley, 68
Largee, 308
Largest gun, 143
Larkin, 227
Larned, 110, 265, 271, 313, 327, 367, 368, 387
Larrabee, 83
Larrenson, 292
Larwill, 229
Laskey, 149, 369
Lassel, 74, 167
Lassett, 205
Last Shift, 37, 38
Latchum, 65
Latham, 170, 183, 219, 233
Lathan, 78
Lathram, 74, 170, 225
Latimer, 204, 341
Latrobe, 35, 131
Laub, 129
Lauck, 329
Laughlin, 142, 161, 217
Laurence, 157, 217
Laurens, 323
Laurie, 4, 40, 184, 237, 268, 283, 321, 339
Laval, 69
Lavallette, 105, 142
Laventure, 9, 24, 65, 133, 152, 188, 393
Law, 24, 142, 184, 185, 192, 303
Lawler, 45
Lawrason, 11
Lawrence, 74, 142, 190, 262, 300, 307, 318, 322, 326, 330, 371
Lawrenson, 202, 208
Lawson, 363
Lawton, 41
Lazenby, 111, 321, 337
Le Grand, 212
Lea, 47
Leach, 21

Leachman, 218
Leaden, 267
Leak's Purchase, 36
Leakin, 292
Lear, 109
Learned, 58
Leary, 32
Leath, 294
Leatherbury, 280
Leavenworth, 356
Leavett, 333
Leblanc, 134
Leckie, 73, 167, 170
Lecompte, 90, 392, 396
Ledingham, 200, 334
Ledyard, 23, 90
Lee, 11, 18, 21, 42, 58, 60, 61, 81, 88, 92, 111, 118, 130, 143, 146, 148, 149, 151, 152, 178, 188, 242, 262, 306, 311, 337, 351, 376, 377
Leeds, 92, 93, 306
Leet, 322
Leete, 340
Lefebre, 85
Lefever, 67
Lefevre, 85
Lefferts, 49
Leftwich, 96, 361, 374
Leggett, 306
Legoux, 78
Leh Manor Head, 35
Leigh, 35, 227, 239, 264, 267
Leighton, 16, 146, 222, 384, 401
Leignher, 378
Leiper, 353
Leipezig, 78
Leitch, 92
Leman, 188
Lemist, 21
Lemmon, 119, 174
Lemon, 51, 221, 289, 400
Lendrum, 179, 193
Lennig, 78
Lenox, 85, 126, 245, 366
Lent, 306

Leonard, 237, 238, 304, 379
Lester, 69, 94, 100, 144, 219, 306, 395
Lestrange, 186
Letcher, 378
Letourno, 302
Levale, 42
Levan, 83
Levi, 157
Levy, 73, 108, 117, 133, 190, 232, 282
Lewellen, 291
Lewis, 20, 33, 47, 50, 93, 108, 154, 155, 163, 206, 217, 220, 247, 254, 267, 286, 287, 291, 306, 370, 393
Lexington, 339
Libby, 201, 328
Libernau, 306
Lieberman, 333, 348
Liefer, 208
Life-boats, 328
Lightfoot, 138
Lilly, 18, 106, 247, 248
Lina, 139
Lincoln, 32, 75, 100, 170, 202, 225, 345, 356
Lind, 318
Linden, 34
Lindenberger, 355
Lindsay, 74, 80, 316, 370
Lindsey, 225
Lindsley, 192, 261, 314
Lindsly, 367
Lineback, 308
Lines, 154
Linfield, 21
Lingham, 235
Linkins, 255
Linn, 99, 101, 261
Linstead, 37
Linthicum, 28, 60, 80, 84, 195, 259, 329, 331
Linton, 153, 159, 230
Lipscomb, 50, 226, 329
Littell, 81
Little, 2, 159, 206, 258, 287, 306, 366, 368, 374

Little Bolton Farm, 69
Littlefield, 263, 275
Littlejohn, 26, 377
Litton, 32
Livermore, 1
Livingston, 44, 73, 78, 92, 102, 164, 251, 262, 305, 306, 377
Llewellen, 39
Llewellen's, 38
Lloyd, 31, 60, 63, 107, 114, 147, 148, 149, 150, 151, 168, 186, 213, 261, 265, 271, 306, 324, 351, 362, 366, 369
Load, 61
Lobdell, 69, 94, 100, 144, 232
Lock's Meadows, 39
Locke, 27, 197
Lockerman, 187
Lockhart, 125
Lockwood, 112, 391
Locust Thicket, 38
Loemis, 145
Logan, 115, 235, 353, 357
Logan's Plains, 37, 38
Lomas, 160
Lomax, 74, 167, 216
Londry, 248
Long, 29, 68, 79, 127, 146, 207, 263, 275, 279, 341
Long Looked-for-come-at-last, 39
Long Meadows, 59
Long Neck, 37, 38
Longacre, 281
Longevity, 79
Longley, 203
Longson, 51
Longworth, 62, 197
Lookar, 197
Looker, 381
Loomis, 68, 355, 393
Looney, 258, 330
Lopez, 264, 386
Loranger, 237
Lord, 58, 77, 133, 238
Loring, 93

Loskey, 81
Lotspeich, 251
Louis Phillippe, 338
Louis XVI, 169, 297
Lounsberry, 304
Lourie, 318
Loutrel, 307
Love, 39, 223
Love's Adventure, 39
Loved, 230
Lovejoy, 21
Lovell, 230, 248, 315
Loveridge, 377
Low, 20, 21, 69, 200, 243
Lowdermilk, 287
Lowe, 88, 177, 206, 227, 244, 248, 255, 303, 368
Lowell, 24, 90
Lowndes, 78, 103, 182, 301, 314, 357, 376
Lowry, 311, 390
Lowther, 78
Loxman, 274
Loy, 49
Loyal Hanna, 68
Loyd, 314
Lucas, 59, 68, 75, 103, 105, 133, 170, 185, 225, 233, 250, 332
Luckett, 215, 239, 248, 302
Ludeke, 183
Ludgate, 39
Ludlow, 264, 307
Lufborough, 117, 143
Lugenbeel, 243, 328, 355
Lumsden, 99
Lundt, 110
Lundy, 148, 150
Lupton, 305, 306
Lurman, 119, 316, 329
Lusher, 248
Lusser, 59, 392, 396
Lutz, 80, 328, 331
Lybrook, 74, 170, 225
Lyddane, 285
Lyell, 306

Lyles, 47, 371
Lyman, 4, 47
Lynch, 29, 104, 136, 149, 150, 235, 281, 349, 372
Lyne, 182
Lynn, 117, 287
Lyon, 73, 106, 128, 151, 171, 233, 306, 384
Lyons, 11, 89, 94, 267, 271, 280, 298, 329
Lytle, 5, 6, 19

M

M'Blair, 176
M'Cauley, 288
M'Caw, 221
M'Cord, 186
M'Culley, 288
M'Donald, 294
M'Intyre, 262
M'Kenzie, 57
M'Naughton, 272
M'Neill, 351
M'Queen, 370
M'Whorter, 162
Ma_in, 244
Mabin, 126
Mabury, 33
Macauley, 178
Macdonald, 325
MacDonald, 231
MacDonell, 286
Macdonnell, 319
Macgill, 149
MacGill, 293
Machen, 228
Machn, 114
Mack, 219
Mackall, 30, 57, 326
Mackay, 88, 133, 223
Mackenheimer, 349
Mackenzie, 103, 128, 151, 152, 164
Mackey, 65
Mackintosh, 13, 131

Maclay, 243, 356
Macleod, 121
MacLeod, 331
Macomb, 6, 70, 123, 193, 230, 243, 244, 264
Macomber, 61
Macon, 3, 219
Macrae, 6, 388
MacRae, 9
Mactier, 101
Macy, 127
Madame Adelaide, 338
Madden, 387
Maddox, 114, 180, 187, 212, 300, 367
Madison, 34, 86, 236, 244
Maeder, 61
Maffit, 154
Magar, 89
Magaw, 37
Magee, 17, 34, 150
Magill, 52, 133, 149
Magness, 307
Magnier, 87
Magnus, 157
Magoon, 75
Magraw, 41
Magruder, 80, 126, 138, 196, 252, 265, 271, 288, 294, 327, 328, 329, 331, 365, 367, 369
Maguire, 91, 104, 270, 288
Maher, 104, 150
Mahoney, 329
Maiden's Fair, 36
Maiden's Lot, 37
Maitland, 18
Malette, 396
Mallen, 225
Mallett, 219
Mallory, 75
Malone, 51
Manchester, 21, 31
Manliet, 222
Manly, 160, 201, 280
Mann, 187, 289
Manners, 137

Manning, 118, 306, 376
Manning's Purchase, 37
Manor, 39, 255
Manser, 98
Mansfield, 16, 112, 197
Maraden, 83
Marbury, 59, 74, 88, 167, 195, 232, 248, 318, 319, 329, 379
Marchand, 79, 322
Marcott, 298
Marcy, 199, 349
Marett, 300
Mark, 47
Mark's Venture, 38
Markins, 94
Markle, 235, 354
Markoe, 352
Marks, 351
Marlette, 392
Marlow, 161, 238
Marmicke, 358
Marquis of Camden, 338
Marrast, 230
Marriott, 179, 372
Marsaque, 64
Marsaqui, 2
Marsh, 16, 41, 127, 204, 306
Marshall, 27, 60, 113, 179, 180, 187, 245, 248, 251, 261, 265, 271, 275, 278, 288, 301, 306, 314, 331, 363, 367, 369
Marston, 306
Martin, 1, 11, 31, 34, 37, 46, 65, 68, 74, 85, 115, 124, 135, 175, 177, 233, 243, 245, 264, 288, 289, 303, 314, 324, 329, 341, 354, 365, 366, 367, 368
Martinez, 50
Maryman, 37, 206, 293, 303, 368
Maryman's Lot & Vowles' Purchase, 37
Masi, 200
Mason, 7, 18, 20, 48, 56, 58, 70, 75, 102, 117, 143, 171, 177, 179, 215,

234, 318, 331, 339, 341, 364, 388, 390
Massey, 34, 270
Massie, 47, 60
Masters, 14, 322
Matchett, 363
Mather, 167
Mathews, 11, 24, 30, 64, 363
Mathieu, 283
Matoaka, 383
Matsell, 306
Mattapony, 39
Matthew, 270
Matthews, 68, 89, 96, 107, 114, 146, 160, 178, 213, 253, 265, 271, 285, 304, 340, 363, 368, 378
Mattingly, 37, 39, 72, 97, 122, 264, 287, 301
Mattison, 21
Maulsby, 179
Mauro, 54
Maury, 63, 66, 152, 163, 173, 179, 237, 247, 265, 271, 324, 331, 369, 396, 402
Mawell, 270
Maxwell, 88, 193
May, 108, 126, 127, 141, 155, 229, 245, 276, 281, 283, 322, 367
Mayer, 111, 277
Mayes, 41, 386
Mayfield, 48, 154
Maynard, 326, 388
Mayo, 216, 230
Mayse, 83
Mazeen, 251
McAchran, 71
McAdam, 283
McAnsland, 122
McArthur, 86, 236
McBlair, 110, 155, 168
McCabe, 124, 202
McCaddin, 306
McCafferty, 306
McCaleb, 152
McCall, 279, 281

McCallion, 317
McCallum, 6, 69
McCants, 67
McCardle, 272, 318, 339, 371
McCarthy, 248, 308
McCarty, 137, 139, 142, 148, 150, 226, 260, 374
McCaskey, 377
McCauley, 11, 31, 76, 93, 148, 149, 150, 151, 206, 245, 368
McCaw, 51
McCeney, 396
McClain, 330
McClanahan, 69, 70, 226, 392
McClay, 315
McCleary, 288
McClellan, 119, 285, 316, 329, 368
McClelland, 80, 126, 152, 179, 245, 324
McClenahan, 99
McClennehan, 209
McClery, 148, 150
McClintock, 60, 141
McCloud, 1, 7, 122, 222
McCluney, 11
McClure, 51, 221, 354, 360
McColgan, 42
McCollum, 99
McComb, 182
McConachy, 312
McConaghy, 346
McConahy, 191
McConiche, 219
McConkey, 277
McConough, 317
McCool, 273
McCord, 385
McCormic, 19
McCormick, 76, 114, 126, 136, 221, 265, 271, 276, 369
McCorry, 63
McCown, 243
McCoy, 43
McCrabb, 5, 6, 111, 113
McCracken, 169

McCrady, 63
McCrea, 241
McCready, 306, 335
McCreary, 389
McCreedy, 158
McCreery, 11
McCrory, 124, 228
McCue, 64, 104
McCulloch, 170, 225
McCullogh, 152
McCulloh, 75, 322
McCullon, 129
McCullough, 209
McCutchon, 316
McCuthcen, 69
McDaniel, 100, 139, 222, 260, 374
McDermott, 148, 149, 150, 306
McDonald, 32, 50, 59, 100, 102, 128, 149, 180, 187, 276, 306, 314, 324, 351, 367, 393
McDonough, 154
McDowell, 3, 121, 165, 213, 271
McDowner, 261
McDuell, 281
McDuffie, 57, 349
McEldery, 27
McEllroy, 168
McElroy, 10
McEvers, 306
McFadden, 238
McFadon, 298
McFee, 318
McGarr, 280
McGheehan, 235
McGill, 245
McGinnis, 318
McGloin, 306
McGlue, 281
McGoffin, 3
McGrath, 306
McGraw, 19
McGregor, 375
McGuire, 16, 114, 189, 223, 359
McGunigle, 281
McGunnigle, 251, 355, 383

McIlheny, 310
McIlvain, 353
McIlvaine, 88, 353
McInnerny, 149
McIntire, 69, 98, 245
McIntosh, 26
McIntyre, 102, 302, 377
McJilton, 111
McKavett, 356
McKay, 52, 79
McKean, 72, 116, 126, 209, 224, 391
McKebbin, 384
McKeehan, 354
McKelden, 111, 126, 173, 245
McKenna, 22
McKennan, 354
McKenney, 60, 80, 247, 282, 299
McKennie, 48
McKenny, 137
McKenzie, 67, 397, 403
McKibbin, 306
McKiernan, 63
McKilten, 351
McKim, 119
McKinney, 164, 230
McKinsey, 122
McKinzie, 133
McKissack, 5
McKnaught, 223
McKnight, 219, 242, 301
McLain, 25, 208, 332, 351
McLane, 168, 379
McLaughlin, 44, 126, 269, 293, 306, 389
McLean, 14, 33, 40, 80, 141, 142, 221, 247, 290, 318
McLehany, 366
McLeod, 99, 126, 173, 204, 234, 240, 340, 392
McMahon, 71, 77, 161, 283, 307
McMaster, 41, 304
McMasters, 49
McMichael, 290
McMillan, 31, 306
McMilton, 83

McMullen, 122
McMullin, 219
McMuster, 83
McNair, 34, 188, 317
McName, 33
McNaughton, 31
McNeal, 147
McNeil, 73
McNeill, 32, 259
McNemar, 88
McNerhaney, 358
McNerhany, 281
McNider, 144
McNides, 105
McNier, 376
McNish, 178
McNutt, 243
McPhail, 243
McPherson, 7, 185, 268, 273, 279, 307, 308, 331, 400
McQueen, 58, 294
McQuintly, 133
McRae, 220
McRee, 5
McRoberts, 90, 189
McSherry, 10, 244, 248
McVean, 321
McVeigh, 291
McWilliams, 37, 60, 103, 172, 245, 289, 352, 368, 376
Mead, 21, 304
Meade, 55, 57, 75, 82, 93, 260, 293, 322, 358, 366, 391
Meadows, 37
Meany, 327
Mears, 217
Mechlin, 97, 113, 140, 152, 230
Medary, 272
Medtart, 145
Meehan, 326, 371
Meek, 386
Meeker, 264
Meggwater, 351
Mehaffey, 317
Melen, 170

Mellon, 74, 222
Melsin, 127
Melvill, 391
Memefee, 288
Menard, 15
Mephistophiles, 174
Mercer, 3, 11, 25, 238, 239, 271, 317, 346, 359, 371
Meriweather, 380
Meriwether, 192
Merriam, 219
Merrick, 183, 248, 346, 362
Merrill, 159, 243
Merritt, 130
Merriweather, 82
Merry, 20
Merryman, 251
Merton, 7, 181
Mervin, 141
Mesereau, 307
Mesick, 262
Mesonan, 337
Messereau, 117
Messerole, 304, 306
Messersmith, 60, 367
Messerve, 306
Metcalf, 16, 48, 244, 301
Meyer, 27
Michard, 259
Mickle, 173
Middleswarth, 68, 354
Middleton, 47, 57, 78, 95, 107, 116, 148, 149, 150, 151, 213, 223, 224, 232, 242, 281, 344, 363, 367
Miesegas, 17
Miffleton, 156
Mifflin, 353
Milan, 351
Milburn, 23, 141, 281
Miler, 216
Miles, 60, 107, 142, 248, 275, 309, 362, 363, 398
Mill, 35
Mill & Mill Seat, 35
Mill Land, 30

Mill Lot, 38
Mill Pond, 35
Mill Race, 35
Millar, 114
Millbank, 50
Miller, 19, 44, 58, 67, 74, 75, 78, 86, 90, 107, 123, 126, 127, 136, 147, 149, 155, 160, 170, 192, 213, 220, 225, 234, 235, 281, 297, 301, 306, 317, 330, 338, 349, 350, 358, 363, 371, 383, 385, 392
Milligan, 68, 181, 293, 379
Milliken, 285
Millikin, 285
Mills, 39, 63, 93, 219, 248, 307
Millwood, 202
Milnor, 73, 108, 123, 134, 215, 233, 286
Milton, 13, 200
Mincey, 286
Mines, 300, 331
Miney, 279
Ming, 306, 307
Minor, 23, 29, 157, 265, 349
Minot, 106
Misroon, 226
Mitchel, 190
Mitchell, 22, 30, 47, 58, 74, 75, 107, 118, 139, 150, 167, 170, 187, 191, 193, 195, 206, 211, 212, 213, 222, 225, 233, 238, 250, 256, 260, 304, 309, 329, 359, 363, 379, 384
Mitts, 69
Mixter, 203
Moale, 204, 333
Mobley, 346
Mockbee, 110, 127, 210, 232
Moeller, 11
Molaisen, 233
Molaison, 74, 167, 175
Molly, 62
Monckton, 62
Moncrief, 47, 307
Mondes, 63
Monette, 57, 124, 232

Monier, 394
Monkus, 297
Monmonier, 111
Monongahela, 68
Monroe, 16, 26, 85, 133, 168, 208, 226, 304, 315
Montamat, 294
Montaubon, 337
Montavo, 157
Montez, 19
Montgomery, 11, 60, 195, 200, 240
Montholon, 337
Montpelier Estate, 56
Moody, 29, 94, 280
Moon, 161, 380
Moor, 307
Moore, 4, 13, 23, 24, 31, 32, 37, 82, 92, 102, 112, 118, 122, 124, 126, 128, 134, 160, 186, 193, 194, 247, 289, 308, 317, 336, 365, 376, 377, 392, 395
Moorman, 224
Mora, 93
Moran, 150, 207, 322, 363, 368, 383
Mordecai, 160, 309, 353
Morehead, 220, 288
Moreland, 62
Morell, 248
Morey, 271
Morfit, 172
Morgan, 2, 15, 37, 52, 57, 59, 63, 68, 97, 99, 105, 125, 126, 129, 135, 218, 219, 221, 250, 254, 272, 282, 296, 349, 392, 395, 396
Moriarty, 14, 58, 280, 331, 340
Morin, 187
Mority, 391
Morley, 92
Morris, 51, 67, 74, 167, 170, 190, 247, 277, 307, 322, 330, 349, 350, 365, 366, 382
Morrison, 1, 16, 46, 144, 188, 235, 299, 314, 344, 354
Morrris, 306
Morrrison, 84

Morse, 189, 238, 386
Morsell, 3, 7, 8, 101, 121, 179, 204, 213, 220, 230, 293, 314, 331, 343, 367, 393, 396, 402
Morton, 34, 44, 52, 80, 107, 114, 188, 203, 208, 222, 285, 326, 329
Morun, 97
Morven, 26
Mosely, 9, 48
Moses, 306
Moss, 192
Mott, 78, 79, 157, 182, 306
Motte, 269
Moulder, 24, 379
Mount, 8, 267, 371
Mountz, 129, 295
Mouton, 160
Mowar, 70
Mozeen, 383
Mt Vernon, 36, 73, 132, 154, 224, 301, 323
Much, 377
Mudd, 56, 107, 114, 140, 144, 148, 213, 363, 374
Mudge, 300
Muhlenberg, 385
Muhlenburg, 318, 370
Muir, 92
Mulgrave, 157
Mull, 120
Mullen, 118
Muller, 327
Mullikin, 141, 150, 383
Mumford, 304
Munding, 224, 240, 274
Mundy, 222
Munro, 150
Munroe, 7, 179, 245, 402
Munson, 238
Murat, 78
Murcheson, 47
Murdock, 7, 117, 179, 297, 402
Muren, 307
Murillo, 207

Murphy, 9, 120, 137, 149, 150, 179, 199, 333, 384, 400, 401
Murray, 74, 96, 104, 149, 150, 151, 170, 181, 215, 225, 252, 318, 372, 389
Murrell, 220
Muruago, 248
Muschitt, 107
Muse, 5
Muspral, 78
Mussleman, 291
Mustard, 288
Myers, 5, 60, 74, 75, 170, 213, 226, 232, 329, 353
Myres, 344

N

N Y Evening Star, 278
N Y Times, 278
Nagel, 120
Nagle, 82
Nailor, 31, 147, 148, 149, 150, 151, 393
Nalle, 155
Nalley, 107, 126, 309, 358
Names not Known, 38
Nantequaus, 362
Nantz, 24, 69, 106
Napoleon, 13, 264, 337, 398
Narcissi, 351
Nardell, 93
Nash, 103, 120, 222
Nathan, 330
Naylor, 24, 25, 77, 93, 129, 236, 259, 290, 291, 321, 322, 390
Neafie, 307
Neal, 79, 133, 212, 392
Neale, 37, 107, 248, 362, 388, 396
Needham, 119, 222, 268, 316, 329
Needles, 217
Needwood, 320
Neel, 74, 170, 216
Neely, 300, 386
Neff, 207

Neighbor's Fare, 37
Neil, 24, 247
Neilson, 111, 118, 119, 306
Nelson, 11, 12, 23, 37, 51, 176, 235, 323, 349, 366, 373
Nesmith, 207
Nestor, 137
Netherton, 359
Neviles, 36
Neville, 139, 261, 349
Nevins, 248, 395
Nevitt, 29, 127, 362
New Design, 36
New Orleans, 46
Newbold, 2
Newby, 304, 305
Newcomb, 75, 166, 390
Newell, 79, 161, 212, 322
Newhard, 321
Newkirk, 116
Newman, 9, 18, 21, 78, 122, 137, 192, 211, 218, 310, 386, 388, 395
Newrisha, 103
Newsted, 157
Newton, 3, 49, 65, 84, 93, 150, 189, 290, 332, 354, 365
Newton's Rest, 38
Nexsen, 307
Nichol's Hope, 38
Nicholas, 16, 69, 370, 403
Nicholason, 130
Nicholls, 16, 58, 60, 80, 259, 301, 322, 328, 394
Nichols, 96, 147, 304
Nicholson, 10, 110, 119, 329, 354, 376
Nicoll, 67, 306
Nicollet, 160
Nicolson, 171
Niebuhr, 305
Niell, 212
Niles, 159, 174, 205, 233, 250, 268
Nimboquint, 38
Nisbet, 192
Niswanger, 163

Nixdorff, 202
Nixon, 17, 34, 93, 99, 269, 308
Nixsen, 42
No Name, 36
Noailles, 323
Noble, 43, 102, 121
Noblit, 278
Nock, 192
Noell, 343
Noer, 149, 150
Noerr, 160, 309
Noland, 230
Nolen, 114
Nones, 167
Norbeck, 312
Nords, 9
Norman, 15, 33
Norris, 37, 76, 118, 125, 181, 208, 238, 285, 339, 384, 403
Norris' Venture, 37
North, 205, 343
Northrup, 10
Norton, 32, 238
Nott, 263, 363
Nourse, 7, 261, 296, 324, 392, 393
Noxon, 144
Noyes, 20, 73, 108, 126, 233, 238, 275, 328
Nugent, 336
Nukirk, 49
Nye, 145, 382

O

O'Brian, 104
O'Brien, 6, 282, 351
O'Bright, 351
O'Donnoghue, 261
O'Hara, 323, 371, 372
O'Kie, 182
O'Mara, 218
O'Neal, 150, 351
O'Neale, 156, 257, 280, 281, 401
O'Neil, 14, 346
O'Neill, 247

O'Sullivan, 247
Oakley, 74, 170, 181, 225, 306, 307
Oatland, 255
Ochiletteree, 9, 349
Odell, 75, 241
Oden, 11, 167, 302
Odenheimer, 361
Odgen, 6
Odill, 49
Offey, 22, 160
Offield, 39
Offutt, 74, 179, 373
Ogden, 6, 31, 260, 262, 304, 305, 320, 350, 377
Oger, 66
Ogilive, 124
Ogle, 60, 276, 322
Ogsburg, 306
Ohola, 347
Okill, 388
Olcott, 304
Oldfield, 290
Oldham, 222
Oldner, 32
Olinger, 51
Oliver, 53, 59
Olmstead, 377
Olney, 74, 170, 188, 225, 266
Onderdonk, 266, 361
Oothout, 304
Opechankanough, 383
Opehankanough, 362
Opie, 316
Orbinson, 400
Orden, 307
Oremieulx, 243
Oris, 389
Orme, 98, 128, 147, 148, 150, 180, 187, 211, 329, 367
Orne, 17
Orr, 235, 281
Orrick, 50
Orten, 297
Orton, 262
Osage Indians, 83

Osborn, 143, 288, 366
Osborne, 25, 69, 94, 100, 120, 134
Osbourn, 253, 284
Osgood, 274, 398
Osteen, 123
Ostein, 28
Ostinelli, 201
Ostrander, 306
Otis, 146, 168, 171, 269
Otterback, 149
Ould, 44, 238, 241
Overly, 112, 222
Overton, 281, 304
Owen, 16, 26, 126, 128, 139, 241, 248, 260, 265, 318, 332
Owens, 113, 157, 223, 371, 372
Owings, 235
Owner, 240, 354
Oxford, 30, 228
Oxford Resurveyed, 30
Oxhard, 293

P

Pablo, 160
Packard, 89, 92, 229
packet *Orleans*, 366
packet-ship *Garrick*, 156
packet-ship *Garrrick*, 157
Paddock, 75, 124
Paganini, 228
Page, 26, 107, 115, 219, 234, 282, 319, 347, 349, 370, 371, 380
Pageot, 297
Pain, 142
Paine, 110, 351, 355, 356, 384
Palfrey, 207
Palmer, 7, 14, 57, 157, 217, 281, 307, 342, 394, 399
Pancoast, 146
Pannill, 104
Parburt, 55
Parcel Enlarged, 97
Paret, 305
Park, 43, 352, 392

Parke, 317
Parker, 7, 12, 13, 15, 41, 50, 70, 74, 75, 115, 116, 117, 132, 159, 167, 177, 217, 222, 229, 238, 254, 269, 280, 294, 399, 402
Parkins, 114, 121, 288
Parks, 103, 120, 171, 194, 208, 344, 378
Parnham's Retreat, 342
Parquin, 337
Parratt, 30
Parrington, 78
Parris, 14, 148, 150, 151, 285
Parrish, 93, 161
Parrot, 221
Parsons, 15, 22, 59, 74, 75, 85, 123, 170, 202, 226, 233, 238, 273, 281
Partnership, 24, 39
Partridge, 35
Paschal, 134, 380, 392, 396
Paschall, 120
Passan, 65
Passau, 133
Passavant, 317
Passeau, 392, 396
Passmore, 353
Pasteh, 382
Paterson, 102
Patrick, 279, 286, 318
Patten, 20, 384
Patterson, 26, 29, 66, 68, 78, 100, 126, 146, 160, 205, 209, 288, 294, 306, 317, 365, 396
Pattison, 78, 307
Patton, 239, 267, 277
Paul, 1, 16, 314
Paulding, 95, 190, 247, 255, 282, 352
Paull, 235
Pavilion, 172
Paxton, 122, 200, 403
Payae, 41
Payn, 377
Payne, 37, 59, 141, 153, 259, 267
Paynter, 321
Peabody, 150

Peace & Quietness, 38
Peacock, 219
Peake, 223, 227, 264, 281, 372
Peale, 35, 60, 318
Pearce, 125, 327, 402
Pearsall, 136
Pearson, 43, 114, 206, 305, 324, 363, 368
Pearsons, 171
Pease, 313
Peay, 347
Peck, 43, 74, 75, 157
Pedrick, 11
Peebles, 48
Pegg, 134
Pegram, 16, 93, 264, 315, 355
Peirce, 4, 7, 17, 18, 143, 259, 331
Peire, 139
Pelicer, 69
Pellett, 17
Pellicer, 49
Peltz, 281
Pendergrast, 226
Pendexter, 21
Pendleton, 88, 115, 197, 239
Penharlow, 391
Penn, 51, 107, 114, 221, 229, 399
Pennel, 133
Pennington, 26, 165
Pennock, 41
Pennsylvania, 68
Pennsylvania Inquirer, 161
Pennybacker, 67
Penrose, 315, 397
Penryn, 39
Pentz, 93
Pentzes, 318
Pepper, 111, 112, 151
Perch Hole Marsh, 36
Perier, 118
Perkins, 14, 46, 86, 87, 201, 224, 232, 235, 259, 321, 360
Pernel, 79
Perrin, 177, 186, 233
Perrine, 269, 278, 289, 380, 389

Perry, 23, 84, 104, 110, 222, 273, 284, 288, 299, 308, 309, 363, 398
Pescud, 240
Peter, 50, 188, 281
Peter the Great, 342
Peters, 18, 21, 50, 63, 105, 155
Peterson, 23
Petit, 248
Petrikin, 33, 322, 331
Pettibone, 261, 371
Pettigrew, 318
Pettingel, 74
Pettit, 149
Pettrich, 45, 174, 249
Peun, 363
Pew, 10, 346
Peyton, 3, 5, 6, 20, 75, 94, 355
Pfouts, 354
Phalen, 52, 224
Phelps, 18, 20, 74, 94, 100, 167, 183, 216, 225, 395
Phil Commercial Herald, 161
Philippe, 108, 118
Philips, 69, 292, 296, 304
Phillips, 24, 32, 149, 179, 193, 203, 221, 253, 267, 273, 281, 285, 292, 296, 306, 356, 369
Phillipson, 119
Philson, 354
Phinizy, 247
Phinney, 184
Phister, 306
Phoenix, 88, 262
Physick, 78
Piatt, 15, 209
Pickell, 287
Pickering, 24
Picket, 21, 28, 197
Pickett, 57
Pickrell, 66, 84, 295, 329, 331
Pierce, 17, 20, 33, 35, 45, 55, 75, 80, 93, 96, 135, 136, 163, 197, 207, 222, 225, 306, 320, 345
Piercy, 319
Pierson, 74, 170, 188, 232, 334

Pigman, 287, 294
Pi-haiokee, 126
Pike, 74, 146, 175, 284, 386
Piles, 288
Piles' Woodland, 36
Pilling, 103
Pinckeny, 267
Pinckney, 229, 237
Pindell, 371
Piner, 9
Piney Neck, 35
Pinkham, 52
Pinkney, 186, 215
Piper, 11, 46, 47, 75, 90, 118, 170, 225
Pipkin, 79
Pirsson, 329
Pitkin, 112
Pitman, 318
Pittman, 301, 308, 398
Pitts, 111, 118, 119, 292, 316, 329, 376
Placide, 92
Plains of Jerico, 39
Plant, 62, 116, 126, 151
Plantt, 207, 368
Plastridge, 238
Plater, 294, 328
Plato, 118
Plauche, 194
Pleasant Levels, 35, 38
Pleasants, 9
Pledge, 372
Plinter, 11
Plowden, 37
Plumb, 158, 222, 391
Plume, 304, 308
Plumer, 322
Plummer, 5, 221
Plummer's Pasture, 375
Plumps, 240
Plumsel, 182
Plunket, 83
Plunkett, 222
Plympton, 355

Pocahontas, 300, 362, 383
Poe, 111, 118, 119, 236, 316, 329
Poinsett, 92, 160, 190, 272, 352
Polhemus, 369
Polk, 51, 110, 160, 208, 221, 312
Pollard, 61, 162, 257, 325, 388
Pollen, 42
Pollitz, 78
Pollock, 139, 235, 238, 261
Pomeroy, 203
Pomfret Fields, 36
Pomroy, 41
Pond, 61, 75, 222
Ponvert, 69, 100, 120, 233, 250
Poole, 5, 6, 75, 82, 170, 225
Poor, 25, 110, 117
Poore, 307
Pope, 78, 95, 110, 162
Poplar Point, 37
Porcher, 78
Pordexter, 18
Portens, 283
Porter, 9, 10, 11, 16, 32, 73, 75, 101, 103, 127, 146, 167, 171, 262, 308, 312, 330, 359, 385
Porto, 248
Posey, 54, 317
Post, 146, 157
Posten, 206
Poston, 220, 338, 368
Potter, 143, 214, 221, 361
Pougnet, 259
Poulson, 2
Pouvert, 94
Poverty Hills, 35
Powell, 5, 28, 148, 149, 150, 155, 156, 223, 280, 301
Power, 194
Powers, 1, 46, 64, 105, 150, 257
Prall, 304
Prather, 274, 299, 379
Pratt, 75, 83, 144, 170, 190, 221, 225, 230, 262, 272, 291, 386
Pray, 16
Preble, 263

Prentiss, 184, 207, 226, 245, 308, 324
Pres' House, 399
Preston, 52, 108, 138, 152, 158, 187, 245, 324, 350, 369, 376
Pretlow, 393
Pretty Prospect, 117
Prettyman, 177, 225, 296
Preuss, 144, 354, 371
Price, 56, 74, 114, 139, 156, 157, 166, 170, 185, 190, 256, 260, 297, 322
Price' Rest, 39
Price's Rest, 39
Priestly, 307, 403
Prieur, 32
Prigg, 176
Prince, 5, 14, 168
Prince Albert, 79, 228
Prince Chas Edw, 359
Prince Jerome, 343
Prince of Canino, 264
Prince of Orange, 337, 340
Princess Augusta Sophia, 326
Princess Victoria, 156
Pringle, 32, 226, 229
Pritchard, 269, 395
privateer *True Blooded Yankee*, 293
Prock, 384
Proctor, 41, 62, 86, 237
Proe, 238
Proffit, 195, 240
Prout, 128, 144, 147, 148, 150, 230
Prouty, 105
Provins, 273
Provost, 358
Prussian Minister, 337
Pruyn, 377
Pryor, 171, 183, 393
Public Lands, 363
Pucket, 155
Pulizzi, 103
Pulling, 280
Pumphrey, 50, 200, 265, 352, 375
Pumphry, 57
Purdens, 310
Purdon, 150

Purdy, 60, 148, 378
Purnell, 318
Pursell, 82, 292
Putnam, 58, 102, 195
Pyatt, 57
Pye, 31, 107, 233, 266, 309, 363

Q

Quackenboss, 44, 259
Quantrill, 47
Quarles, 47
Queen, 150, 247, 248, 314, 324, 363
Queen Charlotte, 326
Queen of England, 79
Queen of Louis, 316
Queen of Portugal, 339
Quimby, 18, 21
Quincy, 292
Quincy, Mass, 179
Quinlican, 34
Quinliman, 9
Quinlivan, 187
Quinn, 51
Quitman, 153
Qunicy, 16

R

Rabb, 3
Rackel, 51
Rackliffe, 96
Rackoon Hills, 37
Radcliff, 150, 189, 223, 227, 304, 324, 367, 370
Rafinesque, 61, 303
Raikes, 387
Raines, 75
Rains, 145, 200
Raley, 37
Ralph, 16
Ralston, 34, 44, 188, 266
Ramage, 359
Ramble, 37, 38
Ramsay, 62, 75, 103, 124, 318, 321, 371

Ramsey, 25, 48, 204, 282, 318, 322, 325, 360
Rand, 41, 65, 158, 225, 392
Randall, 47, 69, 85, 122, 127, 222, 275, 306, 326, 347, 365, 369
Randolph, 3, 29, 73, 152, 187, 197, 261, 298, 346, 357, 367, 368, 380
Rankin, 243, 283
Ransom, 272
Ranson, 124, 243
Ratcliffe, 52, 215
Rathbone, 65, 71, 188, 272, 395, 400
Rathbun, 220
Raub, 146
Rawlings, 126, 144, 186
Rawls, 220
Rawson, 189
Ray, 264
Rayen, 86, 235
Raymond, 32, 43, 153, 204, 306, 326
Rayner, 195, 200, 240
Read, 26, 39, 64, 106, 119, 129, 136, 165, 172, 254, 272, 275
Reader's Purchase, 38
Reardon, 230
Rebeau, 295
Reckless, 101
Recompense, 39
Rector, 10, 397
Redd, 188, 214
Reddick, 156
Reddington, 112
Redfern, 148, 151, 257
Redin, 184
Redman, 36, 261
Redman's Hardship, 37
Redue, 22
Reed, 40, 75, 88, 125, 230, 246, 249, 317, 319, 354, 359, 366, 389
Reeder, 37, 39, 114
Reeder's Adventure, 39
Rees, 123
Reese, 33, 310, 317, 334, 382
Reeves, 15, 142, 165, 169, 186, 235, 242, 268, 332, 366

Reid, 85, 111, 118, 288, 292
Reilly, 100, 104, 105, 128, 205
Reily, 150, 347
Reimily, 147
Reiss, 349
Relf, 385
Relfe, 395
Remainder, 39
Remington, 28, 154, 258
Remsen, 304
Renard, 78
Rennoe, 114, 363
Renshaw, 82, 129, 132
Renwick, 333
Reordan, 248
Resley, 170
Resurrection Manor, 36, 38
Retreat, 291
Revel's Backside, 38
revenue cutter *Wolcott*, 328
Reves, 133
Reynolds, 28, 68, 69, 87, 123, 124, 157, 180, 315, 396, 398
Reynoldson, 262
Rhawn, 330
Rhea, 72
Rhett, 381
Rhinehart, 64
Rhodes, 88, 308, 346, 384
Riall, 218
Ricards, 13, 112, 196
Rice, 61, 74, 167, 225, 233, 246, 288, 291, 357, 390
Rich, 111, 127, 258
Rich Farm, 30
Rich Farm Add, 30
Rich Neck, 277
Richards, 106, 215, 308
Richardson, 83, 119, 206, 207, 210, 308, 316, 329, 368, 371
Richd Maryman's Lands, 37
Richey, 34, 188, 223
Richmond, 48, 134
Richom, 233
Richoux, 74

Ricker, 40, 335
Ricketson, 306
Ridall, 31
Riddel, 90
Riddle, 134, 230
Rideout, 295
Rider, 75, 170, 225, 232
Ridge, 10
Ridgeley, 141
Ridgely, 11, 33, 119, 168, 215, 266, 316, 329, 366
Ridgley, 250, 376
Riell, 307
Riggalls, 207, 368
Riggan, 191
Riggs, 45, 50, 61, 119, 212, 318
Rigney, 219
Rigsby, 160, 176
Riker, 48
Riley, 4, 5, 6, 7, 75, 124, 173, 177, 199, 245, 288, 299, 318, 329
Rindge, 247
Ringgold, 244, 328
Rinker, 46, 51, 75
Riol, 16
Riordan, 90, 365
Ripe, 35
Ripley, 28, 49, 206, 230, 349
Risby, 114
Risley, 216, 225
Riston, 330
Ritchie, 9, 78, 200, 247
Ritner, 353
Rittenhouse, 216, 246
Ritter, 42, 69, 293, 315
Rivard, 2, 30
Rivaud, 393
Rives, 31, 114, 137, 148, 149, 267, 365, 380
Rixter, 253
Rizer, 287, 288
Roach, 69, 79, 146, 255, 351
Roan, 95
Roane, 177, 291
Robb, 68

Robbins, 273, 315, 320, 364
Robbs, 287
Robert, 146
Roberts, 42, 60, 69, 75, 83, 94, 100, 107, 119, 134, 157, 170, 186, 202, 219, 220, 222, 225, 268, 277, 281, 363, 377, 378, 391, 395
Robertson, 1, 9, 13, 43, 69, 72, 87, 105, 107, 114, 123, 131, 149, 206, 243, 244, 251, 302, 306, 311, 368, 370, 383, 394
Robey, 107, 363
Robin, 21
Robins, 140, 308
Robinson, 4, 18, 26, 28, 35, 60, 67, 110, 125, 139, 153, 156, 160, 206, 207, 259, 266, 291, 295, 313, 329, 346, 368, 385, 386
Roby, 52, 171
Rocard, 306
Roch, 93
Rochambeau, 122, 169
Rochat, 150
Roche, 310, 350
Rochester, 37
Rock, 272
Rockwell, 87, 88, 324
Rocky Point, 38
Rodbird, 281
Rodgers, 75, 79, 110, 372
Rodman, 67
Rodney, 5, 6, 214, 379
Roe, 305, 306
Rofferstein, 157
Rogee, 271
Rogers, 41, 51, 87, 92, 106, 112, 122, 139, 189, 221, 222, 243, 260, 302, 312, 371, 379, 384, 403
Rolando, 110
Rolerdeau, 194
Rolfe, 133, 362, 383
Roloff, 140
Romero, 264
Romeyn, 212
Romlin, 58

Ronckendorff, 254
Rooke, 43
Rooker, 68
Roome, 307
Root, 267
Ropas, 92
Rose, 32, 157, 158, 161, 204, 262, 287, 292, 304, 329
Rose Mount, 272
Rosebrough, 238
Rosedale, 117
Roseland & Add, 36
Rosenthal, 150, 388
Roser, 231
Ross, 29, 103, 119, 130, 197, 228, 291, 310, 317, 338, 349, 351, 353, 397
Rossell, 206
Rosseter, 41
Roszel, 99, 289
Rothschild, 207
Rothwell, 223, 227, 282, 367
Roumbport, 239
Roundtree, 376
Rouse, 43, 306
Rousseau, 282
Roussin, 118
Rowan, 128, 199, 308
Rowe, 74
Rowell, 191
Rowlett, 228, 342, 356
Rowlette, 10
Roy, 133, 388
Royall, 61
Rudd, 263, 349
Ruddle, 115
Rudolph, 50, 116, 168
Ruff, 242
Ruffin, 382
Ruffner, 162
Rugg, 87
Ruggles, 329
Ruiz, 19
Rum Point, 341
Rumble, 280

Rumph, 122
Rumsey, 222
Runnells, 233
Ruppert, 150
Rush, 74, 285
Russel, 16, 41, 318
Russell, 37, 46, 222, 228, 240, 288, 381
Russle, 321
Rust, 327
Rutgers, 384
Rutherford, 66, 216
Ryall, 76, 165, 270
Ryan, 104, 135, 385
Ryder, 127, 228, 340
Ryer, 307
Ryerson, 165
Ryland, 11, 90, 101, 113, 256
Ryon, 126

S

Sabin, 24
Sable, 213
Sac, 64, 87, 133, 174
Salem, 20, 36
Salisbury, 168
Salmon, 306
Saloon, 210
Saltmarsh, 3, 123, 158, 380
Saltonstall, 345
Sammons, 7, 51, 79
Samson, 263
Samuel, 78, 214
Sanches, 240
Sand, 21
Sandaman, 157
Sanderlain, 279
Sanderlyn, 145
Sanderman, 156
Sanders, 50, 104, 145, 195, 221, 223, 363, 372
Sanderson, 155, 177, 244, 326
Sandford, 382

Sands, 7, 18, 92, 105, 181, 282, 306, 352, 403
Sandy, 223
Sandy Levals, 37
Sanford, 377, 397
Sangster, 114
Sangston, 32, 135
Sanson, 297
Santander, 242
Santangelo, 302
Sarah's Retreat, 35
Sarchet, 205
Sardo, 148
Sargent, 342
Sarpey, 74
Sarpy, 51, 90, 124, 386, 393
Sartain, 15
Sassean, 337
Sassel, 232
Sassin, 65
Satisfaction, 39
Saugrain, 403
Saugraire, 181
Saul, 75, 170, 202, 225
Saunders, 50, 72, 73, 83, 103, 114, 143, 166, 167, 191, 260, 330, 349
Sausenio, 169
Sauter, 151, 303
Savage, 283, 342
Saward, 163
Sawyer, 7, 11, 45, 49, 112
Saxon, 39
Saxton, 38
Sayers, 293
Sayles, 377
Saylor, 287
Scarborough, 119
Scarce, 2
Scarritt, 5
Scheel, 293
Schenig, 344
Schenk, 75
Schermerhorne, 306
Schleslinger, 78
Schley, 146, 185, 219

Schmeltan, 166
schn'r *Amistad*, 19
schn'r *Archimedes*, 104
schn'r *Buffalo*, 73, 231
schn'r *Butterfly*, 359
schn'r *Byron*, 136
schn'r *Chas Pitman*, 320
schn'r *Deposit*, 379
schn'r *Flirt*, 389
schn'r *Flying Fish*, 229
schn'r *Gen Jackson*, 250
schn'r *Gen Warren*, 163
schn'r *Grampus*, 153
schn'r *Henry Barger*, 336
schn'r *Kewanne*, 163
schn'r *Love*, 359
schn'r *Medium*, 389
schn'r *Pacific*, 83
schn'r *Sarah Ann*, 153
schn'r *Shark*, 201, 254, 255
schn'r *Sylph*, 269
schn'r *Three Bros*, 73, 134
schn'r *Waterloo*, 201
schn'r *Wave*, 269
schn'r *Wm J Watson*, 360
Schneeman, 340
Schneider, 118, 365
Schoeuer, 353
Schofield, 287
Scholmeyer, 76
Schoolcraft, 79, 130, 249
Schott, 161
Schriever, 340
Schuck, 288
Schultz, 20, 21, 92
Schuyler, 59, 171, 260
Schwanck, 305
Schwartz, 318
Scolfield, 338
Scotland, 37
Scott, 9, 32, 34, 44, 47, 80, 85, 93, 124, 133, 139, 140, 169, 178, 180, 189, 195, 197, 200, 202, 220, 222, 234, 241, 246, 258, 261, 267, 282, 318, 329, 370, 380, 385, 393

Scovel, 377
Scovell, 219
Scraggs, 64
Scrivener, 110
Scrubby Oak, 38
Scruggs, 266
Scudder, 142
Seaberry, 258, 277
Seabright, 280
Seaburn, 76
Searcy, 135, 172
Sears, 207, 308, 348
Seaton, 60, 97, 173, 187, 230, 245, 254, 259, 318, 322, 324, 350, 367, 394
Seaver, 387
Second Thought, 375
Security, 37
Seely, 380, 400
Seigle, 124, 228
Seigleman, 75
Seitsinger, 74, 186, 225
Seitz, 326, 383, 394
Seitzinger, 170
Selby, 268, 320, 361, 397
Selden, 60, 101, 151, 185, 257
Sellman, 372
Seminole, 272, 329, 347, 382, 389
Seminoles, 3, 223
Semmes, 7, 60, 148, 156, 159, 179, 220, 230, 247, 293, 294, 326, 328, 393, 402
Semple, 318, 337
Seneca, 41
Seneca nation, 117
Sengstack, 293
Seppings, 159
Sergeant, 321, 361, 379, 385
Serrin, 148, 206, 368
Serrurier, 297
Servery, 114
Sessford, 31, 206, 368, 369
Sevier, 181
Sewall, 35, 99, 275, 276, 371
Seward, 191, 262, 330, 377

Sewart, 367
Sewell, 60, 329
Sexsmith, 44, 126, 390
Seymour, 169, 262, 263, 307, 319, 349
Shackelford, 251
Shackell, 151
Shackerty, 11
Shaff, 218
Shakespeare, 13, 33
Shaler, 59, 165
Shall, 21
Shankland, 305
Shanks, 150, 179, 265, 329, 331
Shannon, 47, 75, 82, 170, 190, 225
Sharp, 262, 311
Sharpe, 166, 377
Shattuck, 231
Shave, 263
Shaw, 70, 78, 160, 203, 290, 296, 362, 382
Shawen, 302
Shawnee, 331
Shay, 75
Shays, 74
Shea, 104
Sheafe, 22
Sheahan, 104
Shearn, 13
Sheckel, 336
Sheckelford, 54
Sheckells, 189
Sheckles, 374
Shedden, 212
Shekell, 186, 261
Shelby, 86, 181, 236
Shelden, 226
Sheldon, 75, 216, 232
Shelpman, 288
Shelton, 73, 155
Shepard, 125, 210, 223
Shephed, 141
Shepherd, 33, 44, 57, 104, 150, 167, 178, 219, 243, 324, 355, 358, 394
Shepherds, 123

Sheppard, 53, 73, 85, 118, 144, 167, 170, 233
Shepperd, 72
Sherar, 219
Sherburne, 54
Sheriff, 130
Sherman, 103, 117, 243, 315
Sherrard, 114
Sherwood, 328
Shields, 31, 71, 312, 378
Shinn, 60, 344
ship *Atlas*, 345
ship *Auburn*, 308
ship *Bienfaisant*, 345
ship *Blanche*, 345
ship *British Queen*, 178, 353
ship *Champlain*, 25
ship *Comet*, 45
ship *Constitution*, 254
ship *Dale*, 381
ship *Delaware*, 57, 173, 312, 372
ship *Discovery*, 345
ship *Encornium*, 45
ship *Erie*, 258
ship *Gen Parkhill*, 328
ship *Genr'l Clinch*, 145
ship *George Washington*, 189
ship *Good Man Richard*, 49
ship *Great Western*, 258, 317
ship *Illinois*, 246
ship *Independence*, 106, 110
ship *Insurgent*, 98
ship *Java*, 57
ship *John Adams*, 44
ship *John Cumming*, 315
ship *Lawrence*, 273
ship *Leopard*, 315
ship *Lexington*, 201, 210
ship *Liverpool*, 397
ship *Macedonian*, 190, 282
ship *Magnificent*, 345
ship *Momtezuma*, 246
ship *Moslem*, 315
ship of the line *Ohio*, 142
ship *Ohio*, 226

ship *Ohio 74*, 66
ship *Oneco*, 216
ship *Ontario*, 184
ship *Philadelphia*, 15
ship *Pique*, 345
ship *Raisonable*, 12
ship *Relief*, 370
ship *Resolution*, 345
ship *Rhone*, 317
ship *Seaman*, 320
ship *Stephen Whitney*, 155
ship *Trumbull*, 49
ship *United States*, 246
ship *Vandalia*, 190, 282
ship *Vesper*, 302
ship *Ville de Lyon*, 17, 164
ship *Ville de Paris*, 323
ship *Wm Penn*, 23
ship *Yorktown*, 381
Shipley, 230, 257, 288
Shirley, 38
Shoemaker, 195, 328, 373
Shoenberger, 46
Shore, 220
Short, 75, 170, 202, 226, 233
Shreeve, 149
Shriver, 287, 288
Shrofe, 75
Shubrick, 16, 92, 282, 372
Shultz, 16
Shulze, 353
Shumate, 287
Shute, 306
Shyne, 296
Sibell, 307
Sibley, 214, 296, 355, 358
Sickles, 307
Sieman, 199
Sigourney, 41, 95
Silden, 157
Sill, 164
Silliman, 153, 397
Silsbee, 7
Sim, 202
Simmes, 247

Simmons, 16, 42, 69, 83, 195, 247, 319, 335, 371
Simms, 26, 27, 80, 111, 148, 149, 150, 151, 174, 223, 242, 268, 278, 290, 302, 331, 354, 364, 366
Simon, 102
Simonds, 272
Simonton, 1, 321
Simpson, 69, 156, 224, 282, 302, 356, 393, 395
Simpson's Supply, 167
Sims, 13
Sinan, 403
Sinclair, 8, 171, 229, 312
Single, 34
Singleton, 47
Sinon, 148, 150
Sinton, 156, 216
Sioux, 61
Sisson, 102
Sisters of Charity, 349
Sitgreaves, 244
Skinner, 41, 57, 78, 172, 173, 184, 372, 376, 377
Slade, 35, 110, 282
Slagle, 46
Slane, 306
Slater, 41, 287, 302
Slattery, 340, 402
Slaughter, 50, 171, 327, 372
Slaymaker, 26
Sleet, 34
Sleeth, 74
Slick, 222
Slicke, 158
Slim, 189
Sloan, 75, 170, 202, 225, 269
Sloane, 33
Sloat, 15, 52, 129, 254, 330
sloop *Key West*, 269
sloop *Mary*, 123, 385
sloop *Merchant*, 18
sloop of war *Boston*, 328, 341, 342
sloop of war *Concord*, 341
sloop of war *Dale*, 372

sloop of war *Levant*, 317, 372
sloop of war *Yorktown*, 333, 372
sloop *Palmyra*, 143
sloop *St Louis*, 201
sloop *Vevilia*, 269
Sloughter, 94
Small, 137
Small Hope, 37
Smallman, 31
Smallwood, 54
Smart, 286
Smick, 353
Smiley, 235
Smith, 2, 3, 9, 14, 15, 20, 21, 22, 27,
  28, 29, 32, 38, 43, 48, 49, 50, 52, 58,
  60, 61, 69, 73, 74, 75, 83, 94, 96, 97,
  100, 101, 105, 108, 110, 111, 119,
  120, 122, 123, 124, 126, 128, 133,
  134, 142, 147, 148, 150, 151, 152,
  160, 167, 170, 185, 188, 191, 194,
  197, 199, 204, 208, 212, 214, 215,
  216, 221, 222, 224, 225, 232, 233,
  234, 237, 245, 247, 252, 254, 256,
  257, 258, 260, 269, 275, 277, 282,
  284, 288, 289, 293, 294, 295, 303,
  306, 307, 309, 318, 322, 327, 328,
  330, 339, 342, 343, 349, 351, 353,
  355, 356, 357, 358, 360, 364, 366,
  369, 373, 376, 378, 380, 383, 384,
  388, 392, 395, 396, 398, 402
Smithson, 164
Smoot, 7, 66, 80, 93, 101, 107, 114,
  126, 147, 150, 179, 195, 284, 299,
  317, 329, 362, 372, 394
Smyth, 72, 209, 306
Snead, 71, 204, 216
Sneed, 265
Sneeling, 234
Snell, 212
Snelling, 86, 234
Snethen, 301
Snider, 221
Sniffen, 308
Snodgrass, 90, 233, 251, 297
Snow, 75, 177, 225, 392

Snowden, 4, 60, 77, 89, 123, 220
Snow-Feather, 383
Snyder, 46, 322, 351
Solms, 230
Somerset Add, 36
Sommerville, 90
Soper, 88, 307
Sortor, 71
Sothoron, 39, 60, 195, 205, 329, 381
Southard, 58, 135, 262
Souther, 240
Southgate, 288
Southoron, 80
Southworth, 29
Spafford, 79, 86, 133, 235, 392
Spalding, 107, 114, 213, 222, 256,
  322, 363, 381
Spalding's Venture, 38
Sparks, 306
Sparrow, 283
Spates, 188
Spaulding, 47
Speake, 128, 293
Spear, 53, 384
Speed, 262, 377
Speiden, 280
Speight, 307
Speiser, 89
Spelman, 352
Spence, 187, 330
Spencer, 38, 93, 101, 153, 156, 197,
  299, 332, 377
Sperry, 308
Spier, 43
Spies, 304
Spilman, 278
Spink's Rest, 38
Sprague, 42, 203, 211, 291
Sprigg, 80, 169, 210, 272, 283, 397,
  403
Spring Tavern, 350
Springsted, 143
Spurling, 138, 383, 394
Srofe, 170
Sroufe, 74, 167, 177

Sryock, 311
St Ann's, 36
St Ann's Freehold, 36
St Augustin, 316
St Clair, 8, 69, 100, 176, 211, 338, 394
St Clement's, 38
St Frances de Sales, 285
St Giles, 36
St Jane Frances, 285
St Jerome's Plains, 35
St John, 23, 93, 208
St John's Mill Seat, 38
St Jos', 37
St Jos' Manor, 35
St Leger, 249
St Matthew's Church, 331
St Mgt's, 37, 38
St Oswald's, 37
St Peter's Hills, 37
St Simon, 323
St Thomas, 328
St Wm's, 37
Staata, 272
Stabler, 57
Stacey, 162
Stackpole, 272
Stacy, 280
Stafford, 118
Stanby, 97
Standerwick, 307
Standford, 204
Stanford, 216, 257
Staniford, 6
Stanislaus, 316
Stanley, 14, 60, 317
Stanly, 236, 262, 317
Stansbury, 244, 304
Stanton, 48, 238
Stark, 107, 108, 215, 233
Starke, 292
Starks, 13
Starr, 49, 361, 363
Starrit, 106
Starritt, 119
Staunton, 157

steamboat *Champlain*, 163
steamboat *Cherokee*, 397, 398
steamboat *Chesapeake*, 131
steamboat *Citizen*, 195
steamboat *Columiba*, 391
steamboat *Commerce*, 91
steamboat *Corvette*, 366
steamboat *De Kalb*, 20
steamboat *Fredericksburg*, 57
steamboat *Grampus*, 169
steamboat *Hyperion*, 49
steamboat *Jewess*, 301
steamboat *John McLean*, 137
steamboat *Jos Johnson*, 91, 279
steamboat *Le Roy*, 342
steamboat *Leroy*, 356
steamboat *Lexington*, 18, 20, 25, 31, 35, 40, 53
steamboat *Monongahela*, 68
steamboat *Odd Fellow*, 359
steamboat *Patuxent*, 202
steamboat *Persian*, 396
steamboat *Phenix*, 333
steamboat *Pizarro*, 30
steamboat *U S*, 163
steamboat *Vesuvius*, 183
steamboats *Albany, De Witt Clinton*, 105
steamboats *Georgia, Jewess, South Carolina*, 333
steamboats *Stanca & Dayton*, 250
steamboats *Stasca & Dayton*, 233
steamer *Columbia*, 116, 146, 218
steamer *Express*, 359
steamer *Forester*, 336
steamer *Fredericksburg*, 116
steamer *Fulton*, 84
steamer *Gen Harrison*, 319
steamer *Genr'l Brady*, 120
steamer *Genr'l Clinch*, 177
steamer *Great Britain*, 253
steamer *Lady Morgan*, 398
steamer *Old Dominion*, 120
steamer *Persian*, 351
steamer *Poinsett*, 349, 372

steamer *Santee*, 389
steamer *Wm Gaston*, 126
steamers *Champion & Kingston*, 252
steamers *Leroy & Charleston*, 252
steam-ship *British Queen*, 156
steam-ship *Great Western*, 78, 92
steamship *N Y*, 125
Stearn, 30
Steed, 30
Steele, 42, 116, 221, 243, 318, 372
Steenbergen, 27, 67
Steene, 102
Steer, 309
Steeves, 43
Steinbergen, 144
Steinman, 353
Steinrod, 158, 395
Stellwagen, 246
Stem, 17, 34
Stephen, 6, 97, 152, 178, 332
Stephens, 119, 192, 226, 232, 328, 394
Stephenson, 85, 226, 261, 265
Stepper, 380, 393
Sterling, 139, 261
Stermott, 317
Stettinius, 101, 126, 147, 148, 401
Steuart, 149, 372
Stevens, 14, 100, 101, 105, 110, 112, 207, 242, 253, 271, 275, 306, 308, 329, 377
Stevenson, 68, 139, 186, 209, 284, 318, 329, 330, 355, 377
Steward, 151, 213, 383
Stewart, 29, 31, 57, 62, 97, 102, 118, 126, 127, 146, 148, 149, 150, 151, 163, 174, 180, 187, 191, 240, 248, 280, 314, 318, 324, 347, 366, 376
Stiggins, 130
Stiles, 23
Stiles' Chance, 35
Stillman, 41
Stilwell, 240, 384
Stimpson, 63, 262
Stimson, 377

Stinnecke, 171
Stinson, 353
Stith, 73
Stobie, 348
Stock, 159
Stockett, 25
Stockman, 32
Stockton, 115, 131, 143, 165, 342
Stockwell, 40
Stoddard, 164, 276
Stoddert, 107, 112, 154, 362
Stoever, 353
Stogdale, 263
Stone, 19, 22, 26, 37, 38, 39, 67, 68, 90, 100, 107, 112, 123, 130, 134, 152, 153, 184, 223, 228, 285, 289, 341, 352, 363, 368, 385, 386, 388, 395
Stonestreet, 179, 247
Store, 227
Storer, 5, 6, 129, 197, 254, 290, 375
Stork, 73
Storms, 306
Storris, 145
Storrow, 78, 327
Storrs, 207, 320
Story, 14, 40, 63, 222, 241, 348
Stott, 29, 127, 148, 210, 302
Stout, 87, 175
Stow, 83, 102
Stowell, 108, 204
Stoy Hill, 38
Strachan, 304
Strader, 7, 123, 396
Strahan, 276
Stratchy, 362
Straton, 41
Stratton, 43, 270
Strawbridge, 4
Streat, 288
Streater, 82
Street, 174
Streeter, 277
Strembeck, 359
Stribbling, 79, 114

Stribling, 333
Strickland, 47, 95, 175, 223
Strife, 39
Stright, 318
Striker, 306
Strine, 330
Stringfellow, 30, 166, 319, 370, 376
Stringham, 341
Strohmeyer, 333
Strong, 74, 75, 158, 170, 171, 190, 192, 202, 222, 225, 394
Strother, 378
Stuart, 31, 189, 282, 285, 306, 357
Stubbins, 280
Stubblefield, 288
Stubbs, 104, 211
Stukey, 68
Stull, 10, 323, 328
Stump, 387
Sturgis, 1, 167
Stuyvesant, 21
Styles, 218
Sugar Bottom Farm, 188
Suit, 127, 350, 401
Sullivan, 27, 59, 89, 115, 151, 154, 202, 304
Sullivant, 163
Sully, 11
Sumerly, 222
Sumerville, 35
Summer Field, 35
Sumner, 312, 332
Sumter, 202
Sumwalt, 273
Suplee, 291
Sure, 306
Surget, 159
Surlls, 65, 194
Surprise, 257
Susanna, 36
Suter, 104, 289
Suttle's Range, 39
Sutton, 222, 333
Suydam, 375, 385
Suydan, 65

Swaitwood, 74
Swamp Island, 38
Swan, 22, 40
Swann, 26, 57, 185, 231, 260, 282, 376, 380
Swart, 74
Swartha, 161
Swartwout, 44, 139, 260, 304, 330
Swartz, 117
Swayne, 377
Sweatt, 106
Sweeny, 60, 107, 126, 359
Sweet, 282, 306
Sweeting, 151
Swift, 70, 306, 330
Swinnerten, 386
Swint, 330
Swords, 308
Sydenham, 325
Sydnor, 324
Sylvester, 171
Symmes, 175

T

Tabbs, 36
Tabele, 307
Tabot, 248
Taft, 102
Taggart, 81, 181
Talbertt, 204
Talbot, 127, 211, 248
Talbott, 111
Talburtt, 291, 292
Talcott, 81, 108, 251
Taliaferro, 71, 381, 382
Tallcott, 102
Tallmadge, 262, 377
Taney, 14, 58, 65, 67, 80, 160, 162, 168
Tanner, 94
Tansey, 241
Tappan, 205, 306, 333
Tarleton, 323
Tarlton, 39

Tarr, 291
Tartar, 231
Tastet, 347
Tate, 126, 179, 278
Taugett, 77
Tauston Dean, 37
Tayloe, 59, 245, 282, 387
Taylor, 3, 7, 14, 43, 46, 52, 60, 62, 69, 79, 92, 94, 100, 106, 114, 115, 121, 127, 132, 133, 139, 141, 153, 156, 157, 177, 191, 200, 205, 214, 220, 232, 239, 251, 255, 260, 261, 263, 267, 275, 288, 306, 311, 314, 326, 330, 344, 357, 371, 377, 384, 392, 400
Tayor, 114
Tazewell, 212
Tea Party, 327
Teackle, 118
Tear Coat, 352
Tebbs, 301
Tecumseh, 174
Tecumsthe, 331
Telfair, 43
Temple, 5, 6
Templeman, 216, 224
Templeton, 318
Tench, 147
Tenney, 341, 392
Terhune, 265
Terrell, 10, 128
Terrett, 5
Terry, 93, 272
Tessier, 99
Tevis, 222
Tewgood, 96
Thatcher, 226
Thaw, 70, 138, 359
Thayer, 5, 211
Thecker, 65, 129, 332
Therber, 18
Thiay, 369
Thiers, 118
Thistle, 196, 257
Thom, 49, 220, 244

Thomas, 31, 38, 47, 70, 75, 89, 92, 102, 113, 115, 140, 169, 185, 193, 203, 204, 209, 222, 243, 250, 256, 263, 275, 280, 282, 288, 304, 318, 329, 335, 356, 358, 364, 371, 391, 395, 402
Thompson, 10, 14, 30, 32, 33, 39, 42, 47, 53, 65, 69, 73, 77, 80, 87, 90, 94, 97, 100, 101, 103, 107, 108, 116, 119, 123, 125, 133, 134, 139, 150, 158, 169, 183, 188, 194, 206, 211, 215, 218, 231, 233, 239, 240, 243, 247, 248, 254, 270, 281, 286, 289, 299, 306, 308, 314, 348, 351, 352, 363, 367, 370, 375, 377, 380, 386, 390, 393, 396, 400
Thompson's Expense, 38
Thomson, 126
Thomspn, 136
Thorn, 8, 181
Thorne, 306, 308
Thornley, 150
Thornton, 99, 156, 176, 178, 212, 226, 230, 260, 285, 293, 296, 330, 370, 400
Thorpe, 327
Three Corners, 36
Three Friends, 36
Throop, 83, 102, 374
Thrun, 316
Thruston, 60, 80, 97, 139, 182, 294, 304, 307, 340
Thucker, 7
Thumlert, 113, 143, 150, 302, 310, 311, 314
Thurber, 102
Thurbur, 21
Thurman, 185
Thurston, 260, 285
Thweat, 47
Thysan, 116
Tidball, 27, 114
Tiers, 69, 94, 100, 128, 232
Tiffany, 75, 105, 170, 202, 225, 232, 304

Tiger-tail, 347
Tilden, 243, 315
Tilghman, 203
Tilley, 169, 219, 332
Tillinghast, 98, 125
Timberlake, 320, 401
Tiner, 39
Tinges, 178
Tippet, 274
Tippett, 194
Tipton, 236
Titus, 75, 258, 306
Tod, 139, 260, 318
Todd, 91, 126, 133, 196, 217, 235, 296, 310, 324, 356, 367
Togno, 342
Toland, 321
Tolford, 4
Tolhouse, 364
Tolson, 35
Tomason, 20
Tombs, 306, 307
Tomlinson, 377
Tompkins, 7, 126, 306, 386
Tongue, 32
Tonkwa Indians, 125
Tooke, 336
Toombs, 192
Torrey, 243
Totten, 352
Toulmin, 274
Tower, 163
Towers, 126, 366
Towles, 89, 265, 310, 388
Town Neck, 39
Townley, 74
Townsend, 58, 306, 377
Townshed, 13
Townshend, 320
Towslee, 87, 171
Towson, 53
Toy, 295
Tracey, 306
Tracy, 122, 176, 262, 279, 377
Tradesman's Lot, 37

Tradle, 105
Trafton, 263
Tranchard, 230
Trangott, 122
Tranquebar, 268
Trapier, 5
Travers, 148, 150, 344
Travis, 12
Treat, 52
Trennile, 382
Trenon, 306
Trent Marsh, 36
Treville, 140
Trevor, 192
Trigg, 311
Trimble, 148
Tringg, 235
Trip, 98
Tripler, 304
Triplet, 117
Tripp, 203
Trist, 42
Troop's Rendezvous, 328
Trore, 106
Truax, 75
True, 377
Trueheart, 266, 360
Trueman's Hunting Qrtr, 39
Truman, 133, 352
Trumbull, 362
Truth & Trust, 35, 36, 38
Tryon, 168
Tschiffely, 237
Tubman, 39
Tuck, 376
Tucker, 73, 95, 101, 108, 135, 137, 150, 157, 171, 202, 222, 262, 278, 282, 303, 305, 311, 338, 341, 348, 350, 386, 393
Tuckerman, 145
Tufts, 41, 355, 356
Tugalla, 40
Tunscott, 157
Tuomy, 307
Tupper, 16, 86, 235, 356, 382

Tupsler, 307
Turish, 307
Turner, 38, 39, 50, 60, 62, 84, 93, 107, 126, 133, 155, 160, 169, 178, 207, 212, 217, 240, 242, 244, 251, 263, 273, 286, 293, 312, 319, 363, 368, 371
Turnpenny, 157
Turpy, 140
Tuston, 141
Tutle, 375
Tutter, 222
Tuylle, 157
Twigg, 248, 288
Twiggs, 199, 387
Twitnam, 37
Two Friends, 37
Tyar, 144
Tyler, 16, 34, 60, 90, 171, 185, 191, 200, 207, 231, 238, 252, 258, 263, 276, 301, 304, 377
Tysen, 70
Tyson, 160, 269, 306, 307

U

Uhler, 341
Ulrich, 340
Ulshoeffer, 54, 105, 305
Underhill, 64
Underwood, 69, 88, 94, 100, 113, 135, 223, 276, 391
Upperman, 129, 183, 390, 394
Upton, 21, 327, 330
Urrea, 295, 341
Usborne, 78
Utter, 306
Uttermuhle, 150, 224

V

V_ger, 168
Vail, 96, 133, 171, 214, 219, 395
Valdenar, 248
Valengin, 67
Vallette, 105

Van Antwerp, 306
Van Benthuysen, 86, 219, 229
Van Beuren, 306
Van Boren, 263
Van Boskerck, 306
Van Buren, 15, 71, 99, 147, 153, 166, 168, 176, 179, 196, 209, 234, 238, 244, 255, 258, 259, 260, 263, 266, 267, 271, 288, 299, 329, 346, 353
Van Coble, 282
Van Cortland, 262
Van Cortlandt, 267, 377
Van Cott, 21
Van den Broeck, 54
Van Dine, 306
Van Dyck, 308
Van Dyk, 306
Van Horn, 102, 153
Van Horne, 328
Van Horseigh, 339, 349, 376
Van Huysum, 228
Van Lear, 358
Van Ness, 5, 14, 23, 49, 224, 282
Van Olinda, 272
Van Renssealer, 350
Van Rensselaer, 151, 222, 255, 377
Van Reswick, 340
Van Riper, 304
Van Schaick, 157
Van Slyck, 122
Van Tassel, 307
Van Tyne, 12, 202
Van Vliet, 243
Van Wyck, 230, 308
Van Zandt, 31, 324
Vance, 24, 43, 283, 301
Vanderbilt, 18
Vanderpool, 304, 305, 308
Vandervoort, 307
Vandeveer, 298
Vansant, 220, 273, 330
Vanyne, 391
Varden, 34, 64, 249, 322, 382
Varian, 223, 330
Vase, 177

Vattemare, 61
Vattemere, 57
Vaugh, 106
Vaws, 106
Veazie, 391
Veirs, 218
Veitch, 220
Venable, 93, 282
Venturo, 78
Vermilyea, 306
Verplanck, 55, 377
vessel *Agnes*, 29
vessel *Eliza*, 133
vessel *Lord Nelson*, 164
Vethake, 306
Vial, 96
Vibeit, 17
Vickory, 48, 75
Vidal, 400
Vigilant, 167
Vigo, 15, 382
Vincent, 192, 219
Vinson, 182
Viomenil, 323
Vivans, 150
Vivien, 118
Vleit, 100, 134, 395
Vliet, 69, 94, 119, 385
Voisin, 337
Voorhees, 75, 377
Voorhies, 262
Vosburg, 304
Vose, 182
Voss, 6, 394
Vowell, 124
Vowler, 271
Vowles Purchase, 36
Vowles' Purchase, 37, 38
Vreeland, 43, 308
Vroman, 41
Vroom, 76, 165, 270

W

Waddam, 112
Waddell, 65
Wade, 131, 137, 188, 263, 353
Wagener, 321
Waggaman, 22, 286, 338
Wagler, 78, 213, 302, 340
Wagner, 253, 384
Wainwright, 183, 349, 400
Walbach, 5, 141
Walcott, 67
Walden, 15, 115, 167, 267, 296
Waldron, 307, 351
Wales, 36, 163
Walke, 11
Walker, 1, 5, 6, 18, 20, 21, 22, 36, 38, 57, 58, 63, 69, 94, 100, 101, 120, 121, 126, 135, 138, 148, 150, 151, 165, 169, 180, 186, 187, 195, 230, 247, 248, 258, 275, 279, 282, 295, 299, 307, 312, 314, 318, 330, 335, 354, 356, 367, 387, 397, 402
Walker's Venture, 38
Walkins, 335
Wall, 104, 114, 256, 367, 373
Wallace, 1, 48, 65, 83, 167, 170, 230, 248, 262, 288, 319, 330, 358
Wallach, 126, 135, 290
Wallen, 243, 355
Waller, 7, 146, 342, 380, 386, 400
Walling, 183
Wallingsford, 35, 62
Wallis, 92, 327, 376
Wallon, 95
Walsh, 11, 17, 118, 119, 307, 316, 329, 349
Walter, 165, 282
Walters, 192
Walton, 214, 330
Walworth, 87, 307
Wannall, 127
Wannell, 134
Waples, 310
Ward, 10, 33, 45, 53, 70, 101, 120, 147, 148, 151, 153, 208, 296, 395
Warden, 230, 364
Warder, 78

Wardle, 129
Wardwell, 41, 105, 135, 222, 238, 244, 356
Ware, 130
Warfield, 60, 164, 195, 297, 329
Waring, 248
Warley, 64
Warner, 15, 22, 41, 156, 195, 219, 232, 307
Warren, 87, 192, 248
Warring, 191, 307
Warrington, 57, 129, 254
Washburn, 238
Washingon, 321
Washington, 3, 34, 40, 59, 61, 66, 72, 76, 77, 88, 127, 129, 130, 145, 210, 211, 213, 224, 235, 249, 256, 323, 336, 376, 377, 400
Washington Park, 37
Wason, 307, 318
Wasson, 133, 304
Water Mill, 35, 38
Waterbury, 21
Waterloo, 40
Waterman, 102
Waters, 56, 81, 126, 151, 155, 175, 183, 190, 195, 204, 206, 282, 300, 304, 328, 344, 352, 368, 400
Waterston, 60
Wathan's Disappointment, 37
Wathen, 172
Watkins, 45, 133, 153, 179, 230, 242, 248, 335, 345, 372, 376
Watkinson, 222
Watson, 28, 39, 85, 95, 113, 124, 128, 143, 220, 223, 262, 282
Watteeston, 137
Watterman, 67
Watterson, 289
Watterston, 245, 289, 344
Watts, 13, 75, 81, 303, 348
Way, 344
Wayland, 392
Wayne, 3, 14, 43, 61, 86, 115, 117, 237, 384

Weademan, 393
Weaklin, 38
Weatherby, 136
Weaver, 141, 346, 359, 378
Webb, 60, 82, 152, 230, 348, 377
Webster, 49, 168, 208, 241, 262, 300, 309, 334
Weed, 1, 40, 127, 330, 377, 380
Weeden, 41, 126
Weedon, 49
Weems, 187, 202, 352, 372
Wegher, 182
Weightman, 60, 172
Weir, 28, 110
Weiss, 84
Welch, 167, 232
Welchman, 157
Weldran, 307
Well Close, 35
Weller, 270
Welles, 219
Wellesley, 185
Wellford, 239
Welling, 306
Wells, 135, 151, 155, 188, 214, 235, 282, 307, 376
Welsh, 38, 74, 84, 185, 298
Wensel, 318
Wentworth, 221
Wenwood, 386
Werner, 69
Wertenbaker, 338
West, 24, 142, 151, 202, 327
Westbrook, 162, 321
Westcott, 165
Westervelt, 307
Westfall, 34, 188
Westfield, 9
Westham, 39
Westlake, 384
Westmacott, 157
Weston, 18, 21, 63
Westtake, 44
Westwood, 134, 271, 351
Wetherill, 353

Wetmore, 49, 304, 330
Wever, 79, 133
Wex, 200
Whailes, 2
Whalen, 177, 282
Wharton, 56, 70, 85, 104, 180, 314, 367
Wheat, 403
Wheatley, 9, 38
Wheatley's Content, 37
Wheatley's Meadows, 37
Wheaton, 377
Wheeler, 35, 38, 87, 99, 114, 201, 208, 238, 262, 263, 307, 321
Wheelock, 40
Wheelwright, 11, 118
Whelan, 91, 187
Wheney, 90
Whetcroft, 215
Whicher, 238
Whipple, 44, 85, 307
Whitaker, 28, 383
Whitall, 328
Whitcomb, 160
White, 7, 20, 25, 44, 47, 49, 58, 61, 64, 68, 72, 80, 82, 104, 108, 115, 127, 143, 148, 149, 150, 178, 179, 209, 240, 262, 278, 294, 310, 311, 318, 331, 350, 357, 380, 382, 386, 390, 395, 400
White Acre, 37
White Cottage, 142
White Plains, 172
White's Neck, 38, 39
Whitehead, 1, 42, 192
Whitehorn, 371
Whiting, 16, 31, 89, 243, 247, 267
Whitler, 259
Whitlet, 75
Whitley, 307
Whitlock, 164
Whitman, 26, 75, 395
Whitmore, 62, 83, 122, 123, 221
Whitney, 78, 110, 125, 230, 332
Whittaker, 386

Whittel, 225
Whittemore, 15
Whittingham, 184, 374
Whittle, 170
Whitue, 83
Wickam, 100
Wickham, 94, 123, 134, 232
Wickliff, 212
Widger, 46
Widow's Down, 39
Widrig, 74, 170, 225
Widsham, 69
Wigfall, 343
Wiggens, 78
Wiggins, 62
Wigginton, 221
Wight, 167, 170, 232
Wilber, 105
Wilburn, 268
Wilcox, 23, 34, 87, 102, 247, 248
Wild Cat, 35
Wilde, 333
Wilderspool, 36, 37
Wildes, 15, 70, 240
Wiley, 74, 79, 170, 188, 225, 264
Wilhelm, 39
Wilkes, 230
Wilkins, 162, 354
Wilkinson, 38, 69, 94, 100, 102, 110, 120, 128, 149, 218, 222, 267, 268, 274, 280, 349, 361, 373, 395, 397
Wilkinson's Industry, 37
Will, 237
Willard, 136, 203
Willet, 47
Willett, 151, 179, 399
Willey, 31, 135, 202, 222
Williams, 1, 3, 17, 19, 21, 25, 27, 32, 33, 38, 41, 44, 49, 58, 63, 67, 73, 78, 81, 82, 87, 89, 90, 92, 97, 105, 114, 117, 119, 133, 135, 140, 146, 149, 155, 158, 162, 164, 181, 188, 218, 224, 230, 233, 254, 262, 268, 269, 282, 316, 320, 325, 328, 329, 351, 352, 355, 369, 374, 377, 382, 384,

387, 391, 392, 393, 395, 398, 400, 403
Williamson, 55, 57, 153, 183, 184, 192, 219, 234, 243, 279, 288, 357
Willing, 98
Willis, 32, 69, 73, 79, 94, 95, 100, 134, 142, 154, 232, 245
Willock, 235
Wills, 105, 107, 362, 363
Willson, 11, 30, 321
Wilmer, 33, 155
Wilson, 2, 16, 18, 22, 27, 31, 35, 60, 64, 75, 78, 113, 118, 122, 129, 133, 134, 160, 170, 173, 176, 179, 180, 183, 184, 187, 190, 195, 197, 205, 207, 209, 210, 222, 223, 225, 253, 263, 265, 272, 280, 282, 287, 296, 301, 310, 318, 329, 333, 343, 354, 366, 367, 369, 372, 377, 382, 383, 391, 403
Wiltberger, 207, 257, 271, 322, 327, 367
Wimberly, 192
Wimsatt, 97, 207, 270, 368, 371, 376
Winans, 307, 331
Winchester, 128, 220, 273, 358
Winder, 110, 243, 244
Wineow, 287
Wingerd, 100, 292, 366
Wingfield, 87
Winn, 113, 174, 223, 335, 342
Winnebago Indians, 203, 273
Winrott, 124
Winsatt, 38
Winship, 243
Winslow, 11, 17, 21, 42, 75, 105, 170, 216, 223, 226, 232
Winston, 74, 181
Winters, 126, 212
Wintersmith, 288
Winthrop, 7, 29, 158, 207, 345, 392
Wirt, 26, 84
Wisbart, 93
Wise, 87, 230, 239, 267, 318, 330, 339, 361

Wiswal, 307
Wiswall, 307
Witherow, 46
Withers, 60, 267, 282, 350
Witter, 208
Wives Wanted, 81
Wm I, 358
Wm II, 337
Wm White, 344
Wm's Endeavor, 38
Wolcott, 167
Woleben, 384
Wolf, 84, 93
Wolfskill, 133
Wollard, 333
Womack, 33, 240
Wood, 5, 11, 27, 43, 57, 65, 73, 75, 104, 114, 116, 133, 141, 142, 158, 167, 170, 190, 197, 202, 203, 225, 233, 235, 271, 282, 304, 307, 309, 324, 363, 368, 379
Wood's, 36
Wood's Enclosure, 39
Woodall, 161
Woodbury, 8, 19, 58, 101, 108, 168, 238, 332
Wooden, 99
Woodhull, 307
Woodis, 396
Woodland, 38
Woodland Plains, 128
Woodlawn, 154, 252
Woodley, 117
Woodman, 263
Woodpecker, 37
Woodruff, 5, 11
Woods, 83, 118, 258, 337
Woodson, 311
Woodville, 138
Woodward, 4, 22, 29, 38, 39, 98, 101, 148, 161, 169, 182, 195, 200, 254, 274, 280, 340, 388
Woodworth, 267
Wool, 124, 179, 193, 392
Wooldridge, 216, 307

Woolesy, 20
Woolley, 43, 157
Woolsey, 18, 74, 230
Woolsey Manor, 35
Wootten, 364
Wootton, 187, 210
Word, 253
Worden, 230
Workington Park, 36
Workman, 58
Wormely, 384
Wornal, 364
Wornell, 302
Worrell, 50, 389
Worth, 42
Wortham, 396
Worthington, 23, 26, 33, 78, 160, 231, 287, 288, 326
Wousten, 42
Wren, 220
Wright, 11, 42, 46, 73, 75, 83, 90, 100, 117, 170, 184, 190, 191, 194, 197, 216, 233, 273, 279, 290, 329, 343, 354, 355, 368, 369, 376, 391, 400
Wroth, 9, 137
Wuker, 43
Wyall, 95
Wyant, 304
Wyatt, 22, 106, 290
Wyer, 224
Wyeth, 142
Wyman, 398

Y

Yancey, 73, 357
Yarnall, 318
Yates, 16, 38, 119, 307
Yeager, 299
Yell, 375
Yerkes, 116
Yieldingberry, 36, 38
Yocum, 263
Yohe, 59
Yoke by Chance, 36, 37
York, 74, 83, 170, 202
Yorke, 270
Yost, 56
Young, 20, 23, 46, 54, 64, 65, 70, 80, 96, 107, 114, 120, 126, 142, 149, 152, 157, 171, 173, 178, 194, 196, 232, 239, 245, 247, 248, 253, 265, 295, 304, 309, 310, 318, 324, 330, 331, 345, 352, 363, 367, 368, 369, 387, 401

Z

Zapata, 136
Zebold, 381
Zelim, 353

Heritage Books by Joan M. Dixon:

National Intelligencer *Newspaper Abstracts*
Special Edition: The Civil War Years
Volume 1: January 1, 1861–June 30, 1863

National Intelligencer *Newspaper Abstracts*
Special Edition: The Civil War Years
Volume 2: July 1, 1863–December 31, 1865

National Intelligencer *Newspaper Abstracts*
Jan. 1, 1869–Jan. 8, 1870

National Intelligencer *Newspaper Abstracts*
Volume 1866–Volume 1868

National Intelligencer *Newspaper Abstracts*
Volume 1840–Volume 1860

National Intelligencer *Newspaper Abstracts, 1838–1839*

National Intelligencer *Newspaper Abstracts, 1836–1837*

National Intelligencer *Newspaper Abstracts, 1834–1835*

National Intelligencer *Newspaper Abstracts, 1832–1833*

National Intelligencer *Newspaper Abstracts, 1830–1831*

National Intelligencer *Newspaper Abstracts, 1827–1829*

National Intelligencer *Newspaper Abstracts, 1824–1826*

National Intelligencer *Newspaper Abstracts, 1821–1823*

National Intelligencer *Newspaper Abstracts, 1818–1820*

National Intelligencer *Newspaper Abstracts, 1814–1817*

National Intelligencer *Newspaper Abstracts, 1811–1813*

National Intelligencer *Newspaper Abstracts, 1806–1810*

National Intelligencer *Newspaper Abstracts, 1800–1805*